LIVES

OF THE

LORD CHANCELLORS OF ENGLAND.

LIVES

OF

THE LORD CHANCELLORS

AND

KEEPERS OF THE GREAT SEAL

OF

ENGLAND

FROM THE EARLIEST TIMES TILL THE REIGN OF QUEEN VICTORIA

BY

LORD CAMPBELL.

SEVENTH EDITION.

ILLUSTRATED.

VOL. IX.

WILDSIDE PRESS

CONTENTS

OF

THE NINTH VOLUME.

CHAP.		PAGE
CC.—Continuation of the Life of Lord Eldon till the permanent illness of George III.,	. . . . . .	1
CCI.—Continuation of the Life of Lord Eldon till the Prince Regent forever renounced the Whigs,	. . . .	27
CCII.—Continuation of the Life of Lord Eldon till the conclusion of the General Peace,	. . . . . .	64
CCIII.—Continuation of the Life of Lord Eldon till the death of George III.,	. . . .	103
CCIV.—Continuation of the Life of Lord Eldon till the conclusion of the Queen's trial,	. . . . . .	134
CCV.—Continuation of the Life of Lord Eldon till the Cabinet was liberalized by the introduction of Mr. Canning and Mr. Huskisson in the year 1823,	. . . . .	158
CCVI.—Continuation of the Life of Lord Eldon till the commencement of proceedings against the Catholic Association,	.	174
CCVII.—Continuation of the Life of Lord Eldon till he was deprived of the Great Seal,	. . . . . .	201
CCVIII.—Continuation of the Life of Lord Eldon till the passing of the Bill to repeal the Test Act,	. . . . .	248
CCIX.—Continuation of the Life of Lord Eldon till the passing of the Catholic Relief Bill	. . . . . .	267

CONTENTS.

CHAP.		PAGE
CCX.	Continuation of the Life of Lord Eldon till after the passing of the Reform Bill,	291
CCXI.	Continuation of the Life of Lord Eldon till his final retreat from politics,	339
CCXII.	Conclusion of the Life of Lord Eldon,	364
CCXIII.	Character of Lord Eldon,	385
Postscript		485

LIVES

OF THE

LORD CHANCELLORS OF ENGLAND.

CHAPTER CC.

CONTINUATION OF THE LIFE OF LORD ELDON TILL THE PERMANENT ILLNESS OF GEORGE III.

LORD ELDON, on being re-appointed Chancellor, thought his tenure of the Great Seal exceedingly precarious; yet he held it continuously for more than twenty years—taking a prominent part in an Administration which, in the midst of unexampled difficulties, skillfully conducted our foreign affairs, and, by the aid of the most consummate General who ever led an English army to victory, overthrew the power of Napoleon, and restored peace to the world.

The first measure of the new Administration was an immediate dissolution of the Parliament, which had only sat a few months. This Lord Eldon strongly recommended, notwithstanding his violent animadversions on the late Ministers for dissolving a Parliament which had sat above four years. The speech delivered by him, closing the session in the King's name, announced the object of this proceeding to be, "to afford to his people the best opportunity of testifying their determination to support him in every exercise of the prerogatives of his crown, which is conformable to the sacred obligations under which they are held, and conducive to the welfare of his kingdom and to the security of the Constitution." This plain denunciation of the Catholics was received with loud applause, and most of the candidates supposed to be favorable to their claims were defeated at the hustings. When the "No-Popery Parliament" met, the note of triumph was sounded in the royal speech delivered by the Lord Chancellor, which boasted of "the numerous addresses which his Majesty had received from his subjects, expressing their firm resolution to support him in defending the just rights of his crown and the true principles of the Constitution."[1]

An amendment being moved, censuring the late dissolution, and the principles upon which the change of Administration had taken place, "the Lord Chancellor said the present Government was stigmatized by the amendment, which accused them of manifest misconduct. He defended the dissolution, which had been found necessary for the safety of the Established Church; and he denied the general doctrine, that Ministers, by accepting office, were responsible for the manner in which their predecessors had been dismissed,[2] although he declared his entire approbation of the principles on which the King had lately called to his councils men in whom not only his Majesty but the nation confided."[3] The amendment was rejected by a majority of 160 to 67.[4]

On a subsequent day, Lord Erskine and Lord Spencer having reiterated the same complaints on the occasion of the second reading of a Bill to indemnify Ministers for an Order in Council rendered necessary by the dissolution of Parliament, "the Lord Chancellor avowed, that, with a view to render the new Administration as firm and as vigorous as possible, he had been a strenuous adviser—probably one of the most strenuous advisers—of that measure. He looked to the Protestant people, whose regard and veneration, once lost to the Government, would at least be but imperfectly replaced by the conciliation of the Roman Catholics. But such a conciliation was not, in his opinion, at all likely to be effected. He concluded by taunting the late Government for confining their measure of relief to officers in the army and navy, and asked why it should not be extended to all professions and all

---

[1] 9 Parl. Deb. 577.
[2] Sir Robert Peel, who will generally be found to lay down sound constitutional doctrine, admitted in the Parliament which met in the beginning of 1835, that in accepting office, after the dismissal of Lord Melbourne's Government by William IV., he made himself responsible for that act, although he was at Rome when it took place, and he was in no respect actually privy to it.   [3] 9 Parl. Deb. 605   [4] Ib. 607.

offices in the state?"[1] In a subsequent stage of the bill he was quite jocular in answering a charge of having been factious when in Opposition, and observed, that "*All the Talents*, as they were called, had been absolutely without any opponents in that House, or he believed anywhere else, until they began to *oppose* themselves."[2]

The only other occasion of his addressing the House during this session was for the purpose of throwing out Lord Holland's Bill from the establishment of Parochial Schools,—on the ground that "it departed from the great principle of education in this country, by taking the business of instruction, in a great degree, out of the superintendence and control of the clergy." He even objected to a provision in the bill giving the Court of Chancery jurisdiction over the funds appropriated to the use of the schools; saying,—what he would not have allowed any one else to say without expressing high indignation,—"It should be recollected how money so intrusted was *sweated* in that court, and how, in the end, when the oyster came to be divided, the parties entitled got nothing but the shells."[3] His will in the House of Lords was henceforth law, and at the prorogation he exultingly returned thanks to them in the King's name, "for the steady loyalty, and the zealous devotion to the public service, which had characterized all their deliberations"[4]—although only a few months had elapsed since his desponding conviction that the King was alienated from him, and that the Whigs, with their new Parliament, were permanently fixed in power. This revolution was in no small degree to be attributed to his own dexterity in turning to account the prejudices of the King and of the people.

Lord Eldon at this time exercised a much greater influence in the Cabinet than had belonged to any Chancellor for a vast number of years. The nominal head of the Government was the Duke of Portland—never a very vigorous statesman, and now enfeebled by age and disease; and Mr. Perceval, leader of the House of Commons, having long practiced as counsel under the Chancellor, still regarded him as his chief. Lord Camden, Lord Westmoreland, Lord Mulgrave, and Lord Chatham, were very little considered; and Lord Hawkesbury, Lord Castle-

[1] 9 Parl. Deb. 778.   [2] Ib. 808.   [3] Ib. 1176.   [4] Ib. 1223.

reagh, and Mr. Canning, though aspiring statesmen, had not yet acquired much ascendency. Lord Eldon continued in high favor with the King and the Duke of Cumberland; and his colleagues, sensible that they chiefly owed their places to his skillful intrigues, were for a while, much disposed to defer to his opinion.

He zealously supported, if he did not suggest, two measures of great energy, but very doubtful justice and expediency—the discussion of which long occupied Parliament and the public—the Orders in Council against Neutral Commerce, and the seizure of the Danish fleet. Napoleon's Berlin and Milan decrees having declared "the whole of British dominions in a state of blockade," and ordained that " every article of her manufacture, or belonging to her, or coming from her colonies, wheresoever found, should be lawful prize," it was judged right, through orders in council, to retaliate, by declaring "that not only the ports and places of France and her allies, and of any other country at war with his Majesty, but likewise all ports and places in Europe from which the British flag was excluded, and all ports and places in the colonies of the King's enemies, should be subject to the same restrictions, in point of trade and navigation, as if they were under actual blockade; and further, that all trade in the produce or manufacture of the said countries or colonies should be deemed unlawful; and that every vessel trading from or to them, and its cargo, and every article of the produce or manufactures aforesaid, should be liable to be captured as enemies' property." Of these orders in council Napoleon had no right to complain; but they were grievously unjust to neutrals, and it is now generally allowed that they were contrary to the law of nations and to our own municipal law.

On the seizure of the Danish fleet, diversity of sentiment still prevails; but, in my opinion, the act was unjustifiable, for the Danes had offered us not the slightest provocation, and it is vain to say that self-preservation required such an outrage upon an independent and friendly people,—the only pretext for it being that, if we did not seize their ships, probably, ere long, Napoleon would have tried to do so.[1]

[1] I have received from the venerable ex-Lord Justice General Hope a letter, in which, after some complimentary expressions, he says, " I differ

The stormy session of Parliament which began in January, 1808, was almost entirely taken up with motions on these two subjects. Lord Eldon repeatedly defended with ability the orders in council. "He denied that they were contrary either to international or municipal law. He admitted that neutrals might suffer some inconvenience by the retaliation which placed them between confiscation by France or by England, but a neutral nation, which, by her acquiescence in an invasion of her rights lent herself to one belligerent at the expense of the other, could have very little reason to complain if the other belligerent protected himself by the necessary measures for rendering such a combination ineffectual. These measures were aimed, not at the neutral, but at the adverse belligerent—the damage to the neutral was only incidental. It might be an evil, but it was not an injury. With respect to America, the chief sufferer, we must recollect the mischief she caused us by acquiescing in the decrees of Bonaparte, as well as the advantage she might bring to us by her trade and friendship; and he hoped that, instead of going to war with us, she would join us in resisting the extravagant pretensions of the common enemy of all civilized nations." It required much suffering to ourselves from the Orders in Council, as well as a long-continued series of attacks against them in both Houses of Parliament, to do away with the effect of such arguments.[1]

The cause of the Danes was warmly taken up by Lord from you respecting the expedition to Copenhagen, and the seizure of the Danish fleet. The fact was this:—Mr. Henry Hope, of Amsterdam, and of the great house of Hope & Co. there, upon the invasion of the French on Holland, came over to this country, and lived in that large house in the corner of Harley Street, Cavendish Square, in which he had that fine collection of pictures. On account of his mercantile and banking proceedings, he was led to have secret agents and banking correspondents in every court of Europe: among others, at Paris in the time of Bonaparte. And by them at Paris he learnt that Bonaparte was at that very time marching small detachments of sailors, under lieutenants, through Germany to Copenhagen, there to take possession of, and man, the Danish fleet. This fact Mr. Henry Hope communicated to my brother, Sir William, who, of course, communicated it to the Board of Admiralty, of which he was then a member, and of course our expedition was undertaken in order to anticipate that of Bonaparte. Now this private history could not be made public at the time; for if it had, Bonaparte would have put to death the one-half of his officials in Paris. In consequence our Government was obliged to let the affair pass as a voluntary and spontaneous movement of ours."—*Note to 3rd Edition.*

[1] 10 Parl. Deb. 149, 641, 1079, 1244.

Ellenborough and Lord Sidmouth, who, having been ejected with the Whigs, were not disposed to view with much favor the measures of the new Government, and who commented severely on this expedition as dishonorable to England and discreditable to those who had advised it. Lord Eldon had been shocked at the carnage caused among the Danes, which, however, he ascribed to "weak pride and false honor," in not quietly submitting. In a letter to Lady Eldon, giving an account of a conversation with some of the officers present, whom he had met at dinner on their return, he says, "The state of the inhabitants in Copenhagen, and their distresses, must have been terrible and tremenduous. In one street our mortars destroyed five hundred persons, principally poor helpless women and children. It seems weak pride and false honor that actuated the Danish commander. From the first he meant to surrender, and yet wished to have the credit of a battle before he did so ; and to this point of military etiquette he sacrificed one-fourth of the buildings of the town, and devoted to destruction property and lives to a terrible amount. It made my heart ache, and my blood run cold, to hear the accounts these gentlemen gave." But now, in the House of Lords, he declared that, "so far from feeling himself dishonored as an Englishman by the measure adopted, he should have felt himself dishonored if, under all the circumstances, he had hesitated to concur in advising it;"—and he scouted the proposal that the ships should be restored to Denmark at the end of the war, saying "that the Danish Government had not even a pretense for demanding a restitution, which had been offered only on the condition of peaceable surrender."[1]

Soon after came the Jesuits' Bark Bill, in opposing which, as counsel, at the bar of the House of Lords, I made my *début* in public life.[2] Lord Eldon behaved with great courtesy to me, and, I must say, seemed impressed

---

[1] 10 Parl. Deb. 656. He used afterwards to relate, on the authority of the King himself, an anecdote showing that on this occasion his Majesty could not have approved of the act of his Ministers. "When Mr. Jackson, our ambassador sent to Copenhagen to demand the surrender of the fleet, was presented at Court on his return, the King abruptly asked him, 'Was the Prince Royal upstairs or down when he received you ?' 'He was on the ground floor,' was the answer. 'I am glad of it, I am glad of it,' rejoined the King, 'for if he had half the spirit of his uncle George III., he would infallibly have kicked you down stairs !'" [2] Ante.Vol. VIII., Ch. CLXXXVI.

by my observations and evidence as to the private injustice which would be done to my client, the owner of several valuable cargoes, which would be embargoed and rendered useless by this measure, directed against the fever hospitals of France. He took no part in the debate, leaving it to others to contend that the bill rested on the principle which justifies cutting off supplies of arms and provisions from a besieged town,—although he was compelled to vote in the disgraced majority of 110 to 44, by which it was carried.[1]

He still continued his intimacy with the Princess of Wales, who was patronized by the King, and not only visited her at Blackheath, but gave her a grand dinner in his own house in Bedford Square. From the following good-natured note, we find that this entertainment had gone off well, although he had not been able to prevail on Lady Eldon to appear at table:—

"Thursday, June 9th, 1808.

"The Princess of Wales desires of the Lord Chancellor to express to Lady Eldon how much she was mortified at not having had the pleasure of meeting her at the Chancellor's agreeable dinner; and trusts that, whenever another opportunity shall offer itself, she may have the gratification of assuring the Lord Chancellor, as well as Lady Eldon, that the Princess will ever be happy of personally assuring them of her highest regard at their house."

The same autumn he received a visit of some days, at his country residence, Encombe, in Dorsetshire, of his steady friend and associate in Cabinet-making, the Duke of Cumberland. An entertaining account given by him, in a letter to his daughter-in-law, of his Royal Highness's gracious demeanor, says, "He was very good-humored and condescending, and we all behaved well. . . . dear Mamma very well, after the flutter which, you know, so rare a scene would occasion. . . . Fanny got an embrace, and we have had some difficulty to get her to allow her face to be washed since, lest she should lose the impression."

The session of 1809 was very inactive with the Lords, who were obliged to look quietly on while the nation was almost convulsed by the proceedings in the House of

[1] 10 Parl. Deb. 1320.

Commons against the Duke of York. Lord Eldon privately gave advice as to the conduct of the defense—and if it had been implicitly followed, the result would probably have been less disastrous. On the resignation of the command of the army, he wrote to his daughter-in-law,— " People in general, as far as I have seen anybody, seem affected and softened in consequence of this step; but whether the bloodhounds of St. Stephen's on Bragge Bathurst's motion to-morrow will or will not continue to hunt him down in his retirement, I can not say; but I have seen so much of injustice that I shall not be surprised to see a good deal of hard-heartedness; and the Duke's measure having disappointed some political maneuvers, the vengeance of politicians may still follow him, when men with hearts would forgive and relent." However, he judged rather harshly of the Duke's prosecutors; for the vote charging him with complicity in the sale of commissions by Mrs. Clarke was not pressed, and the general belief being that his conduct, although censurable on the score of morality, was entirely free from pecuniary corruption, he was allowed, two years afterwards, to resume the command of the army, when, by the admirable management of it, he essentially contributed to the triumphs achieved by England in the Peninsula.

Lord Eldon had an opportunity of showing his abhorrence of innovation, on a proposal being made (which has since been carried into effect) of prohibiting the sale of all offices connected with the administration of justice. As he must be supposed to have read the trial of Lord Macclesfield, he no doubt caused some astonishment when he said, "he believed there was not on record an instance where the patronage bestowed on the Keeper of the Great Seal had been abused, from the Revolution to the present hour, although that patronage was a main link in the chain that fitted each noble person who preceded him in office during that period, to have the personal means of holding rank consistently and suitably with others of their Lordships."[1]

In the House of Lords there was nothing more memorable during the session than the event of Lord Byron taking his seat on coming of age. Those who are ignorant of the careless manner in which such a ceromony is always

---
[1] 14 Parl. Deb. 1016.

conducted, have speculated much, and foolishly, upon the poet's disappointment at not being received with more distinction. We have the following authentic account of it from himself, in one of his note books:—"When I came of age, some delays, on account of some birth and marriage certificates from Cornwall, occasioned me not to take my seat for several weeks. When these were over, and I had taken the oaths, the Chancellor apologized to me for the delay, observing that these forms were a part of his duty. I begged him to make no apology, and added, as he certainly had shown no violent hurry, 'Your Lordship was exactly like Tom Thumb (which was then being acted),

'You did your duty, and you did no more.'"

Parliament was prorogued so early as the middle of June, and Lord Eldon expected a tranquil, long vacation at Encombe; but he was doomed to suffer much anxiety before the return of Michaelmas Term,—and, in the course of a violent and protracted Ministerial crisis, he repeatedly thought that the Great Seal had forever departed from him. The age and declining health of the Duke of Portland showed that the office of First Lord of the Treasury must soon be vacant. The King, referring to this subject, had "expressed himself as thinking the Duke could not remain long where he was, and therefore it was necessary that his other Ministers should look about them."[1] The grand struggle was between Mr. Perceval and Mr. Canning,—the former being patronized by Lord Eldon, and the latter preferred by the majority of the Cabinet, particularly by the more liberal section of it, who had been the personal friends of Mr. Pitt. Canning commenced operations, with a view to establish his own ascendency, by insisting that Lord Castlereagh, although permitted to retain his office, should be removed from the conduct of the War Department, for which he was supposed to have shown himself very unfit, and which was to be transferred to Lord Wellesley. This demand was conceded to him; but it was arranged that the intended change should not be communicated to the party principally interested till after the sailing of the Walcheren expedition (of which he was the author), and that it should then be broken to him by his near relation, Lord Camden. The result of this expedi-

---

[1] Letter from Mr. Perceval to Lord Eldon, 15th Aug. 1809.

tion having been still more disastrous than had been apprehended, Canning insisted that the promise made to him should be carried into effect; and, being told not only that Lord Castlereagh had yet been kept in ignorance of the whole arrangement, but that new difficulties had arisen of which he had not been before apprised, he insisted that his own resignation, which he had before tendered, should be laid before the King. He likewise desisted from any further attendance in Cabinet, although he continued to do the routine duties of his office till his successor should be appointed. The Duke of Portland, feeling his inability to quell the raging storm, announced his retirement, which was immediately followed by that of Lord Castlereagh.

The country being suddenly left without a Government, Lord Eldon was summoned from his repose at Encombe, and, on his arrival in town, found, to his horror, that there was a scheme in agitation by which he was to be deprived of the Great Seal. Canning, by way of getting rid of Perceval as a candidate for the Premiership, had proposed that, after having been Chancellor of the Exchequer for three years, he should return to the profession of the law, to which he had been bred, and should be made Lord High Chancellor of Great Britain,— the further advantage no doubt being calculated upon, of entirely excluding from the Cabinet *him* who not only had a personal spite against the semi-liberal proposer of this ingenious expedient, but who was a decided enemy to all improvement in our institutions. In this state of things, Lord Eldon wrote the following letter to his wife, which places him in a very amiable point of view by proving his affection for her, and the confidence he reposed in her:—

" Monday, Sept. 11th.

"MY DEAREST BESSY,

" We are here in a most singular state.

" As soon as the account came that the expedition could not be pursued, Canning renewed his insistings that Lord Castlereagh should deliver up his situation to Lord Wellesley. The latter[1] magnanimously, but I think most foolishly, said, he considered C—g's services in the House of Commons of so much consequence that he would resign; and accordingly sent his resignation, stating, however, that

[1] Lord Castlereagh must be meant.

he would not condescend to take any other office. This had nearly produced the resignation of Perceval, Liverpool, Camden and Bathurst. They saw plainly, that if the D. of Portland could give way to Canning, so far as to turn out Lord Cas. merely because that gentleman chose it, Canning was really the Minister, the Duke but an instrument in his hands, and that the world must see it too, and that everybody was at the mercy of that gentleman's caprice. This intended measure alarmed the Duke; he thought the King would be deserted; that if some other great nobleman was put in his place we might be all kept together still; and so the Duke sent in a tender of his resignation, and the King accepted it; and he has commanded Perceval, Liverpool, and myself to get him an Administration, which I think we shall not be able to do. For, mark what follows. This well-intended step on the part of the Duke has produced what shows me that I have been right in my conjectures, what from the first had been Canning's objects. Canning instantly wrote to Perceval, to say that some person in the House of Commons must be Minister, and in a roundabout way intimated that he, Canning, could not think of Perceval's being Minister, which of course left Canning the only person to be Minister; and he intimated, that if either there was a Minister in the H. of Lords, or Perceval was Minister, that he (C.) must resign. This quick step appears to me, I own, to have been a mode of trying whether Perceval's attachment to the King would be so far taken by surprise, as to lead him, at the moment, to give way. Little P., however, was upon the alert: he stated his willingness to remain as he was, provided nobody *in the House of Commons* was put over his head, but he would not act under Mr. Canning as Minister, tho' upon equal terms with him he would act. Canning's present suggestions therefore seem to be, that he will resign. I think, however, he will make an attempt, professing to fall in with the purpose of having a Minister in the H. of Lords, to get somebody named who shall be entirely under his own influence; and if that scheme does not succeed, which I think it will not, he will retire; and will thus, in the attempt to gratify his ambition, have contrived to overthrow himself and all of us along with him; and this is called *serving* the King.

"There are but two things which in that case can be

done. The one is to attempt to strengthen the King's friends who hang together, by some junction of parties; the other, to fight it out with such aid as we can get from our own party. I think Liverpool clearly is for the former plan: I think Perceval also is, but not so clearly,—he has doubts. I own I do not like it. In the first place, I think, nobody that joins from other parties, would join unless I cease to be Chancellor; and, in the next place, I have an opinion about this thing called 'junction of parties,' which would disincline me to remain Chancellor. I think it never strengthens anybody, and it does nobody credit. And that body of us who have hitherto thought ourselves strong in public opinion would lose the whole of the good opinion of the public. On the other hand, I think it very clear, that if we stand alone, we must fall after a very short—very, very short—desperate conflict, with the Opposition joined by Canning and his followers. In the latter mode I think the King will oblige us to fight the battle, at all hazards, if he can persuade us—but I am not sure he can persuade enough of us to fight it so. Upon the whole I think it quite clear, either that some junction of parties will immediately take place, or that a change without a junction of parties will very soon take place. What will you think of politicians, when I tell you that it has even been suggested that Perceval should return to the law, and be made Chancellor, and that, to provide for keeping things together in this way, I should retire? Perceval himself told me this: he did not name Canning as proposing it, but I take, upon suspicion, that to have been so; and then, Perceval being Chancellor, Canning might be Minister. Perceval treated this as he ought.

"I thought you would like to know how things go on; and, though, as they *are* going on, I can give no guess when I shall have the blessing of seeing you, it is quite manifest that either I shall return to you without the Seals, which I think very probable,—or, if that is not so, that before Christmas they will not be in these hands. Immediately, therefore, or shortly, those days will commence in which we may, with God's blessing, fear no interruption of our happiness by any future, even temporary, separation between us. *This I write all to yourself.*"

While things continued in this plight, he thus vents his

spleen against Canning and the Duke of Portland in another letter to Lady Eldon :—

"I think the individual who has occasioned all this mischief, is Vanity in a human form. Nothing will serve him but being what he will never be permitted to be.

"And I believe now, such is the imbecility of man, that the old D., who had resigned, is trying, in vain, to get back again."

He continues his bulletins :—

"Thursday (Sept. 14th).

"MY EVER DEAR LIFE,

"One after another, all of us saw the King yesterday : he is more to be pitied than any man in his dominions : and one ambitious man is the cause of all he now suffers. Mr. C. thinks proper, that his determination not to act under a third person, or to do anything else but be himself Minister, should remain unshaken : and his resignation [is] certain. I am just going to a meeting of such of us as have hearts feeling for the King, to see what can possibly be done, as all attempts to bring matters to rights again have finally failed. I can not, for one, see a ray of hope that anything, can be arranged which can have any endurance,—if, indeed, any arrangement, whatever, can be made ; and yet the poor K., in language that makes one's heart bleed for him, urges that we should not run away from him. My head and heart are perplexed and grieved for my old master's sake ; upon my own account I do not care a fig about it."

"Friday morning (Sept. 15th).

"After a great many hours spent in consultations yesterday, to be succeeded by more to-day, among those in whom the King thinks he can still have confidence, we have formed, or shall form, opinions which are to be offered to his consideration, and which he will adopt or reject as he thinks fit. I still think that it can not end in my remaining in office. I use the expression, in whom the King *thinks* he can have confidence, because I am sure there is scarce a man living, of whom he can say that he *knows* he may have confidence in him. I wish to God the thing was settled one way or the other ! If I knew that I was to go out, I would come to you instantly, and stay over Christmas ; if I knew I was to stay in, I could then know when and how I was to see you. Some of the plans proposed are what I do most greatly abhor, and I think they won't succeed. I have offered my office to the King, and told him, for I write constantly when I don't see him, my likings and dislikings. 'For God's sake,' he says, 'don't you run away from me: don't reduce me to the state in which you formerly left me. You are my sheet-anchor!' I fear the effects of his agitation and agony—and I do pray God to protect him in this his hour of distress.

. . . . . .

"May God's best and kindest providence watch over her who has the whole heart of *her*   ELDON."

"Monday, Sept. 18th.

"I proceed to tell you with much feeling, that the train of settlement we seemed to have got into is all undone. Shocked as I am to say it, George Rose has declared his attachment to Canning,—Huskisson has done the same,—Charles Long won't abide by us,—Sturges Bourne has declared for Canning. As these are the four men of business, it appeared to us last night that, without junction, the King must be sacrificed; with it, I do not know how he is to be saved in any degree of comfort. We are to take the resolution as to what is to be communicated to him at a meeting to-day, at one o'clock. I can not help thinking but that it must, that it necessarily must, lead to my being restored to a life of privacy."

"Thursday, Sept. 21st.

"MY EVER LOVED ELIZA,

"After I finished my letter yesterday, I went to the levee, and I had an audience of the King for a full hour. His agitation and uneasiness were such as have left me perfectly agitated and uneasy ever since I left him, though, I thank God, I am quite well. I dare not commit to paper what passed, for fear accident should not bring that paper to the hands of my Eliza; and though I promised her a letter of particulars, the particulars that passed are really so very special in their kind, that I can not communicate them even to her except in conversation—and would I could have that conversation! He would not decide what he would do, but said he should compose a paper at Windsor last night, and require from us written answers to several questions he should put in that paper, and order us to be convened to-day to consider the questions and give the answers: and accordingly we are summoned to meet at one o'clock at Perceval's; and I think it not unlikely, from what I know, that we may sit there till one in the morning. By *we* I mean such of us as have not resigned or tendered our resignations."

The same day had taken place, on Wimbledon Common, the famous duel between Castlereagh and Canning, in which the latter received a pistol-ball in his thigh. The Chancellor continues his bulletins to Lady Eldon:—

"Sept. 22nd, Friday.

"MY EVER DEAREST,

"I had hoped, when I wrote yesterday, that I should have been a great deal wiser to-day than I am. We waited at our meeting to a late hour, but no paper came from the King. I infer from this that he is in a most unhappy state of difficulty, and knows not what to do; and I greatly fear that something of the very worst sort may follow upon the agitation. If it pleases God to avert this greatest of all evils, we shall, I hope, have his paper to-day, and proceed in the consideration of it. But if he has taken *so much* time to consider it, I fear, I must look to those before whom it is to be laid taking *some* before they can make up their minds what answer they shall give to his questions and observations; and thus things train on from day to day, through a period of time which is very long, and seems longer and longer as it is protracted. This dreadful business of the duel between Castlereagh and Canning, while it is to be lamented on every ground, adds difficulty to difficulty, and I have no doubt will create a great deal, indeed of additional uneasiness in the King's mind."

"Saturday, Sept. 23rd.

"After I wrote to you yesterday, I went to the meeting, and I there found that Perceval had received the King's paper, which is one of the finest compositions, and the most affecting, I ever saw or heard in my life. After discussing the strength which any Administration could have that did not include G. and G., he acknowledges that there would be a weakness in it, which a sense of duty to his people calls upon him, by every personal sacrifice not affecting his honor and conscience, to endeavor to avoid: he therefore permits his present servants to converse with them upon a more extended Administration than his present servants could themselves make, but declares previously and solemnly, that, if any arrangement is offered to him which does not include such a share of his present servants as shall effectually protect him against the renewal of measures which his conscience can not assent to, that he will go on with his present servants at all hazards, throwing himself upon his people and his God,—his people, whose rights, he says, he never knowingly injured, and his God, to whose presence he is determined, whenever he is called hence, to go with a pure conscience. He predicts, however, that though he, in duty to his people, submits to this mortifying step, they (G. and G.) will not allow any effect to it; and then addresses himself in the most pathetic strains to all his present servants, calling forth all their courage, their resources, and the discharge of their duty to him. Perceval and Liverpool, therefore, will talk with the two G.'s: and it will either end in the junction, with a good many of the present servants left, or we shall live for about a fortnight after Parliament meets. They can not begin their conferences till about the middle of the week; and I should suppose, if they begin conferences, they will conclude them in the week. I shall not, however, be surprised if these gentlemen, the G.'s, refuse to confer at all with Perceval and Liverpool, and I think they *will* refuse, especially if they have any understanding with Canning. The King has also written a most dignified paper upon the fact of two persons, yet having the Seals of Secretaries of State in their hands, fighting a duel. I doubt much whether he will permit either of them to make their formal resignations in his presence."

. . . .

"September 28th, Thursday.

"I can not bring my mind to think anything so proper or so good for me as to have done with office now, and to spend the rest of my days in some degree of quiet and retirement; but I am afraid, and indeed sure, that unless he is so driven to the wall as to be able to do nothing whatever that he wishes to do, he will make it a most difficult thing for me to quit his service. Yet I shall beg very hard, for in truth the labor of my office is too much for me in the time of business, and what recompense can I have for what—I speak from my present sufferings—for what I undergo, in having my time of vacation ruined as this is?"

"Monday, Oct. 2nd.

"MY EVER DEAREST AND MOST BELOVED,

"I told you in a little note, on Saturday, that I was obliged to go to Windsor: I was compelled to do it, and therefore I could not help myself. I was called up in the night, so as to set off exactly at three o'clock in the morning; and I was with the King from seven till a little after eight, engaged with him in a conversation, the most interesting, and affecting, and important, that I have ever had with man in my life. I shall soon, I thank God, I shall soon be able to state the particulars of it in my dearest Elizabeth's hearing, and these particulars I really dare not commit to paper. The general result is, that we stay in, making such arrangements, without junction, as we can,—standing of course till Parliament meets, and then standing or falling as that body will please to deal with us. I think we had better have resigned; but *that* the King would not hear of for a moment. I think going on, with the certainty of being turned out, would be better than junction: at least to me it is more acceptable; and if we are turned out, as we shall be, I shall have the satisfaction of remembering that I declined being a negotiator for junction, and have stood, throughout, the servant of no man or men, but the King, and determined to abide by him and him only, to his last breath, or to my last breath, as far as I have anything to do with politics. After I left him, the Duke of Cumberland's Encombe servant I found waiting, to tell me that the Duke had just heard that I was there, and had got breakfast for me; and I was shown up to his apartments; and I received a great proof of his good nature and attention, as I thought it, and as he certainly meant it; for he had sent off for and got up William Henry from Mrs. Middleton's,[1] and he breakfasted with us at the Castle. This was a very pleasing incident. I had very little time to stay, and after sitting awhile and shaking hands with William Henry, who is very well, I returned here upon my business. Perceval will be First Lord of the Treasury in the room of the Duke of Portland. That is at present the only appointment settled. Lord Melville is behaving well; so is Lord Sidmouth.

[1] Eton School.

But what is most unexpected, the Prince has really conducted himself towards his father upon this occasion with exemplary propriety. The King showed me yesterday the Prince's letter to him, and his answer; and I'll tell you all about them when I see you.

"At the end of my conversation with him (the King) I asked his leave to return to Encombe. He said I should not go till after his levee on Wednesday, for he must see me there; that I might then put myself in my chaise, come to you without stopping, and stay with you to the end of the month. This was our bargain at parting; and I hope, therefore, to dine with you on Thursday. And of God I have no blessing to ask or pray for with so much of anxiety and importunity, as that nothing may interrupt this. I think nothing will or can. O that I was with you! For ever, and ever, and ever,

"Yours, your own,
"ELDON."

Extracts from two of his letters to Sir William will complete the history of this famous journey to London, and bring him back, still holding the great Seal, to Encombe.

"Oct. 4th, 1809.

"DEAR BROTHER,

"If you recollect at what vast distance men to be talked with are, you'll not be surprised that I have not filled up vacant offices in my correspondence. Melville must either be in office or be satisfied with being out of it. Now a letter to him, and an answer from him, and a reply to his answer, occupies thirteen days and a half. There's a hope that Lord Wellesley will take the Foreign Secretaryship. He is in Spain. I think Bathurst will have it *ad interim*. One infinite difficulty about Sidmouth is, that every person connected with him must have *office* found for him: Bragge, Vansittart, Hiley, Hobhouse, &c. &c. Sidmouth's army are all officers, and no soldiers. I suspect George Rose wants to be Chancellor of the Exchequer. As to calling Parliament soon, that will never do. Bets here go twenty guineas to one, that we never face it. But odds are sometimes lost. I think we shall now have no Parliament on this side of Christmas.

"The silence of such of Cas.'s colleagues who knew of the matter can not be well vindicated. With respect to myself, I feel uneasy; though the period at which I heard it, the personage (the K.) who told it me, and the injunction with which he accompanied a communication which I must needs say he ought not to have made under such an injunction, give me a good deal to say for myself. But, in some degree, all who knew it have been—more or less blamable, but—blamable.

"Nothing can be worse than the Walcheren business. But that business itself will grow worse and worse. The island must be evacuated, and I think you'll soon hear the Army accusing the Navy, and the Navy accusing the Army, as the cause of the failure. There will be warm blood in the two services.

"Harrowby, I think, will go to the Board of Trade, if he continues to exist: he is very ill. If you don't hear from me on Friday, I shall have gone to Encombe to bring my family home, with such leave of absence as the King to-day shall offer me. I shall not ask any; but I have had a hint that he means to press a short absence on me. In fact I have got to the full extent of all the good I can do here."

"Encombe, Oct. 7th, 1809.

"DEAR BROTHER,

"As I intimated it was likely, I set out after the levee, about eight at night on Wednesday, for this place, and I got here late on Thursday, though I did not stop on the road. I lay so long in bed on Friday that I lost the post, and this I write on Saturday evening for to-morrow's post, Saturday not being post-day here. I shall have all things packed up here, that we may all return on a moment's notice to me to come back. After the full explanation I have given of all I have to say on the present business, I do not know why I should be called up, but I take it for granted I shall, and therefore shall have my household as well as myself in a complete packed-up state. The Duke of P. gave me a fair opportunity enough, for he took occasion to tell me, that, let what would happen, I must not leave the King; he would not endure it,—that is, he, the King, would not. I replied, that I thought if there was a junction, the new ones would not endure me, and that I was hurt to find that, among the old ones, those whose confidence I thought I had, had been represented to be ready enough to suggest my separation from office, and therefore from the King, without even the mention of it to me. He was apparently embarrassed, said nothing, and looked foolish. I should have pressed him to the quick, but a man laboring under the torment of the stone at the moment was less an object of pity. Of my fact I am sure: there are so many witnesses to it, that there can be no mistake."

I have thought it best to allow Lord Eldon, in this affair, to be his own historian, and these letters afford the most favorable specimen I have met with of his epistolary style. Once more had he completely triumphed in political intrigue. Perceval, whom he favored, was now Prime Minister; and Canning, who had the audacity to think of a new Lord Chancellor, was, for the present, chased from office—though destined hereafter to have his revenge, by actually putting the Great Seal into the hand of Lord Lyndhurst.

Lord Eldon was known to have had a narrow escape in the late crisis, and his official life was for some time considered very precarious. Of the public opinion upon this subject we have a striking proof in the result of an election for the office of Chancellor of the University of Oxford. Had a vacancy in this office taken place when he was understood to be firmly seated on the woolsack, he must have succeeded to it as a matter of course, combining every possible qualification for it—academical distinction—unspotted private character—high church-and-king principles—and a steady opposition to any relaxation of the laws against Roman Catholics or Dissenters—with the prospect of long continuing to dispose of ecclesiastical dignities. At present, the last and not the least essential was wanting. The "G. and G. negotiation" was well known, and many thought that within a few weeks Lord Grenville would be at the head of the Treasury, with Lord Erskine, or Sir Samuel Romilly, as Lord High Chancellor. In this posture of affairs died the Duke of Portland, Chancellor of the University of Oxford, and Lord Eldon and Lord Grenville were started as candidates to succeed him. The King said "it would be hard if Cambridge had a Unitarian Chancellor,[1] and Oxford a Popish one." This was a strong declaration against Lord

[1] The Duke of Grafton, then Chancellor of Cambridge, openly attended the Unitarian meeting house in Essex street.

Grenville for his advocacy of Catholic emancipation, and Lord Eldon construed it into a pledge to support himself —which he evidently thought had been violated. For some unexplained reason, a party at Court brought forward the Duke of Beaufort, a very respectable nobleman, but having nothing to recommend him except his high lineage, and that he kept near Oxford the best appointed pack of foxhounds in all England. On this occurrence Lord Eldon wrote to a friend:—

"After it was fully understood that the Duke of Beaufort had refused to be a candidate, and some of his nearest connections had canvassed for me, he has become a candidate. This makes confusion more confused; but I shall stand it out, as I have consented to stand—for I can not be made a fool of with my own consent; and therefore, if both the D. of B. and I go to the wall, and Grenville succeeds, my consolation is that I am not to blame."

At the close of the poll the numbers were, Beaufort, 238; Eldon, 393; Grenville, 406. Lord Eldon was more hurt by this disappointment than by any he ever experienced in his life. He declared that he had been atrociously ill used; he suspected that even the King had betrayed him, and he loudly blustered about resigning the Great Seal—of course, without for a moment having had any such intention. The worst of it was, that, in virtue of his office of High Steward of the University, he ought to have officiated at the inauguration of the new Chancellor. Thus he poured forth his grief in a letter to Sir William:—

"I have written to the King, to know whether any part of my conduct could justify the Oxford reports, that I had not his support, or that he was hurt that I did not give way to Beaufort. From him I have had a satisfactory letter. I still think that I can't remain (with the public opinion that I have not been supported) where I am; and I persuade myself that if I feel compelled to retire from my great office because I don't choose to sacrifice the pretensions of a man long laboring for the public, to a fox-hunting Duke, I shall not fail to have your approbation. I have received a letter from the Duke of Richmond, in answer to a complaint of mine, that he had no reason to believe that I had the support of Government!!! As to what I am to do about the High

Stewardship, I am willing to pause : but, upon looking into the statutes and my oath of office, I may be called upon to do what I never will do. The short result seems to me to be, and perhaps the best result, that a few weeks will send me to dear Encombe as a resting place between vexation and the grave."

He asserted that the Duke of Beaufort's committee had turned the election by voting against him; and in a letter to his daughter-in-law he said, " Aristocratic combination beat me, and without combination it could not have hurt me. Of private ingratitude I have seen much, that gives more pain than the gout. Ingratitude bites hard."

Among the ungrateful, it is pretty clear that in his own mind he numbered George III., whom he considered indebted to him for still wearing the crown. The King's letter to him, if his Majesty was quite sincere, ought to have appeased him :—

*Windsor Castle, Dec. 16th, 1809.

" The King has received the Chancellor's letter, and sincerely concurs with him in lamenting the issue of the contest at Oxford, both on public grounds, and from motives personal to the Chancellor. His Majesty desires the Chancellor will feel assured that he has approved his conduct throughout the whole course of this business, as well by allowing himself to be named a candidate, and as continuing so to the close of the poll: his Majesty being very sensible that he could not, with honor or with advantage to the general cause, retire, after his friends had been engaged to support his well-founded pretensions.

"GEORGE R."

Notwithstanding his professions of entire belief in the King's good faith the following letter to Sir William, I think, indicates that suspicions on the subject still haunted his mind, and that he was reconciled to the notion of retaining the Great Seal chiefly by considerations that this course was for his own advantage :—

" If I doubted the King's good faith, I should not hesitate one moment ; but considering what we were pledged to, with reference to *him*, before this unfortunate business was engaged in,—to stand by him on *his* account, and on *that only*,—if he has kept good faith, I doubt whether I can contribute to the *immediate* destruction of the Administration by my resignation and whether then I shall

not be told that I have ruined the K., as I have ruined
the D. of B., more especially as the question of its existence, if I remain, is probably a question of a week or a
fortnight. Independent of this, all my own reasoning, and
every fact you state to me, make resignation the step I
ought to take ; and this I must discuss with you when I
see you. "Yours, "ELDON."

It required little persuasion on the part of Sir William
to drive away this fancy of resignation, by which the
Chancellor himself could not have been for a moment
deceived, for he would quite as soon have put a voluntary
end to his natural as to his official existence.

As long as George III. was able to execute the functions of government, Lord Eldon served him zealously and
faithfully, and perhaps their friendship did not suffer any
abatement ; but I do not subsequently find any marks of
fond intercourse between them as in former times, and the
Chancellor now began to strive gradually to insinuate himself into the good graces of the Prince of Wales.

Certainly the situation of Mr. Perceval's new Ministry
seemed very inauspicious. It had serious dangers to
encounter from the distractions which still prevailed in
the Tory party, and it had to undertake the defense of the
Walcheren expedition, which was not more disastrous than
ill-planned,—while the Orders in Council were rapidly
tending to involve us in war with America.

The last session of Parliament held while George III.
actually sat upon the throne began in January, 1810, and
was very tempestuous. Lord Eldon was suffering from
ill-health, and he took no part in the debates respecting
the Walcheren expedition and the warlike operations in
the Peninsula ; but he was forced up to oppose a bill which
the House of Commons had passed to forbid the granting of
offices in reversion. He said : " Sir Matthew Hale, who
would ever continue to be considered as an ornament, if
not an oracle, to the profession to which he had belonged,
had, he knew, highly disapproved of reversions,—as had
Lord Coke. But still, their authority was not to be
decisive of the question. We ought to be cautious how
we meddled with a system which had been the practice of
the Constitution for three centuries. He did not deny
that some good might be effected by judicious regulation,
—by the curtailment of emoluments in some cases, and

by their total abolition in others. Without inquiry, however, it would not become their Lordships to legislate upon the subject; and no inquiry, he believed, would warrant the House in going to the length proposed in this bill. Whatever the censure which he might incur for his dislike to innovation, he never could consent to legislate in the dark; but he protested against being considered as the enemy of all reform, merely because he was averse to reform which he could not understand. He had himself procured reversions for members of his own family, as former Chancellors had done,—and, certainly, without the smallest conception that he was doing anything of an objectionable nature. Having done this, he now desired to avow it; though, certainly, the value of the offices so bestowed by himself, altogether, was not sufficient to make the validity or invalidity of the gifts a matter of any great uneasiness to the expectants." The bill was thrown out by a majority of 100 to 67.[1]

The Chancellor was next alarmed by a bill of Sir S. Romilly's, which had passed the Commons, to abolish the punishment of death for the offense of privately stealing in a shop to the value of 5s. Commenting upon a very just observation, that "certainty is of more importance than severity of punishment, with a view to deter from the commission of crimes," he chose to represent that those who were for mitigating the severity of the penal code, wished that each offense should invariably be visited by the same degree of secondary punishment,—whereas, they only contended that the highest punishment that it would be proper to inflict in any case should be defined—leaving extenuating circumstances still to have their due weight. After contending for the necessity of some discretion being left in the judge, he said, "I remember a whole family indicted before me for stealing a single sheep. It was a case of peculiar hardship. These poor people were driven to the commission of a capital crime by the pressing calls of famine—exhausted nature, no longer able to bear the restraint of human laws, threw aside every consideration of honesty, and these unhappy wretches committed an offense which subjected them to a capital punishment. Now, my Lords, no man living could say that this was a case where the judge should have no dis-

[1] 15 Parl. Deb. 597, 600.

cretion. There is no man living who could go through such a trial without feeling that he should commit a greater crime than the unhappy wretches themselves, if he permitted the law to take its course.—I shall now mention a case where the principle is applicable the other way. It likewise occurred before me, during the short time I had the honor of to be Chief Justice of the Common Pleas. A man was indicted for stealing a horse, of the small value of 7s. 6d., and which he had sold for that sum to a horse-butcher. The jury found him guilty, and you will be surprised, perhaps, to learn, that for so trifling an offense, I suffered the law to take its course. The punishment of death, for this offense only, might appear extremely harsh; but, my Lords, in this instance I was guided by the nature of the evidence in the course of the trial, the detail of which I have now fresh upon my memory. It appeared, I think, that on the prisoner were found skeleton keys of all the turnpike gates within twenty miles of London, which he had manifestly procured for the purpose of carrying on the regular business of a horse-stealer. When we talk of the severity of the punishment, the objection to the law is much diminished by the practice of it; for it is severe only by its frequent execution, whereas, in practice, its execution is extremely rare. It is needless for us to differ about theories, if the practice reconciles the difference."[1]—He was thus obliged to rely upon the fact that the punishment which the law awarded was not usually inflicted; and he seems to justify the principle that to trespass on a common should be made a capital offense, because the trespasser may have a pistol or a dose of arsenic in his pocket, and ought to be hanged as if convicted of highway robbery or murder. I make great allowance for narrow-minded prejudice: but it would be to confound all the distinctions of right and wrong nor to praise the enlightened efforts of Romilly, and not to censure the systematic opposition of Eldon, by which they were long rendered ineffectual. The bill was of course thrown out,—and, for years following, juries went on finding, on their oath, that goods of the value of £50 were under the value of 5s.,—judges pronouncing sentences of death which they never meant should be executed—in a rare instance, perhaps, a cruel, or fan-

[1] 17 Parl. Deb. 200.

tastical, or careless judge allowing the law to take its course, and bringing great scandal on the administration of justice.¹

I have sincere pleasure, however, in coming to Lord Eldon's able vindication, against Erskine, of the right of the two Houses of Parliament to commit for breach of privilege, in analogy to the right of courts of law to commit for contempt. "He appealed to all the judicial authorities, if the process of attachment for contempts was not as much a part of the *lex terræ* as trial by jury. If a similar power were not allowed to the House of Commons, how could they possibly exercise their inquisitorial functions? He asked if Lord Somers, Cowper, Nottingham, or any of the most illustrious of his predecessors, had ever hesitated to commit in cases of contempt? Nay, a case had occurred of a libel upon a decree of his noble and learned friend (Erskine) when holding the Great Seal, when the distinguished champion of "trial by jury" himself committed the parties—a husband and his wife, with their attorney—to the Fleet; and very rightly, for they had all joined in composing, printing, and publishing the libel."²

The only other subject on which he spoke during the session was one on which I always read his speeches with entire respect, although I do not agree with their reasoning,—for they were spoken with perfect sincerity as well as seeming earnestness, and many most enlightened men continued to share with him the sentiments which he expressed. The Earl of Donoughmore having moved that a petition from the Irish Catholics should be referred to a committee of the whole House, "The Chancellor declared that he was too sensible of the blessings of civil and religious liberty which the country enjoyed to risk them on a speculation of which no one could inform him the grounds. He would continue to support the Protestant Church as by law established, although he might be called a bigot or a monk. He did think it but reasonable to inquire, before going into a committee, what it was intended to substitute in the room of those sacred outworks

¹ While I went the Oxford Circuit, a man was hanged at Gloucester by mistake, from there having been some delay in forwarding the reprieve from Hereford. The sheriff, on account of the trifling nature of the offense, confidently expected that a reprieve would come, and delayed the execution to the last minute. It did come when the executioner was cutting down the dead man from the gibbet. ² 17 Parl. Deb. 591.

and bulwarks of the Constitution thus asked to be removed. At present they knew not even what terms the petitioners would be pleased to accept. The proposed VETO he considered nothing. That, and other securities talked of, could not be conscientiously agreed to by the Roman Catholics, and dishonest men could not be good subjects. The penal enactments against them were not framed to disqualify for religious opinions, but to guard against the political consequences necessarily connected with that faith which acknowledged a foreign supreme authority. He could never consent, on mere speculation, to tamper with the actual state of happiness the country enjoyed—a state of happiness from which the Irish Catholics were not excluded—and which for a century and a half had rendered us the envy of the world. He would not interfere with this in the dark, or go into a committee, in which, for aught he yet knew, propositions might be yet made which would render the Protestants in a few months as much the objects of commiseration to the noble Earl as the Catholics were at present." However, there was now a minority of 68 to 154,[1] and hopes were entertained that the relief prayed for would soon be granted from a sense of generosity and justice—as a boon,—instead of being deferred till it should be extorted by combination and violence, when it would lose half its value, and would lay the foundation of future perils to the empire.

CHAPTER CCI.

CONTINUATION OF THE LIFE OF LORD ELDON TILL THE PRINCE REGENT FOREVER RENOUNCED THE WHIGS.

IN the latter part of the year 1810 it again seemed as if Lord Eldon's official career were certainly drawing to a close. All attempts to induce Lord Castlereagh to join Mr. Perceval had proved ineffectual; and the Whig Opposition, led by Lord Grey and Lord Grenville, was becoming more and more formidable. But an event which was expected to precipitate the fall of the Tories, in the result kept them in power many years. Though they

[1] 17 Parl. Deb. 404–440.

could not have stood much longer under their old patron, George III., they became irresistible under the Regency of the Prince of Wales, who was as yet believed to be impatient for an opportunity of crushing them.

Parliament stood prorogued to the 1st of November. Before that day arrived, his Majesty was laboring under such a violent paroxysm of mental malady as to render it utterly impossible for the Chancellor to pass a commission for opening the proceedings of the session, or ordering a further prorogation. From former experience we may conjecture that if this bold functionary could have obtained the royal signature to the commission, he would have considered himself justified in acting upon it, without trying the royal competency upon the principles which decide the validity of the deeds and contracts of private individuals;[1] but, at an interview which he had with the King, at Windsor, on the 29th of October, to see whether there could not be some arrangement for the march of public business without an open disclosure of the calamity with which the nation was again visited, he found his Majesty under physical restraint in the custody of Dr. Robert Willis and other physicians, and the notion of proceeding by a commission signed by him was necessarily abandoned. The difficulty of treating with him where writing was required was much increased by the circumstance that his eyesight had been long decaying, and that he was now nearly blind.

On Thursday, the 1st of November, the House met, and the Chancellor concluded an explanation of the circumstance of there being no commission by saying, "It remains for me to state that the indisposition of his Majesty has arisen from the pressure of domestic affliction operating upon his paternal feelings; and I have the satisfaction to add, that a confident expectation is entertained of his Majesty's speedy recovery."[2] The King had been much

---

[1] It would have been but a small liberty to have passed this commission, for there had been an order made at a council, at which the King presided, to prorogue Parliament from the 1st to the 29th of November, and to *prepare* a commission for this purpose.

[2] The following touching note from Queen Charlotte to Lord Eldon shows that he had in vain tried to see the King again before going to the House of Lords :—

"Windsor, Nov. 2nd, 1810.

"The Queen feels, more than she has words to express, the attention shown her by the Lord Chancellor and his colleagues, in making an excuse for not

affected by the illness and death of his favorite daughter, the Princess Amelia; but the physicians, when examined before the Privy Council, said "that they could not ascribe his former attacks of the same sort to any particular cause."[1] The House adjourned for a fortnight, and the Lord Chancellor addressed letters to all peers, requiring their attendance.[2] At the end of that period, on his statement that the physicians were sanguine in the hope of his Majesty speedy recovery, although he had actually been supposed to be dying, a further adjournment of a fortnight was agreed to. In answer to an insinuation that a commission might have been produced for proroguing Parliament, Lord Grey said, that "if Ministers had ventured to do any act which by the Constitution can only flow from the personal exercise of the royal functions they would have merited the strongest reprehension of every reflecting man, and that the indignation of the whole country would have been most justly excited."[3] At the next adjournment the Lord Chancellor excused himself for not affixing the Great Seal to a commission without having the sign manual of his Majesty—darkly hinting that he might have done so. "If he had acted wrong," he said, "he wished their Lordships to decide. He had acted unquestionably according to his conscience, and *that* told him he had acted as he ought. Their Lordships would bear in their recollection that the monarchy was hereditary,—that the King of this country was King in his infancy—his old age—in health and in sickness; and if they should transfer the exercise of the royal function from him, they did away with his authority altogether."[4] There was a division on a motion for a further adjournment, which was carried by 88 to 56.

calling upon her yesterday. She is perfectly sensible that the subject it related to would have been equally painful to both parties; and is highly sensible of the delicacy of the conduct of the Lord Chancellor, Marquis of Wellesley, and Mr. Ryder, to whom she begs her compliments.

"Our domestic misfortunes are truly severe; but I trust Providence will carry us through. CHARLOTTE."

[1] There used to be a strong disposition to impute the King's illness to excitement, produced by his resistance to Catholic Emancipation; but in 1765, in 1788, and in 1810, he was struck by the malady when Catholic Emancipation was not talked of, and when his Government was going on very smoothly.
[2] 18 Parl. Deb. 1. [3] Ibid. 6, 14, 18.
[4] The vice of this reasoning is, that it regards only the individual supposed to be on the throne,—utterly forgetting the hereditary nature of the office and the purposes for which it exists.

The Whigs confident in the delusive hope that they were to step into office as soon as the Regency Bill passed were for pushing on proceedings as expeditiously as possible; and the Ministers, with equal certainty considering this as their death warrant, struggled to defer it by all practicable delays.

At last, committees of both Houses were appointed to examine the King's physicians,—when some very curious information was elicited respecting the present and former illnesses of his Majesty, and the manner in which his Ministers had communicated with him.[1]

The mode of proceeding to provide for the exercise of the royal authority being debated the Chancellor strongly argued for following the precedent of 1789, and declared that "for his own part, as the Great Seal was intrusted to him by his Majesty, he therefore, would not give it up till he knew that some one was legally appointed to receive it out of his hands."[2] He denied that the Prince of Wales could have any right to govern during his father's lifetime; he maintained that the office of Regent could only be created by Act of Parliament; and declared that any address of the two Houses to the Prince of Wales, asking him to exercise the prerogatives of the Crown, would be treasonable.[3]

Nevertheless, all the Princes of the blood royal (including the Duke of Cumberland) joined in a solemn protest against these proceedings, "as perfectly unconstitutional, and subversive of the principles that seated their family upon the throne of these realms." This was forwarded to the Chancellor with the following note:—

"Thursday (Dec. 20th).

"MY DEAR LORD,

"I can not without feeling *the greatest regret* inclose to you a paper signed, as you will see, by ALL of us: not from its contents being contrary to the bearings of my mind, which has, God knows, been occupied for some time upon this unfortunate calamity, but from there appearing a difference of opinion between yourself and myself; and I believe you can not doubt, if ever one man is sincerely attached to another from having the highest veneration, esteem, and I may add, a sort of filial love, that man is myself, and it is therefore a most painful

[1] 18 Parl. Deb. 75–229.   [2] Ib. 459.   [3] Ibid. 713.

task for me to differ on this occasion; but I hope and trust that this will be the *only* time. For the hurry and bad writing of this note excuse me, but I am anxious you should receive this as early as possible.

"Believe me
"Yours very sincerely,
"ERNEST."

While this discussion was pending, an incident arose which very strikingly showed how the two Houses of Parliament were usurping kingly power. An issue of money was wanted from the Exchequer for the army and navy, and it could not by law be obtained without the royal sign-manual. Lord Eldon, the prop of the monarchy, and the stickler for ancient rules, joined in a resolution of the Lords and Commons,[1] by which the money was ordered to issue, even, without going through the form of forging the King's signature.[2]

At length the "phantom" appeared; and while the unhappy King was universally known to be under necessary coercion, and wholly unconscious of what was passing beyond the walls of his own apartment in Windsor Castle, the Lord Chancellor ordered the Commons to be summoned, to hear read a commission which he had received from his Majesty; and, when they had arrived at the bar, he thus proceeded:—

"My Lords and Gentlemen: Forasmuch as for certain causes his Majesty can not conveniently be present here in his royal person, a commission has been issued, under the Great Seal, authorizing the Lords in the said commission named to declare the causes of your meeting, and to do, in all respects, in his Majesty's name." He then, "by the authority in his Majesty's commission, and in his Majesty's name, called their attention to the afflicting circumstance of his Majesty's indisposition, and to the necessity of making due and suitable provision for the care of his Majesty,s sacred person, the maintenance of his royal dignity, and the exercise of his royal authority, in such manner and to such extent as the exigency of the case appeared to require."[3]

When the Regency Bill came up from the Commons, and the clause was discussed vesting the patronage of all

[1] A protest against this resolution was signed by all the Royal Dukes.
[2] 18 Parl. Deb. 796.
[3] 18 Ibid. 829.

the household offices in the Queen, Lord Landsdowne moved, as an amendment, that the arrangement of those offices should be made by a separate Act of Parliament, to be subsequently passed. This being strongly opposed by Lord Liverpool, Lord Grey sharply assailed the Chancellor, who was supposed to be trying to defeat a previous resolution, which, against the strenuous efforts of the Ministers, the Lords had passed,—"That the Queen's authority should be limited to the sole direction of such portion of his Majesty's household as should be deemed requisite and suitable for the due attendance on his Majesty's sacred person, and the maintenance of his royal dignity,"—saying, that "the effect of the enactment in its present shape would be to give the Queen about forty-seven appointments, and the Regent only two. The noble Lord, he believed, was actuated by conscientious feelings; the frequency of his appeal to those feelings was evidence of their sincerity, and he besought him, therefore, to indulge the same honorable sentiment in the discharge of his political, as he was proverbially accustomed to do in his legal and judicial, functions. Suppose the case (and he put it directly to the noble and learned Lord, who had high judicial duties to perform in another place) of a person deceased, by whose will a portion of the estate was directed to be applied to the support of the aged widow, while the remainder was to devolve to the eldest son, for the general purposes of maintaining himself and the members of the family in the rank and station to which they belonged. Would the noble and learned Lord interpret the intention of the testator, to be that forty-seven shares (for that was the proportion of the household to be given to the Queen) should belong to the widow, and two to the heir? With respect to that part of the bill which provided for the resumption of the royal authority upon his Majesty's recovery, he would say that no one—not even any of the noble lords on the other side of the House—would more sincerely rejoice at the arrival of that period than himself; but he must have other authority for the fact of such recovery than the mere putting of the Great Seal to a commission in his Majesty's name. Considering what had taken place on two former occasions, when it was notorious that the Great Seal had been employed, as if by his Majesty's command, at a time when he was under the care and actual restraint of a physician, for a malady similar to that by which he was now afflicted, the noble and learned Lord must excuse him for saying there must be better authority produced than *his* declaration, for his Majesty's recovery. Nothing short of an examination of the physicians by their Lordships could afford that proof of it which would satisfy his mind."

The Lord Chancellor left the woolsack, and said,—

"The allusions of the noble Lord were so marked that he could not suppress the feeling they had excited, nor omit to take the earliest opportunity of answering them; aud he trusted, therefore, that the committee would pardon him for trespassing on their attention. If he had occasionally referred to the rule of his own conscience, it was because that was the rule by which, from the outset of his public life to the present hour, he had endeavored to regulate his conduct. Confident in the probity of his intentions, and assured of the integrity with which he had labored to perform his official duties, both to the Sovereign and the public he would now repeat that he not only did not decline, but distinctly challenged, the strictest inquiry into his conduct. Nor would he scruple to declare that no fear, no influence of any kind, should deter him from doing again what he had already done, if he conceived it necessary to the interests of the King, his master, or of the country at large. Of his Majesty he never could speak without gratitude for the favors, the obligations, the King had heaped upon him; nor think without the acutest sensibility of that unhappy malady by which his Sovereign was oppressed. Reports of physicians should not operate, nor threats within or without the doors of that House, to prevent him from exercising his own judgment in whatever regarded the interests of his royal master. Rather than desert his allegiance by shrinking from any step pointed out to him by his duty and his office, he would bear to perish ignominiously on the scaffold. In every case which might arise, he would act upon his official responsibility, and content himself with leaving the consequences to Heaven. In what he had done upon the occasion alluded to by the noble Earl, he had pursued, under the solemn obligation of an oath, the course which his judgment prescribed to him. He felt himself, therefore, superior to the uncalled-for imputation of the noble Earl; and, until his country should tell him he had done wrong, he should rest satisfied with his own conduct in that matter. No man was entitled to charge him with a criminal act. He had long and faithfully served a most gracious master, at the most critical moment this country had ever known." After praising his own exertions to put down treason and sedition, which, with the personal character of the Sovereign, he said had saved the country, he thus continued —' Into the transactions of 1801 and 1804, I again say that I challenge the strictest inquiry. The opinions of physicians, though entitled to great attention, are not to bind me absolutely; I must act, and I have always acted, on my oath and to the best of my own judgment: charges, therefore, and menaces are indifferent to me. Let them come,—I am ready to encounter them: *impavidum ferient*. To the daily scandal poured out against me, I will not condescend to reply; nor will I ask of the noble Lord to trust me. I have been attacked and reviled; but I disregard it. Actions which I have never done have been imputed to me, and actions which I have done have been swollen and distorted by misrepresentation and calumny. In the newspapers I may read to-morrow, as I have often read before, sentiments and expressions attributed to me of which I am totally unconscious; but all this I can view without pain. I never refer to those diurnal publications without discovering errors and misrepresentations as to myself; but the consciousness of rectitude and integrity is sufficient to sustain my equanimity. I have been significantly asked whether I would supersede a commission of lunacy against the opinion of physicians. *I have often done so.*[1] Perhaps I may have been wrong in so doing; but again I repeat, I have acted on my conscience. With respect to the clause now under consideration, I will say, using an expression which I borrow from one well skilled in the science of human nature, that I know not how 'to disquantity the train'[2] of my royal master. I am asked what I would do in the Court

---

[1] A seemingly bold assertion; but I think the true meaning must be, that he superseded commissions of lunacy, some physicians swearing that the party was still a lunatic, while others, on whose judgment he more relied, swore to a perfect recovery. But the King's physicians, whom he rather tries here to depreciate, although eager to give the most favorable account possible, had unanimously agreed in his Majesty's incompetency.

[2] King Lear, Act i. Scene 4.

of Chancery if the present clause came before me in connection with the resolution on which it is founded? I answer, that the resolution is not of such certainty that a *Court* could deal with it at all. If I am asked my own view, I say that I deem *the whole* of the household to be 'requisite and suitable for the due attendance on his Majesty's sacred person and the maintenance of his royal dignity:' those are the words of the resolution, and therefore, according to the principle of that resolution, *the whole* of the household ought, in my sincere opinion, to be in the gift of her Majesty. In saying this, I speak with the same tender regard to conscience as if I were acting in a judicial capacity. I will tell this House,—I will tell every man who hears me,—I will tell all his Majesty's subjects,—that the last thing I would do in the Court in which I sit would be to remove from any man, laboring under an affliction such as has unhappily befallen his Majesty, the comforts which become his condition, and to which he has been accustomed. For myself, let me but see my Sovereign well, and then let me depart in peace. I can not take my heart out of my breast and forget that my most gracious master is a man. Let those who can do so, do it. I am not made of such impenetrable stuff; I have neither the nerve nor the apathy requisite for such stern and unrelenting duty. Until his Majesty shall vacate his throne by descending into his grave, to no other person shall I acknowledge myself a subject. Before I sit down, I must make my solemn protest against the principle upon which the proposed distribution of the household patronage is argued; as if the government of this country could not be carried on, except upon a system the most unconstitutional, the most degrading, and I will even say the most Jacobinical, that was ever suggested by the most inveterate enemies of the Constitution. What! are your Lordships to be told that no Master of the Horse, no Groom of the Stole, no Lord Steward of the Household, has the least consideration for the country,— but that their votes in this House will be controlled and directed by those to whom they owe their respective appointments? If this be the case, I have got, at the end of my life, into such company as I never was placed in at the beginning of it. But I can not believe that the noble persons about me—the descendants of those whose virtues and talents adorn the history of this great country—can be influenced by the unworthy motives thus ascribed to them. The Regent, to be sure, will be subject to restrictions; but the King himself, in this country, is a limited monarch. His Majesty, whatever his mental state, must be King until he descends into the grave. I can never discharge it from my recollection, that the Committee has two objects to accomplish; it has to provide for the stability and security of the government; but it has also to provide for the safe and effectual resumption of the royal functions on the part of his Majesty, whenever his recovery shall be fully ascertained. I feel the importance of the former consideration; but I feel also that, in taking care for his Majesty's restoration to his government, we are providing in the most effectual manner for the true interests and for the ultimate security of the state. Your Lordships, therefore, should not diminish the splendor that surrounds his Majesty, but preserve it in all its plenitude. I remember, and with a satisfaction which will terminate only with my life, the part which I took in the discussions of 1789: I will act on the same principles now. My conduct on that occasion obtained for me the approbation of my gracious master, as I trust will my conduct in the present crisis. I have no reason to change the opinion which I gave in a former debate respecting the probabilities of his recovery. Far from it: for, in addition to what I then said, I have now the satisfaction of acquainting the House that his actual state gives increased expectations of that happy result. I am not ambitious of continuing in place; I am incapable of entertaining any interested views at such a period as the present." The report states, that " he concluded a speech, delivered throughout with peculiar solemnity of manner, by repeating his regard and veneration for his Majesty, and his intention to oppose the amendment." [1]

In spite of these arguments, and the hardy announcement of the improvement in his Majesty's health which was calculated to have still greater weight, the amendment was carried by a majority of 107 to 98.[2]

Three days after, the Chancellor, feeling that he had been rather damaged in his rencounter with Lord Grey, took the opportunity of an amendment being moved by Lord Grenville for the purpose of accelerating the deter-

[1] 18 Parl. Deb. 1016. [2] Ibid. 1026.

mination of the restrictions on the Regent, to renew his defense:—

"I repeat my denial," said he, "of the charge with which I was assailed on a former evening. There are many noble Lords now present who well know how complete a justification I possess against all the accusations aimed at me. Nay, some of those who formed part of an administration with me, and acted with me then, sit now on the bench with my accusers, and must be convinced that all I said in my vindication is strictly true. What I did, I did with the concurrence and with the approbation of all my colleagues; but I would have done it, even had I differed from every man among them. Nay, I say that, acting conscientiously, so help me God, I could not have done otherwise than I did. While I have the approbation of my own conscience, I am ready to incur every risk, and submit to all the responsibility to which I am exposed by the faithful discharge of my duty. But what, I will ask, is the nature of the crime imputed to me? Why, that on the occasions in question I acted in obedience to his Majesty's commands. What would the noble Earl (Lord Grey) have thought of my conduct, if I had refused compliance? What kind of crime would the noble Lord have held me guilty of, if I had dared to disobey the positive commands of the Sovereign? I acted then upon my conscience, and to the best of my judgment: my rule of conduct is the same on this occasion. I will act on my oath, in despite of the opposition of the whole world. It is my opinion, so help me God, that there is a most material amendment in his Majesty. It is little more than forty-eight hours since I had an opportunity of ascertaining this improvement;[1] and I trust in God that my gracious master will live many years, to be, as he has always been, the benefactor of his subjects."

In delivering this very indiscreet address, which takes a false issue on the fact, Lord Eldon really seems to have thought that he was sitting in the Court of Chancery, and

[1] In an account of the same interview, in a private letter to Sir William, he says,—" I saw the King on Saturday for much more than an hour. He is not well, and, I fear, requires time. In the midst of this state, it is impossible to conceive how right, how pious, how religious, how everything he should be, he is, with the distressing aberrations I allude to."—Not quite so encouraging!

lecturing a young barrister who would not dare to reply to him.

Lord Grey, as might have been expected, rose with calm dignity, and, by an appeal to dates and events which could not be controverted, made good his charge. After taunting him with his delusive language about the King's speedy recovery, he thus proceeded:—

"In performing what I conceive to be my duty to your Lordships and to my country, I am bound to arraign the noble and learned Lord for an offense little short of high treason. In bringing this accusation against the noble and learned Lord, I will not conceal that it is my intention to deal as severely with him as I possibly can; but, at the same time, as justly as the importance of the question and the solemnity of the case require. The rigid and impartial line of public duty I shall strictly observe towards the noble and learned Lord, determined that neither his agitation nor his tears shall deter me from arraigning him, if I shall find that he has been guilty of what I can not but consider all but high treason. The noble and learned Lord asks, 'What is the designation of that crime which a public servant would commit in refusing to obey the just commands of his Sovereign?' I acknowledge that would be treason to the Sovereign; but with my answer I beg leave to couple another question: What, I ask, would be the character, what the appropriate punishment, of his offense, who, knowing his Sovereign to be actually at the time incompetent,— who, in the full conviction of his notorious and avowed incapacity, and while he was under medical care and personal restraint,—should come here and declare that there was no necessary suspension of the royal functions;—who, under such circumstances, should, in his Majesty's name, and under the pretext of his Majesty's commands, put the royal seal to acts which could not be legal without his Majesty's full and complete acquiescence? What, I ask, would be the crime of that man who should venture to take such a course? I do not hesitate to pronounce his offense to be treason against the Constitution and the country.—With respect to the conduct of the noble and learned Lord on those former occasions to which I before alluded, it is now in evidence before your Lordships, that, as well in the year 1801 as 1804, the King's name had been used to public acts, and

the royal authority exercised, at a time when, according
to the evidence, his Majesty was personally incapable of
exercising his royal functions. His Majesty's malady began
about the 12th of February, 1801, and continued without
remission till the beginning of March. Your Lordships
will recollect that councils had been held, and members
sworn in, during that interval. The foreign relations of
the country, too, had meanwhile undergone a material
change. Sweden, which had been our ally, assumed a
hostile aspect, and acceded to the Northern Confederacy;
and even considerable expeditions were equipped and sent
out. Subsequent to that date, too, about the 17th of
March, another council was held, and members sworn at
it. Here I must beg the attention of your Lordships to
the circumstance that, about the 14th or 16th of June following,
even after he had been declared to be fully recovered,
his Majesty had a relapse, which, though it did
not last long, required the aid of attendance. All this
took place in 1801.—In 1804 I was a member of the other
House, and, from the anxiety felt by the public upon the
subject, I considered it my duty to put a question to the
noble Viscount on the cross bench (Sidmouth), then a
member of the other House, respecting the state of his
Majesty's health; and, though my noble friend at first endeavored
to shift and evade the question, upon being
pressed he ended with saying that 'there was no necessary
suspension of the royal functions.' To a similar question
put in this House, the noble Lord upon the woolsack returned
a similar declaration. Certainly the noble Lord
opposite (Lord Liverpool) had made such a declaration,
and that was afterwards confirmed by the noble Lord on
the woolsack, in this House. Now, by referring to the
evidence of Dr. Heberden, your Lordships will find that
at that very period his Majesty had been ill, and continued
in that state from the 12th of February, 1804, to the 23rd
of April following, when, I believe, he presided at a council—a
circumstance which most probably was considered as
sufficient proof that his Majesty was well enough to resume
his royal authority. Within that interval, viz., on the
9th of March, a commission was issued under his Majesty's
Great Seal for giving the royal assent to fifteen different
bills which had passed the two Houses. But still more—
the noble and learned Lord had, on the 5th of March, an

interview with his Majesty, in consequence of which, he felt himself warranted in declaring to your Lordships that his Majesty's intellects were sound and unimpaired. But will this House consider a hasty opinion, formed during such an interview, which may have taken place at a lucid interval, sufficient to outweigh the evidence, upon oath, of physicians regularly and constantly in attendance? Will you not, on the contrary, be convinced that it would be a direct breach of the Constitution for the highest officer in his Majesty's service to venture, under such circumstances, even during a lucid interval, to take his Majesty's pleasure upon high matters of state? I will put it even to the noble and learned Lord himself, whether, in the case of a private individual, who should have continued, from the 12th of February to the 23rd of April, in a state of lunacy, and might within that period have been induced by an attorney to make a will, that noble Lord would consider such a will valid? If the transaction should subsequently be submitted to the Court of Chancery, what would be the feelings of the Court? what its just reprobation of the conduct of the attorney?— The charge, therefore, which I have to make upon the noble Lord before your Lordships, and in the face of the country, is this—that he has culpably made use of the King's name without the King's sanction, and criminally exercised the royal functions when the Sovereign was laboring under a moral incapacity to authorize such a proceeding; and with such a transaction in your view, I will ask your Lordships whether you will suffer this bill to pass without making effectual provision to prevent the recurrence of similar circumstances? whether, if you should omit to make such provision, you will perform your duty to the public, whose interest you are bound solemnly to secure and to protect? In the evidence of Dr. Reynolds it appears that, when the King removed to Kew, in 1804, he had himself ceased to attend him,—and for this reason, that 'it would have a better appearance with the public.' It was also apparent from the evidence, that his Majesty was then, and till October continued to be, in such a state as to require medical attendance. I am prepared also to assert, and challenge the noble and learned Lord to deny the fact, that Dr. Simmons and his attendants had not only been in attendance, but exercised control over his Majesty, until the 10th of June. For my own part, I shall never consent to suffer a Lord Chancellor, a Lord Keeper, or any man, or set of men, however great or distinguished, to possess himself or themselves of the royal authority under such circumstances, and exercise the functions of the Sovereign."

Lord Sidmouth took upon himself the responsibility of all that had been done in 1801 and 1804; but Lord Moira renewed the charge against Lord Eldon, and contrasted his conduct with that of Mr. Pitt in 1788, who had never once acted in the King's name when the King was incompetent.

Lord Eldon again rose, and said:—

"I can not forbear to observe how unfair it is to select me individually from the Ministers of 1801 and 1804, and make me the constant object of attack. Noble lords should have done me the justice to state that the course then adopted was upon the opinion, not of myself individually, but of the Administration generally; upon the unanimous opinion, I am proud to say, of many great and honorable men with whom I then acted. I think I could satisfy any candid man of the propriety of my conduct both in 1801 and in 1804. In 1801 I had not been a member of the Government till the 14th of April, when I accepted the Seals in circumstances wherein I could have no motive for it but the commands of his Majesty: and after the 14th of April I knew of no act done which would fall within the objection advanced on the other side. In 1804, several distinguished noblemen, now present among your Lordships, were members of the Cabinet: one of them was a noble Lord opposite (Earl St. Vincent), who was then First Lord of the Admiralty, and who, after being present at the examination of the physicians, concurred with the rest of the Cabinet in the conduct then pursued. The physicians having been all agreed that on the 9th of March his Majesty was fully competent to do the act which they had advised him to perform, the question now is, whether, under that medical authority, I was right in doing what I did for the transaction of most important business, or whether I ought to have left the country to shift for itself. If I had entertained the smallest doubt of his Majesty's competency to direct a commission for giving the royal assent to the bills which then awaited that sanction, I should have done one of two things: either I should have taken upon myself to affix the Great Seal to that commission and have applied to Parliament for an indemnity, or I should have come to the House and made the same declaration as on the 1st of November, 1810. And, even if the evidence of the physicians had been less decided than it was, I assert it to be most important to the Sovereign that a Chancellor be not wholly determined by medical opinions, so as to suspend the royal authority where he himself thinks the King fully competent to exercise it. It does not follow, because the physicians all concurred in the acts then done, that I am guilty of any inconsistency in saying now, that, whatever might be the report of the King's physicians, I would not consent, on that mere report, to dethrone his Majesty, while I myself, in my judgment and conscience, believed the King adequate to the discharge of the royal functions. I must be permitted to state, that the great man who was then at the head of the Administration (Mr. Pitt) afterwards expressed some surprise when he found that *it had been my fixed resolution never to see his Majesty at any time when he could be considered under the control of others, or in presence of any persons who might be considered as exercising any control over him.* My interviews with his Majesty at that time were always in the absence of such persons; and it was my firm conviction that I was warranted in the course that was then adopted. I knew the dangers of this proceeding, but I knew my duty too, and had determined to see my Sovereign, and judge of his complaint, when he was as free from restraint as any of his subjects whom it has been my painful duty to examine under similar circumstances. This was very hazardous to myself; but I did my duty without being deterred by fear of consequences. His Majesty, on the 9th of March, understood the duty which I had to perform better than I did myself; this I believe I can prove. If I *did* act wrong, it was with the best intentions, and those will acquit me in the sight of God, if not in the opinion of my country."

Earl Grey, to justify his selection of a particular Minister, on this occasion rejoined, that—

"The Constitution of the country always selects for responsibility the individual Minister who does any particular act; and it was upon this ground that he had singled out the Lord Chancellor from the rest of his colleagues upon a question of affixing the Great Seal. For this he was individually responsible. The Constitution knew nothing of the committee called a Cabinet. Every individual Minister was responsible for his own conduct. If ever the time should come when it might be thought necessary to call the serious attention of the House to the conduct of the noble and learned Lord, the House must determine simply on the propriety of his conduct, and not upon the purity of his intentions, or the coincidence of other people with his opinions. As to the statement of the noble and learned Lord about his never visiting his Majesty in the presence of persons under whose control he might be supposed to be, he should only observe, that it was not the removal of the persons appointed to control his Majesty from the room in which he saw his Chancellor—it was not their removal from an antechamber, that would justify a Minister in acting as the noble and learned Lord had done. The absence of all *idea of control* from his *mind* was necessary, before the Chancellor could have, in his name, exercised the royal authority, and adopted a line of conduct which, in this case, he could consider as nothing less than usurpation. It appeared from the evidence, that from the 12th of February up to the 23rd of April, and even so late as the 10th of June in that year, his Majesty had been attended by Dr. Simmons and his servants, who did exercise a control over the mind of his Majesty. He did not mean to say that this control was constantly exerted, or that those persons were present when the Sovereign was visited by the noble and learned Lord; but there was a knowledge in the King's mind that those persons were in attendance, and could be brought forward to control him whenever it might be judged necessary. If such had been the circumstances in a former case, he should now call upon their Lordships, as peers of the realm, as hereditary guardians of the Constitution and of the liberties of the people, not to suffer this usurpation to pass without taking effectual measures to prevent the recurrence of such conduct in future. On the 7th of May, 1804, at the time his Majesty was thus under control, the union of the two great political rivals (Mr. Fox and Mr. Pitt) had been in contemplation, but had been prevented. This too was a subject for serious consideration."

Lord Grenville's amendment being negatived by 139 against 122,[1] the clause appointing the Queen's Council came next,—when Lord King formally moved the omission of Lord Eldon's name:—

"The noble and learned Lord," he said, "had been repeatedly charged, in the course of these debates, with a violation of his duty as Lord Chancellor. After the unanswerable manner in which the charge had been established against the noble and learned Lord, it was unnecessary to enter into the subject further than simply to repeat that it had been proved by the evidence of the King's physicians, taken on oath, that in 1804 his Majesty's illness had continued from the 12th of February to the 23rd of April, in which interval the Great Seal was affixed to two commissions, one dated the 9th, and one the 23rd, of March; and that the Lord Chancellor had also signified his Majesty's consent to the Duke of York's Estate Bill, being a public bill affecting the interests of the Crown. The noble and learned Lord, having thus, in consequence of his own erroneous view and strong bias, been instrumental to deceive the House and the country in 1804, was an improper person to be placed on the Queen's Council, because, if appointed to a seat in it, he, from his high station and legal character, would be the party to decide on the competence of the Sovereign."[2]

Hansard represents that Lord Eldon remained silent, and merely gives the numbers when the House divided; but I have been informed by a gentleman who was then standing on the steps of the throne, "that his Lordship, in spite of his usual self-command, was thrown into a transport of passion; that he spoke some words in an angry tone, which were hardly intelligible; that it was an affair only of a few moments, and that, not having time to cool, he rashly called for a division,—thinking that Lord King would walk below the bar alone."[3]

[1] 18 Parl. Deb. 1084. I have been told by a peer who was present at this debate, that Lord Grey having called Lord Eldon on one occasion his "noble and learned friend," Lord Eldon interrupted him, and said, "How can any one call me *friend* who charges me with such villainy?"

[2] Ibid. 1086.

[3] My informant adds,—"I was next to Mr. Hand, the purse-bearer, who

The CONTENTS were 54!!! the NOT CONTENTS 129; and a most bitter protest, fully reciting the evidence of the physicians, and the acts of parliament passed while the Sovereign was incompetent, was signed by Lord Grey, Lord Lauderdale, Lord Holland, Lord Erskine, and other Peers.[1]

In the House of Commons, too, a violent attack was made on Lord Eldon by Mr. Whitbread for having usurped royal authority during the King's incapacity, particularly in the year 1804. His Lordship complained of having been feebly defended by his colleagues; but there was a majority in his favor of 198 to 81.[2]

These assaults upon him were greatly encouraged by the extreme sensibility he exhibited under them. Soon afterwards he said to Lord Sidmouth,—"I am like a thing that is raw; why am I thus singled out?" "First," replied his Lordship, "because you are eminent; and, secondly, because you are sore."[3]

The recollection of these scenes caused to Lord Eldon a distress of mind which shows that he possessed much more sensibility than he had credit for with those who thought that he cared for nothing but present power and emolument. When years had gone by, he was walking with a contemporary, likewise a high dignitary in the law, to whom he said, "No doubt the world regard me as a prosperous and happy man: the *prosperity* I admit; but the *happiness* I deny." Being asked to explain how he could be unhappy in the midst of all his prosperity, he alluded to the division on Lord King's motion, saying, "It makes me very unhappy, as I fear it will lead posterity to entertain a very unfavorable opinion of my conduct and character."[4]

---

[1] 18 Parl. Deb. 1031–1087. In the midst of this badgering he thought himself very ill-used, not only by the Opposition, but by his old colleagues and by the royal family. Thus he wrote to his brother, Sir William:—"I am hardly in my right mind upon what is passing; and when I am attacked day by day, and every man who was with me in Administration in 1804 is obstinately holding silence, and the whole royal family, whose protestations of gratitude my boxes teem with, are among my enemies, God help me, if I had not the means of proving that I have nothing to fear."

[2] 19 Parl. Deb. 87.   [3] Life of Lord Sidmouth, iii. 37.

[4] The gentleman from whom I have the above anecdote shrewdly adds,—"This may have been the indulgence, without any apparent motive, of his habit of canting; but if it contains any portion of truth, it proves that he was greatly disturbed by his master's temper so completely getting the better of his judgment."

I think Lord Eldon would have done better by resting his defense on the necessity of the case, and the difficulties and evils which must have arisen from following a contrary course. The fact that he did allow the King to sign commissions for passing bills,—to swear in privy councillors,—and to do other important acts of state, when his Majesty was wholly incompetent from mental disease, was before abundantly clear, but is now placed beyond all controversy by the correspondence upon the subject recently communicated to the public. For example, the period beginning from the 14th of April, 1801, is one of "the two fits of insanity," in which Lord Eldon, in his letter on the dissolution of Parliament in 1807, says that he "attended him." But I must repeat my humble opinion, that between the acts of an English sovereign, for which there is always a responsible adviser, and the execution of a deed, will, or contract by a private individual, there is no strict analogy; and that, "regard being had" to all the circumstances of the case, both in 1801 and 1804 Lord Eldon deserved well of the country by assuming the competency of the King, instead of suspending the functions of the executive government, conjuring up "the phantom," and having debates on the Regency Bill, which would have been stopped before they had made much progress by the King's entire recovery. Indeed, those ought to be the least scrupulous who think that the constitutional mode of proceeding upon such an emergency is for the Heir Apparent to take the regency upon himself as a matter of right—until the moment arrives when the afflicted Sovereign may be properly superseded. Any such attempt at either of the periods in question to vest in the Prince of Wales the exercise of the prerogatives of the Crown would have produced civil war.

The Regency Bill having passed both Houses, the Great Seal was put to a mock commission for giving the royal assent to it; and the Lord Chancellor, with other dignitaries named in it, having summoned the Commons to the Bar, he said, " My Lords and Gentlemen, by the commands, and by virtue of the powers and authority to us given by the said commission, we do declare and notify his Majesty's royal assent to the Act in the said commission mentioned, and the clerks are required to pass the same in the usual form

not like some we have known, who *seem at least* to be reckless of reputation, present or future."

and words." Accordingly, the Deputy Clerk of the Crown having read the title of the Bill, and the clerk-assistant of the Parliaments having bowed to the empty throne, the words were shouted out, " *Le Roi le veut,*" whereupon the Regency was established.[1]

Lord Eldon had laid his account with being now "restored to a life of privacy at sweet Encombe," of which he talked with seeming delight, but to which he looked forward with real dismay. The Ministers and the Opposition had fought the Regency Bill to its last stage, in the full belief that as soon as it passed they were to change

[1] 18 Parl. Deb. 1124.

At the end of the rule of George III., I may appropriately introduce Lord Eldon's opinion of him, and some anecdotes respecting him, as related to me by a gentleman who lived with Lord Eldon on the most familiar terms for many years:—"He often declared, upon his honor, that he thought his old master had more wisdom than all his Ministers conjointly,—an opinion which I have heard him support by declaring that he could not remember having taken to him any state paper of importance which he did not alter, nor one which he did not alter for the better. But it ought to be added, that this opinion of the superior wisdom of George III. was qualified by the addition, 'Not that I mean to assert that he would have been more wise if his opportunity of gaining knowledge had not been greater than that of any of his servants. But what is the experience of the oldest of them in comparison of his? And though his manner of stating the result of that experience is calculated to mislead casual observers, yet those who will divest his matter of his manner must come to the conviction that it has been gathered by long and laborious application of powers of no ordinary strength.'"

"After the King's mind had become a wreck, and when its native strength could be traced only by the 'method of madness,' Lord E. would sometimes describe it, after he had been at the Queen's Council. The following is an instance of this, of which I retain a perfectly clear recollection :—It was agreed, he related, that if any strong feature of the King's malady appeared during the presence of the council, Sir H. Halford should, on receiving a signal from me, endeavor to recall him from his aberrations; and, accordingly, when his Majesty appeared to be addressing himself to two of the persons whom he most favored in his early life, long dead, Sir H. observed, 'Your Majesty has, I believe, forgotten that —— and —— both died many years ago.' 'True,' was the reply, 'died to you and to the world in general; but not to me. You, Sir H., are forgetting that I have the power of holding intercourse with those whom you call dead. Yes, Sir H. H.,' continued he, assuming a lighter manner, 'it is in vain, as far as I am concerned, that you kill your patients. Yes, Dr. Baillie;—but Baillie—Baillie,' pursued he with resumed gravity. 'I don't know. He is an anatomist; he dissects his patients; and then it would not be a resuscitation only, but a re-creation; and that, I think, is beyond my power.'"

"After his Majesty had, in 1807, changed the Ministry which was so unpalatable to him, I re-appearing as Chancellor in my former official attire, the King asked, in a whisper, 'My Lord, is not that the *old* wig?' and receiving the reply, 'It is, Sir, the old wig,'—the rejoinder was, 'I say, Lord C., why did *you* keep *an old Whig?*'"

places,—the former striving to prolong the interregnum, and to curtail the power of the Regent—the latter, to invest him as soon as possible with the unrestricted exercise of all the prerogatives of the Crown. But to the unspeakable surprise of both parties, on the day before the mockery of giving the royal assent to the bill, his Royal Highness wrote a letter to Mr. Perceval, in which he declared that, "actuated solely by filial duty and affection, and dreading lest any act of his might in the smallest degree interfere with the progress of his father's recovery, he felt it incumbent upon him to communicate his intention not to remove from their stations those whom he found there as his Majesty's official servants."—This intelligence did not cause either high exultation or deep disappointment. The good faith and political steadiness of the Prince were not yet suspected, and it was believed that the change of Administration was only decently deferred till it was seen whether the predictions of the King's speedy recovery would be verified, or at all events till the expiration of the restrictions imposed by the Regency Bill.

Some said that the Chancellor had already gained over the Prince, and a letter was quoted, which his Royal Highness had written to him a few months before, respecting the Princess Charlotte, in which this courteous language occurred: "I trust to the very particular attention which has marked your Lordship's proceedings through the whole of this business, to take the most suitable course of conveying to the King, with the most profound respect and duty on my part, the feelings with which I am impressed on this occasion by his Majesty's most gracious and condescending attention to me." But, in reality, the zealous and factious manner in which Lord Eldon and Mr. Perceval had taken part with the Princess, and had printed "the Book" in her defense, still rankled in the Prince's heart; and they knew that, wishing to be revenged of them, he was only lying by for a favorable opportunity to cashier them. Accordingly, for some months there was undisguised enmity between the Regent and his Ministers. He talked of them disparagingly, and gave dinners at Carlton House to the Whigs. He would not even accept a vote offered him of a sum of money to provide for his household—intimating that he postponed all such arrangements till he could have his "early friends" in office about him. The Queen and Lord Eldon, on the other hand, did all in their power to defeat this purpose,—their most powerful weapon being the King's immediate resumption of his authority. On the 6th of February the Queen wrote a letter to Lord Eldon, thanking him "for the pleasing account of his Majesty's improvement since Friday;" and the physicians, at his request, sent a report to him, to be handed about, in which, considering the unhappy condition of the now dethroned Sovereign in their keeping, they strangely say, "We have it in command from his Majesty to express his personal regard to your Lordship, and the particular satisfaction he has felt from the circumstance of your Lordship being made one of her Majesty's Council,—not by your office of Lord Chancellor, but as Lord Eldon."[1]

But in the course of a few weeks, if hopes of the King's recovery really were entertained, they died away. It was felt that his reign was virtually at an end, and that those who wished to enjoy power must gain the favor of the Prince as if he already bore the title of George IV. Lord Eldon, with his usual sagacity, at once saw that the way to win his affections was by taking part against his wife. It was not very easy for the authors of "the Book" to do so; but soon after Lord Eldon and Mr. Perceval were in the situation of Chancellor and Prime Minister to the Regent, they refused to dine with the Princess at Blackheath,—they cut off all correspondence with her,—and they bought up at large prices the few copies of "the Book" which had got into circulation. When she found herself suddenly "cut" by them, without there having been hitherto any fresh imputation of misconduct against her, she complained loudly of the "baseness of mankind."[2] We shall see how the Regent was softened towards his Ministers, and how he appreciated and rewarded their sacrifices and their exertions in his service.

[1] It would be curious to know whether his Majesty had been informed of Lord King's motion to exclude him from the Council, and what his Majesty thought of it.
[2] There is no evidence of their having changed the tone of their conversation respecting her past conduct, except Lord Eldon's declaration to Lord Grey, "that his opinion was, and always had been, that, though she was not with child, she had supposed herself to be with child." (Life of Sir S. Romilly, iii. 104.)

Meanwhile, they applied themselves with diligence and ability to their official duties, and continued to rise in public estimation.

The session began for regular business on the 12th of February, with a speech delivered by Lord Eldon in the Regent's name, containing this graceful conclusion:—

"We are commanded by his Royal Highness to declare to you that it is the most anxious wish of his heart that he may be enabled to restore unimpaired into the hands of his Majesty the government of his kingdom; and thus his Royal Highness earnestly prays that the Almighty may be pleased, in His mercy, to accelerate the termination of a calamity so deeply lamented by the whole nation, and so peculiarly afflicting to his Royal Highness himself."[1]

The first important matter brought forward in the House of Lords was the abuse of the power of filing *ex officio* informations for libel. Sir Vicary Gibbs, who, in 1807, had succeeded Sir Arthur Pigot as Attorney General, had instituted an immense number of prosecutions against the press; and, when he resolved to punish a newspaper, he made it a rule to include as defendants, who were to be fined and imprisoned, or perhaps pilloried, all persons, without regard to age, sex, or calling, who, under family settlements or otherwise, had any share in the proprietorship.[2] Lord Eldon, when public prosecutor, had never himself done anything personally harsh, and I think he could not have been aware of Sir Vicary's mode of proceeding when he wrote the following letter to Sir William Scott, regretting that there had been too much forbearance in this department:—

"As to the prosecution of the 'Morning Chronicle,' and as to *your friend*, Cobbett, I know what I should have done as to those publications long ago, if I had been Attorney General; but it seems to me that ever since my time it has been thought right to leave the Government's character, and individual character, without the protection

[1] 18 Parl. Deb. 1147.
[2] I remember much compassion being excited by an old widow lady, of the name of Mrs. Mary Vint, who appeared on the floor of the Court of King's Bench, with about fifty others, to plead to informations against them. She had been residing in the country, and never even read any numbers of the journal, from which, under her husband's will, she drew a small subsistence.

of the law enforced, because I had proved its efficacy when it was called into exertion. I am very sore upon this subject; I have growled and grumbled about it till I am weary."

Incited by his own peevish disposition, and encouraged by his superiors, Mr. Attorney had gone on multiplying *ex officio* informations till much public indignation was caused by his severity. Lord Holland now moved for a return of the number filed, and the proceedings under them. He questioned the legality of *ex officio* informations for libel, and he strongly reprobated the manner in which the process had been abused, animadverting upon the statute lately obtained, which enabled the Attorney General to arrest those whom he prosecuted before trial; and, likewise on the partial system of striking special juries which then prevailed.

Lord Eldon ably and successfully defended the right of the Attorney General to prosecute libelers by *ex officio* information; but the rest of his speech I read with regret. He maintained that the power of arresting the defendant when an *ex officio* information was filed was fit to be given, and to be exercised; and he stood up strenuously for the old mode of striking special juries by *selection*, which was afterwards effectually rectified by Sir Robert Peel:—

"He believed that no Attorney General had prosecuted more libels than it had fallen to his lot to prosecute. He acted on a conviction, that the publication of libel was one of the most formidable weapons then wielded against the Constitution, and that it was an engine which was directed to the subversion of the government of the country. It was his decided opinion, that the mere fact of the number of prosecutions having increased was not a sufficient ground for inducing them to accede to the motion of the noble Lord. With respect to including all the proprietors of a newspaper in the *ex officio* information, he was desirous of stating, that the principle which governed him on these occasions was to prosecute all the parties implicated in the publication of the libel; and he had uniformly found, that by extinguishing the papers he got rid of the authors. The present motion was one which he felt it incumbent on him to oppose, because an acquiescence in such a motion would, in some degree, sanction a suspicion that there was something in the administration of justice which the House considered so far improper as to need some interference."[1]

It seems wonderful to think, that so few years ago such sentiments could be uttered by a mild, moderate, and really good-natured man, who justly expected that they would be applauded by a large majority of the audience he addressed. Lord Holland's motion found only twelve supporters.[2] I believe there is no peer who would now hold such language; and I am sure, if there were, he would be equally condemned by both sides. The general improvement ought to make us look with indulgence on the individuals who spoke and acted in a very different state of public feeling respecting libels.—I think no one will deny the improved respectability of the press under milder treatment.

The Lord Chancellor's efforts were next called forth by a dangerous bill,—to take away the punishment of death from the offense of stealing in a dwelling-house to the value of forty shillings. In answer to the reasoning of Lord Holland and Lord Erskine, that the punishment was wholly disproportionate to the offense, and that, if not inflicted, sentence of death ought not to be pronounced, in cases where it was never meant to be carried into execution, he said, "he used to take similar views of the subject, before *observation* and *experience* had matured his judgment: since, however, he had learned to listen to these great teachers in this important science, his ideas had greatly changed, and he saw the wisdom of the principles and practice by which our criminal code was regulated. The Bill having taken away the pain of death, allowed the Judge great latitude of discretion in measuring out the punishments to be substituted for it; but, after the most serious consideration, it was the conviction of his mind, that, as long as human nature remained what it was, the apprehension of death would have the most powerful co-operation in deterring from the commission of crimes; and he thought it unwise to withdraw the salutary influence of that terror."[3] He concluded without intimating any intention of extending the punishment of death—which, to be consistent, he ought to have done—

[1] 19 Parl. Deb. 158.   [2] Ib. 174.   [3] 20 Ib. 296.

to petty larceny and to common assaults. The bill was rejected by a majority of 27 to 10.[1]

Lord Donoughmore's motion for the Catholics was this year supported by Dr. Bathurst, the Bishop of Norwich. On him the Lord Chancellor was particularly severe—taunting him with not paying proper respect to the Book of Common Prayer. He said, "he could hardly tell where he was,—he could not think himself in a British House of Lords when he heard some things uttered that night. He denied that the authority of Archbishop Wake, which had been quoted, was in favor of concession; he had read something of Archbishop Wake (having been himself in early life intended for the Church), and he could quote him page by page. He could also quote Fenelon on some of these subjects."[2] Professing high respect for Mr. Pitt, he declared, rather jeeringly, that he never could discover what the securities were by which that statesman proposed to guard the Established Church; and he scorned the *Veto* which had been lately propounded by Lord Grenville in a "Letter to Lord Fingal."[3] It is creditable to Lord Eldon that his anti-Catholic zeal was unabated, although the Regent was understood yet to retain his early opinions in favor of emancipation. There were certain concessions which he would have made out of loyal deference to the Prince on the throne, but his religious scruples, I am convinced, he never would have sacrificed.

The only other subject on which he spoke during the present session was one in which he was personally interested, and which caused him serious annoyance—the increasing arrear of judicial business in the Court of Chancery, and in the House of Lords. Here he was to blame, but not at all in the way his accusers alleged. Years ago he ought to have spontaneously pointed out the evil and applied a remedy. The country had long outgrown its judicial establishments, and the antiquated procedure

---

[1] 20 Parl. Deb. 303. It is little creditable to the Whig peers that they made so poor a muster, for they all now pretended zealously to support Sir S. Romilly in mitigating the severity of the penal code; but I presume the division did not take place till the approach of the hour for dinner, when a party struggle alone can keep up a decent attendance on either side.

[2] This is a very rare instance of Lord Eldon pretending to a knowledge of anything but law books, for he was greatly above the affectation of universality.   [3] 20 Parl. Deb. 676.

preserved in Westminster Hall was unsuited to a state of society quite different from that in which it had been originally framed. In the Court of Chancery there were still only two Judges, the Lord Chancellor and the Master of the Rolls, as in the time of Edward I., and for ages past not the slightest attempt had been made to render proceedings in that Court more simple, economical, and efficacious,—while its contentious jurisdiction had been greatly extended, and the property administered in it had increased ten-fold.—Again, in the early periods of our judicial history, a few days in a year were sufficient to enable the House of Lords, with the assistance of the Judges, satisfactorily to discharge its duties as the Court of the last resort; but now, from English equity appeals, which were formerly unknown, and the enormous influx of appeals from Scotland and Ireland in consequence of the union with those kingdoms, although comparatively little help could be obtained from the Judges,—the Chancellor sitting in the House of Lords had nearly sufficient occupation there during the whole of the forensic year.

There is not the slightest pretense for saying that Lord Eldon neglected his judicial functions. In critical times of rare occurrence, he naturally considered his *intriguing functions* more important, but the Administration being safe, he devoted himself with the most unremitting assiduity to determine the causes of the suitors which came before him. He often doubted when he might have safely decided, and he might have got through his paper more rapidly—but he actually did dispose of more business than any one judge could reasonably be called upon to undertake. Yet, having been ten years Chancellor, he had introduced no reform, although he daily saw justice denied to hundreds. For a long while, in the Court of Chancery, no cause could be regularly heard by him, the whole of his time being occupied with motions and irregular attempts to force an opinion from him. In the House of Lords there were depending 296 appeals, and 42 writs of error, which could not on a moderate computation be disposed of in less than seven sessions of Parliament.

The outcry was at last so loud, that Lord Eldon slowly and reluctantly referred the subject to a Select Committee of the House of Lords, in which he moved, "That, to reduce the arrear, it would be expedient for the House to sit, for judicial business, at least three days a week during the session; and that, for securing the Lord Chancellor's attendance in the House of Lords, an additional judge should be appointed in the Court of Chancery." Little good being expected from these palliatives, a motion was made in the House of Commons for a similar committee. Sir S. Romilly, in supporting it, bore testimony to Lord Eldon's judicial merits, saying, "The motion would not convey, either directly or indirectly, any mark of censure upon the noble and learned Lord; and he did assure the House that nothing could give him greater concern than to be thought to consent to any motion which could in any way be construed into a desire to reflect upon the conduct of that noble and learned Lord. No man had experienced more uniform acts of kindness than himself from the noble and learned Lord. Indeed, his general attention to the Bar, his conciliatory demeanor, and his strict love of justice, had endeared him to all the gentlemen who practiced in that Court. A man more eminently qualified, in point of talents and learning, for all parts of his profession, he knew not; and he most firmly believed that he never had his equal in point of anxiety to do justice to the suitors of the Court. If he had any fault, it was an over-anxiety in that respect." The committee was carried by the casting vote of the Speaker, but it had made no progress when its labors were terminated by the prorogation.

Lord Eldon was, and to the end of his official career continued, much annoyed by these discussions. He now wrote to his friend Dr. Swire:—

"I need not tell you that I have been sorely goaded and vexed and tormented this session; but I defy all my foes, and a man can not have had the duties to execute in life which I have had to discharge without having many and bitter foes." He then adds (with what sincerity the reader must determine for himself) that he continues, *much against his inclination*, to retain the Great Seal, and to encounter all these evils purely from his attachment to the good old King, and in the hope of again seeing him on the throne, being resolved, as soon as that hope had fled, to retire into private life, and to take *a ride to Eldon*:—

"Of my poor old master I don't despair, though I do not confidently hope, about him. When I give up the Seal, you may look upon that as an act of despair: for though the Regent has certainly conducted himself to *me*, personally, in every respect as well as I could desire, I serve only that my master may find me at my post if he returns to his; and when I give up the hope of that, I have done. I can not quit the expectation of a ride with you yet to Eldon, and nobody can say how soon that may be."

It seems to me that, being at the head of the Queen's Council, and possessing her Majesty's entire confidence, he wished to preserve the state of the King's health a mystery in his own keeping,—to be turned to his own advantage. A letter to him from Lord Ellenborough respecting "the questions which we ought to put to the physicians," shows that he had been trying to repress the inquiries of all the other councillors,—while he had special reports made to himself:—

"MY DEAR LORD,

"I have had some conversation this evening with the two Archbishops. I own I am very much inclined to doubt the propriety of any opinion I may have formed, if it differs from yours; but agreeing, as I fully do, that our declaration to the Privy Council need only contain a brief, true, and distinct statement of the King's health, incumbered with as little further circumstance as possible, still I think that for our own information, and for our justification with the world, if it should be hereafter inquired of us what information we had in fact obtained at the time when our statement was made, that we should distinctly know, by precise questions put and answered, *what the King's ailment actually is, and by what symptoms and circumstances of conversation and conduct it is now manifested*,—and also, what is the description and character which we ought properly to ascribe to the *delusions* (as we call them) and what to the *irregularities* and extravagances of plans and projects of which we hear daily.

"This information, when obtained, is *for ourselves* and *to ourselves* only, unless Parliament should require it of us —and if they do, I own I should be sorry to own that we were possessed of no fuller and more distinct information than we are at present enabled to lay before them on this subject. I should be sorry that we should in the judgment of any appear to have inertly and insufficiently exercised a function of inquiry so important as that is which is delegated to us."[1]

The following minute report from the Duke of York to the Chancellor must have made him think of renouncing the Great Seal, or of changing his resolution to do so when the King's recovery was hopeless:—

"Upon my arrival yesterday morning, I found his Majesty in the Queen's room. He appeared at first very much affected at seeing me, and expressed himself in the kindest and most affectionate manner upon my reappointment to the chief command of the army; but soon flew off from that subject, and then ran on, in perfect good humor, but with the greatest rapidity and with little or no connection, upon the most trifling topics, at times hinting at some of the subjects of his delusion, in spite of all our endeavors to change the conversation. This continued the same during his ride and the whole of the Queen's visit in the afternoon; and though this morning his Majesty was quieter and less rapid in the change of his ideas, yet the topics of his conversation were equally frivolous.

"I was so much shocked at what I had observed both on Wednesday and during the different visits of yesterday, that I took an opportunity, when I left his Majesty yesterday evening, to have a conversation with Dr. Robert Willis, who very candidly stated to me his opinion, that his Majesty had lost ground this week, and that though he thought very seriously of the state of his bodily health, he was much more alarmed at the apparent frivolity, or rather imbecility, of his mind. He added, that something ought to be done; but that, in the present state of his Majesty's mind, it was in vain to hope that any conversation with him would be attended with any good effect."

In reality the unhappy King became worse and worse; and at a Council held at Windsor in the end of August, it was known that he had fallen into a state of incurable imbecility.

"Love oft hopes, when Reason would despair,"—

---
[1] April 3rd, 1811.

and perhaps Lord Eldon still was only desirous that *his old master*, remounting the throne, might find him at his post; but I can not help suspecting that this was a sight he never expected to see, and that he had made up his mind, *for the public good*, to remain at his post under George IV., *if he might*.

He and Mr. Perceval accordingly contemplated the fit measures to be taken at the important crisis when the restrictions on the Regent were to expire—which would be on the 1st of February, 1812, if Parliament had been sitting six weeks previously. Mr. Perceval, in a letter to the Chancellor soon after the last sitting of the Queen's Council, having expressed regret at not being able to have a personal interview with him, thus proceeds:—

"I must, however, content myself with opening the subject by letter, on which I should have had to communicate with you in person if we were to meet. It respects no less a matter than the meeting of Parliament. It must meet and sit, you know, for six weeks before the restrictions of the Regency Bill can expire. The day pointed out in the Act for their expiration is the 1st of February. If Parliament does not meet before Christmas, of course the restrictions must be prolonged from the 1st of February for six weeks from the date of its meeting. Under these circumstances, I think we can hardly pass over the next prorogation without knowing the Prince's pleasure, whether he thinks it so material that the Regency restrictions shall expire on the 1st of February, as to make it necessary that Parliament should meet before Christmas. This is a point so very much of feeling for H. R. H. himself, and in which he is so directly and personally interested, that I can not but think myself he ought to have it submitted to his most free decision, with as little opinion and advice from his servants upon the point as can be. But if he should determine, as he naturally may and probably will, that Parliament shall so meet as that the restrictions shall expire on the day mentioned, it is a pretty material consideration, on which we should form an opinion, whether it should not meet so long before Christmas as to enable us to arrange, before the Christmas vacation, the household and any other questions which Parliament may have to provide for.

. . . . . . "To conclude: upon these questions, and such as may be connected with them, I think it will be essentially necessary that we should have our Cabinet friends meet in force, either in the last week in September, or the first week of October; and they ought to know what the business is, and that it is probable they may be detained for a few days. I should like, therefore, to know from you what time, which would answer these purposes, would best suit you to be fixed for the assembling our Cabinet friends."

The object now was, instead of weakening the influence of the Regent by rumors of the King's speedy recovery, to strengthen it by a disclosure of his Majesty's actual condition. Accordingly, on the 5th of October, the "Declaration of the members of her Majesty's Council respecting the state of his Majesty's health" amounted in reality to a proclamation that there had been a demise of the Crown, and that George IV. had begun to reign—this being its language:—

"His Majesty's mental health appears to us to be materially worse than it was at the time of our last report, and, upon the grounds of the protraction of the disorder, the present state of it, the duration of accessions of the disorder, and the peculiar character which the disorder now assumes, his Majesty's recovery is represented as 'improbable' by one of the physicians, and as 'very improbable' by all the other physicians in attendance on his Majesty."[1]

The Regent, expressing satisfaction at the generous suggestion by his Ministers, of an early meeting of the Legislature, whereby the speediest end might be put to the restrictions which they had imposed upon his exercise of the royal authority, intimated his wish that the session should *not* begin sooner than was necessary for the dispatch of ordinary business.

On the 7th of January, the day appointed, Lord Eldon, in the name of the Regent, decently reminded the two Houses of "the indispensable duty of continuing to preserve for his Majesty the facility of resuming the personal exercise of his royal authority in the happy event of his recovery, so earnestly desired by the wishes and the

[1] 21 Parl. Deb. 50.

prayers of his family and his subjects." But it was well understood on all sides that the Prince of Wales, under the title of REGENT, was as firmly seated on the throne as if his father had been dead; no one thought of proposing a renewal of the restrictions; and it was generally expected that when the six weeks from the meeting of Parliament allowed by the Regency Act for that purpose had expired, all the great offices under the Crown would be in possession of the oft-disappointed Whigs, who at last, after a lapse of above half a century, having a favorable court, would see a return of the halcyon days enjoyed by their party from the death of Queen Anne till the accession of George III.

But, alas! alas! the Regent had secretly made up his mind forever to discard his "early friends," and permanently to retain as his Ministers the men who had long thwarted him in all his wishes, and for whom he had expressed and felt the strongest personal as well as political dislike. Various causes have been assigned for this revolution of sentiment. The most creditable one, and that which we are bound to suppose had considerable weight, was, that the military operations in the Peninsula had been going on prosperously under the present Administration; but this alone could not have prevailed, for Mr. Perceval was not looked upon as a great war minister; and sections of the Tory party, headed by Lord Castlereagh and Mr. Canning, were hostile to him, while he was hardly able to cope with the systematic opposition of Lords Grey and Grenville. A more probable solution is, the effect of the possession of royal power, which was supposed to have disinclined his Royal Highness to any concession to the Catholics or any extension of popular rights, and induced him to look with preference to those who were for carrying to the highest pitch the power of the Crown. His Royal Highness certainly did at a subsequent period manifest an entire change of opinion on the question of Catholic emancipation, and showed that he had become thoroughly reconciled to his father's high-prerogative principles of government; but I am inclined to think that as yet he was actuated only by personal motives. A lady of rank to whom he was now much attached was an enemy to the Whigs and their principles, and was supposed mainly to have induced her admirer to declare against them.¹ Perhaps, however, he was more swayed by hatred than by love. His ruling passion for many years was the desire to expose the failings of his wife—if possible to get rid of her—and at all events to degrade her. Mr. Perceval and Lord Eldon, instead of being the bitterest, most reckless, and most formidable opponents of his plans for this purpose, as they had been while her protector George III. was on the throne, he now sanguinely hoped to convert into partisans against her. They had actually ceased to be her advisers, or to have any intercourse with her. There is no reason to believe that, without fresh indiscretions on her part, either of them ever would have agreed to any prosecution against her; but from their late negative conduct the Regent might not unnaturally have hoped that they would positively assist him in the steps which he contemplated. I believe, likewise, that he labored under an erroneous belief that during the last year her cause had been taken up by the Whigs. One or two distinguished lawyers belonging to that party had been consulted by her when she was cast off by her former advisers; but Lords Grey and Grenville had always remained at a dignified distance from her, and would have spurned at the idea of turning her supposed wrongs into an engine of faction against the Government.

Whatever might be his Royal Highness's reasonings or motives, a few days before the restrictions were to expire he very clearly intimated his resolution to renounce the Whigs, by writing a letter to the Duke of York, in which, after stating that his sense of filial duty had originally induced him to retain his father's Ministers,—adverting to the recent successes in the Peninsula, and declaring his determination to persevere in the contest,—he said, "I

---

¹ Of this opinion was Sir S. Romilly. In referring to the judgment of the House of Lords in Miss Seymour's case, in 1806, he says,—"This decision was attended, some years afterwards, with consequences of considerable importance. It occasioned a great intimacy between the Prince and Lady Hertford, which ended with her entirely supplanting Mrs. Fitzherbert in the Prince's favor; and it produced that hostility towards the Catholics which the Prince manifested when he became Regent, and his determination to place his confidence in those Tory Ministers whom he had always before considered his personal enemies."—*Life of Romilly*, ii. 146. Again, when relating the events in the beginning of 1812, at which we have now arrived, Sir Samuel says, very significantly, "The Prince does not pass a day without visiting Lady Hertford."—Vol. iii. p. 12.

have no predilections to indulge, no resentments to gratify, no objects to attain, but such as are common to the whole empire. Having made this communication of my sentiments in this new and extraordinary crisis of our affairs, I can not conclude without expressing the gratification I should feel if some of those persons, with whom the early habits of my public life were formed, would strengthen my hands and constitute a part of my Government." He authorized the Duke to communicate these sentiments to Lord Grey, with liberty for him to make them known to Lord Grenville; but he added, in a postscript, "I shall send a copy of this letter immediately to Mr. Perceval."[1]

I am surprised that Lord Eldon, with his keen sagacity, did not immediately see that this offer could not possibly be entertained by the Whigs for a single instant, and that it was made with the sole view of rendering the desertion of them less odious. As soon as he was informed of it he wrote the following letter, which I think is very honorable to him, for he peremptorily refused to sanction such a preposterous coalition, although, if it had taken place, the Great Seal would have remained in his custody.

"Saturday.

"DEAR PERCEVAL,

"As it may not be absolutely impossible that, in the course of this day, during my absence at Windsor, something may pass, tending to a proposal to associate me in a talk with Lords G. and G. upon junction, permit me to state, in a few words, that my determination to take no part in that talk is founded upon the following reasons; and, if *necessity* requires it, you may so state to the Regent:—

"That I think it not consistent with my honor to take part in a negotiation for a junction, in which junction I can take no part. I can take no part in it—

"Because, having been twenty-nine years in Parliament without deviating, as far as I can recollect, from my principles with respect to the Constitution of the country and the means of supporting its Monarchy, there appears to have been, in that long course of years, no agreement in those principles between Lord Grey and myself.

[1] 22 Parl. Deb. 39.

"Because there was no such agreement between Lord Grey and Lord Grenville between 1783 and 1801.

"Because there has been no such agreement between them and myself since 1801.

"Because my decided opinion is, that all attempts at making strong Administrations upon broad bottoms must be known, to those who are practiced politicians, to be frauds upon the country originally,—and frauds which, whether such politicians know *that* or not, can no longer be effectually practiced upon the country. The great mass of the people, through many ranks of which I have passed, I know, hold the thing, and the men that are engaged in it, in utter detestation, producing absolute weakness in Government, and of course deeply affecting the interests of the Crown.

"Because the differences with respect to the Catholic question, American affairs, and bullion, are, in my opinion, too deep to be skinned over.

"Because, if that were not so, differences upon most essential points of government, avowed for thirty years, clearly establish that Lords G., G., and Lord Eldon '*non bene conveniunt.*'

"Because my situation is peculiar. Lord G—y said in debate, and Lord G—y, Lord G——e, and others who, if they come into Administration, must come into Administration along with them, have said, in their protest upon the Journals, what I can give no countenance to by coming into their assembly.'[1]

"Allow me to add, that you know how much my heart has been wrung with the difficulties of holding office, when I have been obliged, but I hope justified, in taking the painful part I have had to execute, with regard to the situation of my Sovereign and benefactor, my revered master. "Yours, my dear Perceval,
"ELDON."

He was soon tranquillized by a note from Mr. Perceval, saying, "The answer was a refusal—on public grounds—to have anything to do with us. The Prince sent to me immediately to show the answer, and to authorize me to say that I was to be continued Minister."

What other result could possibly have been expected?

[1] Referring to the protest upon the motion for excluding him from the Queen's Council.

Both parties were agreed upon the necessity of vigorously prosecuting the war against Napoleon, but upon the impending war with America, and upon every other existing question of foreign and domestic policy, they were completely at variance. Instead of a soothing compliment, a wanton insult seems to have been intended to Lord Grey and Lord Grenville, for they were called upon to strengthen his Royal Highness's hands by supporting all the measures of the present Government. "The very proposal, indeed," says Sir S. Romilly, "imports that a total sacrifice of honor and of character was a necessary qualification for entering into the Prince's service. He says in the letter that 'he has no predilection to indulge, and no resentment to gratify'—a most dangerous statement at the commencement of his reign, considering his past conduct and his past professions. It will be understood to mean, that 'there are no injuries he will not forgive, and no services he will not forget.'"[1]

At the time there was an unfounded belief that the offer to the Whig leaders was a subtle contrivance of Lord Eldon's. We certainly know that—"minister-maker" as he was—he had no hand in this intrigue; and there is even some reason to doubt whether, although Mr. Perceval had gained the Prince's unqualified confidence, the Chancellor was not still regarded at Carlton House with some remains of suspicion and dislike—which by his agreeable manners, however, he soon entirely dissipated.[2]

CHAPTER CCII.

CONTINUATION OF THE LIFE OF LORD ELDON TILL THE CONCLUSION OF THE GENERAL PEACE.

ON all occasions Lord Eldon now seemed penetrated with the same respect and affection for his "dear young master," the Prince Regent, which he had professed formerly for his "dear old master," George III. In the debate on a motion of Lord Boringdon's for

---

[1] Life, iii. 11. Sir Samuel, pleased with the attentions he had received from the Prince, had hitherto been inclined to think, and had spoken, well of him.   [2] See Twiss, i. 477, ch. xxxiii.

"the formation of an efficient Administration," in speaking to order, he was led by his zeal to be very disorderly in commenting on what had been said in a past debate, when a question had been asked "whether the letter purporting to come from the Prince Regent to the Duke of York was genuine?" Said Lord Eldon: "When on a former evening I saw a noble Lord stand up in his place with a newspaper in his hand, and proceed to ask questions of a Minister about a private letter written by my royal master, I confess my astonishment at what I conceive to be a most novel and unjustifiable proceeding." Being called to order by the Marquis of Douglas, he persisted in saying, "I again reprobate the production of a newspaper for the purpose of asking whether an article in it was a letter from the Prince Regent; and I declare, if any confidential servant of his Royal Highness had given an answer to such a question, I never after would have entered the same room with that person for the purposes of confidential advice." Lord Holland again speaking to order, the Chancellor said, "I never will act so unbecoming the person placed on the woolsack as to permit such language as I sometimes hear—for I am bold to assert, in the presence of all the noble lords present, that I never witnessed in the course of thirty years' parliamentary experience anything so monstrous and disorderly as the production of a newspaper in that House." [Here his Lordship was interrupted by loud and repeated cries of ORDER!]—*Marquis of Lansdowne.* "I never heard anything so disorderly as the language made use of by the noble and learned Lord on the woolsack,"—*Lord Chancellor.* "I shall always object to any observation being made in the House, having a reference to his Royal Highness, the Prince Regent, which in the strict course of parliamentary proceeding ought not to be applied to the King himself, whose representative he is, and I shall certainly always protest against the production of a newspaper." He was again stopped by cries of ORDER! and Lord Boringdon put an end to the altercation by saying, that "he considered the act of the Prince Regent in writing the letter the act of a responsible adviser."

At a later hour in the evening the Lord Chancellor made a regular speech; and to show that he was not hurt by what had passed, he was very jocular. "The noble Lord," said he, "wishes for a broad-bottomed Administration—in general the most mischievous of all Administrations. [A laugh.] I assure the noble Lords who seem to feel this allusion, that I do not mean to speak ill-naturedly of them. Somehow or other they have been for a long time out of humor with me: I am sorry for it, as I really wish them every happiness. As to the estimation in which the present Administration is held by the public, I believe that the people of this good-natured country are weak and foolish enough to honor us with their confidence. Good-natured people are always weak. But let the cause be what it may, so it happens, that the confidence of the country is possessed by the present Administration; and this certainly is no very good reason for addressing the Prince Regent to change it." He then reiterated his doctrine, that "the King, in choosing his servants, must be considered as acting without any adviser," and that "a Minister is only responsible for what happens *after* his own appointment,"—now generally allowed to be inconsistent with the constitutional maxim, that "the King can do no wrong."[1] Ministers had a majority of 165 to 72, and Lord Eldon saw himself more securely possessed of the Great Seal than he had ever before been; for under George III. he lived in perpetual dread that the mental infirmity of that monarch might so far increase as to render his exercise—real or apparent—of the powers of government impossible,—when a change of councils was always certainly anticipated.

Conscious that Dr. Swire, to whom he had announced his certain resignation, when he could no longer expect to hold the Seal under his "dear old master" must be a little scandalized to find him still in possession of the bauble, he sends his bosom friend the following very entertaining explanation of all that had happened:—

"And now, my dear Swire, allow me to discuss with you my present situation, and the strange, the unaccountable occurrences which have taken place in the last eighteen months. When my *dear old master*, under the severe dispensations of Providence, but such as I humbly must suppose to be right, because they are the dispensations of Providence, could no longer personally execute his great functions, I thought that I should have been as

[1] 22 Parl. Deb. 69.

able, as, most sincerely speaking, I was willing, to quit the labors which no man can endure, unless the same Providence shall sustain him with the blessings of health and composure of mind and temper, which are indeed but rarely to be looked for at any period of life, and at mine, very, very rarely indeed to be looked for.

"The medical men thought his Majesty's speedy recovery highly probable:—the Prince therefore thought that in duty to his father he could not dismiss his father's servants. How was it possible, that while he acted under such a feeling of duty to his father, his father's servants could refuse to act under him as the representative of his father? With wishes as anxious as ever man formed, I could not reconcile to myself the notion, that while the father's son so conducted himself, the father's most greatful servant could refuse to take his share in a state of things, which, for the father's sake, the son determined should remain undisturbed by him. So matters went on through the year of restricted Regency. Before the close of it, the Prince had totally altered his opinion of the men whom he had hated—and I have his own authority for believing that the kingdom produced no man whom he more hated than your friend, the writer of this letter. Though the prospect of his father's recovery had grown more gloomy, and though I fear it will never brighten, I must do him the justice to say, that he has always declared to me that he will never despair till his father ceases to live: and my own real opinion is, that whatever motives his friends or foes may, in their conjectures, ascribe his late conduct to, he has been principally governed by a feeling that, if his father should recover, he would never forgive himself if he suffered him to awake to a scene in which the father should see his servants discarded by his son. The same sentiment appears to me to have governed him with respect to the Catholic question, with regard to which, I believe that, after his father's death, he will act with a due regard to the established religion. But with the possibility before him, though the utter improbability, of his father's recovery, I believe the world would not induce him, as far as he is concerned, to countenance any measure that would shock his father's feelings, if, contrary to all expectation, he should recover. With such determinations, on his part, with reference to his father, daily and constantly proved to be most sincerely adopted by him in his intercourse with me, how could I possibly refuse to consent to what his entreaty pressed upon me, to remain in the service of a son so conducting himself towards the father to whom I owe so much? or how could I break up an Administration, which must be succeeded by another which would overturn all that I think right? God knows that we live in times when public office, if it is not vanity, is literally and truly labor and vexation of spirit, and how I get through ny share of it I know not :—*but God is very kind to me.* I have given you the outline of what has governed me in my conduct, and though I care not at all as to the opinion of the world in general. I should be deeply hurt if YOU could not approve it. Interest, or ambition, or even private wishes, have had nothing to do with it. I have believed myself to have been acting right, and I hope in God that I have been so acting."

I must do Lord Eldon the justice, however, to say that he did not attempt to pour forth such hypocritical cant to his brother, Sir William, whom about the same time he thus addresses with *abandon* :—

"Dear Brother,—Little or no news. The L'Orient squadron have got into Cherbourg. The game of the Princess of Wales is to be the grand sport of the remainder of the session.[1] Her husband [thereby then and there meaning his 'dear young royal master'] is furious indeed with indignation against the 'early friends.' And it is now, as we used to suppose it heretofore, that is, that he knows every word that is uttered at Blackheath or Kensington. Sidmouth is all but President of the Council, and I suppose will be before the meeting of Parliament. Some of the Dissenters are writing against the *Popishers*, and publishing dissuasives against making cause with them. The London clergy petition, and some few addresses, very few, come from different parts in favor of the poor old Church."

Such a gleam of sincerity is most refreshing!

The Prince's changed feelings and conduct towards Lord Eldon had been brought about by a variety of causes of a public and private nature—among which, unques-

[1] He seems to have supposed that Lords Grey and Grenville were coming out with a "book," as well as motions, in her behalf.

tionably, the chief was Lord Eldon's changed feelings and conduct towards the Princess of Wales; but he, ever accounting for events in the manner most creditable to himself, ascribed his recent reconciliation with the Prince, and the friendship which now sprung up between them, to a discovery of his Royal Highness, which must have been made, if ever, as soon as the Regency Bill passed. "His Majesty George IV. has frequently told me," he said, "that there was no person in the whole world that he hated so much as for years he hated me. He had been persuaded that I endeavored to keep him at a distance from his father; but when he came into possession of his father's private papers, he completely changed his opinion of me, in consequence of the part which, from my letters, he found I had always taken with reference to himself. He was then convinced that I had always endeavored to do the direct contrary of what was imputed to me. He told me so himself, *and from that time* he treated me with uniform friendliness."[1]

Lord Eldon had now only one source of uneasiness— the investigation going on before Michael Angelo Taylor's Committee in the House of Commons " on the causes of the delays in the administration of justice in the Court of Chancery;"—but this made him very unhappy. He wrote a long letter on the subject to Mr. Perceval, in which, after blaming the Government for allowing the committee to be re-appointed, he says, "I have now sat in my court for above twelve months, an accused culprit, tried by the hostile part of my own bar, upon testimony wrung from my officers, and without the common civility of even one question put by the committee to myself, in such mode of communication as might have been in courtesy adopted. When I say that I know that I am, and that my officers, and that my successors will be, degraded by all this, I say what I think I do know." He then goes on at great length to justify himself, and to censure the plan of separating bankruptcy from the jurisdiction of the Lord Chancellor, together with other reforms which had been suggested. To pacify him, the committee decided that "they would not examine barristers and solicitors of the Court of Chancery touching the causes of delay in that Court;" and a motion

[1] Twiss, ch. xxxiii.

in the House of Commons to instruct them to do so was negatived by a large majority.[1]

Lord Eldon thought that his cares were over for the rest of this session, and that with the protection of Mr. Perceval, over whom he continued to exercise a sort of control, from the Prime Minister having practiced at the bar under him, he was likely henceforth to enjoy tranquillity.

But in a few days after that victory, Mr. Perceval, who seemed to have before him a long and brilliant official career, who was highly respected and beloved by his own party, and was allowed by his political opponents to be a most amiable and high-minded man, fell by the hand of an assassin—and there arose an almost unexampled scene of political confusion, during which there seemed several times almost a certainty of an entire change of Administration.

Lord Eldon imbibed a notion that he himself had been in imminent danger of being shot by Bellingham; but for this there does not seem to have been any foundation.[2] All classes of the community were dreadfully appalled by this event, and, for many reasons, it occasioned a particular shock to the Chancellor. The Princess Elizabeth wrote a very feeling letter on the occasion to Mrs. Scott, his daughter-in-law, in which, after stating that the Queen had ordered her to inquire after Lord Eldon, she says:—

"Well knowing how deeply he feels, she greatly dreads

[1] 23 Parl. Deb. 61.

[2] Lord Eldon was sitting on the woolsack when intelligence of Mr. Perceval being shot was brought to the House of Lords. Apprehending that there might be a plot to assassinate all the Ministers, he said, "I have just been informed of a most melancholy and atrocious event which has happened in the lobby of the other House. In this situation, I feel it my duty to apprise your Lordships that I shall take care to give the proper directions to the officers that none go out of the doors of this House of Parliament till we have been fully satisfied that they have not the means of doing further mischief." An order was accordingly given to search all strangers below the bar for concealed fire-arms, but it was not carried into execution; and the House, having moved an address to the Regent, expressing their horror at the crime committed, and praying that he would take proper steps for bringing the offender to justice, adjourned.—23 *Parl. Deb.* 161. Bellingham had been in the Court of Chancery the same morning, and was supposed to have looked fiercely at the Chancellor, but seems to have intended no violence at that time. The chief object of his resentment was Lord G. Leveson Gower (afterwards Earl Granville), who had been ambassador in Russia when he had suffered some supposed grievance there, for which he made the Prime Minister responsible.

that the shock of yesterday may have injured his health. It is impossible not to shrink with horror when one thinks of an Englishman committing murder, and doubly striking when one must mourn for the loss of so excellent a man as Mr. Perceval. We live in most awful times: for the loss, both public and private, must be equally felt. We really are so horror-struck, that it is impossible for me to describe our feelings. His family have lost one who has ever proved real affection and attachment, and my beloved father has lost a most upright and conscientious Minister. Our only comfort in the midst of our own trial is, that my father is spared this affliction: for I verily believe, had it pleased the Almighty to have allowed of its being told him, it would have totally overset him. My mother commands me to add, she would herself have written to the Lord Chancellor, but she thought it better to make me write, well knowing his time is precious, and that it was cruel to add to his troubles by desiring an answer."

Lord Eldon did himself reply in the following terms; and in this instance, I believe, expressed not more than he really felt:—

"The Lord Chancellor, offering his most humble duty to your Majesty, while he acknowledges with infinite gratitude your Majesty's gracious condescension and goodness in directing inquiries to be made respecting the Chancellor's health, amidst the afflicting circumstances in which he has been lately placed, takes leave to beseech your Majesty to be persuaded that nothing but the distress of his mind could have so long prevented him from returning your Majesty his heartfelt acknowledgments for the proof he has been honored with, that your Majesty takes some interest in his happiness.

"By the death of Mr. Perceval, the Lord Chancellor has lost a friend whom he valued, esteemed, and loved. His Majesty's people have lost a great and able fellow-subject and statesman, and the Lord Chancellor trusts that your Majesty will do him the justice to believe him when he adds, that his Majesty and his august and illustrious family have lost a servant, whose attachment to them the Lord Chancellor knows to have been the ruling principle in his heart, and whose attachment was rendered important because his virtues were universally known. The Chancellor, as himself a servant of his Majesty, anxious for the honor and welfare of all his Majesty's family, finds it difficult, very difficult, to prescribe bounds to that grief which daily overwhelms him.

"Belford Square, May 18, 1812."

Within a week from the time when the fatal shot was fired, the assassin, with the approbation of Lord Eldon, then at the head of the administration of justice, suffered on the scaffold,[1] although his counsel had earnestly pressed that his trial might be postponed, for the purpose of bringing witnesses from Liverpool to prove his insanity. This precipitation,—after the public mind had recovered its composure, was much blamed; and I can say of my own knowledge that it greatly conduced to lead judges and juries into the contrary extreme, which we have had to lament of late years. Nowadays the commission of an atrocious crime is of itself supposed to afford strong evidence of alienation of mind, and from the vague metaphysical conjectures of physicians who never saw the prisoner, acquittals take place on the ground of insanity, where, at the time when the offense was committed, there was no delusion of the senses, and there was complete consciousness of the nature of the criminal act and of its consequences.

In the ministerial crisis which followed the death of Mr. Perceval, Lord Eldon, really, though not ostensibly, was the prime mover,—displaying the bold decision and consummate skill which always distinguished him on such perilous occasions. He contrived to avoid participating in the numerous discussions which took place in Parliament respecting the negotiations, while they were pending, and no letter of his connected with them appeared before the public till after his death; but we now certainly know, what was before only suspected, that, with the assistance of the Duke of Cumberland, he was throughout the secret adviser of the Regent, and that his intrigues

[1] The shot was fired about five o'clock on Monday afternoon, May 11th; the trial took place on Friday, the 15th; and before nine o'clock in the morning of the Monday following, Bellingham's dead body was lying in the dissecting-room of Surgeons' Hall. He had formerly been confined in a mad-house, and several of his family had been afflicted with madness. Romilly says,—"No person can have heard what the conduct and demeanor of this man has been since he committed the crime, or can have read his defense, without being satisfied he is mad; but it is a species of madness which probably, for the security of mankind, ought not to exempt a man from being answerable for his actions."—*Life*, ii. 36.

achieved the triumph which his party obtained. His conduct at this time has been severely animadverted upon, but I think without any sufficient reason,—except, perhaps, that while he was consulting about offers to be made which might perplex political opponents, and conditions to be demanded which could not be conceded, he shut up the Court of Chancery, instead of trying to clear off his arrear of judgments,—when, apparently, it was his duty to "set his house in order." He was fully justified in doing everything he could to keep out of office Lord Wellesley, Mr. Canning, and the Whigs, for he heartily hated their principles, and he sincerely believed that their accession to power would not only have deprived him of the Great Seal, but would have been the ruin of the empire.

The Regent, still "furious" (as we are told on high authority he had been two months before) "against the *early friends*," was desirous to go on with his surviving Ministers, selecting one of them to be put at the head of the Treasury; and was, above all things, solicitous to exclude Lords Grey and Grenville from his councils. For this purpose, by the advice of the Duke of Cumberland, he very judiciously sent for the Chancellor; and explaining his views to him, commissioned him, first, to try to reconstruct the Cabinet from the existing materials, and if that should be found impossible, the least obnoxious additions were to be made to it. Lord Eldon himself, with a courage which never forsook him in extremity, thought that the present Cabinet, enjoying the entire confidence of the Regent, and not unpopular in the country, although many wished to see it strengthened, might go on without admitting any one, whether Pittite or Whig, who favored the pernicious measure of Catholic emancipation.

But it was necessary to take the opinion of his colleagues; and by the Regent's authority, having assembled them, he put to them, *seriatim*, this question:—"Are you of opinion that without Lord Grey and Lord Grenville, and without Lord Wellesley and Mr. Canning, you can carry on the government?" There is extant the memorandum, in his handwriting, in which he noted their answers and his own.—"*Eldon*. 'It might.' But there was only one other unqualified affirmative—that of the Earl of Westmoreland (not a very great authority), who said simply, 'Yes.' The rest were—'No,' by Lord Mulgrave.—'Doubtful,' by Lord Sidmouth.—'Not,' by Lord Harrowby.—'Dangerous to Prince and country,' by Lord Bathurst.—'Doubtful,' by Lord Buckinghamshire.—'Very doubtful, not desperate,' by Lord Camden.—'Very improbable,' by Lord Melville.—'Doubtful, not desperate,' by Lord Liverpool.—'Extremely difficult,' by Mr. Ryder. —'Doubtful to say the least, *without a proposition,*' by Lord Castlereagh." He next asked them, "if they would join an Administration with Lord Wellesley at the head of it," and with one voice they said "No,"—for he had lately left them on account of their hostility to Catholic emancipation, and their refusal to carry on the war in the Peninsula with sufficient vigor. They were then asked, "If the Prince put *at the head* any member of the *present* Administration, will the rest support him?" They were all at last induced to say that "they would," but they almost all concurred in the sentiment expressed by Lord Castlereagh, that a "proposition" was necessary, for the purpose of showing to Parliament and the public that they had endeavored to render the Government more efficient. They all signed the following declaration, leaving it to Lord Eldon more fully to explain their sentiments to his Royal Highness:—" The Cabinet would feel it to be their duty, if called upon by the Prince Regent, to carry on the administration of the government under any member of the present Cabinet whom his Royal Highness might think proper to select as the head of it. They consider it to be at the same time incumbent upon them most humbly to submit to his Royal Highness, that, under all the present circumstances of the country, the result of their endeavor to carry on the government must in their judgment be very doubtful. It does not, however, appear to them to be hopeless, if the Administration is known to possess the entire confidence of the Prince Regent."

Lords Grey and Grenville were less disagreeable to most of the Cabinet than Lord Wellesley and Mr. Canning, but they could not be pressed upon the Prince till every other resource was exhausted; and with the concurrence of Lord Eldon, a negotiation was first opened through Lord Liverpool, with Lord Wellesley and Mr. Canning, for their accesion to office, upon the basis of Mr. Perceval's policy. While Lord Eldon was ignorant of the result, he wrote to Sir William :—

"Nothing is in any degree settled. The particulars of what has been passing I can not commit to paper. If I am a political coward, as I may very justly be thought, it is, as it appears to me, a very melancholy truth, that I can find nobody among those whom Perceval has left, with respect to whom, upon comparison, I have not a most extraordinary degree of political fortitude. In general, I believe I may say, that attempts are making, with the concurrence of all, to bring Wellesley and Canning into office. If they come, Liverpool will be at the head of the Administration, and Castlereagh to be, among the House of Commons' members of Administration, at the head of them. Most think that W. and C. will not come upon those terms—they will be accepted upon no other. My opinion is, that both are so sick of being out, that they *will* come upon such terms. If they don't, we shall try what we can do without them. Upon this there are three opinions, two among *us:* that is, *I* think, that *that* may and *will go on*—all the rest think that it must be tried, but that it *can not go on*, and that things will fall into the hands of G. and G. nearly forthwith. A third opinion comes from gentlemen in the H. of Commons, who think it will go on—and who are not inclined to support at all, if W. and C. *do* come in. Upon this last opinion, however, it is too late to act, if they bite. Lord Sid. has behaved very well, certainly; so has the Regent."

To Lord Eldon's surprise and joy, Lord Wellesley and Mr. Canning "did not bite." They would not come in on the terms offered, and they proposed, with seeming moderation, "that a Cabinet might be formed on an intermediary principle respecting the Roman Catholic claims, exempt from the dangers of instant unqualified concession, and from those of inconsiderate peremptory exclusion,—and that the entire resources of the empire might be applied to the great objects of the war."[1]

A "proposition" having been made and rejected, it was thought that the old Cabinet might go on without difficulty, and Lord Liverpool was about to be declared Prime Minister; but there was much public dissatisfaction from the belief that the late abortive attempt had not been sincerely made; and Mr. Stuart Wortley (afterwards Lord Wharncliffe) moved in the House of Commons, an ad-

[1] 23 Parl. Deb. 332–392.

dress to the Prince Regent, praying him "to take measures for forming a strong and efficient Administration,"[1]—which was unexpectedly carried by a majority of 174 to 170.[2]

Next day the Ministers all tendered their resignations, and intimated that they only held their offices till their successors were appointed;—but several of them were still sanguine in the belief, that the negotiation for a new Administration might be disturbed, and that they must yet be recalled. Lord Eldon was more constantly closeted with the Duke of Cumberland than ever, and it is supposed that he did not at any moment despair of ultimate success.

Lord Wellesley was now sent for by the Regent, and commissioned to form an Administration. He first applied to the men actually holding office, to know whether any of them would join him,—and, as had been concerted, they unanimously refused to be members of an Administration of his forming. He then had permission to treat with Lord Grey and Lord Grenville; for, although the Whigs were by no means then popular, there was a large class in the community who had a high respect for the great talents and unsullied reputation of these two statesmen, and desired to see them employed in the public service. It was therefore considered necessary that they should not appear to be permanently excluded from office; but Lord Wellesley, though permitted to treat with them, was limited to terms respecting seats in the Cabinet, and other arrangements, to which they could not for a moment listen. In consequence, on the 3rd of June, he stated in the House of Lords, that he had that day resigned the commission intrusted to him for the arrangement of a new Administration, and, in reference to the existing cabinet, "lamented that the most dreadful personal animosities should have interposed to prevent an arrangement which was so essential for the welfare of the country." He declared that he was ready to disclose everything that had passed during his negotiations, but strongly advised their Lordships not to call for the disclosure. This advice was followed,—Lord Liverpool on behalf of himself and his colleagues, disclaiming all personal animosities, and declaring that they had been actuated only by considerations

[1] 23 Parl. Deb. 249.   [2] Ib. 281.

of public principle. Lord Eldon, although strongly alluded to by Lord Grey and Lord Grenville, could not be induced to leave the woolsack for the purpose of communicating information to the House respecting the steps hereafter to be taken.

He was at length of opinion that enough had been done to please the timorous, and he would immediately have started Lord Liverpool as Prime Minister, but Mr. Stuart Wortley threatened another motion in the House of Commons, and several of those, in comparison with whom he had "an extraordinary degree of political fortitude," quailed at the prospect of the coming storm. The Regent was therefore advised to employ Lord Moira to negotiate the formation of an Administration, the basis of which should be "the consideration of the Catholic claims, and the vigorous prosecution of the war in Spain." He was himself only to have an inferior office with a seat in the Cabinet, Lord Wellesley being First Lord of the Treasury, and Lords Grey and Grenville having the principal sway in it.

Notwithstanding Lord Eldon's confident belief that this negotiation would fail, it had very nearly succeeded, and it would have led to his removal from office; but he was saved by Lords Grey and Grenville's unskillful management of a dispute respecting the offices in the household. They were justified in considering that those appointments should form a part of a general ministerial arrangement, and were not to be filled up according to the personal liking of the Sovereign; but they insisted on the preliminary dismissal of the present officers of the household,—who had all privately resolved to resign as soon as the new Administration was formed. The Regent was advised to make his stand upon this point, and even Lord Moira applauded his resistance. The unfortunate issue was chiefly imputed to Sheridan, who concealed from his friends the fact communicated to him, that all the household offices certainly would have been at the disposal of the new Ministers.[1]

It is curious to speculate on the probable consequences

---

[1] Sir S. Romilly exempts Lords Grey and Grenville from all blame, saying that "they very properly refused to be members of the Cabinet, unless the offices in the household, usually appointed to by Ministers, were to be at the disposal of the new Ministers."—*Life*, iii. 41.

of the establishment of the Government which was so near being formed. Lord Wellesley being at the head of it to co-operate zealously with his brother the Duke of Wellington, we may fairly conclude that our military triumphs would not have been less brilliant than those which actually followed;—the unfortunate contest with America would have been avoided by the immediate repeal of the Orders in Council;—and if Catholic emancipation had then been voluntarily granted, we might have escaped many of the evils which arose from its being afterwards extorted by violence.

But the nation took part against Lord Grey and Lord Grenville, and Mr. Stuart Wortley said, "These noble lords have debarred themselves, by their own conduct, from becoming the administration of the country; it was with regret that he saw the nation deprived of the services of such men; but, under the circumstances which had occurred, they were themseves responsible for continuing in a private station."[1]

On the 8th of June Lord Liverpool declared in the House of Lords, that he had been that day appointed, by his Royal Highness, the Prince Regent, First Commissioner of the Treasury, with authority to complete the other arrangements of the Administration as soon as possible; and Lord Moira, in lamenting the failure of his enterprise, said, "there is this consolation, that it is now testified to the world, that on the part of his Royal Highness the Prince Regent, there was in the proposition submitted by his authority to my noble friends no reservation whatever, and that it was made with the most entire disposition to give every effect to the wish expressed by the other branch of the legislature."[2]

Yet Sir Samuel Romilly thought that he had merely been made the tool of a more crafty man; and in his Diary thus sums up his account of this crisis:—

"June 11.—The whole of the negotiations for a new Ministry have been conducted, unquestionably, with a previous determination on the part of the Prince and of those who enjoy his confidence, that they should not end in Lord Grey and Lord Grenville and their friends being in power. The Lord Chancellor has never, from the moment of the address of the House of Commons being carried

---
[1] 23 Parl. Deb. 399.   [2] Ib. 357–359.

shown the least symptom of apprehension that he was to resign his office. During these three weeks that the Ministers had been represented by themselves as holding their offices only till their successors should be named, he has given judgment in none of the numerous causes, petitions, and motions, which have been long waiting his decision; though there never before was an instance of a Chancellor about to resign the Great Seal, who did not hasten to clear away the arrears of his Court. Instead of this, Lord Eldon has been every day closeted with the Duke of Cumberland; and, during several days in the term, the Court has been entirely shut up, while his Lordship was employed in some way never known to the suitors of his Court, or to the public. We have even had the Duke of Cumberland coming down to Westminster Hall, and sending for the Chancellor out of Court. The whole matter has ended pretty much as I expected. It might have been much worse, if Lords Grey and Grenville had not been deterred from taking office by the obstacles which were purposely thrown in their way. They would have been suffered to remain in the Ministry but a very short time; some pretext would have been anxiously watched for, and eagerly seized, to turn them out with the loss of character; or a new cry against Popery would have been raised, and they would probably have been the victims of it."

There was a general opinion that Lord Eldon would, ere long, be called upon, in the midst of new difficulties, to give fresh proofs of his skill in keeping himself and his friends in place, and excluding his opponents; but this Administration, of which he was the real author,—although supposed to be so rickety,—lasted, with some modifications, till the death of Lord Liverpool—a period of fifteen years. The formation of it is a remarkable era in our party annals. Now Mr. Vansittart (Lord Bexley) was placed at the head of the finances; Lord Castlereagh became leader of the House of Commons; and Mr. Peel (our illustrious Sir Robert) began his official career as Irish Secretary, to give assurance to Orangemen that their ascendency would ever be preserved.

The first assault on the new Government was made by Lord Wellesley, who delivered an admirable speech in favor of the Irish Catholics. This was answered by the Lord Chancellor, who said, "There is no wish nearer my heart than to be convinced that I am wrong,—in which case I will, without hesitation, vote for the resolution of the noble Marquis. But it shocks me much to see the descendants of a Somers and a Hardwicke act so oppositely to the principles of their ancestors. If the present motion be carried, the noble Marquis and I may shake hands; but, as I hope for God's mercy, I do not think I shall be living under the same constitution as hitherto." At the same time he was so far softened as to move the *previous question*, "that he might not, by a direct negative, once and for ever, shut the door of conciliation against the Roman Catholics, though he was anxious at the same time not to disguise from them his own objections, on constitutional grounds, to their claims."[1] Such progress had public opinion made on this subject, that it had penetrated the House of Lords, and the previous question (to the horror of the Lord Chancellor, who was observed to be deeply affected as he announced the division) was carried only by a majority of *one*, the numbers being 126 to 125.[2]

He was, if possible, still more annoyed by the proceedings in Michael Angelo Taylor's committee on "the delays in Chancery," and by the complaints on this subject of several members of the House of Commons, who maliciously insinuated that the accumulation of arrears arose chiefly from the Lord Chancellor neglecting his judicial business for political intrigue. Thinking that he was abandoned by his colleagues, he was in such a rage that he threatened to resign, and to leave them to the fate which, without his patronage, would speedily overtake them. Thus he vented his feelings to Sir William:—

"Really, as to the Government, I don't care one farthing about it. *I am mistaken if they do not mainly owe their existence, as such, to me;* and yet I have been, in my judicial capacity, the object of the House of Commons' persecution for two years, without a lawyer there to say a word of truth for me; and though I have pressed, for years past, the importance of being supported there by some individuals in my own department of the profession, not the slightest notice of this has been taken in their arrangements; I have been left unprotected as before,—and so unprotected I can not and will not remain.

"The Prince vows annihilation to the Government if I

[1] 23 Parl. Deb. 833.   [2] Ib. 868.

go; and I suppose would resort to Canning and Wellesley. But I can not feel the obligation I am under of being hunted in the House of Commons without more of protection than I have had—of bearing that the business of the Court of Chancery should be tumbled out at the end of the session, as it was, without communication with me."

However, he was much comforted by having the honor, at the prorogation, of entertaining at dinner his Royal Highness the Regent, with whom he was now a special favorite, and who, enjoying the splendid hospitality and gay good-humor of Bedford Square, forgot that the Princess of Wales had sat in the same room—at the same table—on the same chair—had drunk of the same wine—out of the same cup,—while the conversation had turned on her barbarous usage from her husband, and the best means of publishing to the world *her* wrongs and *his* misconduct.

When the Chancellor retired to Encombe, he wrote the following *résumé* to his friend Dr. Swire—which, if not so rich as that of the preceding year, will be found very characteristic and entertaining:—

"My attention has been utterly distracted by the events of a year which, in their extraordinary nature so far as they respect myself, have surpassed all the extraordinary circumstances which even my checkered life has produced. I could not doubt that at the close of the Regency year, the 18th February, I should have had my dismissal: so sure was I of that, that when the Prince sent for me on the 17th, his commands reached me sitting for my picture *in my robes*. When I went he expressed his surprise that I appeared on a morning in a laced shirt; I told him what I had been about: he then expressed surprise that I could find any time for such a business: my answer was that the fact proved that that was difficult; that the picture had been asked nearly two years for the Guildhall at Newcastle, and that, my countrymen wishing it should be in the Chancellor's robes, I could not delay beyond that day in which I might for the last time be entitled to wear them. He smiled, and next day satisfied me that I needed not to have been in such a hurry. This was curious enough, but is literally a fact. Well, after this poor Perceval was assassinated. By the way, I had a pretty narrow escape. It is said,

> ' Mors sola fatetur
> Quantula sint hominum corpuscula ;'

but I have learned facts of poor Perceval's life, which I never should have learnt but in consequence of his death, and which prove him to have been a most extraordinarily excellent person. Here again, however, I thought I should sing 'Nunc dimittis.' I appointed and attended a Recorder's report, which I thought it unmanly to leave to a successor on a Monday, as I was morally certain that I should not be Chancellor on the usual day, the Wednesday. But whether Grenville and Grey did not wish to be Ministers, or whether they would not be Ministers unless they could bind kings in chains, I don't know. The Tuesday put my wig and gown once more fast upon my head and back, and I am now just as uncertain when I shall see the blessings of final retirement as I was before the King's illness. What a life of anxiety (about myself certainly in no degree such) I led during these scenes, must be reserved, if is to be described, till some happy hour of conversation between us shall be vouchsafed me by Providence. I concluded my stay in town by the Prince Regent's dining in Bedford Square with a man whom he had hated more than any other in his father's dominions, according to his unreserved confession." [After stating his determination to fight to the stumps against Catholic emancipation, he thus concludes:] "And now, dear Sam, I come to a close. Retained in office, with no wish to remain in it, I am praying for some fair opportunity, some honorable reason, for quitting. I grow old; business increases; my ability to discharge it does not improve. These, so help me God, are the reflections which have occupied my anxious thoughts during the last winter, and yet, in this malignant world, while the Regent knows my wishes perfectly, I am supposed to be clinging to office, and intriguing for others who are anxious for it. God forgive them!"

During the autumn, part of his house at Encombe was destroyed by a fire. This, if it did not produce at the time as beautiful a letter as that from Sir Thomas More on a similar occasion, he afterwards described very graphically in his old age:—"It really was a very pretty sight," said he, "for all the maids turned out of their beds, and they formed a line from the water to the fire-engine, hand-ing the buckets; they looked very pretty, *all in their shifts.*" While the flames were raging he was in violent trepidation about the Great Seal, which, although he was not in the habit, like one of his illustrious predecessors, of taking it to bed with him, he always kept in his bedchamber. He flew with it to the garden, and buried it in a flower-border. But his trepidation was almost as overwhelming next morning, for, what between his alarm for the safety of Lady Eldon, and his admiration of the maids in their vestal attire, he could not remember the spot where the *clavis regni* had been hid. "You never saw anything so ridiculous," he said, "as seeing the whole family down that walk probing and digging till we found it."

Considering that Lord Eldon had actually formed the present Cabinet, I am much surprised to perceive the inconsiderable influence he seems to have enjoyed in it, and how little he was consulted by Lord Liverpool, whom he had made Premier. He justly complained that the Attorney and Solicitor General had been appointed without his sanction, and that neither was taken from his Bar;— Sir Thomas Plumer practicing chiefly in the Court of Exchequer, and knowing little of equity; and Sir William Garrow, since he left the Old Bailey, confining himself to the Court of King's Bench, and being, notwithstanding his great natural acuteness, utterly ignorant of law, as well as of equity,—so that they could render him no assistance in the attacks made upon him in the House of Commons respecting delays in the Court of Chancery.

It farther appears, from a letter to him from Lord Liverpool,[1] that the important resolution of dissolving Parliament this autumn was absolutely adopted without any previous communication with him, and he was at once summoned to attend a council, when the proclamation for calling a new Parliament was to be signed by the Regent. The reasons which led to this measure were the mutinous vote of the House of Commons on Mr. Stuart Wortley's motion; the recent victory at Salamanca; a renewed cry against Popery; and a plentiful harvest, which had, as usual, given the people a high opinion of the wisdom of the Government. For these reasons I doubt not that Lord Eldon would have concurred in the

[1] 18th Sept. 1812.

resolution; but it surprises us to find him unceremoniously required to put the Great Seal to writs for the new elections. If he was at all hurt, he must have been comforted by finding that the result of the contests which ensued was generally in favor of the " No Popery " candidates, and that the Government was henceforth sure of a commanding majority in both Houses.

The session was opened with much pomp. For a good many years past, from the infirmities of George III. and the dislike of the Regent to appear in public, the prerogative of the Crown, in Parliamentary proceedings, had only been exercised by commissioners,—but the Regent was prevailed upon to deliver in his own person the speech declaring the reasons for summoning this Parliament, and, to the horror of some over-rigid adherents of hereditary right, by the Chancellor's advice he took his seat on the throne—of course still speaking " in the name and on the behalf of his Majesty." He had to announce the diminished hope of his Majesty's recovery.[1]

"The Orders in Council," found by experience to be so detrimental to our own commerce, had provoked neutrals to set up unwarrantable claims, which would have been fatal to the naval superiority of England,—and we were now at war with the United States of America, who even denied our right to reclaim our own seamen, if they had obtained letters of naturalization from a foreign government. In a debate upon an address to the Regent, to assure him of the support of Parliament in this new contest, Lord Eldon said, " There was no question in the whole course of his political life, on which he had given his opinion more reluctantly, or more decidedly. If the claim of naturalization insisted on by the Americans were allowed, why should it not be made by other countries? If a residence of five years established the right, why not a residence of one month? It would thus be easy, by the offer of impunity, and by the temptation of high pay, to seduce our seamen into the service of rival states. Unless America should think proper to alter her tone, he did not see how the national differences could be settled. As an adviser of the Crown, he would never consent to an armistice on the condition of appearing to hesitate about a right so vitally affecting our honor and our interests as a

[1] 24 Parl. Deb. 12.

nation." The address, though carped at by some Opposition Peers, was carried without a division.[1]

Lord Eldon at last pushed through Parliament a bill which ought to have been passed ten years sooner—for the appointment of a new judge in the Court of Chancery, to be called VICE-CHANCELLOR.[2] This bill was unaccountably opposed by some who had been loudest in complaining of delays in the determination of equity suits; and, I am concerned to say, the most zealous of those was the enlightened and patriotic Romilly. He was far above the prejudice of considering the system of equitable judicature handed down to us from remote antiquity as absolute perfection, and he could not have been swayed by any consideration that his business at the bar was to be scattered among new competitors; yet he spoke and wrote against a necessary and palpable improvement as if he had been fighting against the repeal of the Bill of Rights. Such was the arrear of appeals and writs of error in the House of Lords, that, according to the past rate of despatch, they could not have been decided in less than twelve or thirteen years,—to say nothing of the new arrear which would accumulate in that interval,—and a cause could not be brought to a regular hearing in the Court of Chancery for a good many years after it was ripe for being heard. No better plan was suggested for curing the evil. " Lord Eldon expressed his conviction that when he should be dead and gone, the subjects of this country would feel the salutary and satisfactory operation of a measure which tended to the speedy decision of their appeals to that House, and of their suits in the Court of Chancery. Attacks had been made on his judicial conduct which he would not deign to repel; but he would assert that no man, however experienced, vigorous, and industrious, could get through the business now cast upon the Lord Chancellor. He reminded the House that the visible occupations of that functionary were not alone to be regarded; a Chancellor must give his nights as well as his days to the consideration of his duties; he must pursue them even in the retirement of his house, and in the privacy of his closet, if he meant to do justice."[3]

This prophecy has been amply fulfilled; and the increas-

[1] 24 Parl. Deb. 588, 589.   [2] 53 Geo. 3, c. 24.
[3] Parl. Deb. vol. xxiv, xxv.

ing pressure of business has rendered necessary the creation of two additional Vice-Chancellors—so that at present there is no arrear of appeals or writs of error in the House of Lords; and in the Court of Chancery every cause may be heard as soon as it is ready to be set down for hearing. Nor will anyone who sees how the Woolsack is at present occupied by a consummate Equity Judge, much honor the *clairvoyance* of those who asserted that after the creation of the office of Vice-Chancellor, the Lord Chancellor would be a politician, orator, or man of letters.[1]

Sir Samuel Romilly's spleen, however, induced him to animadvert with bitter, and, I think, unjust severity upon the individual who first filled the office:—

"A worse appointment," says he, "than that of Plumer to be Vice-Chancellor could hardly have been made. He knows nothing of the law of real property, nothing of the law of bankruptcy, and nothing of the doctrines peculiar to courts of equity. His appointment to this office is the more extraordinary, as the Chancellor is fully aware of his incapacity to discharge the duties of it; and as Richards, who is certainly the best qualified for it of anyone now in the profession, and whose politics could raise no objection to his promotion, has been always considered as the Chancellor's most intimate private friend. The Regent certainly can not have made it a point to have Plumer promoted, since he is one of the avowed authors of the Princess of Wales's defense, which abounds with the most injurious insinuations against the Prince. The only explanation of all this is, that, with the rest of the Ministry, Plumer has a very strong interest; that they have earnestly pressed his appointment, and have represented that it would be a great slight upon him if he were to be passed by; and that the Chancellor has not on this, as he never has on any former occasion, suffered his sense of duty towards the public, or his private friendship, to prevail over his party politics."

Sir Thomas Plumer, although he had not enjoyed the advantage of being brought up in the Six Clerks Office, and although he was not a profound jurist, was by no means ignorant of the law of real property, or of the law of bankruptcy, and he had practiced on the Equity side in

---

[1] Surely this cannot be understood as a sarcasm on Lord Cottenham.

the Court of Exchequer for many years. His judgments as Vice-Chancellor, and Master of the Rolls, sneered at by some old Chancery practitioners when they were delivered, are now read by the student with much profit, and are considered of high authority. I do not understand how it would have been any mitigation of Lord Eldon's misconduct that the Regent had pressed the appointment; but if it would, I do not see why he should be so positively deprived of the benefit of it,—for the Chancellor himself, "one of the authors of the Princess of Wales's defense, abounding with the most injurious insinuations against the Prince," had grown into his Royal Highness's special favorite.

I am sorry that the Vice-Chancellor's Bill, which had become indispensable for Lord Eldon's own convenience, is the only instance of his doing anything for the improvement of our institutions. He continued as fierce as ever in his opposition to Romilly's noble endeavors to mitigate the severity of the criminal code, and this session he again threw out the bills for taking away the penalty of death from shoplifting and stealing in a dwelling-house, asking triumphantly, "Is it an encouragement or discouragement in the eyes of any man of common sense, to commit a crime, that instead of being hanged if he commits it, he will at most only be transported?"[1]

But one liberal measure passed—without meeting the smallest opposition, and hardly exciting any notice either in or out of Parliament—the very identical measure which in the year 1807 had turned out "All the Talents," and set the whole country in a flame—the Bill to allow Roman Catholics to hold commissions in the army as field officers! It was introduced into the House of Lords by the Duke of Norfolk, and Lord Liverpool, the Prime Minister, in a short speech said that he entirely approved of it.[2] Nevertheless there are indiscriminate admirers of George III. who still applaud his policy when he not only refused his assent to this measure, but required a written pledge from his Ministers that they never again would propose it to him.

During the present session of Parliament the disputes between the Prince and Princess of Wales again came

[1] 25 Parl. Deb. 525. Two royal Dukes, five Prelates, and three law Lords voted in the majority. [2] 53 Geo. 3, c. 128.

before the public, and at one time seemed likely to lead to a change of the Government. Without any new levity being imputed to her, fresh restrictions were put upon her intercourse with her daughter. To these she would not quietly submit, and she wrote a letter of remonstrance to the Prince, which was thrice sent to Carlton House, and thrice returned unopened. She then wrote a letter to Lord Liverpool to be communicated to the Chancellor, complaining that she was debarred even of the means of stating her wrongs and asking redress. The following answer was returned to her:—

"Lord Liverpool begs leave to inform her Royal Highness the Princess of Wales, that he communicated to the Lord Chancellor, according to her Royal Highness's desire, the letter which he received from the Princess on Sunday night. He has likewise thought it his duty to lay that letter before his Royal Highness the Prince Regent.

"The Lord Chancellor and Lord Liverpool have never declined to be the channel of any communications which the Princess of Wales might be pleased to inform them that her Royal Highness was desirous of making to the Prince Regent through his confidential servants; and they would have been ready to have submitted to his Royal Highness any points in the copy of the letter transmitted by the Princess to Lord Liverpool, which it might have been their duty to have brought under his Royal Highness's consideration, if the Princess had signified to them her intention that the communication to his Royal Highness should have been made in this manner. But it must be for the Prince Regent himself to determine whether he will receive in the manner proposed, any direct communication by letter from the Princess of Wales, or enter into any correspondence with her Royal Highness.

"The Prince Regent has commanded Lord Liverpool to state, that he adheres to the resolution which he has already expressed in this respect, and he has directed Lord Liverpool, therefore, to return her Royal Highness's letter."[1]

Cochrane Johnstone soon afterwards made a motion on the subject in the House of Commons. Mr. Whitbread became the advocate there of the Princess, and her cause

[1] Jan. 19, 1813.

was taken up with warmth by the Livery of London. These proceedings caused much consternation in Carlton House, and the Prince did not think that he was sufficiently supported by his ministers, although they had gone quite as far as any regard to decency would permit in humoring his caprices. In the debate on Cochrane Johnstone's motion, Romilly had spoken merely to defend those concerned in the investigation of 1806—but a hope was entertained that he would zealously take part with the Prince, and the Great Seal was to have been his reward. The negotiation was opened through Mr. Nash, the architect, who was a private friend of the Romillys, and who, since his laying out "Regent Street" and the "Regent's Park," had been patronized by the Regent. He had several times tried in vain to induce Romilly to go to Carlton House, that he might advise his Royal Highness on the course he should pursue in counteracting the schemes of the Princess. The following entry gives an account of a new attempt:—

"March 13th. Mr. Nash called upon me again. He told me that his former visit to me was made at the request of the Regent, and that he had since had much conversation with him; that the Prince was still desirous of seeing me, and said that he had a right to consult me as his counsel, and that as such I was retained for him. I told Mr. Nash that, in all his Royal Highness's private concerns, he had, undoubtedly, a right to command my advice and assistance, but that the conduct of the Princess of Wales had become a matter of state; had been submitted to the consideration of committees of the Privy Council; had been a subject of consideration by the Cabinet, and was as much a matter of public concern as the war with Spain or with America, and that it was impossible for me to advise with the Prince upon it. . . . . He had some more conversation, in which he said that Lord Yarmouth had asked him whether he thought that I was so much of a party-man as on that account to have any personal objection to himself; and he asked, but as entirely from himself, 'Whether I should think it a duty to refuse the Great Seal if it were offered me, unless all my political friends formed part of the Administration?' I told him, that it was not by party motives that I was actuated, but that my opinion was, that no good could be done to the country unless those men who had acted on Mr. Fox's principles were in administration, and that I should not consent to form part of any Administration in which they were not comprehended.

"17th. Mr. Nash called upon me again this morning. He said he came to renew the subject of our last conversation. That he was extremely anxious I should see the Prince; that the Prince had no person who could speak honestly and openly to him; that he thought that if I saw him, what I should say to him might lead to a total change of the Administration; that he was still attached to his former political friends.

"21st. I dined to-day at Nash's. To my surprise, Lord Yarmouth dined there. Before he came in, Nash took me aside, to tell me that everything was in confusion at Carlton House; that this was the moment for bringing about a change of Administration; that he was himself most anxious that it should be effected; and that I was the link by which the Prince might be reunited with his old political friends. I told him that to me this really appeared to be quite impossible. He said that he had, however, thought it right to apprise me of this, and that he had again had a long conversation with the Prince last Friday."[1]

By a letter from Lord Eldon to his brother, written about the same time, it appears that the Prince, while he was striving to lay hold of all the Chancellor's patronage, was quarreling with him for not going far enough about the Princess. This letter is in answer to an application for a Cursitorship:—

"It is absolutely impossible, and I am very sorry for it, that I can avail myself of this occasion to do what you wish. Some one of my own *secretaries* must have the Cursitorship—they have *a right to it*—the Commissionerships are pledged ten deep; and, as to the private secretaryship, that I must dispose of without reference to anybody but myself, if am to continue Chancellor. I doubt whether I am; the Prince having applied for all, and I having refused him all. As to the private secretaryship, it distresses me so much that it is vacant, that I sincerely wish to put an end to my own office. Excuse the haste which I write with from the Bench, and excuse anything

[1] Life of Romilly, iii. 86–94.

improper, for I mean nothing to be so; but my soul is heavy. I am too low, and too ill, to mix with the world, and I therefore absented myself yesterday, and shall do so to-day. The P. has been treating me with so much unkindness, because I won't do so as to his wife and daughter as he wishes—in a way,—that one more such interview as I have had, if it occurs, will save me the trouble of appointing to the secretaryship, or anything else, where the officer goes out of office with the Chancellor."

This storm, however, soon blew over. If the Regent had ever any intention to do more than amuse Romilly, with a view to get a speech from him in the House of Commons, it was abandoned, and his Royal Highness wrote to Lord Eldon such kind and familiar notes as the following:—

"MY DEAR FRIEND,

"Pray give me a call on your way home, when your Cabinet breaks up, as an idea has struck me which I wish to talk over with you for five minutes, in order that you may turn it over in your mind before to-morrow morning. Just send me a line to mention about what hour I may be likely to see you, in order that I may be in the way, and not keep you waiting. "Ever sincerely yours,

"GEORGE, P. R."

A letter to Dr. Swire from the Chancellor shows that by the autumn of this year he had gained a complete ascendency over the Prince, and was very proud of him as a pupil, and a convert. After mentioning as "a piece of Church news" the appointment of Dr. Parsons as Bishop of Peterborough, it thus proceeds:—

"He is a stout fellow, and right, I believe, upon points of modern controversy,—the Catholic question particularly; and my young master, *who is as eager as his father was upon that, and of the same way of thinking*, seems to me to be looking out very sincerely for those who are able and willing to support Church and State as we have had them in times past. What a blessing to himself and to the country it has been, that the Prince did not succeed to government upon the King's demise, but under circumstances which have given him an opportunity of learning what he would otherwise never have known,—or, as the Queen puts it, of enabling her son George to learn that his poor father knew better who were his son's best friends than that son himself did! He is conducting himself really extremely well. His father, he says, often told him not to part with the Chancellor; but he owns to me that he hated me more than he detested any other man in the kingdom. At present many, I believe, think he is too much attached to me, and I am sure that it is impossible for a human being to treat another with more confidence and regard than he does me."

Ever afterwards till the formation of Mr. Canning's Government, there seems to have been the most perfect cordiality between the Chancellor and "his young master," and we hear no more lamentations about "the dear old King."

Although the Regent can not be said to have displayed any very high public or private virtues, and his ministers, with Lord Liverpool as their chief boast, were men much inferior in ability to those who had been at the head of affairs when such disasters befel the country during the American war and in the late coalitions against France,— we are arrived at one of the most glorious and prosperous eras to be met with in English history. Having gained victory after victory, Wellington was descending the Pyrenees into the plains of Languedoc; and Napoleon, having lost amidst the snows of Russia the greatest army ever assembled in modern ages, was gallantly, but vainly, striving to defend his capital against hordes collected from every clime between the River Rhine and the wall of China. At last the advance of the English upon Paris was stopped by a peace which the allies dictated.—Louis XVIII. was king of France and Navarre,—and he who had threatened to make Britain one of his satrapies was hailed as "Emperor of Elba!"—In the general illumination of London to celebrate these successes there were vaunting mottoes in foreign languages, but Lord Eldon, with piety and good taste, displayed, by variegated lamps upon the front of his house in Bedford Square, the words, "THANKS BE TO GOD!" He was much cheered by the mob; and he then little thought that within a year he and his family were to stand a siege in this very house, under serious apprehension of perishing by fire or by the sword!

The session of 1814, which did not begin till the 23rd

of March, was spent almost entirely in votes of thanks and addresses of congratulation. On the 28th of June, Wellington took his seat for the first time in the House of Lords, having been, while serving in the Peninsula, by successive patents, upon gaining fresh victories, created a Viscount, an Earl, a Marquis, and a Duke. Here was an opportunity for eloquence from the Woolsack, exceeding any enjoyed by Lord Cowper in the reign of Queen Anne. I am sorry that the House of Lords' speech of congratulation to "the Hero of a hundred battles" was a most wretched performance, and the meanness of it was the more striking when it was compared with the soul-stirring language in which the thanks of the House of Commons were returned to him, three days afterwards, by Speaker Abbott.[1] I can not understand how the Chancellor, conscious of his own deficiency in literary composition,—from having read nothing but briefs for so many years,—should not have asked his brother, Sir William, to aid him,—as he did when, appointed High Steward of the University of Oxford, he expected to be called upon for a Latin epistle. The only sentence which he uttered above clumsy common-place twaddle was that in which he alluded to "a circumstance singular in the history of that House, that before his introduction he had successively gone through every dignity of the peerage in this country which it was in the power of the Crown to bestow." And here he was inaccurate, for Wellington was made a Viscount when first ennobled, without having previously held the rank of a Baron.[2]

The allied Sovereigns coming to London after the peace, Lord Eldon was presented to them, and several times met them in society; but his ignorance of all Continental languages prevented them having any conversation with him,—which was a great disappointment to some of them, from the high consideration they observed that he held among his countrymen.

He used to relate an anecdote of this visit which, if genuine, he must have heard in a jovial moment from the Regent himself. The Emperor Alexander, scandalized by

[1] 28 Parl. Deb. 490.
[2] Lord Eldon had failed signally (although the occasion was much less memorable) in returning the thanks of the House, in 1810, to Lord Gambier, for the victory won by him in Basque Roads.—See Parliamentary Debates, xv. 355.

the disturbance which the Princess of Wales created at the Opera House and other places to annoy her husband, though himself living on bad terms with the Empress, used the friendly freedom to admonish his Royal Highness to be more regardful of the decencies of domestic life. Next day they were riding together, in the same carriage, through the Strand, in the midst of an immense crowd, who generally sympathized with the supposed wrongs of the Princess,—when a *greasy citizen* actually put his head into the carriage, and hallooed out, "Where's your wife? Go home and live with your wife." Whereupon the Regent, with much readiness, said, "Cela regarde votre Majesté Impériale."

There now arose in the Royal Family another controversy, which, I think, Lord Eldon and his colleagues might, and ought to have prevented. The Regent wished that his daughter should be married to the Prince of Orange, heir apparent to the new kingdom of the Netherlands. Politically, this was not a wise arrangement, it being clearly expedient to select, as the consort of the heiress of the throne of England, a foreign Prince of high lineage and distinguished personal qualities, without any foreign dominions,—that the inconveniences experienced in four reigns, from our connection with Hanover, might never return. A still more serious obejction was, that the Princess Charlotte, from the moment that a hint was thrown out of such a match being in contemplation, testified a deep and insuperable aversion to it, notwithstanding the gallantry of the Dutch Prince. However, all objections were overruled by her father and his ministers. Previously to framing a convention on the subject with the Government of the Netherlands, Lord Liverpool thus addressed Lord Eldon:—

"Upon the principle, I conceive there is no difficulty. One point is indispensable,—that the sovereignty of Great Britain and of Holland shall never be in the same person.

"Another is desirable, but not indispensable,—that the succession to the two sovereignties shall, if possible, go to the descendants in different lines, so that their respective pretensions may not afterwards clash.

"With respect to the Hereditary Prince of Orange, we can not call upon him to give up his rights as future sovereign of the Netherlands. But he will never be King of this country, nor be anything in the country, when he resides here, but a subject. His eldest son, if he lives, will be King of Great Britain. There is no difficulty therefore about excluding him specifically from the sovereignty of Holland. His second son, it is proposed, should succeed to the sovereignty of Holland. If, by the death of his brother, he succeeded to the sovereignty of Great Britain, he of course must give up the sovereignty of Holland. But the question of doubt is, whether, if he succeeded to be *heir apparent* or *heir presumptive* to the sovereignty of Great Britain, he should *thereby* forfeit the sovereignty of Holland.

"Is not this a Dutch question, and might it not be left to the Dutch legislature to determine? All *we* are bound to provide is, that the two sovereignties shall not be in the same person; and we have no objection to stipulate that the first-born son of the marriage shall not succeed to the sovereignty of Holland.

'" Surely there can be no difficulty in providing that all other contingencies as to the sovereignty of Holland shall depend upon the laws of Holland, provided always that the two sovereignties never are vested in one person.

"This can involve us in no difficulty, because it is not proposed to make any alteration in the succession to the throne of Great Britain.

"I wish you would try to draw up a short stipulation in this sense and to this effect; and I am anxious, for reasons that will occur to you, that it should be done soon." [1]

This was a much more difficult "settlement" than any he had been instructed to draw while practicing as a "conveyancer," and it might have given rise to many questions as puzzling as "whether, by the treaty of Utrecht, the issue of the Montpensier marriage be cut off from the succession to the Crown of Spain?"

The political obstacles would have been surmounted, but the young lady was inflexible. We know, on the anthority of Lord Brougham, to whom she applied for advice, that the match continued the subject of unremitting negotiation between her and her father: "An attempt had even been made, through one of his law officers, to persuade

[1] 27th April, 1814.

her that, after receiving some presents, and saying things construed into promises, she could be compelled by a Court of Equity to perform the contract. This strange doctrine, this new kind of equity, she had met with admirable presence of mind, and indeed skill, declaring her ignorance of the law, but offering to believe the proposition thus (by way of threat) laid down,—provided, to prevent all mistakes, they who stated it would put it in writing, and sign their names to it, that she might show it to Mr. Brougham.[1]

No more was heard of this extension of the doctrine of *specific performance;* but still the pressure upon her was so great, that, on the 12th of July, she actually eloped from Warwick House, where she was established, under the care of the Bishop of Salisbury, and tried to find an asylum in her mother's house in Connaught Place. Mr. Twiss says that this was in consequence of the Regent and the Bishop, her tutor, having unexpectedly visited her, and, pronouncing the dismissal of her attendants, having declared that she was to be taken to Carlton House; whereupon, requesting leave to retire, she escaped by the back staircase into the street, and hurried into a hackney-coach; and that the Duke of York and the Lord Chancellor, as soon as the place of her retreat was ascertained, proceeded thither with instructions from the Regent to bring her back.[2] To complete this version of the story, Lord Eldon himself is supposed to have added the following narrative:—

"When we arrived, I informed her a carriage was at the door, and we would attend her home. But home she would not go. She kicked and bounced; but would not go. Well, to do my office as gently as I could, I told her I was sorry for it, for until she did go, she would be obliged to entertain us, as we would not leave her. At last she accompanied us."

" But," says Lord Brougham, " this is a perfect mis-statement, indeed a pure fiction, and there are three persons yet living who know it to be so, and having read the above lines, agree in so declaring it. When the Princess's escape became known at Carlton House (for it is not at all true, as stated by Mr. Twiss, that the Prince and Bishop went to see her at Warwick House, to inform her

---
[1] Law Review, No. XI. 282.   [2] Twiss's Life of Eldon, ch. xxxv.

of the new constitution of her household, and that she asked leave to retire, and escaped by a back staircase), the Regent sent notice to the heads of the law, and of his own Duchy of Cornwall establishment. Soon after these arrived, each in a separate hackney-coach, at Connaught Terrace, the Princess of Wales's residence. These were the Chancellor, Lord Ellenborough, Mr. Adam, Chancellor of the Duchy of Cornwall, Mr. Leach, the Bishop of Salisbury and afterwards the Duke of York. There had already come to join the Princess Charlotte, Miss Mercer, now Lady Keith and Comtesse de Flahault, who came by the Regent's express desire as his daughter's most confidential friend; Mr. Brougham, for whom the young Princess had sent, as a person she had already often consulted; the Duke of Sussex, whose attendance he had taken the precaution of asking, knowing that he happened to dine in the immediate neighborhood; the Princess of Wales too had arrived from her villa at Blackheath, where she was when Mr. Brougham and Miss Mercer arrived; her Royal Highness was accompanied by Lady Charlotte Lindsay, then in waiting. Dinner had been ordered by the Princess Charlotte, and the party, except the Duke of Sussex, who did not immediately arrive, were at table; when from time to time the arrival of the great personages sent by the Regent was announced, as each of their hackney-coaches in succession came into the street. Some were suffered to remain in these vehicles, better fitted for convenience than for state; but the presumptive heiress to the Crown having chosen that conveyance, it was the humor of the party which she was now delighting with her humor, and interesting by her high spirits, like a bird flown from a cage, that these exalted subjects should become familiar with a residence which had so lately been graced with the occupancy of their future sovereign. Exceptions, however, were made, and the Duke of York immediately was asked into a room on the ground-floor. It is an undoubted fact, that not one of the persons sent by the Regent, not even the Duke of York, ever was in any of the apartments above stairs for one instant until the young Princess had agreed to leave the house and return home. The Princess of Wales saw the Duke of York for a few minutes below; and this was the only communication between the company above and those below—of whom all but the Duke and the Bishop remained outside the house. After a great deal of discussion the Princess Charlotte asked Mr. Brougham what he, on the whole, would advise her to do. He said,—'Return to Warwick House or to Carlton House, and on no account pass a night out of it.' She was exceedingly affected—even to tears—and asked if he too refused to stand by her. The day was beginning to break; a Westminster election to reinstate Lord Cochrane (after the sentence on him which abolished the pillory, and secured his re-election) was to be held that day at ten o'clock. Mr. Brougham led the young Princess to the window, and said, 'I have but to show you to the multitude which in a few hours will fill these streets and that Park—and possibly Carlton House will be pulled down—but in an hour after the soldiers will be called out, blood will flow, and, if your Royal Highness lives a hundred years, it will never be forgotten that your running away from your home and your father was the cause of the mischief; and you may depend upon it the English people so hate blood that you never will get over it.' She at once perceived the truth of this statement, and without any kind of hesitation agreed to see her uncle below, and accompany him home. But she told him she would not go in any carriage except one of her father's, as her character might suffer; she therefore retired to the drawing-room until a royal coach was sent for, and she then went home with the Duke of York."[1]

The Princess Charlotte was carried to Carlton House, and was understood to be kept there for some time a close prisoner. In consequence her uncle the Duke of Sussex put several questions to Ministers in the House of Lords, "Whether since her removal to Carlton House, she was allowed that degree of communication with her friends and connections which she had enjoyed in Warwick House?" "Whether she had liberty of communication by letter?" "Whether she was in that state of liberty which persons considered not in confinement ought to be in?" and "Whether, as she had reached the age of eighteen, there was any intention of providing an establishment for her suitable to her rank?" Lord Liverpool having declined to answer any of these questions, Lord Eldon added, "If

[1] Law Review No. XI. 280. See also Edinburgh Review for July, 1838, p. 34.

my noble friend had answered the questions put to him by the illustrious Duke, he would have been guilty of a gross breach of his duty to his Sovereign, and I will tell my noble friend that I never again would have conversed with him. What is meant by the question, 'Whether the Princess is allowed intercourse with her friends and connections (it might as well have been said with her *enemies*) while living under the roof of her royal Father?' Is not this an imputation? But I must look upon it as an animadversion on the Ministers of the Crown with reference to supposed advice. I will now only say that the great person alluded to has the exclusive right to direct the education of his child, and that no man is entitled to interpose between them, and a very strong ground, indeed, must be previously established to warrant the interposition of Parliament upon such a subject. With reference to the whole of the conduct of the great person alluded to in this affair, I have the satisfaction of being able to state in the face of the country, that he is deserving of the applause and not the censure of mankind."[1]

The Duke of Sussex gave notice of a motion respecting the treatment of the Princess Charlotte, but withdrew it, saying, "he had learned that she had been seen riding on horseback in Windsor Park, so that he was inclined to hope that more lenient measures were to be taken towards her." The Lord Chancellor said, "he never had meant to contend that there might not be cases with regard to the treatment of members of the Royal Family, in which it might be the duty of Parliament to interfere, but in the present instance he maintained that no ground had been laid for such interference."[2]

The firmness of the Princess Charlotte relieved her from any further importunity upon this subject, and she afterwards contracted a marriage of affection which the whole country approved, and which promised the most auspicious results, when she was suddenly snatched away to an early tomb.

It might have been supposed that at least in this glorious year, when Lord Eldon had met with so much to gratify him, and so little to annoy him, he might have been tolerably reconciled to the cares of office; but it

[1] 28 Parl. Deb. 755.   [2] Ib. 895.

turns out that all the while he was more eager than ever to get rid of them: thus he wrote to Dr. Swire:—

"I had thought that ere this time I should have been disengaged from the fatigue and oppression (for it begins to be oppressive at my years) of my office. But I have found it more difficult to persuade others than to persuade myself, that it is time for me to go. Providence and the country have bestowed upon me so much more than I could hope or deserve, that I ought perhaps to be somewhat ashamed of quitting my post, when those who are entrusted to judge, think that I may still be useful; but the struggle, between inclination to resign and reluctance to be thought too willing to consult my own ease, can not last much longer, because it must soon become a question about existence."[1]

The general rejoicings for the triumphant peace of 1814 were soon succeeded by dangerous riots on account of the bill to prohibit the importation of all foreign corn till wheat had reached the price of eighty shillings the quarter, and other *cereals* were proportionally dear. Lord Eldon probably thought, like Lord Sidmouth[2] and many other respectable politicians, that foreign corn should at all times be *contraband*, or that the price when importation was to be permitted should have been still higher,—and no blame could have been imputed to him if he had felt and expressed such sentiments. But, in reality, he had taken no part in the corn law debates, except complaining of the violent clamor which had been raised upon the subject out of doors, and very properly resisting a petition from the Lord Mayor and Livery of London to be heard against the bill by counsel at the bar.[3] Nevertheless he

[1] The letter likewise contains much about religion, which I do not copy, that I may avoid all risk of seeming levity upon so awful a subject.

[2] See letter, March 15, 1815, in which he says,—"My apprehension and conviction is, that the protecting price (80*s.*), as fixed by the bill, is not sufficient to give that confidence to the corn-grower which is essential to the attainment of the great object of the bill,—namely, an ample and independent supply." He then goes on to explain that the continual dread of arriving at that price would check the application of capital and labor to the production of grain from our own soil.—*Life*, iii. 127.

[3] On this occasion, while he was saying, "Why must not Bristol be heard —why not Birmingham—why not Cheltenham—why not every town in the kingdom?" the Duke of Gloucester *cheered* ironically and offensively; whereupon Lord Eldon said, with great spirit, "The illustrious Duke cries 'Hear! hear!' I wish he would *hear;* and I now tell him, that as I think all petitioners equal, I know all peers to be so."—30 *Parl. Deb.* 243.

was, for his supposed hostility to free trade, especially obnoxious to the mob. Once he was rescued from their violence by Lady Eldon. At the rising of the House of Lords a great assemblage of workmen and apprentices insulted him, as he was waiting for his carriage to return home; but on finding, when it drove up, that his wife, who had been in the habit of coming to fetch him, was in it,—and had not been deterred from her duty by the fear of their violence,—they gave her three cheers, and allowed both of them to depart in peace.

However, in the night of the 6th of March, his house in Bedford Square was attacked by a large body of the rioters, who broke the windows, tore up the iron railings, and bursting open the outer door, rushed into the hall. There they were checked by a few soldiers, called in through a back entry from the British Museum, which was near at hand. As the soldiers entered in single file, Lord Eldon at their head, he exclaimed, "Guards in the rear, reserve your fire." The panic-stricken mob fled. The Chancellor then gallantly sallying forth, brought in two prisoners, and said to them, "If you don't mind what you are about, lads, you will all come to be hanged." On which one of them said,—as their friends were coming to their rescue,—"Perhaps so, old chap; but I think it looks *now* as if you would be hanged *first*." In telling the story the old Peer would add, "and I had my misgivings that he was in the right. However, I got my wife and children safely into the Museum, and the mob were dispersed by a large reinforcement of soldiers." The morning after the riot the Duke of Wellington called in Bedford Square to compliment the Chancellor on his escape, and being told of the stratagem which had led to victory, he exclaimed, " I am glad, my Lord, that you have taken to act the General only when I have left the field, for you certainly would have beaten me in that career!"

For three weeks his house was a garrison, and during all that time he could only get to Westminster Hall by going stealthily through the Museum Gardens, and diving into all the obscure alleys in which he could find a passage, attended by Townsend, the Bow Street officer, and a rear-guard of policemen. Such were the storie she told, —but I think that, like other great lawyers giving an account of their conflicts with mobs, he must have exaggerated considerably both his perils and his prowess.'

The discussion about the corn laws and all internal disputes were suddenly suspended by the astounding intelligence that Napoleon had escaped from Elba, had landed at Cannes, had been joined by all the troops stationed at Grenoble, had proceeded in triumph to Paris, and was again established at the Tuileries in the place of Louis XVIII., who had fled to Ghent. Although a distinguished lawyer then thought that the world must be regenerated by the subversion of all the old monarchies in Europe, and joyously tossed up his hat at the thought of the coming confusion,—the rightly disposed of all parties in the state at this juncture cordially concurred in assisting the Government to crush our implacable foe, and to maintain our independence as a nation.

It is not mine to record the glories of Waterloo, and there was no memorable occurrence, within my humble sphere, till, on Napoleon being brought captive on an English ship of war to Plymouth, the question arose, how his person was to be disposed of? Lord Ellenborough Sir William Grant, Sir William Scott, and other great jurists being consulted, they gave conflicting and very unsatisfactory opinions with respect to the law of nations upon the *status* of the Emperor,—some saying that he was to be regarded as a prisoner of war—others as a subject of Louis XVIII., to whom he should be delivered up to be tried for treason—and others as a pirate or *hostis humani generis*, carrying about with him *caput lupinum*—while there were not wanting persons so romantically liberal as to contend that, having thrown himself on our hospitality, he was entitled to immediate freedom, and that he should be allowed to range at pleasure over the earth. I think Lord Eldon took a much more sensible view of the subject than any of them—which was " that the case was not provided for by anything to be found in Grotius or Vattel, but that the law of self-preservation would justify the keeping of him under restraint in some distant region, where he should be treated with all indulgence compatible with a due regard for the peace of mankind." Accordingly, St. Helena was selected as the place of his exile; and to put a stop to all experiments in our Courts, by

[1] *Vide* ante, Vol. VIII.

writs of *habeas corpus,* or actions for false imprisonment, an Act of Parliament was passed to legalize his detention.¹ Had the disgraceful disputes been avoided which afterwards took place respecting the number of bottles of wine he should be allowed for dinner, and the domiciliary visits to which he should be liable, I believe that his captivity at Longwood would have brought no impeachment on British justice or generosity, either in his own age or with posterity. As things were managed, I am afraid it will be said that he was treated, in the nineteenth century, with the same cruel spirit as the Maid of Orleans was in the fifteenth; and there may be tragedies on the Death of Napoleon, in which Sir Hudson Lowe will be the "SBIRRO"—and even Lord Eldon may be introduced as the *Stern Old Councillor* who decreed the hero's imprisonment.

CHAPTER CCIII.

CONTINUATION OF THE LIFE OF LORD ELDON TILL THE DEATH OF GEORGE III.

IT will be impossible for the future historian to clear Lord Eldon's fame from the charge of sadly mistaking his duty respecting the institutions of his own country.

Some thought that with peace a new era of improvement would have begun, the answer to all attempts at reform during the last quarter of a century having been—"This is not the time for such projects, when we are fighting for our existence;" but Lord Eldon still obdurately defended every antiquated abuse and absurdity which disgraced our jurisprudence. Sir Samuel Romilly sent up from the House of Commons a bill to subject freehold lands to simple contract debts, for the purpose of preventing this fraud (among others), that a man might borrow £100,000 to buy an estate, and dying, leave it unincumbered to his

---

¹ 56 Geo. 3, c. 22. Lord Eldon very properly resisted a motion of Lord Holland, for a reference to the opinion of the Judges relating to the character in which Napoleon Bonaparte stood after his surrender, and our right to detain him as a prisoner.—8th April, 1816. 33 *Parl. Deb.* 1019.

son—without a shilling of the debt being ever repaid. But Lord Eldon rejected the bill, after a long speech, in which he condemned it as contrary to the wisdom of our ancestors, and subversive of the Constitution under which we had long flourished. I believe he was quite sincere; and the great bulk of his audience listened to him with reverence—insomuch that Lord Grey, who ably advocated the measure, was obliged to give it up without a division.[1] A few years after, I had the pleasure of humbly assisting my friend Mr. John Romilly, the son of Sir Samuel, to pass this very bill through Parliament—when, even in the House of Lords, it met with hardly any opposition. Its justice and expediency are now so universally acknowledged, that people can hardly believe there was so recently a state of the public mind which could permit its rejection.

Strange to say, Lord Eldon countenanced an innovation in the administration of justice in Scotland, although it was most strenuously resisted by many enlightened men in that country, and among others by Sir Walter Scott,— the introduction of trial by jury in civil causes. I must confess that I myself entertain very serious doubts as to its expediency. This mode of trial works admirably well in England, where, from long usage, the procedure is so well understood, and it accords entirely with the habits of the people as well as with the frame of our laws. But where the relative duties of judge and jury were necessarily so little understood,—where issues of fact were to be framed in every cause by an officer of the Court, not always competent to understand on what facts the judgment was to depend,—where the Bench and the Bar were imperfectly acquainted with the rules of evidence,—and "bills of exceptions," "special verdicts," and "new trials," were terms not to be found in all Erskine's Institutes, or in all Morrison's Dictionary,—there might have been a misgiving that the reformation, however plausible, would produce confusion in practice, and occasion much expense and vexation to the suitors. A better plan probably would have been—separating the law from the facts upon the record—still to have reserved the decision of disputed facts for the Court, and to have improved the manner of taking the written depositions, or to have examined the

[1] 31 Parl. Deb. 1037.

witnesses in court *vivâ voce*. Lord Eldon, however, insisted on at once introducing the English system, and required that the jury should be *unanimous*—contrary not only to theoretical reasoning, but to the experience in Scotland of juries in criminal trials. One great object he had in view was to get rid of the immense number of appeals from the Court of Session to the House of Lords on mere questions of fact, by which his time had been most unprofitably and vexatiously consumed. The measure was, without difficulty, carried through Parliament; but the expectations entertained from it have been by no means realized, and before long this new system must either be abolished or reformed.

Lord Eldon was not called upon to come forward in debate during the session of 1816, except in opposing a motion in favor of the Irish Roman Catholics; and in spite of his zealous exertions, he was exceedingly distressed to find it supported by a Bishop, and rejected by the alarmingly small majority of four.[1]

He was further annoyed by the return to office of Mr. Canning, whom he regarded as little better than a Whig. Although Catholic emancipation henceforth became an open question, he had the full assurance of Lord Liverpool and of the Regent that it should not be granted. On this understanding alone would he have consented to remain in the Cabinet. My firm belief is, that, in spite of his professions, by which he tried to deceive others, and perhaps deceived himself, he was strongly attached to the Great Seal; but I am sure that he would have resigned it without one moment of doubt, rather than have agreed to a surrender of any of those safeguards which he considered necessary to preserve our Protestant Establishment. His retention of office was probably rendered doubly agreeable to him by the reflection that he could thereby more effectually watch and counteract the dangerous shemes of his latitudinarian colleagues.

Now he had to arrange the preliminaries of the marriage between the Princess Charlotte and Prince Leopold of Saxe Coburg—destined to be followed by other alliances with that illustrious house, which auspiciously promise to connect it forever with the throne of Great Britain. When the ceremony took place, the Chancellor

[1] 73 to 69. 31 Parl. Deb. 125.

was treated with peculiar distinction by the Regent, and the royal bride and bridegroom.[1]

His graceful manners and skillful tact as a courtier, in which, by intuition as it were, the coal-fitter's son, reared in the purlieus of Lincoln's Inn, excelled all the hereditary nobility of England, had so completely ingratiated him with his "young master," that he was not unfrequently invited as a guest to the private *symposia* at Carlton House,—where, with his Northern-Circuit stories, he was a full match for professed wits, although he wisely took care to testify a conscious inferiority in jovial powers, as much as in rank, to his Royal Highness, who, in his imitations of Lord Thurlow, and in the relation of ridiculous anecdotes of other public characters, really was a very considerable performer. We have a striking proof of the familiarity with which "Old Bags" was now treated by the man against whom "the Book" had been indited a few years ago, in the notes to him from the Regent, which all conclude "Your very affectionate friend, GEORGE P. R.," or "Very affectionately yours, GEORGE P. R.," and particularly in one urging him to complete some law arrangements without further delay—thus concluding with a very good-humored caution, that his Lordship should not be quite contented with his own notions of despatch: "Forgive me also, my dear friend, if I add, and bring to your recollection (and I can hardly do so without its forcing at the same time a smile on my countenance) that a snail's gallop is but a bad thing, and a very poor pace at best, in most of the occurrences of life, and I am sure that you would particularly find it such in the present."[2] The Chancellor knew too well both his duty and interest ever to forget for a moment that it was his sovereign who jested with him; and therefore while

---

[1] The Chancellor and Lady Eldon were likewise present at the wedding of the Princess Mary with the Duke of Gloucester on the 22nd of July following. We have an account of this ceremony in a letter from him to one of his daughters:—"Mamma (Lady Eldon) went through her part of the ceremony capitally well; but dear Princess Mary's behavior was so interesting and affecting that everybody was affected. Even the tears trickled down *my* cheeks; and as to Mamma, she cried all night, and nine-tenth parts of the next day." It is delightful to think that this illustrious lady, whose kindness of disposition and exemplary conduct have ever secured to her the admiration and respect of all classes of the community, is still likely to be long preserved, as an example of the union of the highest rank with the highest virtues.

[2] 2nd May, 1817.

other boon companions were successively cast off, he long retained the favor and the respect of George IV.

The transition from a long war to profound peace, the derangement of our monetary system by the Bank Restriction Acts, and the contemplated return to cash payments, had caused much commercial distress—with want of employment, and a great lowering of wages in many manufacturing districts. The consequence was, a dangerous ferment in the minds of the lower orders. How was this to be met? Said Lord Eldon, Lord Liverpool, Lord Castlereagh, and Lord Sidmouth :—" By suspending the Habeas Corpus Act, by passing a new act against Seditious Meetings, and by making perpetual the Treason Extension Act passed in 1796,[1] which was to expire with the reign of George III." Perhaps they were right; but, after much consideration and experience, having formed an opinion, that for such an emergency the true remedy is a vigorous execution of the old constitutional law, not new measures of coercion, I think that a mistaken policy was pursued—to which may be ascribed the increased irritation and discontent which prevailed for some years —the outbreak in 1819, called the " Manchester Massacre" —and the supposed necessity for the suspension of the Constitution by the passing of the "Six Acts." There was not the smallest ground for the imputation thrown upon the Ministers, that they had a plan for permanently encroaching on public liberty, and suspicion of indirect motive could not reasonably be carried farther than that they wished to strengthen themselves as a party, by spreading alarm that there were really plots against the Government which required a prohibition of public meetings without a license, the detention in prison of persons for political offenses for an unlimited time without bringing them to trial, and more stringent enactments against high treason than the law which had been found sufficient in England for four centuries. However, in the session of 1817 the proposed measures all passed, with the zealous, and, I doubt not, sincere advocacy of Lord Eldon, and he went so far as to defend both the legality and expediency of Lord Sidmouth's famous "Circular" recommending magistrates to hold to bail persons who published libels, without waiting till an indictment should be found against

[1] 36 Geo. 3, c. 7.   57 Geo. 3, c. 6.

them; which, if acted upon, might (contrary to the intention of the framer of it) have filled the jails with persons who had written against the existing Administration. Lord Grey having questioned the law laid down in the "Circular," and censured as unconstitutional the issuing of any instruction to magistrates from a Secretary of State respecting the manner in which they should administer justice to any particular class of offenders, Lord Eldon declared that in his opinion the law was correctly stated in the "Circular," and contended that there could be no impropriety in a correct exposition of the duty of judges coming from any quarter. He defended the suspension of the Habeas Corpus Act; and so alarmed was he by *frame-breaking*, and other enormities of the "*Luddites*," that he who had been Attorney-General in the fervor of the French Revolution, asserted with mnch solemnity, that "the dangers of the country were now greater than at any former period when he had known it to be suspended." He likewise maintained that Government was bound to employ spies, if their aid was necessary for detecting and defeating plots.[1] We shall see that instead of any misgivings as to the principles on which he was acting—when these measures proved ineffectual—he afterwards demanded, and carried, others much more arbitrary.

The melancholy death of the Princess Charlotte in the autumn of this year, threw every family of the kingdom into mourning as the loss of a near relative. Lord Eldon, in a very touching statement of the event, after mentioning his being summoned to Claremont to be present at her confinement, and that a bed had been provided for him, while other lords had to sleep on the carpet, says:—
"When her labor was over, I saw the babe, and a noble infant it was, as like the Royal Family as possible. I then went into the room where the surgeons were consulting what bulletin of the Princess they should send; and they had actually drawn one up, stating that 'she was going on as favorably as possible,' when Baillie came in, and after reading it, he refused to sign it, for such was not his opinion. We returned to our homes about two o'clock in the morning, and before six a messenger arrived to let us know the Princess was dead."[2]

[1] 36 Parl. Deb. 502, 1062.   [2] Twiss, ch. xxxix

This catastrophe at first increased the power of Lord Eldon, and would have done so permanently, if not counteracted by opposite influences. The Princess, though sincerely attached to the Protestant Establishment, was believed to have imbibed a strong opinion that its safety would be increased by relaxing the penal laws against the Roman Catholics; the Duke of York, now the heir presumptive to the throne, entertained an opinion, if possible, more adverse to their claims than his father's. He was known, though of mild temper, to be of inflexible resolution, and he naturally felt the highest possible veneration for the great champion of that cause which he had espoused. During an illness which the Regent soon after had, there were speculations that Lord Eldon would not only be Lord Chancellor, but Prime Minister to Frederic I., and that though advanced in years, he would display the energy of a Ximenes in supporting Orange ascendency in Ireland.

Yet he seems soon after to have been in serious danger of being supplanted by a rival. This was Sir John Leach, who, having in spite of obscure birth and defective education pushed himself into practice at the Chancery Bar, and obtained a seat in Parliament, had gained the notice of the Prince of Wales by advocating his right to the arrears of the Duchy of Cornwall during his minority, had been promoted to be Chancellor of that Duchy, and had become his Royal Highness's private confidential adviser. On a move in the law caused by the resignation of Sir William Grant, he was now appointed Vice-Chancellor, and he resolved speedily to be upon the woolsack. The Princess of Wales, destined so often to be made an instrument of faction and political intrigue, he hoped would accomplish his ambitious purpose.[1]

[1] Sir John Leach was a man of unblemished private honor, and no doubt believed the Princess to be guilty; but his eagerness in pushing forward the proceedings against her, contrary to the wishes of the Ministers, drew forth afterwards, from her eloquent counsel, Mr. Denman, the quotation—
"Some busy and insinuating rogue,—
Some cogging, cozening slave, *to get some office*,
Hath devis'd this slander."
The charge receives some countenance from Mr. Wilberforce's Diary, lately published:—
"27th April, 1820. The Vice-Chancellor Leach has been trying to root out the Ministry; he has been telling the King that his present Ministers are not standing by him, and that he ought to have a divorce."—*Life of Wilberforce*, v. 54.

This unhappy lady had left England in the year 1814, and, in visiting Germany, Italy, and the Holy Land, had certainly conducted herself in a most unbecoming manner, although, from the bad character of most of those who bore testimony against her, there was great difficulty in safely determining to what degree she had carried her violation of the rules of decorum and modesty. As she had been atrociously ill-used by her husband from the moment of her arrival in England, and as she had been finally abandoned by him,—receiving from him what was called a "Letter of License," his Ministers knew that any inquiry into the new charges against her would recoil upon him, would be hurtful to the national morality, and would even be dangerous to the monarchy. They therefore most wisely and properly wished to keep matters quiet between them, and discouraged every suggestion of instituting proceedings of any kind against her. But the Prince was surrounded by "private friends" and flatterers, who made him forget or overlook his own bad conduct towards her, and gratified him with the prospect of actually getting rid of her as his wife. Of these the leader was Leach, who, the more that the proposal of a divorce-suit was resisted by the Ministers of the Crown, the more eagerly recommended it—in the expectation that his Royal Highness would take as the "Keeper of his Conscience" one who gave him such palatable counsel. The death of the Princess Charlotte was urged upon him as removing all objection to the necessary inquiry, and representations were made to him that he might not only redeem himself from the disgrace of his present conjugal connection, which would become more galling when she might claim to be received as Queen of England, but that he might form a happier union, and provide heirs to the crown in a direct line.

In consequence, the Regent still elaborately civil to Lord Eldon, and still expecting to overcome all his scruples, wrote him a letter, which after lamenting that his Lordship had been prevented by indisposition from attending a meeting of the Ministers at Brighton, explained that his Royal Highness was desirous of conferring with him upon the steps to be taken with reference to the conduct of the Princess of Wales, which, he said, "had given great scandal on the Continent, and especially at Vienna, where the Court had refused to receive her" —and thus disclosed his Royal Highness's design: "You can not, therefore, be surprised (much difficulty, in point of delicacy, being now set aside in my mind by the late melancholy event which has taken place in my family) if I therefore turn my whole thoughts to the endeavoring to extricate myself from the cruelest as well as most unjust predicament that even the lowest individual, much more a Prince, ever was placed in."—Inveighing in strong terms against her, and expressing his wish to be unshackled from such a woman, he puts this question: "Is it then, my dear friend, to be tolerated that ...... is to be suffered to continue to bear my name, to belong to me and the country, and that *that* country, the first in all the world, and myself, its Sovereign, are to be expected to submit silently to a degradation under which no upright and honorable mind can exist?"

The particulars of the meeting between the Regent and the Chancellor, on this occasion, have not yet been given to the world, but the result had by no means corresponded with the warm wishes of his Royal Highness; for no ministerial measure was instituted respecting the Princess, and the famous "Milan commission," which then took its origin, was left entirely to the management and control of Sir John Leach.

A paragraph, of which Lord Eldon believed that "his Honor" was the author, appeared in the newspapers, stating that "the Lord Chancellor, on account of his age and infirmities, had resolved immediately to resign the Great Seal, that he might enjoy that dignified repose to which, from his long and meritorious services to the Crown and to the public, he was so justly entitled." The rumor being supposed to receive strong corroboration, particularly from persons connected with Carlton House, was in everybody's mouth, and was generally credited; people varying chiefly as to the cause of the unexpected event—some saying that Lord Eldon was sincerely tired of office—more, that he had quarreled with his colleagues about the Catholic question—and a few of the well-informed whispering that there had been some unpleasant discussions about the Princess of Wales. He himself was thrown into an agony of mortification, and he much resembled, for a time, the old man who had called upon Death to relieve him from his load, when the grisly monarch actually appeared before him. Thus he at last disburdened himself to Sir William, who had written to him to know the truth of the report:—

"DEAR BROTHER,

"While *I* am ignorant of what you hear in all quarters, *you* are not the only person ignorant of it. A paragraph appeared in a morning paper about a week ago, which informed me of my intention to resign. This may have occasioned much of what you have heard. There are other causes, which may have contributed to the gossip of all quarters. There is a malignity, natural enough, and sufficiently manifest, I think, that leads to observations not met in any manner, that a man, who has been sixteen years and upwards in possession of the Great Seal, is no longer fit to hold it; and this acquires a mighty effect when it is seconded by a conviction in the holder's mind, sometimes betrayed (from the fatigue of what is passed and the dread of what is coming) in expressions (of which you have heard more than any other person) that he has become and is becoming more and more unfit, both with respect to himself and the country, to hold it. In addition to this, the public are very well aware that, as I had no assistance from Ellenborough, and little from Redesdale, in Parliament last session, I have none to look for in the next stormy session from any lawyer in the House: and how I was dealt with towards the close of the last Session in the other House, or rather how I should have been dealt with by Brougham and Co., if I had not myself personally interfered to produce something more decent towards myself, I need not mention. These things also suggest probabilities to all quarters. *There are also persons who have strong interest in first making resignation probable by talk in all quarters, and so accomplishing it.* Perhaps too it is pretty well known that, growing unequal to my judicial duties, I have no influence as to other matters and this may induce many to represent resignation as probable. The truth too is, that I have long wished to resign —that I am conscious that I am unable to execute the great duties of my office as they ought to be executed, and that at my time of life my insufficiency must daily increase and be more apparent. Sir William Grant's resignation, too early for himself and much too early for the public, has made a sort of call for my resignation, which I certainly am conscious has been too long delayed. I am, moreover, impressed with a conviction that no presumption can warrant me in supposing that I can, even if I live through another Parliament, live through it with any credit in office. I am likewise strongly impressed with a persuasion that, at my time of life, I should be thinking much oftener and more seriously of another world and its concerns than it is possible for me to address my thoughts to them in possession of the most laborious office in the kingdom. I add, that I wish too for a little more comfort in this world; for I feel the labors of this office to be such, and myself to be growing so unequal to them, as to feel now the necessity of refusing all invitations out of my house, that I can with any decency refuse, that I may have all my time for purposes to which I feel the whole of it to be insufficient. I have made Grant's for Tuesday next an exception to this. The newspaper paragraph has set the world in all quarters a-talking on this subject. Whatever may be my wishes on this subject, when they became fixed purpose, as such, they would have been first communicated to my wife, to you, and the Regent. In truth, till the meeting of Parliament, it would be nonsense to suffer wish to ripen into purpose. If it would have matured into purpose, it should seem as if it would be in vain. When I attended at Carlton House on Wednesday to seal the consent to a royal marriage, the Prince, led by the newspaper paragraph to the subject, held a language to me (as to his confidence that I would not, to use his expression, ' desert him,' repeating that expression often), which I foresee, whenever the attempt is made to 'abolish' *my* 'slavery,' will make it no easy matter to effectuate it. But my time of life will compel it against all difficulties, before much longer time can pass, though the conversation to which I allude may pospone it longer than I like. If, to serve my master, I am compelled to remain somewhat longer, he must prevail upon my fellow-servants to take a little more care of my character in the House of Commons than they have hitherto done."

It certainly is very amusing, after observing his rage against the newspaper paragraph, and his indignant charge against those persons who, having a strong interest, tried to accomplish his resignation by talking about it, to watch the workings of his mind. He was afraid that, in complaining of this wicked fabrication, he had betrayed some fondness for the office, which he did not like to acknowledge to himself, much less to his brother, and therefore he gravely talks of his various reasons for resigning. But, then, with wonderful facility, he overrules them all on the simple request of the Regent, "not to desert him," which he must have known to be insincere; for although Lord Liverpool and his colleagues would have deeply regretted the loss of Lord Eldon, and probably would have refused to admit into the Cabinet the mover of the mischief, his Royal Highness at this time would unquestionably have been delighted to hand over the Great Seal to him who was unscrupulously laboring to gratify the wish nearest his heart. The concluding touch, about the manner in which he had been abandoned in the House of Commons by his "fellow-servants" to his enemies, is particularly racy. Yet, though he continued to be more factiously assailed and more feebly defended in the House of Commons, he was prevailed upon to hold the Great Seal above nine years longer, and then he thought that he was ill-used in being deprived of it.

Ministers remained firmly united as to the line of conduct to be adopted in the dispute between the Regent and his wife, till Mr. Canning generously withdrew, in consequence of the unfortunate resolution at last taken, upon her return to this country as Queen, to dissolve their marriage by Act of Parliament. The session of 1818 went off very smoothly.

In support of a bill to indemnify those who had acted under the Habeas Corpus Suspension Act, Lord Eldon said that, "to that Act he believed the tranquillity of the country had been chiefly owing; it had been a mild and merciful measure, preventive of miseries—not productive of them." That such a measure had been found highly useful in former times, by enabling the Government to send Jacobite leaders to the Tower, and although there was no sufficient legal evidence against them to keep them there till the danger of rebellion had blown over, I perfectly understand; but we can hardly now believe, that under such sensible men as Lord Liverpool and Lord Eldon, it should be applied to putting down riots among starving artisans, excited by persons who had no influence in the state, and who could be brought to trial in the ordinary course of law for the offenses they had committed.[1]

There had lately been several government prosecutions which had signally failed—very much from a feeling that there was a disposition to strain the law both of *treason* and of *libel;* but Lord Eldon in the course of these debates took an opportunity to vindicate all that had been done by the Attorney General, and to ridicule the notion that libels on the law and constitution should be left unpunished, lest the notice of them should give them publicity.[2]

Now began the agitation of the social question, so very important and so very difficult, respecting the duty of the State to limit the hours of labor in manufactories. He must be on arrogant man who would venture to express a very confident opinion upon it. A bill introducing several humane regulations for the protection of factory children,—brought in by Sir Robert Peel the elder,—coming up from the Commons, Lord Eldon, opposing Lord Kenyon, took what seems *prima facie* to be the sound view of the subject, and, this session, succeeded in throwing it out. He said, "he hoped he should not be suspected of hard-heartedness, if he confessed himself one of those who really thought that philanthropy had not taken its right course in modern times. Varied and conflicting interests should be well balanced before a man of discretion and honesty would pronounce a fair decision. The overworking of children was a misdemeanor at common law, and adults should be allowed to take care of themselves." The same bill, however, was passed in the following session,[3] and was found to operate beneficially—so that the principle of State interference was fully established, and the consideration now is one of detail,—*how far* it is expedient to push it.

Lord Eldon strenuously, and I think rightly, opposed Lord Erskine's bill for *declaring* it unlawful for Justices of the Peace to hold to bail for libel before indictment.

---

[1] Nor was the new Treason Law of the slightest benefit. The counts framed upon it gave Sir Charles Witherell a considerable advantage in defending Dr. Watson; and the conviction of Brandreth and his confederates at Derby was under the old statute of Edward III.—See State Trials, vol. xxxii.   [2] 37 Parl. Deb. 713, 788.

[3] 59 Geo. 3, c. 66, which limited the time of labor in cotton mills and factories to twelve hours, for persons under sixteen years of age.

Although Lord Sidmouth's "Circular" urging them to do so might be blameable, the principle of the common law is, that for all misdemeanors supposed to involve a breach of the peace, the offender may be held to bail upon a sworn information before a magistrate; and *libel* clearly comes within this category. The House found that, since the time of Queen Anne, there had been 128 cases in which the Judges of the Court of King's Bench had, as magistrates, held to bail in cases of libel, and the law makes no distinction, for this purpose, between them and common Justices of the Peace. Lord Erskine, therefore ought, at all events, to have his bill *enacting*, not *declaratory;* and I am only surprised that it was not rejected by a larger majority than 31 to 18.[1]

At the close of the session, the Prince Regent in person having delivered a speech in which he not ungracefully drew a contrast between the present state of the country and that in which he had found it when he first began to govern in his father's name, did an act perfectly legal and constitutional,—although not witnessed since the reign of Charles II.,—by actually dissolving the Parliament in the presence of the two Houses, the usual course having been first to prorogue, and shortly after to dissolve by proclamation. But the Chancellor said, "My Lords and Gentlemen:—It is the will and pleasure of his Royal Highness the Prince Regent, acting in the name and on behalf of his Majesty, that this Parliament be now dissolved, and this Parliament is dissolved accordingly." It had lasted above six years, and all parted in good humor.[2]

Lord Eldon, before he retired to Encombe for the long vacation was summoned to be present at the celebration of the auspicious marriage between his Royal Highness

[1] 38 Parl. Deb. 1081–1114.

[2] Ib. 1316 In 1831, when the House of Commons was disposed to reject the Reform Bill, the proceeding more nearly resembled the abrupt dissolutions of the 17th century. On that occasion the King said, "I have come to meet you for the purpose of proroguing this Parliament, with a view to its immediate dissolution."—*Hansard*, 3rd series, vol. iii. p. 1810.

On the 23rd of July, 1847, while I was a member of the Cabinet, the Queen having intimated in her speech from the throne that she meant forthwith to dissolve the Parliament, a prorogation was ordered; and as soon as her Majesty had returned to her palace, she held a council, at which she signed an order for the dissolution,—and all the writs for the new elections went by the post the same evening.

the Duke of Kent and the Dowager Princess of Leiningen, born a Princess of the illustrious House of Coburg; and he lived to see the child of this marriage seated on the throne of Great Britain.

While in the country he was much disturbed by the resignation of Lord Ellenborough. Sir Samuel Shepherd, the Attorney General, who in every other respect would have made an excellent successor, was disqualified by deafness, and much perplexity arose respecting the appointment. The Regent pressed that Lord Ellenborough should be consulted on the subject, but this Lord Eldon very properly resisted, saying, "that if those who possessed under the Crown the great law offices were to be advised with as to the question who should be their successors, a choice, which ought to be made at the time of filling the vacancy, of the best and most eminent men at *that time* in the profession, would seldom be made, and the succession would probably in all cases be settled by management and intrigue." Lord Eldon laudably selected Mr. Justice Abbott, who had been his most useful "Devil" when he was Attorney General, and who as a Puisne Judge had displayed the highest judicial ability. He thus justified his choice in a letter to Lord Kenyon, which I am afraid the common reader may find dull, but which is so full of delightful Westminster Hall gossip, that, for the sake of my professional friends, I have not the heart to exclude it. After stating that he is confined to the house by a fit of the gout, he thus proceeds:—

"I agree with you that, generally speaking, the Chief Justice of the King's Bench should be a Peer, even if there had been no usage upon the subject. But then the state of the profession must admit of it. I have not been able to find (in that state) a person fitter for it than Abbott. Now see the effect of this. Lord Mansfield had had long practice in lucrative situations at the Bar,—he was of a noble family—he was not likely to have descendants, that is, issue. Your father had been, at the Bar, the most eminent lawyer of our times; he had made by his practice, independently of the law offices, a larger fortune than any professional man of his time. When called to the King's Bench I know (I think) myself, that Peerage was one object with him in accepting the office; and if

Providence had not suffered him to live but the shortest time in the office, a peerage would have gone to his children, with ample means to support the dignity. Lord Ellenborough had likewise made some fortune, much less, certainly, at the Bar; but if he had died before Mr. Way, I doubt whether the Peerage *there* would have been either convenient to the family or useful to the public. As to the Common Pleas, when C. J. de Grey went out, they gave him a peerage in order to find a Chief Justice-ship for Wedderburn. You see that peerage has been obliged to be helped out by office. Lord Loughborough had no children; his peerage, therefore, as Loughborough, could not descend; and his office would support him during his life. What he meant, when he left the Chancellorship, by getting an unendowed earldom for his nephew, I can't pretend to say. When I came to the Common Pleas, I had made some fortune in a successful practice at the Bar and in the great law offices, which I held nearly twelve years. Mr. Pitt was unwilling to give me an office which would take me out of Parliament; I could not be in it unless in the House of Lords, and I can assure you that I have often thought that, if I had survived the acceptance of the peerage but a short time, I had accepted what would have been a nuisance to my family, and no benefit to the public. Of our dear friend Lord A., can anybody now say that it was a wise measure on his part to accept a peerage?[1] Now as to Abbott, his practice has been behind the bar. He never had any office, I think not a silk gown: he enters, therefore, upon the office in very moderate circumstances, with a considerable family. The permanent offices of profit, in the gift of the Chief Justice, as I understand, without exception, are not any of them likely to be vacant while he is likely to live or to hold his office—what he can save out of the other emoluments of the office, he did not, and indeed he could not, think would enable him to transmit with a peerage a fully competent fortune to support it; his health is tender, and his eye-sight not in a very safe state: upon the whole, his own difficulty about taking the office, was the apprehension that peerage was

[1] Lord Alvanley. His accomplished son is certainly an ornament to the peerage.

to go with it. He immediately determined, if it was not. As to himself, this determination appears to me to have been quite right. If a contrary determination would, as to the public, have been right in any *other* person at the bar, where are you to find one (in whom, in point of circumstances, it had been right with peerage), to whom this great office could have been offered? The Attorney General, from his deafness, could take neither chiefship; that of the King's Bench could not be offered to so young a man as the Solicitor General. He refused that of the Common Pleas, as not yet having any fortune to leave to his family. Upon the whole, we endeavored to do the best we could: we could not do what really would have been unexceptionable. It was impossible."

Lord Chief Justice Abbott (afterwards created Lord Tenterden) fulfilled the highest expectations that could have been formed of him, and I feel personally grateful to those who advised his elevation. I practiced under him till his death,—having daily fresh reason to admire his profound knowledge of his profession, his extraordinary soundness of intellect, and his invariable and earnest love of justice.[1]

In a few days after Lord Eldon had resumed his labors in Lincoln's Inn Hall, he was dreadfully shocked by the melancholy death of Sir Samuel Romilly, who had been so long by far the first advocate in his Court, and with whom, although they were so much opposed to each other, not only in party warfare, but on all the principles of government and legislation, he had always lived on terms of courtesy and mutual respect. Taking his seat on the bench on the morning after the fatal event,—as soon as he cast his eye on the vacant place within the bar which Romilly had been accustomed to occupy, his eyes filled with natural tears, and exclaiming, with unfeigned emotion, "I can not sit here,"—he withdrew, and the Court was adjourned.

In the same month he lost his old friend Queen Charlotte who ever regarded him as the wisest and honestest of mankind; but she had ceased for some years to have much influence, and her death was chiefly noticed by its render-

[1] While he was Chief Justice, I passed the most agreeable part of my forensic career, before I was tossed on the sea of politics. I was made Solicitor General on his death, in 1832.

ing necessary some arrangement for the custody of the King's person.

This was the first subject brought before the new Parliament, which met in January, 1819. Lord Eldon at last agreed to "disquantity" the train of his old master. The Windsor establishment of lords in waiting and grooms of the bed-chamber was greatly reduced, and the Duke of York was constituted CUSTOS of the King's person, with an additional allowance of £10,000 a year. But a proposal being made that this should be paid out of the privy purse, of which, unfortunately, his Majesty could make no use, and which was idly accumulating, the Chancellor said, " the privy purse was as completely private property in the King as anything belonging to any of their Lordships was private property in them: now the private property of any subject during mental alienation was placed under proper care that it might be forthcoming for his use at the return of his reason,—and he would put it to their Lordships, whether the Sovereign ought to be deprived in his affliction of that which was allowed to the humblest of his subjects—the benefit of the principle which arose from a hope of his recovery. It did not follow, however, that the King's privy purse was liable, like the private property of a subject, to the maintenance of the proprietor during lunacy,—the King being entitled both in health and in sickness to a maintenance from the nation, irrespectively of his privy purse."[1] This reasoning was not considered very consistent or very satisfactory, and the arrangement caused a good deal of disgust in the most loyal bosoms.

The session was an uncomfortable one for the Ministers, who, although omnipotent in the House of Lords, met with several mortifying checks in the House of Commons, insomuch that Lord Liverpool seriously thought of resigning. The monetary question was still the most difficult to deal with. Lord Eldon was much hurt by finding that Peel had sided with the " Bullionists," whom he considered to be almost as dangerous as the " Spenceans," and he could not be made to see the objections to a forced paper currency. He therefore resisted the proposal to return to a metallic circulation; and, standing out in the Cabinet,— seemingly alone,—was for postponing the consideration

[1] 39 Parl. Deb. 1257. Stat. 59 Geo. 3, c. 22.

of the subject for two years. This resistance brought him the following remonstrance from the Premier:—

"I am sanguine enough to think that we have a reasonable chance of success, in carrying the measures which were discussed on Saturday; but whether I may turn out to be right or wrong, as to this I am quite satisfied, after long and anxious consideration, that if we can not carry what has been proposed, it is far, far better for the country that we should cease to be the Government.

"After the defeats we have already experienced during this session, our remaining in office is a *positive* evil. It confounds all ideas of government in the minds of men. It disgraces us *personally*, and renders us less capable every day of being of any real service to the country, either now or hereafter. If, therefore, things are to remain as they are, I am quite clear that there is no advantage, in any way, in our being the persons to carry on the public service. A strong and decisive effort can alone redeem our character and credit, and is as necessary for the country as it is for ourselves. As to a postponement for two years, it would be mere self-delusion, and is far more objectionable in my judgment, in every bearing, than at once renouncing all idea of setting the finances of the country right."

Upon this threat of breaking up the Government, the Chancellor appears to have renounced any intermeddling on such subjects, and to have confined himself to law and religion. He again fought the battle of Catholic emancipation against Lord Donoughmore—and, this year, with better success, having a majority of 147 to 106.[1]

A more formidable assault was made by Lord Grey, who actually introduced a bill to do away with the declaration against transubstantiation, so that Roman Catholic peers might sit in Parliament, as they had done from the Reformation till the latter part of the reign of Charles II. But the Lord Chancellor opposed the principle of the measure as most dangerous. He said that "the law of Charles II. had been re-enacted in the first Parliament of William III., the founder of our civil and religious liberties. It had been thought necessary for the preservation of these that Papists should not be allowed to sit in Parliament, and some test was therefore necessary by

[1] 40 Parl. Deb. 448.

which it might be ascertained whether a man was a Papist or a Protestant. The only possible test for such a purpose was an oath declaratory of religious belief; and, as Dr. Paley had observed, 'it was perfectly just to have a religious test of a political creed.' He entreated the House not to commit the crime against posterity of transmitting to them in an impaired and insecure state the civil and religious liberties of England."[1] To his great delight the bill was rejected by a majority of 141 to 82; and he thought that all danger from such attempts must in future be obviated by the Duke of Wellington's accession to a political office and a seat in the Cabinet.

But the great marvel of this session was, that the Lord Chancellor himself actually proposed a bill to abolish *trial by battle* in real actions, and entirely to do away with *appeals of murder* which were to be decided in this warlike manner. Trial by battle in real actions had been introduced by William the Conqueror, had been occasionally practiced so recently as the reign of Elizabeth, when the lists were erected and the champions sworn in Tothill Fields, before the Judges of the Common Pleas—and it might still be demanded by either party. An appeal of murder had lately been prosecuted in the Court of King's Bench, when I myself saw the appellee, on being required to plead, throw down his gauntlet on the floor, and insist on clearing his innocence by battle,—as the Judges held he was entitled to do. And Lord Holt, Mr. Dunning, and other great lawyers had declared that this appeal of murder, which might be brought after an acquittal before a jury, and in which the Crown had no power to pardon, was "a glorious badge of the rights and privileges of Englishmen." Yet Lord Chancellor Eldon, to the amazement of the House of Peers and of the public, moved the second reading of a bill sent up by the Commons, to reform these practices, which he described as abuses, and, notwithstanding their antiquity, attacked in the most unsparing manner:—

"With respect to civil cases," said he, "the 'trial by battle' was permitted only in real actions, and even in these the parties were not suffered to fight *in propriâ personâ*,—they were compelled to confide their interests to *champions*, on the principle, that if one of the parties were

[1] 40 Parl. Deb. 1063.

slain, the suit would abate. They were, therefore, under the necessity of appointing champions, and these were to fight from morning till the stars appeared in the firmament at night, or till one of them used what the law-writers called the 'horrible word' *Craven*,—and according to the result of the battle the right to the property was determined. Then, as to 'appeal of murder,' he thought it could not be allowed to continue, taking away trial by battle; for, according to the old law, those who made the appeal were obliged to do so at the hazard of their own lives. But he thought it a great absurdity that a man who had been acquitted by the unanimous opinion of a jury should again be put into jeopardy of his life, provided any person standing in a certain degree of relationship to the deceased thought proper, from motives either of vengeance or of avarice, to proceed against him by way of civil suit. Was it not also a very gross absurdity that the Crown, in which the power of pardoning offenses against the public was invested, should not have the power of pardoning in the case of an appeal, and yet that the appellor, if successful in his appeal, might grant life and liberty for a sum of money? Proceeding by indictment, if the prosecutor *compounds the felony*, he is liable to severe punishment; but if he prefers an appeal, he may lawfully stay execution for a bribe. It was indeed surprising that such a law should have continued a part of our system, which in other respects came so near to perfection."

The Lords seem to have been struck dumb with astonishment, for, without another word being uttered, the bill was agreed to, and the House adjourned. I must observe, however, that this was a measure, not concocted by such schemers as Romilly or Mackintosh, but framed by the Attorney General, with the authority of the Cabinet.'[1]— Without any other memorable occurrence, in which Lord Eldon was concerned, he had the satisfaction to terminate the session by a prorogation.[2]

Whether from some misgiving that the Lord Chancellor no longer stood *super vias antiquas*, or from what other cause I know not, the Government was not in good repute even with the Tory party, and it would probably have fallen to pieces soon, had it not been strengthened by the

---

[1] 40 Parl. Deb. 1203-1207.   [2] Ib. 1571.

alarm which the agitation of a few contemptible demagogues now spread through the country.

But before I come to scenes so disgraceful, I have to record a joyful event, of which the Chancellor was officially called upon to be a witness—the birth of the Princess Victoria. The Duke and Duchess of Kent had been traveling on the Continent, when her Royal Highness gave hopes of presenting an heir to the throne, and they most happily resolved, in spite of some difficulties to be overcome, that the "auspicious babe" should first see the light in the happy Island which it might one day have to govern. On the 24th of May, 1818, Lord Eldon was summoned to Kensington Palace, according to royal etiquette, to attend the accouchement. He had the happiness to return home to Lady Eldon with news of the birth of a fair Princess, and that all was going well both with mother and child. It is said that, rubbing up his recollection of Shakspeare, he exclaimed,—

> "This royal infant (Heaven still move about her!),
> Though in her cradle, yet now promises
> Upon this land a thousand thousand blessings,
> Which time shall bring to ripeness.—
> In her days every man shall eat in safety,
> Under his own vine, what he plants, and sing
> The merry songs of peace to all his neighbors."

Notwithstanding the coercive measures of 1817, the discontents in the manufacturing districts had seriously increased, and Mr. Henry Hunt and other mob-orators were holding meetings in different parts of the country, which were dangerous to the public peace. These meetings most undoubtedly ought to have been prevented or dispersed, and the ringleaders ought to have been prosecuted and punished. For such salutary purposes the existing law of the land, and the civil force, if vigorously and judiciously applied, would have been abundantly sufficient. But Ministers were at first supine, and then indiscreetly active. Lord Eldon was early alarmed by the danger: but instead of warding it off by constitutional means, he was for resorting to his old recipe, and instituting prosecutions for high treason. Thus he wrote to Sir William:—

"Your exhortations to the King's servants, I doubt, can't reach many of them, for, with the exception of Liverpool, Castlereagh, Sidmouth, Wellington, Van, and myself, they are all, eight in number, in different parts of Europe. We meet daily, but can resolve upon nothing. In fact the state of our law is so inapplicable to existing circumstances, that we can't meet the present case: and I am as convinced as I am of my existence, that if Parliament don't *forthwith* assemble, there is nothing that can be done but to let those meetings take place, reading the Riot Act, if there be a riot at any of them. Prosecutions for *sedition* spoken at them, we have now in plenty on foot—and they may come to trial nine months hence. They are not worth a straw: and blamed as I was in 1794 for prosecuting for *High Treason*, all are convinced here that *that* species of prosecution can alone be of any use. I think, however, that it won't be attempted: the case is as large and complicated as mine was in 1794, and nobody has the spirit to attempt it."

A meeting of a clearly illegal nature had been advertised to take place at Manchester, on the 16th of August. It was improperly allowed to assemble, without any warning from those appointed to preserve the public peace, and a disturbance arising, a regiment of yeomanry cavalry was very indiscreetly employed to charge the multitude,—in consequence of which several lives were lost. This tumult, called by the vulgar the "Battle of Peterloo," and the "Manchester Massacre," caused much excitement all over England, and the conduct of the magistrates, under whose orders the military had acted, was severely condemned. The Government probably did right in supporting them; but might have done so with more moderation. Lord Eldon thought that a still more energetic course should be taken, and urged in vain, that now, at last, with such *overt acts*, Hunt and his associates ought to be prosecuted and punished as traitors:—

"Neither the Prince nor most of his Ministers," he writes to Sir William, "seem to act as you think they should. He came here late on Thursday evening—rather night—and went off again to the Marquess of Hertford's, I *believe;*—that he went there or elsewhere is certain. Eight out of fourteen Ministers, I believe, abroad—in that there is no harm: the other six are full as many as can usefully converse upon any subject. So, at least, I think experience has taught me. Of the six, five are at their villas, and I alone am here. They come, however, daily: not that I can see that there is much use in it. There are but two things to be done—to treat what is passing as high treason, or as misdemeanor; and when the Law Officers have said what THEY can do, what more is to be done? They decide for misdemeanor; and who will be bold enough to command them to institute prosecutions, such as they think they can't maintain? Without all doubt, the Manchester magistrates must be supported; but they are very generally blamed here. For my part, I think if the assembly was only an unlawful assembly, that task will be difficult enough in sound reasoning. If the meeting was an overt act of treason, their justification is complete. That it was such, and that the Birmingham was such, is my clear opinion. Under Edward's statute, I know very well it would be difficult to maintain that; but, under my act of the 36th of the King, in force at this moment, a conspiracy to levy war —a conspiracy to depose him—or a conspiracy by force to make a change in either House of Parliament,—manifested by an overt act,—is treason. Can any man doubt, connecting Birmingham and Manchester together, that these meetings are overt acts of conspirators, to instigate to such specific acts of treason, or some of them? I can't doubt it. But how ridiculously shall I be reasoning in Parliament, if the prosecutions are for misdemeanor! An unlawful assembly, *as such merely*, I apprehend, can't be dispersed; and what constitutes *riot* enough to justify dispersion is no easy matter to determine, where there is not actual violence begun on the part of those assembled."

In a few days after he again wrote to Sir William, in no degree tranquillized:—

"The accounts in general, from the disturbed districts, very gloomy, portending storms, and those not afar off. The better sort of people in the kingdom are, as it seems to me, insane: they are divisible into two classes; the one insane, and manifesting that insanity in perfect apathy, eating and drinking, as if there was no danger of political death, yea, even to-morrow; the other, your Cokes, your Bedfords, &c., hallooing on an infuriate multitude to those acts of desperation and fury which will first destroy those who encourage the perpetration of them. We are in a state in which the country must make new laws to meet this new state of things, or we must make a shocking choice between military government and anarchy. Lord Clarendon, I think, speaks of Lord Keeper Coventry as fortunate in not living to see the civil broils of his country: I am excessively fearful that no man can now hold the Great Seal for any material portion of time, and live without seeing what Coventry did not see."

The Chancellor was overruled in his scheme of a trial for high treason,—all the rest of the Cabinet concurring in the opinion of the Attorney and Solicitor General, that the prosecution could only be for a misdemeanor; but he was comforted by finding that in arguing the necessity of new laws, he had made an impression on at least one member of the Cabinet. Lord Sidmouth, the Home Secretary, sent him a letter, saying, " These considerations have convinced me, though they have not convinced others, that the laws ought to be strengthened, and the military force of the country augmented, without delay; and for these purposes Parliament should be assembled in the month of November, at the latest. It is, however, determined to wait and see—a determination, believe me, wholly unsuited to the exigency of the present moment." Lord Eldon wrote back in answer:—

" The great question is, what is to be done? I can say no more upon that, than I have said. In thinking what laws may be necessary to be enacted, it occurs me to recollect that, at the time of union with Ireland, I told Mr. Pitt that I thought the great objection to it was, that it would perhaps introduce into this country sedition and treason, in their Irish modes and forms; that, if such should be the case, we should have to attempt passing, at Westminster, such laws as Ireland had enacted; that my belief was, that no Parliament at Westminster ever would pass such laws; that if they would not, Great Britain, as a land of anarchy, would be a land in which it would be impossible to exist; and if they would pass such laws, it would be a land of necessary tyranny, in which existence would not be to be wished. Treason and sedition do now appear in such modes and forms. We shall see whether I was right as to what the consequences must be. As sure as I am living, nothing but Parliament can attempt a remedy for present evils. Whether that attempt will succeed, I know not; but if Ministers will not try it, they ought to make way for other Ministers, who either will try it, or some other measure which may occur to them and does not occur to me. God bless you, and may his Providence avert the evils which seem impending over us."

Before Parliament met, that most amiable, excellent and loyal nobleman, the late Earl Fitzwilliam, was dismissed from his office of Lord Lieutenant of the West Riding of Yorkshire, becanse he had joined in calling a meeting of freeholders to consider of a petition to the Crown and the two Houses of the Legislature, upon the present position of affairs—in terms supposed to reflect upon an answer recently given by the Regent to an address from the City of London. This news was exultingly conveyed in the following letter to Lord Eldon ;—

"Richmond Park, Oct. 21st, 1819.

"MY DEAR LORD,

"I had not a single moment, before I left town to-day, to tell you that a messenger has been despatched to Wentworth, with a letter informing Lord Fitzwilliam that the Prince Regent has no further occasion for his services as Lord Lieutenant of the W. Riding of Yorkshire. This was a necessary act of insulted authority; we shall now be abused by our enemies; if we had shrunk from it, we should have been despised by our friends, and perhaps by our enemies too. The clouds in the North are very black, and I think they must burst. "Ever truly yours,

"SIDMOUTH."

It is most refreshing to find here a striking illustration of the lines of the poet :—

"With secret course, which no loud storms annoy,
Glides the smooth current of domestic joy."

Lord Eldon, during this time, was happy, and spreading happiness around him, at his retreat in Dorsetshire, and wrote the following charming letter to his grandson, the present Earl of Eldon, then a boy of fifteen—which must make us love the old peer, in spite of his passions for coercive acts and prosecutions for high treason :—

"Encombe, Sept. 12th, 1819.

"MY VERY DEAR JOHN,

"We have not yet been a week here, but I have now had time to see all that is to be seen here.

"And first, Grandmamma and Fan send, with me, the warmest love to you. I hope you got mamma's letter safe: and we shall be most happy to hear that you are well.

"There are a great many partridges, a great many hares, and, I think, a fair quantity of pheasants. The ponies, Diamond and Dancer, are quite stout, and fat as butter. Aunt Fan's little pony, Dapper, in endeavoring to open for itself a stable door, got its head between the door and the side of the door where the lock is, and has very nearly hanged himself. He is much hurt, but seems in a fair way of recovery.

"The greyhounds, Messrs. Smoker, Spot, Smut, and Fly (the two latter I should call Mesdames), are all as they should be; so are also Messrs. Don, Carlo, Bill, and Bob, the pointers. Bill and Bob have been very good and diligent in their winter education, and I think will be towards the top of my dog-college.[1] Don is a freshman, sent down here a few days before we came, but he is a capital performer in the field. Poor old Mat, whom you may remember, a pointer, seems quite superannuated, and I think will see no more service.

"Your friends at the farm, Mr. and Mrs. Parmiter and their family, are all well, and they and Mr. Willis inquire much after you. Mr. Parmiter's dog Tiger is in excellent condition, and, when taken out, finds hares and rabbits in abundance.

"And now for great Cæsar. He is amazing fat, looks very handsome, is more affectionate than ever, and is particularly careful in his attendance at the breakfast-room window, when the good things for the teeth and palate are there: as to the loves between him and Aunt Fanny, they are endless—such endearing, such salutations, such pettings, as no Dorsetshire or other Christian has the good fortune to be honored with.

"In the course of the winter I have had a beautiful vessel built—a sailing vessel of good size—in which we

---

[1] In another letter to the same correspondent he thus contrasts the characters of Bob and Bill :—" Bob has considerable natural merit, but he has contracted such a stubborn self-will, that we are obliged to administer discipline very frequently; as soon as it is over, he is just as much as ever untractable, whereas Bill, after flogging, feels that sense of degradation, and regret that he deserved it, which is a great security with men as well as dogs for virtuous, honorable, and good future conduct."

went by sea yesterday, to Lulworth and back, with all sails bent, and colors flying at the mast-head and other parts of her,—a very excellent and beautiful vessel.

"We have had a great piece of good luck in fishing, having caught in one fishing about twenty-four mullet, whitings, &c., &c., of large size.

"And now, my dearest John, do you ask me why I enjoy all these things so much? It is because, as your friend Horace has it, they lull one into the 'Solicitæ jucunda oblivia vitæ.' It is because one enjoys them by contrast with meritorious labor at other times: and depend upon it, neither Encombe nor any other place will have any lasting charms, unless, in the period of life spent in education, a great stock of information is laid in in the mind, and a great stock of virtuous and religious feeling is implanted in the heart. That you may be diligent in acquiring both in youth, in order that you may be truly happy when you grow up to manhood, is the heartfelt wish, and will be the prayer offered up daily to Heaven on your account, of your truly affectionate
"ELDON."

Parliament met on the 23rd of November; and on the first day of the session, Earl Grey having moved an amendment, pledging the House to inquire into the proceedings connected with the late Manchester meeting, the Lord Chancellor said:—

"However much, as an individual, I may wish for inquiry, to vindicate the magistrates and the Government, I must, in my public capacity, declare that it can not be granted consistently with the spirit of English law. Considering that proceedings are in progress before the criminal tribunals, I am reluctant to deliver an opinion upon a question which will be regularly decided there; but when I read in my law books that numbers constitute force, that force constitutes terror, and that terror constitutes illegality, I feel that no man can deny the Manchester meeting to have been an illegal one. The two Houses of Parliament did, I admit, inquire and publish Reports before the treason trials of 1794; but that was not with the view of biassing the opinion of judges or juries, and I object to parliamentary inquiry during the pendency of prosecutions except where some continuing danger creates a state necessity for such inteference.

I am sure that the Government will be found to have done its duty; and if the magistracy have erred at all during the late excitement, their error has been rather on the side of remissness than of undue vigor. I will not now give any opinion on the proceedings at Manchester, as all the facts are to be laid before a jury. This only I owe it to myself to say,—that it is my fixed, my unqualified opinion, that the meeting at Manchester, on the 16th of August, was, in every sense of the word, an illegal meeting."

Such a declaration of the law, while inquiry was denied, I think was very exceptionable. One bad consequence which it produced was, that when Mr. Hunt's trial came on, Mr. Justice Bayley, a very learned and honest, but not very strong-minded, judge—to show his independence, expressed considerable doubts respecting the character of the meeting, and actually advised Sir James Scarlett, who was leading counsel for the Crown, after the trial had lasted some days, to give up the prosecution. Indeed, it was owing to the firmness and extraordinary ability of that gentleman, who considered himself bound to exert himself the more from being politically opposed to the Government, that justice was not defeated by an acquittal.[1] What would have been the consequence if the Lord Chancellor's advice had been taken, and the indictment had charged Mr. Hunt with "traitorously imagining the death of our lord the King, and levying war against him in his realm?"[2]

Now was passed the unconstitutional code called "The Six Acts," the latest violation of our free Constitution, and I believe the last, for we have seen, both under Whig and Tory rule, considerably greater danger from tumultuary meetings and secret associations, and yet on these occasions tranquillity was restored and preserved, and protection was afforded to life and property, by a skillful and vigorous use of the ordinary powers of the law. The

---

[1] When Sir James Scarlett returned to London, he was warmly thanked for his exertions by Lord Liverpool, who acknowledged to him, that if Mr. Hunt had been acquitted, there must have been a change of Administration.

[2] Being convicted of a misdemeanor, he was very properly sentenced by the Court of King's Bench to imprisonment for two years in Dorchester jail. An attempt to have him hanged, drawn, and quartered would have insured him an ovation, amidst the plaudits of hundreds of thousands, all over England.

most obnoxious bills, then passed, which fortunately have all expired or been repealed, were—to prevent public meetings without the license of magistrates,—to permit a search in private houses for arms,—to impose a high stamp duty on newspapers, for the avowed purpose of checking their circulation,—and to subject to transportation beyond the seas any person who should be convicted a second time of publishing a libel. These, I presume, were all suggested by the Lord Chancellor, and they were all gallantly defended by him. "I ask the House," said he, "what they think England would be like if these bills should *not* pass? The *Arms Bill* does not authorize the searching of a house on the mere information that the owner of it has arms in his possession; such possession must be 'for a purpose dangerous to the public peace.' The principle of the right of the King's subjects to possess arms for their defense is not quite so broad as it has been frequently represented; it is accompanied with the qualification that 'the arms so to be possessed by them are suitable to their situation in life.'[1] If the object of the persons to whom these bills are to be applied is to give to their meetings, by the collection of great numbers, the quality of physical force for the purpose of procuring, by the display of that physical force, any alteration in the government in Church or State,—I must declare that such a proceeding is an over act of high treason." With respect to the bill for the transportation of libellers, he said, "I maintain, my Lords, that it is necessary for the suppression of libels, that the courts should have the power which we now propose to vest in them. As the law stands, if a man, between the times of his prosecution and his judgment, think proper, day by day, and hour by hour, to repeat his offense by means of his servant, his wife, or some other authorized person, there is nothing to prevent him. Until a great lawyer, and a great reformer of laws [meaning poor Michael Angelo Taylor, who had not only introduced the Pillory Abolition Bill, but made a yearly motion on the delays in Chancery], had thought proper to take away the punishment of the pillory, there was some check on this species of pertinacity; but now the Court can only imprison and

---

[1] He might have added,—and I wonder that he did not,—another condition specified by the Bill of Rights,—"that the King's subjects who claim to use arms in their defense are *Protestants*."

fine, and often the fine is imposed where it can not be paid.[1] It is true that each of these publications may form the subject for a distinct prosecution; but if they extend to the number of 500, or 1000, or 1500, is it possible for the duration of human life to afford a sufficient space for a punishment equal to the incalculable mischief which their circulation will effect? I vote for these measures because I consider them as tending to secure the peace, and to promote the happiness, of the people." The alarm caused by such language was very great,—so that for a time the Ministry was strengthened, and the bills were all carried by vast majorities. I make no doubt that Lord Eldon acted conscientiously in proposing and supporting them; but in doing so he showed at once a total disregard of the principles of the English Constitution, and entire ignorance of the feelings of the English people. The "Six Acts," bringing unspeakable odium on the Government, increased and prolonged the ferment which they were intended to suppress.

The two Houses finished their work with unexampled despatch, and were, on the 29th of December, adjourned to the 15th of February following.

Before that day arrived, the aspect of public affairs was greatly altered by Death, who impartially visits the cottage and the palace. On the 22nd of January, 1820, expired his Royal Highness the Duke of Kent,—a prince who had continued to keep aloof from party politics, but, performing in an exemplary manner all the duties of his station, was universally beloved and respected.

Seven days afterwards, George III., whose mind was too much weakened to allow him to be conscious of his bereavment, was himself released from suffering. This event produced a deep sensation, although it was not likely to be attended with any political change, and ten years ago his reign had in reality terminated. But his name had still been preserved in all public acts; his image appeared on the coin; the nation still considered itself under his auspices; much sympathy had been excited by the thought that a mighty monarch, reduced to a state of mental imbecility and blindness, was cut off even from

[1] This would be contrary to Magna Charta, and the Chancellor can hardly have thrown such an imputation on the Judges. The inefficacy of fines legally imposed proceeds from their being paid by a subscription.

the intercourse of his own family, to whom he had been so tenderly attached; and, his faults being forgotten, people were disposed to think only of his singleness and sincerity of purpose, his determined resolution, and his truly English heart. He certainly was a prince possessed of very valuable qualities; and it is only fair to state, that everything discovered concerning him since his death has tended to raise our opinion both of his abilities and of his generosity.[1]

CHAPTER CCIV.

CONTINUATION OF THE LIFE OF LORD ELDON TILL THE CONCLUSION OF THE QUEEN'S TRIAL.

ALTHOUGH the day on which the death of George III. was announced was a Sunday,—according to the requisition of the statute 6 Anne, c. 7, both Houses of Parliament met on that day. Lord Eldon merely appeared on the woolsack, and as soon as prayers were read the House of Peers was adjourned.

Shortly after, a council was held at Carlton House, when the usual ceremonies were observed as upon the commencement of a new reign. On this occasion all the Ministers delivered up the emblems of their different offices, and were all graciously re-appointed.[2] Of Lord

---

[1] I have had an opportunity of reading his private correspondence with Lord North, which conveys a wonderful idea of his activity, familiarity with business, and knowledge of character. His steady attachment to that Minister is highly creditable to his heart. With a better education, he might have been one of the greatest sovereigns who ever filled the throne of England.

From a *mot* of his, recorded by Lord Eldon, he might even have displayed a talent for delicate sarcasm:—" On one occasion George III., when he came out of the House of Lords, after opening the session of Parliament, said to me, 'Lord Chancellor, did I deliver the speech well?' 'Very well indeed, Sir,' was my answer. 'I am glad of that,' replied the King, '*for there was nothing in it.*'"

I remember being told, when I was a boy, although I never saw the anecdote in print, that having knighted a gentleman of the name of *Day*, at a levee held on the 29th of September, he said, "Now I know that I am a King, for I have turned DAY into *Knight*, and made LADY-DAY at *Michaelmas*."

[2] "30th January, 1820.—Memorandum, that the Right Hon. John, Lord Eldon, Lord High Chancellor of that part of the United Kingdom of Great Britain and Ireland called Great Britain, delivered the Great Seal to his Majesty in Council, at Carlton House, when his Majesty was graciously

Eldon's part in this ceremony we have an account from himself in the following letter from him to his sister-in-law, Mrs. H. Ridley:—

"London, Jan. 31st, 1820.

"DEAR FANNY,

"I have lost the master whom I have long served, and whom I have most affectionately loved.

"The Acts of Parliament now in being would have continued me in office till the Royal pleasure should remove me; but I determined that, as I was acting under the appointment of him who was no more, I owed it as matter of respect to him, and as matter of respect to his successor, to consider my office as determined by the death of him who gave it me, and that I ought not, with respect to the latter, to leave him to the pain of removing me if he thought that fit—and especially as I know, and to his credit I say it, that he kept us, and me among the rest, originally, only because we were his father's servants.

"I therefore yesterday resigned into his hands the Seals; and, as I told him, I hoped unsullied by any act of mine. Out of office, he thought proper to call me back into it; and now I am in the very singular situation—that of a third Chancellorship.[1]

"Remain in it long I can not—to be restored to it I did not wish; but I could not for the present withdraw from the offer graciously made to me by the son of my greatest benefactor, who certainly has behaved with great kindness to me, though he had been taught heretofore to hate me. With our love to you all—to you all—

"Believe me affectionately yours,
"ELDON."

pleased to re-deliver to him the said Seal, with the title of Lord High Chancellor of Great Britain; and on the 1st day of February, his Lordship, between the hours of ten and eleven in the forenoon, went into the Court of Chancery, at Westminster, attended by Masters Campbell, Stratford, and Alexander, and, standing in his place there in open court, took the oaths of allegiance and supremacy, and also the oath of the Lord Chancellor, which oaths were read to him by the Deputy Clerk of the Crown, Master Campbell, the senior Master present, in the absence of the Master of the Rolls (who was prevented from attending by indisposition), holding the book, which being done, the Attorney General moved that it might be recorded, which was ordered accordingly."—*Min. Book*, No. 2, fol. 118.

[1] His immediate successor has been four times Chancellor, and Lord Cottenham three times. He was probably not aware that one of his predecessors had been Chancellor five times.

It is amusing to observe how he enhances the delight he felt at the commencement of his third Chancellorship by protestations that he was reluctantly induced again to accept the worthless bauble, lest by declining it he should be chargeable with ingratitude.

Parliament again met for a few days, but only to vote addresses of condolence and congratulation; for this House of Commons having been several times a little refractory, the resolution was taken to get rid of it as soon as possible. The Marquis of Lansdowne pointed out that there was not the usual reason for a dissolution which occurred upon a demise of the Crown; but Lord Eldon explained that, at common law, the Parliament died with the Sovereign in whose name it was called, and although by the statute of William III. it might sit six months longer, it was liable to be dissolved sooner; and constitutionally it ought to be dissolved as soon as public business will allow—so that noble lords who started any business to delay the dissolution would be obstructing the due exercise of the royal prerogative. He, as Lord Commissioner, concluded the session by delivering the Royal Speech, which deplored the loss of a Sovereign, "the common father of all his people," and praised the prudence and firmness with which the Lords and Commons had counteracted the designs of the disaffected.[1]

Yet the new laws were insufficient to prevent the formation of the most diabolical and the most preposterous plot recorded in our annals—"the Cato Street conspiracy,"—by which it was intended to upset the monarchy by assassinating the Lord Chancellor and all his colleagues while assembled together at a Cabinet dinner. One Thistlewood, who had been a subaltern officer in the army, with about a score of others,—butchers, shoemakers, and of such low trades,—had agreed that when the Cabinet Ministers were dining at Lord Harrowby's, one of the confederates should gain admission at the outer door by pretending to deliver a letter; that all the others should then rush in, and, having executed their bloody purpose, they should constitute themselves the Government of the country.[2] But two of them having "'peached,"

[1] 41 Parl. Deb. 1642.
[2] This plot bears a considerable resemblance to that of Caliban, Stephano,

they were all apprehended in their conclave in Cato Street, when about to set forth for Lord Harrowby's. Being speedily brought to trial, the charge of high treason was satisfactorily made out against them, and five of them were executed.

I do not think that Ministers deserved any censure for the manner in which they conducted themselves in this affair, unless that they somewhat unscrupulously yielded to the temptation of arguing that the plot was a justification of their recent coercive laws, and of pretending to infer from this insane scheme that there was a revolutionary spirit generally prevailing in the country. Lord Eldon, who considerably overrated his actual danger, piously wrote to a lady of his family: "For the past, thankfulness and gratitude, I trust, will relieve all other feelings: as to the future, I trust there is something to be hoped for of protection in human caution, and that we may all fully depend upon that Providence to which we are so largely indebted."

The new Parliament met on the 21st of April, and the session promised for some weeks to be very dull,—no subjects more stirring being brought forward, or announced, than the settlement of the Civil List, the discharge of insolvent debtors, the suppression of Sunday newspapers, and the reading of the Athanasian Creed,—when a political storm was excited, such as had not been known in the country for a century, by a sealed green bag being laid upon the table of the House of Lords and of the House of Commons, with a message from his Majesty, that "in consequence of the arrival of the Queen, his Majesty had communicated certain papers respecting her conduct, which he recommended to their immediate and serious attention."[1]

At the commencement of the reign of George IV., Ministers were placed in a situation of much embarrassment with their royal master, who, ruling "*proprio jam jure, animo paterno,*"[2] became much more unmanageable than he had before been, and more inclined to listen to "private friends" than to his constitutional advisers. They first had a difference with him on arranging the Civil

and Trineulo, in "The Tempest"—to murder Prospero, and make themselves Kings of the Enchanted Island.

[1] 1 Hansard, 886.   [2] Motto on the Coronation medal.

List; but this was easily accommodated, and was thus jocosely alluded to in a letter from Lord Eldon to his daughter: "Our royal master seems to have got into temper again,—as far as I could judge from his conversation with me this morning. He has been pretty well disposed to part with us all, because we would not make additions to his revenue. This we thought conscientiously we could not do in the present state of the country, and of the distresses of the middle and lower orders of the people, to which we might add, too, that of the higher orders."[1]

But a far more difficult subject remained behind; and, rather than not have his way here, he was ready to peril his crown,—at any rate to try how far he might succeed with another Cabinet. He had resolved that his wife, although now by law Queen of England, and entitled to the well-defined privileges of that high station as much as *he* was to wear the crown, without regard to personal character,—should enjoy none of them, and that she should be degraded from her royal rank, even if the tie of marriage between them should not be dissolved. Till the death of King George III., she had been prayed for in the Liturgy as "Princess of Wales;" but King George IV. insisted that she should now be entirely excluded from it, and his Ministers very improperly yielded to his arbitrary will, contenting themselves with saying, that "they would take no other step against her while she consented to remain abroad." They feebly defended themselves by alleging that she was prayed for under the words "the rest of the royal family;" but, as her counsel, Mr. Denman, afterwards pathetically observed, "the general prayer in which she was embraced was, 'for all that are desolate and oppressed.'"

When the news of this insult reached her in Italy,—as might have been foreseen by Lord Eldon, who from his long intimacy with her was well acquainted with her spirit,—she announced her intention of immediately revisiting England, to claim her legal rights. For some time he flattered himself that this was a vain boast, or that her courage would fail; and thus he wrote to his daughter: "Our Queen threatens approach to England; but if she can venture, she is the most courageous lady I

[1] 20th April, 1820.

ever heard of. The mischief, if she does come, will be infinite. At first she will have extensive popularity with the multitude; in a few short months or weeks she will be ruined in the opinion of the world."[1] On a subsequent day, when the Queen must have been almost in sight of the shores of England, he again wrote: "I saw my royal master, as usual, yesterday. The committee to settle the forms of the coronation have reported to him that, as there is to be no crowning of a queen, peeresses should not be summoned to attend, and so all former precedents, in like cases, appear to have been. But he says that, as Queen Elizabeth, though a lady, had both peers and peeresses, so he, though he has no queen, will have both ladies and gentlemen to attend him. I think, however, he will not persist in this. The town is employed in nothing but speculation whether her Majesty will or will not come. Great bets are laid about it. Some people have taken fifty guineas, undertaking in lieu of them to pay a guinea a day till she comes, so sure are these that she will come within fifty days; others, again, are taking less than fifty guineas, undertaking to pay a guinea a day till she comes,—so sure are they that she will not come. Others assert that they know she will come, and that she will find her way into Westminster Abbey and Westminister Hall on the Coronation, in spite of all opposition. I retain my old opinion, that she will not come *unless she is insane.* It is, however, certain that she has appointed maids of honor,—ladies to whom she is pleased to give that appellation."[2]

In a few hours, news was received that her Majesty had arrived at St. Omer's, and a negotiation was opened with her there;—but, indignantly refusing £50,000 a-year under the condition of not using the title of Queen of England, or any other title attached to the British royal family, on the 6th of June she entered London amid the plaudits of the multitude. The following is Lord Eldon's account of this ovation:—

"Contrary to all expectation, the Queen entered London yesterday in an open carriage, with the Alderman and Lady Anne Hamilton, and amidst a vast concourse of people in carriages and on horseback, who had gone out to meet her and to hail her approach. She drove to

[1] 10th April, 1820. [2] 29th May.

Alderman Wood's house in South Audley-street, where she exhibited herself and the Alderman from a balcony to all who chose to take a peep at them, the multitude in the street requiring all who passed by to make their reverences and obeisances to her Majesty. In the mean time messages were sent to both Houses of Parliament, which may be considered as the forerunners of long parliamentary proceedings relative to her conduct. These parliamentary proceedings are likely to be warm on both sides. At present one can only *conjecture* what is to happen,—and conjecture deserves little confidence when this lady's arrival has robbed conjecture of all credit."[1]

In a few days after, he wrote to his daughter:—

"The lower orders here are all Queen's folks; few of the middling or higher orders, except the profligate, or those who are endeavoring to acquire power through mischief. The bulk of those who are in Parliament are afraid of the effect of the disclosures and discussions which must take place, if there is not some pacific settlement; the Queen is obstinate, and makes no propositions tending to that—at least as yet;—the King is determined, and will hear of none—of nothing but thorough investigation, and what he, and those who consider *themselves* more than him, think and talk of—thorough exposure of the Q., and divorce. To this extent Parliament will not go; but, amidst this mess of difficulties, something must arise in a few days; or it will happen, I think, in a few days, that the K. will try whether he can not find an Administration which can bring Parliament more into his views than the present Ministers. I don't see how matters can go on a week longer with the present Administration remaining; I think no Administration, who have any regard for him, will go the length he wishes, *as* an Administration—and if they will, they can not take Parliament along with them. That body is afraid of disclosures—*not on one side only*—which may affect the monarchy itself. There is certainly an inclination to disquiet among the lower orders; but it is so well watched, that there is no great cause for uneasiness on that account."

From the foregoing letter it appears that hitherto Ministers had resisted the King's wish for a Divorce Bill. This was the utmost extent to which he had ever proposed to go;

[1] Letter, 7th June, to Honorable Mrs. Banks.

and according to the doctrine afterwards solemnly laid down, he could not even on the completest proof of her infidelity, have attempted to make Caroline of Brunswick share the fate of Anna Boleyn and Katherine Howard,—her supposed paramour being an alien, and the alleged adultery having been committed beyond the seas, so that neither party was guilty of high treason. It is deeply to be regretted that Ministers, from selfish motives or from defective judgment, did not continue steadily to protect the Sovereign from the effects of his own waywardness. Although Lord Eldon was to blame in concurring in the measure which was at last adopted, I am sorry to think that the responsibility of it chiefly attaches to Lord Liverpool, a statesman whose general character is most respectable, and whose administration is a brilliant portion of our history. But he was afraid to act with sufficient boldness in combating his Sovereign's inclination on this subject; and he followed a middle course, which is sometimes the most disastrous, instead of being the safest. Although he would not take up the divorce as a Ministerial measure when he was pressed to do so in 1818,—that he might not utterly quarrel with the Regent, he allowed Sir John Leach privately to frame the "Milan commission," he provided funds for defraying the expenses of it, and he from time to time read the *ex parte* evidence which the commissioners collected from very suspicious sourcces. He discussed it with the Prince, and he could not deny that if it were believed, it established the guilt of the Princess. Thus, while he refused to originate any proceedings, he kept alive in the mind of his Royal Highness the hope of a divorce, and he prevented a settlement which might have saved the parties and the nation from the unheard of disgrace now to be cast upon them.[1] I do not find that Lord Eldon took any part in these proceedings, from the formation of the Milan commission till the accession of George IV. The evidence being then laid before him, he most unfortunately joined in the resolution to exclude the Queen's name from the Liturgy; and believing that she never would return to England, he consented that, if she did, some proceedings should be insti-

---

[1] Some have supposed, probably without any sufficient reason, that Lord Liverpool had a personal grudge against the Princess because she had strongly exerted her influence against him for Mr. Canning.

tuted for the purpose of exposing her misconduct: but he still resisted the notion of a divorce, seeing that, according to all principle as well as precedent, this would open the door for recrimination, and might be dangerous to the monarchy.

Before the plan of operation was finally agreed upon, a motion was made in the House of Lords to refer the papers contained in the Green Bag to a secret committee. This being strongly opposed by Lord Lansdowne and Lord Holland, and other peers, Lord Eldon said,—

"The object of Ministers, in proposing a secret committee, was to prevent injustice towards the accused. That committee would not be permitted to pronounce a decision: it would merely find, like a Grand Jury, that matter of accusation did or did not exist. Such matter, even if found to have existence, could not be the subject of a *judicial proceeding*, strictly so called. The offense of a Queen Consort, or Princess Consort of Wales, committing adultery with a person owing allegiance to the British Crown, would be that of a principal in high treason, because, by statute, it was high treason in him; and as accessaries in high treason are principals, she would thus be guilty of high treason as a principal. But as the act of a person owing no allegiance to the British Crown could not be high treason in him; so neither could a Princess be guilty of that crime merely by being an accessary to such a person's act. There were likewise great difficulties in a Sovereign seeking a divorce in the Ecclesiastical Courts according to the ordinary rules of law.[1] Yet although, for this reason, there could be no judicial proceeding in such a case, there might be a legislative one, and the existence or non-existence of grounds for such legislative proceeding, was a matter into which it would be fit that a secret committee should inquire. In no case could injustice be done, because that committee's decision would not be final."[2]

The motion for a secret committee was carried without a division.[3]

But all reasonable men were alarmed at the delirium of the King and Queen, by which the British nation was to

---

[1] Henry VIII. was divorced from Catherine of Arragon by the Ecclesiastical Court—and also from Anne Boleyn between the day of her conviction and execution. [2] 1 Hansard, new series, 896. [3] Ibid. 902.

be punished; and, by a motion in the House of Commons, proceedings were stayed, in the hope of a compromise, which was to be attempted between the Duke of Wellington and Lord Castlereagh acting as plenipotentiaries for the King, and Mr. Brougham and Mr. Denman for the Queen—upon the basis that she admitted nothing, and he retracted nothing, of what had been charged against her. While this was pending, Lord Eldon expressed his sentiments upon it in a letter to his daughter:—

"It seems to me that both Houses of Parliament are determined to have an end of this business between the K. and Q. without inquiry and disclosure. All seem to be agreed that she shall not live in this country; but there is nothing but difference of opinion how she is to be treated abroad. The Ministers will be compelled to give way to Parliament,—and they are in a pretty case: if they give way, the K. will remove them; if they do not, they will be outvoted in Parliament, and can not remain. At least I do not see my way honorably out of this difficulty. . . . To-morrow will be a very busy day, if the Q. means to make any propositions for arrangement. The K. will make none,—and if he can find an administration that will fight everything to the last moment at any risk, he will *receive* none."

Such an Administration, after many cabinet councils had been held upon the subject, his Majesty seems to have thought that he already possessed; for his plenipotentiaries, by his orders, not only required that the Queen should ever after live abroad, but still insisted on excluding her name from the Liturgy, and refused the concession that she might be introduced officially at some one foreign Court, which she might select for her residence. The negotiation was accordingly broken off before a single article had been agreed to, and both parties prepared for war *à l'outrance*. The Queen's first move was to intimate to the Lord Chancellor, that she meant to come in person to the House of Lords when her case should be next discussed there—meaning to go in state, with half the population of London at her heels. He sent her back word that, as Speaker, he could not permit her to enter without the authority of the House, for which she must previously apply. She then desired that he would deliver a message to the House in her name, but he told her that "the

House did not receive messages from anybody but the King, unless they were sent as answers to addresses from the House." So far he was correct; but I think he was quite wrong in refusing to present a petition from her to the House of Lords. By the Constitution, every subject has a right to petition either House of Parliament, and a petition can only be presented by a member of the House. I have therefore always understood the rule to be (and I have myself always acted on this rule), that if a petition is respectfully worded, and is upon a subject within the jurisdiction of Parliament, any member, when asked, is bound, in the discharge of his parliamentary duty, to present it, however much he may disapprove of its prayer. The Lord Chancellor, although Speaker of the House, has in all respects the duties and privileges of other peers. Lord Eldon stated in a letter written at the time, " When they brought a petition from her, to be presented to the House by me,—this I declined also ; and for this Messrs. Grey, Lansdowne, and Holland abused me pretty handsomely. However, I don't think that I suffered much by all that, and I am resolved I will not be employed in any way by this lady."

The Queen's petition being presented by Lord Dacre, with some observations upon the manner in which the duty of presenting it had been cast upon him, an entire stranger to her Majesty, " the Lord Chancellor declared upon his honor, that when he declined to present the petition, he entertained no objection to its being submitted to the consideration of the House ; but it appeared to him better that it should be presented by any other noble lord rather than by himself ; a due regard to the situation in which he stood, induced him to pause, and he had not had three minutes for the consideration of the question : he would sooner suffer death than admit any abatement of the principle, that a person accused is not therefore to be considered guilty."[1]

Mr. Brougham and Mr. Denman, her Majesty's Attorney and Solicitor General, were then called in to support the petition, which prayed that their Lordships would not prosecute a secret inquiry against her,—and they began that series of orations in her defense, which raised the reputation of British forensic eloquence.

[1] 1 Hansard, 1325, 1327, 1329.

The following day, Earl Grey, in the hope of saving the country from the disgrace about to be heaped upon it, having moved to discharge the order for the appointment of the secret committee, which had hitherto suspended its operations,—the Chancellor ably vindicated the propriety of inquiry after the communication from the Throne, and thus *more suo* concluded : " For my own part, my Lords, if after this inquiry further proceedings should be deemed necessary, I shall enter upon them in the spirit so ably described by an eminent English judge,[1] who declared that 'he had made a covenant with God and himself, that neither affection nor any other undue motive should ever make him swerve from the strict line of his duty.' In that spirit I have always continued to act during the past, and I shall endeavor to act for the future. The consciousness of doing so will be the best consolation I can possess, if I should appear to the friends whom I esteem to act wrongly, and will form my best title to pardon at the hands of that God before whose tribunal all mankind must sooner or later stand to be judged."[2] Lord Grey's motion was negatived by a majority of 102 to 47.[3] This was the first division on the proceedings against the Queen, and gave great confidence to the King's party.

The secret committee proceeded to open the Green Bag, and in a few days reported to the House, "that allegations, supported by the concurrent testimony of a great number of persons in various situations of life, and residing in different parts of Europe, appeared to be calculated so deeply to affect the character of the Queen, the dignity of the Crown, and the moral feeling and honor of the country, that it was indispensable that they should become the subject of a solemn inquiry, which would best be effected in the course of a legislative proceeding."[4]

Lord Dacre having next day presented another petition from the Queen, praying to be immediately heard by her counsel, the Chancellor said, " he would be glad to know where in the history of Parliament it was to be found that counsel were admitted to be heard against a measure of some kind or other not yet submitted to their lordships, but which some noble lord was expected to propose. Their Lordships differed from the practice of the other

[1] C. J. Crewe.   [2] 2 Hansard, 24.   [3] Ib. 49.   [4] Ib. 167.

House of Parliament, by allowing a peer to lay a bill on the table without asking previous leave to do so; and would they now hear counsel against this privilege of the peerage?"[1] The motion that counsel be called in, was negatived without a division.[2]

Lord Liverpool forthwith introduced the "Bill of Pains and Penalties against her Majesty," which, reciting that "she had carried on an adulterous intercourse with Bergami, her menial servant," enacted that "she should be degraded from the title and station of Queen, and that her marriage with the King should be dissolved." After her counsel had been heard at the bar against this mode of proceeding, the bill was read a first time, and was ordered to be read a second time on the 17th of August,—when the preamble was to be proved, and the "trial" was to begin.

In the meanwhile, Lord Erskine having made the very reasonable motion, that the Queen should be furnished with a list of the witnesses to be produced against her, the Lord Chancellor resisted it in a long speech, in which he pointed out the inconvenience which this practice produces in trials for treason,—insisted that it should not be extended to other cases,—and, reminding their lordships that the rank of the party accused should not weigh with them—in spite of his early failure in quoting Shakespeare, exclaimed—

> "The poor beetle that we tread upon
> In corporal sufferance feels a pang as great
> As when a giant dies."[3]

He might have recollected that the Queen was substantially charged with high treason, and that in Scotland (of which she was Queen as well as of England) no criminal of any degree can be brought to trial without the advantage which she claimed.

I think he likewise erred in resisting a motion afterwards made by Lord Erskine, that as the charge in the preamble of the bill extended over several years, and over many countries in Europe and Asia, she should, for the purpose of preparing her defense, be furnished with a specification of the times and places when and where the offense was supposed to have been committed. The Chancellor said, "there was no analogy between the com-

---

[1] 2 Hansard, 199.   [2] Ib. 207.   [3] Ib. 440.

mon law of this country and a proceeding before Parliament; and his noble and learned friend had not pointed out a single instance in which, in a proceeding like the present, their lordships had gone the length to which their lordships were now requested to go: the demand for a specification was unsupported by any principle, and unsanctioned by any precedent."[1] But surely he had not consulted his oracle, Sir William, that great Consistorial Judge, who would have told him that in an ordinary divorce suit the libel must articulately set forth the charges—with time and place—and that to these charges the proofs are confined. Indeed, by the standing orders of the House of Peers, a Bill to dissolve a marriage for adultery can not be introduced till there has been a sentence of divorce *a mensâ et thoro* in the Ecclesiastical Court, after such specific allegations established by evidence.

These violations of the sacred principles of impartial justice excited much sympathy in favor of the party accused, and inclined the public to be incredulous to the formidable case that was afterwards made out against her.

When the trial actually began, and during the whole course of it, Lord Eldon's conduct as President of the Court was such to be admired; displaying not only dignity and ability, but impartiality and candor. In the midst of great provocation, he always preserved his equanimity; and while he firmly checked the irregularities of counsel when they exceeded the latitude to be fairly expected in the discharge of their arduous duty, he treated them with uniform courtesy. He summoned to his aid the Judges of the land, and upon the many difficult questions of evidence which arose he always decided according to their opinion. I must, likewise, point out his high merit, by which every good lawyer must be struck, in framing the questions to be submitted to these sages. It should be remembered, that, being only *advisers*, there is a jealousy in putting to them in the *concrete* the very point which the House is to decide, and that they are generally consulted by an *abstract* question arising out of a supposititious case. Some dexterity may be evinced by the framing of such questions, so as to obtain an answer which may

[1] 2 Hansard, 576.

meet the wishes of the framer; but Lord Eldon—in his imaginary ejectments and trials upon indictments—with the greatest fairness and felicity submitted the exact matter in controversy for their advice, without the slightest regard to the manner in which their answer might operate.[1] Amidst the humiliation caused by the proceeding, it was consolatory to observe, not only the unexampled display of talent at the Bar, but, though the contending parties were so unequal, the strict regard to the rules of law and to the principles of enlightened criminal procedure exhibited by the Court.

When the evidence for the prosecution had closed, Lord Eldon very properly resisted the proposition made by Mr. Brougham, in his laudable zeal for his client,—that he should then be allowed to open the evidence for the defense, with a delay of some weeks, to enable him to adduce it;—or that he should be allowed to divide his address into two halves—one commenting on the evidence already given, to be spoken immediately—and the other opening the evidence for the defense, to be spoken after the adjournment. The natural anxiety was, that the powerful summing up of the King's case, by the Solicitor General, Copley, should not remain so long unanswered; but the alternative was very fairly given, to adjourn at the conclusion of it for as long a time as her Majesty should require to prepare fully for her defense, or to proceed continuously till her defense should be closed. A delay till the 3rd of October was asked by her Majesty's counsel, and to that day the House adjourned.

While Lord Eldon was exhibiting so much coolness on the woolsack, he had been the subject of some very absurd attempts personally to annoy him by the worst-judging section of the Queen's friends, who (among other schemes) projected purchasing for her use the house next to his, in Hamilton Place, where it was intended that she should keep a court, the mob mounting guard over her.

Having heard that the Lords of the Treasury intended, on a specious representation, to assist her in procuring this place of residence, he actually wrote the following letter to Lord Liverpool, threatening instantly to resign if they did:—

[1] Our Law of Evidence was much enriched by the decisions in the "Queen's Case,"—although two or three of them have since been doubted.

"MY DEAR LORD,

"I understand upon inquiry that the transaction as to the Hamilton Place house can not take effect without Government making themselves a party to it. I should be very unwilling to state anything offensively, but I can not but express my confidence that Government will not aid a project which must remove the Chancellor from his house the next hour that it takes effect, and from his office at the same time. I am confident that I can satisfy you that it could not reasonably be expected of me that I should adopt any other conduct if this matter takes effect, much as I should in every way wish to prove myself

"Yours most truly,
"ELDON."

Lord Liverpool withdrew the assistance of the Government from the scheme; but it was about to be completed by means of a voluntary subscription,—when it was defeated, after the terms had actually been agreed upon, by Lord Eldon himself becoming the purchaser, at an advanced price. In consequence, he wrote to his daughter, —" I had no other means of preventing the destruction of my present house as a place in which I could live, or which anybody else could take. The purchase-money is large; but I have already had such offers, that I shall not, I think, lose by it."

He now went to enjoy some repose at Encombe. On his journey thither he was constantly saluted by cries of "Queen Caroline for ever!" and in the country he found that public opinion was all against the King, the people saying sweepingly, "Italians are not to be believed." He was still confident, however, in his tribunal, if it had not been for one misgiving—the dread of recrimination. On this subject he wrote the following letter to Sir William, in which his reasoning is most sophistical, and is evidently at variance with his own private conviction:—

"I have long thought that the *effect* of recrimination will be produced, even if *evidence* of recrimination should be refused. But I wanted some scrap, to enable me to argue the point whether it should be refused, for I can hardly escape being called upon to say something about it. In ordinary bills of divorce, they are not tendered to the House in the first instance by a lord: the husband petitions for leave to have a bill brought in: the proceeding is therefore in the nature of *his* suit. As *against him*, it is fair to show that *he* ought not to be relieved; he is a party, in somewhat of a strict sense, in the proceeding; he has therefore no right to complain if his actions are examined in that proceeding; of his actions, Commons, Lords, and King are to judge. But in *this* proceeding, the King is no petitioning party (more than one foolish thing has been said by those who should not have said it, attending to this circumstance)—the bill is not brought in upon leave *at his suit*—a lord brings it in upon his own responsibility—might bring it whether *he* would or not—he has not, as a petitioner placed himself in a situation in which *he* has *submitted* his actions to examination in a proceeding in which he can repel imputation by proof, even if, as a King, he could submit his actions to examination—he has nothing to do, in form and upon principle, with the proceeding, till the bill is tendered to him for his assent to what Commons advise and Lords advise: they can't try his conduct. The received notion, that this would be treason if committed here, is to be looked to. Suppose it had been committed here, adultery on his part would have been no defense—could not have been given in evidence. See, then, what would be the case;—she is convicted—does he pardon, so as to save her life? If he can't have a divorce, because of adultery on his part, he must either let the law take its course against her, and divorce by execution, or take the pardoned traitor to his arms to love and to cherish. Notwithstanding all that can be said, I should, if I were to decide to-day, argue the case as if recrimination had been proved. But it is very essential to settle the point whether it should be admitted: for, whatever notoriety there may be in *this* case, it would be monstrous in *a possible* case to admit it: the case for instance in which, *after* shameful notorious adultery in a wife, the husband, suing for a divorce, had in a single instance, in an unfortunate moment, sinned,—righteous altogether before his wife's adultery."

He here admits, that if the bill had been introduced at the King's suit, recrimination could not be refused; and he is obliged to resort to the miserable subterfuge, that the bill was brought in by a lord, on his own responsibility —forgetting, that in point of form, even, as well as substance, the King was the petitioner, or *actor*, by the message he had sent along with the "green bag." Then the supposition, that the proceeding was like a criminal trial on a capital charge, where the personal conduct of the prosecutor, unconnected with the specific offense charged, would be irrelevant, was at variance not only with the fact, but with all his own reasoning in the prior stages of the proceeding. To such inconsistency was he driven by his original want of firmness in combating the inclinations of the Sovereign, who, according to the law of God and man, had forfeited all claim to the remedy his Ministers were now obsequiously struggling to obtain for him.

When the House met, after the adjournment, it again assumed the aspect of an enlightened and impartial court of justice—which it maintained till the evidence had been closed, and everything had been urged by the counsel on either side, which could be suggested by zeal, learning, and genius. The question being then put, "That this bill be now read a second time,"—

The Lord Chancellor, leaving the woolsack, delivered a long and able speech in support of it. After vindicating the mode of proceeding by "Bill of Pains and Penalties," which he said was very favorable to the accused party, and arguing that the Queen had not been prejudiced by a refusal of "a list of the witnesses," or a "specification," such as she had demanded, or by any of her supposed grievances, he took a masterly view of the evidence, and contended, that while there was no sufficient reason to disbelieve the witnesses whose credit had been impeached, —according to all the rules of inference by which courts of justice were guided in the investigation of truth, the case was abundantly established by evidence allowed to be sincere. Without having once shed tears, or appealed to his conscience, he thus concluded in a very manly and dignified strain :—

"One word more, my Lords, and I have done. As to what has passed, or is passing out of doors, I will take no notice of it, for I am not supposed to hear it, or to know anything about it ; only this I will say, that, whatever has happened, or whatever may happen, I will perform my duty here. But in the course of this solemn inquiry, your Lordships have heard from the bar of this House what I was very sorry to hear, and what I believe was never before addressed to a court of justice. Something like a threat was held out to your Lordships, that if you passed judgment against the Queen, you would never have the power of passing another judgment. I do not profess to use the words of the speaker, but the impression is distinct upon my mind. My Lords, however that may be, I will take upon myself to declare, than an address of such a nature, such an address of intimidation to any court of justice, was never until this hour considered to be consistent with the duty of an advocate; and that such an address, whether an advocate has a right to make it or not, ought to have no effect whatever upon your Lordships. You stand here as the great and acknowledged protectors of the liberties, the character, the honor, and the lives of your fellow-subjects, and you can not discharge that high trust a moment longer than while you can say to one another,—and for myself, if I had not a moment longer to live, I would say to you,—'Be just, and fear not!' My Lords, I know the people of this country. I am sure that if your Lordships do your duty to them, by preserving their liberties and the Constitution which has been handed down to you from your ancestors, the time is not far distant when they will do their duty to you; when they will acknowledge that those who are invested with the great judicial functions of the state ought firmly to meet all the reproaches to which the faithful performance of those functions may expose them; to court no popularity; to do their duty, and to leave the consequenees to the wisdom and justice of God, who guides the feelings and actions of men, and directs the course and consequences of all human affairs."[1]

On the division, after a debate of four nights, the second reading was carried by a majority only of 28.[2]

Lord Liverpool, and most of his colleagues, now cried "Craven;" but Lord Eldon, whose courage ever grew with difficulty, like a stout champion, was eager to continue the combat, and thus unbosomed himself to Sir William:—

"Dear Brother,

"I complain not only of a deadly want of energy in the public, but a want of it in the Administration. Most expressly I complained of the latter want. I think, if the

[1] 3 Hansard, 1439.   [2] 123 to 95.

latter did not exist, we should not see quite so much of the former; whereas most of those who are infected with the latter, attribute their own conduct, I think erroneously, to necessity arising out of the apathy of the former.

"How is it possible that Ministers can help the propagation of reports? How is it possible that they can avoid determinations, in given cases, to go out? Their friends, as they call themselves, are constantly complaining that the Cabinet don't let them know how much they make a point of this or that matter, excusing their lukewarmness and their non-attendance, because they were not informed that this or that point was material; if they had been so informed, oh! they would have been in their places, and have given the most entire support! Ministers are, therefore, driven to state upon what they put their existence, to those they believe to be their friends; but it does so happen that some of those whom they fancy to be such are living with all parties, wishing to be well with all parties, and therefore some studiously and some by surprise upon themselves, giving to the opponents of Ministers the information which Ministers meant to give exclusively to friends, and which they have been compelled to give them. It is some such friend who has told Brougham, or the person whoever he may be, what has been told to Lady ——, who has been as willing as anybody to keep herself out of a scrape, of being a witness on a late occasion. If Ministers do mean to insist upon the Queen's being kept out of the Liturgy, could they permit all whom they call friends to be pledging themselves before Parliament meets, that they, their friends, will make no point of the Liturgy? The King may be false, but he has told me twenty times, and within these forty-eight hours once, that he will take no Ministry that will introduce her into the Liturgy. I have no reason to be believe, nor do I believe, that the King has sent for Lord Spencer.

"I only add, that I know the Ministers think they have been driven by lukewarmness of friends (excusing it by complaining that communications were not made by them of points on which they put their existence) to communicate what it may now be represented to have been very foolish to communicate. I think withdrawing the bill, if anything has that effect, is what will destroy the Administration, to whatever cause the friends or foes of Administration, or neutrals, may attribute it."

Lord Eldon prevailed so far, that the bill was carried through another stage; but in the committee it encountered fresh difficulties, from a religious scruple respecting the divorce clause, on which the Right Reverend Prelates were divided in opinion—the Archbishop of Canterbury and the Bishops of London and Llandaff speaking for it; and the Archbishops of York and Tuam, and the Bishops of Chester, Worcester, and Peterborough, against it. In sad perplexity, Lord Eldon proposed to omit the divorce clause altogether, so that the bill might only degrade the Queen from her royal rank and dignity, without dissolving the marriage: but many of the King's friends objected to his being placed in the unprecedented condition of continuing the husband of a woman convicted of adultery; and some of her friends said that, though they believed her innocent, they would vote for the clause, that the bill might be defeated by it.

The Committee dividing on the question, "That the divorce clause stand part of the bill," the CONTENTS were 129, the NOT CONTENTS 62,—Lord Eldon, Lord Liverpool, and all the Ministers voting in the minority.[1]

When the division was over, Lord Holland seated himself beside Lord Eldon on the woolsack, and said to him, —"Lord Chancellor, your bishops have made but an indifferent figure to-night,—one half of them saying that a man will be damned if under certain circumstances he lives with his wife, and the other half that he will be damned if under the same circumstances he puts her away." *Lord Chancellor:* "I am only certain of one thing, which is—that these Bishops will *all* be damned."

Undismayed, he was for pushing the bill forward, and sending it to the House of Commons, notwithstanding the strong opposition with which it was threatened there; but, at a Cabinet held in the evening of the 9th of November, Lord Liverpool peremptorily declared his resolution not to proceed farther with the measure. Lord Eldon maintained his own opinion with boldness, and some hot words seem to have passed between them. It was finally agreed to feel the pulse of the House by taking a division on the third reading, the Chancellor having first tried to

[1] 3 Hansard, 1726.

fix waverers by again reminding them of the evidence of the unimpeached witnesses, and the necessary inferences to be drawn from it.

He accordingly spoke very emphatically in the debate on the third reading, contending that no peer who had voted for the second reading, and thus declared his conviction of the Queen's guilt, could now be justified in withdrawing his support from it. He said:—

"Are there any of your Lordships who, on such a subject, will not be satisfied with circumstantial evidence? Murders are proved to the satisfaction of juries by circumstantial evidence. I recollect a case in which a man was found dead in the highway—shot through the head—the wadding of the pistol clotted in his hair; on the head being washed, a piece of paper was found unconsumed; this proved to be part of a ballad; and the remainder of it was found in the pocket of another person, who was apprehended on suspicion of being the murderer. Was not this a safer ground for conviction than the oath of a man swearing that he saw the shot fired? Suppose a lady and gentleman are interrupted in a criminal purpose, and afterwards lock themselves up in a room for some hours, or are found sleeping in the same apartment, what inference is to be drawn? Laying aside the evidence of Majocchi, Demont, and that class of witnesses,—if there is not enough remaining to establish the charge, I have grievously erred in allowing divorce bills to pass through this House. But, looking at all the circumstances, I think it would be very difficult for any of your Lordships to lay your hands on your heart, and say, 'Not guilty, upon my honor.'"[1]

When he sat down, Lord Liverpool threw to him a slip of paper, with the following words:—"Most admirably! I am much obliged to you for it—and sorry if what I said last night gave you pain."[2]

Nevertheless, upon a division, the third reading was carried only by a majority of nine.[3]

---

[1] 3 Hansard, 1739.
[2] On the back of this was found the following memorandum:—"Liverpool asked me to speak in the House of Lords upon circumstantial evidence on the last day of the Queen's trial. I did so. He then handed this to me, apologizing for angry language at the Cabinet the night before, when he communicated his intention of relinquishing the business."
[3] 108 to 99. 3 Hansard, 1744.

Thereupon Lord Liverpool, instead of moving "That this bill do pass," said, that, "Had the third reading been carried by as considerable a number as the second reading, he and his noble colleagues would have felt it their duty to persevere in the bill, and to submit it to the other branch of the legislature. In the present state of the country, however, and with opinions so nearly balanced—just exemplified by their Lordships—they had come to the determination to proceed no farther with it." He accordingly moved, "That the farther consideration of the Bill be adjourned to this day six months."

Lord Eldon put the question from the woolsack, and with an abject countenance said, "The contents have it."

Heartily dissatisfied with the issue, and with his brethren of the Cabinet, he thus addressed his daughter:—

"I thought it wholly inconsistent with the dignity of the House of Lords to close the most solemn inquiry ever entertained in that House by doing nothing. The bill should either have been rejected or passed. But to have upon our Journals four different resolutions, all founded upon our avowed conviction of her guilt, and then neither to withdraw those resolutions, nor to act upon them, appears to me perfectly absurd, and, both to the country and to her, unjust. To her surely, it is so. We condemn her four times; she desires at our bar that we will allow her to be heard in her defense before the Commons; we will neither do that, nor withdraw our condemnations; for, though the bill is withdrawn, the votes of condemnation remain upon our Journals. This is surely not pretty treatment for a lady. Report says that in a petition, which Lord Dacre would have presented if the bill had not been withdrawn, she signs herself thus—

'CAROLINE, QUEEN IN SPITE OF YOU.'

This thing, which has so long kept the country in a state of agitation, will probably die away like all other nine days' wonders—except that, when Parliament meets, Ministers will be abused heartily, and some witnesses on both sides will be prosecuted for perjury."

He was mistaken in supposing that the memory of this scandalous proceeding would so soon pass away, for it produced a deep disgust in the public mind, which was not effaced during the current reign;—and not until examples of purity and of all the domestic virtues had afterwards been displayed on the throne, was it that the people of this country were again affectionately attached to the monarchical government under which they and their forefathers had so long flourished. Lord Eldon himself, though little given to change his opinion, or to confess that he had been wrong, seems in his latter days to have regretted "the proceedings upon the Bill of Pains and Penalties against Queen Caroline"—which he goes so far as to denominate—"proceedings, *perhaps*, more *just* than *prudent*."[1] Happily, I am not called upon to offer any opinion upon the guilt or innocence of the party accused, or to say how far her disregard of the opinion of others, and her habitual refusal to submit to the conventional restraints imposed upon her rank and sex, may, in her case, repel the inference usually drawn from certain transgressions of the rules of delicacy, and so redeem her from the highest imputation of misconduct. Had it not been for the ill-usage she experienced in the early part of her married life, there probably would have been little hesitation in coming to an unfavorable conclusion upon the evidence produced against her, and in that case, whatever the fact might be, she would have had no just reason to complain, for a woman must be prepared to see the inferences drawn against her which naturally arise from the situations in which she chooses to place herself; and if she has raised a general belief of guilt, it is really not very important to others that she retains a consciousness in her own breast of not having actually consummated her infidelity.

This was the most wretched part of Lord Eldon's life. His sufferings must have been materially aggravated by the consideration that the individual whom he was now called upon to vilify and to degrade was the same Caroline of Brunswick who received him so hospitably at Blackheath—and he must have felt some envy when he saw Mr. Canning sacrificing office, and daring the King's displeasure, rather than assist in the proceedings against her.

[1] Anecdote Book.

CHAPTER CCV.

CONTINUATION OF THE LIFE OF LORD ELDON TILL THE CABINET WAS LIBERALIZED BY THE INTRODUCTION OF MR. CANNING AND MR. HUSKISSON IN THE YEAR 1823.

DURING the Christmas vacation which followed the Queen's trial, Lord Eldon enjoyed a short repose at Encombe, and after the exciting scenes in which he had been engaged, he took delight in meditating for hours together on the hearth, "with the fancy very busy in finding out likenesses of the human visage in the fire." He concludes a letter to his daughter, giving an account of this "sleep of the mind," by announcing his speedy return to the turmoils of business: "In an hour's time I shall be among the lawyers, who are no favorites of yours; and I would much rather see my pointers, &c., and listen to the sounds with which they express their joy at seeing their master, than to the eloquence of the most eloquent of the babblers, to whom now, for a long time possibly, I must lend unwilling ears. I say possibly, because, till the temper of Parliament is tried in the subsequent week, our fate remains mighty uncertain."

The zeal of the Whigs in opposing the "Bill of Pains and Penalties," no doubt had been sharpened by the hope that the Ministry would either be beaten in Parliament by persisting in it, or would quarrel with the King by abandoning it—so that either way their gain was certain. But Lord Liverpool baffled them completely. The King, upon reflection, became satisfied that more could hardly have been done to gratify him; and his Majesty looked with some displeasure on Sir John Leach, by whose sanguine prophecies he had been buoyed up. For his present servants he had no great regard; but he decidedly preferred them to the "early friends," against whom he was now much exasperated, as they had defeated him in the object nearest his heart, and he imputed their conduct to purely factious motives. The Queen's popularity likewise considerably declined when her dangers were over: the excesses of the multitude enlisted in her cause had excited alarm in the minds of moderate men, and a general feeling prevailed that it was necessary, for the sake of public tranquillity, to rally round the Government.

For these reasons the session of Parliament, which was expected to be so stormy, and to which Lord Eldon had looked forward with so much apprehension, was one of the quietest known for many years. Sir Charles Wetherell delivered a very elaborate argument in the House of Commons to prove the illegality of the continued exclusion of the Queen's name from the Liturgy: but a resolution to that effect was there negatived by a large majority,[1] and, when the subject came to be mentioned in the House of Peers, Lord Eldon, giving no reasons, contented himself with dogmatically asserting the contrary doctrine, "after having obtained every information that could be acquired, and applied to it the deepest research."[2]

The only serious difficulty to be encountered was "Catholic Emancipation," which began to assume a very formidable aspect. Hitherto there had been only debates on petitions from the Roman Catholics, or resolutions for taking their claims into consideration at a future time. But a bill for removing all their disabilities had passed the House of Commons, and (horrible to relate) was actually put into the hands of Lord Eldon, at the bar of the House of Lords, by Mr. Plunket, its author. His Lordship behaved on the occasion with composure and self-command. On his return to the woolsack he recited, with an unbroken voice, the title of the bill to which the concurrence of their lordships was asked; and he calmly declared, that "although he feared it would be impossible for the promoters of the measure, by any modifications, ever to induce him to acquiesce in it, he would bestow his best reflection on the subject before the discussion on the second reading."

When the motion for a second reading of the bill came on,—after inducing the Duke of York to make a very bold declaration against any change in "the Protestant Constitution of 1688," he himself delivered what is considered his greatest anti-Catholic speech, concluding, after praising the old Whig Peers, who had framed the Act of Settlement, with this earnest prayer: "May the posterity

[1] 4 Hansard, 219.   [2] Ib. 799.

of those noble lords find, in the preservation of our present laws, in those wise and fundamental laws which require the Throne, the Government, and the Church to be unalterably and forever Protestant, that solid security for their liberties which they can never find in excluding a Papist from the throne, but surrounding a Protestant King with Popish advisers!" The bill was rejected by what was considered the auspicious majority of THIRTY-NINE.[1]

Next day Lord Eldon wrote to Sir William: "The Duke of York has done more to quiet this matter than everything put together. It has had a great effect. I have nothing further to delay your drinking to the 'THIRTY-NINE, who saved the THIRTY-NINE ARTICLES,'—a very fashionable toast." Shortly after, being requested by him to correct and publish his speech, he wrote back an answer, showing his uneasy suspicions of Lord Liverpool's sincerity, and his own resolution, which, being really founded on principle, ever proved indomitable: " I have no great appetite for printing.[2] At the same time, the papers have printed such nonsense, that I am uneasy about it. As to Liverpool, I do not know what he means. To please Grenville, he makes a Regius Professor,—friend to the Catholics. To please Lansdowne, he makes a Bishop of Bristol and Regius Professor,—friend to the Catholics. He, therefore, I dare say, will not stir a step beyond pronouncing in words his speech. I am not quite content with this—and yet I don't know what to do. But what he does or does not do, I think should not regulate me. Can a man who makes such a Secretary for Ireland as we have, and two such Regius Professors and such a Bishop, be serious? With me this thing about the Catholics is not a matter of consistency, but of conscience. If there is any truth in religious matters, I can not otherwise regard it."[3]

[1] 159 to 160. 5 Hansard, 356.
[2] It was published in a pamphlet as corrected by himself, and it is reprinted in Hansard, v. 285.
[3] In the same letter, referring to an application for a place for an idle young lawyer, he gives such admirable advice that I cannot refrain from copying it:—"The truth is, that upon F. there must be impressed the necessity of his working for himself. These lads, who give each other great dinners, with their claret, champagne, &c., must learn that this will not do, if they are to pursue a profession; and they must learn that if they want the aid of a profession, they must submit to the privations which young men,

The only other measure which excited much interest during the present session was the bill for disfranchising the borough of Grampound. This Lord Eldon strenuously opposed, although it was supported by his colleagues. He said that "the present bill was completely irreconcilable with the law and constitution of this country. It was 'a bill of pains and penalties,' and an *ex post facto* law, for it inflicted on innocent men the punishment due only to the guilty, and a severer punishment than any existing law provides for the guilty."[1] However, on the ground, not of punishing crime, but of taking the elective franchise from a place which could not be permitted to enjoy it longer without serious detriment to the public, the bill passed, and formed a precedent for the bill to disfranchise Sudbury, soon after carried through with the sanction of Sir Robert Peel.

As the session drew to a close, preparations began to be made with a view to the coronation of George IV., which the Queen's arrival had interrupted the preceding year. On this occasion Lord Eldon was very fitly raised to an Earldom. He said that "George III. and George IV. had previously often pressed the dignity upon him, and that even now his 'young master' was obliged to say, 'If you will not make out your own patent, I will get some one else to do it; and when I send it to you, I will see if you dare to return it.'" He sent a formal letter of thanks to his Majesty, and received an answer testifying the favor in which he was then held:

"Hamilton Place, Saturday, July 7th, 1821.

"The Lord Chancellor, having been informed that your Majesty has been pleased to sign the warrant for his promotion in the peerage, can not permit himself to delay the expressing to your Majesty his most grateful thanks. He is too sensible of the many imperfections which, during the vigor of life, have occurred in his attempts to discharge the duties of that great station, in which his gracious Sovereigns have been pleased to place, and so long to continue him, not to feel that he is wholly and entirely indebted for this distinction to royal favor; and he can not hope, in the decline of life, to render any services which can be in any degree an adequate return for it. He trusts that your

---

who are to get forward in professions, have always submitted to. This is a truth of which they are not aware." [1] 5 Hansard, 695.

Majesty will permit him to offer to your Majesty his warmest gratitude, to tender to you the duty and attachment of a devoted servant, and the homage and loyalty of a faithful subject."

"Carlton Palace, Saturday night, July 7th, 1821.
"MY DEAR FRIEND,

"I must thank you for your affectionate letter, which is very acceptable to my feelings: God grant that you may long live to enjoy the honors so justly due to your eminent talents and distinguished services! I shall hope to see you early in the morning, as I have much to say to you. "Always, my dear friend,
"Very affectionately yours,
"G. R."

The patent was dated the 7th of July, 1821, the consideration recited in it being "the distinguished ability and integrity which he had invariably evinced in administering the laws in his office of Chancellor during the period of nineteen years." Two days afterwards he took his seat in the House of Lords as an Earl, and received the warm congratulations of peers of all parties; for, on account of the striking amenity of his manners, he was very generally beloved in that assembly.[1]

On reference to the Heralds, it was resolved that the

[1] The following is the ceremonial of his installation as recorded in the Journals:—" The Earl of Liverpool signified to the House, that his Majesty had been pleased to create John, Lord Eldon, Lord High Chancellor of that part of the United Kingdom of Great Britain and Ireland called Great Britain, a Viscount and Earl of the United Kingdom of Great Britain and Ireland, by the style and title of Viscount Encombe and Earl of Eldon. Whereupon his Lordship, taking in his hand the purse with the Great Seal, retired to the lower end of the House, and having then put on his robes, was introduced between the Earl of Shaftsbury and the Earl of Liverpool (also in their robes); the Gentleman Usher of the Black Rod, Clarencieux King of Arms (in the absence of Garter King of Arms), carrying his Lordship's patent (which he delivered to him at the steps of the throne), and the Deputy Lord Great Chamberlain of England preceding.

"His Lordship (after three obeisances) laid down his letters patent upon the chair of state, kneeling, and from thence took and delivered them to the clerk, who read the same at the table.

"The said letters patent bear date the 7th day of July, in the second year of the reign of his present Majesty. His Lordship's writ of summons was also read." (Here follows the writ verbatim.) "Then his Lordship, at the table, took the oaths, and made and subscribed the declaration, and also took and subscribed the oath of abjuration, pursuant to the statutes, and was afterwards placed on the lower end of the Earls' bench, and from thence went to the upper end of the same bench, and sat there as Lord Chancellor, and then his Lordship returned to the woolsack."—*Journ.* liv. 572.

title of " Viscount Encombe," at the same time bestowed upon him, should be borne by his grandson ; and he communicated the intelligence in a dreadfully long, stiff, and prosy epistle[1] to the promising youth, whose excellent disposition was proof against all the temptations to pride, idleness, or extravagance arising out of his new rank.

At the same time the house of Scott was further honored by Sir William being created Lord Stowell—with the universal approbation of the public. His judgments in the Court of Admiralty had conferred a lasting obligation on his country, and his elegant accomplishments and delightful social qualities had endeared him to a large circle of private friends. The public—although much given to envy, yet not without generosity—were pleased to see two brothers, who had raised themselves from obscurity by their own merits, both invested with the highest dignities of the state.

There were serious apprehensions that the coronation would be disturbed by the Queen. She claimed to be crowned at the same time with the King ; but Lord Eldon and a committee of the Privy Council, after hearing Mr. Brougham on her right, unanimously reported against her. She then, against the strong remonstrances of her more prudent advisers, resolved to force her way into Westminster Abbey, and insist on a crown being placed on her head. Rumors of this project caused much uneasiness, but the ceremony went off auspiciously, as we may know from the following lively notice of it from the Earl of Eldon to his daughter, the Lady F. J. Banks :—

" July 20th, 1821.

" It is all over, quite safe and well. The Queen's attempt to make mischief failed. She sent a message to say, that she would be at the Abbey by 8 o'clock. To take the persons there by surprise, she came between 6 and 7. After trying every door of the Abbey in vain, she came to the Hall ; there she was also denied entrance. A few of the mob called ' Queen for ever ! ' I am informed that, on the other hand, there was great hissing, cries of ' Shame, shame, go to Bergami ! ' and a gentleman in the Hall told us, that when her Majesty got into the carriage again, she wept. Yesterday must have informed her how

[1] Twiss, ii. 438.

fleeting is popular favor. Her friends broke Londonderry's windows, Montrose's, and various other people's windows, who were preparing illuminations. We had a very handsome illumination : John Bull spared us ; indeed his family were very civil to me, in the course of my transit from the Hall to the Abbey. The business is certainly over in a way nobody could have hoped. Everybody went in the morning with very uncomfortable feelings and dread. I think the fatigue of it would have killed dear Mamma. William Henry was a capital figure in the dress of an ancient Baron of the Cinque Ports. He looked amazingly well, and performed his duty well. John's delight, I think, was the Champion, and the Duke of Wellington and the Marquis of Anglesea going on horseback for, and returning on horseback with, the King's dinner."

The new Earl's fatigues at the coronation brought on a fit of the gout. He would have been almost completely consoled by the following most gracious note from his "young master," if he could have placed entire reliance on its sincerity :—

"Thursday evening, 6 o'clock, July 26, 1821.

"MY DEAR CHANCELLOR,

"I delay not a moment thanking you for your affectionate note. I have known you, and, with truth I do add, that I have loved and esteemed you as a friend, much too long for a moment to entertain a thought that you would not have presented yourself both at the levee yesterday, as well as the drawing-room this day, if it had been morally possible for you to have done so. If there be any blame, it rests with me, for not having sent to inquire after you, but which I desire you will not impute to forgetfulness on my side, but to the constant *worry* and hurly-burly I have been perpetually kept in for the last fortnight. "I remain, my dear Lord,

"Always your most affectionate friend,

"G. R."

"P. S. I shall rejoice, if you are able to come to me, to see you on Sunday as usual."

But he had to suffer, along with the twinges of the gout, the dread of speedy changes in the Cabinet; and, while still confilned to his room, he thus wrote to Lord Stowell :—

"Somebody brought to my ladies a report that all the

Ministers were going out but Lord Sidmouth and the Chancellor. That any changes have been determined upon, I take to be quite unfounded; that many must take place soon, if the King and Liverpool continue in the temper in which they respectively are, I have no doubt, though the thing may wear on as it is till his excursions are over. The bulk of the Ministers are, I think, convinced that the K. means, and that my neighbor[1] will induce him, to change them; and I should not wonder if, in a too great confidence that he has this meaning, they were to retire before he knew how to execute it. It is impossible but that the thing must fall to pieces. This is so strongly the conviction of the greatest part of the Administration, that I think that conviction will of itself almost produce the change."

However, the King, without making any change, set forth on his visit to Ireland, when he heard of "the greatest of all possible deliverances,"[2]—the death of the Queen. This threw his Ministers, as well as himself, for some time into a transport of joy, but Lord Eldon was soon disturbed by accounts that his Majesty in Ireland was showing marked kindness to the supporters of Catholic emancipation,—and that Mr. Canning, on whom he himself looked with more and more aversion, and from whom he thought he was forever safe, by the part which this "emancipator" had taken in favor of Caroline,—was again coming into office. In sad perturbation he thus wrote to Lord Stowell:—

"DEAR BROTHER,

"I think there is a great alteration in the opinions of some where I did not look for it" (the King) "about Canning, and even Sidmouth thinks the death of the Queen has removed, in a great degree, all objection to Canning. But suppose the King and Liverpool can not settle their differences, what is to be done? Who is to be at the head? In the House of Commons you'll say Londonderry" (Lord Castlereagh, now, by the death of his father, Marquis of Londonderry) —"but that won't do. For many of the peers, who have great parliamentary interest, will not support, as Prime Minister, any person who stands pledged to remove Catholic disabilities, and I have per-

[1] The Marchioness of Conyngham.
[2] Letter from Lord Castlereagh to Lord Eldon.

suaded myself that they, with the Duke of York at the head of them, will never agree to that. If you go to the House of Lords, who can you have? Sidmouth's last determination as communicated to me, was, that, whether there were or were not any other changes, he would not, in any office, meet the Parliament at its next meeting. They talk of the Duke of Wellington; but I have reason to believe that, if there were no objections, he would have nothing to do with it. Indeed, I think he is, the most of all of us, convinced that the King is inclined to sweep the cabinet room of the whole of us, and that he feels very strongly that we have all experienced, and are likely to experience, treatment not very easy to bear. If Sidmouth goes, I shall go. With a new Secretary for the Home Department, a new Chancellor, a change of Prime Minister,—who can suppose things to be in a settled state? In truth, I don't see how we can go on without some explanation as to what all the occurrences in Ireland mean—as to the Catholic question, unexplained. With a determination in many in the Cabinet to resist claims to the utmost, we are continuing parts of a Government apparently daily in every way encouraging them.

"I understand the King was particular and lavish in his attentions to Plunket: he certainly means, if he can, to bring him into office —another Papist!"

It turned out, that although the King, in his exuberant spirits, arising from a late event, and captivated by the novelty of the enthusiastic popularity which he experienced, had incautiously given hopes to the Irish Roman Catholics that the hour of their deliverance was at hand,—he had no serious thoughts of changing either measures or men.—and his visit to Ireland, instead of bringing about an equality of civil rights in that country by quiet and constitutional means, soon caused deeper discontents, and quickened the agitation which in a few years mischievously extorted what might sooner have been beneficially conceded. On his return he gave Lord Liverpool assurances that he would continue to preserve the ascendency of the anti-Catholic part of the Cabinet, and that upon this principle alone would he admit any addition to it.

When Christmas came round, he sent the following

invitation to the Chancellor, which places his Majesty in a most amiable point of view, and makes us deeply regret that his good qualities were not always so conspicuous:—

"Brighton, Dec. 26, 1821.

"MY DEAR FRIEND,

"You flattered me that when you had relaxation from business, you would make me a short visit. It strikes me that next Monday and Tuesday are the two most probable days to afford you such an opportunity: therefore, if this should be so, and unless you have formed any pleasanter scheme for yourself, *pray come to me then*. I believe it will be necessary for you to swear in one or two of my state servants, the most of whom you will find assembled here; therefore pray be properly prepared. I hope it is not necessary for me to add how truly happy I should be, if our dear and good friend Lord Stowell would accompany you. A hearty welcome, good and warm beds, turkey and chine, and last, though not least in love, *liver and crow*,[1] are the order of the day.

"Ever, my dear Lord,
"Most sincerely yours,
"G. R."

"P. S.—N.B. No church preferment will be requested upon the present occasion."

The negotiations for strengthening the Government ended in the accession of the Grenville party; and Mr. Peel was placed in the office of Secretary of State for the Home Department. This last appointment was very agreeable Lord Eldon, for he had not yet found out, what was ere long proved, that the new Secretary was a law reformer,—still less did he suspect the dangerous liberality of his principles upon other subjects.[2] But our Chancellor was much chagrined by the interloping of the Grenvilles, who had been contaminated by the Whigs, and with whom he had been at enmity almost ever since he held the Great Seal. He wrote to his daughter: "This coalition, I think, will have consequences very different from those expected by the mem-

[1] A Newcastle dish, more savory than delicate, to which the Chancellor was much attached.
[2] Now began the official correspondence between Lord Eldon and Mr Peel, from which, through the kindness of the latter, this and the two following chapters are much enriched.

bers of Administration who have brought it about. I hate coalitions." And he subsequently send her the following *mots* against their new allies,—the first alluding to the number of offices they had required, and the other to a personal defect of one of them, who was, nevertheless, a very able as well as honorable man: 1. "Lord Holland says, 'All articles are now to be had *at low prices*, except *Grenvilles*.' 2. Lord Erskine, alluding to Charles Wynn's voice, which prevented him from being elected *Speaker* as he would have been called "*Mr. Squeaker*," says, 'Ministers are hard run, but they still have a *squeak* for it.'"

Lord Eldon had rejoiced much that Mr. Canning had been kept out of office on the late Ministerial arrangements, but was soon alarmed by a notice which this *quasi* Whig—animated by private resentment as well as public principle—gave in the House of Commons, of a motion for leave to bring in a bill to reinstate Catholic peers in their legislative privileges. The move was very skillful, for Catholic peers had been allowed to sit and vote till they were disfranchised by a factious effort of the profligate and irreligious Shaftesbury in the reign of Charles II.; and the present representatives of the Catholic families, with the Duke of Norfolk at their head, were distinguished for their loyalty not less than for their ancient blood. The Chancellor, who thought that this measure would be as dangerous as allowing a Roman Catholic to be upon the throne, wrote to Lord Stowell, with more point than is usually to be found in his epistles: "Peel is studying much the objections to Canning's motion. Canning says the peers should be first restored, because they were last excluded. The *Papist King* was the *last* excluded."[1]

He was sadly distressed that the Bill was to be considered by a mixed Cabinet, and was to be left "an open question." To his daughter, Lady Frances, he now writes: —"I am going, as usual, to Carlton House; the King is still confined by the gout. How he is to manage, with

---

[1] He seems to have been in a happy vein at this time. In reference to applications to him for livings, he adds, " My applying clergy may be divided into two classes—applicants who have begot twelve children, and applicants who are most anxious to marry in order to beget twelve ; and every man of each class thinks the Chancellor bound to provide for him and his, that are and are to be." From a most exaggerated notion prevailing of the ecclesiastical patronage belonging to the office of Chancellor of the Duchy of Lancaster, which I have now the honor to hold, I can easily conceive how he was appealed to by the married and the marrying.—1848.

some Ministers servants of the Pope, and others foes of his Holiness, I can't tell; but if I was a King, I would have my servants all of one mind. . . . . . Great uncertainty as to the event of next Friday on the Catholic business. I think it will pass the Commons, and while individuals are voting for it *there* under a conviction that it will be lost in the Lords, there is reason, very much, I am sorry to say, to doubt that,—for lords are beginning to think it foolish to be the instruments by which other persons may vote dishonestly."

The bill having passed the Commons,[1] was brought up to the Lords, and allowed to be read a first time; but a strenuous resistance to it was to be made upon the second reading, with respect to which Lord Eldon was unnecessarily very nervous. He wrote to Lady Frances:—"I am sorry to hear that your Bishop (the Bishop of Norwich) is coming, though I am far from wishing him to be indisposed. He brings his own vote, and the Bishop of Rochester's proxy; and *two* is *two too* much."[2]

When the day came, he made a very able speech against the bill, dwelling with much force upon the fact that the exclusion of Roman Catholic peers was re-enacted at the Revolution as essential to our liberties. Having gone over all the statutes on the subject, and observed that if Catholics were allowed to sit in the House of Lords they could not be excluded from the House of Commons, he thus concluded:—"Will the mover of this bill abrogate any of those enactments, with respect to religion, which affect the Sovereign? Will he allow the King to marry a Papist? If, from a conscientious feeling, he would prevent his Sovereign from marrying a Papist, he must equally, from a conscientious feeling, object to the introduction of Papists into this House. I am quite sure that if I agree to this measure, I can resist no other. It is neither more nor less than a motion for general emancipation, and therefore I can not consent to its adoption. In a short time, it will be of very little consequence to what I do consent, or to what I do not; but while I retain the power, I will endeavor to discharge my duty firmly. It is con-

[1] 7 Hansard, 475, 673.
[2] He subsequently wrote in a very kindly strain respecting the same Prelate:—" The Bishop of Norwich is a very agreeable man, and always talks delightfully about you. If the days of Popery should return, we will vote him into the Papal chair."

stantly urged that the question of emancipation will be carried, sooner or later. I do not believe it; and I think that the oftener the assertion shall be made, the less will be the chance of its being fulfilled. Though these were the last words I had ever to speak, I would still say that, if this measure be carried, the liberties of my country as settled at the Revolution, the laws of my country as established by the securities then framed for the preservation of her freedom, are all gone; but I shall have the pleasure to reflect that I have not been accessory to their destruction. Those laws and liberties of England I will maintain to the utmost; and therefore I will give my decided opposition to this measure."[1] The second reading was negatived by a majority of 171 to 129.[2]

The only other bill on which Lord Eldon spoke, during the session of 1822, was a most excellent one—to validate marriages celebrated in the face of the church, without certain required formalities,—where the parties believed that they were regularly contracting matrimony, and continued for a certain time to live together as man and wife. This he unaccountably opposed, and he was quite furious against the clause giving it a retrospective operation, which he said was an invasion of the rights of property. He divided the House against it, and, to his great surprise and mortification, being left in a small minority,—after declaring the numbers, he exclaimed:—"My Lords, ten days ago I believed this House possessed the good opinion of the public, as the mediator between them and the laws of the country: if this bill pass to-night, I hope in God that this House may still have that good opinion ten days hence. But, to say the best of this measure, I consider it neither more nor less than a legal robbery, so help me God. I have but a short time to remain with you, but I trust it will be hereafter known that I used every means in my power to prevent its passing into a law."[3]

He became rather sulky with his colleagues, and, when he had any decent excuse, declined attending Cabinets. Thus he wrote to Mr. Secretary Peel:—"I have received your summons to attend a Cabinet on the Alien Act, on Friday next, at two o'clock. I can not possibly attend it, the orders of this House requiring me on Mondays, Wednesdays, and Fridays, to be upon the woolsack, in

[1] 7 Hansard, 1230.   [2] Ib. 1262.   [3] Ib. 1141, 1198, 1373, 1453, 1455.

this place, hearing causes from ten till four. My absence, however, can be of little, and possibly of no consequence." [1] These *orders of the House* have not been considered by his successors as preventing them from attending a Cabinet, and *he* would very little have regarded them if he had been summoned by the Duke of Cumberland to deliberate on the formation of a new Government.

As soon as the session was over, the King set forward on his voyage to Scotland, and, on his arrival in Leith Roads, received the melancholy news of the death of Lord Castlereagh, who, with all his faults of oratory, had proved himself a very useful Minister, and had, for a number of years, creditably supported the important part of Government-leader in the House of Commons. Lord Eldon, on this occasion, feelingly wrote to his daughter, Lady Frances:—" Our own country and Europe have suffered a loss, in my opinion quite *irreparable*. I had a great affection for him, and he deserved it from me, for to me he showed an uniform kindness, of which no other colleague's conduct furnished an example. I learn, upon the best authority, that for two or three days he was perfectly insane; and the medical men attribute that fact to the operation upon his head of the unceasing attention to business, which the last harassing session to him called for."

He again wrote on the day of the funeral:—" This morning I have been much affected by attending Lord Londonderry to his grave. The concourse of people between St. James's Square and the Abbey was very great, the great bulk of them behaving decorously, some behaving otherwise; but I protest I am almost sorry to have lived till I have seen, in England, a collection of persons so brutalized, as, upon the taking the coffin at the Abbey door out of the hearse, to have received it with cheering for joy that L. was no more."

The remodeling of the Administration now caused the Chancellor perplexity. He deeply regretted that Mr. Canning, who had accepted the office of Governor General of India, and was preparing for his departure, had not actually set sail, although he did not think that there could be any very serious danger from a man who was not only looked upon with suspicion by the ultra-high-church

[1] Peel MSS.

party, but who was supposed, from his intimacy with Queen Caroline, to be personally obnoxious to the King. Hitherto, upon such emergencies, Lord Eldon had shown peculiar skill in bringing about an arrangement according to his own wishes, and still he was in good hopes that he should be able to strengthen the Protestant interest.

The first check he received was a letter from George IV., who, after lamenting Lord Castlereagh's death, thus admonished him: "My great object, my good friend, in writing to you to-night, is to tell you that I have written to Liverpool, and I do implore of you not to *lend yourself* to any arrangement *whatever*, until my return to town. This, indeed, is Lord Liverpool's own proposal; and, as you may suppose, *I* have joined *most cordially* in the proposition. It will require the most *prudent foresight* on *my* part relative to the new arrangements that must now necessarily take place. You may judge of the state of my mind."[1]

In consequence, deeming himself bound by his allegiance, under such a strict injunction, to obey—he actually did abstain from political conversation and correspondence till the King's return. Although his sittings in the Court of Chancery had closed, he continued in London to await the event, trying to work up some judgments which were in arrear, but thinking more "who was to be leader of the House of Commons?"—and "how the Church Establishment might be protected?"—with, perhaps, now and then a wandering thought towards his *own security*. During this interval he wrote a letter to a lady of his acquaintance, who expected a visit from him in the country: "The busy world, having nothing better to think about, has employed itself lately in informing me and others what are likely to be my political movements, and my corporeal movements; and as to both, that busy world has suggested much that I am yet a stranger to. I wish to go to Encombe. I have had no thought of going to Eldon. I neither know, nor ever heard, one syllable about political movements. I have spoken to nobody upon the subject, nor is it my intention to say one word about them to anybody, unless my royal master forces a word out of my mouth when he comes. I can

[1] 15th August, 1822, dated from Leith Roads.

not quit this place till he does come; and when he and Sir William Curtis are to cease exhibiting in the full Highland garb, I can not be sure."[1]

The King having returned from his northern metropolis, the Chancellor was about to press upon him the promotion of Mr. Peel, who had won high distinction in the late debate upon the Catholic Peers,—when, to his unspeakable chagrin, he found that Lord Liverpool had not only himself resolved to prefer Mr. Canning, but had succeeded in overcoming the dislike to him in the royal bosom, by representations that this was the only arrangement effectually to exclude the Whigs, and by an assurance that Catholic emancipation, though left an open question, should be resolutely opposed.

The unhappy Chancellor's mortifications did not here end; for, without having been once consulted upon the subject, he read in a newspaper that there was to be another addition to the Cabinet,—if possible, more disagreeable to him. He thereupon, in a towering fit of indignation, wrote to Lord Stowell :—

"DEAR BROTHER,

"The 'Courier' of last night announces Mr. Huskisson's introduction into the Cabinet—of the intention or the fact I have no other communication. Whether Lord Sidmouth has or not, I don't know; but really this is rather too much. Looking at the whole history of this gentleman, I don't consider this introduction, without a word said about the intention, as I should perhaps have done with respect to some persons that have been or might be brought into Cabinet,—but turning out one man and introducing another in the way all this is done, is telling the Chancellor that he should not give them the trouble of disposing of him, but should (not treated as a Chancellor) cease to be a Chancellor. What makes it worse is, that the great man of all has a hundred times most solemnly declared, that no connections of a certain person's should come in. There is no believing one word anybody says—and what makes the

[1] 28th August, 1822.—To the mother of the Reverend C. Stuart, of Sunning Dale, Berks, from whom I have received the original.—In the last sentence Lord Eldon alludes to the King having assumed the Stewart tartan at Edinburgh, and having been imitated by Sir William Curtis, the fat Alderman of London, who accompanied him,—to the great amusement of the public and benefit of the caricaturists.

matter still worse is, that everybody acquiesces most quietly, and waits in all humility and patience till their own turn comes.

"I have written to Liverpool (before this news came, and therefore not on the ground of this fact) that I have no wish to remain Chancellor; and, to say the truth, I think those who do remain, and especially that officer, stand a very good chance of being disgraced."

One would have thought that this was rather a favorable opportunity for his retiring to that repose for which he had been long panting. In a letter written to his brother before the storm arose, he had said, in the most unqualified terms, "As Chancellor, I will not meet another session of Parliament." We have no direct information, and it would be wrong to conjecture with any confidence, respecting the means used to shake his resolution. We are bound to believe that, if he had only consulted his own inclination, he would instantly have resigned; but that he was persuaded—for the good of his country—to pocket the affront, and to consent to sit in the Cabinet,—with Canning on his right hand, and Huskisson on his left!

CHAPTER CCVI.

CONTINUATION OF THE LIFE OF LORD ELDON TILL THE COMMENCEMENT OF PROCEEDINGS AGAINST THE CATHOLIC ASSOCIATION.

LORD ELDON sacrificed no public principle by remaining Chancellor, and it was still well understood that the *Government* was to be anti-Catholic; but I can not help thinking that it would have been more for his dignity if he had now resigned. He had not only been thwarted, but slighted, in these late arrangements,—and he might have seen that his influence was gone.

Accordingly, while Catholic emancipation continued to be steadily opposed till the year 1829,—from this era there was in other respects, a marked alteration in the internal policy of the country. We have no more suspensions of the *Habeas Corpus;*—"the Six Acts" were allowed to expire or to fall into desuetude;—soon after began the Attorney Generalship of Sir John Copley, during which, while plenty of libels were published, not one single criminal information was filed;—and, although not much was yet done to reform the law, the horror of correcting ancient abuses was sensibly declining, so that men could descry the dawning of a better day. Lord Eldon's colleagues continued to treat him with perfect courtesy; and, respecting his character, and valuing the credit which his name brought to them, notwithstanding motions about his delays in Chancery, and sarcasms upon his antediluvian theories of government, they were desirous of humoring him as far as they decently could;—but henceforth the dread of shocking his prejudices was considerably diminished, and, very little consulted in politics, he was left almost entirely to the task of trying to work off his Chancery arrears.[1]

It is pleasing to observe that the improved spirit of the age made some impression even upon *him*, and that, if he still resisted all mitigation of the letter of the criminal law, he was much softened with respect to the manner in which it ought to be enforced,—showing himself in advance of at least one man in the kingdom. Being asked to look over the cases of capital convictions at the Old Bailey before they were submitted formally to the King, he wrote to Mr. Secretary Peel: "I think, from the Recorder's communication to me, he is much more bloody minded than I am, after three times reading all the cases. . . . . . Times are gone by when so many persons can be executed at once, as were so dealt with twenty years ago."[2]

I am likewise grateful to him for the good advice which he gave when consulted about one of the excellent judicial appointments in Scotland, which distinguished the Secretaryship of Mr. Peel:—"For aught I know, the individual named may be a very fit person at a period when, I believe I am justified fully in saying, nothing can be of more consequence to the lieges of Scotland than selecting for the Bench the ablest man at the Bar, let his politics be what they may, if he does not act upon them in the seat of

---

[1] One who had a near view of what was going on, although not a member of the Cabinet, writes to me,—"I was struck with the indications of great want of cordial good-will to Lord E. on the part of his brother Ministers."

[2] Nov. 1822. Peel MSS.

judicature. To the credit of the English Bar, when you give the ermine to an opposition lawyer, you never make an opposition judge: but whether this would also be the case if you make a Scotch opposition lawyer a judge, is what I can't answer for. I am sure much mischief has been done in Scotland by their old system of party and particular families filling the Bench. To do Lord Melville justice, in his time there have been some very fit appointments of lawyers to the Bench, not altogether addicted to Administration, but acting on the Bench ably and impartially."[1]

The session of 1823 passed off very quietly, the chief measure brought forward having for its object to facilitate the hearing of appeals in the House of Lords. Lord Liverpool stated, that since 1813, when the plan of the Chancellor sitting to hear appeals three days in the week was established, the number of new appeals entered much exceeded the number of old ones decided, and that it would take several years of continual sitting to hear those from Scotland alone.—The subject was referred to a Select Committee, who in their Report recommended that the House should sit on appeals five days every week during the session, and that, to enable the Chancellor to attend in his own court, a Deputy Speaker should be appointed in the House of Lords.

When resolutions to this effect were moved, Lord Eldon took the opportunity to vindicate his own judicial conduct, which had been much questioned on the score of *doubts* and *delays*, and to repel the indecent attacks which had long been yearly made upon him in the House of Commons. He said that—

"When they were deciding causes in the last resort, and their decisions were to give the law to other Courts, they could not be too cautious. The time was fast approaching when his natural life must terminate; and for his judicial life, it had already been too long: but when the termination of his natural life did arrive, that degree of caution, which was called *doubt* and *hesitation*, would be his greatest comfort; because, by means of that caution, he had reversed decrees, and prevented the injustice of A keeping possession of property which of right belonged to B. If their Lordships would compare his

[1] Peel MSS.

conduct during the twenty years which he had sat on the judicial bench, with the conduct of any of his illustrious predecessors—and he did not fear the comparison, on the contrary he invited it—he was sure that the comparison would not turn out to his discredit. On that account he could not but feel indignation, when he was informed of the language in which his conduct had been arraigned in another place, by those who ought to have known better. It had been publicly asserted, that appeals in the House of Lords were nothing more than appeals from the Lord Chancellor in one place to the Lord Chancellor in another. He should like to know whether the persons who dealt in such assertions were aware that there were many appeals to their Lordships from the Chancellor in cases which had never been heard at all by the Lord Chancellor, but which had been decided by the Master of the Rolls or the Vice-Chancellor? He would undertake to say, that not one of the distinguished characters who had sat before him upon their Lordships' woolsack had shown the slightest reluctance to reverse his judgment when it was shown to be incorrect; and he would fearlessly ask, whether he himself had ever exhibited any unwillingness to reconsider before their Lordships any of the decisions to which he might have previously come in another place? He could say most conscientiously that he never had; and for that very reason, the insinuations which had been thrown out against his judicial conduct were as cruel and vexatious as they were unfounded and unjust. He had never upon any occasion declined,—on the contrary, he had made it his continual practice, to state at length the various grounds upon which he rested his decisions, in order that the Bar might be enabled to declare to their clients whether those decisions were correct or not. And he defied any man to point out a single case where the correctness of them had been doubted in which he had not expressed his gratitude to the party who suggested the doubt. If persons acquainted with the practice of his Court had made upon his conduct the observations which had been made upon it by those who were totally unacquainted with it, he should indeed have felt them acutely; but he was happy to say, that those observations did not proceed from those who had the best opportunities of marking his conduct. They came from those who knew

IX.—

little or nothing of the subject, who had scarcely ever put a foot into his Court, and who were not, therefore, particularly well qualified to judge of its proceedings. He would add that, upon that very account, they were bonnd, in common honesty, to abstain from throwing out random insinuations, which were calculated to hurt, in the opinion of the King's subjects, an individual, who, if he was not a great judge—and he did not venture to call himself a great judge—at least filled a great judicial situation."

The resolution passed, and Lord Gifford was appointed Deputy Speaker. With a view of simplifying and improving the forms of procedure in the Court of Sessions in Scotland, and thereby to lessen the number of appeals, a bill was introduced for the appointment of commissioners to examine the matter. When this bill came to be debated in the Commons, Mr. Brougham replied with great freedom to the Chancellor's late speech in the House cf Lords :—

"This bill," he said, "had been carried through the other House with the support of a noble and learned lord, who would have done well to consider whether its principles might not be applied to the administration of justice in another part of the United Kingdom ; for he believed the forms of process in Scotland were not more prolix or objectionable than those of the English Court of Chancery. When the noble and learned lord at the head of that Court did, in the other House, in carrying the resolutions on the appellate jurisdiction, evince a great anxiety to facilitate the proceedings of Scotch law, he ought not to have forgotten that the process of the Court over which he himself presided was as fit an object for inquiry as that to which those resolutious referred. But perhaps the noble and learned lord would not agree with him, that inquiry, like charity, ought to begin at home. Yet he ought surely to have kept in view the Christian maxim ; and before he proceeded to remove the mote out of the eyes of our Scotch brethren, he should have taken the beam out of his own. Why had not the Attorney General and the great ornaments of the Court of Chancery been called upon to state their ideas of its abuses and of the remedies? In looking over the report which he had mentioned, it was curious to observe how summarily it disposed of a matter of grave dispute, which elsewhere was still *vexata quæstio*. It declared, unreservedly, that it was impossible for the Lord Chancellor to discharge all his duties in the House of Lords and in the Court of Chancery. Such had not been the opinion of Sir S. Romilly. In 1813, Sir S. Romilly had not thought that a Vice-Chancellor was necessary, but a new Chancellor: he had admitted the great legal talents of Lord Eldon, but denied his fitness for the office he filled: he had complained that Lord Eldon did not confine himself to his judicial duties, but that his ministerial duties crossed and jostled them on the way, and interfered with their progress; he had objected that Lord Eldon was required to be not only in his own Court, but in the Cabinet, in the Privy Counsel, and in the King's closet; in short, that his other avocations took up so much of his time, that Lord Eldon could not devote his high talents and his unequalled learning to the cases of suitors in Equity. He (Mr. B.) joined in these sentiments most heartily. He wished to speak with all due respect of the incorruptible integrity of the learned lord in the discharge of ordinary judicial business. A man who stood exposed to the eyes of all the world could not well be guilty of any acts of corruption; but the appointments made by him to judicial offices formed quite a different question. There the politician interfered, and it was the opinion of all Westminster Hall that Lord Eldon carried the politician too much in court, in disposing of the patronage attached to his station. Let it be remembered, also, that he had taken upon himself another office, namely, that of Prime Minister." "As to Lord Liverpool being Prime Minister" (continued the learned gentleman, not aware of the ascendency Lord Liverpool had lately acquired, and of Lord Eldon's declension), "he is no more Prime Minister than I am. I reckon Lord Liverpool a sort of member of Opposition; and, after what has recently passed, I should designate him as 'a noble lord in another place, with whom I have the honor to act.' [*A laugh.*] Lord Liverpool may have collateral influence, but Lord Eldon has all the direct influence of the Prime Minister. He is Prime Minister to all intents and purposes, and he stands alone in the full exercise of all the influence of that high situation. Lord Liverpool has carried measures against the Lord Chancellor. So have I;

therefore I say that we act together. If Lord Liverpool carried the Marriage Act, I carried the Education Bill; and if Lord Liverpool succeeded against Lord Eldon in some points on the Queen's trial, I say that I totally defeated him on that odious Bill of Pains and Penalties. I might just as well call myself Prime Minister as Lord Liverpool. He has no more claim to the distinction than I have. He acts with me, and I with him; and I call him 'my noble coadjutor,' and I trust we shall enjoy a long course of co-operation. I am sincerely glad of it; and, long as I have sat and fought on this side of the House, I never welcomed a recruit to our body with greater satisfaction. With such powerful assistance, I should not wonder if we were to make head against our opponents, and in time turn out the Minister."

While the Chancellor was thus thought by others to be Prime Minister or Dictator, he was himself laboring under the consciousness of diminished influence, and was actually afraid of being ejected from the Cabinet. He particularly dreaded the rising consequence of Canning. The following letter from him to Lord Stowell shows that this affectionate brother had been trying to soothe his uneasiness, and had quoted to him the advice, "Tu ne cede malis, sed contra audentior ito,"—but that a masterly stroke (as he conceived it) of his chief enemy had almost driven him into despair:—

"The appointment of Lord Francis Conyngham in the Foreign Office, has, by female influence, put Canning beyond the reach of anything to affect him, and will assuredly enable him to turn those out whom he does not wish to remain in. The King is in such thraldom that one has nobody to fall back upon. The person that has got . . . ., after having in conversations, I believe, uttered nothing that was kind about Canning, was one of his voters for his cabinet office. The devil of it is, there is no consistency in anybody. Again, upon 'ne cede malis,' it is better to go out than to be turned out!! which will assuredly be the case. God bless you!"

It should be stated, however, to Lord Eldon's credit, that, eager as he had ever been for carrying on the late war till Napoleon was laid low, he now entirely approved of Mr. Canning's pacific policy upon the foolish invasion of Spain by a French army, about the present time.

When this measure was threatened, and many exclaimed that England should send an opposing army to the Peninsula, the worthy old peer thus sensibly addressed his grandson :—

"I have nothing new to tell you. France and Spain are so foolish as to go to war with each other, and probably they may both sorely repent it before it concludes. I hope old England will have the good sense to know the value of peace and quiet, and not suffer its repose to be disturbed. Dr. Johnson, in a pamphlet written many years ago, says, that men forget the actual miseries of war—the expenditure of blood and treasure—and delude themselves by supposing that it consists wholly in a 'proclamation, a battle, a victory, and a triumph.' Of the soldiers' widows and the soldiers' orphans after the fathers and husbands have fallen in the field of battle, the survivors think not."[1]

When Parliament met in the beginning of February, 1824, there seemed to be a dangerous storm rising against the Lord Chancellor. With little blame personally imputable to him, beyond not providing a legislative remedy for the evils daily before his eyes, the state of business in the Court of Chancery was still most deplorable, and there really was a denial of justice to the suitors there. This grievance afforded a plausible ground of attack to the political opponents of the Government, who were particularly pleased with an opportunity of wounding the man who had so zealously and so sucessfully thwarted all their efforts to return to power. The effect of the annual motion against him in the House of Commons had been considerably impaired by the ridicule attached to the character of the mover, Mr. Michael Angelo Taylor, who was known by the *sobriquet* of "Chicken Taylor," and of whose pomposity many laughable stories were familiar to his hearers.[2] But a notice of

---

[1] March 31, 1823.

[2] On some point of law which arose in the House of Commons, Mr. Taylor had answered the great lawyer, Bearcroft, but not without an apology, "that he himself, who was then but a young practitioner, and, as he might phrase it, *a chicken in the law*, should venture on a fight with the cock of Westminster Hall!!" He then acquired, and he never lost, the name of "Chicken Taylor." Although very short in stature, he was of athletic proportions, and Lord Ellenborough said that his father, who was a skillful artist, had produced him as "a pocket Hercules."—But he was more celebrated as an Amphitryon, and I can testify that he gave the best dinners of any man in

moving for a committee to inquire into the delays of the Court of Chancery was now given by Mr. John Williams,[1] a lawyer of eminence on the Northern Circuit, who had distinguished himself as one of the Counsel for Queen Caroline, and as author of several excellent articles in the Edinburgh Review on the eloquence of Demosthenes.

Lord Eldon did not like to intrust his defense against this formidable antagonist to Mr. Canning, the leader of the House of Commons, but applied to one whose sentiments he considered more congenial to his own, and whose rise he had patronized. In a letter to Mr. Secretary Peel, after observations respecting the Recorder's report, he said, "I hope you will be so good as to take some care of the Court of Chancery in the House of Commons. It is not possible to go on in my office, the object of constant attack,—which will never cease till the present Chancellor is removed. It is a nuisance, therefore, to the Administration."[2]

Forthwith he received the following kind answer:—

"MY DEAR CHANCELLOR, "February 10, 1824.

"I shall be most happy to confer with you on the motions respecting the Court of Chancery.

"Every consideration, arising out of my sincere esteem for you, and my knowledge of the motives of those who attack you, would induce me zealously, at least, to co-operate with more able and competent defenders in resisting these attacks.

"Depend upon it, my dear Chancellor, they can make no impression. Men ask themselves who is the ablest and the honestest man who ever presided in the Court of Chancery, and the decisive answer to that question, if it does not silence malignity and political hostility, at least disarms them of the power to rob you of your hardly-earned and justly acquired honors.

"Believe me,
"With sincere attachment and regard,
"Most faithfully yours,
"ROBERT PEEL."

London. One of these was the ruin of a great motion for Parliamentary Reform; for while the leading patriots were partaking of it, the House of Commons was counted out. The occurrence gave rise to a very scurrilous, but very witty, song in "John Bull," written by Sir Alexander Boswell, afterwards killed in a duel for a similar production.

[1] Afterwards a Judge of the Court of King's Bench.
[2] 10th Feb. 1824. Peel MSS.

On the day before the motion was to be made, a long consultation was held on behalf of the Chancellor,—as we know from the following good-humored note to his daughter, showing that his equanimity was undisturbed, and exciting an interest in his favor:

"Monday (February 23rd, 1824).

"Sir Thomas Lawrence has had two hours of my company, and Mr. Peel and four lawyers two more: the former, to make my face look as well on canvas as might be; the latter to be enabled to make me *look as well* as might be in the debate on Chancery to-morrow night, which will be carried on with great acrimony on one side, and, I think, with much zeal on the other."

Mr. Williams certainly did lead on a merciless onslaught, but was defeated by the dexterity of Mr. Peel, who, affecting a convenient ignorance of details,—" only to be understood by a professional lawyer,"—dwelt upon the profound learning, unsullied integrity, and earnest desire to do justice, which distinguished this venerable magistrate, —and intimated that, for the purpose of thoroughly investigating the subject, a commission was forthwith to be issued by the Crown, upon which some Chancery practitioners not in Parliament might be placed, and which would be much better qualified to sift the evils of the present system, and to suggest the proper remedies, than a committee of the House of Commons. After speeches from Mr. Abercromby and Mr. Brougham, admitting the personal good qualities of the Chancellor, but pointing out the enormous grievances which had accumulated under him,—by their advice Mr. Williams withdrew his motion, in the hope that some good would arise out of the promised commission.[1]

Next morning, while not yet quite correctly informed of what had passed, the Chancellor wrote to his daughter:—

"Wednesday (February 25th, 1824).

"Mr. Williams made his attack last night, as savage as the Dey of Algiers, with whom we are gone to war. He told a great many . . . . which dissatisfied attorneys had thrown into his mouth, and a great many things which neither I, nor any person interested about me, ever heard of before, mentioning, however, some things which, in the

[1] 10 Hansard, 372-437.

lazy moments of twenty-two years, appeared like (and, perhaps, really constituted) negligence on my part, which, however, could not much affect or sully the tenor and character of a long industrious life. He then abused all the Masters of the Court, and, indeed, everybody belonging to the Court; and then moved for a committee to inquire into the misdeeds and misdoings of all of us.

"In June last, I had communicated to the House of Lords my purpose of having—not a Committee of Inquiry and Vengeance, but—a commission to inquire whether any and what improvements could be made for the future in the practice of the Court of Chancery, or any part of it, and whether the Chancellor could be relieved of any part of his business by sending such part to other Courts. At my instance, therefore, Mr. Peel, in a most admirable speech, moved for such a commission, as a great merit on my part in aiming at improvement, instead of this Committee of Vengeance; and this threw Mr. Williams, &c. upon their backs, and they did not venture to divide. So for the present *this storm* is over, and matters will be tolerable *till the next begins to rage.*"

On a subsequent day [1] he wrote to her: "I have reason to think that the debate in the Commons has done me much good. Peel's speech was, I understand, most eloquent, and, towards me, expressive of regard amounting to affection:—Lord Stowell came out of the House of Commons in tears,—he was so affected by it. The speech did much good,—by informing the House that the Chancellor's income was hardly more than a third of what nine-tenths of the members thought it was—by informing them how much I had paid out of my own pocket to save the public. The newspapers, too, had charged me with hearing lunatic and bankrupt petitions rather than other matters, in order to get money. He let the House of Commons know that I had, for twenty-two years, administered all matters in lunacy without receiving *one farthing;* and as to petitions in bankruptcy, 12s. 6d. was all that was paid for a petition, which sometimes occupied four, five, six, seven, eight, or even ten days.[2] In short, he set me up, in the

---

[1] Thursday, 26th February, from the bench.

[2] This is an amusing instance of "dressing up a case for the House of Commons." I most potently believe that the charge against Lord Eldon, of preferring to dispose of bankruptcy business, because it was more profitable, was a calumny; but this business undoubtedly was very profitable to him.

public opinion, against what I hold in utter detestation, being influenced by sordid motives and feelings; and so do I detest such meanness, that being set right in this view of my character will render me happier than I have been as long as I live." . . . "Saturday, 28. Peel tells me that the people he lives with most are quite astonished to find the Chancellor's income so very far short of what they had always believed it to be; and he will have it, that the late House of Commons business has been a most fortunate thing for *your* father. How that may be I can not be sure; but I am sure that he could not have taken more pains about it if I had been *his* father. I still regret, however, that there was no division, notwithstanding that before they could have got to a division there must have been an immense quantity of foul abuse. There are thoughts of publishing, in a small pamphlet, contradictions to Williams' and Abercromby's misrepresentations. I was surprised at the language of the latter. Upon his father's fall in Egypt, I sent him a commissionership of bankrupts, which he keeps to this hour. He might, therefore, have been commonly civil, if not just.

The "next storm was to rage," after a very short lull. Lord Eldon had been much irritated by having been truly told, that, on Mr. Peel's announcing the intended commission, Mr. Abercromby had said their opponents had "capitulated at the opening of the campaign;" and it so happened that on this very Saturday, while he was sitting on the bench in Lincoln's Inn Hall, a newspaper was put into his hand, containing an inaccurate account of Mr. Abercromby's speech, in which the learned gentleman was represented to have averred that the Chancellor had been in the habit of deciding appeals and re-hearings from Sir John Leach, the Vice-Chancellor, *on fresh evidence.* He thereupon very imprudently and unwarrantably burst out with the following invective: "With respect to appeals and re-hearings, it is supposed that I have heard them *on new evidence*, and thereby brought discredit on some part of the Court. IT IS AN UTTER FALSEHOOD! On *re-hearings* it

Although his fee on the "petition" was only 12s. 6d., his fees upon the mass of "affidavits" for and against it might amount to £20. Then, one would suppose that part of the consideration for which he received his *salary* as Chancellor was "administering matters in lunacy"—a labor he is supposed to have undergone gratuitously for twenty-two years!

is always competent to read the evidence *given* in *the cause*, though it was not read in the Court below, either by the counsel or the Judge. Further than *that* the Court does not go. On *appeals* it only reads what has been *read in the Court below*, and that practice I have never departed from in any one instance. Therefore, really, before things are so represented, particularly by gentlemen with gowns on their backs, they should at least take care to be accurate, for it is their business to be so."

Mr. Abercromby, who was known by all present to be aimed at, happened at that moment to be attending the Court of Exchequer in Gray's Inn Hall, but was soon informed by his friends of what had happened in Lincoln's Inn Hall. Thereupon, with the firmness, decision, and high sense of honor which have ever distinguished him, he instantly resolved to bring the matter before the House of Commons as a breach of privilege, although not unaware of the injury likely to be done to his own professional prospects by such a *fracas* with the Lord High Chancellor,—and he called on Master Courteney, now the Earl of Devon, requesting him to communicate the intended motion to his Lordship, that he might be prepared to meet it by his friends. Next day he wrote the following letter, fully explaining his purpose—that it might be shown to the Chancellor:—

" New Street, Sunday night.

" MY DEAR COURTENAY,

" The interval which has elapsed since I communicated with you yesterday at your office, has only tended to confirm my conviction that a due sense of what I owe to myself and to the profession to which I belong, imposes on me the necessity of complaining in Parliament of what the Lord Chancellor said on the bench in Lincoln's Inn Hall on Saturday. I must therefore entreat you to have the goodness to mention to the Lord Chancellor that such is my fixed determination; and this I do in order that he may apply to you or to any other person to report to him faithfully what I shall feel it to be my duty to state. I am very happy that I applied to you as early as I did, because it will enable you to state that the resolution I have taken is the result of the sense I have of the injustice that has been done, and of the duty which is imposed upon me of vindicating my character from the stain that has been attempted to be fixed upon it.

"I do assure you, upon my honor, that I have not consulted any man living upon the fitness or unfitness of defending my own reputation, although it is true that I have consulted others as to the parliamentary course of proceeding in such a case.

"I find myself in a situation which can not fail to be distressing to any person who has an interest in his profession, however small; but I think that the principles which ought to govern my conduct are plain, and by them I shall be guided. I shall certainly feel that I must express myself strongly; but my best defense for that will be found in the terms that have been applied to me. If, in the execution of the commission you have so kindly undertaken, you think that it will afford you any facility to show or read this letter to the Lord Chancellor, you may do so, for I have nothing to conceal, as I think I shall be able to show that I have nothing to fear.

"Yours ever truly, &c.
"J. ABERCROMBY."

Lord Eldon thought, that to offer any apology then might be construed into timidity, and the motion was made.

Mr. Abercromby thus began:—

"Sir, a sense of the duty I owe to myself as an individual, a sense of the duty I owe to the House of Commons as one of its members, and a sense of the duty I owe to the profession of which I have the honor to be a member, concur to impose upon me the task of complaining to this House of one of the most gross and unwarrantable attacks that was ever made on the freedom of debate—made from the seat of public justice, by the Lord High Chancellor of Great Britain." After detailing what he himself had actually said in the debate, what Lord Eldon had imputed to him, and the other facts of the case, he proceeded:—"Lord Eldon says, that with respect to appeals and re-hearings, he does not hear them on new evidence. Not appeals from decrees, and further directions, certainly. I never said that he did. Quite the contrary. I put them in distinct contrast to motions, which I again declare the Lord Chancellor frequently hears on fresh evidence. I think, therefore, Sir, that the House will agree with me, that Lord Eldon, at the very moment when he says I have been guilty of 'an utter falsehood,' puts into my mouth not only what I did not say, but the very reverse of what I did say. [*Hear, hear!*] The noble and learned lord altogether abstains from noticing my distinctions, and confounds that which I stated on the subject of motions with that which I stated on the subject of decrees. Lord Eldon has, therefore, falsely put into my mouth what I did not utter; and has declared, that in what I felt it to be my duty to state, in my place in Parliament, I imposed on the public. These, Sir, are the facts. But are there no aggravations of them? I ask when it was, and where it was, that Lord Eldon uttered this foul calumny against me? Was I present? Had I any notice of the noble and learned lord's intention? Before whom did he utter the calumny? Before persons whose unfavorable opinion, if I had no means but what I derive from my profession, must effect my entire ruin. [*Hear, hear!*] In what form did this calumny go forth to the people of England? In that of a report made by a reporter in a court of justice, attending on behalf of the public, who took down the words as soon as they were uttered, and sent them to an office where they were printed before the ink with which they were written was dry. Such was the place, such was the occasion, and such were the means, by which the Lord High Chancellor of England sought to vilify an individual, one of the humblest members of his own Court. If, Sir, I had chanced to be in the Court at the time, what might have happened? I hope, and I believe, I should have been able to control my feelings. If, however, I had not done so, it would have been in the power of the noble and learned lord to silence me. If I had persisted in addressing him, he might have committed me to the Fleet. If the noble and learned Lord had stopped me, would it not have been an act of the grossest injustice and indecency, after having calumniated a member of his own profession and of his own Court, by doing what he could to induce the public to believe that that individual had been guilty of an 'utter falsehood,' to prevent him from replying to so monstrous and injurious an accusation? But if Lord Eldon had thought fit—as he could not have abstained from doing without the grossest injustice—to allow me to reply to him, what a

spectacle it would have been, to have seen the Lord
Chancellor of England engaged in a controversy with one
of the humblest practitioners in his own Court, respecting
words used in the House of Commons! Lord Eldon
thought fit to impute to me, that I did not use due
caution before I made those statements which he attributed to me. In which case was the defect of caution
most signal? In the case of myself, Sir, who was speaking in the presence of honorable and learned gentlemen,
every way my superiors, especially in the knowledge of
the practice of the Court of Chancery, who, if I had been
guilty of any misrepresentation, would have instantly
detected and refuted it to my utter confusion and shame,
—or in the case of Lord Eldon, who, invested with all the
power, and patronage, and authority of the office of Lord
Chancellor, presumed, on the seat of justice, to take advantage of a false representation of the words of an humble
individual, to pronounce upon him, without inquiry, the sort
of censure best calculated to destroy his fame, and at a
time when no one had the means of interfering to avert
the effect of that most unjust censure? [*Hear, hear!*]
We have heard a great deal, Sir, of the delicacy of Lord
Eldon, of his anxious desire for justice, of that amiable
weakness of mind, too sensitive to the fear of possible
wrong to others, and too cautious to decide lest he should
decide erroneously. If this had been a case in which the
right of private parties had been concerned, there would
have been, no doubt, argument after argument, affidavit
and supplemental affidavit, months and years would have
passed, and the 'too sensitive' mind of Lord Eldon would
have abstained from settling those claims which it is his
duty to decide on. But what, Sir, was his mode of
proceeding, when there was an occasion to pronounce
from the seat of justice an anathema founded on a false
statement of facts, to destroy the character of an
individual whom he supposed to have censured himself?
Then, indeed, to the just mind of the just Lord Eldon,
there seemed no room for caution—no time for inquiry.
[*Hear, hear!*] He at once proceeded to decide, to
pronounce, and to execute his sentence. From whom, I
should be glad to know, did Lord Eldon receive his
information? From what legitimate source did he derive
it? The Attorney and Solicitor General were present

in the House: neither of them could have given the learned lord the statement which he dared to attribute to me. My honorable and learned friend the member for Exeter (Mr. Courtenay), and my honorable and learned friend whom I saw just now in the House, the member for Tewkesbury (Mr. Dowdeswell), were also present during my speech; and if the Lord Chancellor had chosen to resort to them for information as to what had passed in these walls, he would have learned how unlike what I uttered was that which he attributed to me. [*Hear, hear!*] But now, Sir, let me ask, what authority, what right, has the Lord Chancellor of England, or any other Judge, to undertake to comment, on the judgment-seat, on the debates of this House? Where does Lord Eldon, who is so cautious, find a precedent for this? How can he say he is not guilty of a gross breach of the privileges of this House? It is not a formal, but a substantial breach of privilege,—a direct attack on the security and freedom of debate, which is the only legitimate object of privilege. What is the situation of any member of this House, if the Lord Chancellor, or Lord Chief Justice of the King's Bench, may presume to put false statements into his mouth, and send him forth a disgraced, and, as far as the authority of the judgment-seat can go, a ruined individual? By what tenure shall we then hold the freedom of debate, but at the will and caprice of any Lord Chancellor and any Chief Justice? If this condition be intolerable to all the members of the House, how much more fatal must it be to those members who also belong to the profession of the law, if they are subject, for what they say in this House, to be denounced by the Lord Chancellor from the bench—if any of the Judges, when anything is uttered in the House which touches their feelings, are to denounce in the Court where he practices a man who exists only by his honest exertions in his profession, and to destroy, in a moment, by a false statement, his character, not only as a professional man, but as a gentleman and a man of honor? [*Hear, hear!*] If the House do not protect its members from this tyranny and despotism (for what can be greater tyranny and despotism I can not conceive),—nay, if it do not secure itself against all control of this kind,—if Lord Eldon be allowed to extinguish any member of this House, by uttering things of him from the judgment-seat,—of what avail is the freedom of debate—particularly to any man who shall at once be a member of the House and of the profession of the law? If the House shall think the facts that I have stated to be clearly proved (and I will adduce evidence to put them out of doubt), it must be incumbent on it to take decided and vigorous steps to secure its own privileges, to vindicate the freedom of debate, and to put on a secure footing the independence, the spirit, and the usefulness of Parliament. If, on the other hand, the House pass by this gross violation of its privileges without interfering, how, I ask, can we expect that there shall remain any vestige of independence, public spirit, or usefulness in this House? If my appeal be neglected, what wrong can be offered to a member of this House against which he can think there is any hope in calling on the House for protection? The result will be to lay the Bar of England prostrate at the feet of Lord Eldon. The conduct of Lord Eldon, which I shall substantiate, is a gross attack on the freedom of debate; for if I had uttered a thousand falsehoods in this House, the Lord Chancellor has no right to animadvert on them on the judgment-seat. It is on this ground that I offer the conduct of the Lord Chancellor to the notice of the House, and if the House be prepared to pass it by, let it say distinctly that there shall be no longer freedom of debate."

The feelings of all present were much roused by this appeal, and party was nearly forgotten in the general excitement—so that Mr. Canning had a difficult task to perform when he rose to put a negative on the motion. But he very skillfully explained, and mitigated, and soothed, without at all compromising the honor or dignity of the party accused:—

"We have not here," he said, "a great officer of the Crown attempting to intimidate a member of the House of Commons—but an individual, feeling, perhaps too sensibly, for his character, after a public life of great, and spotless, and irreproachable merit, and of whom it may be said that he wears his heart upon his sleeve 'for daws to peck at,' and dreads too much every trifling attack, as striking at the vitals of his reputation. It is a fault to be so sensitive—it is a fault in a public man—but it will be hard on public men that it should be so severely visited as the honorable and learned gentleman proposes: for I am sure that the course he points out can lead us to little less than an accusation of the most serious kind. I certainly wish that a different course had been taken by the noble and learned lord, and that in the time that elapsed between the debate in this House and the end of the week he had recurred to other testimony, which might have set him right as to the words actually uttered by the honorable and learned gentleman. [*Hear, hear!* from the Opposition.] That it is to be regretted that the noble and learned lord neglected this precaution, I admit; but that he could treasure up the mis-statement to take an opportunity of wreaking his vengeance on an individual, is what no man would believe of another, and what any one who knows the character of the noble and learned lord will not dream of attributing to him."

The motion was finally rejected by a majority of 151 to 102.[1] "Lord Eldon's sufferings on that memorable night formed a sufficient atonement for his precipitation. During an eager and protracted debate he was seen hovering about the lobbies in a state of the most anxious suspense. On the explanation of Mr. Abercromby, however, and the failure of his motion, the Chancellor resumed his wonted equanimity and good humor, the sudden departure from which had startled the public like a flash of sheet-lightning on a calm summer's day."[2]—I am happy in being able to lay before the public for the first time a letter which he wrote to Mr. Abercromby next morning, and which redounds highly to his honor:—

"Tuesday morning.

"MY DEAR SIR,

"When Mr. Courtenay communicated to me the sub-

[1] Parl. Deb. x. 571.
[2] 2 Townsend's Twelve Judges, 440. The feeling of the usual supporters of Government seems to have been strong against the Chancellor on this occasion—and there must have been a difficulty to prevail upon them to vote for him. Mr. Wilberforce in his Diary gives us the following interesting sketch of the scene :—

"March 1, 1824. Abercromby came forward with a case of breach of privilege against the Chancellor for charging him on the bench with falsehood. Brougham spoke admirably, and Abercromby excellently; indeed, Scarlett also, and all the lawyers, did well. Canning spoke admirably in mitigation, and Peel defended as well as could be, but the case was too strong to be put by without an authorized apology. So, though I longed to go away, I staid and voted, 102 to 150. I seldom recollect—certainly not for many years—suffering so much pain."—*Life of Wilberforce*, v. 214.

stance of your letter to him, I expressed then what I wish to state to you now. I could not authorize him to represent at that time what I did then so express, because I thought it did not become me to prevent that step being taken which I understood it to be your purpose to adopt. At present, I shall relieve my own feelings by assuring you that I have too long known the respect which is justly due to you, to forbear representing that I regret, that, among the words which fell from me, I should have used an expression, which, if applied to you, I ought to retract, as inconsistent with all the feelings towards you with which I am, "Dear Sir,
"Yours truly,
"ELDON."

The following is Mr. Abercromby's answer:—
"New Street, Tuesday evening.
"MY LORD,
"I hasten to acknowledge the receipt of your letter, which I found on returning home this afternoon. I appreciate as I ought the motives which induced you to delay writing to me until this morning; I can derive nothing but pleasure and satisfaction from the sentiments you have been pleased to express, and I assure you that my personal feelings shall always remain as untainted by any recollection of the words to which you allude, as if they had never been used.
"I have the honor to be,
"My Lord,
"Your most obedient and faithful servant,
"J. ABERCROMBY."

The writer of this letter, who has since filled the chair of the House of Commons with distinguished ability, and now, as Lord Dunfermline, enjoys the universal respect of his countrymen, in kindly communicating to me the above correspondence, concludes with the gratifying statement —"In all my subsequent intercourse with Lord Eldon, I perceived neither any unusual constraint in his manner, nor any failure of courtesy."

Lord King, not knowing how this matter had been accommodated, attempted to taunt the Chancellor into some indiscretion by saying, in the course of a discussion on the manner of hearing appeals in the House of Lords, 'The noble and learned lord is a very great friend to the

Church; but what would he say to a rector who, wishing to be relieved from the burden of his clerical duties, should get a curate to perform them for him, and, instead of paying the curate out of his own emoluments, should leave him to be paid by the parish? What would be thought of a bishop who should declare from the pulpit that a person whom he disliked had stated *an utter falsehood?* What would the noble and learned lord think of the right reverend dignitary who should thus express himself respecting the character of another, in a place where what he said could not be answered? I am sure the noble and learned lord would be the last man in the world to give his approbation to such conduct."[1] The noble and learned lord, however, very prudently remained silent.

I wish, for his fair fame, that he had observed the same course when the Dissenters' Marriage Bill was debated, as the sentiments he then uttered expose him to the charge of bigotry, intolerance, and an entire ignorance, or disregard, of the best interests of the Established Church and of true religion.

The object of this measure, which the Archbishop of Canterbury and several other pious prelates supported, and which has since, with more extensive enactments, been carried almost unanimously, was to enable those who objected to be married according to the rites of the Church of England to be married by their own pastors, in their own places of religious worship, lawfully licensed. But, after it had been ably supported by the Primate, the Chancellor declared that, "notwithstanding his sincere respect for the Most Reverend Prelate, he could not concur with him on this occasion. The bill contained principles which were not consistent with the protection of the Established Church. On account of the Dissenters themselves he should oppose it, as there could not be enlightened toleration without the Established Church. It was said that the persons calling themselves 'Unitarians' had real scruples of conscience on the doctrine of the Trinity. So had Deists, Atheists, and others. If he understood the doctrines of the Church of England at all, it was impossible that there could be a greater repugnance between any doctrines than there was between the doc-

[1] 10 Hansard, 641.

trine of the Church of England and that of the Unitarians. The Unitarians must think the Church of England idolatry. What, therefore, would be the sort of comprehension that it would effect? Their lordships might pass the bill, but he had discharged his duty in giving his opinion on it; and he thought a worse bill had never been submitted to Parliament."—He succeeded in throwing it out by a majority of 105 to 66.[1]

The ascendency he now enjoyed in the House of Lords was strikingly illustrated by his successful opposition to the next liberal measure brought forward there, although it was supported by the Prime Minister. This was a bill which the Marquis of Lansdowne introduced merely to give to Roman Catholics in England the right of voting for Members of Parliament,—which Roman Catholics had enjoyed in Ireland since the year 1793. The Lord Chancellor, however, represented this concession as highly dangerous to the Protestant Establishment, and confirmed his opinion by an historical statement of the struggles between the two religions from the reign of Henry VIII. downwards. He said, "If they gave to the Catholics of England a portion of the privileges conceded to the Irish Catholics, they must go on and give them all the other privileges which the Irish Catholics possessed, and he saw no reason why more mischief should be done now because there had been some mischief done before. For the last twenty years there had been incessant attempts to take the Church of England by storm; these shocks it had withstood: let it now be destroyed by sapping and mining."

Lord Liverpool said, "he did not yield to his noble and learned friend on the woolsack in his zeal to maintain the Potestant Establishment, or the principle of the supremacy of the Crown; but, although he still maintained the necessity of having a Protestant Parliament, he saw no danger from the present measure; nay, he believed that the granting of such privileges to the Catholics of England would strengthen the Protestant Establishment, —as a cause of discontent would thus be removed, as a reproach perpetually thrown in their teeth would be taken away, and as by these safe concessions strength would be obtained to resist dangerous encroachments." However,

[1] 11 Hansard, 78–438.

upon a division, the bill was rejected by a majority of 139 to 101.[1]

Lord Eldon's speech on this occasion called forth from advocates of Roman Catholic claims some very free remarks. To these (which had not been accurately reported to him) he thus indignantly refers in the "Anecdote Book:"—" In the House of Commons Mr. Canning or Mr. Plunket, or both, thought proper to treat this as a sort of speech which an *almanack maker*, reciting past events, might make ; and which, therefore, might deserve no answer. And Canning, I think, called it a 'pettifogger's speech,' as he thought all lawyers' speeches were." After some remarks, proceeding from an entire misconception of the beautiful allusion to an *old almanack* which had really been made,[2] he proceeds: "As to Mr. Canning's 'pettifogging lawyers,' I should have treated that, if the terms had been applied to me in my presence, with the scorn and contempt which insolence merits. Politicians are fond of representing lawyers as most ignorant politicians: they are pleased, however, to represent politicians as not being ignorant lawyers, which they most undoubtedly generally are—and this was never more clearly demonstrated than by Mr. Canning's speeches on the Roman Catholic question."[3]

I am quite at a loss to account for Lord Eldon's conduct with respect to the next measure which was brought forward, and it furnishes almost the only instance in which his consistency can be questioned during his long and eventful life. In the late debate he not only had generally warned the House against any concessions to the Roman Catholics, however small, but he had specifically expressed a strong opinion against allowing the Duke

---

[1] 11 Hansard, 817–842.

[2] Mr. Plunket, instead of calling Lord Eldon an "almanack maker," had, without even referring to him, uttered one of the pointed sayings which will make him forever remembered. After showing how governments should watch and direct the changes of public sentiment, he observed, "If this were not the spirit which animated them, philosophy would be impertinent, and *History no better than* AN OLD ALMANACK."—7 *Hansard*, 808.

[3] In a letter which he wrote soon after to his daughter, Lady Frances, he says—" Pugilists, you will read in the papers, when they have got a great advantage over their adversaries, say they have 'put them into Chancery.' I could have put Canning, as to some of his points, *into Chancery*, if I had had a *set-to* with him. But brother Ministers in the House of Commons don't seem to like hitting hard against each other, and yet nothing but determination will do in a contest of this kind."

of Norfolk, a Roman Catholic, at the head of the English peerage, to exercise his hereditary office of Earl Marshal, without taking the oath of supremacy and making the declaration against transubstantiation,—stating his objection to be, that "if their lordships were to go step by step, taking a little here and taking a little there, they would be doing gradually what they could not have done at once, and creating danger without the salutary alarm which should precede it."[1] Yet within a little month he actually sanctioned a bill introduced by Lord Holland for this express purpose. When the second reading was moved, although he could instantly have thrown it out without the smallest difficulty, he contented himself with mildly suggesting that it should be postponed to a future session, in consequence of which only 10 voted against it, —and the third reading he allowed to pass without any show of opposition. This naturally alarmed his "young master," who had never once been consulted upon the subject, and who seems, from the following very stern note, in which nothing is to be found about "liver and crow," really to have thought that the worthy old Chancellor had all of a sudden forgotten his duty both to the altar and the throne:—

"Carlton House, June 23rd, 1824.

"The King desires to apprise the Lord Chancellor that the King has learned, through the evidence of the newspapers, what has been passing in Parliament relative to the office of Earl Marshal of England.

"The King can not suppose that the Lord Chancellor of England can approve of the King's dispensing with the usual oaths attached to that or any other high office; but if the King should be mistaken in this supposition, the King desires that the Lord Chancellor will state his reasons in writing, why the King should be expected to give his consent to such an unusual and unprecedented measure. "G. R."

The Lord Chancellor, by what means we do not know, contrived to satisfy both himself and the King, that in this instance a Roman Catholic might exercise a high office without danger to the Church; for the bill, having passed both Houses, received the royal assent,[2] and he moreover took an opportunity expressly to declare his

[1] 11 Hansard, 839.   [2] 5 George IV., c. 109.

good opinion of it when Lord Holland brought before the House the very intemperate terms in which the Duke of Newcastle and the Earl of Abingdon had entered a protest against it. He said,—" that if the House was supposed to have acted hastily in passing the act, the only course now was to bring in a bill to repeal it. He was far, however, from insinuating that such a course would be proper in the present case; his opinion was decidedly otherwise." He then made a most important statement, which I am most anxious that all true friends of the Church should bear in remembrance: " With respect to the *Oath of Allegiance* to be taken by the Earl Marshal, I must say as a lawyer, that it contains in it everything included in the Oath of Supremacy, and that the Oath of Supremacy was, in fact, added as an explanation of the *Oath of Allegiance*, or, as Lord Hale has expressed it, ' was passed to unravel the errors that had crept in.' "[1] Upon such high authority, I do trust that we shall ere long return to the *Oath of Allegiance* as all sufficient to testify the duties of a good subject, and that such idle, I had almost said irreligious, oaths as abjuring the descendants of James II., who have been extinct ever since the death of the Cardinal of York, in the year 1807, and all declarations distinguishing between religious persuasions as a qualification for civil offices, will be entirely swept away!"[2]

However, Lord Eldon soon recovered from this fit of liberality by an alarming proposal made to him by Mr. Secretary Peel, that a Roman Catholic nobleman should be placed in in the commission of the peace. The following was his answer:—

" Upon inquiry I find there are very few Catholics in the existing commissions. My inquiries into that are not finished, but there is a notion afloat that some of them have contrived to procure the capacity of acting without taking the oath of supremacy, and this is said of the Duke of Norfolk. I do not hear the same of any other of the R. Catholic nobility, who for compliment are put into some of the commissions, but don't act. But, if they can acquire an acting capacity without taking the oath of

---

[1] 11 Hansard, 1992.
[2] This is the advice given by the able commissioners appointed to consider the subject by Lord Lyrdhurst, and approved by him.

supremacy, and trust to the annual Indemnity Bill, all is over; for if this can be done with justices of the peace, then in the case of every magistrate, where, though there is constant usage, there is not an express law requiring that oath, and every person holding office, where there is no such express law requiring that oath to be taken *before* they act, the whole policy of England of supporting the King's supremacy is gone, or may be gone."[1]

Being further pressed, however, he yielded—in the hope that his concession would be unmeaning ceremony:—

"If Lord Pembroke recommends Lord Arundel to be placed in the commission, I shall not refuse to insert his name. I find the considerable Catholics in Dorsetshire and Devonshire are in the commission, but, by reason of the Act of Supremacy, have not qualified to act; and the case may probably be the same with this nobleman if his name is inserted."[2]

In consequence of this anti-Catholic steadiness and zeal the Chancellor again basked in the sunshine of royal favor. Sending an account to his daughter of a grand dinner he had given soon after to the Duke of York, the Duke of Wellington, and other "celebrities," he says—"The King sent me a message by the Duke of York that he would have dined with me if he had been asked. He should certainly have been asked if I had been aware that he would have condescended to permit me to send him an invitation. I have not heard, however, of his dining out since the crown descended upon him. Perhaps it is better, great as the honor would have been, that I did not know that he would have conferred it; for as to these things, such a condescension would have excited a good deal of jealousy in some men's minds; for there are such feelings in the minds of some (notwithstanding all the prayers they offer up to be delivered therefrom) as feelings of malice, hatred, envy, and uncharitableness; and that, too, where there is no ground or excuse for harboring such feelings."

His Majesty's late ebullition against the Earl Marshal's bill must have inspired the highest confidence in his Protestant zeal; but in other respects the Chancellor still thought him unequal to his father. Giving an account of a review in Hyde Park on a very rainy day, Lord Eldon

[1] Sept. 1824. Peel MSS.   [2] Ib.

says to his daughter—" Our sovereign lord the King did not attend. No weather would have prevented George III. from being at the haad of his troops." Again: stating, soon after, how the Duke of York had been cheered at another review in Hyde Parke, he adds,— " My royal master was in Carlton House, *i. e.* within half a mile of this scene, but did not approach it. It is astonishing what is lost by this sort of dealing, and it is grievous that the popularity which might be so easily earned and acquired, at so small an expenditure of time and trouble, should not only not be secured, but a feeling of disgust and reproach be engendered towards a person with respect to whom a very different feeling most easily might and ought to be created." Nay, the wary Chancellor seems even to have had serious doubts as to his " young master's " sincerity, and to have anticipated that a time might come when he would prefer a " Keeper of his conscience " with no predilection for " liver and crow," or for " Protestant ascendency." Thus he treats royal civilities:—"At about eleven Sir William Knighton called upon me—ordered, he said, ' to give me the King's affectionate regards;' and, if all Sir William said is truth, *very affectionate indeed they must be!* " [1]

[1] About this time the Chancellor was obliged to behave very discourteously to a lady claiming to be the legitimate daughter of the Duke of Cumberland, brother of George III., and styling herself the Princess Olivia of Cumberland. She at last presented a " Petition of Right " to the King, praying that her title might be recognized; and the Chancellor, being consulted as to how this ought to be dealt with, wrote back to Mr. Secretary Peel:—" Instead of a *Petition of Right*, this looks like a case for Monro or Warburton to be asked to take care of that illustrious personage."*

It has been said that whenever a Petition of Right is presented, the Sovereign should be advised to write upon it " Soit droit fait," whatever may be the prayer of it—leaving it to the Chancellor or other Judges to say whether it discloses any ground for relief. But, with great deference, I deny this doctrine. By the law and constitution of England, a suit can not be maintained against the Sovereign without the Sovereign's express consent. That consent can not be properly withheld where there is any feasible ground of suit, but ought to be withheld where clearly and certainly no relief can be given. The Attorney-General is answerable to Parliament for the advice he offers upon this subject, as he would be respecting the granting of a writ of error or a *nolle prosequi.* There is no authority for the contrary doctrine;— it is not at all supported by the analogy of a writ sued out by one subject against another,—and in some instances, without the possibility of any advantage to the petitioner, it may lead to a grievous waste of public money and of public time.

* Nov. 1824. Peel MSS.

CHAPTER CCVII.

CONTINUATION OF THE LIFE OF LORD ELDON TILL HE WAS DEPRIVED OF THE GREAT SEAL.

WHEN Parliament was about to assemble in the beginning of 1825, considerable alarm was excited by the proceedings of the Catholic Association in Ireland, which from oft-deferred hope had become very dangerous. The day before the opening of the session, the Chancellor wrote to his daughter. "To-day we have a cabinet in Downing Street and council at Carlton House, to try if we can make a good speech for the King. But there are too many hands at work to make a good thing of it, and so you will think, I believe, when you read it." He continued: "It is to be regretted that associations should exist in Ireland, which have adopted proceedings irreconcilable with the spirit of the Constitution, and calculated, by exciting alarm and by exasperating animosities, to endanger the peace of society and to retard the course of national improvement." Next morning, before going down to the House, he thus describes the result of their joint labors: "The King's speech was settled yesterday in the ante-room to his bed-room,—he having too much gout to come down-stairs. I don't much admire the composition or the matter of the speech. My OLD MASTER, the late King, would have said that 'it required to be set off by good reading.' It falls to my lot to read it, and I should read it better if I liked it better."

In the House of Lords the debate on the Address went off very smoothly, and there was no personal allusion to the Chancellor; but, in the House of Commons, Mr. Brougham forcibly pointed out, that relief from the penal laws was the only cure for the Catholic Association; and, having advised the section of the Cabinet favorable to the measure to act with vigor, he thus proceeded to pour forth the phials of his wrath on the devoted head of the Lord Chancellor:—

"Of what are they afraid? What is their ground of alarm? Are they apprehensive that the result would be

the resignation of any of their colleagues? Do they think
that any one of their coadjutors, some man of splendid
talents, of profound learning, of unwearied industry, would
give up his place? Do they think he would resign his
office? that he would quit the Great Seal? Prince Hohenlohe is nothing to the man who could effect such a
miracle. [*Hear! and a laugh.*] A more chimerical apprehension never entered the brain of a distempered poet.
Anything but that. Many things may surprise me; but
nothing would so much surprise me, as that the noble and
learned individual to whom I allude should quit his hold
of office while life remains. A more superfluous fear than
that of such an event never crossed the wildest visionary
in his dreams. Indeed, Sir, I cannot refrain from saying,
that I think the right honorable gentlemen opposite
greatly underrate the steadiness of mind of the noble
and learned individual in question. I think they
greatly underrate the firmness and courage with which
he bears, and will continue to bear, the burthens of
his high and important station. In these qualities the
noble and learned lord has never been excelled,—has
never perhaps been paralleled. Nothing can equal the
forbearance which he has manifested. Nothing can equal
the constancy with which he has borne the thwarts that
he has lately received on the question of trade. His
patience, under such painful circumstances, can be rivaled
only by the fortitude with which he bears the prolonged
distress of the suitors in his own Court. But to apprehend
that any defeat would induce him to quit office, is one of
the vainest fears, one of the most fantastic apprehensions,
that was ever entertained by man. Let him be tried. In
his generous mind, expanded as it has been by his long
official character, there is no propensity so strong as a love
of the service of his country. He is no doubt convinced
that, the higher an office, the more unjustifiable it is to
abandon it. The more splendid the emoluments of a
situation,—the more extensive its patronage,—the more
he is persuaded that it is not allowed to a wise and good
man to tear himself from it. I contend, therefore, that
the right honorable gentlemen opposite underrate the
firmness of their noble and learned colleague. Let them
make the experiment; and, if they succeed in wrenching
power from his gripe, I shall thenceforward estimate them

as nothing short of miracle mongers. His present station the noble lord holds as an estate for life. That is universally admitted. The only question is, whether he is to appoint his successor. By some it is supposed that he has actually appointed him, and I own I have observed several symptoms of such being the case. If it be so, I warn that successor, that he will be exceedingly disappointed if he expects to step into the office a single moment before the decease of its present holder. [*A laugh.*] However, I do intreat that the perseverance of this eminent person may be put to the test. Let the right honorable gentleman say he will resign if the Catholic question *is not* carried in the Cabinet; let the noble and learned lord say that he will resign if it *is* carried,—I am quite sure of the result. The Catholic question would be carried: but the noble and learned lord would retain his place. He would behave with the fortitude which has distinguished him in the other instances in which he has been defeated; and the country would not be deprived, for a single hour, of the inestimable benefit of his services. [*A laugh.*] To return, however, to the state of Ireland. The speech talks of *Associations* in the plural. That is not without an object. I warn the House, however, not to be taken in by the contrivance. The little letter *s* is one of the slyest introductions that Belial ever resorted to, in any of those speeches which are calculated to

> ' make the worse appear
> The better reason; to perplex and dash
> Maturest counsels; for his thoughts are low.'

I am perfectly aware, Sir, by whom that *s* was added. I know the handwriting. I know the reflection which passed through the mind of the writer,—' I must put the word in the plural; it will then be considered as applicable to Orange as to Catholic Associations, and the adversaries of both will be conciliated.' Let not that little letter *s*, however, deceive a single person. However it may be pretended to hold the balance between the Catholic and the Orange Associations, depend upon it, it will be only a nominal equity. It will be like one of those 'subtle equities,' so well known in the Court over which the noble and learned Lord, to whom I have been alluding, presides. Let the proposed measures be carried, and the Catholic Association will be strongly put down with one hand, while the Orange Association will receive only a gentle tap with the other.[1]

I introduce this satire upon the Chancellor to show the characteristic sensitiveness and good-nature with which he bore it. Thus he comments upon it, in a letter to his daughter :—

"Saturday (Feb. 5th, 1825).

"Since I last wrote, I have seen the debates of the Commons on Thursday night. When you read them, you will see that Brougham has had no mercy upon the Chancellor. Laughs and cheers he produced from the company, repeatedly, with his jokes: which, however, he meant to play off in bitter malignity, and yet I could not help laughing at some of the jokes, pretty heartily, myself. No young lady was ever so unforgiving for being refused a silk gown, when silk gowns adorned female form, as Brougham is with me, because, having insulted my master, the insulted don't like to clothe him with distinction, and honor, and silk. In the straightforward discharge of my public duty, I shall defy all my opponents : their wit, their sarcasms, their calumnies, I regard not, while conscious I have a great duty to perform ; and *that* I have now, in the support of the Constitution in Church and State. I shall do what I think right—a maxim I have endeavored in past life to make the rule of conduct—and trust the consequences to God.

"Now for digression from the serious to the lighter matters, — having first noticed that Canning answered every part of Brougham's speech, except what concerned his colleague, myself. But this is what I should have expected." . . .

The Chancellor strenuously defended the Bill to put down unlawful Associations in Ireland, although he declared that he had taken no part whatever in drawing it. He said, "he would not endure that a Roman Catholic body should assume a representative character—that they should proceed to tax the people of Ireland, and that they should exercise a control over the administration of justice : as the bill applied to all associations, it would equally put down any disposition to violence which might be displayed by Orangemen, and would show that all classes of the community must pay obedience to the law."[2]

[1] 12 Hansard, 51. [2] Ib. 866.

I ought not to pass over the humane and enlightened sentiments which he expressed in favor of a bill which passed the House of Lords almost unanimously, but was thrown out by the 'squires in the House of Commons—to prevent the setting of spring-guns to shoot poachers. He said "he wished to see property protected, but he should be sorry to be thought an advocate for spring-guns. There had been no occasion for these engines in former times; but now, every plantation was turned into a poultry yard, and a sportsman was thought nothing of unless he could kill his thousand birds a day; and thus arose the demand for these new sorts of protection. Now that so many plantations had been made, and so well stocked with pheasants, how could their lordships expect that people who had a taste for game—and he never knew an Englishman who had not—would not go and look for it where it was to be found? Poaching was the consequence of game being preserved and protected. He, for one, never could defend the practice of setting engines to endanger the life of a fellow-creature, for the sake of a partridge or a pheasant."[1]

The Duke of York's celebrated declaration now made against Catholic emancipation, concluding with a solemn oath "THAT HE NEVER WOULD ASSENT TO IT IN WHATEVER SITUATION HE MIGHT BE PLACED," was generally supposed to have been written for him by Lord Eldon; but his Lordship, although he exceedingly rejoiced in it, denied all previous knowledge of it, and it can not be supposed that he would have advised a step so very unconstitutional and improper.[2]

In spite of the vow of the Heir Presumptive, which was justly supposed not to be disagreeable to the King on the throne, a bill to remove the civil disabilities of the Catholics soon after passed the Lower House by a majority of 21. A single touch in a letter from the Chancellor to his

---

[1] 12 Hansard, 939.
[2] He thus wrote to Lady Frances:—"If the D. of Y.'s speech was imprudent, it has nevertheless, on account of its firmness and boldness, placed him on a pinnacle of popularity." But he was not blind to the failings of the "Protestant Hero," for he adds, "The D. of Y. is at Newmarket. It is to be regretted that, in his highly important and lofty situation, he spends so many days with blacklegs, and so many nights at cards,—among which we know there are *knaves*, as well as, what are better company for him, *kings* and *queens*."

daughter, enables us to form a lively notion of the scene when the bill was brought up to the Lords: "The Commons stared me very impudently in the face when they delivered to me the Catholic bill at the bar of the House." He has his revenge by adding,—"This bill, however, I think those gentlemen will never see again!"

The prophecy was verified at the close of the debate on the second reading—when the bill was rejected by a majority of 48.[1] Lord Eldon's speech on this occasion was more than usually zealous; and he had an advantage, of which he dexterously availed himself, in the circumstance that the accompanying measures called the "wings," then considered essential, had not yet been agreed to by the House of Commons.[2]

This must have been a very happy period of his life. He received letters of congratulation and thanks from several dowager duchesses, and he was universally *feted* by all the Protestant grandees. The following is his account of one of these entertainments:—

"We had a most sumptuous and splendid set-out at the Duke of York's on Saturday—twenty-four rejoicing Protestants round the table—and such a magnificient show of plate as even eclipses the King's exhibition of that article, and, as it appears to me, eclipses all of the same article which all the monarchs of Europe have presented to the Duke of Wellington. We drank the 48,—the year 1688,—and the glorious and immortal memory of William III.—but without noise or riot. I saw the King yesterday, who is much better, and not a little relieved in point of anxiety by the vote on the Catholic question." But—

> ———" pleasures are like poppies spread—
> You seize the flower—its bloom is shed;
> Or like the snow-fall in the river,
> A moment white—then melts forever;
> Or like the Borealis race,
> That flit ere you can point their place;
> Or like the rainbow's lovely form,
> Evanishing amid the storm:"—

Lord Eldon soon apprehensively wrote to his daughter: "My old foes, Mr. Denman and Mr. Williams, are, on next Tuesday night, to attack the Chancery and the Chan-

[1] 178 to 130. 13 Hansard, 766.   Ib. 762.

cellor. Wishing to live the rest of my time in the shade, I had rather be excused this annual attack; for, though I care not what they say of me as a political character, I am very nice and touchy about my judicial fame."

Forthwith he made this appeal to the Home Secretary, on whose aid he chiefly relied:—

"(Confidential; in haste.)

"DEAR MR. PEEL,

"I observe that Mr. W^{m} is again moving upon the subject of the Court of Chancery. I thank you cordially for what, I learn from the papers, passed upon his mention of the subject. I can not forbear, however, troubling you for a few minutes upon this subject: not upon the motion, whatever it may be, merely, but upon what I can not but think is a matter much more material to the public than anything which may affect my individual character. Can it possibly be endured that a barrister, because he happens to be a member of the House of Commons, instructed, for so the fact may be (I will not say that I have reason to believe it is), by a person (his character I say nothing of) in an inferior rank of the profession, is to hold a *surveillance* over the highest court of justice in the kingdom, and, *de anno in annum*, to attack the characters of the Judges of that court? and call upon the Judges anually to explain their conduct, which he can't possibly understand? Can any man remain a Judge in that court under such circumstances? Is he to go into court, day by day, to attend to his duty, not in the persuasion that, if he decides immediately, or takes time, be it short or be it long, in intricate and difficult cases, to be sure that he is right before he decides, with a conviction that he is watched by those who are, annually, to bring him before the public upon charges of delay, who can not possibly know the causes which have operated, and should operate, to determine him as to what his conduct should be; and where, unless he is brought forward, or comes forward, as a person accused and under trial, he can not possibly explain that conduct, either to those who are present when the annual attack is made, or to the public? What would have been said in Lord Hardwicke's time, if he had been called upon by a barrister, aided by a solicitor, the worst or the best in his court, to account why he had delayed his judgments, in particulars cases, for so long a time, as it appears from the printed Reports he thought some cases required consideration before he gave his judgments?

"It is impossible to submit, with any comfort to this sort of degradation; but the personal consideration is as nothing, when one attends to the consequences of bringing into hatred and contempt the tribunals of the country, with the co-operation of the House of Commons, or suffering them to be brought into contempt because John William hates John Scott.

"His motion, as I read it in the papers, is calculated to do all possible mischief, without its being possible to prevent it. When he moves for a List of Causes, he knows that in my department, so full have been my hands of other important business, that *causes* have hardly been brought before me in the period he mentions.

"When he asks how causes, or, if he asks it, how other business has been disposed of, he means to argue from what he can't explain, and what no other man in the House can sufficiently explain, as to what are the reasons which have delayed the finishing of the several matters that have been brought before the Court, and which have not been finished.

"The extreme nicety and difficulty of some questions, involved in what has been before the Court, the imperfect manner in which the pleadings have been brought before the Court, to give scope to the chance of finishing matters in litigation by amicable arrangement, the discovery by the Court of matters which had escaped the attention of the Bar, and which calls for an entire new consideration of the case, the necessity for new evidence, the interruption of the Judge's attention to judicial matters, from his obligation to attend to other matters;—in short, the innumerable matters which, in equity causes, retard decision, render it impossible to answer imputations without much time employed to answer them, and utterly impossible to answer them without much reason to despair whether the answers be understood, except by persons skilled in equity practice. In the mean time the Judge, the Court, and the general administration of justice, is cruelly calumniated; the business can never be set right—quite right—in public opinion, and when Parliament dismisses it the calumny continues to be propagated in pamphlet after pamphlet, review after review, &c. &c.

"'You may hear that I have heard nothing but motions, and this is not very far from being true. Then it is said, motions are matters of course. Now, many of them have occupied, before me, two or three, I believe some four, days,—and the matter of the cause in which the motion has been made has been decided on the motion, while decision could not have been had in the hearing of a cause, as a cause, for years. A motion, for instance, is often made to stay proceedings upon an appeal from a decree from the Rolls or the V.-Chancellor, because it is appealed from to the Chancellor, and because the proceedings would be expensive and thrown away, if the Chancellor reverses the decree. Now, when such a motion is made, the merits of the decree appealed from must be entered into, because, if the appeal has not sufficient merits, the proceedings ought not to be stayed. It happens, therefore, that I give my opinion upon the appeal by my judgment upon the motion, and there is an end of the appeal; and yet a common lawyer, as ignorant as a post of equity proceedings, publishes to the world that the appeal is not disposed of.

"At all events, if this annual motion to the dishonor of the Judges and the Court is to be granted, it is expedient that one should know what it is, that it may be added to or amended, in order to make the return to it as creditable to the Judges and the Court as it can be: to do justice to them in any return to it is absolutely impossible.

"Yours, dear Sir, most faithfully,

"ELDON."[1]

The attack was made by Mr. Williams, according to the fashion of that time, on presenting a petition; and a long debate was terminated by the motion being carried. "That this petition do lie upon the table." Several unaccountable cases of a delay of judgment after the hearing had been concluded were brought out; but the attempt failed to impute to the Chancellor the general arrear of causes which stood for hearing. He was ably defended by Mr. Secretary Peel, who excited the hopes of the country by declaring himself a friend to rational reform, and explaining the measures which he had in contemplation for improving the criminal code.[2]

The Chancellor had scarcely recovered his composure

---

[1] Peel MSS
[2] 13 Hansard, 959–1008

when it was again ruffled by the Dissenters' Marriage Bill once more coming up from the Commons, and by finding a considerable accession of Prelates in its favor. He gives his daughter the following indignant account of its reception and its fate:—" The Unitarian Bill came on in the House of Lords last night. Both Archbishops, the Bishop of London, the Bishop of Bath and Wells, the Bishop of Exeter, the Bishop of Norwich, voted for it. Shameful, surely! However, we threw out the bill, 56 to 50. It would have been about 100 to 50, if we had divided upon the third reading instead of the second; but our good orthodox friends were absent—most at Ascot—so that how a horse runs is much more important than how the Church fares."

It appears from Hansard, that, although he spoke after all the Bishops who supported the bill, he boldly denounced it as mischievous, and took the untenable ground, that, although the statute of William rendering it penal to deny the doctrine of the Trinity had been repealed, such a denial was a misdemeanor at common law.[1]

The only other occasion which called upon him to come forward, during this session of Parliament, was to correct certain exaggerated statements of his official gains—when he represented himself as a sufferer, in a pecuniary point of view, by holding the Great Seal. He said, "that in no one year, since he had been made Lord Chancellor, had he received the same amount of profit which he enjoyed while at the Bar: had he remained at the Bar, and kept the situation he held there, he solemnly declared he should not be one shilling a poorer man than he was at that moment, notwithstanding his office."[2] By what mental reservation he reconciled this statement to his conscience, I am wholly at a loss to conjecture; for his fee-book proves that the largest sum he ever received in any one year, while Attorney General, was £12,140 15s.—the average receipt being little more than £10,000; whereas, the returns he made to the House of Commons of his official income as Chancellor shows that in 1810 it reached £22,730, and that, subject to all deductions, it exceeded

[1] In Lady Hewley's case, the clear opinion of the House of Lords was, that *since* the repeal of the statute of William, Unitarians are on the same footing as other Protestant Dissenters; and on this principle proceeded Sir Robert Peel's admirable measure of the "Dissenters' Chapel Bill" in 1844.

[2] 13 Hansard, 1379.

on an average £17,000 a year—to say nothing of the lucrative offices and reversions he had been able to bestow upon his family. He now alleged, that the misrepresentation, respecting the emoluments of his office, was the reason for reluctantly retaining it. "Perhaps it was thought," he said, "that this mode of calumnious misrepresentation was the way to get me out of office: they are mistaken who think so; I will not yield to such aspersions, nor shrink from asserting what I owe to myself. Had I been treated with common justice, I should not now, *perhaps*, have remained Chancellor; but I will not be driven from my office by calumnious attacks. Let me only be treated with common justice, and in five minutes my office will be at anybody's disposal."[1]

Parliament was prorogued, and the long vacation arrived; but Encombe had lost all its charms, by reason of an order made by the House of Commons, at the very close of the session, on the motion of Sir Francis Burdett, without any opposition by the Government,—"That there be laid before this House a list of all causes that have been heard by the Lord Chancellor during the last eighteen years wherein judgment had not yet been given, specifying the time when heard; comprising all petitions in cases of bankruptcy already heard, and not decided."

He first wrote the following letter to the Home Secretary:—

"(Private.)   "July 30, 1825

"DEAR MR. PEEL,

"I have given orders about Lord Verulam, and shall duly attend to what you mention as to the Recorder's report.

"I avail myself of this opportunity of thanking you for your kindness on many occasions towards me in the House of Commons, when *unjustly*, I think, attacked. I have not yet intimated to any other person that I have *almost* come to a determination, after employing myself in my vacation so as to be able to dispose of all my arrears in November, to request permission to place the Great Seal in his Majesty's hands. Sir Francis Burdett's motion, unopposed by any lawyer, and relating to the transactions of eighteen years, in its terms has held me up to the public, as probably a great delinquent, for at least six months

[1] 13 Hansard, 1379.

to come. If you meet with Courtenay, he will tell you how much or how little I have to apprehend from the information to be given in consequence of that motion; but my character is suffering in the mean time, and communications from all parts daily satisfy me that such is this case. I feel great pain about giving way to unmerited abuse, but, upon principle, I *begin* to doubt whether an abused and calumniated Chancellor can, upon a just view of his duty to the public, as well as of that due to himself, remain in office. Time was when the law officers of the Crown would not have suffered a person in that station to have been exposed to unjust surmises in the public mind, or have failed to have the grounds of such a motion shown to be weighty before it was granted. I am aware that it might be mere inattention that the matter passed *sub silentio*—and confidently believe that no unkindness was meant. But this has been a very unfortunate and distressing transaction, and I know it has occasioned much remark.

"Perhaps I may see you at the Recorder's report—if not, I only add, that if the Cabinet, about the meeting of Parliament, requires, in your opinion, may attendance, pray let me know. "Yours sincerely,
"ELDON."[1]

Mr. Peel seems to have referred him to the Prime Minister, to whom he wrote several times during the long vacation, without receiving any satisfactory answer. At last, on his return to town, he sent the following letter, conditionally tendering his resignation:—

"DEAR LORD LIVERPOOL,

"In our little correspondence during the vacation, you advised me not to trouble myself about Sir Francis Burdett's motion. I can most sincerely assure you that I feel the greatest uneasiness on account of the trouble which my colleagues and friends endure on my account. If your Lordship recollects for how many sessions I have been assailed in the House of Commons, and looks to the effect, as I know it, of its proceedings upon the business of the Court and upon the minds of the public, you may make some estimate of their effect upon myself. If that motion, as made in the last session, is to command obedience from the officers of my Court, that obedience must either

[1] Peel MSS.

be paid to it, or the order must be rescinded: if the order is to be considered as falling at the close of the session, and is to be renewed by Sir F. B., with the concurrence of the House, obedience must then be given to it. Now, my dear Lord, allow me to say, with perfect kind feeling, that I cannot reconcile it to any notions which I can form of my duty to the public, to sit at the head of one high court of justice in the kingdom, if I either continue to be, or am again, placed in such circumstances as that order placed me in, or a renewal of it will place me in. It is impossible to consider it otherwise than as a resolution accusatory in its nature, and meant to be, if the result of the inquiry will authorize it, the foundation of a positive and express accusation. If this be so, how can I, with honor, continue to preside in the Court in which I sit, prejudiced and damaged in public opinion by a vote of the House of Commons, unopposed by any individual in it? Or how can I continue to sit in that Court, with all the subordinate officers employed in collecting the materials, under an order of the House of Commons, for an accusation against the person at the head of the Court, aided by the bitterness of every solicitor or counsel whose conduct I have had occasion to reprehend? As to the abuse of the public prints, the licentiousness of which, against the Judges of the land and Chancellor, appears to me, as to all matters, sanctioned by the sufferance which is given to it—and the correspondence which this vote of the House of Commons brings to me every day from every part of the kingdom, more blameable than the licentious press, if possible,—I repeat that they would rather provoke me to remain in office, if permitted, than to think of quitting it. But, my Lord, I find myself placed in *my Court* by this proceeding in a state in which it is unfit that a Chancellor should be placed; and, with respect to the public, I fear I am doing very wrong, in letting down the dignity and respect due, not to me, but to the Chancellor, who holds an office which should be filled with a person respected by the public, and protected, if he deserves so to be, against resolutions which clearly mean to impute, or to lay the grounds of imputation against him. I do assure your Lordship that I have every feeling of good will and kind regard towards every individual with whom I am associated as a servant of his Majesty;

and I trust I need not mention what are my feelings towards yourself,—but to all of them and to you I owe it as a duty to take care that the abuse thrown upon me daily should not, through me, affect their and your utility. What obedience to that vote might furnish, of information with respect to my conduct, I know not,—but if it furnished all that I could wish, the mischief that must be done before its result could be known is incalculably great. That in the course of eighteen years, for such is the period to which this vote refers, I cannot doubt (I cannot, however, but hope that they may be such as my general conduct in office might atone for) that there may be many things represented as omissions of duty during eighteen years which are not such, but which it is impossible to find the means at this day of satisfactorily accounting for, must be obvious: I cannot doubt that the multiplicity of my engagements may have led to omission and neglect as to some of them.

"Under these circumstances, my dear Lord, I wish very much to know, and to know *now*, whether the motion of Sir F. B., if it does not require renewal, is to be attempted to be discharged by Government by any proceeding when the House meets; or, if it does require renewal, whether it is then to be suffered to be renewed, without opposition on the part of Government. My object in seeking this now, is, that I may so apply myself (without engaging further than I *must* in new business) to what is depending, as to be able to retire about the time of Parliament's meeting, if the King will graciously please to dismiss me, and not then to leave causes which have been heard to be either heard over again, or the judgments of a retired Chancellor to be given in fact though not in form, as I myself have formerly assisted in acting for a retired Chancellor. I know well that Sir F.'s motion was passed (at least I sincerely so believe) without, on the part of Government or its friends, any ill-will, I can almost say without any positive inattention, to me, but by actual surprise. The effects, however, the evil effects of it, are very great —as great as if the causes of it were different,—and many have been the mortifying inquiries made of me, by those who do not know how this happened,—how I account for not having, as they supposed, one person in the House of Commons to say one word against such a proceeding; for of the fact that this was effected by surprise, *the public* cannot be conusant. If out of office, I can't take the situation of Deputy Speaker of the House of Lords—but I should attend the Scotch causes, and I might be voted into the chair as a Peer."

Lord Liverpool's answer, though civil, very distinctly shows that the Chancellor's colleagues thought there was some foundation for the complaints made against him; that they were highly dissatisfied with the delay which had occurred in the proceedings under the Commission appointed nearly two years ago; and that they were determined to suspend the deprecated "order" over his head *in terrorem*, for the purpose of obtaining a Report from the Commission:—

"This order was made without notice, on the 30th of June, one of the very last days of the sitting of the House of Commons, in the absence of *all* the Ministers and of the law officers of the Crown. The motion has, however, certainly *dropped* with the session. It must be renewed to have any force; and, considering how it was carried, you are, I think, perfectly justified in waiting for its renewal before you act upon it.

"Mr. Peel assures me that he would have opposed it if he had been in the house, and that he will be prepared to oppose the renewal of it if it is again brought forward in the beginning of the next session. But, in order to make it *possible* for him to carry his intention into effect, the Report of the Commission of Inquiry as to the Court of Chancery must be ready, and be laid before Parliament immediately upon its meeting.

"In saying this, I am not giving you Mr. Peel's opinion *only*. Some time before I received your letter I was urged by others, well acquainted with the House of Commons, to take measures for securing the production of this Report, as the point upon which would turn all the difficulties or facilities of the next and last session of Parliament.

"Let me entreat you, therefore, to spare no effort for the completion of this Report without further delay. It is really become a question of vital importance, and there is *no inconvenience* that ought not to be incurred for the attainment of this object.

"Independent of the complaint of *neglect*, and of the

suspicion which the very delay in making the Report occasions, the Report is really necessary in order to enable Ministers in the House of Commons to resist effectually the unjustifiable attacks daily made upon the Court of Chancery.

"The business of that Court is not like other business, of which every person may be supposed to have, or may easily acquire, at least a superficial knowledge. Except persons engaged in the profession of the law, all others are wholly ignorant of what relates to Chancery; they do not even know where, or how, to obtain information.

"The Report would not only speak with more or less of authority to the House, but it would inform your friends, and would furnish them with a *text* upon which they could defend you.

"I hope I do not appear to press this matter with too much importunity, but I am so *deeply sensible* of its importance, that I should not do my duty if I did not urge it in the strongest manner.

"Let us but have the Report, and all other difficulties may be fairly encountered; but, without that, no person (in the present heated state of the public mind upon the subject) can answer for the consequence."[1]

During the last long vacation Mr. Peel had ventured to consult the Chancellor on the bills which he had framed for the improvement of the criminal law. These, without introducing much change into its provisions, most usefully and laudably condensed and methodized the scattered and disjointed statutes upon the subject, which had been passed in a long succession of ages. More could not at that time have been prudently attempted, and even so much seems not a little to have alarmed the Chancellor, —though coming from one in whom as yet he reposed such confidence, and to whom he felt himself under deep obligations. The following was his courteous but very cautious answer:—

"Wednesday evening.

"DEAR MR. PEEL,

"I was so convinced that I should see you before this day, that I delayed troubling you with any communication about your bills, the heads of which you sent me, till we met, as I supposed we should meet, in town. I see no

[1] Nov. 16th, 1825

objection to your laying them before, and procuring the benefit of the opinions of the Judges upon them. Indeed I think that absolutely necessary, for they have a degree of information upon such subjects, derived from their termly meetings upon criminal cases, not publicly argued, which may make their opinions very important. I venture to take the liberty of saying that I should be glad to have an opportunity given to me, after they have formed their opinions, of conversing with some of them; for it does so happen, that, though as a criminal lawyer I have very little knowledge, I have lived so much longer in the profession than all the Judges but one, that on some subjects I can give them information derived from eminent lawyers now deposited in the urns and sepulchres of mortality, which it would do them no harm to receive. It may be so even with respect to the Criminal Law.

"I have not heard what were the prevailing reasons as to dissolution or no dissolution. I hope it was fully understood that we were not to be assailed upon the R. C. question. We shall have, in a last session, mischief enough without that.

"We have very few partridges here this season, and those few very wild. I am, dear Mr. Peel,

"Most faithfully and sincerely yours,

"ELDON.

"I kill nothing but—as Lord Stowell formerly reported of me—Time." [1]

When Parliament met, the Report of the Commission was announced to be forthcoming, and the promise of it stopped the motion for a renewal of the dreaded order. At last, on the 28th of February, the Report was actually presented to both Houses, and ordered to be printed. As it was awfully voluminous, with a massive Appendix of evidence, there was a general disposition to give a reasonable time for considering it; but, there being a petition presented to the House of Commons from a person very properly committed for a contempt of the Court of Chancery, Mr. Joseph Hume, sometimes more zealous than discreet, created a strong feeling in favor of the Chancellor, by declaring that "the greatest curse which ever fell on any nation was to have such a Chancellor and such a Court of Chancery." [2] The Chancellor, rather pleased with

[1] Peel MSS. [2] 15 Hansard, 303, 537.

this attack, treated it thus merrily in a letter to Lord Encombe:—

"You see Mr. Hume called your grandfather *a curse to the country*. He dignified also the quietest, meekest man in the country with the title of *a firebrand*, i. e. the Bishop of London. I met the Bishop at the Exhibition, and as it happened to be an uncommonly cold day, in this most unusually cold weather I told him that *the curse of the country* was so very cold that I hoped he would allow him to keep himself warm by sitting next to *the firebrand;* and so we laughed, and amused ourselves with this fellow's impertinence."

Mr. Peel, desirous that some relief should be given to the suitors in the Court of Chancery as soon as possible, wrote to Lord Eldon :—

"I have spoken to the Attorney-General on the subject of the Report, and entreated him, as the first law officer of the Crown in the House of Commons, to take into his own hands any measures which may necessarily grow out of the Report, should it be fitting for those measures to originate in the House of Commons."

A bill was accordingly prepared for improving the process of the Court of Chancery, and rendering proceedings there more rapid and less costly. This was brought in by the Attorney-General, on the 18th of May, and opened by him in a very luminous manner, but, I am afraid, without any satisfactory explanation why it had not been prepared, brought in, and carried twenty years before by Lord Eldon himself, who then knew of his own knowledge all the material facts stated in the Report of the Commissioners.

The bill was only introduced that it might be printed and stand over till another year. Parliament was about to come to a termination by lapse of time, and there was, as usual under such circumstances, a strong desire to put off all measures of consequence, for the purpose of avoiding disagreeable discussions on the hustings. Lord Eldon was not called upon to oppose a "Catholic Relief Bill," or a "Dissenters' Marriage Bill," or a "Criminal Code Mitigation Bill," during the session, which was brought to a close on the 31st of May. The time of both Houses had been almost entirely taken up in devising measures to meet the commercial distress caused by the unexampled panic in the money market which had occurred in the autumn of the preceding year; and the Chancellor had never been called upon to take part in debate.

Mr. Peel, naturally desirous to keep him in good humor, and to soften his opposition to the plan for reforming the penal code, wrote him the following letter, giving, perhaps, a disproportionate importance to a common incident :—

"(Private and confidential.)   "Whitehall, June 23rd, 1826.
"MY DEAR CHANCELLOR,

"I can not help reporting to you the manner in which your health was received the other day at a meeting of about 700 persons, who were assembled at the mayor's dinner at Norwich.

"I never witnessed a stronger manifestation of attachment and respect — a more decided proof that the calumnies of disappointed lawyers, and a malignant press, have not abated one jot of the real estimation in which you are held. I wish you could have been present.   Ever yours,
"ROBERT PEEL.

"The dinner comprised the whole of the respectability of the city of Norwich, and many of the first families of the county."

The Chancellor, much gratified, returned the following answer :—

"(Private and confidential.)
"DEAR MR. PEEL,

"Many thanks to you for your letter—and for another proof of that attention to my character and comfort, for which I have been so often and so much obliged. I am as much aware as any other person can be of my defects as a Judge, and I am so often angry at myself that I ought not to be surprised to find that others are not pleased with me. As to my political conduct, it has been all right or all wrong, for, in the forty-three years in which I have been in Parliament, there has been no change, I think, in the character of that conduct, or the principles by which it has been regulated. The proceeding at Norwich is a most comfortable set-off, as we lawyers should say, against the malignity which has been so bitter as in some measure to defeat its own purposes.

"Set-offs I don't, at present, like. In peerages and in

elections we see nothing but set-offs of Paptists against Protestants—and which I fear will lead to propositions about compromises in Parliament, which will either lead to a dissolution of it, or to adoption of some concessions to the Catholics which will give them the place whereupon they may stand, and hereafter remove from its foundations our Protestant Establishment.

"Yours, dear Sir, most truly and sincerely,
'ELDON.

" 24th June, 1826."[1]

Little was it then foreseen that within three years these distinguished men, now so cordially united, were to act such opposite parts on a subject which hitherto had formed the great bond of union between them!

Parliament not sitting, the Chancellor had now only to attend to his business in the Court of Chancery, which he seems to have done with much vigor. Thus, on the eve of the long vacation, he wrote to Lady Frances:—" I have worn out my counsel pretty completely. They seem all as tired as a pack of hounds at the end of a long chase, while I remain, like a well-disciplined and well-trained huntsman, not the least fatigued with the labor of keeping up with them. They wish, perhaps, to make the world think that I put an end to business. I heartily wish it was at an end; but I had rather that the world should believe that the cessation of work is their doing."

His colleagues, pleased to have got through the last session so quietly, and looking forward with some dismay to *Chancery Reform* being used as the grand "battle horse" in the new Parliament, earnestly urged on the projected measure, and wrote the following letters:—

Mr. Robinson[2] *to Mr. Peel.*

'August 26th, 1826.

"MY DEAR PEEL,
" I am satisfied that we shall be involved in inextricable difficulties, and much public mischief will follow, if we have nothing to propose next session upon the subject of Chancery; and, if the satisfactory arrangement of that something depends upon the readiness of the Treasury to find pecuniary means, the means must be found."

[1] Peel MSS.
[2] Now Earl of Ripon, then Chancellor of the Exchequer.

Lord Liverpool to Mr. Peel.
"Fife House, Sept. 2nd, 1826.

"MY DEAR PEEL,

"I return the inclosed papers, and I can entertain no doubt that it is our duty, at the very earliest practicable period of the next session of Parliament, to bring in measures for giving effect to the recommendations of the Chancery Commissioners.

"There may, undoubtedly, be points on which there may be difference of opinion; but in all cases where we have not the most clear and satisfactory reasons to urge against the opinion of the Commissioners, we ought in this, as we have done in other commissions, to assume that the Commissioners are right.

"Indeed the value of such commissions is, that they are a mode of bringing points of difference to a decision, which are never likely to be decided in any other way.

"With respect to the necessary funds: it will be the duty of the Chancellor of the Exchequer, and of myself, to propose to Parliament whatever may be requisite for any just and equitable purpose. Judging from the past, I do not think there would be any disposition in Parliament to be illiberal on this head; but, if we should be mistaken, let the blame then lie with Parliament, and do not let us bring it upon ourselves."

Mr. Peel to the Chancellor.
"Whitehall, Sept. 7th, 1826.

"MY DEAR CHANCELLOR,

"I sent to Lord Liverpool and the Chancellor of the Exchequer the letter which was addressed to you by Courtenay, and which you sent to me.

"I begged their immediate consideration of that part of Courtenay's letter in particular which referred to the expense which the adoption of some of the recommendations of the Chancery Commission might entail.

"Enclosed are copies of the answers which I received from them. They intimate readiness on their part to provide the pecuniary means of giving effect to the Report of the Commission.

"You will perceive that Robinson suggests that the Suitor's Fund might possibly, without injustice, be drawn upon; but should there be valid objections to the appropriation of that fund to the purposes in question, neither he nor Lord Liverpool would, I am confident, object to propose to Parliament to make the necessary provision out of the public funds.

"The enclosed letters appear to me to give full authority to proceed in making such arrangements as can be made without the intervention of Parliament's authority; of course I mean so far as considerations of expense are concerned."

It would seem that in consequence of this urgency, or for some other mysterious reason, Lord Eldon had again sent in his resignation, but probably not with more seriousness than upon Queen Caroline's being about to purchase the house next door to him in Hamilton Place, or upon Sir Francis Burdett's order for a return of Chancery arrears. There had been a rumor of Lord Gifford being his successor, and this arrangement at some very distant day he probably would have preferred to any other: but I can not believe that as yet he had any serious design to retire. His health and vigor were unimpaired; he must naturally have desired to superintend the measures for the reformation of his court; and if personal abuse required him to remain in office, that motive must now have operated with double strength. But, while affecting, or really entertaining, the purpose of resigning, he heard the melancholy news of Lord Gifford's death. The first letter he received on this subject was the following from Lord Liverpool:—

"Coombe Wood, Sept. 5th, 1826

"MY DEAR LORD,

"You will of course have heard the melancholy and unexpected death of Lord Gifford. He is a very great loss at this time, both public and private. I send you the accounts which I have received of his illness, which I will be obliged to you to return when I see you.

"I shall be in town to-morrow morning: may I request of you to call upon me either at one or two o'clock, as may best suit, or, if anything should detain you at home, I would come to you in Hamilton Place.

"I promise you that I will speak to no one upon the *consequences* till I have seen you. Having, however, received, by the attention of my friend Mr. Latham of Dover, an account yesterday of Lord Gifford's extreme danger, it was impossible I should not turn in my mind, during the night, what was to arise if we were so unfortunate as to lose him.

"I confess to you the present inclination of my mind is, that the Attorney General should be *made* to accept the Mastership of the Rolls. He has no competitor at the Bar, at least on *our side*, nor any on the Bench, who can compete with him in the highest honors of the profession. Indeed I know not what else can be done which would not increase all prospective difficulties to an immense degree.

"Do not return any answer to this letter, or at least to this suggestion; but turn it well over in your mind, and let us talk of it when we meet to-morrow."

Lord Eldon, at this time, was on the most cordial terms with the Home Secretary, who happened to be then at Drayton Manor, his seat in Staffordshire, and to him he wrote the following letter:—

"(Most private and confidential.)

"MY DEAR MR. PEEL,

"The death of the M. Rolls is a great private and public loss. I think he would, if he had continued to live, have corrected that opinion in the public mind which had certainly, in a degree, lately laid hold of it; and which, perhaps, poor fellow, was generated in it by the industry of some who envied his rapid professional advancement, more than by any other assignable cause. But he is no more—and I am mistaken if you don't find him much lamented, and his qualifications for professional situations, whatever they might be, now almost universally acknowledged.

"Of course, the Min^r. is now looking for a successor— he naturally looks to Copley. I doubt extremely whether he will accept the office of M. R., even with the prospect of possessing the Great Seal. His professional emoluments must be very great;—the object for him naturally to look to is the King's Bench, and report, as to the health of the Chief Justice, does not represent the prospect of attaining that object as at a distance. I have stated to Lord L., who has conducted himself to me, as to this, very respectfully, my apprehensions that he will decline the Rolls—he ought not perhaps—yet a man of his eminence in that part of the profession in which he has been engaged may probably feel unwilling to go into a Court of Equity as a

Judge, never having been in one as a counsel—and especially in that Equity Court in which much business is rather business of form, than requiring the exercise of a powerful intellect.

"I don't know why I have written what you have read before you reach this part of this sheet. My purpose was only to tell you, that I thought it my duty to the public to mention to Lord L. that, as it was impossible that at my time of life I could remain long in office, even if I wished to do so, it might be worth his considering whether it might not be useful, if both the Chan^r. and the Office of the Rolls were vacant, and a general arrangement as to the Chancery Offices should now be made, instead of that interim and partial arrangement of filling up the Rolls only for a time. He stated some weighty objections to this, and continues to object to it. He thinks that Copley would go better to the Chancellor^p with a little experience gained at the Rolls; and I think he feels an unwillingness that my departure should precede what may come forward upon the Catholic question —there could, too, be no objection to Copley's going from the Rolls to the K. B., as Kenyon did. He has always refused briefs in Scotch causes—which looks as if his views were directed to the K. B., and not to the office of Chancellor, who must hear so many Scotch causes.

"Unfortunately, he is out of town, so that it has been impossible, and the rather because it is not known where he is, to learn what his feelings are.

"The notion is that he should remain, if he takes the office, in the H. of Commons, at least till the Chancery Bill is got through there. You will excuse the trouble which I am now giving you, and giving you in perfect confidence. But I wished to state to you, that I should certainly feel it to be my duty not to allow any consideration respecting myself to obstruct, impede, or delay any arrangement which should be thought for the public interest. I do feel a great anxiety to protect myself upon this occasion from the imputation of clinging to office, and that too in my 76th year. I write this from the Office over which you preside—not finding you here. I say what I learnt in my schoolboy days: 'Quod dicere non potui scribere jussit amor.' You will please to construe this word *amor* as Latin for cordial and affectionate respect. I have detained you too long. I have no wish to remain in office, and therefore I sacrifice nothing by counteracting any wish, if, for the purpose of the most desirable object, I retire. I shall be abused for remaining even some short time longer; but the same considerations of public duty, which would determine me for the public to retire, will determine me also, if that be right, to remain for awhile, if those whom I respect think that I ought so to do for the public interest; and in their good opinion I shall seek for shelter against the storms of abuse, which represent me as unreasonably and improperly clinging in old age to office.

"I am, dear Mr Peel,
"Y^r. faith^l. and affec^{te}. servant and friend,
"ELDON."

Mr. Peel, good-naturedly professing to believe that the Chancellor really wished to retire, and was only reluctantly induced to hold the Great Seal a little longer for the public good, sent him this answer:—

"Drayton Manor, Sept. 10th, 1826.

"MY DEAR CHANCELLOR,

"I am confident, that on every account, public and private, you have determined wisely in not now pressing your resignation. By private account, I mean that you have consulted what is due, not to your ease, but to your high and unblemished character, by consenting, for a time, to give to the public the continued benefit of your knowledge and experience, rather than subject them to the inconvenience of having two new Equity Judges at the same time.

"Supposing Copley to accept the Rolls, what must be done as to the Attorney and Solicitor General? Anything which you may write to me on that head I will, if you shall wish it, consider most strictly confidential. Believe me, my dear Chancellor, no man, whose good opinion you value, will hear of your continuance in office with any other feelings than those of satisfaction.

I doubt whether under present circumstances you could overcome the King's reluctance to lose your invaluable services—I really doubt whether he would accept the Seals from your hands."

These solicitations were not to be resisted, and Lord Eldon once more *multa gemens*, suffered the Great Seal to remain in his hands. He thus (I think with ill-suppressed glee) announced to Lady Frances the violence that had been practised upon him:—

"Copley is to be the new Master of the Rolls. He has accepted. Upon this occasion, as I thought it more for the public interest, and certainly for my comfort and happiness, that they should attempt a general and permanent arrangement of the law offices, instead of making appointments from time to time as vacancies happen, I have *strongly* and *repeatedly* pressed for my own retirement *now* from the labors I undergo; but, notwithstanding all my efforts, I am unable to succeed, and, abused and calumniated as I have been, they are puzzled how to supply my place if they let me go. So I suppose I must wait awhile longer."

At the same time the Lord Chancellor sent to the Home Secretary the following account of the result of his negotiations with the Attorney General:—

" (Most private and confidential.)

"MY DEAR MR. PEEL,

. . . . .

"With respect to Copley, he accepted the office, and, it appeared to me, without any doubt about accepting it. Indeed, though I doubted whether he would accept, as he never had been in a Court of Equity at all, and never would take a brief in a Scotch cause, yet, recollecting that the Chancellorship and the Chief Justiceship of the King's Bench may be soon open, and, on the other hand, a change of Administration may not be a thing so impossible in the meantime, as to make the acceptance a foolish thing, of an office and house worth £8000 a year for life, which may be accepted without prejudice to his moving to either of the above offices, if they happen to be vacant in due time,—I think he has acted very imprudently, especially taking into the account that he goes to school in the lower form (the Rolls) to qualify him to remove into the higher, if he takes the Chancellorship.

. . . . .

"His emoluments at the Bar were very considerable before he was Solicitor—they have of course since (for such always happens with a Solicitor-General) been less —but I have no doubt, that if he quitted that office, such emoluments would be very considerable. During the several years in which I was Solicitor, I received annually considerably less than my profession brought me before I accepted the office. I may venture to say much beyond £2,000 a year less. It is, therefore, much to be attended to that you should not discourage gentlemen from taking the office of Solicitor by not allowing them to have the fair advantages which vacancies of higher offices may offer. Indeed, such encouragement should generally be given to the law officers, as may lead the profession to think that when they arrive at those offices they are 'heirs to all things good,' as they have always been reported to be.

    "Yours, my dear Sir, most faithfully,
              "ELDON."

This arrangement being completed, and Copley, Master of the Rolls, remaining in the House of Commons, Lord Eldon took (as it were) a new lease of office—likely to last during his natural life. The cry about *Chancery Reform* had been quieted by the new bill, based upon the Report of the Commissioners;—there seemed no other annoyance for him to dread,—and if there had been no change in the Premiership, the probability is, that, often again talking of resignation, he would have extended his Chancellorship much beyond the quarter of a century.

On account of the dreadful scarcity which prevailed in the autumn of this year, accompanied by severe commercial distress, an order in council had been made, with the concurrence of the Chancellor, for the introduction of foreign corn duty free,—and Parliament was called together in November to indemnify Ministers for the violation of law, to which the safety of the people had obliged them to resort. The bill of indemnity was carried with little opposition, and the short session passed over very quietly,—without the Chancellor being ever called upon to open his lips, unless, as Speaker, to put the question, and to say, " the contents have it." [1]

In the House of Commons, Mr. Canning had thrown out some sneers against ultra-Toryism,—which induced Cobbett thus to address him:—" If the Chancellor be sound wind and limb, and thus continue (as I am told he is likely to do for several years longer), he will beat you and any other enterprising free-trader, whatever may be

[1] Parl. Deb. xvi. 1–336.

the quantum of noise that nature has enabled him to make with his tongue. The Lord Chancellor—and his brother still less—is not a great talker; they never shone much in the art of haranguing; but they have had three-fourths of the governing of this country in their hands for a great many years; and while the Chancellor has the full confidence of a very great majority of the noblemen and gentlemen, he has at his back, sticking to him everlastingly, that body called the *Church*, of which you, great talker as you are, appear to think so little."

The Chancellor was very happy in such anticipations; but on the very day of the adjournment a notice was given in the House of Commons, by Mr. J. Williams, "That, early after the recess, he would move for a return of the state of business in the Court of Chancery,—with an account of all cases argued and not yet determined, specifying the number of times that judgment had been promised to them—and postponed."

The Chancellor's peace of mind was again disturbed; and, in great agony, he thus addressed the Home Secretary :—

" (Private and confidential.)

" Sunday night.

"DEAR MR. PEEL,

. . . . .

"As to J. Williams's motion, experience has taught me that you will do what is right, and I most gratefully acknowledge the protection your kindness has hitherto thrown around me. The object of such a notion as he has given notice of cannot be mistaken. I do not mean to say that, overwhelmed with work as I have been—my attention drawn from one subject before it was disposed of, to another, and so to a third, and a fourth, &c., &c.— counsel absent, parties not prepared—some blame may not justly be imputed to me; it is equal to that which might be imputed to my predecessors. It is utterly impossible, however, that, if such a motion is granted by the House of Commons, I can find the time, *while in office*, to look into the vast mass of business which has been before me, so as to be able to amend the motion, and render it somewhat more just, or, if the motion passes, to be able, while in office, to get together the materials necessary to give information, such as, if given, I am satisfied would reduce my culpability to far less than that which might be imputed to some who have gone before me, if not to reduce it entirely, while I have completed a quantum of work much greater, I believe, than they have done. But to do this, employed in the constant duties of office, is impossible.

"But there is one view of such a motion as this, which allow me to exhibit. It is of very inferior consequence what becomes of the character of *Lord Eldon*, with respect I mean to the public, compared to what becomes of the character of the *Chancellor remaining in office*, with respect to the public.

"I am ashamed of myself when I think how long I have remained in office under the circumstances in which I have been so often and so many years placed by the House of Commons—first, by M. A. Taylor's committee; secondly, and repeatedly, by motions, which, till you took me under your protection, were neither opposed nor grounded upon any reasons given.

"Ministers with whom I have been acting have said nothing in opposition, and all that I could obtain as a reason why they did not, was, that they did not understand the matter. But did it require great exertion of mind to be satisfied that the First Law Officer of the Crown could not possibly be maintained in the respect that was due to him for the sake of the public, if attorneys, solicitors, &c., perhaps those whom in the due execution of his duty he had had to reprove, were day by day laying complaints before Taylor's committee for the dishonor of the Lord Chancellor, and if, in almost every year since that committee was defunct, all the officers and dissatisfied practicers of the Court in which the Chancellor presides have been employed in getting together the materials in obedience to the order of the Commons, founded on the motion of some discontented lawyer who had obtained a seat in Parliament, which materials were to be used to his disgrace? How can the Court go on with the magistrate so disgraced at the head of it in the opinion of all the officers of his Court, who should have no feeling towards him but that of unqualified respect? I can not deny that reflections of this nature have often made me extremely miserable, though that misery has been softened by a conviction that it required more than even these proceedings to destroy that just feeling towards me which I believe all the respectable part of my Bar and all the officers of my Court entertain, notwithstanding the persecution I have endured for years. The lawyers in the House of Commons have not adverted to this view of the subject—they have endeavored, and for that I am deeply indebted to them, to answer case by case, or rather to explain the cases brought forward,—a thing, however, almost impossible to be done with sufficiency, when matters, long ago occurring, have been forgotten, and neither time nor means can be procured for enabling a correct understanding to be formed respecting them.

"I have agreed to lend myself for a short time (at the period of life which I have reached, it can not be but for a very short time) to assist in the difficulties to which Lord Gifford's death has contributed; but my strength decreasing, my ability to labor not now being equal to the demand upon me for labor, my powers of struggling against the vexations, which injustice and calumnies can not but occasion, not remaining such as they were, my conviction being strong that I owe it to the country no longer to exhibit to it a Chancellor unable to proceed with his business, because those whose assistance and respect is necessary to the forwarding of business year after year are called upon to employ themselves in collecting materials upon which censure or disgrace is intended to be inflicted on the person at whose feet they sit;—all these and many other considerations lead me to say that I must, if Mr. W.'s motion passes—not for my own gratification—but from a sense of duty to the public—remove the Great Seal from the hands of a person who, if it is just thus to treat him, certainly ought not to have that Seal in his hands. To you let me again express my gratitude. I sincerely hope your father is recovered. I write this from my bed-room—rather better than I have been.

"Yours faithfully,
"ELDON."[1]

Mr. Peel promised his zealous support, and the Chancellor hoped that, with the aid of the "Chancery Reform Bill," to be introduced by the new Master of the Rolls, "Williams & Co." might be put down, and he might again tide over the session.

[1] Peel MSS.

But from events over which man had no control, his official career was now rapidly drawing to a close. The first of these was the death of the Heir Presumptive to the throne, who had vowed eternal resistance to Catholic Emancipation, and who was naturally much attached to the venerable champion of the anti-Catholic cause. Lord Eldon alludes to this melancholy subject in a letter to his grandson, dated January 2nd, 1827:—" The poor Duke of York still exists, contrary to what medical men said, as long ago as Sunday last, could be the case. My account last night from Arlington House[1] intimated, that his constitution was still so strong, that his existence might endure for some days. His resignation, his composure, the fortitude with which he bears his present state, are very, very great. Now his death is certain, there is an universal gloom, I understand, everywhere in this town, very striking. His death must affect every man's political situation,—perhaps nobody's more than my own. It may shorten, it may prolong, my stay in office. The 'Morning Chronicle' has, I hear, advertised my resignation."

Lord Eldon had been often with the Duke during his illness, and enjoyed his confidence to the last. He was much affected when he heard of his death on the 5th of January, and some years afterwards entered in the "Anecdote Book" this affectionate testimony to his memory:—

" His death occasioned an irreparable loss to the nation. His own personal example, as to great political questions, would have done much for the country. He had, moreover, great influence with his Majesty; he showed me a correspondence he had had with his Majesty upon political questions, and the proper persons to be continued or to be appointed his Ministers, in which, as well as I could judge, his judgment was much governed by what had been, and what he thought would be, the conduct of each person as to the Catholic claims. This was shown to me shortly before his death; and very shortly before his death he predicted that change of Ministry which soon after his death took place. I firmly believe that that change would not have taken place if he had lived. We never shall look upon his like again. His existence appeared to me to be essential to the effectual counter-

[1] The house in which his royal highness died.

acting that influence, which soon after his death prevailed, to place at the head of the Administration the great advocate in the House of Commons of the Roman Catholic claims, to whom the greatest aversion had been often expressed in the highest place."[1]

Lord Eldon attended the Duke's funeral in St. George's Chapel, Windsor, at serious risk to his health from the cold and damp of the season and of the place, but effectually protected himself, while younger men suffered, by laying his cocked-hat on the flag-stones and standing upon it. A relic of the deceased was treated in Hamilton Place as if it had belonged to a Saint and would operate as a charm against all evil :—" We had a lock of the Duke's hair sent us," says the Earl to his grandson, " and we have each had some put into a little gold case, which we wear with our watch-chains. Mamma [Lady Eldon] would not trust the lock of hair out of the house, and, therefore, had a person from Hamlet's come to the house to put the hair into the golden receptacles."

This calamity was soon followed by another, which produced more immediate consequences in the government of the country. Lord Liverpool, who, without brilliant talents, well understood how to manage the mind of George IV., as well as Parliamentary majorities, was universally respected for his spotless integrity, and delicately trimmed the balance between the Catholics and the Protestants in the Cabinet,—but, while little past the middle period of life, and with health, although impaired, permitting the full exercise of his official functions, he was suddenly struck with apoplexy. The following account of the catastrophe was next day sent to Lady Frances Bankes by her father,—already haunted by the dread of Canning :—

"We are at present, from Lord Liverpool's state, in great trouble. Poor fellow! yesterday morning, after breakfast, the servant, surprised that he did not ring his bell, went into the room and found him on the floor in a violent apoplectic fit, quite senseless. I never saw him better or more cheerful than he was on Friday afternoon in the House of Lords.

[1] There is added a sarcasm on Mr. Canning, for having, a short period before his advancement, courted those whose principles (save on the Catholic question) he, as an Anti-Jacobin and Anti-Radical, had been combating in youth and in manhood.

"He is very little, perhaps a shade better to-day; but his life is very uncertain, and it is quite certain that, as an official man, he is no more. This is a tremendous blow, *under present circumstances*, to the public, and its effects upon individuals must be important. Heaven knows who will succeed him. Peel went down to Brighton to inform the King of the event; at the time I write he is not returned. If other things made it certain that he would otherwise succeed him, I should *suppose* Canning's health would not let him undertake the labor of the situation. But ambition will attempt anything."

To a similar statement which Lord Eldon sent to his grandson, he adds:—

"This, at any time, would be an event of importance: so immediately after the Duke of York's death, and upon the eve of the days when the great questions of the Corn Trade and Catholic Emancipation are to be discussed and decided, it is of importance so great, that nobody can be certain whether it is not of so much importance as to render almost certain wrong decisions upon those vital questions.

"Nobody knows, and nobody can conjecture with probability, how soon the illness of the Minister will, as it seemingly must, dissolve the Administration, or how another is to be formed and composed. Speculation, as to this, is very busy, and politicians are all at work. The Opposition are in high spirits, and confidently expecting to enjoy the loaves and the fishes. They may—but they also may not—be disappointed."

Lord Liverpool languished some months, but his recovery was known to be impossible, and a ministerial crisis arose,—one of the most remarkable in the history of parties in England. Although accounts were given out to the public that the Prime Minister was better, and business proceeded in Parliament for some time as if he had only been disabled by a temporary indisposition, all connected with the Government knew his true situation and the necessity for appointing a successor. Mr. Canning conceived that he himself had the best claim to the vacant post, as since the death of Lord Castlereagh he had been the leader of the House of Commons, and been considered the second in the Cabinet,—but he was obnoxious to the Anti-Catholic party on account of his principles, and he was personally disliked by Lord Eldon. Mr. Peel from the beginning of the controversy resolved that he would not form part of an Administration with Mr. Canning as its chief, but did not propose to step over his head; and professed a wish that, to preserve the system which had prevailed under Lord Liverpool, an Anti-Catholic peer, fit for the situation, should be appointed, the other Ministers retaining their offices. But where was such a peer to be discovered? for as yet the Duke of Wellington declared that it would be " worse than madness for him to aspire to be Prime Minister."

Lord Eldon was keenly hostile to Canning; though by no means determined not to serve under him: but he did not venture to propose Peel; and, seeing the difficulty of fixing upon another Anti-Catholic chief, contrary to his habit on similar occasions he remained long inactive, while Canning and Peel were bringing forward their separate pretensions and views. The King in his heart decidedly favored the principles of the Anti-Catholic section of the Cabinet, but he was under influences which inclined him, on personal considerations, to their opponents; and if it had not been from his standing considerably in awe of Lord Eldon, he probably would early have declared for Canning. His object was to combine both advantages, and, selecting the Pro-Catholic candidate for Prime Minister, with an Anti-Catholic pledge, to induce his Anti-Catholic colleagues to submit to him. Of Lord Eldon he had good hopes when it should come to the pinch; and the grand effort was to bend the inflexibility of Peel.

As yet no notice had been taken in Parliament of Lord Liverpool's illness, and the business of both Houses proceeded as usual. On the 27th of February, Sir John Copley, as Master of the Rolls, introduced into the Commons the Bill for reforming the proceedings in the Court of Chancery, which had been much improved since the preceding session; but it made no further progress. A motion was then made, directed against the Lord Chancellor, for "a return of all the arrears in his Court, specifying the cases standing for judgment —with the periods which had elapsed since the hearings were finished —and the number of times they had stood in the paper for being finally disposed of."

This motion, again, caused great alarm to the object of it, but it was speciously resisted by Mr. Peel, on the ground that all useful information respecting these matters was to be found in the Report of the Chancery Commission, and it was rejected by a majority of 132 to 66.[1]

In the House of Lords, too, the Lord Chancellor was "turned out for a day's sport," as some styled it,—or, as he himself said in the Newcastle phrase, was "hauled over the coals." In allusion to the pending negotiations, he was represented as the great obstacle to a satisfactory arrangement being made, and the House was taunted with being governed in all its resolves by his influence. In answer he said: "God forbid that it should be the fact! His own confident opinion was, that their Lordships' decisions were those of a Protestant House of Parliament in a Protestant empire,—paying only a proper attention to the honest declarations of the opinions of one of the members of that House—for he was too well acquainted with his own imperfections (and he said this as a man approaching to his grave) to suppose that their Lordships were guided by his authority in a matter of such great importance. He only wished so to conduct himself, that the subjects of a Protestant King, and a Protestant Parliament, might be convinced that he went to the grave without having lessened the security which the country had for the enjoyment of civil and religious liberty."— Becoming deeply affected, he exclaimed: "No man in the kingdom is a greater friend to toleration than I am. Upon this ground I hope and trust (I should say so if these were the last words I shall ever utter,—and I am approaching quickly to the end of my days)—I hope and trust your Lordships, both for the sake of the Protestant and of the Catholic subjects of this empire, will preserve that Constitution which has been earned by the exertions of your ancestors. In conclusion, I will state to the Roman Catholics, that, with my consent, they shall have everything, except power, in a Protestant state."[2]—This was the last time he ever addressed the House as Chancellor.

In the beginning of April the public became dissatisfied with being so long without a Government, and notice was taken in Parliament[3] of the unreasonable delays, which

[1] 17 Parl. Deb. 265.   [2] 16 Hansard, 1285.   [3] 17 Hansard, 280, 391.

had occurred from the conflict of contending factions. Lord Eldon, seemingly much disturbed, thus addressed his daughter:—

"Wednesday.

"This must be a short scrap. I can not help it in the distressed state in which the unsettled state[1] of Administration is, and the necessity of *speedily* settling it. I think—who could have thought it?—that Mr. Canning will have his own way. I *guess* that I, Wellington, Peel, Bathurst, Westmoreland, &c., will be out."

And a few days after, when his apprehensions were still more raised, he wrote:—

"There seems again to be some uncertainty whether Lord Lansdowne and a few Whigs have joined Mr. C.; but it *will* be so, I have no doubt.

"The whole conversation in this town is made up of abusive, bitterly abusive talk, of people about each other —all fire and flame. I have known nothing like it.

"To be sure never was so piebald an Administration as this is likely to be, if it is finally formed by the junction of some of the Whigs."

He had now several interviews with the King, who employed him to negotiate with Mr. Peel. In consequence, he saw this resolute Minister on the 9th of April, and afterwards received from him the two following letters to be laid before his Majesty:—

"Whitehall, April 9th, 1827.

"MY DEAR CHANCELLOR,

"To prevent misconception, allow me to commit to writing the purport of what I said to you this morning.

"My earnest wish is to see the present Government retained in his Majesty's service on the footing on which it stood at the time of Lord Liverpool's misfortune. I am content with my own position, and wish for no advancement or change. Differing on the Catholic question from every one of my colleagues in the Government who is a member of the House of Commons, still I have been enabled to act cordially with them, and much to my satisfaction, on other matters. I esteem and respect them, and should consider it a great misfortune were his Majesty to lose the services of any one of them, but particularly of Canning.

[1] Sic in orig. and so printed by Mr. Twiss.

"I can say with truth, that on all matters of domestic and general policy (with the exception of the Catholic question) my opinions are in accordance with theirs. In regarding the interests of the country, and the position of the Government, I can not confine my views to the Catholic question alone. Our differences on that question are a great evil; but they ought not to make us forget that on other subjects, some of not less importance—Parliamentary Reform, for instance—we are united. On the Catholic question the House of Commons recently divided, 276 to 272. Is not such a division an answer to those who demand an united Government, either in favor of, or opposition to, the Catholic claims?

"You informed me that the King had mentioned to you yesterday, that I feared I should have great difficulty in remaining in office if Canning were placed in the situation of Prime Minister. As his Majesty has mentioned this to you, I may, in writing to you now, break that silence which I have hitherto maintained on a subject of so much delicacy.

"The difficulty to which his Majesty referred arises out of the Catholic question, and I must say out of that alone. If I agreed with Canning on that question, or if his opinions had been the same with Lord Liverpool's, I should not have hesitated to remain in office, had his Majesty commissioned Canning to form a Government, and had Canning proposed to me that I should form a part of it.

"My own position, with respect to the Catholic question, and with respect also to the particular duties which my office devolves upon me, is a peculiar one. I have, for many years, taken a leading part in the House of Commons in opposition to the Roman Catholic claims; and for the last five years (God knows not without serious difficulty and embarrassment) I have filled that office which is mainly responsible for the administration of affairs in Ireland.

"Can I see the influence of the office of Prime Minister transferred from Lord Liverpool to Canning, and added to that of leader of the House of Commons, without subjecting myself to misconstruction with respect to my views on the Catholic question? Can it be so transferred without affecting my particular situation as Secretary for the Home Department, and my weight and efficiency in the administration of Irish affairs? It is with deep and unaffected regret that I answer these questions in the negative. You will perceive, at the same time, that no small part of my difficulty is a peculiar and personal one. It arises partly from the very marked course I have taken on the Catholic question—partly from the particular office in which circumstances have placed me, and the particular relation in which I stand to Ireland and Irish affairs. Others of my colleagues, who concur with me generally on the Catholic question, may not feel this difficulty. I will not seek, directly or indirectly, to influence their judgment: my first wish is to see the present (perhaps I should rather say the late) Administration reconstituted precisely on the footing on which it stood when Lord Liverpool was at its head. If this be impossible, can it be reconstituted by Canning, I alone retiring?

"If it can, I shall retire in perfect good humor, and without the slightest disappointment, though certainly not without regret.

"I shall continue, out of office, to act upon the principles on which I have hitherto acted; and can not but feel that, if the Government shall remain in the hands of my former colleagues, I shall be enabled, in conformity with those principles, to give it a general support. I have written this in great haste; and as you are so soon to see his Majesty, I have hardly had time to read it over.

"Ever, my dear Lord,
"Most faithfully yours,
"ROBERT PEEL.

"P.S.—I hope that I explained, entirely to your own satisfaction, the reason why I had not opened my lips to you on the subject of the present state of affairs as connected with the position of the Government until this morning.

Mr. Peel to the Lord Chancellor.

"Whitehall, April 9th, 1827.

"MY DEAR CHANCELLOR,

"What I said with respect to a Protestant peer at the head of the Government was this,—that if a peer of sufficient weight and influence could be found whose general principles were in accordance with those of Lord Liverpool,—the appointment of such a peer to be head of the Government would be quite unobjectionable to me, so far as I am personally concerned. It might be difficult to find such a person, because I think he ought to be a peer of name and character, and ability also sufficient to sustain the part of Prime Minister.

"I certainly did say to his Majesty that I could not advise the attempt to form an exclusive Protestant Government; that I could not be a party even to the attempt, should it be contemplated: but his Majesty was, I am confident, of the same opinion.

"I said, also, that I was out of the question as the head of a Government, under that arrangement which I consider by far the best that could be made—namely, the reconstitution of the late Administration; because it was quite impossible for Canning to acquiesce in my appointment.

"I wish to remain as I am, acting with him, he being leader of the House of Commons, with the just influence and authority of that station, subject, of course, to what I stated in my first letter. "Ever yours,
"ROBERT PEEL."

Lord Eldon had another audience of the King on the morning of the 10th, when his Majesty intimated to him that, although Mr. Peel was inflexible, and his valuable services for the present must be lost, yet, as there seemed no way in which the Government could be reconstructed on the principle he suggested, his Majesty had resolved to commission Mr. Canning to lay before him the plan of a new Administration, of which himself was to be the head. It is a curious fact, that Lord Eldon not only did not then disclose any intention of resigning, but actually gave the King reason to believe that he would continue in office and support the new Prime Minister. Still more curious is it, that the same day, he held the same language to Mr. Canning himself. He is, therefore, entirely free from the charge—afterwards most pertinaciously brought against him—of having combined with other Anti-Catholic members of the Cabinet to deprive the King of the choice of his Ministers by a threat that, if Mr. Canning were put at the head of the Treasury, they would all resign,—although he seems by no means entitled to the credit he took to himself—of having resolved from the beginning that he never would hold the Great Seal under a Pro-Catholic Prime Minister.

What changed the purpose which he certainly appears

to have entertained on the 10th of April, we can only conjecture; for the next fact which we positively know is, that early on the 12th, without any previous communication of his intention, he sent his resignation to Mr. Canning,—who received it when he was actually in the King's closet, about to kiss hands as First Lord of the Treasury. The probability is, that Lord Eldon, in the intermediate time, had formed his resolution to resign—finding that not only Sir Robert Peel, but all the Anti-Catholic members of the Cabinet, had resigned, so that he could not remain with any decency,—and believing that, upon such a general defection, Mr. Canning could not stand,—so that they must all be speedily restored.

There can be no doubt that he might have continued to hold the Great Seal if he had been so inclined; for George IV., at this time being strongly Anti-Catholic, it was arranged that he should have an Anti-Catholic "Keeper of his conscience,"—and who so fit for that purpose? But no further attempt was made to retain him, and the resolution was formed to offer the Great Seal to Sir John Copley. This distinguished man, although he was understood formerly to have strongly condemned the practice of making religious belief the test of fitness for civil employment,—luckily happened at the present juncture—of course without any reference to the requisite condition of Anti-Catholicism in the new Chancellor—to be much alarmed by the danger to the Church from any further concession to the Catholics,—and he at once magnanimously accepted the offer—thus submitting to the imputation of bigotry and inconsistency that he might save the sinking state.

It was accordingly stated to Lord Eldon, with all the forms of civility, that his resignation was accepted; and he himself announced from the bench that he only held the Great Seal for the purpose of giving judgment in cases which had been argued before him.

He continued to sit in the Court of Chancery nearly three weeks—the time being prolonged from the difficulty Mr. Canning had experienced in filling up his Cabinet. When he understood that the ministerial arrangements were nearly completed, he courteously wrote to Lord Lyndhurst to congratulate him, and to inquire when it would be convenient that the transfer of the Great Seal should take place. He received the following becoming answer:—

'George Street, April 26th.

"MY DEAR LORD,

"I thank your Lordship for your kind congratulations with respect to the change of the custody of the Seal. Nothing more has been stated to me than a wish that it should take place before the meeting of the House of Lords. I beg your Lordship will, in every particular, consult your own convenience, to which it will be my greatest pleasure to conform. If your Lordship will permit me, I will wait upon you after I have made the necessary inquiries, and inform your Lordship of the result. Believe me, my dear Lord (with the deepest sense of your uniform kindness to me), to remain, with unfeigned respect,

"Your Lordship's faithful servant,
"LYNDHURST."

The Great Seal was actually delivered up by Lord Eldon, at Carlton House, on Monday, the 1st of May, 1827. We have an account of this ceremony from himself, in the following letter to his daughter:—

"May 2nd, 1827.

"MY EVER DEAR FRANCES,

"I took my final leave of the King on Monday. The King to me personally behaved with kindness. He sent for me on the Sunday, as he said he could not prevail upon himself to part with me having only the short interview which the hurry of Monday, when the whole change was to be made, would admit. His conversation to me was very kind, certainly; and it discovered a heart that had such affectionate feelings as one can not but deeply lament should, from intrigue and undue influence, not be left to its own operations upon the head. Bessy will have told you of the memorial of his feelings towards me, which he has sent me; and the pen I think more likely to describe its beauties than mine would be, and so I leave that subject.

"To-night, I presume, we shall have some account to give of our conduct in the House of Lords, as Peel did last night of his in the Commons, in a speech you will of course see in the papers. We who are to account to-night, are Wellington, Bathurst, Melville, Westmoreland, and myself. Mine will be short, but I hope satisfactory to those who I should wish should be satisfied with my conduct.

"I have now taken my farewell of office. Johnson, in the 'Rambler,' or 'Idler,' I forget which, in his *concluding* essay, speaks of every person's being affected by what is '*the last*,' by the finishing of his labors. Is the mind so constituted that it can not be otherwise than that, for a short season, the change from a station of labor and vast importance, to a state of comparatively no labor and no importance, must feel strange? I bless God, however, that He has enabled me, in that state of change, to look back to a period of nearly half a century spent in professional and judicial situations and stations, with the conviction that the remembrance of the past will gild the future years which His Providence may allow to me, not merely with content, but with that satisfaction and comfort, and with such happiness, of which the world can not deprive me."

Notwithstanding the conviction of Lord Eldon that the complacent remembrance of the past would gild his future years, I can not help suspecting that when he drove home from Carlton House, without the Purse to bear him company, he suffered under what he considered a sad bereavement, and that when he awoke next morning, and looked to the chest in which the bauble had been so long carefully guarded by him, he felt a bitter pang at the recollection that it was gone, and that he should see its face no more. What a sinking of the heart must have come over him when the hour arrived for his train-bearer and his mace-bearer to announce to him that the carriage was ready to take him to Westminster Hall, and instead of the bustle of the daily procession, he was left undisturbed in his breakfast-parlor, to pore over a newspaper giving an account of the installation of the new Ministers! Now he would have been pleased to endure the eternal " din of the tongues of counsel," though more grating than the drone of a Scottish bagpipe.[1] Called upon to sign

---

[1] 1st Aug. 1824. " I have some and no small comfort to-day in having my organs of hearing relieved from the eternal din of the tongues of counsel. I am sometimes tormented by the noise of Lady Gwydir's Scotchmen playing under my windows upon the Scotch instrument vulgarly called the *bagpipes*; but there is music in that droning instrument compared to the battle of lawyers' tongues."—*Letter to Lady Frances.*

his name—having written Eldon, he inadvertently added C.; and when he blotted out this letter, the thought came into his mind that signatures would no longer produce fees, and that quarter-day would come round without bringing a gale of salary.—But what must have been his sensations when he entered the House of Lords, and walking, as if by instinct—from the habit of twenty-five years—to the woolsack, he actually found it occupied by another, and he had to take his seat on the Opposition bench, which he had so long viewed with contempt and abhorrence! Great must have been his agony in seeing a Pro-Catholic the organ of the government in this as well as in the other House of Parliament—notwithstanding the vaunted *steady orthodoxy* of his successor on the woolsack.

Nature kindly mitigates our severest sufferings; and I suspect that Lord Eldon, in the sharpness of his grief, found some consolation by anticipating the speedy downfall of Mr. Canning, and—all Papists being banished from power—the establishment of a purely Protestant Cabinet.

Yet he was dreadfully shocked by the valedictory harangue of Mr. Peel, "which," he said, "might have come from the mouth of the vilest Whig." "The fact is undeniable," boasted the retiring Secretary, "that when I first entered on the duties of the Home Department, there were laws in existence which imposed upon the subjects of this realm unusual and galling restrictions; the fact is undeniable that those laws have been effaced. I have the further satisfaction of knowing that there is not a single legislative measure connected with my name which has not had for its object some mitigation of the severity of the criminal law,—some prevention of abuse in the exercise of it,—or some security for its impartial administration. I may also recollect with pleasure, that during the severest trials to which the manufacturing interests have ever been exposed, during the two last years, I have preserved internal tranquillity without applying to Parliament for any measures of extraordinary severity."[1] So much was Lord Eldon alarmed by such latitudinarian sentiments respecting Suspensions of the Habeas Corpus Act, Coercion Bills, and the mitigation of the Criminal Code, that he said to an old friend,[2] "You and I may not live to see it, but the

[1] 17 Hansard, 411.
[2] Mr. Pennington, the apothecary, who physicked Westminster Hall for half a century.

day will come when Mr. Peel will place himself at the head of the democracy of England, and will overthrow the Church."

Mr. Canning, in his explanation in the House of Commons, stated distinctly that "he did not understand from the Lord Chancellor on the evening of the 10th of April, that it was his intention to resign, and that, so far from anticipating his resignation, the King and himself were each under the delusion that there were the best reasons to expect the support of his services in the new arrangement; the resignation of the noble and learned Lord, with that of Lord Bexley, only reached him when he was in the King's Closet, on the 12th of April, the day when he kissed hands as First Lord of the Treasury." He added, "It is bare justice to Lord Eldon to say, that his conduct was that of a man with the highest feelings of honor, and that throughout it had been above all exception."[1]

Lord Eldon, in his own explanation, was at great pains to refute the imputed charge of "combination" between him and some of his late colleagues, which he denominated "a base and gross falsehood." He said, "he had for years been meditating whether it was not his duty to resign. Allowing the King to have a constitutional right to choose his Ministers, every subject must consider whether, under the selection made, he could usefully serve the public." Having at great length vindicated his opinion on the Catholic question, he observed, that "though he found it possible to serve in an Administration having such a man at the head of it as Lord Liverpool, yet in an Administration headed by the present Prime Minister (to whom he gave full credit for sincerity of opinion) he could not serve." The letter which informed him who was to Prime Minister, stated that the Administration was to be formed on the same principle as Lord Liverpool's, but he never could agree that it was so,—Lord Liverpool being a zealous opponent of Catholic Emancipation, and the present Prime Minister its most zealous advocate. He trusted that, as he had never doubted the sincerity of noble lords while they were supporting opinions opposed to his own, their lordships would not doubt at present of the sincerity of his motives." He gracefully concluded

[1] 17 Hansard, 446, 522.

with expressing thanks to the House for "the kindness with which they had always supported him in the discharge of the arduous duties from which he had just been relieved."[1]

In a few days after he wrote to his grandson:—

"We ex-Ministers have been as much abused, for cabal and conspiracy, as if we had formed another Cato Street gang; and we were tried in the House of Lords, as if we had been a band of culprits. We all pleaded not guilty, and I believe we were all, in the opinion of all, most honorably acquitted. The fact is, that, with my principles, to remain in office under a Prime Minister of different principles (either his principles or mine being, *but both* certainly *not being*, consistent with the support of the pure reformed established religion of the country, and the support of its political liberties) appeared to me to be unworthy conduct on my part, being satisfied that my own principles were right. I look back to forty-four or five years spent in Parliament with perfect consistency in conduct—no deviation whatever—I have been either always right or always wrong, *Servetur ad*, &c. &c. Not that consistency in error is otherwise than most blamable, if the person, observing that consistency, has discovered that he has been in error. This discovery I have not been able to make; and the line that I have taken in the support of the religion and political constitution of my country, after a most anxious endeavor to inform myself aright upon subjects so interesting, I think, upon severe reflection, was the line I ought to pursue in the discharge of my duty to myself, my descendants, my fellow-subjects, their descendants, my Sovereign, and the Throne; and, with all due humility, I add, my duty to God. *Esto perpetua*, is my prayer as to the Constitution in Church and State. I tremble somewhat when I see a Prime Minister supported by those individuals who have been thought to hold Jacobinical and Radical doctrines for years past, and when I see some of our supposed Whigs joining them. Can this long endure? My defensive speech, I have reason to believe, did me and my family no discredit, and I think it will do none to my memory. The House was much surprised with the ability, clearness, judgment, and power with which the Duke of Wellington spoke.

[1] 17 Hansard, 450.

"The king parted with me in a very kind and affectionate manner. The piece of magnificent plate which he has presented to me upon parting, will, I think, very much please you; and it is certainly a very valuable family possession."[1]

In his high hope at the outset of the new Government, that its duration would be very short, and that he himself would speedily be restored to office, he wrote to Lady Frances:—

"I think political enmity runs higher, and waxes warmer, than I ever knew it. God bless us all!—to think of our Prime Minister's principal supporters in the House of Commons being Burdett and Brougham! Surely such things can't remain long. I still think that the Minister must either fall, or be borne up by the Lansdowne party. That, however, seems very small, as one looks at them when congregated in the House of Lords. Think of Lord King sitting among the Bishops! I am afraid that that Bench, as to some of them, will do themselves no credit."

He was right as to the duration of the Government, for the hand of death was upon its chief; but his own official career had terminated forever. He ought to have been contented, however, as he had held the Great Seal longer than any Chancellor, clerical or lay, since the Norman Conquest.[2]

It is unaccountable that, on his final retirement, there was no address to him from the Bar, by whom generally he was very much respected and beloved, although some members of the body, particularly among the Tories, were much dissatisfied with the stingy manner in which he had distributed professional honors among them.[3]

---

[1] This consisted of a tankard of silver gilt, its lid having an "accession medal" of the King placed in it, and bore the following inscription:—
"The Gift of His Majesty King GEORGE IV.
to his highly-valued and excellent Friend
JOHN EARL OF ELDON,
LORD HIGH CHANCELLOR OF ENGLAND, &c.,
upon his retiring from his Official Duties in 1827."
The key of the case in which it stood was put into Lord Eldon's hand by the King himself.

[2]
	Years.	Months	Days.
From 14th April, 1801, to 7th February 1806.	4	9	24
From 1st April, 1807, to 30th April, 1827.	20	0	29
Total duration	24	10	23

[3] I myself never felt personally aggrieved, although he had refused me a

The Masters in Chancery, all of whom he had appointed, sent him a touching address, to which he returned the following answer:—

"May 7th, 1827.

"Lord Eldon has received with great satisfaction the letter which the Masters in Chancery have been pleased to address to him.

"He reflects with great pleasure upon the fact, that he has given to the public the benefit of the services of all these gentlemen.

"Separated from them, as being no longer in a judicial situation, he trusts that he may carry with him in retirement their good opinions; and he assures them that, in what remains to him of life, he shall most anxiously promote, as far as he can, their honor and welfare."

I may here likewise appropriately mention a grand dinner afterwards given to him in London by the Northern Circuit, which was attended not only by the existing members of that distinguished body, but by contemporaries of Jack Scott, who, having been initiated in its mysteries, had long left the Bar. All were eager to do honor to their illustrious guest, and he was as merry and as boyish as he had been when assisting to play off tricks on Jack Lee and Jemmy Boswell half a century before.[1]

---

silk gown when I had been for years leading the Oxford Circuit in "stuff." There were zealous political adherents, and even personal connections of his own, who, from as strong claims being as little attended to, were very bitter against him. I was included in a batch of King's Counsel made by the new Chancellor, which, with one exception, was supposed to include all, whatever their politics, who had a fair claim to this distinction. Mr. Denman was still proscribed; but justice was soon after done to him through the firmness of the Duke of Wellington, who is entitled to our gratitude for gallantly giving good advice to the Sovereign as well as for leading our armies to victory.

[1] I have heard many amusing anecdotes of the sayings and doings at this memorable meeting; but the Court sat *foribus clausis*, and I am not at liberty to disclose them. From the records of the Circuit it appears that the following late or present members attended :—" Earl of Clarendon " (the late Earl, who was at the Bar when a younger brother); " Lord Auckland " (now First Lord of the Admiralty); " Sir Nicholas Tindal " (late Chief Justice of Common Pleas); " Sir John Beckett " (late M. P. for Leeds); " Sir James Allan Park " (late a Judge of Common Pleas); " Sir John Hullock " (late a Baron of the Exchequer); " Sir Joseph Littledale " (late a Judge of King's Bench); " Sir James Parke " (now a Baron of the Exchequer); " Hon. G. Lamb " (late Under Secretary of State); " Raine " (late a Welsh Judge); " Brougham " (my noble and learned friend the Lord Brougham and Vaux); " Pollock " (now Chief Baron of the Exchequer); " Williams " (late a Judge

CHAPTER CCVIII.

CONTINUATION OF THE LIFE OF LORD ELDON TILL THE PASSING OF THE BILL TO REPEAL THE TEST ACT.

WE are again to view Lord Eldon in the trying situation of an ex-Chancellor, in which my heroes have differed much more than in office,—where they were almost all alike engrossed in the common objects of retaining power, and doing as much good to their country as was consistent with their own ease and aggrandizement. It would have been very delightful to me if I could have recorded that this, the last of my series, taking Lord Somers for his model, had now devoted himself to literature and science,—and had eclipsed his great judicial reputation by reforming the laws and improving the institutions of his country. It really might have been expected, that the pupil of Moises, and the brother of Sir William Scott, would eagerly return to a perusal of the classics, when duty no longer required him to pore over the interminable tomes of Equity Reports; and that although hitherto—his eyes being dazzled by the bright beam of royal favor—he had been blind to the faults of the system over which he had presided, he would at last distinctly see them in all their deformity, and would struggle to remove them. But, alas! he had forever lost all taste for any reading more recondite than the newspapers,—complaining even that "nowadays they are too bulky, and presume to discuss subjects which should be left to pamphlets and reviews." Instead of framing a reformation of Chancery procedure, to be known by posterity under the title of "Lord Eldon's Equity Jeofails Act," he gave himself no further trouble in carrying out the Report of the Chancery Commission; and though he had been driven by pressure from without to show it some countenance, he probably thought that its suggestions were dangerous innovations, which, in their remote

of the Queen's Bench); "Alderson" (now a Baron of the Exchequer); "Coltman" (now a Judge of the Common Pleas); "Patteson" (now a Judge of the Queen's Bench); "Cresswell" (now a Judge of the Common Pleas); "Wightman" (now a Judge of the Queen's Bench); "Dundas" (now Solicitor-General).—1847.

consequences, might lead to the subversion of the monarchy.

When the "Advertisements" in the "TIMES" had been exhausted, I am afraid that he had no resource except counting over the money in his chest—and receiving gossiping visits from a few old professional friends, who flattered him with reminiscences of his former greatness, and censures of the proceedings of his successor. The listless day appeared dreadfully long to him, and he must often have been impatient for the hour of dinner, when he could soothe his inaction with a bottle of "Newcastle Port."

But the full misery of idleness, awaiting a mere lawyer in retirement, was not experienced by him till after the formation of the Duke of Wellington's Government, in the beginning of the following year—when he considered himself abandoned by all his political associates, and he certainly knew that he never was again to be in office.

For the present he was excited by the hope of seeing the usurpers of power turned adrift, and of assisting in that occupation in which he took such pleasure and had often displayed such skill—the formation of a "downright Tory Government."

He forgot all he had suffered in giving up the Great Seal when he heard the Duke of Wellington's explanation —which was very damaging to Mr. Canning,[1]—and he was thrown into raptures by Lord Grey's tremendous attack upon that Minister which soon followed, although a considerable section of the Whigs were supporting him.[2] Hating all coalitions, he thought that there was little danger of a coalition between these leaders, for Lord Grey on this very occasion had renewed his pledge to support Catholic Emancipation, and had assigned the promise of the new Chief to postpone it—with the appointment of a professing Anti-Catholic Chancellor—as strong reasons for withholding confidence from the present Government; but he hoped that without *concert* there would be *co-operation* between them, and, knowing the King's increased dislike to the "early friends," he anticipated that

[1] 17 Hansard, 454.
[2] Ibid. 720. This is said to have made the new Premier so angry, that he actually wrote a letter to the King, asking a peerage that he might come and answer it, and that it was not till after the lapse of several days that his friends could drive him from this purpose,

in the course of a few months the true old genuine Tories would be in possession of undivided empire.

He was made more sanguine when Mr. Canning's foreign policy, particularly with respect to Portugal, was condemned by these opposite leaders; and still more so when, by their simultaneous though independent efforts, the Government bill for a relaxation of the corn laws, which had passed the House of Commons, was defeated in the House of Lords.[1]

The only alloy to these joys was, that the Dissenters' Marriage Bill again coming up from the Commons,—although the ex-Chancellor abused very handsomely the measure itself and the Bishops who supported it—upon a division there was now a majority in its favor,[2] and it actually went through a committee; but, the prorogation being at hand, the Government agreed that, for the purpose of receiving some amendments, it should stand over till another session.

Parliament being prorogued by Lord Chancellor Lyndhurst, Lord ex-Chancellor Eldon immediately retreated to Encombe,—the hall of which was no longer crowded by King's messengers, carrying Cabinet boxes—by breathless applicants for injunctions and commissions of bankruptcy—by royal visitors to concert measures for Protestant ascendency—nor by parsons with twelve children, coming in quest of livings. The tranquillity of the place, which in former vacations would have seemed so desirable, was now felt by Lord Eldon, like the tameness of the surrounding animals by Robinson Crusoe, as "awful." But while, in

[1] Ibid. 984, 1217, 1258.—I regret very much that, in a note which I carelessly appended to my Life of Lord Northington (Vol. VI. p. 333),—in comparing Lord Rockingham's first Administration in 1766 to Mr. Canning's Administration in 1827, I used language from which it might be supposed that I represented the Duke of Wellington and Lord Grey acting against Mr. Canning in *concert*, with a view to turn him out. Lord Grey, retaining all his own high principles, did (I think erroneously) express a very unfavorable opinion of Mr. Canning and his measures; but it is well known that he grounded that opinion upon his belief that the manner in which Mr. Canning had acted would tend to retard the accomplishment of Catholic Emancipation and other necessary reforms. Hence, he thought that he could not support an Administration of which he had formed this judgment, and still less could he enter into any alliance with those who were as deeply pledged against Catholic Emancipation as Lord Eldon himself. I could hardly be supposed, by any one who knows me, to intend to cast any reflection on the honor or consistency of Lord Grey,—having formerly been proud of him as my political chief, and now venerating his memory.

[2] 61 to 54. 17 Hansard, 1424.

the terms of an indictment for murder, he "languishing did live," the newspaper of the 10th of August unexpectedly brought him the melancholy intelligence of the death of the Prime Minister.

His strong political feelings were instantly rekindled within him, and, in imagination, he was constructing a new Cabinet. He expected to be immediately sent for to London; but no summons was received. He then became alarmed that the Whigs were to enter through the door opened to them by Lord Lansdowne, but was greatly comforted by hearing of an arrangement which he was sure could not last, and which must ere long make way for the true Tories—that Lord Goderich (now Earl of Ripon) should be placed at the head of the Treasury, without any real accession of strength in the Cabinet.

He was a good deal disgusted, however, by an occurrence which immediately followed—the Duke of Wellington consenting to resume the office of Commander-in-Chief, which he had indignantly refused to hold under Mr. Canning. The ex-Chancellor thus betrayed his uneasy thoughts to Lord Encombe:—

"You have seen that the Duke of Wellington, now poor Canning is dead, has taken the command of the army. He holds that this connects him no more with Ministers than if he took the command of the Horse Guards, as I hear. This *is not* inconsistent, though it will *seem* to the public to be so, when it may be said, 'If it does not connect him with Ministers, why did he not keep it under Minister Canning?' I happen to know that there is a very satisfactory difference between those two cases. I wish that I was as sure that it does not connect him with Ministers. I am sure he thinks it does not; for an honester man does not live. But—I say no more."

He felt so uncomfortable in his suspicions of the Duke not being quite steady in his opposition to the existing semi-liberal Administration, that he wrote to him on the subject, and received the following explanation, which did not by any means quiet his apprehensions:—

"Strathfieldsaye, Sept. 1st, 1827.

"MY DEAR LORD ELDON,

"I am very much obliged to you for your letter; and as I had not heard from you on the subject of that one which I had desired Lord Fitzroy Somerset to show you,

I intended to write to you. I certainly thought and wished that there should be no mistake in regard to the principle upon which I accepted the office of Commander-in-Chief, and to the relation in which its acceptance would place me to the politics of the Government. In regard to the acceptance of the office itself, I had declared myself in public as well as in private, and in writing to his Majesty and to his late Minister; and I had likewise declared in Parliament the relation in which I should stand to the politics of the Government. With these declarations before them, the King and his Minister called upon me to give my service, on the ground of the public interests requiring it; and, in accepting, I have again declared my principle. I may have placed myself too high, and, like others, fall from the difficult position which I have assumed. But this is quite clear, viz., that I *have* assumed that position; and there I will remain as long as I can do any good in it.

"I am not astonished that the friends of the Administration should consider this arrangement as a great gain. In one sense it is so. If, on the one hand, the Administration have no claim upon my services out of my profession, I, on the other, can be of no counsel or party against them; and they are certain that one great branch of the service will be conducted according to their wishes."

Laboring under a groundless belief that Lord Goderich's Administration might be durable, so as to endanger the Church, and destroy his own prospects of returuing to office, he despatched the following letter to his grandson:—

"Though I am perfectly satisfied that, in the present circumstances of the country, the Duke of Wellington could not refuse to accept the command of the army—and though he is not in the Cabinet, and disapproves, I believe, thoroughly, the formation of an Administration composed of persons of such opposite public principles, that, if they are all honest in their professed opinions, they never could agree in any interesting public matter,—yet that acceptance can not but be, I think, a strong prop to the Administration, as the present Opposition can not possibly, I think, have the benefit of his counsel and advice against the Administration, if they choose to adopt measures which he may think ought not to be adopted, but which the Commander-in-Chief may be obliged to execute. Besides this, all experience proves, that when individuals come frequently into company and contact with each other, they soon like each other better than they did before; they soften as to their differences; and the oil and vinegar begin to lose their repugnant properties, and to amalgamate with each other as if they were substances of the same nature. Among those who, towards the end of the session, were the determined friends of Wellington, Peel, and Eldon, the opinions, as to W.'s acceptance, are various. Some think he ought not to have accepted,—some, that he ought,—some, that he should have made conditions,—and some, that he should have told his Majesty plainly, that he must change his Administration, and take the late Ministers, and that upon that condition only he would command the army. This last opinion, I am sure, is wrong; for I have seen enough of the feelings of the people of this country to be sure that they will have their King (let them ever so heartily dislike measures) talked to *as* a King,—that they will not bear any person's dictating to him,—that they will not endure a Sovereign over their Sovereign,—and, particularly, that they would never endure a person's holding such language to the King, whom they would consider as a military man, confiding in the attachment of the army to him; which army he, as a good subject, should, by every proper means in his power, endeavor to attach to the Sovereign. After all, though I think he could not refuse to accept, because the country has not another man in it fit to command the army, I think the acceptance, though unavoidable in my opinion, will nevertheless be the cause of much that, with my principles, I shall have to lament. The members of the motley Administration and their adherents think they have gained a vast advantage. So much as to the *salus publica.*"

When November came round, and, according to the usage of near sixty years, he ought to have celebrated the "Morrow of All Souls" in Westminster Hall, it seemed most strange to him to find himself still in the country; and he was evidently much depressed, although he tried to put a good face upon it by writing to his friends:—
"The loneliness of the place is far from being an object of distaste to me. We are now here already some days

beyond the day to which in any former year we could remain here. It is at least as pleasant as sitting in Lincoln's Inn Hall, among the lawyers."[1]

He came to London a few days after Christmas, hastening his journey on account of rumors of a dissolution of the Ministry. He went, with some, by the name of the "Stormy Petrel," being supposed to delight in such convulsions. The newspapers seem to have prognosticated a coming change from his appearance, and to have somewhat misrepresented his proceedings,—as we learn from the following paragraph in a letter to Lady Frances:—

"I believe the world here are now pretty well satisfied that I have not come here for the sole purpose of intrigue, cabal, and holding conclaves for political purposes, the Ministerial [papers] having, when they stated me to have political meetings in Hamilton Place, unluckily brought company together of many who have not been in town."

Various attempts having been made to strengthen the Administration, Lord Goderich lost courage altogether; and,—not venturing to meet Parliament,—on the 8th of January, 1828, he resigned. The same day, the Duke of Wellington, whose confidence in himself had greatly increased by several excellent speeches he had made while in Opposition, agreed to be First Minister, and was formally authorized by the King to lay before him the list of a new Administration. This was joyful news for our ex-Chancellor, who believed that he had mainly contributed to bring things to this pass, and who expected, from the Duke of Wellington's inexperience in civil affairs and great reliance upon him, to become more powerful than he had ever been under Lord Liverpool. But dreadful disappointment was in store for him, and he was about to suffer more severe mortification than at any period of his life.

At first all seemed to go smoothly. The Duke wrote to him a very civil note, announcing the commission he had received, and actually called upon him in Hamilton Place. Lord Eldon then expressed his readiness to re-

[1] In this letter he is very severe upon his old friend, poor Sir Anthony Hart, who had accepted the Irish Great Seal without consulting him, and for whom he makes this excuse: "Indeed, commencing a Chancellorship at seventy-three is so foolish a business, that perhaps he thought it most advisable to be silent." But he himself would not have been at all sorry to commence a new Chancellorship when considerably above that age.

sume the Great Seal if this should be wished,—although if they had any one else to hold it (which he no doubt thought impossible) he did not set up a claim to it—but he clearly and distinctly intimated his desire to be included in the arrangement, and to fill a Cabinet office. There seems to have been some embarrassment in the manner of the Duke, who talked much of the difficulties in which he was involved from the pretensions of conflicting claimants. They parted without further explanation.

From that hour he knew nothing of what was going on till about a fortnight after, when he saw in the newspapers a list of the new Ministry, beginning thus:—
"CHANCELLOR, LORD LYNDHURST."
The only other offices which he could have filled, the Presidentship of the Council and the Privy Seal, were, according to this record, to be held by Lord Bathurst and Lord Ellenborough,—and his own name was nowhere to be found or alluded to. I must own that, considering his age, the riches and honors already heaped upon him, and the danger of his obstructing any liberal measures which the progress of public opinion might render necessary, they would have been fully justified in respectfully declining his offer of future official service; but nothing can justify or palliate the neglect with which he was treated. As might be expected, he was in a furious rage, and he was not at all sparing in the epithets he bestowed upon the new Cabinet collectively, and upon the individuals who were to compose it.[2] In a subdued tone he wrote to his daughter:—

"You will observe Dudley, Huskisson, Grant, Palmerston, and Lyndhurst (five), were all *Canningites*, with whom the rest were three weeks ago in most violent contest and opposition. These things are to me quite marvellous. How they are all to deal with each other's conduct as to the late treaty with Turkey and the Navarino battle, is impossible to conjecture. As the first fruits of this arrangement, the Corporation of London have agreed to petition Parliament to repeal the laws which affect Dissenters."

[1] I do not find him yet making any personal complaint of his " Young Master ;" but, when he received the TANKARD, he little expected to be so cast off by him on the return of his party to power.

His revilings and threatenings getting abroad, and influential peers of the old school having expressed an opinion that they were all insulted in his person, some alarm, and perhaps some remorse, arose in the breasts of his old colleagues.

Mr. Peel tried to soothe him by the following epistle :—

"Whitehall Gardens, Jan. 26th, 1828,
Saturday night.

"MY DEAR LORD ELDON,

"It was not until this day that my appointment to the office of Home Secretary of State was completed by my taking the oaths in Council.

"My first act is to express to you my deep regret, that any circumstances should have occurred carrying with them the remotest appearance of a separation from you in public life. All the impressions of affectionate regard and esteem for you, derived from long and unreserved intercourse, are much too deeply engraven on my mind to be ever effaced or weakened.

"I am grateful to you for the uniform kindness I have experienced from you from my first entrance into public life, proud of having possessed your confidence, and most anxious to retain, without reference to politics, your personal good-will and esteem.

"My return to public life has been no source of gratification to me. In common with the Duke of Wellington, hitherto at least, I have had nothing to contemplate but painful sacrifices, so far as private feelings are concerned.

"For the last ten days, except when I was *compelled* to disregard the commands of my physician, I have been confined to the house. I hope, however, to be able to call on you very soon. It shall be the first visit I pay.

"With the sincerest prayer for your health, and that every comfort and happiness may attend you,

"Believe me, my dear Lord Eldon,
"With true esteem and affection, most faithfully yours,
"ROBERT PEEL."

"The Right Hon. the Earl of Eldon, &c., &c., &c."

The Duke of Wellington likewise had an affecting interview with him. Of this we have an interesting account in the following letters to his daughter :—

"Jan. 30th, 1828. (Wednesday.)

"MY DEAREST FAN,

. . . . . .

"The day after the D. of W. received his Majesty's commands to form an Administration, he sent me a note informing me of that event, and telling me that he would wait upon me. I sent an answer, saying, that if he would name any time for my waiting upon him on that or any other day, I should do so. However, on Friday, I think a fortnight ago last Friday, he called upon me, and after he had sat down some time, he proceeded to state the difficulties he found himself involved in, from the various conflicting claimants to office,—and being sure that I could not be mistaken in what this was to lead to, I told him that, as I thought he was coming to make mention of the Chancellorship, I desired him not to consider me as a conflicting claimant *for that office*,—that if they had any proper person to fill it, it was obvious, from what I said upon the resignation of it, that I could have nothing to do *with that office* (indeed, no serious offer, after that, could be made of it). No offer, therefore, was made to me of *it*, and the Duke left me without more said, except something of repetition as to his difficulties about conflicting claims generally.[1] From the moment of his quitting me, to the appearance in the papers of all the appointments, I never saw his Grace. I had no communication with him, either personally, by note, letter, by message through any other person, or in any manner whatever—and for the whole fortnight, I heard no more of the matter than you did at Corfe —some of my old colleagues in office (and much obliged to me too) passing my door constantly on their way to Apsley House without calling upon me. Indeed, no one of them called upon me, except on the last day but one before the settlement was in the papers; but after all was settled, Melville called upon me; but, upon this subject, his lips were not opened. In the mean time rumor was abroad that I had refused *all* office; and this was most industriously circulated, when it was found there was, as there really does appear to me to

---

[1] I believe that at the time when the Duke was first commissioned to form a Government, it had been definitively settled that Lord Lyndhurst should continue to hold the Great Seal, a strong wish to this effect having been expressed by the King himself.

have been, very great dissatisfaction among very important persons on my account, as neither included in office, nor at all, not in the least, consulted. Rumor again stated that I was too obstinate a Tory to be consulted or included. Rumor again stated that the interference of a lady had interposed her all-influential veto. However, there was a degree of discontent and anger among persons of consequence, which, I suppose, working together with its having been somehow communicated that I was much hurt at this sort of treatment, brought the D. of W. to me again—and the object of his visit seemed to be to account for all this. He stated in substance that he had found it impracticable to make any such Administration as he was sure I would be satisfied with; and, therefore, he thought he should only be giving me unnecessary trouble in coming near me, or to that effect. I observed, that I supposed that he had not found out this impracticability at the time he came to me about the Chancellorship; if he had, THAT visit would have been only a visit of 'unnecessary trouble.' That with respect to its being impracticable to form an Administration that I should be satisfied with, I knew no reason, founded on any former conduct of mine, which should have led him to conclude that I should urge impracticabilities; and that, at any rate, it would have been not too much to expect, that, during a whole fortnight, I should [not] have been left ignorant of what was going on, and that I was not to suppose that in that I had any concern [1]—that though I should have been gratified if an offer had been made to me of the Presidentship of the Council, I did not know that I should have accepted it, and that I was sure that, if the offer had been made, and accompanied with an intimation that my accepting it would embarrass them with respect to any other person, I would not have accepted it. He mentioned as a probable proof that I would not have fallen into his views as to the Administration, that he doubted that I did not approve of it as formed. I told him he was right there, and that I thought it a—(I must not put the word in a letter, to a lady, or anybody) a — bad one. We conversed together till, as it seemed to me, we both became a good deal affected; he mentioned some things that he proposed to my acceptance as propitiatory — not of much consequence — as

[1] Sic in orig.

to which I told him I would consider of it; for I can do nothing which can authorize the public to think that I can deem anything that could be proposed as compensating for undeserved neglect. I think I have given correctly the substance of what has passed—the very words it is impossible to give. I found it likely that they were not going to restore Wetherell to the Attorney Generalship, which he resigned nobly when we resigned, and by which step he has lost the Vice-Chancellorship. The D. has sent me word that, as he understood that I wished that Wetherell should be restored to that office, he is reappointed. I am satisfied that, with the country, all this has raised me; and as I don't want office, I care not about not having it. Lord Bathurst has, at length, been also with me, protesting in the most strong terms against any intention of disrespect, and expressive of the greatest concern that any part of their proceedings should have hurt me. I have not the least doubt that they have heard from some, if not from many, remonstrance upon the seeming, if not real, ill-treatment of me, and that there is at least something like contrition on that account. With respect to the part I have begun to take and to pursue in Parliament, it does not become me to appear angry or discontented, or to thwart the measures of Government by treating the Administration, as I think of it, as not a desirable one, at a time when I think, as I avowed last night in the House of Lords, that a person sincerely anxious for his country must feel it to be his bounden duty to interpose nothing that can delay for a moment the most active measures to secure the peace of Europe, likely to be interrupted by the occurrences with the Sultan, and which *perhaps* may be secured, if the present moment is employed for that purpose, instead of being lost in a sort of war at home about places and offices."

"(February 2nd, 1828.)

"All the newspapers seem to be employed in representing to the public that I, in a conversation with the Duke, when he waited upon me, spontaneously waived all office, and all sort of consultation about public arrangements or matters. Nothing can be so utterly false—there is not even the semblance of truth in it—but, there having been a great deal of public feeling upon this subject, the underlings of Administration have resorted to these means of quieting it. They begin in the papers devoted to Government and in its pay, and the matter is copied into other papers. I don't think that what has passed has done me any harm. I have been very busy in receiving and returning the calls of many very respectable persons, and in receiving and answering the letters of others of the same class of persons. I think those who have treated me with apparent disrespect are very sorry for it, and as much (at *least*) hurt about it as I have been. What is the real reason for what has happened, I know not; and it probably neither is, nor ever will be, avowed. A lady, probably, has had something to do with it. At the same time there may be something in the Duke's saying that some of my opinions had something to do with this, for nobody can read the late speeches of Lord Palmerston and Vesey Fitzgerald without being apprehensive that most dangerous concessions are about to be thought of to the Catholics, such as, shortly and surely, will shake the foundations of the Protestant Church."

. . . . .

"I don't know whether I told you that Princess Lieven asked me, at the Duchess of Kent's, why I was not a Minister. An impertinent interrogatory! She asked me for a sincere answer. I told her I would give her a sincere answer. My answer was, 'I *don't know* why I was not a Minister!'"

. . . . .

"It is not because office was not offered me that I complain—it is because those with whom I had so long acted and served, did not, candidly and unreservedly, explain themselves and their difficulties to me. And they were not mine adversaries that did me this dishonor, but mine own familiar friends, with whom I had, for so many years, taken sweet counsel together."

He now considered himself ill-used, not only by his old colleagues, but in a higher quarter. I must admit that he considerably overrated his services there; for he really seems to have thought that George IV. was indebted for his crown to Lord Eldon, instead of Lord Eldon being indebted for the Great Seal to George IV.

That he should not have been eagerly recalled to be "Keeper of the Royal Conscience," when this step seemed so easy and so natural, he could not comprehend. Daily and hourly he had expected a summons to Windsor, during the formation of the Ministry; but when he found that the King, without making any communication to him, had consented to his being entirely excluded from the Cabinet, he exclaimed, " Put not your trust in princes.'

He was too loyal, however, publicly to show his resentment; and if he was no longer to be squeezed in the royal embrace, and to be bedewed with tears of affection from royal eyes, he was determined to pass before his Majesty in the crowd of a *levée*, and to make him a bow. We have, from his own pen, the following subdued but touching account of his reception:—

"Friday (March 28th, 1828).

"I went to the levée yesterday—form requiring that ceremony at the first levée after quitting office. The multitude there was very great. The King, I thought, did not look well. He could not, or did not, stand up to receive his company, but each person passed him sitting in a great chair; and, as it appeared to me, the ceremony between him and 99 out of 100 of the company was no more than their merely bowing their heads to him as they passed, and he in return bowing his head to them. It came to my turn to pass. I thought he appeared a little of what I should call, for want of a better word, 'flustered;'—he could not, I think, see that I was approaching him till I was close to him. When I made my bow, he held out his hand to me, and shook hands with me, and said, ' My Lord, fresh air seems to have done you a great deal of good.' I then moved on, and that was all that passed with me at that moment or afterwards. In due time, Encombe, who was to be introduced, and who was most gaily and handsomely dressed, but had been by the multitude well squeezed, to the detriment and injury of his laced ruffles, and whom the pressure of the company had made not a little hot, arrived towards the King, and the Marquis of Winchester having announced him, he kissed hands, and was moving off, when the King, recollecting him, as he was withdrawing with his face towards his Majesty, as the usage is, nodded to him, with apparent earnestness, and, as well as I could hear, asked very kindly how he was, and obviously meant to show him attention and kindness. And so ends my account of the ceremonials of the day, upon which I forbear comment."

However, he, by degrees, reconciled himself to his fate; and when he saw some of the measures which the new Government brought forward or supported, he derived some comfort from finding that he was at full liberty to offer them a determined opposition.

He was first horrified by the news, which for a long time he declared he could not believe, that Lord John Russell having brought a bill into the House of Commons to repeal the Test Act, Mr. Peel, after a slight show of resistance, had declared his readiness to agree to it, provided that, in the place of taking the sacrament according to the rites of the Church of England, there should—for the safety of the Church—be substituted a *Declaration* which might be made by Dissenters and Roman Catholics as well as by Churchmen.[1] There was only one division on the bill in the House of Commons, when there appeared a majority of 45 in its favor,[2] and, the *Declaration* being very properly agreed to, it passed through the Lower House without difficulty. In a state of consternation and despair, Lord Eldon thus wrote respecting its approach to the House of Lords:—

"(April, 1828.)

"I suppose the Dissenters' Bill will pass the Commons to-day,[3] and be brought up to the House of Lords, where, I presume, we shall not debate it till after the holidays. We, who oppose, shall be in but a wretched minority, though the individuals who compose it will, as to several, I think, be of the most respectable class of Peers: but the Administration have—to their shame be it said—got the Archbishops and most of the Bishops to support this revolutionary bill. I voted as long ago as in the years, I think, 1787, 1789, and 1790, against a similar measure; Lords North and Pitt opposing it as destructive of the Church Establishment—Dr. Priestley, a dissenting minister, then asserting, that he had laid a train of gunpowder under the Church, which would blow it up; and Dr. Price, another dissenting minister, blessing God that he could depart in peace, as the revolution in France would lead here to the destruction of all union between Church and State. The young men and lads in the House of Commons are too young to remember these things. From

[1] 18 Hansard, 676.   [2] Ib. 781.
[3] The bill for the repeal of the Test and Corporation Acts.

1790 to 1827, many and various have been the attempts to relieve the Catholics; but through those thirty-seven years nobody has thought, and evinced that thought, of proposing such a bill as this in Parliament, as necessary, or fit, as between the Church and the Dissenters. Canning, last year, positively declared that he would oppose it altogether."
" (April, 1828.)

* * * * * *

"The Dissenters' Bill is to be debated in the House of Lords on the 17th—we, who oppose, shall fight respectably and honorably; but victory can not be ours. All the Whig Lords will be against us: as Government began in the Commons by opposition, and then ran away like a parcel of cowards, I suppose Government also will be against us;—but what is most calamitous of all is, that the Archbishops and several Bishops are also against us. What they can mean, they best know, for nobody else can tell—and, sooner or later,—perhaps in this very year—almost certainly in the next,—the concessions to the Dissenters must be followed by the like concessions to the Roman Catholics. That seems unavoidable, though at present, the policy is to conceal this additional purpose. But I must weary you on this subject."
" Saturday, April 12th, 1828.

"We, as we think ourselves, sincere friends of the Church of England, mean to fight, as well as we can, on Thursday next, against this most shameful bill in favor of the Dissenters, which has been sent up to us from the Commons—a bill which Peel's declaration in the House, as to the probability of its passing in the Lords, has made it impossible to resist with effect. As the bill is constructed, it operates not merely for Protestant Dissenters; but, unless the language of it can be materially altered in the Lords' House, it appears to me to be equally favorable to Roman Catholics, Deists, Infidels, Turks, Atheists. How the Bishops can have overlooked its extensive and deplorable effects, is to me the most strange thing possible. If the Lords won't, at least, alter it, which I don't believe they will, I don't see how, if the Commons act consistently with themselves, Sir F. Burdett can fail in his motion on the 29th, in favor of the Roman Catholics. The state of minds and feelings in the Tory part, and aristocratical part, of the friends of Liverpool's Administration, is, at present, excessively feverish, and they support Ministers because they know not where to look for others. It's obvious that the Ministers who were Canning's followers, to use a vulgar phrase, 'rule the roast,' or at least have too much influence."

In the debate on the second reading of the bill, Lord Eldon animadverted very strongly on the conduct of Ministers in the other House, who had acquiesced in the bill, although they pretended to disapprove of it; but he said, "he should perform his duty by acting on his own conscientious conviction, even if there should be a majority of both Houses against him. Much as he had heard of the 'march of mind,' he did not believe that the *march* could have been so rapid as to induce some of the changes of opinion which he had witnessed within the last year. The preamble recited that the bill was '*expedient*,'—a term resorted to when nothing else could be said in defense of a bad measure. But their Lordships must not be satisfied with the bare assertion of the supposed *expediency*. Repealing the laws for safeguard of the Church could not be the way to preserve it. The proposed *declaration* was no security: it might even be made by a Jew or an infidel. The Sacramental Act though often assailed, had remained ever since the reign of Charles II., and the annual indemnity took away all its harshness. The obnoxious act did not interfere with the rights of conscience, as it did not compel any man to take the sacrament according to the rites of the Church of England, and only deprived him of office if he did not. The proposed enactment, he was prepared to show, would endanger the Established Church. A question was put 'Why pass Annual Indemnity Acts rather than sweep away the test?' But the Indemnity Acts were a recognition of its necessity. He had voted against such a bill before some of their Lordships now supporting it were born; and he might say the same of some of the Right Reverend Prelates who were so strangely showing their attachment to the Church. The last time the question was agitated in the House of Commons was in 1790, when there was a majority of 187 against it. Nothing had occurred since to make it less mischievous. His prayer to God was, that the individuals who supported it might find that, as they intended no mischief to the Church, no mischief had ensued. Giving them credit for sincerity, he claimed a similar allowance for himself when he solemnly said, as he then did from his heart and soul, NOT CONTENT." The Duke of Wellington followed, handling the noble and learned Lord rather roughly, and defending the measure with admirable good sense. The second reading was carried without a division.[1]

However, Lord Eldon, on a subsequent day, opposed the motion for going into a committee on the bill. In answer to the objection that such tests were degrading, "he reminded their Lordships that his Majesty was obliged to take the sacrament before he began to exercise the royal functions. He entreated those who were the guardians of the Church to pause before they allowed her to be stripped of these safeguards by which she had been so long protected, lest those miseries from which she had been so happily rescued should return, in which case they would have to look again to the restoration of the Constitution such as it was established in the reign of Charles II., and look perhaps for such restoration in vain."

In the committee he had a very sharp altercation with Bloomfield (then Bishop of Chester, afterwards translated to London), who, pointing out the inconsistency of some of his amendments, was recommended by him "to attend to his own inconsistency, and not gratuitously to tender advice to others."

Lord Eldon's main amendment was to exclude Roman Catholics from the benefit of the bill, by inserting in the declaration, "I am a Protestant."

Being now accused by Lord Lyndhurst, the new Chancellor, of "exercising his talents, his zeal, and his influence mischievously in opposing this bill," he said, "I trust I have too long engaged the attention of noble lords in this House, not to receive from them a patient hearing, while I reply to such a charge, coming from such a place, and such an authority. I have served my country to the best of my abilities; I have endeavored to be a useful servant to my Sovereign, and if I am now engaged in anything calculated to be *mischievous* to the interests of the public, I pray to God that I may be forgiven; —but I solemnly declare my belief, that I can **never** be

[1] 18 Hansard, 1497–1517.

engaged in anything so *mischievous* as the forwarding of this measure. I am well aware of the fate of the amendment which I now propose; but such is my conviction of the evil consequences of this bill, in its present form, that, if I stand alone, I will go below the bar and give my vote against it; and were I called upon this night to render my account before Heaven, I would go with the consoling reflection that I have never advocated anything *mischievous* to my country. I cast back the imputation which has been sought to be thrown upon my conduct, by the noble and learned Lord on the woolsack, with all the scorn of a man who feels himself injured."

The amendment was negatived by 117 to 55. But so eager was he for it, that he renewed it on the third reading of the bill, when the CONTENTS were 52, NOT CONTENTS 154. Still he entered on the Journals a violent protest against the bill, in which he was joined by the Duke of Cumberland and nine other peers.[1]

He soon forgave Lord Lyndhurst, but he continued highly incensed against the Bishops, from whom he had expected better things. After the bill had passed, he thus wrote to his daughter:—

"I am hurt, distressed, and fatigued, by what has lately been passing in the House of Lords. I hope reflection may enable me, but I fear I can not reasonably hope that it ever will, to account rationally for the conduct of the Bishops. It is not rationally accounting for it to say that they were afraid that something worse would happen if they did not agree to this measure: fear and timidity produce, in state matters, the very consequences which they are alarmed about. In Charles I.'s time, Mr. Hyde, afterwards Lord Clarendon, expressed his astonishment to the virtuous Falkland, that he could give a particular vote against the Church. The answer was, in the very language of this day, 'Indulge the enemies of the Church in this vote, and they will ask no more.' Such is the very talk, the foolish talk, of this day. The historian observes, that after this was granted, everything more was asked that could be asked; and though Falkland had also said that the friends of the Establishment would successfully oppose everything more that was asked, they durst not

[1] 18 Hansard, 1573–1616; 19 Ib. 39, 109, 156.

venture opposition to any one further demand of the discontented. History is written for our instruction; but we may as well not trouble ourselves with reading the pages of history. . . . I have fought like a lion, but my talons have been cut off.

"The bill is, in my poor judgment, as bad, as mischievous, and as revolutionary as the most captious Dissenter could wish it to be."

Were he now alive, he would be obliged to acknowledge that by the repeal of the Test Act we have got rid of the desecration of the most solemn rite of our religion,—freedom of conscience has been protected,—and the Church of England has become more popular and more secure than at any time since the Reformation.

As soon as this measure was carried, all the world acknowledged the Duke of Wellington's sagacity in declining the offer of Lord Eldon to return to office; for if that sturdy adherent to ancient prejudices had been Lord Chancellor or President of the Council, the Government must either have been speedily dissolved by internal dissensions, or overthrown by a vain resistance to the popular voice.

CHAPTER CCIX.

CONTINUATION OF THE LIFE OF LORD ELDON TILL THE PASSING OF THE CATHOLIC RELIEF BILL.

THE Duke of Wellington's next move was highly agreeable to Lord Eldon, but it must now be regretted by all staunch Conservatives, for it certainly led to the Reform Bill. Had he consented to the transfer of the forfeited franchise of East Retford to Manchester,—with an intimation that the right of sending members to Parliament would gradually be taken from the decayed boroughs and vested in the great unrepresented manufacturing towns,—he might have continued at the head of affairs for many years, to carry this plan into effect. But, now making a stand against all change in the representative system, he threw himself upon the exclusive support of the high Tory party, without being able to satisfy them; and, being driven to yield Catholic Emancipation, he fell,—to make way for eleven years of Whig rule, and measures of innovation which might otherwise have been postponed for a century.

The first effect of this error was the resignation of Mr. Huskisson, Lord Palmerston, Lord Dudley, and Mr. W. Lamb,—afterwards himself Prime Minister. Lord Eldon was well pleased to see the Cabinet purged of some of those whom he considered its most dangerous members,—but he prophetically wrote to his daughter, in communicating this intelligence,—" The Minister will have great difficulties to struggle with. The Whigs, the Canningites, and the Huskissonites will join and be very strong. With the exception of Lord Lonsdale, the great Tory parliamentary lords are not propitiated by the new arrangements, and many of them will either be neuter or adverse."

Soon after, he found himself associated (and for the last time) with his old Tory colleagues in resisting the claims of the Roman Catholics. The question being again brought forward, in the hope that, from the spirit displayed in the late debates on the Test Act, it might even pass the House of Lords, the Protestant champion's courage rose as the danger thickened, and he defended what he called the "bulwarks of the Church" with increased energy. He said "he would hazard the risk of being again taken for an '*almanack-maker*,' when he had Lord Bacon to share the honor with him;"—and having given a history of the penal statutes, he thus continued: " A noble lord has alluded to the necessary rejection of the Duke of Norfolk, on account of his faith, should he present himself in that House, to assume the right of his ancestors. With respect to myself, individually, I can only say, that a more painful duty than that suggested could not, by possibility, have been imposed upon me while I had the honor to preside upon the woolsack. But if the Sovereign himself had appeared here, without having previously taken the oaths, and made the declaration against transubstantiation, as required by law, I should have been constrained to inform him that he was *ipso facto* incapacitated from discharging the constitutional duties of King. Touching the coronation oath, I will say that if, in this Protestant state—for such the Acts of Parliament warrant me in calling it—his Majesty should think that, consistently with his duty, he could not give his consent to bills for the relief of the Roman Catholics, he would be under as solemn an obligation as any man could ever be placed under, to refuse that consent, although those bills should have passed both Houses."[1] He had the fleeting satisfaction of finding the motion rejected by a majority of 181 to 137.[2] But this was the last division in either House of Parliament against our Roman Catholic fellow-subjects.

The vessel of state being at this time on the Conservative tack, Lord Eldon entertained a sanguine hope, although he had been cruelly thrown overboard,—that, struggling in the waters, he might be picked up by his old messmates.

While such meditations were passing through his mind, he was much excited by a message from his "Young Master," who had hitherto wholly neglected him since his resignation, intimating that "he should call upon him as a friend." He no doubt thought all his influence in the royal closet was about to be revived, but he came away grievously disappointed. Having told his daughter that he had a conversation of some length with the King, he adds: "It had, however, no matter in it, but civil speeches and professions of friendship and regard ; *but no word to account for what I don't think very consistent with such speeches and professions.* So much for that which I mention, because it is not unlikely that the papers may make mention of my visit, with many conjectures and guesses what it could be about."

His hopes were nearly extinguished by a slight which he soon after experienced, and to which he thus refers :— " The King gives a grand dinner on the 12th [of August] at Windsor Castle. He has not, as one of his guests, invited a person of whom I can be bold enough to say that the King is more indebted to him than he is to any other subject he ever had in a civil department,"—adding, by way of showing a little modesty, the old expression, "'though I say it, who should not say it.'"

In the following month he was thrown into absolute despair by a rumor that the Earl of Westmoreland, who had been omitted in the original formation of the Ministry,

---

[1] 19 Hansard, 1279.　　　　[2] Ib. 1294.

was now to have an office. "If this appointment of Westmoreland takes place," says he, "Lord Eldon seems to be the only person in our Cabinet, formerly working with the present Minister, totally set aside. These things naturally made London very disagreeable and irksome to me. You mention a person you have seen at Worthing very shy as to talking politics. That forms a sample of the uncomfortably cold treatment one meets with from persons, all over attachment and love, as it were, some little time ago. I love grumbling here in solitude, when my own mind happens to turn to the contemplation of these things—at least I prefer it to having that grumbling called forth in every street where one meets an old political brother workman."[1]

A rumor was soon after spread, that he was actually about to re-enter the Cabinet. To this he refers in the following letter to his brother-in-law, Mr. Surtees:—

"I hear nothing from town, except what I know there is no foundation whatever for, viz.—that it is reported that I am to come into office:—I mean reported in town, for, except that I learn from London correspondence that it is so reported, I have heard nothing respecting any such matter. Indeed, if any such offer was made, there is much to be explained before I would give any answer. That no such offer will be made I am as certain as I can be of anything that I do not positively know,—and I am so because I think I can't be mistaken when I believe that the inflexibility of my opinions respecting the Catholic claims was, with those who are not inflexible as to those claims, the reason, or at least one of the reasons, that produced that silence towards me, which took place on the change of Administration, and it remains very well known to be the fact that *that inflexibility can not be shaken.*"

I doubt not that he would have proved—

"The man resolv'd, and steady to his trust,
Inflexible to ill, and obstinately just."

But he was evidently most cruelly mortified in waiting in vain for an attempt to be made upon his virtue.

He was further disturbed by hearing, that, in compliance with a recommendation of the House of Commons, Mr. Peel had issued two commissions with a view to juridical improvement,—one to examine "the Procedure of

[1] Letter to Lord Stowell, Sept. 1828.

the Courts of Common Law," and the other "the Tenure and Transfer of Real Property,"—more particularly when he was told that at the head of the latter commission was placed a Whig who had lately received a silk gown from Lord Lyndhurst.[1]—He considered such proceedings as unsettling the foundations of all law, and as subversive of all principle.

But a much more immediate danger now threatened the State from Mr. O'Connell's election for the County of Clare. With the political prescience which certainly belonged to Lord Eldon, he thought that Ministers would speedily give up further opposition to the Catholic claims, and thus he wrote:—

"Nothing is talked of now, which interests anybody the least in the world, except the election of Mr. O'Connell, and the mischief that it will produce among debaters in the House of Commons, and the more serious mischief it will, in all human probability excite in Ireland. As O'Connell will not, though elected, be allowed to take his seat in the House of Commons, unless he will take the oaths, &c. (and that he won't do, unless he can get absolution), his rejection from the Commons may excite rebellion in Ireland. At all events, this business must bring the Roman Catholic question, which has been so often discussed, to a crisis and a conclusion. The nature of that conclusion I don't think likely to be favorable to Protestantism.

. . . . . .

"O'Connell's proceedings in Ireland, which you'll see in the papers, and the supposed or real ambiguity which marked the D. of W.'s speech, have led to a very general persuasion, that Ministry intend, or at least that the Duke intends, next session, to emancipate the Roman Catholics, as he has the Dissenters; and the world is uneasy."

. . . . . .

"I look on the Roman Catholic question as, bit by bit, here a little and there a little, to be ultimately, and at no distant day, carried. I have no conception that even Oxford will struggle effectually against the great Church interests which will patronize that question, and those who support it in Parliament."[2]

The only kindred spirit that he found was the Duke of

[1] Mr. Campbell, afterwards Lord Campbell.   [2] Letters to Lady Frances.

Newcastle, whose letter to Lord Kenyon against any concession to the Catholics pleased him much. He says,—

"It is well worth reading. He must expect, that while many people will admire his spirit, and think his observations very just, multitudes of Radicals and Liberals will abuse him unsparingly; while the friends and foes of Ministers will praise him and blame him with all zeal and earnestness. He is a fellow, at all events, of good spirit, and no flincher—he speaks out most boldly. Whatever one party may think of him as a politician, no party can refuse to him the character of a most excellent and virtuous man in private life. If, in these times, it is a fault to be much attached to the Established Church, as some seem to think, he is certainly as much attached as anybody living to it. Whether he will persuade his countrymen to rally round that Church, as he desires to persuade them, is another matter. I, who think that the State is as much aimed at by the enemies of the Church as the Church itself, am afraid that his countrymen have been so long fast asleep, that it will be no easy matter to awaken them."

He went to Encombe in the autumn, and continued there several months, lamenting the evil times which he had lived to see. One of his letters, in this interval, to Lord Stowell, states very forcibly and plausibly the objection to the removal of Roman Catholic disabilities:—

"If, as the Liberals say, religious opinions ought to have *no* influence on the exercise of political power, why should the Sovereign's professing the Roman Catholic religion, or marrying a Roman Catholic princess, be, as by law it is, a forfeiture of the crown? If this be a just principle, how can opposition to restoring to the Roman Catholics that establishment which formerly belonged to them and their priesthood be justified? If, on the other hand, you say that religious opinions *ought* to have such influence where the religious opinions may lead persons to do what is wrong; still, if making both Houses of Parliament replete with Roman Catholics (nothing religious opinions withstanding) would not lead *them* to do wrong, why is it to be *taken for granted* that *a King*, being of the same religious persuasion as his Parliament, will do wrong? The project of emancipation seems to me to be founded on assumptions which, if just, render much which was done in 1688, and the Act of Settlement on the Princess Sophia and the heirs of her body, *being Protestants*,—the forfeiture of the crown by conversion or marriage,—altogether unjust; and that, if the Ministers of the Crown advise his Majesty to consent to emancipation, as it is asked, they advise him to give his assent to a libel on his title to the throne."

But he was summoned from solitary reveries to repel what he considered a deadly assault upon the Church, led on by the Duke of Wellington and Mr. Peel. These chiefs, it is believed, had become convinced, ever since the Clare election in the preceding summer, of the necessity of Catholic emancipation for the safety of the empire; but it was quite impossible that they could with any propriety make known their altered views till they had gained the King's consent to the measure, and Parliament was about to assemble. After much difficulty the King's written consent to it, signed with his own hand, was given,—and on the first day of the new session, these thrilling words were spoken by Lord Chancellor Lyndhurst, to the two Houses of Parliament: "His Majesty recommends that you should take into your deliberate consideration the whole condition of Ireland, AND THAT YOU SHOULD REVIEW THE LAWS WHICH IMPOSE CIVIL DISABILITIES ON HIS MAJESTY'S ROMAN CATHOLIC SUBJECTS."[1]

Lord Eldon lost no time in expressing his high disapprobation of the intentions thus announced. In the course of a long and animated speech, in opposition to the Address, he said,—

"I should betray my duty to my fellow-subjects, and to the principle of Protestantism as established at the Revolution—which it now appears was conducted by bigots in religion and politics (your Lordships will also permit me to say, *there may be bigots in liberality and laxity*)—if I do not protest against the proposed measure; if I do not raise my voice loudly and earnestly against it. Since the Bill of Rights, no measure so important has been submitted to Parliament by the ruling authority in the state. The barriers of our Constitution, then established, are to be broken down; and the law, the religion, and the liberty of the country are to be subverted. But, if the people

[1] 20 Parl. Deb., p. 4.

will rouse themselves, a hope still remains, and it shall not be my fault if they are not made conscious of the dangers which surround them. If I had a voice that would sound to the remotest corner of the empire, I would re-echo the principle, that, if ever a Roman Catholic is permitted to form part of the legislature of this country, or to hold any of the great executive offices of the Government, from that moment the SUN OF GREAT BRITAIN IS SET FOREVER. [*A laugh.*] My opinions may be received with contempt and derision—opprobrium may be heaped upon their author—but they shall not be stifled; and whatever calamities may befall the nation, it shall be known that there was one Englishman who boldly strove to avert them."[1]

There was no amendment moved to the Address—upon the understanding that every one was to be at liberty, on *reviewing* the laws which impose civil disabilities upon the Roman Catholics, to contend that they ought to be continued without any relaxation; and there was no trial of strength between the contending parties till the election for the University of Oxford—the result of which gave new spirit to the Anti-Catholics. When Mr. Peel chivalrously vacated his seat in the House of Commons, as representative for this learned body, it was at first proposed, out of compliment to the Protestant champion, to bring forward as a candidate his grandson, Lord Encombe, who naturally and laudably inherited his opinions, and had made himself very much respected while resident as an under-graduate. Lord Eldon thereupon wrote to him:—

"I am told, here, that some well-wishers had written to Oxford to think of you on the vacancy. This was entirely without my knowledge; for, though my warmest affections and best wishes will ever attend you, I should not have thought that such a proposition, at your standing and time of life, would do in opposition to Mr. Peel (if anything would do in opposition to him), and it is very essential that the attempt to change their member at Oxford should not fail. But infinite exertions of great men will be made for that purpose."

The young nobleman was gallantly ready to enter the lists, but, upon consideration, it was thought advisable to

[1] 20 Hansard, 15.

start an opponent to Mr. Peel of more experience and weight; and Sir Robert Inglis was selected—a thorough Church-and-King politician of the old school, who was universally beloved for his social qualities and genuine goodness of heart. This arrangement could not be censured by Lord Eldon; but it disconcerted him a little, and he wrote to his grandson:—

"I grieve that things have been so unluckily managed about Oxford. I quite approve of your consenting to be nominated; I think you did quite right. But I am very anxious to stand acquitted of any inattention to you. Since the idea was dismissed, I have been informed that people here thought of it, and now think that you might have succeeded, and that Sir R. I. will not. Your statement and conduct fully justify the conviction that, if you were ever in Parliament, you would oppose in the House of Commons the present Catholic measures. They will commence again there after Mr. P. for some place—Oxford or some other—is returned to Parliament."

It is well known that Mr. Peel was defeated at Oxford, and was driven to take refuge in Westbury. Lord Encombe was soon after returned for Truro, and he represented that place till after the passage of the Reform Bill, supporting his grandfather's principles with much steadiness and modesty.

The preliminary measure—to put down the Catholic Association—passed through both Chambers very quietly. Lord Eldon could not well offer it any opposition, although he knew to what it led; but he would not vote for it, and he absented himself when it was discussed in the House of Lords.

A war of petitions went on here for several weeks, while the Catholic Relief Bill was depending in the Lower House. Lord Eldon was supposed to have presented about a thousand against the measure, and in presenting them he made many speeches to explain and enforce the sentiments of the petitioners. In these skirmishes he seems generally to have had the advantage, though sometimes (according to his own phrase) "his head was put into Chancery." One petition which he presented was from the Company of Tailors at Glasgow. LORD LYNDHURST (aside, in a stage whisper, while sitting on the woolsack): "What! do the *tailors* trouble themselves about such *measures?*" LORD ELDON: " No wonder; you can't suppose that *tailors* like *turncoats.*" [*A laugh.*]

On another day, after presenting an immense number of petitions, he at last said, " I now hold in my hand, my Lords, another which I do not know how to treat. It is a petition signed by a great many ladies. I am not aware whether there be any precedent for admitting ladies as petitioners to your Lordships' House, but I will search the Journals, and see whether they have ever been prevented from remonstrating against measures which they consider injurious to the Constitution." LORD KING: " Will the noble and learned Earl inform the House, as it may materially influence your Lordships' decision, whether this petition expresses the sentiments of *young* or of *old* ladies?" LORD ELDON: " I can not answer the noble Lord as to the exact age of these petitioners; but of this I am sure, that there are many women, both young and old, who possess more knowledge of the Constitution, and more common sense, than some descendants of Lord Chancellors." [*A laugh.*]

Lord Eldon having on several occasions alluded to the inefficiency of oaths prescribed to Roman Catholics as a security to the Church, Lord Chancellor Lyndhurst, after ably vindicating them from the charge of refusing or disregarding oaths, thus proceeded: " The charge is not made in direct terms against the Roman Catholics; but my noble and learned friend did insinuate that the Roman Catholics are unwilling to swear that they will support the Protestant succession to the crown of these realms. My Lords, I deem it my imperative duty, considering the *insidious* manner in which these insinuations are thrown out day after day, not to suffer them to pass without notice. I maintain that the Roman Catholics of Ireland are ready to support the Constitution as strenuously as the Protestants of Great Britain. It is on account of my confidence in them that I will, by every means in my power, uphold the measure which my noble and learned friend so loudly condemns."

Lord Eldon, after answering at great length certain arguments of Lord Plunket, said, " I offer no answer, my Lords, to what has fallen from the noble and learned Lord on the woolsack. If that noble and learned Lord says that my honest opinions are uttered with an *insidious* design, my character—known to my country for more than fifty years—is, I feel, more than sufficient to repel so unfounded a charge."[1]

At last the bill was to be delivered, at the Bar of the House of Lords, into the hands of Lord Lyndhurst. The messengers of the Commons recollected that while he sat among them he had strenuously opposed the measure, and that he had been made Chancellor as an Anti-Catholic, yet they knew that he had seen the error of his ways. Accordingly, instead of the scornful grins and dark scowls which had formerly been witnessed on similar occasions in Lord Eldon's time, there was now a reciprocation of nods, and becks, and wreathed smiles, as the purse with the Great Seal was rested on the bar, and the announcement was made, "The Commons have passed a bill to relieve his Majesty's Roman Catholic subjects from their civil disabilities, to which they pray the concurrence of your Lordships." This message being gaily recited by the Chancellor, on his return to the woolsack, Lord Eldon shook his head and looked melancholy, having the worst anticipations of the result. Resolved, nevertheless, to do his duty, he opposed the first reading, although he did not divide upon it; and he made a struggle for postponing the second reading to a distant day. He was by no means satisfied with what "agitation" had yet done to stir up resistance to the measure, and was highly indignant at what he considered the general apathy. Thus he addressed Lady Frances:—

"The newspapers seem all employed in endeavoring to rouse the country to petition against the Roman Catholic relief measures, and the language those papers address to the public on this matter seems proof enough that the country cares very little about the matter. We fear there is a falling off in the Lords which will reduce the former majority. Some say, 'After what you have done for the Dissenters, the republicans, we won't vote against the Roman Catholics, who are, at least, friends to monarchy:' other lords say, 'We can't continue forever in a contest of the kind we have been so long engaged in: and though some folks tell us that there is a great Anti-Catholic feeling in the people, we perceive no signs of it; and it looks as if, ere long, the great body, who belong to the Estab-

[1] 20 Hansard, 1027-1042.

lished Church, will wake some morning from their sleep, and, hearing the news that the Roman Catholics have succeeded, will dispose of the matter with, Oh dear, who could have thought it?'"[1]

When the debate on the second reading came on, there was a contest between the Chancellor and the ex-Chancellor, which should have the advantage of following the other. The former, being often personally appealed to by Anti-Catholic speakers, was forced up, and outdid the ability of his admirable speech on the other side, for which he was supposed to have been a good deal indebted to the pamphlet of Dr. Philpotts. He now very boldly charged Lord Eldon with *inconsistency*, in having agreed to several bills giving benefits to Roman Catholics when he was Attorney General under Mr. Pitt; and more particularly with having made such an outcry against the Whig Bill in 1807, to allow Roman Catholics to hold commissions in the army, and afterwards, when he held the Great Seal, cordially agreeing to the very same measure. He then laid stress upon the fact that for a century after the Reformation, and during five Protestant reigns, Roman Catholic peers had been allowed to sit and vote in that House. LORD ELDON: "Did the noble and learned Lord know that fact last year?" LORD LYNDHURST (with most enviable coolness): "I must own, my Lords, that I did not; but I have since prosecuted my studies. I have advanced in knowledge and in wisdom, and perhaps my noble and learned friend might improve himself in the same way, and with the same result."

When Lord Eldon rose, he is said to have been much exhausted, and to have been suffering from a fit of the gout, but he still displayed spirit and energy. He retorted the charge of *inconsistency*, showing the rapid changes of his accuser under Lord Liverpool, Mr. Canning, and the Duke of Wellington. He added,—" I ceased to call the noble and learned Lord on the woolsack ' my noble and learned friend,' because he accused me of disingenuous insinuations and a designed mystification of the articles of the Union with Scotland—this the noble and learned Lord did in language which I felt to be extremely disre-

---

[1] This is somewhat like the prophecy in the reign of Charles II.: "We Protestants shall awake some morning, and find our throats all cut by the Papists."

spectful. But, if the noble and learned Lord can make up the difference between himself in the House of Commons and himself in this place respecting the present measure, I am ready to be reconciled to him, and to forget all that has passed. I feel, in making these remarks, that there is a sort of indecorum in such a dispute between a Chancellor and an ex-Chancellor, but I can not refrain from expressing my astonishment that the noble and learned Lord should attempt to show that he himself had been *consistent* by preferring a charge of *inconsistency* against me. I have read the speech of the Attorney General—not Sir Charles Wetherell, one of the most honest and independent men in the profession—but of the noble and learned Lord now on the woolsack, Attorney General in June last. From that speech I have drawn almost all the arguments I have used in defense of the Corporation and Test Acts, and to prove the ruinous consequences of the concessions now proposed. Since then there is no change in the circumstances of the country, although there is a great change in the circumstances of the noble and learned Lord. His sudden conversion may be sincere and disinterested, but surely he is not the man to taunt me with *inconsistency*. Laying my account to encounter obloquy while I was in office, I hoped to have escaped it when I retired into private life; but I regret to find that it is still thought a pleasant thing in Parliament to have a dash at the ex-Chancellor. This brings to my mind an anecdote which, though not perhaps well suited to this serious question, I will, with the patience of the House, take the liberty to mention. I was once at Buxton with my venerable friend Lord Thurlow, who went there for the benefit of the waters. I called on him one evening at the inn where he was residing, when he told me that he had heard there were six or eight persons in the house who meant to have a dash at the ex-Chancellor in the bath the next morning. I asked him what course he intended to take, and he replied prudently, 'that he meant to keep out of the way.' The misfortune is, I have not been able to keep out of the way of those who have been anxious to have a dash at me." [*Hear, and a laugh.*] He then referred to the different concessions to the Catholics to which he had assented, showing how trifling they were, "whereas the present sweeping measure was more monstrous than any Whig Government would have dared to propose."[1]—He did not explain how he came to support the very measure on which he had contrived to turn out "All the Talents."— After three nights' debate the second reading was carried by a large majority.

In the committee Lord Eldon was very pathetic upon the clause which dispensed with the necessity of an oath from Roman Catholics, *that the Pope has no spiritual jurisdiction within this realm.* "I beg your Lordships," said he, "to think indulgently of me, who have sworn over and over again—aye, forty times—that his Majesty has the supremacy now denied to him;—I beg your Lordships to think indulgently of me if I can not presume to take away a supremacy which has been recognized as an indisputable right of the Crown ever since the reign of Edward the Confessor. I can not—I will not—break the oath which I have taken." This reasoning was most undoubtedly fallacious, and Lord Eldon ought to have known that it was so. Lord Lyndhurst strongly animadverted upon it, and intimated that Lord Eldon had been arguing against his better knowledge: "Now, my Lords," continued he, "are we to be overborne by the talent, the learning, and the name of the noble and learned Lord, who comes down here and deals with subjects of so much importance in this way?" LORD ELDON: "My Lords, the authorities would, I think, fully support my reasoning. I have now been twenty-nine years in this House, and have on all public questions spoken my opinions—sometimes perhaps in language too strong—but always with sincerity;—and I have now to tell the noble and learned Lord on the woolsack that I never borne down the House, and I will not now be borne down by him nor twenty such."[2]

The Duke of Wellington having moved the third reading of the bill,

"Lord Eldon addressed the House,—probably, he said, for the last time. After five-and-twenty years of conscientious opposition to measures like the present, he was anxious to take this final opportunity of stating his opinion and the grounds of it. He assured the House that after this bill should have passed, strong and deep-rooted as were his objections to it, he should feel it his duty to

[1] 21 Hansard, 41–394. [2] 21 Hansard, 468–619.

endeavor, by every means in his power, to soothe down the agitation which it had created, to let his countrymen know that it was their duty to obey the laws, however they might have been opposed to them while in their progress through Parliament. It was not his desire—God forbid!—to add in any way whatever to the agitation which he knew existed in the country, to an extent at which he was affrighted. He would be satisfied to pass the remainder of his days in retirement from public life—satisfied that during the many years in which he had been engaged in public life he had endeavored to do his duty, and that he had done it sincerely and conscientiously in opposing the present bill. During a long course of years he had considered the nature and tendency of such a bill as this with all the attention in his power; and though he admitted that consistency in error was one of the greatest blots which could attach to the character of a statesman,—and though he should be ashamed to claim credit for consistency in any opinion if he could for an instant see that it was one which he could not justify,—yet, with every disposition to discover the error in his opinion, if error there was, he had considered this question over and over again in every possible point of view; and after all that consideration, he would say that, so help him God! he would rather perish that moment than give his consent to the bill before their Lordships. He thought this bill the most dangerous that had ever been presented to the consideration of Parliament. Could it be a matter of pleasure or of comfort to him to stand in the situation he did, in opposition to the noble Duke and those other friends from whom he now differed so widely on this point? He owned it would have given him pleasure to support them, if he could have done so conscientiously."

After reviewing, and insisting upon, the settlement made of the Constitution by the Revolution of 1688 and the Act of Union with Scotland, and indicating his doubts respecting the fitness of the Irish enfranchisement which was intended to accompany this relief bill, he protested against the present measure as fraught with ruin to the purest Church and the purest system of Christianity which the world had ever seen. Thus he concluded, with much emotion:—

"I believe that I know something of the Catholic clergy,

and of their feelings towards our Protestant Church; and though it is late in life for me to alter my opinion, I should be willing to think better of them if I could. But I do declare, my Lords, that I would rather hear at this moment that to-morrow my existence was to cease—an illustration, however, which I put as of no great force, since I should look upon that event as anything but an affliction—than to awake to the reflection that I had consented to an act which had stamped me as a violator of my solemn oath, a traitor to my Church, and a traitor to the Constitution!"

Nevertheless, the third reading was carried by a majority of 213 to 109.[1] A strong protest against it, which Lord Eldon drew, was signed by him and many other peers.

Nothing more could be done within the walls of Parliament; but, in his zeal, he was determined to act upon the doctrine he had promulgated—that the King, if he personally disapproved of the bill, ought to put his veto upon it, although it had passed both Houses. Accordingly he had two audiences of George IV.,—to present petitions praying that his Majesty would withhold the royal assent from the bill,—and to advise him to comply with this prayer. The attempt was by no means a desperate one, for the King, notwithstanding his early prepossessions in favor of the Roman Catholics, had of late years formed a strong opinion against removing their disabilities; and, although he had given in writing a promise to support this bill, he he had been told that such a promise was contrary to his coronation oath, and was not binding. The ex-Chancellor alone thought that he could reject the bill on his own scruples, without the advice of responsible Ministers; but a plan was pointed out to him for rejecting the bill constitutionally,—for he might dismiss his present Ministers,—call in others who had a due respect for the Protestant Establishment,—and, saying *Le Roi s'avisera*, he might dissolve Parliament; there might be a rebellion in Ireland, but the 'No Popery cry' was now so strong in Great Britain that he might safely rely upon a Protestant House of Commons being returned, who would save the Church, if the Empire should be dismembered.

We have, from Lord Eldon's own pen, a very interesting account of these conferences. Of the first, which took

[1] 21 Hansard, 619–697.

place on the 28th of March, and lasted four hours, he says,
—" His Majesty employed a very considerable portion of
his time in stating all that he represented to have passed
when Mr. Canning was made Minister, and expressly stated
that Mr. C. would never, and that he had engaged that he
would never, allow him to be troubled about the Roman
Catholic question. He blamed all the Ministers who had
retired upon C.'s appointment; represented, in substance,
that their retirement, and not he, had made C. Minister.
He excepted from this blame, in words, myself."—The
memorandum, after using the freedom to question this
representation respecting the appointment of Mr. Canning
as Prime Minister, goes on with the grievances suffered
by his Majesty from the Duke of Wellington:—

" That, at the time the Administration was formed, no
reason was given him to suppose that any measures for
the relief of the Roman Catholics were intended or
thought of by Ministers—that he had frequently himself
suggested the absolute necessity of putting down the
Roman Catholic Association, of suspending the Habeas
Corpus Act, to destroy the powers of the most seditious
and rebellious proceedings of the members of it, and particularly at the time that Lawless made his march,—that
instead of following what he had so strongly recommended,
after some (the exact time I can not recollect that he
mentioned, but some) time, not a very long time, before
the present session, he was applied to to allow his Ministers to propose to him, as an united Cabinet, the opening
the Parliament by sending such a message as his speech
contained:—that, after much struggling against it, and
after the measure had been strongly pressed upon him as
of absolute necessity, he had consented that the Protest-
tant members of his Cabinet, if they could so persuade
themselves to act, might join in such a representation to
him, but that he would not then, nor in his recommendation to Parliament, pledge himself to anything. He
repeatedly mentioned that he represented to his Ministers
the infinite pain it gave him to consent even so far as
that. . . . .

" He complained that he had never seen the bills—that
the condition of Ireland had not been taken into consideration—that the Association Bill had been passed through
both Houses before he had seen it—that it was a very

inefficient measure compared to those which he had, in vain, himself recommended—that the other proposed measures gave him the greatest possible pain and uneasiness—that he was in the state of a person with a pistol presented to his breast—that he had nothing to fall back upon—that his Ministers had threatened (I think he said twice, at the time of my seeing him) to resign if the measures were not proceeded in, and that he had said to them, 'Go on,' when he knew not how to relieve himself from the state in which he was placed :—and that in one of those meetings, when resignation was threatened, he was urged to the sort of consent he gave, by what passed in the interview between him and his Ministers, till the interview and the talk had brought him into such a state, that he hardly knew what he was about, when he, after several hours, said 'Go on.'—He then repeatedly expressed himself as in a state of the greatest misery; repeatedly saying, 'What can I do? I have nothing to fall back upon;' and musing for some time, and then again repeating the same expression. . . . .

"In this day's audience, his Majesty did not show me many papers that he showed me in the second. I collected, from what passed in the second, that his consent to go on was in writings then shown to me. After a great deal of time spent" (still in the first interview), "in which his Majesty was sometimes silent—apparently uneasy—occasionally stating his distress—the hard usage he had received—his wish to extricate himself;—that he had not what to look to—what to fall back upon;—that he was miserable beyond what he could express—I asked him whether his Majesty, so frequently thus expressing himself, meant either to enjoin me, or to forbid me, considering or trying whether anything could be found or arranged, upon which he *could* fall back. He said, 'I neither enjoin you to do so, nor forbid you to do so; but, for God's sake, take care that I am not exposed to the humiliation of being again placed in such circumstances, that I must submit again to pray of my present Ministers that they will remain with me.' He appeared to me to be exceedingly miserable, and intimated that he would see me again.

"I was not sent for afterwards, but went on Thursday, the 9th April, with more addresses. In the second interview, which began a little before two o'clock, the King repeatedly, and with some minutes interposed between his such repeated declarations, musing in silence in the interim, expressed his anguish, and pain, and misery, that the measure had ever been thought of, and as often declared that he had been most harshly and cruelly treated—that he had been treated as a man whose consent had been asked with a pistol pointed to his breast; or as obliged, if he did not give it, to leap down from a five-pair of stairs window. What could he do? What had he to fall back upon? . . . .

"I told him that his late Majesty, when he did not mean that a measure proposed to him should pass, expressed his determination in the most early stage of the business. If it seemed to himself necessary to dissent, he asked no advice about dismissing his Ministers. He made that his own act. He trusted to what he had to hope for from his subjects, who—when he had placed himself in such circumstances, and protected them from the violence of party, if party, meaning to be violent, should get uppermost—could not leave him unsupported. That, on the other hand, there could not but be great difficulties in finding persons willing to embark in office, when matters had proceeded to the extent to which the present measures had been carried—as was supposed and had been *represented—after full explanation of them to his Majesty*, and he had so far assented.

"This led to his mentioning again what he had to say as to his assent. In the former interview it had been represented that, after much conversation *twice* with his Ministers, or such as had come down, he had said, 'Go on;' and upon the latter of *those two* occasions, after many hours' fatigue, and exhausted by the fatigue of conversation, he had *said*, 'Go on.' He now produced *two papers*, which he represented as copies of what he had written to them, *in which he assents to their proceeding and going on with the bill*, adding certainly in each, as he read them, very strong expressions of the pain and misery the proceedings gave him. It struck me at the time that I should, if I had been in office, have felt considerable difficulty about going on after reading such expressions; but whatever might be fair observation as to giving, or not, effect to those expressions, *I told his Majesty it was impossible to maintain that his assent had not been expressed*, or to cure the evils which were consequential—after the bill, in such circumstances, had been read a second time, and in the Lord's House, with a majority of 105. This led him to much conversation upon that fact, that he had, he said, been deserted by an aristocracy that had supported his father; that instead of forty-five against the measure, there were twice that number of peers for it; that everything was revolutionary, everything was tending to revolution, and the peers and the aristocracy were giving way to it. They (he said more than once or twice more) supported his father; but see what they had done to *him*. I took the liberty to say that I agreed that matters were rapidly tending to revolution; that I had long thought that this measure of Catholic emancipation was meant to be and would certainly be a step towards producing it; that it was avowed as such with the Radicals in 1724, 1725, and 1726; that many of the Catholic Association were understood to have been engaged in all the transactions in Ireland in 1798; and what had they not been threatening to do if this measure was not carried, and even if it was carried? But I thought it only just to some of the peers who voted for the bill, to suppose that they had been led, or misled, to believe that his Majesty had agreed and consented to it.

"He then began to talk about the coronation oath. On that I could only repeat what I before said, if his Majesty meant me to say anything upon the subject. Understanding that he did so wish, I repeated that, as far as his oath was concerned, it was a matter between him, God, and his conscience, whether giving his royal assent to this measure was 'supporting, to the utmost of his power, the Protestant reformed religion.' That it was not my opinion, nor the opinions of the archbishops, bishops, or lay peers (*all which he must know*, as well the opinions in favor of the measure as those against it), that were to guide and govern him; but he was to act according to his own conscientious view of the obligations under which such an oath placed him.

"Little more passed, except occasional bursts of expression: 'What can I do? What can I now fall back upon? What can I fall back upon? I am miserable, wretched; my situation is dreadful; nobody about me to advise with. If I do give my assent, I'll go to the baths abroad, and from thence to Hanover. I'll return no more to England; I'll make no Roman Catholic peers; I will not do what this bill will enable me to do; I'll return no more; let them get a Catholic king in Clarence.' I think he also mentioned Sussex. 'The people will see that I did not wish this.'

"There were the strongest appearances certainly of misery. He more than once stopped my leaving him. When the time came that I was to go, he threw his arms around my neck and expressed great misery. I left him about twenty minutes or a quarter before five.

"I certainly thought, when I left him, that he would express great difficulty, when the bill was proposed for the royal assent (great, but which would be overcome), about giving it. I fear that it seemed to be given as a matter of course."

Lord Eldon's hopes had been high, but when the commission for giving the royal assent to the bill came down to Windsor, the King had not the courage to refuse to sign it,—and, on the 13th of April,—instead of "*Le Roi s'avisera*,"—the words were pronounced over it, "*Le Roi le veut.*'—Next day Lord Eldon wrote to his daughter :—

" (April 14th, 1829.)

"The fatal bill received the royal assent yesterday afternoon. After all I had heard in my visits, not a day's delay! God bless us, and His Church!"

He had the poor consolation of finding that the King had acted contrary to his own strong inclination, and that he was much enraged against his Ministers and their supporters:

Soon after, the ex-Chancellor wrote to Lady Frances :—

"I went to the levée in conseqence of a communication that it was much desired that I should do so by the King. I was grieved that my visit was a visit of duty to a Sovereign whose supremacy is shared by that Italian priest, as Shakspeare calls the Pope. But I heard that he much wished it, and I understood that it would be a relief if I would go. I was certainly received with a very marked attention. I followed those who are in the high places of office, to whom one bow was made. When I was about to pass, expecting the same slight notice, he took me by the hand and shook it heartily, speaking with great kindness. It was very much remarked that he showed to the late minority a degree of attention not manifested to those who, I understand, he much complained of, as having forced him to the late disastrous measure. I have been told this morning, that, at his dinner, he expressed great pleasure at having had his friend Lord Eldon by the hand at his levée. . . . .

" He is certainly very wretched about the late business. It is a pity he has not the comfort of being free from blame himself. The ladies to-day are swarming to the drawing-room: but I don't go to-day, my visit of yesterday being occasioned by particular circumstances, which I have mentioned."

. . . . . .

" The universal talk here is about the manner in which the King, at the levée, received the voters for the Catholics—most uncivilly—markedly so towards the Lords spiritual, the Bishops who so voted,—and the civility with which he received the Anti-Catholic voters, particularly the Bishops. It seems to be very general talk now, that his Ministers went much beyond what they should have said in Parliament as to his consent to the measure. Consent, however, he certainly did; but with a language of reluctance, pain, and misery, which, if it had been represented, would have prevented a great deal of that ratting which carried the measure.

" The Duke of Cumberland dined with me yesterday. No company but Mamma and Bessy."

The following is his last letter upon the subject, containing prophecies which I hope never will be verified:—

" If your scrap, laudatory of your father, which came in your letter, is not returned in this, you may be assured it will be returned in some other epistle. I fought as well I could, but I am not what I was; and I never was what a statesman—an accomplished statesman—ought to be. Indeed, a lawyer hardly can be both learned in his profession and accomplished in political science. The country will feel—deeply feel—the evils arising from this late measure. Not that those evils will be felt in its immediate effects. Those in whose favor the measure has taken place are too wary—far too wary—to give an alarm immediately; but few years will pass before its direful effects will be made manifest in the ruin of some of our most sacred, and most reverenced, and most useful establishments."

Had the measure been carried as proposed by Mr. Pitt, in 1801, at the time of the Union, it would have been safe and efficacious. The long delay certainly impaired its healing tendency, and rendered it dangerous by the example of successful agitation; but we may yet hope to see Protestants and Roman Catholics enjoying equal rights, and equally attached to the Constitution.

Those who differ in opinion with Lord Eldon on the question of Catholic Emancipation must respect the sincerity and admire the energy with which he opposed it. There is no ground for imputing to him any fanatical attachment to Protestantism, or horror of Popery. He viewed it much more as a political than as a religious question, and his great object was to prevent power from passing into the hands of those whom he thought would abuse it. In the fervor of his Anti-Catholic zeal, and when actually within hearing of the Bishops, he persisted in the habit of profane swearing, to which he, along with most of his contemporaries, was addicted. "In one of the debates on the Catholic question," says Lord Byron, "when we were either equal or within one (I forget which), I had been sent for in great haste to a ball, which I quitted, I confess, somewhat reluctantly, to emancipate five millions of people. I came in late, and did not go immediately into the body of the House, but stood just behind the woolsack. Lord Eldon turned round, and catching my eye, immediately said to a peer who had come to him for a few minutes on the woolsack, as is the custom of his friends, 'D—n them! they'll have it now! By G—, the vote that is just come in will give it them!'"[1]

The noble poet afterwards, in some lines which he wrote as a continuation of the "Devil's Walk," showed that he had taken a very unfavorable view of the ex-Chancellor's feelings and wishes on this subject:—

> "And he saw the tears in Eldon's eyes,
> Because the Catholics would not rise,
> In spite of his tears and his prophecies."

But, in truth, I believe the noble and learned Lord was

---

[1] Moore's Life of Byron.

well pleased to find that his prophecies were falsified. Thus he very good-humoredly refers to one of them:—

"I don't know what state you are in, in London, but here, one should think that a second deluge has been ordained: and a tenant of mine, of a house in Kingston here, says, 'It is all owing to the bill in favor of the Romans:' like unto what was reported of a maid-servant of Lady Goderich, who, complaining of wet weather, was informed by the servant, 'Why, madam, you know that Lord Eldon said, if the bill passed, THE SUN OF GREAT BRITAIN WAS SET FOREVER.'"[1]

Meanwhile, he was the idol of the Anti-Catholic party throughout the United Kingdom. For his extraordinary exertions in the cause, he received the freedom of Dublin, Cork, Bristol, Exeter, and many other cities and corporations; many children were named after him by pious parents; addresses were sent to him from bodies of the clergy, hailing him as the truest friend of the Church; a school was endowed at Vauxhall "to commemorate his able, zealous, and constant defense of the Protestant reformed religion against every innovation;" and the "Eldon Law Scholarship" was founded by a munificent subscription in the University of Oxford.

I am glad to relate that, by an administration of reciprocal flattery, the sharp disputes between the Chancellor and the ex-Chancellor, which had arisen during the discussions on the Catholic Relief Bill, were adjusted, and they were again designated the "noble and learned friends" of each other. Towards the conclusion of the session, during a debate on the bill for the appointment of an additional equity judge, Lord Lyndhurst said, very handsomely,—

"I owe it to the noble and learned Lord to observe, that the same evil exists, to the same extent, in my time, as it existed in his. It is impossible for me,—notwithstanding the political differences which now divide us,—it is impossible for me, I say, having once mentioned the name of that noble and learned Lord, not to add, that no man, sitting on the same bench which he so long filled, and considering the nature of his decisions, can refrain from admiring his profound sagacity, his great erudition, and his extraordinary attainments. It has been often

---

[1] Letter from Encombe to Lady Frances Bankes, Sept. 1829.

said in the profession, that no one ever doubted his decrees except the noble and learned Lord himself. I am sure, from the short opportunity which I have had of judging of them, that none of his predecessors ever had a more complete command of the whole complicated system of equity than that noble and learned personage. I therefore feel myself bound to say, that I do not ascribe the delays which have taken place in the Court of Chancery to the noble Earl, but to the system established in that Court. I say that there has *never* been sufficient power in the judge, to dispose of causes when ready for hearing, since the first establishment of the Court of Chancery."

Lord Eldon, after requesting that time might be allowed for a due consideration of the measure, adverted to the complimentary language employed by the Lord Chancellor, and said, that "whatever might have been the political differences between himself and the noble Lord, he was not the person unwilling to be reconciled; particularly when more had been said in his praise then he deserved. He had, indeed, done all in his power to administer justice with industry, diligence, and fidelity: beyond that, he must claim no credit."—Further, in reference to the narrow-minded notions of some Chancery practitioners, that the present Chancellor was unfit for the woolsack because he had not been brought up to draw bills and answers in an equity-draughtsman's office, the ex-Chancellor emphatically said, "SOME JUDGES FROM THE COMMON LAW COURTS HAVE FORMED *almost* AS GOOD JUDGES IN CHANCERY AS ANY THAT EVER SAT IN THAT COURT."[1]—Lawyers' are like lovers' quarrels.

CHAPTER CCX.

CONTINUATION OF THE LIFE OF LORD ELDON TILL AFTER THE PASSING OF THE REFORM BILL.

A LULL succeeded the tempest created by the Catholic Relief Bill; and the session which commenced in February, 1830, was comparatively quiet. The only measure on which Lord Eldon took a prominent

[1] 21 Hansard, 1274, 1492.

part, was the excellent bill prepared by Sir James Scarlett, then Attorney General, for abolishing the jurisdiction of the Courts of Great Sessions in Wales,—for increasing the number of the Judges in the Courts at Westminster,—for enabling these Judges to go circuits in Wales, as in England,—and for introducing several other palpable improvements in the administration of justice. This was of course opposed by Lord Eldon. Although Welsh judgeships, from being considered political appointments, had produced a very demoralizing effect among lawyers in the House of Commons, and the Welsh Courts were almost unanimously condemned as inefficient, insomuch that some said landed property in Wales was worth several years' purchase less than in England on account of the consequent insecurity of title,—he gallantly defended them, because they had both a legal and an equitable jurisdiction—asserting that they had long satisfactorily brought home justice to the doors of the inhabitants of the Principality.[1] However, he did not venture to divide against the bill, being afraid of walking out alone.

But, his courage rising, he did call for a division against the bill for appointing a new Vice-Chancellor;—when the Autocrat who for a quarter of a century dictated the decisions of the House of Lords found himself in a minority of *four!* [2]

This was his last appearance in the House of Lords during the reign of George IV. There had been no intercourse between him and his "young master" since his appearance at the levée on the passing of the Roman Catholic Relief Bill,—and after a burst of ill-humor, his Majesty had become entirely reconciled to the Ministers who advised that measure. Lord Eldon was deeply hurt at finding himself neglected by him whom he had faithfully counselled on many trying occasions; but he never, for supposed wrongs to himself, relaxed from his loyal attachment to the person as well as the authority of the Sovereign. He was greatly distressed by the accounts now received from Windsor, indicating that a demise of the Crown could not be far distant; and he assisted in suggesting amendments to the bill allowing the use of a stamp for the King's signature, to be applied to documents which, by the ordinary law, required the sign manual.

[1] 22 Hansard, 925. 23 Ib. 829.   [2] 24 Ib. 1128.

He was comforted by observing that some symptons of a coalition between the existing Ministry and the Whigs, which had alarmed him very unnecsssarily,[1] now entirely disappeared, and that a pure Tory Government was likely to be restored in the new reign. Although the "early friends" had continued excluded from *office*, he complained that during the latter years of George IV. they had been in the enjoyment of *power*;—and he yet hoped to live to see the day when an effectual check should be given to innovation,—libels should be again prosecuted with due severity,—and, in case of any danger to the public peace, he might rejoice in the suspension of the "Habeas Corpus Act" and in other wholesome measures of coercion. The heir to the throne, on whose vow he had fondly relied, was gone; but although he had no personal acquaintance with the Duke of Clarence, who was next in succession, he had good hopes of him from the part which his Royal Highness had formerly taken along with himself in defending the slave trade.[2]

On the 26 of June George IV. expired—not very deeply regretted by any class or any party in the state. Possessing great natural advantages, both of person and of intellect, along with his exalted rank,—if he could have exercised self-control, he might have been respected and

---

[1] In June, 1829, he had written to Lady Frances Banks,—"We understand that Lord Rosslyn is to be Privy Seal. It is believed that the wish was to have Lord Grey; but *that* not being likely to be agreed to by the King, they took Rosslyn as another Whig." He had likewise been much perturbed by the appointment of Mr. Abercromby, a notorious Whig, as Lord Chief Baron of the Court of Exchequer in Scotland.

[2] However, it would appear that his Royal Highness had spoken very slightingly of the fast friend of the Duke of Cumberland. Lord Eldon, only a year or two before his own death declared that he had never conversed with William IV. except twice,—adding this curious anecdote of the SAILOR KING:—"I went with Dr. Grey, the late Bishop of Bristol, to present an address. After it had been presented, as I was passing, the King stopped me, and said, 'My Lord, political parties and feelings have run very high, and I am afraid I have made observations upon your Lordship which now——' I immediately said, 'I entreat your Majesty's pardon; a subject must not hear the language of apology from the lips of his Sovereign,'—and passed on."—*Twiss*, ch. iii. It must be very hazardous to criticise the *tact* of such a consummate master of courtly arts; but to the uninitiated it would seem better if the *Subject* had not abruptly stopped the *Sovereign*, and, assuming superiority, prevented him from finishing a prepared speech, which might have been as pointed as that of James II., when he said that "a King of England must not remember the quarrels of a Duke of York."

beloved—but, giving way to every inclination and caprice, he disgusted his subjects by an utter disgregard of the duties of domestic life, and he displayed no firmness in maintaining any principles of government. The glories of his Regency the people ascribed to the happy auspices of the King, still supposed to be on the throne; from the time that he began to reign in his own right, he had been engaged in the unhappy contest with his wife; and of late years, shut up in his palace, and as much as possible shunning the public gaze, he had been regarded as a heartless voluptuary.

At the accession of William IV. there was general joy, from his popular manners, his straightforward character, and the appellation given to him of the " Sailor King." Lord Eldon, who had been the Chancellor of the two preceding Sovereigns, was in hopes that he should have been specially noticed at the commencement of the new reign, and probably restored to the Cabinet.

The Great Seal, I really believe, he now would have declined, *unless it had been forced upon him;* but he would still have been highly pleased to be President of the Council. He had the satisfaction to observe that William at first showed no inclination for the Whigs; but at the same time he was disappointed and mortified in finding that he himself was not sent for to be consulted at Court, and that his old colleagues seemed entirely to stand aloof from him. Under these circumstances he entered fully into the feelings of the other leaders of the Ultra-Protestant party, who deeply resented what they called the *treachery* of the Duke of Wellington and Mr. Peel respecting the Catholic question, and, exclaiming "NUSQUAM TUTA FIDES!" vowed revenge,—even at the risk of the Whigs being for a time being admitted to office. He believed that this must be a short-lived evil, and he declared that an obnoxious party, whose bad principles were avowed, would be less formidable to the Church than her pretended friends.

An opportunity soon arose for our ex-Chancellor to show his propensities; and, for the first time in his life, he was heard londly cheering the leader of the Whigs.

In answer to William IV.'s maiden message, recommending the two Houses to enter upon no new business, and to wind up that which was already before them as soon as possible, as his Majesty intended speedily to dissolve Parliament,—the Duke of Wellington having proposed an address of acquiescence, Lord Grey pointed out the propriety of forthwith passing a Regency Bill, on the ground that, before a new Parliament could assemble, there might be a demise of the Crown,—and in that event (so much to be deprecated, in the present state of the royal family) the greatest public confusion might arise.[1] Suggesting that the subject had entirely escaped the attention of the Government, he moved that the debate be adjourned, to give time for consideration. This was opposed by Lord Chancellor Lyndhurst, who pointed out the improbability of such a misfortune, and said: " If it should unfortunately happen, on the accession of an infant to the throne, the same course would be adopted as on that of a Sovereign of mature years. Proclamation would be made of the accession of the new Sovereign in the same form which their Lordshids had witnessed a few days before. The infant would have the power of continuing or changing Ministers, and the same responsibility would rest upon them as at present."

Lord Eldon: " I feel it to be my duty to support the amendment of the noble Earl. If it be supposed that I have any objection to an early appeal to the people, in order to give them an opportunity of expressing what they think of the conduct of Government, there can not be a greater mistake. I wish that the people enjoyed such an opportunity this very night, if it were compatible with the safety of the state. If the people are satisfied with the conduct of the present Government, they ought to have an immediate opportunity of expressing that satisfaction. If perchance they are dissatisfied, they should also have the like opportunity of declaring their feelings. I have heard a great deal, by report, of dissatisfaction among the people at the late measures of the Government, and of its expression in words; I should wish them to have an opportunity of showing it by acts; if it is expressed only in words, and not by acts, I would

---

[1] William IV. had no surviving child by his Queen, but she might still have been expected to bring children. The heir presumptive was the Princess Alexandrine Victoria, daughter of the Duke of Kent (her present Majesty), then in her eleventh year.

say they had better hold their tongues, and be contented. But the safety of the state is compromised by this hurried dissolution. The arguments of the noble Duke, and of my noble and learned friend on the woolsack, are all in favor of the amendment. They rely upon the acts of William III. and Queen Anne, which continue the existence of Parliament for six months after a demise of the Crown; but these acts prove the necessity for the contingencies arising in the new reign being immediately provided for. I have listened, with some surprise, to the observations made upon an infant Sovereign coming to the throne—a little King that one may dandle and play with. I agree with my noble and learned friend, that this occurrence may not be disagreeable to the Minister who happens then to be in office, for he is converted into the Sovereign. For my own part, if I were Prime Minister, there is nothing I should like more. It would, no doubt, be much more convenient than to have a Sovereign who would not submit to dictation. THE NOBLE DUKE KNOWS VERY WELL TO WHAT I ALLUDE.[1] But I ask your Lordships whether, if an infant Sovereign is likely to be on the throne, some provision ought not to be made beforehand for the administration of the government. If an infant Sovereign were to be on the throne, whose head, if he were laid in the integument which covers the head of my noble and learned friend, could not be seen over it, he would, by a fiction of law in favor of royalty, be supposed to have as much sense, knowledge, and experience as if he had reached the age of three score and ten; but, admitting the truth of the supposition in a constitutional sense, is it unreasonable to ask that there should be some party acting for the Sovereign during what may be termed his natural, though not his political, minority? There is yet another case, for which it is the duty of Parliament to make some provision—the supposition of a successor to the throne, though not yet visible, being in existence at the demise of the Crown. Cases in some respects analogous are of no uncommon occurrence. I will suppose, for example, that another Guy Fawkes should succeed in blowing up this House, and that my noble and learned

---

[1] I am sure I do not know to what he alludes; for the Duke, while Prime Minister to George IV., had carried everything his own way; and upon the Catholic question the King had at last submitted implicitly to his advice.

friend on the woolsack, destined to another end, is the only one who escapes; I know that, before writs are issued to those who are to succeed many of your Lordships, my noble and learned friend would have to inquire whether such of your Lordships as had no children born had left widows, and whether those widows were in that state which offered a prospect of an heir. If they were, no writ of summons to a collateral could issue until that question is decided by the birth of an heir; and till such time has elapsed, to put the question of issue beyond doubt, he would have to ascertain whether there was any little peer, not then visible—but who might be so in due course of time—and until that was determined, the title would be, as it were, in abeyance. Now, would it not, à fortiori, be still more necessary to institute the same inquiry in case of the event to which allusion has been made? Is it not necessary to make some provision for such a contingency, which is, in present circumstances, by no means a remote one? In any measure adopted after a demise of the Crown, in case none be adopted before, it would be necessary to have recourse to the authority of some party exercising the power of the Sovereign. There must be a real or a phantom King; and it is just the same in principle whether this little King is not able to speak or walk, or whether he is only *en ventre sa mère*. To prevent the difficulty to which this would give rise, recourse should be had to the authority of a Regent, who is really, as well as constitutionally, able to exercise the prerogatives of the Crown. So convinced am I that some early provision should be made for such a contingency, that I must vote for the amendment of the noble Earl."[1]

Upon a division, there appeared, for the amendment, 56; against it, 100; but Lord Eldon carried with him,

[1] 25 Hansard, 740. In his zeal to embarrass the Government, he mis-states. for he could hardly misapprehend, the constitutional doctrine upon this subject. If a peer dies, leaving his widow *enceinte*, most undoubtedly the peerage would be in abeyance; but the public safety does not allow this doctrine to apply to the Crown, which cannot be in abeyance. If a childless King were to die, leaving his widow *enceinte*, the next collateral heir would mount the throne *ad interim*,—his title being defeasible by the Queen giving birth to a child; whereupon he would descend from the throne, and the child would be proclaimed King. This doctrine was fully recognized on the death of William IV., when we swore allegiance to her present Majesty Queen Victoria, " saving the rights of any issue of his late Majesty King William IV., which may be born of his late Majesty's consort." See stat. 1 Will. 4, c. 2

into the minority, the Duke of Newcastle, and the Earls of Winchelsea, of Harrowby, of Carnarvon, and of Mansfield, with other Tory peers, and this was felt as a heavy blow to the Government.[1]

The dissolution soon after followed, and the different parties struggled eagerly to strengthen themselves in the Parliament by which the complexion of the new reign was to be determined. William IV. had already made himself very popular by his frankness and condescending affability to all classes of his subjects, and it was understood that, without personal antipathies or partialities, he was resolved to rule on constitutional principles.

On account of the impaired state of Lady Eldon's health, which required the best medical advice, Lord Eldon remained with her in London during the whole of this summer and autumn—having his sad, listless hours a little enlivened by the stirring political events which were going on, both at home and abroad. The feelings with which he surveyed these, we learn from his letters to different members of his family. On the dissolution, he wrote:—

"All the world here is engaged about elections and contests, of which it is said there will be a vast many, and I hear that seats in the next Parliament are very high-priced indeed—much beyond any price in former Parliaments. So much for corruption!"[2]

The returns to the House of Commons proving favorable to the Liberal side, Lord Eldon was very indignant, and thus he vented his spleen in a letter to Mr. Surtees:—

"If the injury done to the Established Church and the religion professed in it can be repaired, God grant that it

---

[1] 25 Hansard, 767.
[2] In the same letter he refers sneeringly to what I think was a rational taste of William IV.—to see congregated before him particular classes of the great functionaries of the state, as "all the Judges," &c. :—

"Our lord the King came to the Chapel Royal yesterday, to take the Sacrament, as the proof that he is in communion with the Established Church. He took great pains to secure the attendance of the Archbishops, and laid his wishes before, if not commands upon, them, to bring all the Bishops they could muster."

Soon after he wrote, rather harshly, "I hear the condescensions of the K. are beginning to make him unpopular. In that station such familiarity must produce the destruction of respect. If the people don't continue to think the King somewhat more than a man, they will soon find out that he is not an object of that high respect which is absolutely necessary to the utility of his character."

may be! The great calamity of the times is, that the conduct of some men—perhaps more especially of Bishops —while it has shaken public confidence in all public men —has worked still more evil by inducing many to take it for granted that men do not really believe the doctrines they preach.

"The passage in the K.'s last speech—although the Catholic Relief Bill, probably, never *will* be revoked— which declares that bill to be *irrevocable*, is one of the most impudent and unconstitutional passages that a Minister ever ventured to advise his Master to utter. The Parliament that could revoke the settlement of 1688 surely *can*, if it be right, revoke that of 1829!

"What is to happen in France who can tell? There is a very considerable republican party in that kingdom, and, if the royalists, who, by the way, are not agreed who shall be King, should quarrel—whether Orleans or Bourdeaux—and the republicans should get uppermost—the kings, in countries neighboring upon France, may tremble. I fear we shall soon hear of such scenes passing in Spain and Portugal—perhaps in the Netherlands—as have taken place in France.

"In nine places out of ten—I am afraid the proportion may be greater—the electors who petitioned, in the very strongest language, against the Catholic Relief Bill have again re-elected the very same members, who voted, to their *most strongly avowed* dissatisfaction, for that very bill. Be assured the electors of this kingdom are, to say the least, as corrupt—I think more so—than their members elected;—nobody votes but as it serves his own interest to vote.

"All my prophecies as to what was to happen in this country have been realized—I forsee great increasing miseries probably to happen, and at no very distant period.

"Hume member for the great metropolitan county of Middlesex! Brougham for the great county of York! Neither with an acre of land!!!"

The "Three days of July" placed Louis Phillippe, the Citizen King, on the throne of the Bourbons—to surround Paris with fortresses, and for a time to enjoy more authority than any hereditary Sovereign of France since the time of Louis XIV. Lord Eldon displayed much sagacity by foreseeing the consequences of this revolution, both in France and in England:—

"19th August, 1830.

"To get a thorough insight into the effect of the French Revolution here, you have only to read the proceedings at meetings in London, and all that is stated in them. It will require a master head, such as Pitt had and nobody now has in this country, to allay what is brewing, a storm for changes here, especially for Reform in Parliament. Everybody here seems to think that the borough members of Parliament can scarcely be preserved until another Parliament. Such a change, considering that the present system is the support of a floating aristocracy, must, if it takes place, deeply affect the higher orders, and perhaps the monarchy itself. My head is full of thought upon this sebject. I care not who rules, provided our system of government can be preserved."

"23rd August, 1830.

"The Frenchmen are making, what can't long exist, a Republican Government, with a King at the head of it. They will soon find that such things can't co-exist, and revolution has not yet done its work in that country, I persuade myself."

"1st September.

"Marmont, who has been in London, has declared that he had no reason to suppose that there was to be any such mischief as happened in France till the morning on which it happened, and he was in this state of ignorance though the person who was to command the military in Paris. That a Ministry should think of measures so indefensible, and preparing no means calculated to carry them into execution, is one of the most astonishing things that ever happened. This French business has all possible bad effects here: it poisons the minds of multitudes among the different orders in the country and town."

"11th October.

"Report insists that a negotiation is going on between Ministers and Palmerston and Co. I incline to believe it. I hear that it is also reported that a pledge has been given that there shall be a partial parliamentary reform, and some kind of a parliamentary measure about tithes."

These rumors were entirely devoid of foundation, for, notwithstanding Mr. Brougham's return for the county of

York, and many indications of the wish of the people for a correction of the existing inequalities and abuses in the representation of the people, the Government resolved against making any concession, and vainly attempted by a contrary policy to reunite the whole of the Conservative party.

On the meeting of Parliament all aid from Liberals was repudiated rather ostentatiously by a paragraph in the King's Speech, lamenting "that the enlightened administration of the King of the Netherlands should not have preserved his dominions from revolt;" and by a declaration of the Duke of Wellington in the debate on the Address, that "the existing system of the representation was absolutely perfect, and possessed the entire confidence of the country."[1]

But while all liberals were thus forced in active opposition, the Ultra-Tories were in no measure conciliated; and while notices of motion for parliamentary reform were given by the former party, the latter still announced unabated hostility to those who, long professing to be guardians of the Church, had carried the Catholic Relief Bill, and from whom measures still more dangerous might be dreaded.[2] The difficulties of the Government were increased by the prædial disturbances and incendiary fires raging all over the country, and by the dangerous spirit prevailing among the populace of London, which prevented the King from dining at Guildhall according to ancient custom on Lord Mayor's day. It was evident that retirement must be desirable to Ministers themselves, and the only doubt was as to the question on which there might be a division enabling them to tender their resignation without discredit. This came sooner than was expected, by the motion of Sir Henry Parnell for a committee upon the Civil List,—when, to their satisfaction, there was a majority against them of 29,—composed of both sections of their opponents.[3]

Now was formed the Whig Government, which was at first expected to be very short-lived, but which, with a short interruption and some modifications, lasted eleven years,—which carried the Reform Bill, with other measures for improving our institutions hardly less important, —and which will ever make the reign of William IV.,

[1] Hansard, 2nd series, 52.   [2] Ib. 196.   [3] Ib. 548.

though unillustrated by warlike exploits, one of the most interesting in the annals of our Constitution.

Lord Eldon was rather appalled when he beheld the monster that he had helped to call into existence. Although I have no authority for saying so, the probability is that he already repented the factious opposition which he had recently offered to the Duke of Wellington's Government. He supported a motion for a committee on the distress of the country, brought forward by Lord Wynford with a view to embarrass the new Ministers in their schemes for reform; and Lord Radnor imputing the distress of the country to Tory rule, he took occasion to announce that his Conservatism remained untainted, by saying, " It is among the greatest of my consolations, in a retrospect of my political life, that I have always maintained principles the reverse of the noble Earl's."[1]

With all his blandness of manner, and all his self-command, it was a severe trial to him to see the Attorney General of Queen Caroline, in the Chancellor's robes, presiding on the woolsack; and, although he could not deny the extraordinary powers which were now exhibited there, he must certainly have felt that he and his successor were "*magis pares quam similes.*" Lord Chancellor Brougham having, with dignity and propriety, repudiated the advice that extraordinary laws should be enacted to put down the present disturbances, and afterwards suggested that lords-lieutenants of counties should recommend to him some additonal magistrates for the commission of the peace, with an intimation that there were persons who, notwithstanding their station, their character, and their activity, had been passed over on account of politics,—the Ex-Chancellor took occasion to read him a long lecture on the rights and duties of the Great Seal respecting the appointment and removal of magistrates,—concluding with an account of his own practice for the twenty-five years of his Chancellorship, which certainly deserves much commendation—particularly in not allowing the name of a magistrate to be struck out of the commission without proof that he had been guilty of some grave offense.[2]

Lord Eldon was beginning to be a little relieved from his apprehension of the Whigs by reason of some financial

[1] 1 Hansard, 3rd series, 828.   [2] Ib. 681.

mistakes they had made, and a notion impressed upon the public mind that their officials were not practical men of business,—so that their dismissal seemed to be at hand, —when it was hoped that the whole party would cordially reunite in support of pure Tory principles.

But the face of affairs was suddenly changed by the sweeping plan of Parliamentary Reform proposed on the memorable 1st of March. Notwithstanding the assurances of Earl Grey as to the character of his coming measure, the admirers of the existing system had flattered themselves that he wanted courage materially to interfere with it, aud that public disappointment on this subject would precipitate his fall. The consternation now felt by Lord Eldon may be conjectured by the following letter from him to his daughter:—

"3rd March, 1831.

"There is no describing the amazement this plan of reform, which before this time yon will have read in your paper, has occasioned. There are divers opinions, whether it will or not pass the Commons. Generally it is thought that it can not;—but what the result of the operation of fear of the consequences that will follow, in the minds of revolutionary men, if it does not pass, and of fear, in the minds of sober-minded men, if it does pass, there is no saying."

At the end of the week he was still more alarmed.

"Thursday morning (10th March).

"The system of threatening persons who don't vote for reform, is carried to a shocking length. Whether the members of the Legislature have nerves to withstand it, is very doubtful."

The second reading being carried by a single vote, and a majority of the existing House of Commons being undoubtedly adverse to the bill in their hearts, many thought that the danger had blown over,—but Lord Eldon, more clear-sighted, still trembled when he thought of the manly enthusiasm of the supporters of the measure, and still more of the apathy and inactivity of its opponents. Thus, during the Easter recess, he wrote to Lord Stowell:—

"(April, 1831.)

"DEAR BROTHER,
"I shall be glad if I am able, by my notes, to give you

either information which may amuse you, or acquaint you with what you can not find in your newspapers. At present, however, that is impossible; for, though Parliament begins to sit again next week, and, to save the country, the present week ought to be speut in making arrangements to defeat the mischievous projects now on foot, every person, whose counsel and co-operation would be of use for that most pressing and desirable object, are gone out of town to amuse themselves during the Easter holidays, with as little concern about public affairs as if we lived in the happiest moments that old England ever knew.

"All will be lost by the confidence with which people act, and with which they persuade themselves that all will be safe. Our feiend Lord Sidmouth, on the day on which the second reading of the Bill was carried, spoke to me of the majority by which it would undoubtedly be lost and negatived. And now the few, very few individuals here whom I see, speak of the rejection of the Bill as if it was certain to be rejected, though no two persons agree as to what shall be the course of measures by which its rejection can be accomplished. The folly with which people act is inconceivably provoking.

"The members for counties will, some keep silence —many vote against rejecting the reform—they are afraid of losing their seats—they have not the sense to see that, if the measure is carried, they must lose their consequence, their rank, and most assuredly their property.

"You will that observed by the Minister, who says that he will stand or fall by his measure,—that he will brave consequences,—has gone the length of stating that the connection between England and Ireland may be preserved, and be as equally useful to both, if there are different Church Establishments, as if there were the same Church establishments in the two islands—in one Protestant, in the other Roman Catholic.

"And yet all the petitioners, or many of them, whose petitions I presented against the Catholic Relief Bill, are petitioners for the Reform Bill; for, say they, a House of Commons which could vote for the Emancipation Bill can not be such a House of Commons as ought any longer to exist. Such is the folly and insanity with which people are acting.

"You will perceive that at the Lord Mayor's Easter Monday dinner all the Ministers—one after another—declared the K.'s entire confidence in them, and determination to support them. This was all perfectly unconstitutional, and there are here some persons who do not believe one word of what they said. I can not say that I am altogether so incredulous."

This terrible misgiving as to the royal inclination turned out to have too much foundation. Till the resistance which the Reform Bill experienced from the Peers, King William IV. very heartily supported it; and a majority of the existing House of Commons having shown their hostility to it by carrying the resolution moved by General Gascoyne, that the number of English representatives should not be diminished, he eagerly agreed to an abrupt dissolution of Parliament, expressing his readiness to go in a hackney-coach from his palace to the House of Lords, there to announce his purpose of appealing to the sense of his people on this great question.[1]

Lord Eldon was not present when Lord Wharncliff's motion for an address against a dissolution of Parliament was interrupted by his Majesty's arrival to dissolve it, or his authority would probably have prevented the indecent struggle which then took place; but at a meeting of the Pitt Club, held a few days after, he, in very mild and touching language, warned the multitude of what he considered the consequences of the course they were pursuing. He said, " The proposed bill must be fatal to the aristocracy; and the aristocracy once destroyed, the best supporters of the lower classes would be swept away. In using the term *lower classes*, he meant nothing offensive. How could he do so? He himself had been one of the lower classes. He gloried in the fact, and it was noble and delightful to know that the humblest of the realm might, by a life of industry, propriety, and good moral and religious conduct, rise to eminence. All could not become eminent in public life,—that was impossible; but every man might arrive at honor, independence, and competence."

[1] Never shall I forget the scene then exhibited in the House of Commons,—which might convey an adequate idea of the tumultuary dissolutions in the times of the Stuarts. The most exciting moment of my public life was when we cheered the guns which announced his Majesty's approach.

Lord Eldon had the mortification to hear, that in the midst of exaggerated statements of the evils arising from the existing system of representation, and delusive hopes of the transcendent benefits to be conferred upon all classes from the proposed change, a new House of Commons had been elected prepared to carry "the bill, the whole bill, and nothing but the bill."

While looking forward with dismay to what he considered the mad proceedings now to be anticipated, he forgot for a while all his apprehensions for the public, being plunged into the deepest grief by a heavy domestic affliction with which he was visited. His steady and enthusiastic devotion to her who had engaged his early affections constitutes the most amiable trait of his character. When "Bessy" was no longer young or beautiful,—when by her peculiar tastes and habits she gave him much annoyance, and almost entirely cut him off from hospitable intercourse with his friends,—contented with seeing that her heart still was his, he continued to behave to her as a lover, when half a century had elapsed since their flight into Scotland. With others he might be selfish, and he might be insincere; but her happiness he ever studied in preference to his own; and the language of endearment and tenderness in which he spoke of her, inadequately expressed his genuine sensations. She had been long in a declining state of health, and he had watched the vicissitudes of her sickness with the most anxious solicitude. He must long have forseen its fatal termination; but when the blow came, it almost overpowered him. He wrote the following letter to Lord Stowell on the day of hea death—

"The first dark day of nothingness."

"MY EVER DEAR BROTHER,

"Your letter reaches me in a flood of tears, and a sort of burst of agonizing feeling. I submit as well as I can—I fear not as well as I ought—to God's will. But I will do my utmost to acquire the means of doing my duty. I am quite sure that our meeting as yet would overpower me; and I fear also, you—that you are the person who is the object of all my affections and anxieties along with my offspring.

"When I can have the strength and fortitude in person to say to you 'God Almighty bless you,'—as I now say it

in correspondence,—I shall in person assure [you], that I am, as I have [been] through life, and [have] had so much reason to be, [your]   Ever affectionate
"ELDON."

Lady Eldon's remains were deposited in a family vault which he had caused to be constructed in a piece of newly consecrated ground adjoining the ancient cemetery of the chapel of Kingston, in the parish of Corfe Castle, in which Encombe stands.[1]

A few weeks after, the bereaved husband indulged his grief in a visit to the last resting-place of his beloved wife —where, life's fitful fever being over, he was soon to repose by her side. His feelings during this melancholy pilgrimage he portrays in two letters to Lord Stowell, written the same day:—

"Encombe, Monday (29th August, 1831).

"DEAR BROTHER,

"I arrived here last night. My first approach to this place, so often the scene of great happiness in former days, has, at present, most deeply and painfully affected me. I shall have many trials during my short stay here, which I know not how to bear. I have, however, designedly exposed myself to this present state of suffer-

---

[1] The following is a touching account of the ceremony of the consecration, from the pen of the present Earl of Eldon :—" The Bishop arrived on the spot about seven. After hearing prayers, his Lordship proceeded to the burial ground (which was perambulated), and signed and sealed the deed under a marquee erected in the centre. Then the sentence and the prayer of consecration were read, and three verses sung—and the Bishop gave his blessing. Returning from the ground, the Bishop looked at the people, who had ranged themselves quietly and respectfully round the railing and the walls of the churchyard, and asked me whether he should say a few words to them of Lord Eldon, whom he supposed to have been often at church there. I write them down from memory :—

"' My Friends,

"' You have, this evening, witnessed the consecration of a piece of ground destined to be the burial place of a great and good man, who has lived among you,—who has for many years supported the laws and liberties of your country with firm and undeviating integrity. Having deposited here the mortal remains of the companion of his life, the beloved object of his constant affection and attention, he would that here also his own ashes should repose. Long may it be yet before he shall come to lie here—but, in the meantime, you will hold sacred a spot which he has chosen to be the place of his interment : and many will, even now, come to look at the future grave of Lord Eldon. For you, who have so often seen him coming to worship God with you in this village church, I have only to bid you, remember this,—and lead such good and holy lives yourselves, as may (through His grace) fit and prepare you for the hour of death, and the day of judgment ; and so, good bye to you all !'"—*Twiss*, ch. liv.

ing, because, some time or other, if I live, I must meet what I have at present exposed myself to.

"I pray God, daily and incessantly, for all that can contribute to your health, comfort, and happiness, and am, with all possible affection,   Yours, dear Brother,
"ELDON."

"MY DEAREST BROTHER,

"I write a short line, being unable to do more. I have this morning visited the spot where the remains of my ever dear departed are deposited, and where, when God pleases to summon me hence, I shall repose till the Day of Judgment. I have been nervous, and in some degree hysterical, through the day, but am better this evening. I have been constantly reproaching myself for not having attended the funeral, and my mind has been ever at work in representing to me the spot, which I have seen to-day, and the seeing of which, however painful to memory, is less so than contemplation before having seen it. I am now satisfied, from vision, that all has been respectfully done that the sad occasion would admit of. I am sorry to write you a melancholy letter—but I can not help it. May God's best blessings ever attend you.
"Yours, with all possible affection,
"ELDON."

These effusions are no less remarkable for the devotion which they show to the memory of his deceased wife, than for the ardent affection which they prove still to have subsisted between the two brothers, notwithstanding the chill of age, and the hardening tendency of long prosperity.

But I must hurry back to the noisy scenes which were now acting on the political stage. Lord Eldon did not long yield to unmanly sorrow—recollecting the calls which his country had upon him in her hour of peril.

The new Parliament having met on the 18th of June, the English Reform Bill, without any abatement in its stringency, was forthwith introduced, and large majorities divided in favor of its principles and all its details; but, on account of the gallant resistance made to it by the Conservatives, it did not pass the Lower House till the 22nd of September. The Lords were meanwhile amusing themselves with Reform skirmishes, originated by petitions,—and with discussions on matters of a comparatively trifling nature.

Lord Chanceller Brougham, making extraordinary efforts to clear off the arrears in the Court of Chancery, had been holding evening sittings, which prevented him from appearing on the woolsack in the House of Lords. Lord Eldon thereupon remarked, that, " according to the standing orders of their Lordships, the paramount duty of the Lord Chancellor was to be in his place in that House during their Lordships' sittings, and not to be employed elsewhere; and there were many precedents where permission to attend elsewhere during the sittings of that House had been refused. He had no doubt whatever that his noble and learned friend had been most usefully employed, but his noble and learned friend had no power to dispense with the standing orders of the House." Their Lordships, however, were satisfied with Lord Brougham's assurance of the absolute necessity of his attending elsewhere, and with the hope which he held out of being speedily able to clear of all arrears both in that House and in the Court of Chancery.[1]

On a subsequent day, the complaint being renewed by another noble Lord, and the Lord Chancellor having excused his absence on this occasion by the necessity for recruiting his health after his severe labors in clearing off arrears—Lord Eldon, being hurt probably as much by the excuse as by the alleged breach of the standing order, reminded the House of the instance where Lord Chancellor Macclesfield had pleaded, as a reason for his absence, that he had been sent for by the Sovereign, but the House voted that this was no sufficient reason, and that it was his paramount duty to be in attendance on the woolsack.[2] He pointed out the disrespect shown to their Lordships by the Chancellor's absence without any previous leave, adding, that " if the Chancellor were absent, even for justifiable cause, he should give notice to the Deputy Speaker—and not leave their Lordships to exercise their privilege of choosing a Speaker by their own authority. It was necessary that the Lord Chancellor or Deputy Speaker should attend to protect the prerogatives of the Crown. In the absence of the Lord Chancellor, one of the most eminent judges of Westminster Hall should perform the duties of Speaker." He then defended himself from the charge that the

[1] 6 Hansard, 3rd series, 453.   [2] Ante, Vol. V. p. 266.

arrears in the Court of Chancery, and in the judicial department of that House, had arisen from any default of his—and concluded by giving notice of a measure which he should bring forward in the next session of Parliament, to enforce the attendance of the Lord Chancellor in the House of Lords. But he never afterwards revived the discussion finding that the Lord Chancellor sedulously devoted himself to his public duties, and that their Lordships were not unwilling to submit to the occasional privation of his presence among them, whether he was clearing off arrears in the Court of Chancery, or recruiting himself in the country after his fatigues.[1]

On Lord Brougham's Bankruptcy Bill coming before the House of Lords, Lord Eldon felt considerable alarm. It contained most salutary enactments for the appointment of a small number of permanent commissioners, instead of SEVENTY who had been hitherto casually employed,—and for substituting official assignees, in the place of friends of the bankrupt, to manage the estate which ought to be divided among the creditors:—but it miscalculated the judicial power requisite in the Court of Review, by constituting a new tribunal of four judges, who were to sit all the year for the transaction of business, the whole of which one of the Vice-Chancellors, it is now found, can do in a few days without interfering with his own proper functions. Lord Eldon opposed it indiscriminately. He first addressed a letter to the Lord Chancellor respecting a claim to compensation for the sinecure office of "Patentee of Bankrupts," about to be abolished. After stating that he took an interest in the matter out of gratitude to Lord Thurlow, to whom, during fifty years, he had been under great obligations, he thus continued:—

"You are probably aware, also, without my mentioning it, that my humble opinion is, that the proposed change in the administration of law in matters of bankruptcy is a change that ought not to be adopted. And it seems respectful to you here to mention, that, if it becomes necessary, I shall be obliged, as at present advised, however reluctantly, to express that such is my opinion. I am aware that that opinion will now have little weight.

"The grants that appear to have been made from time

[1] 7 Hansard, 3rd series, 646-662.

to time of this office, bear date at different periods from the 14th James I.,—grants by different Sovereigns, to the families of Chancellors, at different periods.

"The grant under which Mr. Thurlow claims, bears date in November, 1792, the immediately antecedent grant being made to one of Lord Cowper's family, and one of Lord Hardwicke's.

"It will be found, I believe, to be a fact, that, before the time of Lord Loughborough, there was no retiring pension for a Chancellor. Lord Thurlow had no pension. Loughborough should have provided a better retiring pension for a Chancellor, unless, like Lord Eldon, a Chancellor happened to hold the office insufferably long.

"Lord Camden was very fortunate—being Chancellor not, I think, four years complete. His family was provided for by a grant of a Tellership of the Exchequer, when it was a most extremely valuable office. After a considerably long enjoyment of it as such, he[1] very handsomely gave up the excess of the old profits above the modern profits of the present day; but before that took place, he had held it at the original great value, I think, for many years.

"There seems to have been an understanding that, whenever Lord Thurlow quitted the Chancellorship, he should have a Tellership, with the then usual benefits of it, great and ample as they were; and I think I remember Mr. Fox saying, in the House of Commons, that he ought to have that, if he would declare that he had bargained for it. Such a declaration Thurlow refused to make. Whatever the fact was, he could not avow that he had made a bargain. He had no pension; and as the peerage and title was, by a re-grant, to be extended to his brother's family, he granted the office of bankruptcy, as his predecessors had done, to two of his family; of whom Mr. Thurlow is the survivor, and now in possession of the office."

When the merits of the bill came to be debated, the Lord Chancellor having stated, as an apology for bringing it forward so speedily, that if he had waited longer, like other persons who had gone into the Court with a determination to improve it, he should have found himself so hampered by a temporary tolerance of abuse as to be able

[1] Not Lord Chancellor Camden, but his son.

to do nothing,—the ex-Chancellor, stung by this sarcasm, and showing a wonderful blindness to abuses, said :—

"My Lords, I feel it a duty to my country to declare that I will accept no such apology for my conduct. I knew well what had been the practice of the Court of Chancery many years before I became a judge in it. It was my duty immediately to have set about correcting its abuses if I had believed that any existed. My opinion is, that such abuses do not exist. The noble and learned Lord's bill may have been prepared with great pains,— but is it necessary? This question the House should not leave to any individual, however well qualified, but should decide after patient inquiry before a committee of its own. The proposed change is extensive and violent; and although its professed object is to prevent uncertainty, expense, and delay,—from my experience I am convinced that it will aggravate uncertainty, accumulate expense, and augment delay. No change is necessary; and if change were advisable, that recommended from the wool-sack can not be beneficial."—In the course of a long speech he alluded to the emoluments and patronage of the Great Seal which he defended; although denying all abuse, he somewhat inconsistently admitted that it was very objectionable that these emoluments should be partly derived from fees, " as this arrangement led to the suspicion that business was delayed or despatched with a view to fees, and it would be far better if the Chancellor's income were put on the same footing as that of the Chief Justices of the King's Bench and Common Pleas, who had a fixed salary." [1]

We may ask, then, why he did not many years ago, silence the calumnies about his preferring bankruptcy business because it was most profitable, by introducing this improvement, which every Prime Minister under whom he served would have gladly sanctioned? The dislike of innovation probably operated with him more than the dread of loss from a fixed salary. His predictions as the working of the Bankruptcy Act [2] were completely falsified; for, although the Court of Review has been abolished, the permanent commissioners and official assignees have undoubtedly rendered the administration of the bankrupt law much more pure, cheap and expeditious than it was in his time.

[1] 7 Hansard, 3rd series, 251.   [2] 1 & 2 W. 4, c. 56.

At last, Lord John Russell, attended by Lord Althorp and a great body of the most distinguished Reformers, appeared at the bar of the House of Lords, and handed the English Reform Bill to the Lord Chancellor, praying the concurrence of their Lordships.[1] This scene, which has been made the shbject of a great historical painting, Lord Eldon had anticipated, as we learn by a note written by him the same day to Lord Stowell:—

"Thursday (Sept. 22nd, 1831).

"The Reform Bill passed the Commons at an early hour this morning. For it, 345; against it, 236—majority, 109. I presume we shall have it brought up, with as much pomp and ceremony of attending members of the House of Commons as may be, *this* day, when the day proposed for the second reading in the House of Lords will be fixed."

After an indecent cry of *Hear! hear!* from some members of the House of Commons, which was put down by a cry of *Order! order!* the bill, without any opposition or remark from Lord Eldon or any Conservative peer, was read a first time, on the motion of Earl Grey, and ordered to be read a second time on the Monday se'nnight.[2]

In an intervening discussion on the presentation of a petition in favor of the bill, as the Marquess of Westminster had indiscreetly asserted that having passed the Commons, to which it peculiarly belonged, the Peers ought not to interfere with it, Lord Eldon very properly rebuked him, saying, that "the proposition that the Peers of England had no interest in this question was the most absurd one that had ever been uttered or propounded, here or elsewhere. He hoped and believed, that when that question came to be discussed by their Lordships they would do their duty fearlessly and manfully, and at the hazard of all the consequences. He should be utterly ashamed of himself if he should give way to the imputation of being prevented by fear from doing his duty. He would discharge his duty with regard to it, because he believed that in it were involved, not only their Lordships' interests, but the interests of the Throne. Bred as he had been in loyalty, living under the law, and revering the Constitution of his country—now that he had arrived

---

[1] 7 Hansard, 479.   [2] Ib.

at the age of four-score years, he would rather die in his place than suppress his indignation at such sentiments."[1]

It is difficult to imagine the consternation now felt by him who had successfully resisted such mild reforms as taking away the punishment of death from the offense of stealing to the value of 40s. in a dwelling-house, or 5s. in a shop, when he regarded the triumphant progress of a measure which was to operate a revolution, by the transference of political power, under the form of a legislative act to be passed by King, Lords, and Commons.

He sent the following account of the first night's debate on the second reading of the bill in the Lords to his grandson, who had lately been most auspiciously married to a daughter of Lord Feversham :—

("Oct. 4th, 1831.)

"MY DEAR ENCOMBE,

"Accept my kindest thanks for your letter this moment received. I repeat to you, and I beg you will state on my behalf, to the lady whom I have now the happiness to call my grand-daughter, my heart's best wishes for the felicity of both.

"I got to bed about a quarter before three, much fatigued, and oppressed beyond measure with the heat of the House, and my head is in a bad state this morning.

"My own conjecture is, that our debates will not terminate before Thursday evening. It may, however, be, that they will finish on Wednesday.

"Lord Grey spoke very well; but his speech, I thought, betrayed an opinion that he would be in a minority.

"Wharncliffe did very well; but made a sad mistake in moving that the bill be 'rejected;' a word that seemed to many to be too strong as to a bill passed by the Commons, and a great deal of time was spent in getting the House to agree to change what he had moved into a motion, 'That the bill be taken into consideration on that day six months.'

"Lord Mansfield spoke most ably and admirably against the bill. Lord Mulgrave *acted* his part tolerably. . . .

"Then we all retired. My head is painful. I hate the sight of food. All seem to think the bill will be lost."

The debate lasted the whole week. Before it was

[1] 7 Hansard, 887.

resumed on the Wednesday, there was a conflict respecting the legality or illegality of public meetings, between the Chancellor and the ex-Chancellor, in which, according to the printed accouut of it, the latter had the advantage. A Peer, on the presentation of a petition, stated " that at a meeting of the Birmingham Union, attended by many thousands, an orator who addressed them advised them, if the Reform Bill should be rejected by the Lords, to refuse to pay taxes any more;—that he called upon those present who would support this resolution to hold up their hands,—and that thereupon a forest of hands was held up amidst an immense cheer." The Lord Chancellor is represented, after expressing disapprobation of such proceedings, to have added, " Nevertheless, as a lawyer, I must say that all those hands may have been held up, and yet I can not say that there was any breach of the King's peace, nor any offense that the law knows how to punish. I can not help it. Such is the law." LORD ELDON: "I should be ashamed of myself, if, after living so long in my profession, I did not now offer a few words. I fully admit that a meeting is not answerable for the declarations of an individual; but if, by holding by their hands, or in any other way, the meeting endangers the peace of the country, I know no reason for believing that they have not made themselees responsible to the laws. As a lawyer, I would ask the Chief Justice of the King's Bench (Lord Tenterden), and the late Chief Justice of the Common Pleas (Lord Wynford), whether, if those hands could be proved to have been held up in the manner described, every individual responding be not as much answerable for the language used as the man who used it? And I beg to tell the noble and learned Lord, with the greatest respect, that his seat on the woolsack will not be a seat which any one can maintain for six months, if the doctrines now circulated through the country, and placed every morning under the review of every one, are suffered to be promulgated any longer. That is my opinion; I alone am answerable for my opinions; and for this I am prepared to answer at all hazards."

Except in the heat of debate, no lawyer could doubt that a meeting so passing a resolution to violate the law by refusing the payment of taxes was illegal and riotous. The Lord Chancellor afterwards said that " although no breach of the peace had been committed, pernaps an indictment might be preferred for an offence of a different nature; upon which he would give no opinion."[1] The debate then proceeded, and Lord Eldon next morning wrote to his brother:—

"I got to bed last night about half-past two—much fatigued and overcome with heat, &c.

"We had some excellent speakers—Lord Dudley and Lord Haddington quite surprised me. They spoke admirably against the bill.

"Lansdowne and Goderich spoke for it; in their speeches, however, rather contending for going into a committee to amend and alter it, than for passing the bill in its present shape. From all I can judge upon such information as I have, the bill will be thrown out by a majority greater than I had, till yesterday, heard mentioned.

"As yet, none of the profession to which I belonged have spoken, and I suppose the House will have enough of us before we have finished. Some think the vote will take place on Friday, some on Saturday, and some on Monday; I can't conjecture on which. God bless you. I am very weak."

On the Friday morning he sent Lord Stowell the following sketch of the preceding evening's debate :—

"We have survived one more fatiguing night, passed in hearing some heavy, some moderate, one most excellent speech, which surprised me, from Lord Carnarvon, and one, not very excellent, from Lord Plunket, from whom I expected something better. In the course of the evening I tendered myself to the House; but Lord Carnarvon, stating his just pretensions to be heard, as he was too ill to hope to speak at any other time, I was obliged to give way, and I was too ill to speak at a later period of the night.

"We adjourned to five o'clock this evening, and in case the debate does not finish to-night, we are to attempt to finish it to-morrow (Saturday) by meeting at one o'clock instead of five, and sitting till near twelve on to-morrow (Saturday) night; if we do not then finish, the debate, I think, must conclude on Monday. At present I have all the reason which, in such matters, we can have to be confident that the bill will not pass. Making new peers to

[1] 7 Hansard, 3rd series, 1328.

pass it has been much talked of; but, unless our calculation of numbers is erroneous, and most grossly so, audacity itself could not venture to attempt a sufficient supply of new peers."

The fifth night of the debate was occupied by the lawyers. Lord Eldon, following Lord Wynford and Lord Plunket, spoke as follows :—

"My Lords, if I did not feel it an encumbent duty on me, I can assure your Lordships I should have spared you, and not encountered the hazard and difficulty which I feel in addressing you, in consequence of my age and of that infirmity which has been occasioned in some degree by my constant attendance on this House. I well remember that on another question—and I would take this opportunity of declaring, before God and my country, that on that question—I mean the Roman Catholic question—I took no part which I did not feel it my duty to take both to God and my country,—but I very well remember that, at the period when that measure was under discussion, I stated that it was probably the last opportunity of which I should ever avail myself of addressing your Lordships. I thought so at the time, and, considering that I was then advanced to fourscore years, I had scarcely any right to expect to have been able again to address your Lordships; but as the kind and indulgent providence of God has allowed me to continue in the enjoyment of a certain degree of health for a short period longer, I am able again to take my seat in this House. My Lords, I was taunted for appearing again before your Lordships, after the declaration I had made; but I felt myself called upon by a sense of duty which I could not resist,—from the moment when my Sovereign called me to a seat in this House, as long as my strength permitted me,—to offer myself and my opinions to the suffrages and approbation, or to the dissent and reprobation, of my fellow-subjects.—Doctrines have now been laid down, with respect to the law of this country and its institutions, which I have never heard of before, although I have spent a long life in considering what the law of this country is, and some time in considering how it might be improved. Those considerations, my Lords, have satisfied me that alterations are not always improvements; but when I find it stated, in the preamble of this bill, that it is *expedient* that all the acknowledged rights of property, that all the rights arising out of charters, that all the rights of close corporations, and the rights of corporations which are not close, should be swept away,—though it does come recommended by the name of reform, I find it impossible to give it my assent. I do not think this property can be taken away, and I never can consent to hear the principle of expediency put forward as the justification of a measure which is not consistent with the principles of British law and of the British Constitution. I know, my Lords, and I am ready to agree, that there is a popular notion with respect to the boroughs in this country, that they are not property, but trusts. I say, my Lords, that they are *both* property *and* trusts. Those old-fashioned gentlemen, whose names will be held in lasting remembrance after the delirium of this day shall have passed away,—I mean such men as my Lord Holt and my Lord Hale,—what have they said with respect to those unpopular things called boroughs? My Lords, they said they were both a franchise and a right. Now let me ask your Lordships what is to be the consequence with respect to property of any species whatever? —for there is no property in the country which is not accompanied with *some* trust for its due application. Is it possible for any man to have the boldness to say that property is secure, when we are sweeping away near one hundred boroughs, and almost all the corporations in the country, because we have a notion that those who are connected with them have not executed their trust properly? Will you not hear the individuals against whom the allegation is made, as well as those who made it? Will you not hear the matter argued in your presence, and allow the right of calling witnesses, on whose evidence you may decide? This new doctrine, I repeat, affects every species of property which any man possesses in this country. I have heard, in the course of the last two or three months, a good deal about close corporations. I will now say, that close corporations are hereditary rights, held by charter from the Crown; and they have as good a right to hold their charters under the Great Seal, as any of your Lordships have to your titles and your peerages.—I do not object to the courtesy of creating peers on the occasion of the Coronation. I should, on the contrary, be happy to see individuals introduced to the House, if the members so created had not already voted for the bill in the other House, and then come here to vote for it again: and I should be still more happy to find that they did not vote at all on this question. But there is a rumor abroad, that the opinion of this House is to be, somehow or other, finally overruled. My Lords, I do not credit it. I do not believe that the noble Earl, to whom I have been opposed throughout the whole course of my political life—honestly on my part, and honestly on his, because I know his opinions are as honest as mine,—I do not believe that that Minister, whose name will be illustrious in future generations, whatever may be the fate of this bill, will ever taint his character by recommending a measure which means neither more nor less than what, if you pass this bill, will be done in due time—namely, to annihilate this House. With respect to the proposition of his Majesty's Ministers, or any object connected with it, I hope, before the Lords of this House strip off their robes, they will let their Sovereign know their sentiments.—Now, my Lords, let us suppose for a moment that there are some corporations in which a few influential individuals elect the members of Parliament. Has it ever been heard of in the history of this country, or will it ever be heard of in the history of this country, that the Lords of this House should take upon themselves, on a bill stating it to be expedient to do so and so, to destroy that Constitution which has been preserved from age to age, and which it has never been thought *expedient* to destroy, until this experiment was proposed,—that now you are about to sweep away all the corporations in the kingdom, because they are close, and there may be abuses in them? My Lords, I am a freeman of Newcastle-upon-Tyne. I hold it to be one of the highest honors which I possess, and I consider that it ought to be an encouragement to all the young rising men of that place, that any man of this country possessing moderate abilities, improved by industry, may raise himself to the highest situations in the country. For God's sake, my Lords, never part with that principle. You may ask me what application I make of this argument. My Lords. I will tell you the application. I received my education in the corporation school of that town, on cheap terms. As the son of a freeman, I had a right to it; and I had hoped that when my ashes were laid in the grave, where they probably soon will be, I might have given some memorandum that boys there, situated as I was, might rise to be Chancellors of England, if, having the advantage of that education, they were honest, faithful, and industrious in their dealings. But this bill, which is, it seems, founded in part on population, and in part on something else, which I can not tell,—this bill is to do away with corporations."

After giving a long history of the representative system in this country, he thus concluded:—

"A thousand other considerations, of enormous weight on my mind, might be added on such a momentous occasion, without traveling into the details of minor objections; but I am not disposed to reiterate what has been in many cases so ably argued, or fatigue the House. It is, I confess, my Lords, an all-engrossing subject; and the bill will be found, I fear from my soul, to go the length of introducing in its train, if passed, Universal Suffrage, Annual Parliaments, and Vote by Ballot. It will unhinge the whole frame of society as now constituted. Will you then, my Lords, consent to introduce into the Constitution a measure which is at war with the preservation of that Constitution, and which is more particularly remarkable for being altogether incompatible with the existence of a House of Lords? I, my Lords, have nearly run my race in this world, and must soon go to my Maker and my dread account. What I have said in this instance, in all sincerity, I have expressed out of my love to your Lordships; and in that sincerity I will solemnly assert my heartfelt belief that, with this bill in operation, the Monarchy can not exist, and that it is totally incompatible with the existence of the British Constitution."

The House divided in the morning twilight of Saturday, and Lord Eldon sent his brother the following account of the result:—

"Saturday (Oct. 8th, 1831).

"The debate began last night, continued till between six and seven this morning, and I got to my bed about half-past seven, and left it about noon to-day, fatigued beyond all belief, bodily. You will see from the papers that our division was against the second reading of the bill. The fate of the bill, therefore, is decided. Those for the bill were 158; against it, 199,—leaving a majority of votes against the bill of 41; which, I have reason to believe, exceeded by one-half of what Ministers thought it would. I voted for you, by your proxy, against the bill.

"The night was made interesting by the anxieties of all present. Perhaps fortunately, the mob would not on the outside wait so long as it was before Lords left the inside of the House."

As a member of the House of Commons, I was myself present on the steps of the throne during this memorable debate, and heard Lord Eldon's impressive speech, which was listened to with the most profound attention on all sides. Nothing could be more affecting than the allusion, by the octogenarian ex-Chancellor, to the days when he was a poor boy at the Free Grammar School of Newcastle-upon-Tyne; and no one considered whether he proved, very logically, that the Reform Bill would cut off from others the chance of following in the same illustrious career. He was much exhausted before he sat down, and a noble Earl from a distant part of the House very indecorously requested him to *raise his voice;* but this interruption excited a strong expression of sympathy and respect in his favor, as well from those who thought that he was haunted by delusive terrors, as from those who believed that his vaticinations were inspired by the mystical lore which gives to the wizard, in the sunset of life, a glimpse of coming calamities.

His countenance brightened up when, upon taking the votes of the peers present, the rejection of the bill was secure.[1] He was evidently in a state of great delight when the ceremony of "calling proxies" was gone through to increase the majority; and when the clerk said: "John Earl of Eldon hath the proxy of William Lord Stowell," he exclaimed, "*Not content!!!*" with much emphasis and exultation. After the fatigue of five nights' debate, and his own great effort, he was hardly able to support himself when he rose to return home; but he was conducted to his carriage by his friends, who seemed to be congratulating him on his share of the great triumph which had been achieved.

On reaching Palace Yard, the circumstance to which he

---

[1] Contents, 128; Not-contents, 150.

refers in his letter to his brother was very striking,—that the mob had entirely dispersed, their patriotism being cooled by a long drizzling October night; and although it was now broad day, no sound was to be heard except the rolling of the carriages of the peers, who, whether Reformers or Conservatives, passed along Parliament Street as quietly as if they had come from disposing of a Road Bill.

But although the rejection of this gigantic measure by the Lords had been anticipated,—when the event was certainly known, it created deep disappointment, and riots took place both in the metropolis and in the provinces, which threw much disgrace on the cause of Reform. Lord Eldon describes these riots with some exaggeration (which was very natural) in the following letter to his daughter, Lady Frances:—

" October 13th, 1831.

"Our day here yesterday was tremendously alarming. Very fortunately for me, the immense mob of Reformers (hardly a decent-looking man among them) proceeded first to the Duke of Wellington's, and set about the work of destruction. This, after some time, brought to this end of Piccadilly some hundreds of the police in a body; and the Blues coming up from the levée, the appearance of this large body of force was a complete protection to me, dissipating the multitude that were a little higher up Piccadilly. They had also probably heard that the soldiers had behaved with great firmness in or near St. James's Square. The civil power being on the alert and the military being known to be ready, the night was passed most unexpectedly quiet hereabouts; and now I think we have nothing to dread. Londonderry has been very seriously hurt. We hear that the mob (but I can not answer for the truth of it) hanged in effigy the Duke of Wellington[1] and the Duke of Cumberland at Tyburn. The Duke of Newcastle's house, Lord Bristol's, &c., &c., and all other anti-reforming lords, have been visited, and left without glass in their windows. All the shops in town were shut yester-

[1] Happily the rumor of this atrocity was quite unfounded. Too discreditable was it that some of his Grace's windows were actually broken, of which we had long after a mortifying memento in iron blinds which presented themselves to view at Apsley House,—when low and high were all, with equal fervor and unanimity, eager to evince their gratitude to the Hero of Waterloo.

day. The accounts from Derbyshire, Nottinghamshire, and other places are very uncomfortable. I heard last night that the King was frightened by the appearance of people on the outside of St. James's. As to myself and my house, as we have escaped the first night, I have no apprehensions at all now—none. Some friends very usefully spread a report (not true, however) that there was a large armed force stationed in my house."

During the short parliamentary recess which followed, Lord Eldon paid a visit to Encombe. Of his supposed perils on his journey, and while residing there, we have an account in the following extracts of letters from him to his brother: " I stopped to change horses at Poole; and I was glad when that change was over, because people were collecting a little about the door of the inn and the carriage. However, the change of horses was soon effected, and I was driven off without disturbance." . . . .
" The contest in this county is a matter of great public consequence,¹ both as it shows great reaction of opinion here touching reform, and an example of what may be done almost everywhere, if gentlemen would act as if they were not in a sound sleep." . . . . " I don't like my correspondent IGNIS: when I recollect that I have repeatedly, when in London, communications that my house and buildings here should be burnt to the ground, I own that I do not think the threats, even of the lowest of the low, other than extremely alarming; and as well as I can recollect, the handwriting of the correspondent of several months ago being the same as that of my present correspondent, I can not bring myself to think that the letter of my correspondent is not a fair ground of alarm." . . . .
"The thing that I most feel to be dangerous is the formation of bodies of men under the name of political unions, which I see are forming in London, in every part of England, and in Ireland—the latter, professedly, to support English reform, as necessarily leading to the attainment of Irish objects as well as English objects. As to these political unions, I am confident, that if Parliament does not do what it did between 1789 and 1794,—put them down by Act of Parliament,—they will put down the Parliament itself. I have seen a great deal of mischief going forward

[1] The Conservatives had beaten the Reform candidate, after a fifteen days' poll.

in the country; but till those institutions were becoming general, and till the Government, by connivance and apathy, can be said rather to encourage than discourage them, I have had hopes that matters might get right. The crisis is formidable, because of those unions."

It is said that the Pool mob really had meditated an expedition into the Isle of Purbeck, with a view of an assault upon Encombe, but that they were frustrated by a worthy Conservative brickmaker having bored holes in the bottoms of canoes which were to carry them across a ferry; and Lord Eldon, unmolested by IGNIS, had the satisfaction of comfortably receiving a visit from his old friend the Duke of Cumberland,—when they talked over their former exploits in constructing Administrations, and expressed a cheering hope that, upon the speedy expulsion of the Whigs, they might assist in bringing into office men who not only would put a stop to further innovation, but would restore the Constitution to the state of perfection in which it had attracted the admiration of all truly wise men before the dangerous sway of such Ministers as Canning and Peel. These bright prospects, however, were soon overclouded. The Whigs, after a violent convulsion, actually remained in office till they had carried the Reform Bill, and had been supported for two years by overwhelming majorities in a reformed House of Commons. What was more galling still, when they were for a short time actually ejected, Lord Eldon and the Duke of Cumberland were never consulted respecting the new arrangement, and saw principles of government propounded by Sir Robert Peel which they considered little less objectionable than those of Lord Grey and Lord Melbourne.

After a very brief repose, Parliament again met in the beginning of December for the avowed purpose of reconsidering the question of a reform in the House of Commons.[1] Lord Eldon was at his post, and a noble Lord having referred, with some regret, to the fate of the rejected Reform Bill, he observed that "with that bill their Lordships had no concern at present. It was indeed, he said, an irregularity to have referred to it at all in this discussion, inasmuch as it had not been mentioned in the speech from the throne. There was no reason to believe that *the same* bill would be proposed again. If it should,

[1] King's Speech, 9 Hansard, 3rd series, 1.

the House would be bound to reconsider it, and it would be the duty of any noble lord who, on such reconsideration, should think he had mistaken his duty in opposing it before, to retrace his steps. In reference to that part of the speech which touched upon the necessity of punishing the violators of the law, he must mention to the House a publication which, if he had not seen that it was left unpunished, he could not have believed endurable. He spoke of a thing called the 'Black List.' There he was put forward as receiving £54,000 a year, out of the taxes, and his elder brother, whom this accurate list described as his nephew, was represented as receiving a pension of £4,000 a year. The noble Lords who, in the last session, had voted against the Reform Bill, were held up in this paper as receiving millions of money among them out of the taxes. He felt it fair, however, to add, that some of the Reformers were included in the same list. As he understood that many thousand copies of this publication had been sold, he must think it matter of just complaint that some means had not been taken to stay the circulation of such falsehoods."

Earl Grey excused the forbearance of the Government, on the ground that "the contents of the paper in question were too stupidly false, too extravagantly absurd, to influence any honest or intelligent man in the community;"[1] and surely any credulous persons who believed such an extravagant misstatement of ministerial gains, would only have believed it the more, had Ministers attempted to contradict it by calling in the aid of the criminal law.

With respect to prosecutions for libel, and all such proceedings, the ex-Chancellor most conscientiously entertained and unflinchingly expressed the same sentiments which induced him, in the year 1792, to cause a gentleman to be sentenced to the pillory for words overheard after dinner in a coffee-house, and in 1794 to convert speeches for parliamentary reform into overt acts of high treason. He now wrote:—

"Lord Grey said, last night, that he has no further measures to propose about the Unions; indeed, I do not know how he should, having been once himself at the

---

[1] 9 Hansard, 3rd series, 24.

head of a political association, which was, in fact, a political union."

Although he stood almost alone as an expounder of such antiquated notions, in resisting the Reform Bill he co-operated with a very numerous, enlightened, and independent portion of the community; and his opposition to it will never lower him in the estimation of posterity, even if all his apprehensions respecting its fatal consequences should happily prove groundless.

In deference to the peers who, after readily disfranchising hundreds of thousands of Irish forty-shilling freeholders, had expressed a sacred regard for the rights of the most corrupt portion of the old English constituencies, the third bill on this subject, now introduced, enacted "that the hereditary franchise of *freemen* in corporations to vote for members of Parliament, should be preserved, without regard to their substance or situation in life;" but Lord Eldon was in no degree mollified, and next day he thus wrote to Lord Stowell:—

"December 13.

"At present I can make no other observation upon it, except that Ministers, who, at the end of the recess, have been obliged to confess that they were, before that recess, pressing for the passing of a bill of the utmost importance, upon imperfect information as to so many things which required that they should have the most perfect and complete information,—that such Ministers deserve impeachment."[1]

While this Reform Bill was passing through the House of Commons, the Lords were much occupied with discussing a measure for the commutation of tithes in Ireland, which has worked very beneficially by at last entirely

---

[1] Some of Lord Eldon's letters without news or incident for biography are, to my own taste, the most agreeable and interesting. Thus, on the 1st of January, 1832, he, being himself above eighty, addresses Lord Stowell, verging on ninety:—

"Dear Brother,—I trouble you with this, to wish you on New Year's Day all the health and happiness that a brother's affection can possibly lead him to wish you may enjoy. God bless you, is my anxious, heartfelt wish and prayer.

"You will hear from me again very shortly, as to my intended movements from hence. Beautiful weather here.

"Yours, most affectionately yours,
"ELDON.
"New Year's Day."

extinguishing one of the most fruitful sources of discord in that unhappy country. But Lord Eldon was for adhering to the old system of payment of tithes in kind, although the occupier of the land who was to pay them was generally a Roman Catholic, and the receiver a Protestant clergyman—often without any congregation. He thus wrote upon the subject to his brother:—" The Irish tithes are matters infinitely difficult to manage; and, from all I can learn, the day is approaching, and fast approaching, when laws of all sorts in that country will give way to force and arms." In the House of Lords he said, that " when a measure was brought forward which went directly to the annihilation of Church property, and when they were not even told by those who brought such a measure forward what they would substitute for that property, he was very much disappointed not to see a single member of the Right Reverend Bench rise to defend the interests of the Church now so vitally at stake, and to protest against a measure of such a description as the present. There was no argument which applied to the extinction of Church property in Ireland, but what was equally cogent against Church property in England. He thanked his God, however, that he should not be amongst either the ecclesiastical or the lay supporters of this motion. He would not give his assent—his opposition, he saw, would be useless—to a measure which went to deprive the Ministers of the United Church of England and Ireland of that which constituted their entire support, and to which they had as much right as there existed to any lay property in any part of England. It was perfectly absurd to suppose that what would take place in Ireland in this instance would not be sure afterwards to take place in England also."[1]

Notwithstanding Lord Eldon's rebuke to the Bishops, the Commutation Bill for Ireland passed quietly, and, as he foretold, it has been followed by a similar measure in England—which has not only added to the revenues of the clergy, but which has contributed to the present extended popularity and usefulness of the Established Church.

Lord Eldon was now much irritated by a conversation in the House of Commons, in which his name, as he

[1] 10 Hansard, 3rd series, 1269.

thought, had been wantonly and invidiously introduced. A motion having been made respecting the alleged accumulation by Lord Plunket, the Chancellor of Ireland, of places and reversions on his own relations, Mr. Spring Rice, in his defense, referred to the Report of a Committee of the House of Commons, from which it appeared that six legal offices of profit were held by Lord Eldon's son, the Honorable W. H. J. Scott;—adding that, " if there had been six sons, thirty-six offices would have been distributed among them; and that, with such a record open for inspection, it was wonderful that any member should reserve his virtuous indignation for the Lord Chancellor of Ireland." As soon as Lord Eldon heard of this attack, he formed the resolution, which he thus announces to Lord Stowell:—

" 8th March.

" Before you receive this, you will have seen in the papers a speech in the House of Commons of Mr. Rice, justifying Lord Plunket's appointments for the benefit of the Plunket family—and justifying him by the example of Lord Eldon's conduct in giving offices to his son. Neither I, nor any friend of mine, had any notice of that gentleman's intent to say one word relative to me and my son.

"I am going down to the House of Lords, though very ill able so to do, to seek an opportunity of saying something upon the subject—and, though this sort of business is very unpleasant, I have no doubt that when my explanation is made I shall be very triumphant."

He hurried to the House and gave his notice, saying, that " he had no other object but to set himself right in the opinion of his countrymen, to whom he would leave to decide whether his conduct, while he filled the office of Chancellor, had been right or wrong? He had discharged his duty, invariably, to the best of his ability, and he would allow no man, unanswered, to arraign him."[1]

According to Hansard, Lord Eldon delivered a very in different speech—making many protestations of disinterestedness—relating again how the Great Seal had been forced upon him—and asserting that he had conferred the offices on his son only in obedience to the repeated commands of the King, and to show his respect for the Crown,

[1] 10 Hansard, 3rd series, 1268.

—the value of them all being very inconsiderable.¹ But he appears to have been indistinctly heard by the reporters; and we have from himself the following satisfactory account of the result:—

" March 13th, 1832.

"The business of last night went off very well. My voice is too weak to have anything that proceeds from it well reported.

"Publications here, wicked and diabolical, have represented W. H. J. as receiving, under a patent in bankruptcy, £12,000 a-year. I proved to the House that, under that patent, he did not receive one farthing.

"I proved to the House also, that, instead of greedily laying hands on all sources of income in the office, I had, out of my own pocket, supplied, in ease of the suitors, sixty-two thousand pounds.² I think I can assure you that all sides of the House were very well satisfied. Even many who, for various reasons, wished me to withdraw my intention of moving, came to me after I had done, expressing their delight that I had refused to attend to those wishes. The Chancellor stated that I had acted in my communications with him with perfect liberality, and that W. H. J., in the office that connected him with the Chancellor, had conducted himself entirely to his satisfaction."

He sometimes raised an ungrounded suspicion by his *professions*, but, in truth, there is no reason to suppose that he ever made any unfair profit himself, or that he ever improperly conferred any offices on his family.³

When the new Reform Bill had nearly run its course through the House of Commons, all other topics were forgotten in the speculations as to its reception by the Peers. Lord Eldon wrote to his brother:—"It seems to me now too clear that the opponents to the Reform Bill will split upon the question about reading the bill a second time, or rejecting it upon the second reading. If they do,⁴

---

¹ 11 Hansard, 3rd series, 94.
² I do not understand how this is made up, except by his contributions to the salary of the Vice-Chancellor; but, on such occasions, he did not consider himself bound to adhere too rigidly to Cocker.
³ There could not possibly have been a better appointment than when he made Mr. Farrer—connected with him by marriage—a Master in Chancery.
⁴ *i. e.* "allow it to be read a second time." And I think he was right. The opponents of the bill would have had a better chance by throwing it out again on the second reading, then trying to strangle it in the committee.

I fear the bill will pass. I attribute much to affright, and fear of mobs. I don't wonder that there should be such affright and fear. The numerous most *violent* and *furious menacing* letters which I receive are enough to affright persons less accustomed than I am to receive them. I am myself sure, that those who are afraid of the immediate consequences of rejecting the bill will ultimately suffer much more by passing it—the Bishops particularly."

On the 26th of March the bill was brought from the Commons. Lord Eldon was observed to eye the scene with a sorrowful countenance, denoting a foreboding heart,—but he did not take any share in the brief discussion which preceded its being read a first time, and ordered to be read a second time on the 9th of April.[1] In this interval he made a tour for the benefit of his health, that he might be strengthened for the fatigues which were before him.

Speaking on the fourth night of the debate on the second reading, he said:

"That, during the fifty years of his public life, he had never suffered such deep pain as on seeing the House of Commons come to the bar of that House with the bill now upon their Lordships' table. Looking at that body as representing the constituency of the country—the light in which all great constitutional authorities held that they ought to be viewed—he could not but feel a deep sense of humiliation in recollecting the *pledges* under which they had permitted themselves to be returned to the House of Commons. At the time of the Revolution of 1688, when the Convention came to pass an Act of Parliament by which the best rights of the subject were secured, they set out by a declaration, affirming that they were not delegates from this place or from that place, but, clothing themselves with a character more elevated and a higher duty, they declared that they were the representatives of all the commons of England. To convert a member of the other House of Parliament into the mere representative of the particular place for which he was returned, instead of the representative of the whole of the commons of England, was a perversion of one of the best principles of the Constitution; and if there were members of the other House who would indeed submit to the deg-

[1] 11 Hansard, 3rd series, 858–870.

radation of being called to account by their particular constituents, it was high time to take measures to prevent such men from continuing to sit in Parliament.—He had heard much of an exercise of the royal prerogative, by which the passing of this bill was to be secured. He did not deny the right of the Sovereign to the free exercise of that prerogative. He would admit that, at the next Recorder's report of persons condemned at the Old Bailey, the Sovereign possessed not only the right to grant a free pardon to any number of such convicts, but to make peers of them if he pleased. At the same time he contended, that no censure would be too severe, no punishment too great, for any Minister who should advise his Sovereign to destroy the House of Lords by an enormous creation of new peers. It had been proposed by some of those who wished to set aside the Constitution as it existed, that writs should be issued by the Sovereign to new boroughs and great towns, and that the writs which had been usually issued should be withheld from others; and he would say, without hesitation, that, if the advice given by one of the newspapers to swamp that House with a number of new peers was adopted by the Minister, he would not pursue a course less unconstitutional than if he was to advise the King to exercise his prerogative with respect to the writs in the manner he had stated. Borough property was a species of property which had been known in this country for centuries; it had been over and over again made the subject of purchase and sale in all parts of the kingdom; and they might as well extinguish the right of private individuals to their advowsons, as their right to exercise the privileges which they derived from the possession of burgage tenures.—He could not separate from this bill the two bills for amending the representation of the people in Scotland and Ireland. If he had those bills with him, he could demonstrate to the conviction of all who heard him, that the Scotch bill would create a perfect revolution in Scotland, and that the Irish bill would destroy all those bulwarks which were essential to the safety of the Protestant Establishment in Ireland.—He maintained that, during all these discussions, the name of the King had been shamefully and unconstitutionally used. The Sovereign was constitutionally advised to recommend the consideration of this measure to his Parliament; but he was not constitutionally advised when he was brought forward, almost personally, to say that he was determined to have it carried into law. For the sake of the higher, the middle, and the lower orders of society, —for all of whom, and more particularly for the last, he considered himself a trustee,—he was determined, as far as in him lay, to preserve the blessings of that Constitution under which they had all been born and spent their lives, which had rendered them happier than any other people on God's earth, and which had given to their country a lustre and a glory that did not belong to any other nation in the world." [1]

After an admirable reply from Earl Grey, which was not concluded till after six in the morning, the House divided. During this ceremony intense anxiety prevailed, for it was uncertain which side would have the majority,—and the excitement did not subside when it was announced that, of the peers present, there were 128 CONTENT and 126 NOT CONTENT. Proxies were then called, and Lord Eldon gave a tremulous and desponding *Not Content* for Lord Stowell, as, before his name was called, it had been ascertained that the proxies increased the majority from two to nine.[2]

I was again present at this division. The victory was borne with great moderation by the Reformers within the House; but a very different spectacle presented itself in Palace Yard from what had been witnessed there in the dawn of the 8th of October preceding. It was a beautiful spring morning, and the sun, already high above the horizon, shone upon immense masses who had all night been inquiring news as to the different speakers in the House, and the probable result. When the event was known, they rent the air with their acclamations. However, they were all in good humor; and, while Lord Grey was rapturously cheered, I saw Lord Eldon led to his carriage and drive off, looking more dead than alive, but without receiving insult or annoyance.

The committee on the bill stood for the 7th of May, and then the real opinion of the peers was disclosed. Lord Lyndhurst having moved that the clause disfran-

---
[1] 12 Hansard, 3rd series, 390.
[2] 56 to 49: so that the numbers were 184 to 175. 12 Hansard, 3rd series, 454.

chising the rotten boroughs enumerated in Schedule A, which was the essence of the measure, should be postponed, his motion was carried by a majority of 151 to 116. This indiscreet display of undisguised hostility brought on the most memorable crisis in our constitutional history since the Prince and Princess of Orange were placed upon the throne.[1] Ministers were now furnished with a plausible ground for proposing a creation of peers, as this was the only mode of controlling the irresponsible power of the House of Lords, and the Reform Bill, which the nation demanded, seemingly could not be carried by other means.

The conduct of William IV. on this occasion ought to make his memory respected. He still behaved with entire good faith to his Ministers. Although he had expressed his approbation of the Reform Bill, he had warned them that he only wished to see it carried by constitutional means. Now he very reasonably observed, that "he did not consider a large creation of peers, to overpower the recorded opinion of the House of Lords on a pending measure, to be in accordance with the principles of the Constitution; the attempt might fail by giving offense to the body of the peerage; and at any rate it would establish a dangerous precedent, which would soon be the ruin of one branch of the legislature, and utterly upset the balance of the Constitution."

Earl Grey and his colleagues had no course to take but to resign; for it was utterly impossible for them to remain in office and to see their measure mutilated and destroyed by its adversaries. Their resignation was accepted, and for some days it was thought that a Government might be formed by a section of the Conservative party, who, although of opinion that our representative system was absolutely perfect, suddenly professed themselves ready to remodel the existing bill, and to grant a large measure of reform. This proceeding, however, not only drew forth a dangerous burst of public indignation, but was not satisfactory to Lord Eldon and many of the high Tories, who thought that all change in the representation should still be resisted; who considered the modified reform equally

---

[1] If the bill had *bona fide* been allowed to go into committee, with a view to considering its different clauses, there can be no doubt that it might have been considerably modified, in spite of all the efforts of the Government.

destructive with the plan in its original extravagance; and who declared that the Whigs ought in no degree to be relieved from the awful responsibility they had incurred. The new Government, therefore, could not proceed; and, without ever having been formally installed, it fell to pieces, after having existed about eight-and-forty hours. The King was driven to recall his old servants on their own terms, and he gave a written promise to create the requisite number of peers,—an operation which, it was hoped, might not produce permanent inconvenience, as there was an intention to call up, by writ, the eldest sons of existing peers, and to select a considerable number of childless old gentlemen, of respectable birth and character, whose titles would die with them.

There can be little doubt that if Lord Eldon and the party who supported him had persevered in their fierce resistance to the Reform Bill, this most hazardous experiment would have been made; but we were saved from it by the address of the King, and the moderation of the great bulk of the Conservatives. His Majesty caused a letter to be written to them, plainly stating the situation in which he was placed,—disclosing the promise he had given, and recommending that, to obviate the necessity for carrying it into execution, they should absent themselves from the House during the subsequent stages of the bill. Lord Eldon, before the crisis was over, had zealously argued that "although the existence of the King's prerogative to create peers could not be questioned, the House might question the fitness of its exercise on any particular occasion," and had protested against the application of it for the purpose now threatened, as being "at once injurious to the people and perilous to the Crown;"[1] but when he saw that the threat, if necessary, really would be carried into execution, and calmly surveyed the circumstances in which the nation was placed, he prudently judged that the less evil would be to suffer the bill to pass without further opposition, as thereby the fate of the peerage might be postponed, and a remnant of the Constitution might be saved. Accordingly he absented himself from the House till the English Reform Bill had passed, nor did he join in any of the protests against it;

---

[1] 12 Hansard, 3rd series, 1097.

and much as he disapproved of the like bills for Scotland and Ireland, he offered them no opposition.[1]

A deep debt of gratitude is due to those who thus sacrificed inclination to a sense of duty. Had they obstinately forced on a violent creation of peers, there is considerable doubt whether the Reform Bill would have been carried, or an immediate public convulsion would have been avoided, while no one can deny that a dangerous wound would have been inflicted on the Constitution.[2] We should have been still more obliged to these conscientious men, if, participating in enlightened public opinion, they had in due season been convinced of the necessity for reform, and, by spontaneous compliance with measures for adapting our representative system to the altered circumstances of the nation, they had prevented the existence of the difficulty which they afterwards assisted to remove. But we who co-operated in the revolution by which power was transferred, in this country, from an oligarchy to the middle classes, should regard with sincere respect the sentiments of those who opposed it, bearing in mind that, while the prophecies of the sudden ruin it was to bring upon the state have fortunately proved fallacious, there has been a considerable shortcoming in the benefits it was expected to confer, and that, if the nation has got rid of the scandal of rotten boroughs and the reproach of great cities unrepresented, a very serious inconvenience has arisen from the difficulty of introducing into Parliament young men of promising talents, and likewise experienced statesmen the best fitted to serve the Crown ;—while, with splendid exceptions, the representatives of the newly enfranchised constituencies have not added much to the reputation of the House of Commons, either for eloquence or the effective despatch of parliamentary business. It must likewise be admitted

---

[1] The English Reform Bill was read a third time and passed in the House on the 4th of June ; the Scotch Reform Bill on the 13th of July ; and the Irish Reform Bill on the 30th of July.

[2] See Lord Brougham's " Political Philosophy," part iii. p. 307, where the noble author expresses a doubt whether—although a list of eighty new creations had actually been made out, " upon the principle of making the least possible permanent addition to our House and to the aristocracy, by calling up peers' eldest sons ; by choosing men without any families ; by taking Scotch and Irish peers,"—Lord Grey and his colleagues, if the Conservative peers had persisted in opposing the bill, would not rather have allowed it to be lost than resort to such a violent measure. But I confess it seems to me that they had gone too far to recede.

that corruption at elections has been in no degree repressed.

During the present session Lord Eldon was likewise called upon to resist changes, which he considered very dangerous, in the criminal law, in the law of real property, and in the procedure of the Court of Chancery. He once more, but now ineffectually, opposed bills to take away the punishment of death from the offense of stealing in a dwelling-house, and of horse-stealing—when he reiterated his arguments upon the salutary tendency of the dread of a capital sentence, even where it is not to be inflicted, and the danger to property from a sudden relaxation of the severity of the penal code.[1]

The Real Property Commissioners appointed by Sir Robert Peel had, with incessant labor, and with the aid of the most eminent men in the profession of the law, prepared a bill whereby, for the tedious, harassing, expensive, and perilous system of fines and recoveries by means of fictitious actions in the Court of Common Pleas, was substituted a simple deed, to be executed by the parties interested,—a bill allowing a brother of the half-blood of the purchaser of an estate to succeed to it rather than a distant collateral relation,—a bill to simplify conveyances, and to clear titles by regulating the law of dower,—and a bill giving uniformly an indefeasible title to land by an adverse possession of twenty years, whereas the period of prescription before was in some cases five years, and in some cases might be extended to five hundred. These bills were introduced this session into the House of Commons by the gentleman who was at the head of the Commission.[2] Here they were received with general applause, and they seemed likely to pass quietly through the House of Lords. But when they stood for a second reading there, "the Earl of Eldon said, he wished to call the attention of his noble and learned friend on the woolsack to the bills at present in progress through Parliament for making essential changes in the law of real property, and to suggest whether it would not be expedient to refrain from proceeding any further with the bills in the present session. The bills proposed to make most extensive and essential changes in the law. They were founded on the Reports of the Commissioners on the Law of Real

[1] 13 Hansard, 3rd series, 987.   [2] Mr. Campbell, then M. P. for Stafford.

Property, but, recollecting what these Reports were, and the great importance of the alterations, he thought that time ought to be given to consider the subject till the next session; and his advice would be to every proprietor of land, in Parliament, to take home with him an eminent lawyer, and an able solicitor, in order to ascertain what was to become of his property under the provisions of these bills, if they should pass into laws." [1]

The Lord Chancellor, in deference to such high authority, very properly agreed that the bills should stand over, but they passed in a subsequent session without the alteration of a single word being made in any of them in either House of Parliament;—and I believe, that if Lord Eldon were now alive, he would admit that they have operated beneficially.[2]

He finally expressed his high disapprobation of the last reforming measure of the session, which was to abolish a large number of sinecure offices in Chancery, and to simplify some of the proceedings of that Court. "The Earl of Eldon lamented that such a bill should have been brought forward at this period of the session. He could not agree that all these offices were sinecures, and great inconvenience might result from their abolition before a proper provision was made for the performance of the duties. He had filled the office of Lord Chancellor

---

[1] Against the "Limitation of Actions Bill," that most salutary statute, which swept away between fifty and sixty species of actions, his argument resolved itself into the lamentation "that professional men, if these measures were carried, would have to begin their legal studies over again." 2 Townsend, 463. That statute it fell to my lot to prepare. But my labor was light compared to that of my friend Mr. P. B. Brodie, who prepared the statute for substituting a *Deed* in the place of "Fines and Recoveries." This I do deliberately pronounce to be one of the most wonderful efforts of the human mind. The very learned and acute Sir Edward Sugden, late Lord Chancellor of Ireland, not unreasonably pronounced the plan impossible, and recommended that there should merely be some more simple forms which should be declared to have the same operation as Fines and Recoveries,—perpetuating that complicated and abstruse and most artificial head of learning. But Mr. Brodie, comprehensively viewing all that was before done by Fines and Recoveries, has admirably made provision for the same being done directly by Deed between parties,—without, in any respect, shaking the security of titles, and without varying, by a shade, the power of cutting off entails which before existed. All who are acquainted with the subject must be aware of the tremendous difficulties which he had to encounter. Landed proprietors who now re-settle their estates—when they consider the enormous expense and vexation from which they are rescued—ought to exclaim, " Thanks be to God and Peter Bellinger Brodie!"

[2] 14 Hansard, 3rd series, 900. Stat. 3 & 4 W. 4, c. 74, c. 106 c. 105, c. 27.

for seven-and-twenty years, with only a very short interval, and he had been practicing at the bar of the Court for many years; could it, then, be possible for that which was called '*Chancery Reform*' to have escaped his attention, and that of his many noble and learned predecessors? and their impression certainly was, that improvement in the Court of Chancery was not to be brought about by the sudden introduction of a ready-formed system, but by propounding reforms and making orders, as the necessity for them should from time to time arise."[1] Unfortunately, in spite of the most glaring necessity and of repeated warnings, he had propounded no reforms—he had made no orders to correct acknowledged abuse; and the feeling on this occasion was so strong against him, that all sides supported the bill, and it passed without difficulty. He was so much annoyed by such defeats, that he wrote to Lord Stowell:—

" August, 1832.

" I do not *think* I shall be able to persuade myself to go down to Parliament again. God knows I have strength little enough left to be able to afford wasting any portion of it in an attendance utterly, absolutely, and hopelessly useless. Uneasiness of mind, produced by observing *what* is there going on, and *how*, weighs me down more than I can endure, and I rather think that I shall not again think of enduring it."

He was at present likewise haunted by the dread of " Political Unions," which he prophecied would soon " suppress the House of Commons, and the House of Lords too, and the third and higher branch of the legislature into the bargain."[2] He particularly reprobated their doctrines of free trade. " The Unionists," says he, " are, it seems, unanimous for a repeal of the corn laws. The abused and misled lower orders are all for this. It will ruin them. Suppose the repeal lowers rents one-half —what is the consequence of that? The landed gentlemen can neither keep one half of the number of servants they now keep, nor spend one half of what they now spend with tradesmen and manufacturers. Of course the tradesmen and manufacturers must lower the wages, one half, of all the servants and workmen they employ, or only employ one half of them.—The system that the

[1] 14 Hansard, 3rd series, 1177.   [2] Letter to Lord Encombe.

working class and servants are now pushing must ruin themselves."[1] These sentiments are probably still approved by many; and it should be remembered that, when they were uttered, Lord Eldon entertained them in common with a vast majority of the intelligent and independent statesmen of this country.

CHAPTER CCXI.

CONTINUATION OF THE LIFE OF LORD ELDON TILL HIS FINAL RETREAT FROM POLITICS.

SOON after the conclusion of this session of Parliament, which Lord Eldon considered so disastrous, he had the misfortune to lose his second son, William Henry, who, although disqualified for steady application to business by his sinecures, had much natural cleverness, insomuch that his father said, "If I had not been Chancellor, William Henry might."[2]

The bereaved parent, to divert his melancholy, undertook a journey to visit his estate in the county of Durham, which he had not seen for many years. He fixed his head-quarters at the inn at Rusheyford. Being pressed to go on to Newcastle, he said, "Ay, I know my fellow-townsmen complain of my not coming to see them; but how can I pass that bridge?" He referred to the bridge

[1] Letter to Lord Stowell.
[2] The young gentleman had likewise a considerable share of dry humor. He once told me that, while a member of the House of Commons, he made it a rule to be always present at the *division*, and never at the *debate*; adding,—"I regularly read the arguments on both sides in the newspapers next morning, and it is marvelous that I uniformly find I have been right in my votes."
While this sheet is passing through the press, I have heard a noble peer relate the following anecdote, for the purpose of illustrating the characters of Lord Eldon and his son William Henry:—"They were walking together in Piccadilly, when a gentleman, driving past them in a smart cabriolet,—(with a "*tiger*" behind,—took off his hat and made a low bow. 'Who is that?' said Lord Eldon, 'who treats me with respect, now that I am nobody?' 'Why,' said William Henry, 'that is Sir John Campbell, the Whig Solicitor-General.' 'I wonder what they would have said of me,' cried the ex-Chancellor, 'if I had driven about in a cabriolet when I was Solicitor-General.' 'I will tell you what they would have said, dear father,' replied William Henry, 'they would have said, There goes the greatest *lawyer* and the worst *whip* in all England.'"—*1st Edition*, 1847.

across the Tyne looking on the house where "Bessy" had lived with her parents, and from which she had eloped with him.

After his return to Encombe he was cheered by finding, on the dissolution of Parliament, to which, after a good deal of hesitation, William IV. had agreed, at the pressing request of his Ministers,[1] that there were still some Conservative returns, and particularly one for his native county. Thus he gayly and gracefully congratulated the lady of the new Member:—

"DEAR MRS. BELL,

"The heart of an old gentleman of eighty-two is so overjoyed by the intelligence you have been so kind as to send him, that he is quite renovated in youth, health, and spirits; and he thinks if he had you for his partner, he could go down a country dance, as in days of yore, to the tune of Bonny Northumberland."

The opening of the first Reformed Parliament, in January, 1833, when Mr. Manners Sutton, though a keen Conservative, was placed in the chair of the House of Commons, and the Irish Coercion Bill was introduced into the House of Lords, gave much contentment to Lord Eldon,—while it was not quite satisfactory to all the Liberal supporters of the Government. As might be expected, he highly lauded the measure by which courts-martial were to be substituted for trial by jury, in the disturbed districts in Ireland; and he cautioned Lord Gray so to word it, that offenses committed while it was in operation might be punished after it had expired.[2] When the bill came back from the Commons with some mitigation of its severity, he cavilled at the amendments which had been made in it.[3]

All the other bills brought forward by the Government he strenuously opposed. That founded on the Report of

[1] I happened to be called into the King's closet to kiss hands and to be knighted, on my appointment as Solicitor-General, a few minutes after this consent was given; and the excited state in which I found them has since been explained to me.

[2] 15 Hansard, 3rd series, 750.

[3] 16 Hansard, 3rd series, 1294. He secretly believed Catholic Emancipation to have caused all the mischief. In a letter to his daughter while the bill was pending, he says,—"The Duke of Wellington made a good speech; but neither he nor Grey could very easily, and certainly not at all get out of the scrape, by the Roman Relief Bill being the cause of all the disorders and miseries now to be checked and remedied if possible."

the Common Law Commissioners, authorizing the Judges to make rules for regulating pleading as well as practice in their Courts, he condemned, as conferring upon them a legislative power, and he insisted that all the proposed amendments should be specified and defined by Act of Parliament.[1] Yet it passed.[2]

He likewise opposed Lord Brougham's bills for regulating the Judicial Committee of the Privy Council as a court of appeal, and for the establishment of County Courts,—and wrote thus disparagingly of both of them to Lord Stowell:—

"April, 1833.

"The Chancellor must think the Privy Council, as heretofore attended, has been a sad tribunal; for he has brought a bill into the House of Lords, in which he makes all the Judges, and even the principal commissioner of the new Court of Bankruptcy, additional members of a Committee of Privy Councillors, to hear ecclesiastical appeals, prize court appeals, &c., &c. Either he or I am becoming very foolish.

"He has brought in another bill for establishing permanent courts in the different counties, with sergeants or barristers of ten years' standing, constantly sitting with juries, in like manner as the Judges when they go the Spring and Summer circuits throughout the kingdom,—each county as it were having through the year a county Westminster Hall of its own. This odd scheme is at first to be tried only in two or three counties, to see how it answers. I hope he won't select, as his trial or experiment counties, Durham or Dorset; perhaps you would not wish him to take Berks or Gloucestershire. But there are no Lords attending the House upon such matters, and he will have his own way."

Again, respecting this last measure, he thus writes to his daughter:—

"I went down yesterday[3] to denounce a most abominable law bill of the Chancellor's; spoke as strongly against it as an old lawyer's mind and body could enable him to speak, and moved to put off the bill for six months. *His* friends brought together a majority against me;—those—many—who ought to have been *my* friends, to many of whom I

---

[1] 16 Hansard, 3rd series, 1060.   [2] 3 & 4 W. 4, c. 42.
[3] See 18 Hansard, 3rd series, 1105.

had been a friend indeed in past life, would not take the trouble to come, or to stay,—and I was beaten; a thing I don't relish much, and the less because the measure I opposed is, I think, one of the most objectionable I have ever seen proposed to Parliament. I shall attend on the day when a third reading of it will be proposed, vote against it, and record my opinions and objections in a protest. That done, I shall attend no more, except when the Church Reform Bill comes to us, as to which, I think, nobody is acting discreetly and prudently on either side. I know I am gone by, and can do no good; but I will not, in so very important a matter, shrink from making an attempt, however feeble or useless it may be, to do my duty."

The Judicial Committee Bill passed this session, to the great benefit of the community; but the Local Courts Bill was lost in a subsequent stage by the powerful opposition of Lord Lyndhurst.

Lord Eldon was most incensed against Lord Stanley's Irish Church Temporalities Bill, by which ten bishoprics were suppressed, and their revenues were to be applicable to the maintenance of parochial clergy, and the payment of church cess. When it came up from the Commons, although without the famous "appropriation clause," he thus wrote to his daughter:—

"Our news, domestic, is very bad. The Duke of Wellington, and a lot of adherents who act with him, mean to vote for, and not against, the Church Reform Bill to-morrow on the second reading. The few of us who can't consent to Church spoliation will vote, from our hearts, against it; but beaten we must be, as this most unexpected change has taken place. What is to become of all that is worth preserving, is known only to Him who ruleth in heaven. I shall fight for my old principles to the last.

"The fatigues of the debate, which may be long, and perhaps night and night, to me will be, probably, very fatiguing indeed; but I shall nurse myself in the day-time, and keep in as good order as I can. In some part of the proceedings I shall speak."

He did attend, and made a very impressive speech, saying "that, conscious of the approach of that time when, in the course of nature, his existence must close, he felt himself, upon his oath and his honor, imperatively called on to occupy their Lordships' attention for some short space, while he stated the grounds of his opposition to this measure; and he trusted their Lordships would receive his sincere acknowledgments for the uniform respect and attention which they had bestowed upon him during the very long time for which he had sat upon the woolsack. It was a fallacy to talk of the Irish Church as something distinct from the English; from the time of the legislative union between the two countries, there was ONE UNITED CHURCH of England and Ireland. He urged the objections founded on the King's coronation oath, and on the engagement with Ireland and Scotland at the respective times of the two unions. With respect to the union of England and Ireland, the King, when he gave his consent to that Act, was called on, by the most solemn rites and ceremonies, not merely to say, '*Le Roi le veut*,' but he was also called on to say, in the most solemn manner, 'So help me God! I will maintain this Act.'" "And so help me God," his Lordship exclaimed, "I will not consent to any Act of Parliament that will disturb or affect the interests of that Establishment to which I have vowed my constant and eternal attachment. I must be allowed to say, whatever consequences it may expose me to, that if the Great Seal had been in my hands at the present time, which would have bound me to tender my humble advice on this subject to his Majesty, and if the King had declined accepting that advice which in my conscience I might have given, so help me that God before whose tribunal I have soon to appear, I would, with all dutiful respect, have said, 'Sire, it is my duty to assume that you understand that which I think your duty better than I do. The advice I have given is from my soul and conscience what I ought to give you. I am bound to defer to your judgment, but I can not entangle myself with the consequences which, in my after-life, must attach to other advice, and I can not go out of this room without resigning into your hands the seals of office, which compel me to tender you my advice. I have given my Sovereign my best advice, according to my humble judgment, and as it is not approved of, it is my duty to resign.' Can your Lordships suppose, knowing as you must what is going on in this country, that this measure is the limit to which you will be obliged to go, if you accede to it? The present bill destroys the church rates as now collected in Ireland; and every man who reads the newspapers must perceive that the moment is not far distant when no more church rates will be collected in England."[1]

The second reading of the bill was carried, however, by a majority of 157 to 98.[2] On the third reading, Lord Eldon returned to the attack with renewed energy. He said " he founded himself on the experience of a long life in affirming that the prosperity of this country was inseparably interwoven with the maintenance of an established religion. The Protestant religion he considered to be the best form of religion; and he had no more doubt than he had of his own existence, now drawing very near to a close, that the present bill was calculated to undermine the established religion of this country. He hoped the argument, that this was a measure calculated to strengthen the Church by its liberality, would not prevail in that House. He held religious belief to be a thing between God and a man's own conscience; but it must, at the same time, be allowed that a man, having acquired the liberty of his own conscience, was not therefore permitted to disturb the national peace and the national conscience. Whatever might be the opinion of their Lordships as to the religious feeling of the community, they might rely upon it, that if the principle of non-payment of rates because of a difference in religious belief were once established, many would be found to leave the Church for the purpose of evading the burthen. The union between the two countries never would have taken place if this measure could have been foreseen. This bill was a direct fraud upon the Protestants of Ireland,—he could give it no other name. He declared that he would rather forego his existence than support a bill which, in his opinion, was calculated to destroy the Established Church of Ireland."[3]

The bill passed by a great majority;[4] and although I am afraid that, from the mismanagement of property vested in commissioners, little practical good has been done by it, I do not believe that it has worked any injury to the Church, either in England or Ireland.

While Lord Eldon was now considered rather an old-

---

[1] 19 Hansard, 3rd series, 918.   [2] Ib. 1016.
[3] 20 Hansard, 3rd series, 114.   [4] 135 to 54. 20 Hansard, 3rd series, 114

fashioned politician, there was a due appreciation of his steady adherence to his principles,—and, the envy raised by the enjoyment of power having passed away, and the disappointments which must be occasioned by the exercise of great patronage being forgotten, he received tokens of respect and good-will from all classes of the community.

The following is an account of his reception by the Benchers, Barristers, and Students of the Middle Temple:—

"Yesterday being the grand day in Trinity Term at the Middle Temple, on which it is usual for the Judges and other distinguished members of the Society to dine in the Hall, the Earl of Eldon, who has not been present on this occasion for several years, dined at the Bench table. The venerable Earl was in excellent health and spirits. In the course of the evening he proposed as a toast, 'The Bar;' and shortly afterwards an intimation was made to the Bench, that the Bar then present were desirous of testifying their respect for the distinguished member of their Society and of the profession who had that day gratified them by his presence. 'The health of the Earl of Eldon' was then drunk with unexampled enthusiasm. The hall rang with acclamations, Bench, Bar, and Students appearing to vie with each other in their manifestations of respect.—The Earl of Eldon rose, evidently under the influence of considerable emotion, to return thanks. He observed 'that he could not but feel deeply sensible of the honor, or he would rather say the kind feeling, which the Bar had just shown towards him, when he called to mind that a period of half a century had elapsed since he first became a member of that Society. Long, he trusted, might the Bar continue to maintain that high, and honorable, and independent character, which was essential to the pure administration of justice, and which, he would take leave to say, was one of the main sources of the prosperity which this country had hitherto enjoyed. So long as the profession maintained that high character, he was sure that the people of this country would always look to Westminster Hall for the maintenance of their just rights,—and, looking to Westminster Hall, it is impossible,' said the noble Earl, turning towards the window of the Middle Temple Hall, which is decorated with the armorial bearings of Lords Clarendon, Somers, Talbot, Hardwicke, Ashburton, Kenyon, Tenterden, &c., 'that they can ever forget the Middle Temple.' The venerable Earl was, at the conclusion of his speech, and on retiring from the Halll, greeted with enthusiastic and continued cheering by the whole Society."

His own notice of this dinner, in a letter to his daughter, is still more touching:—

" I yesterday, being much pressed so to do, dined at the Middle Temple, at the Benchers' anniversary dinner. It was right that I should conquer, if I could, my great reluctance to everything of that sort, and I was repaid for my struggle to conquer that reluctance, by my reception. All the younger members of the Society dined, as well as the old ones, the Benchers; and, as I walked down the great Hall in which we dined, there was a general sort of acclamation of kindness from them all,.which cheered an old gentleman."

It happened that in a few months after he was subpœnaed as a witness in the Court of Exchequer in an action for false imprisonment, brought by an attorney of the name of Dicas against Lord Chancellor Brougham. The plaintiff proposed to prove, by the evidence of the ex-Chancellor, that the warrant under which he had been committed to the Fleet by the noble and learned defendant was contrary to the practice of the Court of Chancery, and therefore illegal. I give the rest of the story in the words of my excellent friend, Mr. Horace Twiss :—

"When Lord Eldon appeared on the Bench, which is the usual place for peers visiting a court of justice, the whole Bar respectfully rose, with one accord, from their seats. When he stood up to be sworn, the Bar again simultaneously rose. He was interrogated by Mr. (afterwards Baron) Platt, the leading counsel for the plaintiff, about his recollection of certain points of practice as they had been in his own Chancellorship. He stated that he could not distinctly recollect these points at such a distance of time ; but that he could not hope to have so conducted the business of his Court as not to have made some mistakes in a period of almost five-and-twenty years, during which he had held the great Seal, though he was not aware of any particular instance in which errors had been committed by him. At the close of his examination in chief he added, 'I am not a willing witness. I thought it my duty to comply when I was summoned by a subpœna; but, at my age and the distance I was at, I should have hardly been willing to come, unless I had considered it to be a duty between man and man.' It fell to Sir John (afterwards Lord) Campbell, at that time Solicitor General, who led for the defendant, the then Lord Chancellor, to cross-examine Lord Eldon. The learned Solicitor began by saying, 'Allow me, in the name of the Bar, to express the satisfaction we all have in the honor of seing your Lordship:' and then proceeded with his cross-examination. When it concluded, Lord Eldon, who had given his evidence in a low tone of voice, retired; and, as he withdrew, the Bar again expressed their reverence by rising from their seats as before. This was, probably, the only case in which it ever happened that a Lord Chancellor (Lord Brougham) was defendant; an ex-Lord Chancellor (Lord Eldon) a witness; another ex-Lord Chancellor (Lord Lyndhurst) the judge; and a future Lord Chancellor of Ireland (Lord Campbell) the counsel."[1]

But no attentions to himself could soothe his solicitude about public affairs — on which, shortly after this, he wrote to a friend:—

"When I look at the state of the country, and see, or think I see, the Monarchy, the Peerage, the owners of property, sinking—I fear inevitably sinking—under the rule and domination of Democrats, I have no comfort in looking forward."[2]

Yet his spirit remained unbroken, and he resolved to embrace any opportunity that might present itself for striving to serve his country—

> . . . . "though fall'n on evil days,
> On evil days though fall'n, and evil tongues;
> In darkness and with dangers compass'd round."

I now reach the year 1834, which is memorable in our party annals, and which before its termination witnessed the dismissal of the Whigs. But, after a short-lived Government conducted on principles which Lord Eldon could not applaud, they were re-called, and they remained in office till he was removed from a world made sad to him by such mortifying vicissitudes.

[1] Chap. lvii.   [2] Letter to Commissary Gordon, 13th Dec. 1833.

It was generally thought that on the death of Lord Grenville he would at last have become Chancellor of the University of Oxford, his principles being in such exact accordance with those of that learned body. However, I do not find an instance of an ex-Lord Chancellor of England being elected Chancellor of either University. Stoutly as Lord Eldon had fought for Church and King, he was now *emeritus*, and there was hardly a possiblity that he should again be possessed of power and patronage. The Duke of Wellington was not only the hero of a hundred battles, terminating with Waterloo, but was expected before long to resume his station as Prime Minister. His Grace being brought forward by a more influential party, Lord Eldon immediately gave way, but was at first evidently not a little hurt that the author of "the Roman Catholic Bill" should be preferred to the champion of Protestant Ascendency; and thus he wrote to his daughter:—

"I take it that the Duke of Wellington will certainly be the Chancellor of Oxford. It is singular that the warmest supporters of the author of the Roman Catholic bill seem to be those who, on account of that Anti-Protestant measure, threw out Peel from his situation of M. P."

His chagrin was soon dissipated, and he joined in the general wish to do honor to the choice which the University had made,—as we learn from the following letter to his daughter:—

"The new Chancellor of the University of Oxford gave his dinner yesterday, upon being sworn into office. Being asked as High Steward, I thought it right to go. The Duke of Wellington proposed my health in a very handsome speech, and I addressed the company in an answer of thanks, in a way I hope tolerably good, and very well received. The attendance was fatiguing, but to-day I am not the worse for it. I was invited as High Steward to attend the great ceremonial in June at Oxford; but that would be too much for me, and I should have no pleasure in it."

Nevertheless, when June came round, he actually did attend the installation, and from the respect shown to him he had as much reason to be gratified as if he had actually worn the robes of Chancellor of the University. He thus explains his motives and his adventures:—

"The earnest desire expressed to me by so many of the University, that I should at least make my appearance there on this occasion, and the reasons, of a public nature and with reference to public interests, are so strong for my doing so, that repairing there has appeared to me *unavoidable;* but, after I have been there enough to satisfy the reasons for my going at all, I shall quit, and not stay the business throughout." [After describing the difficulty he experienced in finding post-horses on his journey:] "I did arrive, however, at the Vice-Chancellor's in time; and, a little after, arrived also at the Vice-Chancellor's the Duke of Wellington. He, as well as I, was obliged to make his entrance into Oxford with only a pair of poor miserably tired hack post-horses. We were both lodged, throughout the whole time, at the Vice-Chancellor's house, and our parties in it were comfortably small. The next morning was a fine morning, and the procession from University College to the Theatre was all on foot, through countless multitudes in the streets, cheering and huzzaing as we passed along. In this procession were almost all the doctors in divinity and law, except the bishops; and in this, as there are generally are in such spectacles, some very well-dressed pickpockets, one of whom contrived to empty the pockets of Lady Sidmouth's maid, who unfortunately had a good deal of cash in it,—I believe about fifteen pounds. This genteel pickpocket was dressed in academical gown and robes.

"The dinner that day was given, and a very splendid dinner it was, in University College. I *conjecture* that we had thirty peers or more at our banquet. The hall of University College has been put, by repairs, and ornaments, and embellishments, in a state of perfect beauty. We had some good speeches after dinner, and I did, in that way, as well as I could. The company sat long, and afterwards most of them went to the concert, but I did not adventure so to do."

Lord Encombe, with several other persons of distinction, was on this occasion to receive the honorary degree of Doctor of Civil Laws, and the following is an authentic account of the ceremony:—"When it came to his turn to be presented, there was great applause, and the looks of all were turned to Lord Eldon, whose eyes were fixed upon his grandson. Dr. Phillimore, as Law Professor, taking Lord Encombe by the hand, presented him to the Chancellor and Convocation with these words:—'Insignissime Cancellarie, vosque egregii Procuratores, præsento vobis prænobilem virum, Johannem Scott, Vice-Comitem Encombe, e Collegio Novo, Artium Magistrum, et Honoratissimi Comitis de Eldon——' This name had scarcely passed the professor's lips when there arose a universal shout of loud and enthusiastic cheering. Lord Eldon had stood up when his grandson approached, but was quite overcome by this burst of kind feeling toward himself and his family. Leaning his arm on the cushion of his desk he covered his face. When the first applause had subsided, the Professor resumed—"Comitis de Eldon"—but a second burst drowned his voice for several minutes longer. Dr. Phillimore found that it would be quite impossible to get on if he mentioned this name again, so when silence was obtained he continued—'unicum Nepotem, ut admittatur ad gradum Doctoris in Jure Civili, honoris causa.' The Duke of Wellington, as Chancellor, rising and taking off his cap, according to the usage, pronounced the formal admission: 'Vir honoratissime, ego, auctoritate mea et totius universitatis, admitto te ad gradum Doctoris in Jure Civili, honoris causa.'—Upon which Lord Encombe, advancing, ascended the steps of the Chancellor's chair, to receive his hand. The cordiality of the Duke's manner in welcoming his young friend drew fresh cheers from the assembly; and when Lord Encombe, instead of proceeding at once to his place among the Doctors, turned aside and, taking Lord Eldon's hand, bowed himself respectfully and affectionately upon it, the expressions of sympathy with the young nobleman were repeated by the spectators more warmly still. The aged Earl, after gazing on his grandson for some moments with overflowing eyes, again sank his head upon the desk before him, amid continued peals of applause, and covered his face with his hands from the view of the enthusiastic multitude."[1]

Lord Eldon, in writing to his daughter, Lady Frances, thus naturally expressed his own great delight:—

---

[1] This scene has been made the subject of a fine painting by Briggs, which has been beautifully engraved by Finden.

"Wednesday night (June 11th, 1843).

"This has been a very gratifying day—I have been quite overcome by the treatment I received in the Theatre to-day; it almost authorizes me to say that I have spent a life so as to gain a degree of estimation which I had no idea I possessed. It affected me extremely. The multitude in the Theatre quite uproarious: Down with all Whig pickpockets, &c., &c."

"Thursday (June 12th, 1834).

"It is quite overpowering to have met with the congratulations of multitudes, great multitudes, here, upon the reception of my name in the Theatre yesterday over and over again. When Encombe had his degree the manner in which the Duke of Wellington received and handed him up to me, the people calling out 'Eldon,' was affecting beyond anything I ever met."

When he returned to London, he said with honest exultation, "I will tell you what charmed me very much when I left the Theatre, and was trying to get to my carriage;—one man in the crowd shouted out, 'There is old Eldon,—cheer him, for he never ratted!' I was very much delighted, for I never did rat. I will not say I have been right through life—I may have been wrong—but I will say that I have been consistent." All mankind must admit the claim he here makes, which, perhaps, is as much to be respected as that made for candor by sudden "convertites."

But I must now return to the thorny path of politics. Before the installation at Oxford, Lord Eldon had enjoyed the satisfaction of seeing the Whig Ministers disagree among themselves as to the extent to which the property of the Irish Church might be interfered with by the State. This dispute can not yet be discussed as a matter of history, and for obvious reasons I abstain from touching on recent party transactions, except in as far as the subject of this memoir was personally concerned in them. He expressed unbounded delight when Lord Stanley, Sir James Graham, the Duke of Richmond, and Lord Ripon resigned; and he declared that "the misrule under which the nation had been suffering for some years must now be at an end." But, to his great surprise and mortification, Lord Gray's Government rallied from this blow, and for a little time recovered its popularity. The Whig Attorney-General, who, on his promotion, had been thrown out at Dudley on account of Irish coercion and the ministerial support of the Pension List, was, in a few days after, returned triumphantly for the City of Edinburgh; and the different sections of the Liberal party showed a disposition to reunite,[1]—so that Lord Eldon expressed a fear that "the restoration of the TORIES was indefinitely postponed." He always manfully adhered to this old, respected, time-honored name of his party, under which for near two centuries they had so gallantly defended the altar and the throne,—talking rather contemptuously of the upstart appellation of "Conservatives,"—among whom he foretold would be found some of very lax notions both respecting religion and politics.

Although watching anxiously the vicissitudes which seemed favorable or adverse to what he considered good government in the country, and although he still attended regularly in his place in Parliament,—on account of his declining strength he took very little part in the debates during the session; and when he did speak, he complained that he was not heard, and that he was misreported:—

> . . . . "his big manly voice
> Turning again toward childish treble."

He took occasion to denounce the supineness of the law officers of the Crown in not putting down "Trades Unions," whose meetings and processions he declared to be illegal;[2] and he once more inveighed against the unjust practice of disfranchising boroughs for corruption.[3] On the much agitated question, whether any surplus revenue of the Church of Ireland, after providing for the spiritual wants of all the members of the Church, might lawfully be applied to the general education of the people, he said with great earnestness,—" If there be any of your Lordships, or if there be any portion of my countrymen, who regard my opinion as an old lawyer, I do here in this place solemnly deny that the State has any right to meddle with the property of the Church at all. If there be any who will value my opinion when I am gone from among you, I now leave it behind me as my

---

[1] The news of these resignations reached Edinburgh during the night preceding the poll by an express from the Carlton Club, and was announced in handbills, posted all over the city before daybreak, as "*the utter ruin of the Whig cause;*" but it operated favorably for the Whig candidate.
[2] 23 Hansard, 3rd series, 96.   [3] Ib. 368.

solemn and deliberate declaration, that no lawyer on earth can prove that, according to any known principle of law, the surplus in question can be appropriated to any other purposes than those approved of by the Protestant Episcopal Church of Ireland." [1]

He was much excited by an affront which he thought had been offered to the administration of justice. The twelve Judges had been summoned to attend the House of Lords, to assist their Lordships in determining a writ of error from the Court of Exchequer Chamber, in a case which turned on the validity of the notice given of the dishonor of a bill of exchange. When the venerable sages of the law appeared in their robes, there was no Lord Chancellor, or other Speaker of the House, to receive them, and a scene of lamentable confusion ensued. At length the attendance of some lay lords was obtained, and one of these (the Earl of Abingdon), being elected Speaker, took his place on the woolsack—ordered the counsel to be called in—after the conclusion of the arguments at the bar, put a question to the Judges respecting the sufficiency of the notice of the dishonor of the bill,—and received their answer.[2]

At the next meeting of the House, "the Earl of Eldon said he wished to call the attention of their Lordships to a subject of much importance to their character. The attendance of the twelve Judges had been required by that House to give their opinion upon some question relating to a writ of error. Upon that occasion neither the Lord Chancellor, nor the Deputy Speaker, nor any law lord, was present to receive them. This, he could not help remarking, was most irregular,—contrary to the forms of their Lordships' House, and contrary also to their dignity and interests." "I recollect a case," said he, "wherein, the twelve Judges having given their opinions, the Lord Chancellor satisfied the House that they were all wrong. I recollect another case wherein the Lord Chancellor satisfied the House,—not that the opinions were wrong,—but that it would be wrong for that House to act upon them.[3] In the present instance, I believe, the Judges

[1] 24 Hansard, 3rd series, 268.
[2] Lords' Journals, 17th June, 1834. The noble Earl was long after addressed by his friends as "Lord Chancellor," and it is very doubtful whether I am not bound to write his life.
[3] In Mr. O'Connell's case, in 1845, the House of Lords thought that the

were right; but, with such instances on record, was it proper that the Judges should be left with a lay lord only to guide them? I will venture to say that the esteem and respect of the subjects of this country for the House of Lords, as a court of judicature, is greater than for any other tribunal in the country. For the sake of your Lordships and of the suitors, I shall move, on a future day, that the opinions of the twelve Judges shall never be received in this House, unless the Lord Chancellor, or one of the lords mentioned in the commission of Deputy Speaker, be present." The Lord Chancellor said that he himself had been engaged in the Court of Chancery, and that Lord Denman was expected to attend, but had been detained in the Court of King's Bench; whereupon Lord Eldon intimated that, in the hope that such an unfortunate occurrence would never again happen, he should waive the notice of motion which he had given.[1]

He would not oppose the New Poor Law, because it was warmly supported by the Duke of Wellington and almost the whole House of Lords; but he refused to vote in its favor, or to attend any of the discussions upon it, and thus he expressed himself respecting it to his daughter:—" Heaven grant that this new mode of treating the poor and needy may not bring forth those fruits which I for one anticipate! They are to proceed in this hazardous measure to-night; but 'unto their assembly mine honor shall not be united.' "

The last time that Lord Eldon ever spoke in Parliament was on the 25th day of July, 1834; and although the occasion was not a very important one, it enabled him to show his adherence to the principles which had guided him through life. Railroads he denominated, with some truth, "*dangerous* innovations;" and he was very glad to join in a vote rejecting, on the second reading, a bill, which had come up from the House of Commons, for the making of "the Great Western Railway." The majority against it being declared, Lord Wharncliffe said "he feared that the determination, to which the House had come, would lower the respect of the people for their Lordships." The *Earl of Eldon:* " I beg to tell the noble Lord that I have given my vote on *conscientious* grounds; and I am not to be told,

majority of the Judges were wrong, and decided according to the opinion of two dissentient Judges. [1] 24 Hansard, 3rd series, 597, 600, 604.

by him or any other noble Lord, that such a vote will be injurious to your Lordships in the estimation of the people."[1]

He resolved, now, to refrain from any effort of public speaking, but he still hoped to serve his country by his counsels; and, if asked, he would not have been unwilling even to take a seat in a Cabinet, the principles of which he entirely approved, if such an one should happily again be established before his eyes were closed. A sudden gleam of hope was created by the resignation of Earl Grey, but this was immediately overcast by the appointment of Lord Melbourne to succeed him, and Whig domination seemed firmly established under the admirable good sense, discretion, tact, and temper of the new Premier. A most stormy session closed in tranquillity.

For a while our ex-Chancellor forgot his political disappointments, by making another visit to his estate in the county of Durham, and gathering round him all his Northern relations. He even talked of having some merry-making beyond the Tyne; observing to his grandniece, "Well, Ellen, when you and I meet in the Newcastle Assembly Rooms, we will open the ball." *Ellen:* "Yes, uncle; remember, you are engaged to me." *Lord Eldon:* "I will not forget, and we will call for '*Jack's alive*,'—that will be the proper tune,—'*Jack's alive!*'"

In a letter to this young lady, on his return into Dorsetshire, he said:—

"I had a very dull journey from Rusheyford; how should it be otherwise? I had left those I liked to be with, and I had no company except that of an individual now generally spoken of as 'Poor old Eldon.' Here I arrived, however, at last, and got home to my cottage, which, being situated in a deep valley, is not seen till you reach the door of the house. I remember Dr. Warren, when he once came here upon a medical visit, exclaimed, 'Well, I have got to your *den* at last!' In that den I have been pretty generally confined since I entered it; I am, however, as well as I can expect to be."

While confined to his den, and rather in a desponding state of mind from thinking of the great majorities which the Whigs still commanded in the House of Commons,

[1] 25 Hansard, 3rd series, 467.

and the feeble resistance offered to them in the House of Lords, he was astounded by the intelligence, which he could not for some time believe to be true, that during the recess of Parliament—public affairs being in a state of profound tranquillity—King William had dismissed his Ministers, on the ground that Lord Althorp had succeeded to the title of Earl Spencer. "Now, at last," cried he, "the good old times must be restored, and I must be sent for." He was the more confident in this last expectation because Sir Robert Peel, not dreaming of changes of Government, was employing himself in viewing the curiosities of the Vatican. But a week having rolled away without summons or communication to him of any sort, in a letter to his grandson, dated Sunday, November 23rd, he thus betrays his disappointment: "To the moment I am writing I have had no letter from those who would heretofore have courted my advice, or been civil enough to pretend to ask it." However, having detained the letter till next day, he says in a postscript, "Since I wrote what precedes this, I have had a very civil letter from the Duke of Wellington. It tells me nothing material; and, until Peel comes, it *could not* tell me anything material."

He was evidently chagrined at being put off with mere civility, and he had serious misgivings from considering to whose hands the formation of the new Government was to be left; but still he had good hopes of him who had long successfully combated Catholic Emancipation, and having yielded to it from an overruling necessity, had since partly redeemed his character by a gallant resistance to the Reform Bill. Meanwhile, in writing to his daughter, he thus affected indifference, but disclosed anxiety, respecting what was to happen on the arrival of the Premier-elect:—

"The 'Standard' of yesterday contains, in an article from some other paper, that the intended arrangement for the Earl of Eldon has failed. No such arrangement could have failed, for no such was intended; and Lord Eldon is too old, and too wise, again to mingle in ministerial arrangements. I think nothing will be done, as to any such, with respect to anybody, till Peel comes home."

Lord Eldon was much hurt to find that the Cabinet was

filled up without his having the refusal of a seat in it, and without his having had the slightest concern in its formation, more than if he had never gone by the name of the "great Tory cabinet-maker." He now really cared little about place, but he was most seriously alarmed when he read the "Tamworth Manifesto,"[1] which spoke of acquiescing in the Reform Bill,—of respecting the rights of conscience, —and of relaxing restrictions upon commerce. Doubting whether the reins of government might not almost as well have remained in the hands of Lord Melbourne, who probably never seriously meditated any heavy blow to the Church, and might have been effectually restrained from inflicting any, he inveighed even more loudly against this new Government than he had against the Duke of Wellington's in 1828.

Sir Robert Peel now—as then—tried to soothe him by a civil letter:—

"Whitehall Gardens, Jan. 1st. 1835.

"DEAR LORD ELDON,

"Your long experience in public life and your devotion to your public duties will, I hope, have found an excuse for me, if, under the circumstances under which I was called to England, and the incessant and most harassing occupation in which I have been since engaged both night and day, I have appeared deficient, through my silence, in that respect which I most sincerely entertain for you, and which, but for the circumstances to which I have referred, ought to have and would have dictated a much earlier communication to you on the subject of the position of public affairs, and the course which I proposed as the King's Minister to pursue.

"That course has been now sufficiently indicated by the *public declarations* which I have been called upon to make, and by the *appointments* which have taken place, on my advice, to the chief offices of the King's Government. It only remains for me, therefore, to apologize to you for a seeming inadvertence and inattention which would be wholly at variance with my real feelings, and to express an earnest hope that the Administration over which I preside will entitle itself by its acts to your support and confidence.

[1] Sir R. Peel's Address to his Constituents.

"Believe me, my dear Lord, with the sincerest respect, and best wishes for your continued health and happiness,
"Most faithfully yours,
"ROBERT PEEL."

The very brief and stiff reply is silent respecting the "*appointments*" which had taken place by the advice of the Premier, but conveys marked disapprobation of his "*public declarations*":—

'DEAR SIR ROBERT PEEL,
"I don't delay acknowledging the receipt of your kind letter, which being directed to Encombe, did not reach that place till after I had left it, and has been returned from thence.

"If I forbear to enter into any statements respecting the subjects mentioned in that letter, I might be thought disrespectful in delaying my acknowledgments for the kindness and respect you have been pleased to express towards me,—a delay which might not be thought sufficiently apologized for, by observations which could only apply to subjects which I understand you to have been already fully determined upon. "I remain
"Yours very faithfully,
"ELDON."

He was consoled, however, by a carricature, meant for the gratification of all true Church-and-King politicians of the old school, which, while he was excluded from the new Cabinet, represented him as the fittest man in England to guide it. To this he refers in a letter to Lord Encombe:—"There is come out a print of Diogenes, with his lantern, searching the world for an honest man. He appears highly delighted in finding poor LORD ELDON, whose image he is holding forth in a stronger likeness of that poor old gentleman than I have yet seen."[1]

[1] Some may suspect me of maliciously misrepresenting Lord Eldon's wishes at this period of his life, and may believe that he contentedly courted retirement; but a very impartial observer, who knew him well, and cannot be misled by any party bias, writes to me :—" His love of power, and even office, survived the pardonable age. Even when the Duke of Wellington was called on to form his Administration in 1828, and very early communicated on the matter with Lord E., the latter (I have good grounds to believe) *offered* to resume the Great Seal, saying something very disparaging of his eminent successor. This is a point, however, on which I write with some restraint, by reason of its delicacy. I strongly surmise that this was a principal cause of the want of further communication from the Duke on this occasion, of which he loudly complained.

Although by no means contented with the present Government—upon a little reflection he pronounced it much preferable to anything that could be expected from the recall of the Whigs, who were now pressing for Municipal Reform, for a Dissenters' Marriage Bill, and even for the Appropriation of the Surplus Revenues of the Irish Church to the purposes of General Education. On the day after the meeting of the new Parliament he wrote to Lord Encombe:—

"Let anybody read the notices of motion given in the Commons last night, and avoid seeing, if it be possible, the danger of negligence about their political duties. I sat last night in the House of Lords till between twelve and one—till all in that House was over. I certainly would much rather have sat by my fireside quietly, and enjoying the comforts of conversation; but as one individual, I will not belong to the assembly of those who look only to personal ease, enjoyment, and comfort, and will not see what the intentions of some appear to be, as affecting their posterity, and, it may be, themselves ere long."

Thus he sneers, however, at the "Conservatives," whom he evidently considered as little better than Whigs:—

"The new Ministers certainly have the credit, if that be creditable, of being inclined to get as much popularity by what are called *reforms* as their predecessors; and if they do not, at present, go to the full length to which the others were going, they will, at least, make so many im-

" He certainly entered immediately with zeal into the bitterest counsels of the most infuriate Tories,—counsels marked not only by rashness and indiscretion which were discreditable in very young men, but were positively disgraceful in a veteran.

" I know that Lord Sidmouth resisted his urgent solicitations to join him in this opposition after the great event of 1829, even to the extent of almost quarrelling with him. The *revolution* (as I call it,—the *reform*, as you, by a pleasant euphemism, are pleased to designate it) of 1831-32, was the fruit of this fatal policy—policy for which few men were so deeply answerable as Lord E. Considering the great and habitual deference paid to him by all the Tory lords, we cannot doubt that he might have calmed the suicidal frenzy which marked all their conduct from February, 1829, to the same month in 1831, when even they could blind themselves no longer to the destructive consequences of their madness.

" A year or two after the Reform Act passed, he and a younger member of the aristocracy expressed together something like *indignation* against Sir R. Peel for having spoken of that Act in Parliament as one which it would be folly to attempt to repeal, and to which, therefore, it was necessary that practical statesmen should accommodate their views."

portant changes in Church and State, that nobody can guess how far the precedents they establish may lead to changes of a very formidable kind hereafter."[1]

During the residue of "the hundred days," things remained very quiet in the House of Lords while the deadly struggle was going on in the House of Commons. This was terminated by the majority of thirty-three in favor of Lord John Russell's motion for a "committee of the whole House to consider the temporalities of the Church of Ireland,"—which led to the resignation of Sir Robert Peel, and the formation of Lord Melbourne's second Ministry.

Lord Eldon now enjoyed the consolation of voting steadily against all ministerial measures, although he had the mortification to find that some of them, which he most severely condemned, were supported or but feebly opposed by a large section of "Conservatives." The Municipal Reform Bill, which had passed the House of Commons with plaudits from Sir Robert Peel, was the object of his special abhorrence. "He protested loudly against it in private, with feverish alarm, as leading directly to confusion. Its interference with vested rights shocked his sense of equity even more than the sweeping clauses of the Reform Act. To set at naught ancient charters as so many bits of decayed parchment, and destroy the archives of town-halls, seemed in the eyes of the old magistrate, for so many years the guardian of corporate rights, a crowning iniquity. Pale as a marble statue, and confined to his house in Hamilton Place by infirmity, he would deprecate equally the temerity of Ministers and the madness of the people; and his vaticinations, like the prophet's scroll, were full to overflowing with lamentations and woe. His correspondence, for some years previously, had borne marks of the troubled gloom with which he viewed the changes gradually darkening over all he had loved and venerated, till he felt almost a stranger to the institutions of his native land."[2]

Thus he describes to Lord Encombe what he considered the iniquitous proceedings of the Upper House in passing the Municipal Reform Bill, the operation of which is universally allowed to be very salutary:—

"I found, with hardly any exceptions, that the House

[1] Letter to Lady F. Bankes, March, 1835.   [2] Townsend, ii. 490.

of Lords, notwithstanding all I could say for the information of those who formerly would have listened to my humble advice, were determined to pass the bill, such as it has now become; and,—though I admit that Lyndhurst's amendments do him great credit,—to the shame of the House of Lords, the bill furnishes us one of the worst precedents, and as dangerous at least a precedent as any, to be found in the Journals of the proceedings of that House. They may call it, if they please, a bill for the Improvement of Corporations. I must maintain that it is no other than a bill of Pains and Penalties passed by the House of Lords in its *judicial* and *legislative* character, without any evidence before it, whether we consider the King's commission appointing commissioners of inquiry into corporations as *legal* or *illegal*. If the commission was illegal, evidence taken before commissioners under an illegal commission could never, according to law, be considered as legal testimony anywhere. If the commission was legal, and the examination of witnesses under it produced a crop of lawful evidence, the House had not the evidence before it, so acquired,—for not only did not the commissioners annex evidence or the testimony of witnesses examined, but, as I understand, if there was any such testimony on examination, the production of it was refused to the House of Lords. And it is whimsical enough to see that House beginning with the examination of Charley Wetherell in *defense* of his clients, before there was one single word of evidence *against* them before the House, or, as I believe, there yet is.[1] That the House should allow this,—that some lords, of whom I hoped for better things, should agree to this,—that I should be unable to go down to the House, from infirmity, to grapple with such proceedings,—has destroyed that quiet of mind within me, which is so essential to health. Save my country, Heaven! is my morning and evening prayer; but that it can be saved, it can not be hoped. 'Quos vult perdere dementat prius.'"

Encouraged by Lord Lyndhurst's successful opposition in the Lords to several clauses which Sir Robert Peel had warmly supported in the Commons, the undaunted Peer thus wrote to his old friend Sir Robert Vaughan:—

"The House of Lords seems at last to have thought that

[1] See 30 Hansard, 43-180.

it ought to do its duty. I think the Houses will be involved in collision when they meet.[1]

"I trust the cause of my country to that GREAT BEING, who alone can say to the madness of the people as He can to the raging waves of the ocean, 'Hither shall you come, and no further.'

"Let us begin to do, and persevere in doing, our duty; and then, discouraging as the prospect is, we may hope for better days."

However, the Municipal Corporation Bill, with some mutilations which have a little obstructed its working, did pass,[2] and soon after he wrote thus despondingly to the same correspondent:—

"Many, many thanks for your kind remembrance of me. Your kindness gives a support to my constitution, almost worn out by age, and which, nevertheless, will survive, I fear, if it has not already survived, the constitution of my country."

At the close of this melancholy session of Parliament, in which he had seen measures carried which he thought so unjust and mischievous, without having strength to lift up his voice against them, he retired to Encombe to brood over the public misfortunes and the degeneracy of mankind. While there, he was comforted by a kind letter sent to him by that most warm-hearted and excellent man the present Lord Kenyon, containing some strictures upon a statement by Sir John Campbell, made in the House of Commons, respecting the arrears which had been cleared off under Lord Chancellor Brougham, in the Court of Chancery and in the House of Lords, and thought, very groundlessly, to have been meant as a reflection on his great predecessor.

The following is Lord Eldon's answer:[3]—

[1] Their differences, on Municipal Reform, did lead to an "Open Conference," or *viva voce* debate, between the managers of the two Houses, in the Painted Chamber—the only instance of such a proceeding since the Revolution.   [2] 30 Hansard, 962.

[3] 25 Hansard, 3rd series, 1260, 1262. Sir John Campbell had moved for a return of the number of bills filed in the court of Chancery and appeals entered in the years 1825 to 1833 inclusive, together with the number of appeals undecided when the present Chancellor came into office, and of those undecided at his last sitting; but he said "he did not mean to cast any reflection on any other Judge of the Court by the observations he had made, and that, on the contrary, he believed that the other Judges had discharged their duty with the greatest assiduity,—meriting, by their exertions, the highest praise he could bestow."—25 Hansard, 3rd series, 1270.

"Saturday (Nov. 14th, 1835).

"MY VERY DEAR LORD,

"I ought long ago to have thanked you for the comfort I received from my daughter Elizabeth reading a letter, which I think you sent, respecting the velocity, the comparative velocity, of Brougham and Eldon, in Chancery and in Appeals. It is quite obvious that the number of decisions, in a given time, proves nothing of the sort which Lord B. and the present Attorney suppose it to prove. In making a comparison, you must, necessarily, not merely advert to the number of decisions, but the nature of the cases in which the decisions were pronounced. There have been no such matters, since my time, as a Queen's trial, the trial of a Berkeley Peerage, or of the various questions in the great Roxburghe Peerage and estates, in the last of which I think three days were employed in delivering my judgment: cum multis aliis. On a subject of this nature, however, my mind is at rest, though a very fidgety mind. I am mistaken, if, after I am gone, the Chancery records do not prove I decided more than any of my predecessors in the same periods of time. Sir Lloyd Kenyon beat us all. "Your faithful and affectionate
"ELDON.

"For the country's welfare my hopes are gone. I see leaders of all parties sacrificing principle to expediency. They create the expediency, and then they sacrifice all principle to it. Surely it is difficult to support a denial, that all sides, as to leaders, have gone too far in acting on this most mischievous doctrine."

He even seems to have had a foreboding of what he would have considered the last calamity that could be sent to overwhelm the country; for, writing, about this time, to his brother-in-law, Mr. Surtees, then turned of eighty, he observes, that good crops, of which there was then a prospect, were of no avail, "as the corn imported from abroad is already, in quantity, so great, that we can not sell so as to enable the farmer to get a price which will enable him to pay his taxes and his rent;" and thus concludes: "As to the political changes which are going on abroad, and which are leading to political changes here, it seems by no means improbable that even you and I may live to see England without a rag left of the Constitution under which we have so long lived." It would have been a great felicity in his lot if he could have witnessed the indignant rejection of the free-trade measures brought forward by the Whigs in 1841, and then had been snatched away from the evils that were to come.

CHAPTER CCXII.

CONCLUSION OF THE LIFE OF LORD ELDON.

ALTHOUGH Lord Eldon's natural existence was prolonged more than two years, he was now politically defunct, and henceforth he not only entirely abstained from attending in Parliament, but in despair he turned away his eyes from the political occurrences which were happening around him, and he thought only of his family and his private affairs. After having viewed his parliamentary career above half a century, I can not part without regret from this respectable impersonation of genuine old Toryism. Neither we nor our children shall ever look upon his like again. In the middle of the nineteenth century he appeared a living specimen of a species of politicians long extinct. As a public man he was not only interesting from the rarity of the qualities he exhibited, but it is impossible to have been in his company so long without feeling kindness and even veneration for one who, in the midst of constant changes, had remained unchanged—who, if liable to the imputation of cherishing, when turned of eighty, all the prejudices of eighteen, could not be charged, like many others, with having been led to renounce his principles by false philosophy, or by fashion, or by interest.

To prepare for that event, which, in the course of nature, could not long be delayed, he about this time devoted a morning to the examination of his papers, and very properly destroyed much confidential correspondence. There is a class of letters, which, though in some sense confidential, may, after a certain lapse of time, be published without impropriety, and which are the best materials for history; but there are others, written on the implied understanding that they are to be burned as soon as read. Unless such letters may be safely written, government can not be carried on; and to preserve them for the purpose of gratifying the curiosity of a future generation would be as great an atrocity as to leave for publication a statement of all the deliberations of a Cabinet. Perhaps Lord Eldon went further than was necessary, and assisted in concealing what might have afterwards been legitimately made known; for, after dinner, when giving an account of his morning's work, he added: "I have been a member of a good many Administrations, and there are many things connected with them which I do not wish to come out." At the same time it must be acknowledged that he spared much which a cautious regard for his own reputation might have induced him to suppress.[1]

He was much afflicted by the sad state of things under the roof of his brother at Earley Court. William Scott, Lord Stowell's only son, was dying; and Lord Stowell himself, from being one of the most intellectual of men, had fallen into mental imbecility. He thus wrote to Lord Encombe, during the last illness of his nephew:—

"The intelligence I receive is, that W. S. may linger a *little* longer; but the worst may be looked for, and soon. Hopes are not entertained. It is impossible to say how this distresses me. If the worst does happen, and soon, I could be of no comfort in such a state as Earley Court would be in. Not to go, however, might be very distressing to myself, and painful to those to whom I ought, if possible, to avoid giving pain. Contemplation on this subject is to me torture."

Lord Eldon escaped the acute pain he must have suffered from a visit to Earley Court; and, in the course of a few weeks, received from Lord Sidmouth, who had married Lord Stowell's daughter, the following melancholy notices of the decease both of the son and of the father:—

"The vital powers are nearly exhausted, and not likely, it is thought, to hold out another day. Lord Stowell is unconscious of what is passing and impending, but in bodily health is as well as when you last saw him." . . . .

"The ceremony of this day and all the arrangements

---

[1] I take this opportunity of declaring my opinion of the fairness and boldness with which his correspondence has been given to the world by Mr. Twiss, under the sanction of his grandson.

connected with it were conducted with the utmost propriety. Lord Encombe was chief mourner. He was received yesterday by Lord Stowell in a manner that was extremely affecting; and it was evident that Lord S. continued pleased with his guest till they parted, at half-past six; though I am confident that all consciousness of who he was did not last many minutes after their first meeting.

"Under other circumstances, your presence and advice would have been most welcome and acceptable to us; but, under the present, such a journey would have been highly imprudent and hazardous, and such a risk would have added greatly to our distress." . . . .

"The scene is closed. At half-past two, this afternoon, I was called to the bed-chamber, and witnessed the last sigh (for it was no more) of your beloved brother, and of my highly-valued and respected friend."

When the first pang caused by the sad news was over, Lord Eldon was comforted by the thought that his beloved brother was released from a state in which he could have had no enjoyment himself, and in which he was a melancholy spectacle to his friends. The great scholar who had been the boast of Oxford,—the great wit who had been the honored companion of Dr. Johnson,—the great judge, or rather legislator, the author of a code of international law, which defines the rights and duties of belligerents and neutrals, and which is respected over the whole civilized world,—had, for some years, hardly been capable of recognizing his nearest relations, and had been nearly unconscious of all that befell them. Lord Eldon continued to write to him when even the hope of being understood by him had fled. Thus he tried to announce to him the birth of a child of Lord Encombe:—

"MY DEAR BROTHER,

"I learn by letter, that my grandson, Lord Encombe,—who is the only son, you know, of my deceased eldest son, poor John, whose beautiful epitaph you wrote,—has had a daughter born the other day, whose birth renders me a great-grandfather, a title that makes me of venerable years.

"Believe me, from my heart, dear brother,
"Yours most affectionately,
"ELDON."

It is mortifying to think that, amidst the amiable feelings arising in the mind of Lord Eldon on his brother's death, there should have been one of a different character. The deceased had made a very reasonable disposition of his property, by which, upon the death of his daughter, Lady Sidmouth, without issue, his large estates in Gloucestershire were to come to Lord Encombe. Strange to say, Lord Eldon, at his advanced age and with his enormous wealth, was dissatisfied that he should not at least have had a life-interest in them, and expressed his resentment so loudly, that Lord Encombe wrote him a soothing letter, concluding with this request: "I beg that you will, during our lives (should we survive Lady Sidmouth), take entire possession in the amplest manner of every right and power over the Stowell estates which is in the will bestowed on me, not for my own merits, but as being your grandson." This prudent step quite melted the octogenarian's heart, and he wrote back: "Of your kindness and liberality I never could think of availing myself in the smallest degree. If, in events which may happen, I live to see you in possession, you may depend upon my best advice to enable you to enjoy that possession and assistance, if I have the means of rendering that assistance and giving that advice."[1] However, like a sovereign who is apt to be jealous of his successor, Lord Eldon, notwithstanding his grandson's devoted attachment to him and incessant solicitude to please him, viewed him, in his latter days, with some distrust, and in his treatment of him showed the irritability too often produced by age and infirmity in the kindliest natures.

He came to London before the meeting of Parliament in 1836, but was not once in his place in the House of Lords during the whole session. I am afraid that he was now wretchedly at a loss for employment, and that he had much reason to regret his neglect of those studies which are the delight of old age. He only looked into books, ancient and modern, to find that he had "no pleasure in them." His ANECDOTE BOOK he had long closed; and he had almost entirely ceased to write letters, except to the members of his own family. Of late years he had amused himself with receiving accounts of the proceedings in the Court of Chancery,—blessing Heaven,—"that

[1] 14th April, 1836.

he himself was inclined to the *cunctative*." When he heard that Lord Cottenham was made Chancellor, he regretted that such a man should be connected with Whigs, and acknowledged that he was exceedingly well fitted to be an Equity Judge.

During the mornings, which were dreadfully long, he wished he were again writing letters in Lincoln's Inn Hall, while he seemed to be listening to the oft-repeated tale of the counsel; but his only relief from weary thoughts was an occasional call from an old friend to whom he could repeat old stories, and complain that bad men ruled the state:—not feeling much reconciled, however, to a private station, and often saying with a sigh, "Now I am nobody." In this state of *ennui* he was apt to be fretful, to attach importance to trifles which he would formerly have disregarded, and even to be dissatisfied with the most tender attentions of those around him. But when the hour of dinner arrived, and the Newcastle Port—of which, with a constancy that marked all his sentiments and habits, he never took less than three pints —began to cheer his heart, existence still had charms for him; and, going back to the good old times when he was Attorney-General and prosecuted traitors and libellers, he forgot for a while that the Roman Catholics had been emancipated,—or that the House of Commons had been reformed,—or that Fines and Recoveries had been abolished,—or that stealing to the value of five shillings in a shop had ceased to be a capital crime.

In the month of July he paid his annual visit to the North, establishing himself at the inn at Rusheyford, nearly in the center of his Eldon Estates. He was pleased to find that it continued to be kept by Mr. Hoult, the old landlord, who in 1835 had announced his intention of "resigning," on account of his age and the fortune he had made, and to whom he had pleasantly given this advice:—"I hear, Mr. Hoult, that you are talking of retiring from business; but let me advise you *not* to do so. Busy people are very apt to think a life of leisure is a life of happiness; but believe me, for I speak from experience, when a man, who has been occupied through life, arrives at having nothing to do, he is very apt not to know what to do *with himself*. I am interested in this advice, Mr. Hoult, for I intend to come here every year for the *next thirty years*, and I hope to find you still the landlord. And now, good day; and I trust, if God spares me, we shall all meet again next summer."

When relating this anecdote, Lord Eldon used to say, 'Next year, when I again visited Rusheyford, the landlord told me he had taken my advice, and determined not to give up his inn. It was advice given by me in the spirit of that Principal of Brasenose, who, when he took leave of young men quitting college, used to say to them, 'Let me give you one piece of advice: Cave de resignationibus.' And very good advice too."[1]

Having collected his relations round him for some days, at this inn, he was kind to them as usual; he recovered his cheerfulness, and he retained the remarkable self-complacency which never forsook him to his last hour. His grand-niece, Mrs. Foster, a lady of great talents, to whom the world is indebted for many interesting anecdotes concerning him, was of this party, and she says:—

"My dear uncle's conversation at Eldon was partly serious; but the greater part of the time, full of fun, joke, and anecdote. Neither in this nor any former years did I ever know him omit to speak seriously of what his thoughts and feelings ought to be at the very great age he had now attained,—the uncertainty of his ever reaching Eldon again,—the examination of his past life, which the leisure of the last few years had enabled him to make,— *the satisfaction that arose from a consciousness of not having sought honors, but of having endeavored to act in every case from pure motives,*—his prepration for death, which must soon take place. 'I have employed the leisure of my latter years,' he said, 'in looking back upon my past life, and I hope I may say, without presumption, that my mind is at ease. I may have been in the wrong; but I always tried to judge and to act, by the best powers of my mind, unswayed by any impure motive.' Having created the impression on his hearers, which, as a Christian, he appeared to wish to make, he would then turn to lighter subjects, and, by his wit and his anecdote, keep every one amused the whole of the evening."

[1] He might have added old Henry Dundas's advice to Ministers of State: "Beware of resignation; for when you are once out, the Lord Alm'ghty only knows when you may get in again."

As usual, he gave a dinner at the inn to his tenants, and after dinner joined them for a little while and socially sat among them. His health being given, "with three times three, and one cheer more," he made them a speech, —of which we have the following report from an intelligent friend of his, who was present :—

"Gentlemen,—I thank God, that it has pleased him to allow me, once more, the happiness and pleasure of meeting you all again. It also gives me great satisfaction to tell you that I have been informed, by those from whom alone I can receive accurate information on the subject, that you have, all of you, made improvements in the management of your farms. For this I thank you: and I can not but attribute these beneficial effects, in a great measure, to the alteration which you have made in the tenure of your farms, in taking them for a term instead of from year to year. It is evident to me, as it must, I think, be to you all, that a tenant who is liable to be removed in a year from his farm, can not, satisfactorily to himself, make those improvements which he will do when he is sure that he can remain on his farm long enough to reap the benefit to himself of those improvements. I thank you all for your improved management. I will come among you as long as it shall please God to allow me. I wish you all, yourselves and families, health and happiness; and I shall never, while I live, cease to consider my tenantry as part of myself."

Having, in "merry pin," sent a kiss to a young married lady, he desired that it might be given to her "*privately*, in the absence of her husband," and she having written back instructions to give him a "French kiss" in return, adding, "it is what no English lawyer can object to, it being only justice to make both sides of the face equal,"—he said, with a hearty laugh, "I thought I should have lived and died an Englishman; but really, in the article of *osculation*, I must become a Frenchman."[1]

These were the harmless flashes of lightning in the midst of a dark night. He felt that the hand of death

---

[1] He was very fond of such *badinage*, in which the old school seem to have greatly luxuriated. At a still later period of his life, having after dinner given the health of Captain Best, R. N., wishing that he might soon get a ship and go to sea, he took Mrs. Best's hand, and said to her gayly, "Depend upon it, when he goes to sea, I shall stay on shore."

was upon him; but he looked forward, without dismay, to the "inevitable hour." On his return to London, he had some conversation, respecting the disease under which he was suffering, with Mr. Pennington, his medical attendant, who told him he had never known it cured, although there were persons who said they could cure it —expressing a wish that he would call in other medical advice. With a mixed look of benevolence and archness, he emphatically replied, "I have lived by Pennington, and *I will die by Pennington.*"

He passed the autumn at Encombe, which, unless when enlivened by the presence of his grandchildren, was now a very dreary abode for him. His sporting days were over; he took little interest in farming or gardening; and his only reading, besides the newspaper, was a chapter in a copy of the Bible which he had received from his friend Dr. Swire. His mornings he spent in an elbow-chair by the fire-side in his study—called his *shop*—which was ornamented with portraits of his deceased Master George III., and his living companion Pincher, a poodle dog.

His attachment to this animal was very affecting. He used to say, while he caressed him, "Poor Pincher belonged to poor William Henry; and after I last took the Sacrament with him when he was dying, he called me back as I was leaving the room, and said, 'Father, you will take care of poor Pincher.' The dog was brought home to me when all was over; and in a short time he was missed. He was immediately sought for, and he was found lying on the bed beside his dead master." Then followed a long story of Pincher being afterwards decoyed away by a dog-stealer, and recovered by the ex-Chancellor compounding felony with the thief. In consequence of a letter signed "AN AMATEUR DOG-FANCIER," a negotiation was opened, which led to Lord Eldon sending an servant with a five-pound note to a house in a street at a distant part of the town called *Cow Cross Street*, where Pincher was found. The man, being dealt with "on honor," freely disclosed the secrets of his trade, and, in answer to a gentle reproach, exclaimed, "Why, what can we do? Now that Parliament has put a stop to our trade of procuring bodies for the surgeons, we are obliged to turn to this to get an honest livelihood."

Pincher is introduced into several portraits of his

master, who said, "Poor fellow, he has a right to be painted with me, for when my man Smith took him the other day to a law bookseller's, where there were several lawyers assembled, they all received him with great respect, and the master of the shop exclaimed, 'How very like he is to *old Eldon*, particularly when he wore a wig!'—but, indeed, many people say he is the better-looking chap of the two." For this faithful companion, Lord Eldon made a testamentary provision, bequeathing him to Lady Frances Bankes, with an annuity of eight pounds, during the term of his natural life, for his maintenance.[1]

Although Lord Eldon's reasoning powers remained vigorous to the last, his memory, particularly of names, sometimes strangely failed him. This autumn he said, "When I was in office, we wished the Parliament should meet before the day fixed by the prorogation. We felt great difficulty about it. I explained the law to the Cabinet, and told them that, unless there was some strong ground for it, *such as a disturbance or riots of the people*, it could not be done. 'Oh!' said Henry Dundas, afterwards Lord —— (I forget his name, but never mind that); 'if that's all, I can soon get up a very *pretty riot for you in Scotland.*'" He had for the moment forgotten, not only the name of Lord Melville, once so familiar to him, but an Act of Parliament which he himself, when Attorney-General, had introduced into the House of Commons,—whereby Parliament may be required at all times, by proclamation, to meet in fifteen days.[2]

Yet, a few weeks after, he wrote the following most excellent advice to a grandson about to be entered at Oxford:—

"It will depend much upon yourself what degree of benefit you may reap there. Of the young it has been said, 'Gaudent equis, canibusque, et aprici gramine campi,' or something to that effect. Of extravagant gratification of that passion in young men, I well remember the pains which were taken in Oxford to restrain it. What are

---

[1] After Lord Eldon's death, he was painted by that consummate judge of the canine race, Mr. Edward Landseer, who said, "He is a very picturesque old dog, *with a great look of cleverness in his face.*" He is represented listening to the ticking of a watch, given to the Chancellor by George III.

[2] See 37 Geo. 3, c. 127; 39 & 40 Geo. 3, c. 14.

precisely the rules of the University in this respect now, I can not say: but so much I can say, that, after long and great experience, I never knew a young man who had indulged too much in these amusements at Oxford, to the neglect of very diligent if not severe duty, who ever afterwards in life graced his friends, family, or country, as I hope and pray you may hereafter grace them: and I never knew one who signally devoted his time at Oxford to study, who did not in after-life become a blessing and ornament to his family and country. Be very select in the company you keep at Oxford, and never forget what so many forget, that the University is not a place of amusement, but of constant study,—to be interrupted only by *necessary* attention to health."

He returned to London some time before the meeting of Parliament, in January, 1837, not with the hope of again taking part in public affairs, but that he might enjoy the charm of an old Solicitor or a Master in Chancery dropping in to chat with him and while away the time till the hour of dinner should creep on. But he was much alarmed by an announcement in the King's Speech that further measures would be submitted to Parliament " for the improvement of the law and of the administration of justice;" and when the "Wills Bill," which we, the Real Property Commissioners, had prepared after years of labor, was laid on the table of the House of Lords, all his former horror of innovation was revived, and he declared that " he would still attend in his place and lift up his voice against it." Formerly, freehold land, of the minutest value, could not be devised without a will signed by the testator, attested in a particular form by three witnesses,—while copyhold land worth £100,000 a year, as well as personal property to any indefinite amount, might be disposed of by a memorandum in an old almanac, without any witness, and without even being signed by the testator. We proposed to do away, for testamentary purposes, with the distinction between real and personal property, so that a will might not be void as to one, and valid as to the other,—and to require that all wills should be signed by the testator, and attested by two witnesses. This change he wished to denounce as revolutionary, and fatal to the security of all property, real and personal. I really believe that he would have been contented, after the example of Lord Chatham, to have died on the floor of the House of Lords in opposing a measure which he considered so unjust and disastrous. But he then labored under a sharp attack of the gout, which rendered him wholly insufficient for the effort; and he had the mortification to hear, that, notwithstanding some pamphlets against the bill, it passed with unanimity through both Houses of Parliament, all the law lords (Lord Cottenham, Lord Lyndhurst, Lord Brougham, and Lord Langdale) expressing their high approbation of it. He had one consolation—that it was only to operate upon testamentary dispositions executed after the 1st of January, 1838; and he resolved that before that day all his testamentary dispositions should be complete, so that no part of his property should be subject to its enactments.[1]

Unable to preside at the anniversary meeting of the Pitt Club, he was ably represented by his grandson; and there his health was still drunk with unabated enthusiasm, all present loudly cheering the sentiment that "attachment to Lord Eldon was part of the Constitution of the country." He was much affected by the account he had of these proceedings, and he wrote back to Lord Encombe,—"I have received, and read with difficulty, your letter, and another from Lord Kenyon, whilst tears are flowing from my old eyes, and trickling down my cheeks."

He cared little about the demise of the Crown, which soon followed. Although so intensely favored both by George III. and George IV., he had received no notice from William IV., and he was now almost indifferent to changes of Government; for, except that the "Conservatives" were forever pledged to stand by the Corn Laws (and, after what had happened, he placed no great faith in such pledges), they were in his estimation hardly to be distinguished from the Whigs. He therefore heard without dismay that Lord Melbourne was still Prime Minister, with increased influence; and he expressed deep regret that he was unable to attend the first council of Queen Victoria at Kensington,—not joining that section of politicians who, in their disappointment, did not scruple openly to declare a preference for the Salic law, and a wish

---

[1] 9 W. 4, and 1 Vict. c. 28.

that the King of Hanover might have been entitled to mount the throne of England.

Next day he contrived to be carried down to the House of Lords to take the oaths to the new Sovereign. He was highly pleased with the reception he met with, and said on his return,—" The kindness they showed me affected me to tears; the peers, the officers of the House—all were so kind!"

When Parliament was dissolved he paid another visit to Rusheyford, and had a "gathering" of his Northern relations. He was observed to be considerably altered since the preceding year, and there was a presentiment among them, which turned out to be well founded, that when he had taken leave of them they should see his face no more. However, although dejected and disposed to dwell on disagreeable family occurrences, "at other times he was not only cheerful, but lively, and entered into a joke with great fun, carrying it on from day to day."[1] Forgetting Mr. Pitt's letter which he had clandestinely delivered to the King in 1804, with the view of turning out Mr. Addington,—his worship and his persecution of Caroline of Brunswick,—and his many anxious and able intrigues in conjunction with the Duke of Cumberland to exclude the Whigs and to keep down the ascendency of Mr. Canning,—he made this solemn declaration, which, he himself, perhaps, believed to be sincere: "I can assure you, all the honors that have been heaped upon me always came unsought by me: I may safely say, that I never stepped across the kennel out of my way to secure preferment."

He now once more hospitably entertained all his tenantry, and, after dinner, delivered to them the last speech he ever made. With unfeigned piety, he thus began:—" My first acknowledgments are due to that great Being whose pleasure it has been to afflict me with a painful illness, and to continue that infliction for a lengthened period, insomuch that I did not hope to have been able to have seen you all again. So long as it shall please God to allow me, it will ever be my happiness, as it is my duty, thus to come among you.' After again pointing out the advantages of the "leasing system" above "tenancies at will," although it was an innovation, he

[1] Mrs. Foster's account of the visit.

alluded to a contest for the county, and said, most liberally and handsomely, "My sentiments are known, but I shall leave it to my tenants to exercise the franchise which Parliament has given them in such a manner as shall appear to them to be right, and according to good conscience, and as most likely to uphold the Church, in which the purest doctrines of our religion are taught in the best manner." He then bade them, what turned out to be, a last farewell:—"Gentlemen, I repeat the great thankfulness I feel in having been allowed once more to come among you. In taking leave of you, gentlemen, I say from my heart, may God bless you and your families!"

When he returned to Encombe, he wrote a very desponding letter to Lord Sidmouth, in which he said:—

"Though I have been moving through a long journey and return from it, I am in precisely the same state of actual constant weakness and pain which I have now undergone for nearly two long years. I cannot stir without help, and from the moment I am helped into my carriage in a morning I never stir out of it till evening. Pray give my dear niece my most affectionate regards and good wishes. Accept the same yourself. I shall, if God pleases, return to town very soon, and to that as probably my last earthly place of abode."

In about a fortnight after writing this letter he left Encombe, and within three months all his gloomy anticipations were realized. But, not ignorant of what was soon to happen, he preserved his cheerfulness in private society, and was even desirous, as far as his strength would permit, of performing his public duties.

On the meeting of the new Parliament, he qualified himself to be present when the young Queen of eighteen should deliver her speech from the throne—a ceremony which he expressed a strong desire to see before saying "Nunc me dimittis." Mr. Farrer, who had married his daughter-in-law, and regarded him with filial reverence, has given an interesting account of his last appearance in that House where he presided so long:—
"Lord Eldon went down in his chariot to the House of Lords, to take his seat. I met him as he got out of his carriage. Mr. Butt, who had been Lord Eldon's macebearer, and Smith, his butler, assisted him up the stairs.

About half way up, Mr. Butt had a bottle of sherry, and persuaded his old master to take a glass of it. When we came to the door of the House, Smith requested me to support Lord Eldon into the body of the House, which I did. He went up to the woolsack, and said to the Lord to Chancellor (Lord Cottenham), 'My Lord, I am happy to take this opportunity of assuring you that everything I hear of you entitles you to my sincere respect.' He then went to the table, took the oaths, and signed the roll."

But he was excessively fatigued when he returned home, so that he was obliged to give up all notion of being present when her Majesty opened the session in person —which he regretted the more when he was told of the beautiful manner in which she had read her speech, and particularly of the sensation she had created by the delivery of the concluding sentence of it: "The early age at which I am called to the sovereignty of this kingdom renders it a more imperative duty that, under Divine Providence, I should place my reliance upon your cordial co-operation, and upon the love and affection of all my people."[1]

He was now busily engaged in setting his house in order before the much-dreaded day should arrive when the odious "Wills Bill" was to come into operation— of which he professed greater and greater apprehensions. He revised all his testamentary dispositions, and rather capriciously revoked a very reasonable power which he had conferred on Lord Encombe of charging his estates with a sum of 50,000*l.*, for the portions of daughters— leaving the following explanatory paper:—

"Memoraudum. On consideration, I have thought myself perfectly justified, in case of a failure of Lord Encombe's issue male, in preferring, to the fullest extent, my own daughters to the daughters of Lord Encombe, and, therefore, I have revoked the power of charging which I had given to Lord Encombe by my will, considering also that his daughters are otherwise provided for.— ELDON, 6 Decr. 1837. *This is not testamentary.*"[2]

[1] 39 Hansard, 3rd series, 15.
[2] By these words he inadvertently pays a compliment to the bill he so severely condemned; as formerly there were innumerable disputes whether loose memoranda should be considered *testamentary* or not; whereas now

The will and all the codicils being executed according to the old STATUTE OF FRAUDS,—bidding defiance to the Real Property Commissioners and all their conundrums, he said "he could now die in peace."

From that time he sank rapidly, so as to give some countenance to the vulgar notion that a man hastens his end by completing his will. Dr. Philpotts, Bishop of Exeter, who was connected with him by marriage, hearing of his weak state, called upon him and prayed with him. Not having touched on any topic that was distasteful, this visit passed off most satisfactorily. The next time Mr. Pennington appeared, the patient said, "I have had another doctor since I saw you." "I am glad of it," answered the worthy apothecary. "Oh, but," said Lord Eldon, "he was a *spiritual* doctor, not a *medical*. The Bishop of Exeter paid me a visit, and after sitting a little by me, and observing me look very ill, he got up and bolted the door, and knelt down by me. 'Let us pray,' he said. He did pray, and such a prayer! I never heard such a prayer." A few days subsequently, as was gathered from Lord Eldon's own statement, the Bishop repeated his visit, and, after some religious conversation with him, was alarmed by finding the entire self-satisfaction with which he looked back on the whole of his past life, and his great seeming reliance upon his own merits. In the true spirit of a faithful Christian pastor, who must not regard the rank or station of a dying man, the Bishop tried, in mild terms, to remind him that we have all followed too much the devices and desires of our own hearts; and that, confessing our faults, we ought to look elsewhere for pardon than to the recollection of the good works which we may rashly impute to ourselves. The old peer thereupon became very refractory, thinking that some personal disrespect was shown to him, and that a slur was meant to be cast upon his conduct as a public man, which he had ever regarded as most spotless as well as consistent. He was particularly indignant at the thought of such a charge coming from one whom, notwithstanding a show of outward civility, he had regarded with some secret suspicion from the part at last taken by the Right Reverend Prelate respecting Catholic Emanci-

the simple criterion is applied—of their being signed by the testator in the presence of two witnesses.

pation; and he considered it particularly hard to bear taunts from such a quarter.¹ As the ex-Chancellor displayed some impatience, and even resentment, the pious divine in vain strove to make him understand that the only object of this conference was to call his attention to spiritual things,—and, having exhausted all the means which the acutest intellect, the deepest knowledge, and the most winning manners could supply, was obliged to retire, without, in any degree, making the impression which he desired. Next day Lord Eldon received the following most beautiful letter, which, no doubt, brought him to a right frame of mind, and which may be perused with advantage by persons of all ages and all conditions of life, whether in health or in sickness:—

"MY DEAR LORD,

"I take blame to myself for having, as I fear, obtruded on you some important matters of consideration at a time when you were not prepared to admit them; or in a manner which may have been deemed too earnest and importunate. That you pardon the intrusion, I have no doubt, and that you ascribe what may have been ill-timed, or ill-considered, to the true cause—an anxious wish to lead a highly gifted mind like yours to those thoughts which alone can satisfy it.

"Before I leave this place, instead of again trespassing on you in person, I have resolved to commit to paper a few considerations which your own powerful mind will know how to improve, and which I humbly pray the Holy Spirit of God to impress, so far as they accord with His truth, on the hearts of both of us. I contemplate in you, my dear Lord, an object of no ordinary interest. I see a man full of years and honors, honors richly earned (ay, were they tenfold greater than they are) by a life which,

¹ He had, upon a former occasion, patiently allowed even a layman to reason with him on this subject. "I remember," said Mr. Alfred Bell, his solicitor, "that one day after dinner, in the library in Hamilton Place, he beckoned to me to sit by him; and immediately entering into conversation, among other things spoke of his judicial life. He observed that 'it was a source of great satisfaction to him to reflect that he had never given a judgment in any cause without first anxiously satisfying himself that it was right.' 'It is a happiness to me,' he said, 'to reflect that I never gave A the property of B. This is a satisfaction to a man at the last, and in looking to the day of judgment.' Upon my observing upon this, to the effect that 'no reliance could be placed upon anything, but upon the merits and blood of Christ alone,' he fully acquiesced in the truth of the remark."

protracted long beyond the ordinary age of man, has been employed, during all the period of service, in promoting, strengthening, and securing the best and most sacred interests of your country. I see in you the faithful, zealous, and most able advocate of the connection of true religion with the Constitution and Government of England. I see in you one who has largely benefited the generation of which you have been among the most distinguished ornaments. Seeing and feeling this, I am sure you will pardon me if I exhibit a little even of undue eagerness to perform to you the only service which I can hope to render—that of exciting such a mind to those reflections by which, after serving others, it can now do the best and surest service to itself. In truth, those reflections are few and brief, but most pregnant. In short, my dear Lord, I would seek most earnestly to guard you against the danger which arises from the very qualities which we most admire in you, and from the actions for which we are most grateful to you. That danger is, lest you contemplate these matters with too much satisfaction —lest you rest upon them as the grounds of your hope of final acceptance with God. Oh! my dear Lord, the best of the sons of men must be content, or rather must be most anxious, to look out of themselves, and above themselves, for any sure hope—I will not say of justification, but of mercy. Consider the infinite holiness and purity of God, and then say whether any man was ever fit to appear at His tribunal. Consider the demands of His law, extending to the most secret thoughts, and wishes, and imaginations of the heart; and then say whether you, or any one, can stand before Him in your own strength, when He cometh to judgment. No: it is as sinners, as grievous sinners, we shall, we must appear; and the only plea which will be admitted for us is the righteousness and the merits of our crucified Redeemer. If we place any reliance on our own poor doings, or fancied virtues, those very virtues will be our snares, our downfall. Above all things, therefore, it is our duty, and pre-eminently the duty of the purest and best among us, to cast off all confidence in ourselves, and thankfully to embrace Christ's most precious offer on the terms on which He offers it. He will be our Saviour only if we know, and feel, and humbly acknowledge that we need His salvation. He will be more and more our Saviour in proportion as we more and more love and rely upon Him. But surely the more we feel and deplore our own sinfulness, the more earnest will be our love, the firmer our reliance on Him who alone is mighty to save. Therefore it is, that, in preparing ourselves to appear before Him, the less we think of what we may fondly deem our good deeds and good qualities, and the more rigidly we scrutinize our hearts, and detect and deplore our manifold sinfulness, the fitter shall we be, because the more deeply sensible of the absolute necessity and of the incalculable value of His blessed undertaking and suffering for us. One word only more—of ourselves we can not come to this due sense of our own worthlessness; and the devil is always ready to tempt our weak hearts with the bait which is most taking to many among us—confidence in ourselves. It is the Holy Spirit who alone can give us that only knowledge which will be useful to us at the last—the knowledge of our own hearts, of their weakness, their wickedness—and of the way of God's salvation, pardon of the faithful and confiding penitent for His dear Son's sake. Oh! my dear Lord, may you and I be found among the truly penitent, and then we shall have our perfect consummation and bliss among the truly blessed.

"I am, my dear Lord,
"With true veneration and regard,
"Your Lordship's most faithful servant,
"And affectionate brother in Christ,
"The Earl of Eldon."   "H. EXETER.

From the great strength of his constitution he might have languished several years longer, and even have reached the years of Lord Stowell, had it not been for the setting in of an unusually intense frost, which carried off a great number of aged persons. He had had in his most vigorous days a tendency to cough, which Lady Eldon would tell him was only *a trick*—when he would smile and answer, "You know, my dear, I have had a cough these fifty years; but I am none the worse for it." He had now some symptoms of pulmonary consumption, although of a mild type—but his disease may be considered a wasting away of the frame by old age. On some subjects he had erroneous impressions, while on others his intellect remained clear and correct, and his pleasantry, though it very visibly waned, sparkled from time to time so as to recall the memory of its former brilliance. His daughter, Lady Frances Bankes, was now living with him; and Lord Encombe, although occupying a house at Shirley, near Croydon, visited him daily.

On the 20th of December, being asked how he was, he answered, " Very poorly—very poorly: it can not last long. God's will be done; it is my duty to submit."

Till Wednesday, the 10th of January, he came down daily to breakfast, at a late hour, but on that day he did not leave his bed till the evening. When he got up, and with assistance he tried to walk, his strength entirely failed him. However, he was carried down stairs to the dining room and placed at table; but he had a shivering fit during dinner, and it was necessary to carry him back to his bed-room. He was immediately placed in bed, which he never again left. His daughter, Lady Elizabeth Repton, and his grandson, Lord Encombe, were sent for, and were most assiduous in their attentions to him. Next day he was so far better that he could occasionally enter into conversation with those around him, and he smiled when reminded of the anecdote of King George III. having told his court, " I have what no previous King of England has had—an Archbishop of Canterbury,[1] and a Lord Chancellor, each of whom ran away with his wife." He was amused likewise by being reminded of the opposite fates of himself and the Metropolitan; for, while he himself, destined for the Church, had been driven by poverty into the law, Dr. Howley, who had once a longing for the Bar, had entered the Church because he could not afford the expense of a legal education.[2]

On the Friday the frost was dreadfully severe, and he was worse. His family, therefore, were not permitted to be with him; but Mr. Pennington took Lord Encombe into his bed-room to see him a few minutes, and said to him: " It is a cold day, my Lord;" to which Lord Eldon replied, in a low and placid voice: " It matters not to me, where I am going, whether the weather here be hot or cold." These appear to be the last words he ever uttered.

[1] Dr. Manners Sutton.
[2] The Chancellor might have made a very good Archbishop; but all must rejoice in the circumstances which drove the Archbishop from the wrangling of the Bar to that high station which he so eminently ornaments by his mild virtues.—1847.

He languished till a quarter past four o'clock in the afternoon of the following day, Saturday, the 13th of January, 1838, when he expired without a groan, in the eighty-seventh year of his age, and his eyes were closed by his affectionate grandson, the heir of his titles, his estates, and his more amiable qualities.

Although Lord Eldon had sunk a good deal from public notice for several years, his death caused a considerable sensation,—reviving the recollection of what he had been, and of the important part which he had acted with many great men who had been swept away long before him. When his remains lay in state in Hamilton Place, large numbers of all classes went to see the solemn scene; and when the funeral procession, attended by the carriages of the Princes of the blood, many of the peerage, and all the dignitaries of the law, blackened the way,—dense crowds stood uncovered, respectfully gazing at it as it passed. The private carriages having returned to London, when a halt was made near Hammersmith, the procession moved on towards Encombe, the present Earl being chief mourner, and the other near relations of the deceased accompanying him. It rested the first night at Bagshot, the next at Winchester, the third at Wimborne, and the following morning it reached the family mansion in Dorsetshire. The body again lay in state there, and on Friday, the 26th of January, was deposited, according to the directions of the deceased, in the vault which he had constructed in the burying-ground of the chapel at Kingston, by the side of his beloved " Bessy." The appropriate service was read by the clergyman of the parish, with great solemnity, in the midst of an immense assemblage of rustics from the surrounding country, the younger part of whom, when hoary headed, will boast to their grandchildren of having been present at the funeral of the great Lord Chancellor Eldon.

The present Earl has raised, in Kingston chapel, a handsome monument to his memory, with a likeness of him by Sir Francis Chantrey, and an inscription enumerating all the offices which he held, and the honors which were conferred upon him.

The fortune he left behind him, exceeding in amount half a million of money, was all made most honorably. When at the Bar he was always contented with the *hono-*

rarium voluntarily offered to him; and on the Bench, although he took some pains to conceal his official income, he never increased it by unfair means. He bought some land, and laid out considerable sums on mortgage,—though, like his brother, Lord Stowell, he preferred for his accumulations "the elegant simplicity of the three per cents;" but he declared "that his purchases into the stocks, and his sales out of the stocks, were never made (as his bankers could testify) except in the simple and usual course of business,—never by way of speculation, or with reference to any particular public event."

He disposed of these vast possessions by a will and codicils, in his own handwriting, occupying seventy-four sheets. Being drawn by such a conveyancer, we may hope that they will never give rise to any doubt, although many of the most important points in the law of real property have been settled in suits upon the construction of the wills of eminent judges. He gave his Dorsetshire estates to Lord Encombe for life, remainder to Lord Encombe's first and every other son successively in tail male; and for default of such issue, they are settled in moieties upon the testator's two daughters, Lady Elizabeth and Lady Frances,—with remainders in tail to sons in succession, and then to daughters as tenants in common in tail,—and cross-remainders in tail between the families of Lady Frances and Lady Elizabeth. The Durham estates, subject to the settlements of them before made on the marriage of Lord Encombe and on other occasions,—under which they were settled upon Lord Encombe for life, with remainders to his first and every other son successively in tail male,—are given to the same uses, in favor of Lady Elizabeth Repton and Lady Frances Bankes and their families, as the Dorsetshire property. The leasehold house in Hamilton Place is given to Lord Encombe for life, with remainder to his first and other sons successively; and, in default of such issue, becomes part of the testator's personal residue. Several large sums of stock are settled upon the testator's two daughters and their issue. To Lady Elizabeth and Lady Frances are left also some specific articles; and life annuities are given to each. After the bequest of Pincher, described as "my favorite dog," to Lady Frances, he continues: "And I direct that I may be buried in the same tomb at Kingston in which my most beloved wife is buried, and as near to her remains as possible; and I desire that the ring which I wear on my finger[1] may be put with my body into my coffin, and be buried with me." He adds various legacies to servants and others. The general residue of his personal estate he directs to be invested in the purchase of lands, to be settled to the same uses as the Dorsetshire estates. A schedule is annexed, enumerating various articles, which the will directs to descend with the estate in the nature of heirlooms, and to which the first codicil makes some additions. These heir-looms are chiefly busts, portraits painted and engraven, letters of the Royal Family, the watch, chain, and seal given to him by King George III., various snuff-boxes, the salvers having the Great Seal set therein, the tankard given to him by George IV., addresses and other testimonials and tributes to his public character, his law books, the robes and lace worn by him as a Judge and as a Peer respectively, and the service of plate which he had on his appointment as Lord Chancellor.

CHAPTER CCXIII.

CHARACTER OF LORD ELDON.

I CAN not conclude this work without attempting to sketch the character of Lord Eldon.

"Extremum hunc, Arethusa, mihi concede laborem."

The task is the most difficult which has yet been imposed upon me. I am relieved from the scruples which I should otherwise have felt in writing freely of one so recently removed from among us, by the consideration that a "Life" of him, minutely describing his whole career, and professing to appreciate all his qualities, as a public man and as a private individual, has been given to the world, with the full sanction of his family.[2] Thenceforth he became "historical," as much as any of his predeces-

---

[1] The mourning-ring for his wife.
[2] Twiss's "Life of Lord Eldon," to which the present Earl has not only contributed his grandfather's papers, but many valuable observations of his own.

sors who have reposed for centuries in the tomb. As it could not be expected that elaborate encomiums were to be bestowed upon him, without the liberty of pronouncing censure till the present generation had passed away, truth sternly requires that the feelings of his surviving relations and friends should now be entirely disregarded, although it is impossible to suppress regret when pain is inflicted.

My embarrassment arises from the political principles and party connections of the author being so different from those of the subject of this memoir. I have heard it said, that "the most delightful of all employments must be to write the life of an opponent." To me it is most distressing. I have no vengeful propensities to be gratified by warring with the dead, and I am haunted by the apprehension that, in dealing out censure, I may be supposed to be actuated by personal spleen, or by a desire to attack measures and sentiments which I disapprove by disparaging him who was their greatest champion.[1]

I must proceed, however, according to my own sense of duty,—taking care that I do not sacrifice the praise of being just to that of being generous.

Of course Lord Eldon excites most interest as an Equity Judge. It is very unfortunate for him, that here, where he was so eminent, it is so difficult for the biographer to convey an adequate notion of his merit. Were I to try to analyze the thirteen volumes of Vesey, junior, which record his decisions, with the camel-loads of them furnished by other reporters (Beames, Cooper, Merivale, Swanston, Jacob, Walker, Turner, Russell, Rose, Buck, Glynn, Jameson, Dow, and Bligh), however well I might succeed in assisting the law student, or facilitating the researches of the Chancery practitioner, or marking the advance of the science of Equity during the first quarter of the nineteenth century,—I should present something which would be "caviare to the general." Delighted should I be, under favor of the Muses who inspire lawyers,—

" Quarum sacra fero ingenti percussus amore,"—

to travell chronologically from Easter Term, 41 George

[1] I fear that I may be accused of imitating Dr. Johnson, who, in talking of his "DEBATES," said, "I always took care that the Whigs should have the worst of it;" or the Whig blacksmith, who, as often as the horse of a Tory was brought to him to be shod, was sure to lame him.

III. (1801), to Hilary Term, 8 George IV. (1827), and to show how injunctions were granted and refused,—whence sprang the doctrine of illusory appointments,—when the *scintilla juris* is sufficient to feed uses,—what is the effect of trustees to preserve contingent remainders joining in a settlement or sale,—and whether an equitable estate tail is well barred by a fine and recovery. Such lucubrations would be more akin to my pursuits, and would please me far more than detailing parliamentary debates and political intrigues, or narrating personal anecdotes. But, if I were to indulge my legal vein, it is quite certain that my book instead of being found on the ladies' toilettes, and being fought for at clubs, would experience the usual destination of "learned works," in the shop of the trunk-maker or the grocer,—so that the attempt would redound as little to the advantage of my hero as of myself. Renouncing all lofty aspirations, therefore, I must be contented with a few desultory remarks on Lord Eldon's qualifications and performances as occupier of the "marble chair."

I begin with lamenting his defects. But let it be understood at once, that I honor him as a great magistrate, and that, instead of comparing him with excellence which has actually been exhibited, I am considering how near he approaches to an imaginary standard of perfection, or the *beau idéal* of a Chancellor.

Although endued with wonderful acuteness and subtlety of intellect, with a retentive memory, a logical understanding, and power of unwearied application, he was utterly devoid of imagination, and of all taste for what is elegant or refined. His acquirements, even as a jurist, were very limited. He was familiarly acquainted with every nook of the municipal law of this realm; but all beyond was to him *terra incognita.*

Could he have combined with his own stores of professional learning his brother Lord Stowell's profound knowledge of the Civil and Canon Law, of the Law of Nations, and of the Codes of the Continental States, he would have been the most accomplished judge who ever sat on any British tribunal. But while he was reading *Coke upon Littleton* over and over again, and becoming thoroughly versed in all the doctrines laid down by Chief Justices and Chancellors in Westminster Hall, we are not told that he ever dipped into the Code, the Pandects, or the Institutes of Justinian; or that he found any pleasure in Puffendorf or Grotius, or that he ever formed the slightest acquaintance with D'Aguesseau or Pothier. Nor, in any of his arguments at the Bar, or judgments from the Bench, does he, as far as I am aware, ever refer to the civil law, or any foreign writer, as authority, or by way of illustration.[1] Considering that our system of Equity is essentially derived from the Civil Law, when any doubtful question in it arises we rejoice to see it traced to its source. Sir William Grant — "sanctos ausus recludere fontes"—by this practice gives force and beauty to *his* judgments, which, in traveling through the dreary tomes of Vesey, we now and then encounter with delight, like oases in the desert.

As a misfortune to Lord Eldon's judicial reputation, I must likewise point out his utter relinquishment of literature, from the time when he began to study the law. This cost him no sacrifice; he wrote no "Farewell to his Muse;" and he never even felt a wish to resume his liberal studies. He once astonished the Bar by saying that, during the Long Vacation, he had read "PARADISE LOST;" but it was shrewdly suspected that he only skimmed it over,—trying to find out "the *charging part;*"[2] and certain it is that, for many years, his reading was confined to bills, answers, depositions, affidavits, and the

---

[1] Sir Edward Sugden, in his very valuable treatise on "The Law of Vendors and Purchasers,"*—commenting on the case of Paine *v.* Mellor, 6 Vesey, jun. 349, in which Lord Eldon held, that, "upon the sale of a house, if after the day for completing the contract, and after the title has been accepted, but before the conveyance has been executed, it is burnt down, the loss falls on the buyer,"—says, "Lord Eldon's decision in Paine *v.* Mellor exactly accords with the doctrine of the civil law. Indeed, this very case is put in the Institutes. 'Cum autem emptio et venditio contracta sit, periculum rei venditæ statim ad emptorem pertinet tametsi adhuc ea res emptori tradita non sit. Itaque si aut ædes totæ vel aliqua ex parte incendio consumptæ fuerint emptoris damnum est, cui necesse, est, *licet rem non fuerit nactus,* pretium solvere.'"—See Inst. lib. iii. tit. 24, 3. But there is no reason to think that Lord Eldon took his doctrine from the civil law, and, indeed, he proceeds on different reasoning; for he seems to have been actuated by the consideration, that, in equity, the property had passed, although in the civil law, as well as in the Scotch law, the property remains in the seller till delivery.—"Periculum rei venditæ" is a very curious head in the civil law.

[2] Jockey Bell, the famous Chancery pleader, having said that he read all the new novels, and being asked how he found time, answered, "I soon find out *the charging part,*"—wherein lies the virtue of a bill in Chancery.

* 2nd edition, p. 333.

more trifling articles in the "John Bull" newspaper. The intellect can not be confined to such fare without injury. I do not now speak of his loss of that caste to which the Somerses, the Cowpers, and the Talbots, the companions of Swift, Addison, and Pope, had belonged—not to his neglect of fame—but to the depravation of taste which he displayed. Having forgotten his modicum of classical lore, and remaining wholly unacquainted with modern authors, he had no images in his mind, and no turns of phraseology, beyond what he picked up from perusing deeds and equity reports. In his latter days he could neither speak nor write grammatically—insomuch that people would not believe he had gained a prize at Oxford for English Composition; and he was actually compared to the *roué* Duke of Orleans, who said of spelling, "We quarreled at the outset of life, and never made up our differences." This vandalism impaired not only the grace but the efficiency of his high judicial qualities, and not only deprived him of the benefit of knowing something of public opinion and of the progress of improvement, but really hindered him from arranging and expressing his thoughts so as to do justice to the right conclusions at which he had arrived. The celebrity of Lord Mansfield and Lord Stowell, as judges, is in no small degree owing to their having continued to refresh and to embellish their professional labors by perusing the immortal productions of poets, historians, and moralists.

I am next obliged to regret that Lord Eldon, while sitting in his Court, often wasted his time, or, I should rather say, the time of the public. I know well how difficult it is to join the suavity of manner, which he ever preserved, with the energy required for the steady despatch of judicial business. The combination is, perhaps, only an ideal excellence; but although, for the popularity of the Judge with the Bar, the greater object may be never to give offense, it is most important for the suitors that their causes should be decided; and for this purpose the advocates must be kept under control, and it must be made disagreeable to them to wander from the question in hand, to repeat what has been before said, and to talk nonsense. Lord Eldon never complained of irrelevance,—he rather encouraged prolixity and the approach to absurdity he never checked by a rebuke, a sneer, a sarcasm, or even a look of exhausted patience or of suppressed ridicule. He himself was gradually corrupted by this habit of forbearance.

If, when he took his seat in the Court of Chancery, he had followed the course which, from his great experience and authority, was easily open to him, of never hearing more than two counsel in the same interest, and of requiring pure questions of law to be argued only by one counsel on a side, ordering a second argument if necessary —and had exercised a proper control over the discussion, while he devoted his whole attention to it,—he would have done thrice as much business as he actually got through, and his decisions would not only have been more rapid, but would have been, if possible, more satisfactory. His remissness constantly grew upon him. It was utterly impossible that, when the sixth and seventh counsel for the plaintiff were going over the same arguments and authorities which had been exhausted by Sir Samuel Romilly and Mr. Leach, his attention should really be engaged, although he seemed to listen. In reality, he was writing a gossiping letter to Lady Frances, his daughter, or Mrs. Ridley, his sister-in-law.[1] He found this occupation very agreeable, and he was pleased to have undisturbed leisure for it,—laying the flattering unction to his soul, that while he was sitting on the bench, and counsel were speaking in his hearing, he could not be accused of neglecting his duty. When arrears were multiplied to such a degree that, upon a moderate calculation, many years would be necessary to clear them off,—like a man deep in debt, who becomes recklessly prodigal, he grew more and more indifferent respecting the efficient employment of the hours appropriated to forensic labor: and if the appearance of arguing causes were kept up in his Court, however drowsily, the less he was called upon for an effort of thought, the better he was pleased.[2] At

---

[1] When attending the Assizes and Quarter Sessions at Gloucester, where Mrs. Ridley, the wife of Dr. Ridley, a prebendary of the cathedral, resided with her husband, I have several times been shown these letters, which were written on long slips of foolscap paper, such as a Judge uses in taking notes of an argument.

[2] It is said that traps were sometimes laid for him to prove his want of attention to the arguments,—as a junior, about to repeat an argument for the fifth time, would say, " Now, my Lord, I am about to venture upon a new view of the case, which may, perhaps, be deserving of consideration,"—when

last he seemed to be under a sort of infatuation upon the subject; and after the motions against him in the House of Commons, and the appointment of the Chancery Commission, he was still more dilatory and inefficient.

The heaviest charge brought against him in his lifetime was his habit of delaying judgment after the cause had been heard. This, although by no means without foundation, was dreadfully exaggerated. He lived in factious times, and being himself a very keen and successful politician, he excited a good deal of envy and hatred among his opponents. "When Lord Eldon had passed the fifth part of a century in office, and made no sign of retiring, letters of marque were issued by the Whig Opposition to burn, sink, and destroy the old first-rate that lay so obstinately in the very mouth of the harbor, and obstructed their entrance."[1]

Besides the annual motions made against him in the House of Commons, which I have mentioned, there was a constant succession of attacks upon him in pamphlets, reviews, and newspapers, and the grand topic was his "denial of justice by refusing to decide." This was boldly asserted as a fact, and to this mainly was attributed the enormous accumulation of arrears in the Court of Chancery, with all the evils, real and imaginary, prevailing there. Bands of litigants, wan, weary, and wasted, whose suits, after many years of expectation, had been finally heard, were represented as still wandering about Lincoln's Inn Hall, and exclaiming,—

> "Ah! little know'st thou, who hast never tried,
> What hell it is in suing long to bide;—
> To lose good days that might be better spent,
> To waste long nights in pensive discontent;
> To speed to-day, to be put back to-morrow,—
> To feed on hope, to pine with fear and sorrow;
> To fret the soul with crosses and with care,—
> To eat the heart with comfortless despair."

Nay, it was asserted that many, who had large sums undoubtedly due to them, locked up in Chancery, had, by the doubts and delays of the Lord Chancellor, actually died of penury, or of a broken heart, and that their ghosts

---

the Chancellor, having laid aside his pen for a time, would say, "That new view of the case does deserve and shall receive consideration."

[1] 2 Townsend, 410.

might be seen between midnight and cock-crow, flitting round the Accountant-General's office. Ludicrous stories were likewise invented of one cargo of ice having melted away, and another cargo of fruit having all become rotten, while he was doubting what judgment he should pronounce on motions for an injunction.[1]

On the other hand he was zealously defended in all that he did, and in all that he omitted to do—and if his advocates reluctantly admitted that at times he was a little given to the "cunctative," they exclaimed,—

"Tu maximus ille es
Unus qui nobis *cunctando* restituis rem."

Many returns on the subject were ordered by the House of Commons, and many volumes were written, invidiously or complimentarily comparing Lord Eldon with Lord Hardwicke[2] and his predecessors, and with Sir John Leach and his contemporaries.

But the interest of the controversy has almost entirely evaporated. It is very certain that Lord Eldon did defer his judgments most unjustifiably and unaccountably, although the blame to which he was liable for this habit was so much overcharged. It is the duty of a judge, in grave and difficult cases, to take time to consider; but it is his duty, as soon as is consistent with due deliberation, to make up his mind, and to deliver judgment,—further delay not only unnecessarily prolonging the suspense of the parties interested, but rendering the judge less and less qualified to decide rightly, as the facts of the case escape from his recollection, and the impression made upon him by the arguments at the Bar is effaced—to say nothing of the double time and labor required from him in vainly trying to make himself master, a second time, of what he once thoroughly understood. Lord Eldon, as soon as he had been informed of the circumstances of a case, formed a decided opinion upon it, and at the close of

[1] There is no better foundation for these stories than what is to be found in Cousins *v.* Smith, 13 Vesey, 542, where the *fruit* was landed in good order and sold,—the injunction applying to the *proceeds.*

[2] The great controversy was, whether the business of the Court of Chancery had increased since Lord Hardwicke's time? Notwithstanding some returns, showing the number of bills filed, I cannot doubt that it had increased most enormously, considering the increase in our population, commerce, and wealth; and that the sum of money in Court belonging to the suitors had certainly increased more than tenfold.

the arguments he would intimate this pretty plainly. Yet he not unfrequently expressed doubts — reserved to himself the opportunity for further consideration—took home the papers—never read them—promised judgment again and again—and for years never gave it—all the facts and the law connected with it having escaped from his memory. I shall give a few instances of this infirmity.

On one occasion, having spoken very luminously for two hours on the merits of a case which he had heard, and having intimated a strong opinion in favor of the defendant, he finished by saying, "However, I will take home the papers and read them carefully, and will tell the parties on a future day what my judgment will be." Sir Samuel Romilly, rising from his seat and turning round to the juniors, said, "Now is not this extraordinary? I never heard a more satisfactory judgment; and yet the Chancellor professes that he cannot make up his mind. It is wonderful; and the more so, because, however long he takes to consider a cause, I scarcely ever knew him to differ from his first impression."

The history of two cases between *Ware and Horwood*, is detailed in the following letter, which was written by the solicitor for the plaintiff to the Lord Chancellor:—

"Ware *v.* Horwood, } My Lord,—My clients have
    Same *v.* Same.   } great reason to complain of the great injury suffered by them in consequence of these causes not keeping their station at the head of your Lordship's paper, agreeably to your Lordship's order, repeatedly given in my hearing. It is now nearly seven years since they have been waiting for your Lordship's judgment; and upwards of two years ago they had arrived at the top of the paper, at which pace I humbly entreat they may, until you can decide upon them, remain. There is a fund of 10,000*l*. and upwards locked up in court until your Lordship decides in these causes, and it is therefore matter of great importance to my unfortunate client that your Lordship's decision may not be delayed by the circumstances to which I have above alluded. It is painful to me to state to your Lordship that I have learnt, from authority which I have no reason to doubt, that the infant, for whose benefit these suits were instituted twenty years ago, *died of a broken heart on account of being kept out his property*, and

that I have to contend against the bitter feelings of his relations. Under those distressing circumstances, knowing that your Lordship will pardon the liberty I have taken in thus addressing you, and which nothing but the imperious necessity of the case could have induced me to have done, I have the honor," &c.

It is said by Lord Eldon's friends, that upon investigation the sum locked up was found to be greatly overstated, and that the death of the infant of a broken heart, turned out to be a fable; yet, strange to say! the solicitor, instead of being committed to the Fleet Prison for a contempt of court, in fulfillment of a denunciation lately uttered by the Chancellor against the practice of writing private letters to him about pending suits, was sent for to the private room of the Chancellor, where he was most courteously received,—and his bill of costs to his client contained the following item, which, when read aloud, caused a deep sensation in the House of Commons:—

" To attendance on the Lord High Chancellor of Great Britain in his private room, when his Lordship begged for further indulgence from me till to-morrow,
16s. 4d."

His Lordship having begged and obtained a further respite, was at length as good as his word, and, with the spur in his side, actually did make a decree.

But in the following case, verified by the oath of a member of Parliament before the Chancery Commission in August, 1825, it would appear that no decree was ever made: " In a friendly suit, the sum at stake not being more than 2500*l*., the Chancellor declared in November, 1816, that 'he would give judgment in a few days.' The parties died and after three years, the solicitor for some of the representatives, becoming impatient, followed the precedent in *Ware* v. *Horwood*, and wrote the following note to the Lord Chancellor:—

"'*Erskine* v. *Gartshore*.—The solicitor for the representatives of the parties in the cause is desired on their behalf humbly to entreat the Lord Chancellor's judgment in the above cause. The subject-matter in question came on to be heard before his Lordship in the shape of exceptions to the Master's Report on the 20th and 22nd November, 1816.—May 22nd, 1820.'

"In two or three days the Chancellor returned the following answer:—

"'In the case of Erskine v. Gartshore, the papers were long ago taken from my table. I have desired Mr. Hand to make due inquiry for them, and, understanding from your note that I have been mistaken in supposing that the cause was arranged, as soon as I get the papers I will dispose of it.   Yours, with much respect,
"'Eldon.'

"I have only to add," said the witness, "that, notwithstanding the promise contained in his Lordship's note, the cause still stands for judgment in his paper, and is still undisposed of." It has been asserted that "the materials for judgment were gone; the papers could never be recovered."[1]

I will only mention one other case of this class.[2] Under a will it was doubtful which of two sons of the late Earl Somers on his death would be entitled to a considerable estate, With a view to his own will he wished the question to be decided in his lifetime, and for this purpose he directed that a friendly suit should be instituted in the Court of Chancery. The case being most learnedly and elaborately argued, the Chancellor promised a speedy judgment; but term rolled on after term, and year after year, without any judgment being given. Lord Somers several times spoke to him privately, saying that he had no bias on the subject, but that it was of great consequence to his family to have a decision one way or the other. "That you shall," said the Chancellor, "and I take so much time to consider it that you may have one that will stand." Several times was a day appointed for giving judgment, and as often, on some pretense, judgment was postponed. At last, the case being in the paper for judgment, once more Lord Somers attended in person, in the hope of extorting it, and the Lord Chancellor actually began by reading the bill, the answer, and depositions, when he showed that he had utterly forgotten what the question was, and declared that, being obliged to attend a meeting of the Cabinet, he must postpone the judgment to a future day. Lord Somers thereupon intimated to

[1] 2 Townsend, 413.
[2] I am not sure whether there be any notice of it in print, but I have it from an undoubted source.

him that he thought it would be better to allow the question to stand over till after his own death, and that he did not desire that any judgment should be pronounced.

The cause, or perhaps the pretext, for these delays was a principle on which he professed to act, " that it was always his duty to read the bill, answer, depositions, and exhibits, and to consider not only the facts stated and the points made at the bar, but all the facts in the cause, and all the points that might be made on either side." " I know," said he, " it has been an opinion—a maxim—a principle—ay, an honest principle, on which several of those who have presided in this Court have acted,—that a judge is obliged to know nothing more than counsel think proper to communicate to him, relative to the case. But for myself I have thought and acted otherwise; and I know, yes, I could swear upon my oath, that if I had given judgment on such information and statements only as I have received from counsel on both sides, I should have disposed of numerous estates to persons who had no more title to them than I have; and believe me that I feel a comfort in that thought—a comfort of which all the observations on my conduct can never rob me."[1]

" During my Chancellorship," says he, in his ANECEOTE BOOK, with his usual self-complacency, " I was much, very much blamed for not giving judgment at the close of the arguments. I persevered in this, as some thought from obstinacy, but in truth from principle, from adherence to a rule of conduct, formed after much consideration what course of proceeding was most consonant with my duty. With Lord Bacon, ' I confess I have somewhat of the cunctative,' and, with him, I thought that ' whosoever is not wiser upon advice than upon the sudden, the same man is no wiser at fifty than he was at thirty.' I confess that no man ever had more occasion than I had to use the expression, which was Lord Bacon's father's ordinary word, ' You must give me time.' I always thought it better to allow myself to doubt *before* I decided, than to expose myself to the misery, *after* I had decided, of doubting whether I had decided rightly and justly. It is true that too much delay before decision is a great evil; but in many instances delay leads eventually to prevent delay; that is, the delay which enables just decision to be made accel-

[1] Quarterly Review, xliv. 102.

erates the enjoyment of the fruits of the suit ; and I have some reason to hope that, in a great many cases, *final* decision would have been infinitely longer postponed, if doubts as to the soundness of original judgments had led to rehearings and appeals, that it *was* postponed, when infinite care, by much and anxious and long consideration, was taken to form an impregnable original decree. *The business of the Court was also so much increased in some periods of my Chancellorship, that I never could be confident that counsel had fully informed me of the facts or of the law of many of the cases;* and there may be found not a few instances in which most satisfactory judgments were pronounced, which were founded upon facts or instruments with which none of the counsel who argued the cases were acquainted, though such facts and instruments formed part of the evidence in the cause."

Once he observed in the House of Lords,—" It will be a consolation to me, during my remaining life, knowing that it has been said that I have been dilatory in decision, that I have, by looking at the original instruments, saved to the right owner many a landed estate, which would otherwise, probably, have been given to his adversary."[1]

In a private company he said,—" Lord Abergavenny told me he compromised a suit, because his attorney had told him there was in his case a weak point, which, though the opposing parties were not aware of it, *that old fellow* would be sure to find out if the case came before him. It is quite necessary never to trust to the lawyers. It is their business to make a good case for their clients; it is mine to administer justice."

Conversing on these subjects with Mrs. Foster, he said to her : " I was often accused of slowness in my decisions, but really it was sometimes incompatible with justice to decide quicker. Now I will tell you what happened in one case : it was a cause where one party had sold an estate, and the purchaser had afterwards declined completing the bargain, and the estate was thrown back on the seller's hands; this was a suit to compel the completion of the sale and the payment of the purchase-money. Well, it was argued before me at great length, and extracts from various documents were read in Court, and I was then pressed by the counsel to deliver my judgment the

[1] Ruscombe *v.* Hare, 6 Dow, 16.

following day. I refused to do this, stating that I made it a rule to read over and consider *all* the written documents brought into Court; and that, as there was an important question to be discussed that night in the House of Lords, I should be unable to do this before the next morning."

Again he says in the ANECDOTE BOOK: "I thought it my indispensable duty, as a Judge in Equity, to look into the whole record, and all the exhibits and proofs in causes, and not to consider myself as sufficiently informed by counsel. This, I am sure, was right,—not only because, in causes originally heard before me, I learnt much of what was necessary, of which counsel had not informed me, but because, upon rehearings of causes before me, which had been originally heard by others, this, my opinion, was strongly confirmed."

Finally, in a letter to his brother-in-law, Mr. Surtees he says:—

"My habits of doing judicial business I have formed and adhered to upon principle and conviction that they were right; I have done much good by adhering to them, —infinite good.

"As to what I hear of my *doubts*, from persons who, having no doubts upon any subjects, however intricate and difficult, set up as the Ductores Dubitantium, I console myself by recollecting what a most eminent Chancellor in France (D'Aguesseau) said to his son: 'The truth is, I don't like to risk, by velocity, transferring property from those to whom it belongs, to those who may apparently, but not really, have a title to it.'"[1]

Having heard him so fully in his self-glorification, and in the inculpation of others, I must be allowed very respectfully to question the propriety of this professed judicial habit. In the first place, it is impossible. In the vast majority of cases which come before a Judge, whether

---

[1] This is probably the passage to which he refers:—"My child," said the Chancellor, "when you shall have read what I have read, seen what I have seen, and heard what I have heard, you will feel that if, on any subject, you know much, there may be also much that you do not know; and that something even of what you know may not, at the moment, be in your recollection:—you will then, too, be sensible of the mischievous and often ruinous consequences of even a small error in a decision; and conscience, I trust, will then make you as doubtful, as timid, and consequently as dilatory, as I am accused of being."

in a Court of Common Law or Court of Equity, he must take the contents of written documents from the counsel, —trusting to their honor and accuracy, and to their reciprocal supervision. Secondly, it would be exceedingly dangerous for a Judge to be in the habit of deciding upon facts or points of law of his own discovering; for, if noticed at the bar, they would very likely have been found capable of being easily answered or explained away. Thirdly, such a habit must breed a morbid propensity to doubt; and it holds out a tempting bait to procrastination, by affording a ready excuse for idleness.

Sir S. Romilly, in his DIARY, gives a striking view of Lord Eldon's practice of deferring judgment:—

"8th of March, 1811.—What has passed to-day, in the Court of Chancery, affords a strong exemplification of my assertion of yesterday, that the Lord Chancellor was *overanxious* to decide properly. He has, for a long time, had a great number of cases which have been argued before him, waiting for his judgment to be pronounced,—some original causes, and many more motions and petitions. The distress which is occasioned to many parties by this, is hardly to be conceived. On this day three cases were, by his order, put into his paper, for him to deliver his judgment. Of two of them he merely directed that they should stand over till the following Monday, without giving any reason. The third was a case of *Forster* v. *Bellamy*. It was a bill filed by a pauper to redeem a very old mortgage,—the plaintiff alleging that he was heir-at-law to the mortgagor. The defendant disputed the fact of his being heir, and the plaintiff had gone into evidence to prove his title; but the evidence was so unsatisfactory, that all that I, who was counsel for the plaintiff, could do, was to ask that an issue might be directed to try the fact of his being heir. Of this case, which had been argued before the long vacation, the Lord Chancellor said to-day, that he had read all the evidence over three several times, and that he did not think there was sufficient proved to warrant his directing an issue, but that, as it was the case of a pauper, he would go over all the evidence once more; and for that purpose he directed the cause to stand over generally, without appointing any time for his final determination. He thus condemns all the other impatient suitors to continue waiting in anxious expectation of having their causes decided, till he shall have made himself quite sure, by another perusal of the depositions, that he had not been already three times mistaken."[1]

I must confess that I am uncharitable enough to suspect that he had not read the evidence over once, and that he deferred the judgment till he should do so. According to the theory of "white lies," which he patronized, this would be a much less offense than, after having three times read over the whole of the evidence, seeing that the plaintiff did not make out any *primâ facie* case, he should have indefinitely postponed judgment, to the great prejudice, and perhaps the utter ruin, of the defendant.

I really believe that Lord Eldon considerably overrated his labors in private and his discoveries. Several times in the course of a long life, by minutely examining the records, and poring over deeds, he did hit upon matters which had escaped the attention of counsel; but whoever reads through the voluminous reports of his decisions will see that, in 999 times out of 1000, he decides cases upon points made before him at the Bar; and when he had the assistance of such counsel as Romilly, Leach, Bell, Pepys, and Sugden,—distinguished for their industry as well as their deep professional learning,—if he listened to their arguments in Court, it is not at all likely that the "papers," when read at home, would present to him much that was both new and material.[2]

But, in weighing the defenses to which he was driven, we must remember the preposterous charges brought against him. Many persons were so absurd as to impute all the arrears in the Court of Chancery and in the House of Lords to his remissness, and expected that he should pronounce a final decree in every case which came before him;—whereas a motion was frequently made to obtain his opinion in an interlocutory shape—whereupon the parties were satisfied, and the suit was compromised.

But it is impossible to deny that his habit of deferring his judgments, did produce most serious injury to the

---

[1] Memoirs of Romilly's Life, ii. 371, 372.

[2] According to the "Anecdote Book," he claims a mighty discovery in Johnson *v.* Legard, of which not a trace is to be found in the very full and elaborate report of the case by Turner and Russell. See p. 281.

suitors in his Court; and we are tantalized when we think not only how capable he was of being above all reproach in this respect, but that on some occasions he actually was so. Mr. Wilberforce, in his Diary, giving an account of his going into the Court of Chancery, to converse with Sir Samuel Romilly, says, "Lord Eldon saw me, and beckoned to me with as much cheerfulness and gayety as possible. When I was alone with Romilly, and asked him how he was, he answered, 'I am worn to death: here have I been, sitting on in the vacation from nine in the morning untill four, and when I leave this place I have to read through all my papers to be ready for to-morrow morning; but the most extraordinary part of all is, that Eldon, who has not only mine but all the other business to go through, is just as cheerful and untired as ever.'" Again, Sir Samuel Romilly, in his own Diary, under date 23rd August, 1811, says, "The Chancellor ended his sittings. In the last fortnight he has done more business than in all the rest of the year. He has heard nearly 300 petitions in bankruptcy, and has decided as well as heard them. In the last week he sat every morning from nine till four and in the evening from half after five till ten; and he has not only done the business expeditiously, but with very great ability. It should seem as if his object had been to exhibit the most striking contrast imaginable to his usual mode of administering justice."

In lamenting that he was not always equally energetic, we must remember Sir Robert Peel's apology for him:—
"If Lord Eldon's delay had been one arising from his indulgence in pleasure or in frivolous amusements, it would have been a subject of just reprehension; but where a man was seen devoting twelve out of the twenty-four hours, without remission, to the public business, and allowing himself no longer a vacation than three weeks out of fifty-two, it would be but fair to pass with a light hand over the venial fault of him who decided slowly, from the peculiar constitution of his mind, and his ultra anxiety to decide justly."[1] We should likewise ever bear in mind, that when the decree was at last pronounced, it was sure to be right. It may be said of Lord Eldon, that he never wronged a suitor or perverted a principle. "I begin to think," said Sir Samuel Romilly,

[1] Debate in the House of Commons on the Court of Chancery.

after the erection of the Vice-Chancellor's Court, "that the tardy justice of the Chancellor is better than the swift injustice of his deputy."[1] It was said that "*Eldonian doubting* might give a good illustration of ETERNITY;" but there was a limit to the process in his own imagination. Thus he began his judgment in "Radnor v. Schafts:"[2]—"Having had doubts upon this will *for twenty years*, there can be no use in taking more time to consider it." Strange to say, notwithstanding his doubting propensity, he was never known to change the opinion he originally formed when the case was first fully stated to him.

Among minor defects, I must mention his habit of carping at almost everything said by contemporary judges, and his gross partiality in speaking of his immediate predecessors. He might be excused in complaining of the haste of Sir John Leach, who decided without hearing; but he would disparage the judgments of Sir William Grant, without venturing to reverse them; and he gave such offense to the Common Law Judges, by criticising their "reasons," that for many years, when he sent a case for their opinion, they refused to do more than drily to answer affirmatively or negatively the questions he submitted to them. Then, he most extravagantly overrated the authority of his great patron, Lord Thurlow; while he was constantly sneering at Lord Mansfield,—a judge equal to himself in professional learning, and infinitely his superior in eloquence and scholarship.[3]

---

[1] The Chancellor's Court used to be denominated, by certain wits, that of *oyer sans terminer*, and the Vice-Chancellor's that of *terminer sans oyer*.

[2] 11 Vesey, jun. 453.

[3] In addition to his dislike of Lord Mansfield as a supposed favorer of Christchurch men (*ante*, Vol. IX. p. 370), he bore him a grudge *ratione originis*, thinking that one born on the banks of the Tyne had a right to push his fortune in London, but that one born on the banks of the Tay coming to London was an intruder (*ante*, Vol. IX. p. 436). "*Scotchman*" he used as a term of reproach. Being offended with a speech of Mr. Joseph Hume in the House of Commons, he observes, "This same *Scotchman* cares not a farthing what he says;" and when the late Mr. Millar published his ingenious book "On the Civil Law of England," he said, "Now comes out another *Scotchman* at the Bar of the name of Millar, who has abused the Chancellor *black and blue;* and this gentleman, who has made no progress yet in his profession, conceives himself at liberty to calumniate the highest Judge to the utmost of his power also." (June, 1825.) Mr. Abercromby was another Scotchman with whom he had a *passage of arms;* and to Mr. Brougham's Northern education no doubt he imputed much of what he considered objectionable in that gentleman. I must acknowledge, however, that to me, a Scotchman and a Whig, he always behaved with great courtesy, and I hope that no one

In the vain lamentation that Lord Eldon, as an Equity Judge, did not come up to our notion of ideal perfection, I have only further to express a wish that his judgments, while they invariably did justice between the parties, had been more methodical, had been better composed, and had abounded more in general principles. The faults of his judicial style are very much to be ascribed to the circumstance, that, in delivering his opinion, he always extemporized,—not even making use of notes. If the advice of an individual so humble as myself could have any weight hereafter, I would most earnestly implore judges, in all cases of importance, to prepare written judgments. This habit not only insures a minute attention to all the facts of the case, and a calm consideration of the questions of law which they raise, but is of infinite advantage in laying down rules with just precision, and it has a strong tendency to confer the faculty of lucid arrangement and of correct composition. How inferior would Lord Stowell's judgments have been, if blurted out on the conclusion of the arguments at the bar, and taken down by a reporter! Sir William Grant's, hardly inferior in merit, were recited as if the product of his mind at the moment; but it is now ascertained that they had been carefully written out, revised, and committed to memory. Unless in one or two cases, which Lord Eldon decided by consent of parties after he resigned the Great Seal, he never put pen to paper in preparing his judgments. In consequence, it has been remarked by a severe critic, that "Lord Eldon's judgments lie, like Egyptian mummies, embalmed in a multitude of artfully contrived folds and wrappers;"[1] and even Mr. Twiss candidly says, "It may at once be admitted, that as literary compositions they are faulty enough,—inconveniently parenthetical, and over-abundant in limitations and qualifications.

It was interesting to hear him deliver a judgment; for his voice was clear, and, notwithstanding his Newcastle burr, very sweet; his manner was earnest and impressive; he helped out the involution of his sentences by change

will suspect me of ever trying to be revenged on him for his injustice to my country or to my party.

Lord Eldon had a peculiar spite against his immediate predecessor, whom he was in the constant habit of *vilipending;* but he would say that, "although Thurlow was the most powerful reasoner he had ever heard, Wedderburn was the ablest stater of a case."   [1] Edinburgh Review.

of emphasis, and the varying expression of a most benevolent and intellectual countenance; and as he was justly considered infallible, there was a disposition to receive with respect everything that fell from his lips. But very few of his judgments can be perused without a most painful effort, and even the professional reader has often much difficulty in discovering the principles on which they rest, and the doctrines which they establish. They proceeded neither upon the footing of his audience previously knowing, nor being ignorant of, the circumstances of the case. His statement of facts to be found in them is desultory and slovenly, and is often mixed up with propositions of law; he is occasionally very illogical, and you can not tell from what premises he draws his conclusion. Unfortunately he dwells so much on the "specialties" of each particular case, that no one can tell whether the decisions can ever again be applied in any other case; and it has been wittily and correctly observed, that "they will be of special use when the old Ptolemaic cycle shall begin a second time to run, and all things shall happen over again in the exact same order which we now behold."[1] Then his ear was as dull to the music of language as to the notes of Catalani. Not from any hesitation or embarrassment in his delivery (for he was always collected and fluent, and seemed always to be able to select the expressions which he preferred), but from depraved taste, or utter negligence, he would repeat the same word half a dozen times in the same breath, sometimes with a different meaning; and he would tautologically multiply words to which the same meaning was to be affixed, as if he had been dictating deeds of "lease and release;" he had no regard to congruity or balance between the different members of his sentences, and he was as well contented to end with two mean monosyllables, as if he could have introduced the favorite termination of Cicero, "*esse videatur.*"

But with all these defects, which I enumerate to show that I do not view him with blind admiration, and to give some value to my praise of him, I do not hesitate a moment to place him, as a Judge, above all the Judges of my time. For law he really had a natural genius, which was improved by long, severe, and unwearied discipline.

[1] Article in Edinb. Rev. by Mr. Justice Williams.

The law of real property was his *forte;* this he knew more profoundly, more accurately, and more familiarly than any man in the profession, either on the Bench or at the Bar; and there was no branch of the municipal law of England the principles of which he did not thoroughly understand, so as easily to make himself master of any question which might arise respecting it.[1] Although he had never been in an equity draughtsman's office, in which it is now supposed that equity lawyers must be reared, he was superior in the lore of Bills, Pleas, Demurrers, Answers, and Exceptions, to any trained equity draughtsman who practiced before him; and although he had never meddled with special pleading while at the Bar,—if a special pleading point arose on a writ of error while he was presiding on the woolsack, he could handle it as well as a Holroyd, a Richardson, or a Littledale.

In the absence of a political crisis, his whole soul was in his profession. If he had no literature, at least he was not diverted by its blandishments from his judicial duty; and it is much better, if they can not unite, that a judge should have law without literature, than literature without law. I doubt whether he ever entered a theatre three times after he was called to the Bar; his only amusement was frightening partridges for a few weeks in the autumn; and although, for sixty years, he daily drank as much port wine as would disable any two ordinary men for intellectual occupation, it only stimulated him to see abstruse legal distinctions with more acutenesss and accuracy.

I need not mention his unsullied purity,—a praise to which all English judges are now equally entitled. A Welsh woman once attempted to bribe him by sending him a goose,—expressing a grave hope that " her munifi-

---

[1] He himself ascribed his knowledge of the law and his success,—1st, to his practice as a conveyancer; and, 2ndly, to his having so long gone the circuit. I am concerned to hear, that notwithstanding his earnest advice to young equity counsel to go the circuit "for a good many years," they now never go at all. But they should remember his solemn admonition : " I know, from long personal observation and experience, that the great defect of the Chancery Bar is its ignorance of common law and common law practice; and, strange as it should seem, yet almost without exception it is, that gentlemen go to a bar, where they are to modify, qualify, and soften the rigor of the common law, with very little notion of its doctrines or practice."
—*Letter to Mr. Farrer,* 1807.

cence would not incline him to favor her, as she did not mean it as a bribe." In writing an account of this to his daughter, he said, "I think, Taffy, the Welsh woman, will be much surprised when she receives my letter, informing her that, being a judge, she might as properly apply to her goose for advice as to me."[1]

Among his qualifications for the judgment-seat, must be reckoned his fine temper and delightful manners. Mr. John Williams, who had so bitterly assailed him in the House of Commons, had to plead before him at great length respecting an issue tried on the Northern Circuit, and when retiring from Lincoln's Inn Hall he exclaimed, "Your Chancellor is an abundantly agreeable Judge!" He certainly was most courteous to the Bar, to the solicitors, and to all who approached him. Even "upon those unhappy persons, *the afflicted in mind, body, or estate*, who sometimes broke through the trammels of Chancery etiquette to make their grievances known in person, his singular kindness of manner acted with the force of a spell. However irregular the application, or however unbecomingly pertinacious the applicant, Lord Eldon listened with most patient attention, until the object was discovered, and then advised with gentleness, or softened refusal with complacency."[2]

He always maintained his dignity, and effectually checked any unbecoming familiarity. When he had finished giving his judgment in a case that had stood many years in the paper, and put a question respecting the form of the decree, Mr. Heald said,—"I know I was counsel in this case, but whether for the plaintiff or defendant, and whether the judgment is for me or against me, I have not at this distance of time the most remote conception." "I have a glimmering notion it is for me," exclaimed Mr. Horne. Supposing, from the titter running through the Bar, that there was a disposition to jeer at his delays, he restored universal gravity by saying, with some sharpness, "I beg that counsel will not make me the subject of their observations."

But the weapon he usually employed in self-defense was good humor. A very old, very learned, very uncouth Chancery barrister, whom I recollect under the name of "*Hun* HALL," having querulously concluded an unsuc-

[1] 8th January, 1821. [2] Townsend.

cessful argument by observing, "But now, my Lord, I find that I know no law;"—"Mr. Hall," said Lord Eldon, "if you know no law, I can say of my own knowledge, that you have forgot a great deal since I sat in those rows in which you now sit." The Hun's face spreading wider and wider, and his eyes filling with morning dew, he attempted to say something in reply, but, to the amusement of the whole Court, without being able to finish the sentence, sat down in a state of tender suffocation.

My most valued and witty friend, Sir George Rose, when at the Bar, having the note-book of the regular reporter of Lord Eldon's decisions put into his hand with a request that he would take a note for him of any decision which should be given, entered in it the following lines as a full record of all that was material which had occurred during the day:—

"Mr. Leech
Made a speech,
  Angry, neat, but wrong:
Mr. Hart,
On the other part,
  Was heavy, dull, and long.
Mr. Parker
Made the case darker,
  Which was dark enough without:
Mr. Cook
Cited his book,
  And the Chancellor said—' I DOUBT.'"

This *jeu d'esprit*, flying about Westminster Hall, reached the Chancellor, who was very much amused with it, notwithstanding the allusion to his doubting propensity. Soon after, Mr. Rose having to argue before him a very untenable proposition, he gave his opinion very gravely, and with infinite grace and felicity thus concluded:— "For these reasons the judgment must be against your clients; *and here, Mr. Rose, the Chancellor* DOES NOT DOUBT."

But his great merit was his earnest desire to do justice between man and man. Notwithstanding all his professions and all his tears, this he really felt, and by this he was steadily actuated. There have been judges (in former days) who cared not in how perfunctory a manner they did their duty—with no anxiety but to keep their places and to avoid open censure—who would on no account have done anything positively dishonorable, but who were rather indifferent as to the arbitrary rules of right and wrong as established by prior decisions, and who cared nothing for the credit of the system of jurisprudence which they administered, beyond their own time. Lord Eldon had a disinterested, a passionate wish to decide rightly,—and to gain his object there was no labor that he was not willing to undergo. This made him disregard the politics of the litigant, and the personal dislike he might entertain for the advocate. This made him even despise the censure to which he was exposed as a doubting and dilatory Judge. He certainly carried the fear of erring to excess, and by degrees it assumed a morbid shape in his mind; but we should remember the salutary effects which have sprung from it, and bear in our recollection the injury to individuals and the general confusion which would be produced by a succession of indolent and reckless judges. It should likewise be remembered, that, if he sometimes frittered away the benefit of his decision as a precedent by dwelling upon the minute circumstances of the particular case, he never sought to save himself trouble by arbitrarily adapting all the facts to some one convenient ruling principle, as judges of ease-loving though powerful minds are too apt to do; but he diligently had regard to all the considerations which each case presented,—seeing patiently how they affected each other, — and deducing the just result from the whole. I must likewise in fairness observe, that although his judgments are unsystematic in their structure, they are instinct with the true principles of equity, and that from the reports in which they are recorded an equitable code might be constructed, —as we may extract almost all the rules of life from Shakspeare, who had no thought of teaching morality.[1]

[1] The original of the following letter of Lord Eldon has been recently communicated to me, and I have much pleasure in publishing it. A letter had been sent to him by the post, asking his advice in favor of a poor widow, who had lost her all from the bankruptcy of an executor. Most judges would have thrown it into the waste-basket, but he took the trouble to return this good-natured answer :

" Sir,—I have received your letter, which is addressed to me under the influence of a very natural and very common mistake, but, as Chancellor, I have no power to interpose in any such case as you mention, unless in the regular forms of court, upon a petition regularly presented, and openly heard, after notice to all persons interested. It will follow that, as I can only act *as a judge*, it is contrary to my duty to give *advice* respecting a

I should now wish, according to my practice, to lay before the reader some of Lord Eldon's most interesting and important decisions; but, by copying largely from his multitudinous reporters, I should do no justice to his merits, and I should convey to the general reader no notion of his powers. His manner was so diffuse, his arrangement so immethodical, and his style so repulsive, that I have in vain searched for specimens of his judgments which might be perused with pleasure. Not even when he is discoursing on the management of theatres, or on copyright in libelous publications, or taking the custody of children from an immoral parent, is he readable without a fee; and were I to present at length any of his judicial lucubrations for admiration, I should be suspected of selecting them maliciously.[1] His later reporters were very able men, and if they had felt themselves at liberty to methodize and condense,—accurately preserving the substance and the spirit of the original,—they would have done much more justice to him, and conferred a much greater benefit on the public; but I have been told that he highly disapproved of any proposal for reporting him on this plan, and that he was best pleased when he saw himself in the transcript of a short-hand writer.

None of his biographers have ventured on giving an entire judgment as delivered by him. The following have

matter which may be litigated before myself for determination. The parties, if they want *advice*, must apply to professional persons. I would readily give it, where I could do so without a breach of judicial duty. I may mention, generally, that, where an executor becomes bankrupt, not having in his hands at that time the very property, the specific property, which was his testator's, legatees can only come in with the bankrupt's other creditors;—if, at the time he became bankrupt, he had in his hands property of the testator's, as for instance the testator's goods, chattels, leases, &c., unconverted, the law will apply such property to the benefit of the testator's creditors and legatees, and not to those of the bankrupt; but that can only be enforced by regular formal proceedings, as to which my *judicial* situation will not allow me to give any advice.

" I am, Sir, respectfully,
" Your obedient servant,
" ELDON.

" 10th January, 1820.
" To Mr. Robert Bland, Darlington."
—*3rd Edition.*

[1] I was in great hopes that his judgment in Wellesley *v.* Duke of Beaufort, 2 Russell, 17–45, would have been found an exception, as I have been told by those who were present when it was delivered that it was very interesting to hear; but to call upon any one to read it would be unkind to the memory of Lord Eldon.

been presented by those most friendly to his memory as favorable passages: After expressing doubts as to the soundness of the doctrine that the writer of a letter has a sufficient property in it to prevent its publication, he says, " But it is my duty to submit my judgment to the authority of those who have gone before me; and it will not be easy to remove the weight of the decisions of Lord Hardwicke and Lord Apsley. The doctrines of this Court ought to be as well settled, and made as uniform, almost, as those of the common law, *laying down fixed principles*, but taking care that they are to be applied according to the circumstances of each case. *I can not agree that the doctrines of this Court are to be changed with every succeeding Judge.* Nothing would inflict on me greater pain, in quitting this place, than the recollection that I had done anything to justify the reproach that the equity of this Court varies *like the Chancellor's foot*."[1]

Upon the subject of giving relief against bargains made with expectant heirs, he observed, " I am aware that, during my whole time, considerable doubt has been entertained, whether that policy, with regard to expectant heirs ought to have been adopted; and although Lord Thurlow repeatedly laid it down, that this Court does shield heirs expectant, to the extent of declaring a bargain oppressive, in their case, which would not be so in other cases, and imposes an obligation on the parties dealing with them to show that the bargain was fair, yet he seldom applied that doctrine without complaining that he was deserting the principle itself, because the parties dealing with the heir expectant insured themselves against that practice, and therefore the heir made a worse bargain; but he certainly, like his predecessors, adhered to the doctrine, though not very ancient. It is not the duty of a Judge in Equity to vary rules, or to say that rules are not to be considered as fully settled here as in a Court of Law."[2]

Upon the question whether a trust should be executed by the Court he said, " It struck me at first as a point of considerable doubt, whether the Court should execute such a trust. If it was unprejudiced by decision, *that doubt might be maintained by strong argument;* but

---

[1] 2 Swanston, 414. [2] Ib. 162.

it is too late now even to state it; for *there is authority binding my judgment entirely upon that.*"¹

As to the power of a married woman over estates settled to her separate use, he said, " If it is asserted, that though Lord Thurlow, following his predecessors as far back as the doctrine can be traced, repeatedly decided upon this principle, this court has now a right to refuse to follow it, I am not bold to act upon that position."²

Thus he lectured the Judges of the Court of Session in Scotland :—" As to the observation made with respect to the case of feoffees of Heriot's Hospital, that the judgment of this House in that case was one to be *obeyed, not to be followed*, I must take the liberty to say that this would be a course which, if pursued, would call for some attention. For, although every court may say that, if a case varies in facts and circumstances, it is at liberty to proceed upon these different circumstances, I do not recollect that it ever fell from a Judge in this country, that he would obey the judgment of this House in the particular case, but not follow it in others. That is not a doctrine to which we are accustomed."³

Thus he declared himself against allowing even the probable intention of a devisor to overrule the general principles of legal construction :—" Judging as a private individual, there can be no doubt that when he (the testator) executed the will, he meant that instrument and these two letters should have their effect; but unless the rule of law allows me, I cannot establish the letters."⁴

In reference to a question upon conditional legacies, he said, " After the doctrine has been so long settled (though with Lord Kenyon, I think the distinction such as the mind cannot well fasten upon), it is better the law should be certain, than that every judge should speculate upon improvements in it."⁵

To show that although a doctrine may seem at variance with principle, yet, if the decisions upon it were clear, it ought not to be shaken, he said : " If this doctrine has been settled by decision, I shall be no more inclined to disturb it than the decisions upon the Registry Act; as it is much better to rest upon decision, than to hazard, especially upon the subject of title, undoing what has been settled,

¹ 10 Vesey, 342. ² 11 Ib. 321. ³ 6 Dow, 112.
⁴ 6 Vesey, 566. ⁵ 8 Ib. 497.

though perhaps not to be perfectly reconciled to principle."[1]

In the case of the Queensberry leases, he said, in advising the House of Lords upon the judgment they should give,—" All law ought to stand upon principle; and *unless decision* has removed out of the way all argument and all principle, so as to make it impossible to apply them to the case before you, you must find out what is *the principle* upon which it must be decided."[2]

On the petition of certain elders of Jewish congregations, praying a declaration of the admissibility of Jews in common with Christians to the benefit of the Bedford Charity, Lord Eldon, in giving judgment against the petitioners upon the construction of the charter and of the Acts of Parliament bearing upon it, which construction, he said, formed the simple question for his determination, observed, that many arguments had been addressed to him from the Bar on the practice and principle of toleration; but, added he, I apprehend that it is the duty of every Judge, presiding in an English Court of Justice, when he is told that there is no difference between worshiping the Supreme Being in chapel, church, or synagogue, to recollect that Christianity is part of the law of England; that in giving construction to the charter and Acts of Parliament, he is not to proceed on that principle further than just construction requires; but to the extent of just construction of that charter and those acts, he is not at liberty to forget that Christianity is the law of the land."[3]

But, instead of trying to multiply these "Elegant Extracts," I shall best discharge my duty by noticing in general terms, the great improvements which Lord Eldon introduced by his decisions into our sytem of Equity, —and for this purpose I avail myself of a panegyric written by a warm but discriminating admirer. After enumerating the titles of the sixteen collections of his Reporters, he says, "Such is the long list of Lord Eldon's reported judgments,—to be read, marked, learned, and inwardly digested by the laborious student, before he can form any adequate conception of his merits as a Judge. Nearly fifty closely printed octavo volumes which, if all his judgments and decrees had been pre

---

[1] 16 Vesey, 429. [2] 1 Bligh, 486. See Twiss, ch. lxiii. [3] 2 Swanston, 52.

served, would be doubled in number; and every individual case so well sifted, every decree so well weighed, that it may serve as a valuable precedent! What other Judge has left such a monument to his memory?" .... "The reference of title to the Master, when nothing but title is in dispute, is an invention of Lord Eldon's, by which an infinite number of suits have been stopped *in limine*.[1] Prevention of mischief by injunction, is a head of Equity, upon which instances few and far between are to be found before his time. Lord Thurlow would hardly grant an injunction where the parties had a remedy at law. Before his time, there are not more than half a dozen instances of each species of injunction; and in these, relief was as often denied as granted. Now injunction is, it is well known, the right arm of the Court, pervading the workshop of the artisan, the studio of the artist,—entering alike the miner's shaft and the merchant's counting-house. Almost all the principles upon which this relief is granted or refused,—the terms and conditions upon which it is dissolved, revived, continued, extended, or made perpetual,—are to be found in Lord Eldon's judgments alone. The rules of ordering money into court, and appointing receivers on behalf of all parties, are powerful instruments of justice, of which Lord Eldon showed first the perfect use. The inspection of the subject-matter in dispute, pending litigation, is another of the powers to which Courts of Equity have become entitled through his means.[2] These and many other topics will show that the Court of Chancery, under Lord Eldon's superintendence, was not a clog and a burden upon the rank, wealth, and industry of the country."[3]

I must further observe that he distinctly defined the boundaries of legal and equitable jurisdiction; and, while he fully upheld the maxim that agreements must receive in Equity precisely the same construction as in a Court of Common Law, he adhered to the great doctrine that the equitable circumstances by which it might be fitting to regulate the performance of agreements so construed were matters for the consideration only of Courts of Equity.[4]

[1] Fullager *v.* Clarke, 18 Vesey, 482 ; Brooke *v.* Clarke, 1 Sw. 551.
[2] See Kynaston *v.* East India Company, 3 Swan. 248 ; 3 Bligh, 153.
[3] Law Review, No. IV, p. 282. This article is disclaimed by the editor as being from the pen of Lord Brougham.
[4] Wykham *v.* Wykham, 18 Ves. 415 ; Clarke *v.* Parker, 19 Ves. 21.

He established a practice having a strong tendency to check vexatious actions for defamation, although it may produce hardship in particular cases, by granting a commission to examine witnesses abroad, for the purpose of proving a plea justifying the truth of an alleged libel, with an injunction till the return of the commission.[1] He ruled no fewer than sixty-six points on specific performance, by which he threw much new light on that perplexing subject.[2] He admirably illustrated the principles which determine the rights of successive mortgagees, as affected by the delivery or non-delivery of title-deeds;[3] and he much simplified the doctrine of "marshaling of assets," which will, nevertheless, be difficult in the application, as long as there is a difference between specialty and simple-contract debts, and between charges on the heir and the executor.[4] With respect to the advancement of illegitimate children by the putative father,—depending upon whether he is to be considered *in loco parentis*,—he laid down a rule which has since been found most useful, and has been implicitly followed.[5] He adhered to and strengthened the salutary doctrine that deeds obtained by the undue exercise of spiritual ascendency will be set aside as fraudulent.[6] His decision that the Chancellor has authority to take a child from the custody of an immoral parent, to be placed under a guardian appointed by the Court, was violently attacked, and certainly would be mischievous if acted upon, unless in very rare and extraordinary cases; but, upon appeal, it was affirmed by the unanimous judgment of the House of Lords.[7] I will only mention one more of the doctrines

---

[1] Macaulay v. Shackell, 1 Bligh, new series, 96. This case was affirmed on appeal in the House of Lords, when the Chancellor said he had received an anonymous letter, assuring him that "all the men of eminence at the Bar thought this decision wrong, and that it is produced by the affection which the Chancellor is supposed to have had for some Mr. Shackell [printer of 'John Bull'], or some such gentleman," adding,—"If I had complained of that as a libel in a civil action, I should certainly have said that the writer was very well entitled to file a bill of discovery, and to have had a commission to examine his witnesses abroad ; for I do not believe he would have found one in the country in which I have the honor to administer justice, knowing what had been my practice, who would have confirmed by his testimony a slander so base as that is."   [2] See Index to Vesey, entitled vol. xx. p. 180.

[3] Evans v. Bicknell, 6 Ves. 174.

[4] Aldridge v. Cooper, 8 Ves. 382 ; Bootle v. Blundell, 19 Ves, 494, 1 Mer. 193.   [5] Pye exparte, 28 Ves. 149.

[6] 14 Ves. 273 ; Hugenen v. Beaseley. This is the case in which Sir S. Romilly made his best speech.   [7] 2 Russell, 1.

he established, which was, perhaps, the most useful of all, that the *procedure* of the Court of Chancery must accommodate itself to the growing necessities of society,— upon which he relaxed the strict rule, that all individuals interested must be made parties; and, in spite of his horror of joint-stock companies, he allowed a bill to be filed by several persons on behalf of themselves and all others the proprietors of an unincorporated institution.[1]

Although much more in the habit of doubting than overturning judgments brought before him on appeal, he did not shrink from his duty when he was clearly convinced that they were wrong. Thus, upon the abstruse question, whether a *power* could consist with the *fee*, Sir William Grant having rejected the seeming absurdity of giving a special power where there was already an absolute dominion, Lord Eldon, more deeply versed in the laws of real property, held that the two things might be united in the same individual; and his decision was approved of by the profession.[2] So, the same respected Judge having

[1] 16 Ves. 321. This case is highly praised by Lord Cottenham. 1 Mylne & Craig, 636.

A distinguished Equity counsel, very familiarly acquainted with all Lord Eldon's decisions, and fully competent to appreciate their merits, has been good enough to point out to me the following, which are considered by him as the best calculated to show the noble Judge's extraordinary powers:—

Crowley's Case, 2 Swanston, 1, respecting the issuing of a writ of habeas corpus by the Chancellor in vacation, and commitments by Commissioners of Bankrupts.

Gee *v*. Pritchard, 2 Swanston, 402, respecting the right of a person who addresses letters to another to obtain an injunction against the publication of them.

Gibson v. Jeyes, 6 Vesey, 266, respecting dealings of purchase and sale between a solicitor and his client.

Aldrech *v*. Cooper, 8 Vesey, 381, respecting the right of simple contract creditors to come upon the real estate in the marshaling of assets.

Morice *v*. Bishop of Durham, 10 Vesey, 522, respecting the effect of a bequest in trust for "objects of benevolence and liberality," without specifying them.

Mills *v*. Farmer, 1 Merivale, 55, respecting the effect of a bequest for a *charitable purpose*, without specifying it: and

Exparte Rawson, Jacob, 274, in which he held that, "where part of the account between two mercantile houses which become bankrupt consists of bills that may be proved against both estates, there can be no proof in respect of those bills as between the two houses, unless there is a surplus after satisfying the holders of the bills."

This indication may be useful to the student. I had intended at all risks, to enter much more elaborately into the consideration of Lord Eldon's decisions, but want of space entirely debars me from the attempt, having already exceeded my original limits by several volumes.

[2] 10 Ves. 246.

held that a charitable trust was too vague for the Court to execute, Lord Eldon ruled that it came within the class of privileged legacies, saying: "To give effect to a bequest in favor of a charity, the Court will supply the place of an executor, and carry into effect that which in the case of individuals must have failed altogether. This distinction has proceeded partly, perhaps, on the principles in the Roman law which we do not at this time perfectly comprehend,[1]—and partly, no doubt, on the religious notions which formerly obtained in this country, according to which it fell to the ordinary's province to distribute in case of intestacy."[2] In the famous case of *Cholmondeley* v. *Clinton*, he was unwilling to take upon himself the reversal of Sir William Grant's decree; but, when it had been reversed on a rehearing before Sir Thomas Plumer, he heartily concurred in the salutary doctrine, that "adverse possession for twenty years is a bar to equitable relief as well as to an ejectment,"—on which rests the recent statute of limitations.[3]—Sir William Grant had held, that no appointment under a power to divide settled property among children could be set aside as illusory,—thus reasoning very powerfully: "To say that an illusory share must not be given, or that a substantial share must be given, is rather to raise a question than establish a rule. What is an illusory share, and what is a substantial share? It is to be judged of upon a mere statement of the sum given, without reference to the amount of the fortune, which is the subject of the power? If so, what is the sum that must be given to exclude the interference of the Court? What is the limit of amount at which it ceases to be illusory and begins to be substantial? If it is to be considered with reference to the amount of the fortune, what is the proportion, either of the whole or of the share, that would belong to each upon an equal division? In terms, the power, though limited as to objects, is discretionary as to shares. A Court of Law says, no object can be excluded; but there it stops. Every instrument must receive the same construction from every Court. Whatever must be its true

---

[1] If he had condescended to look into the writers on the civil law, he would have found these principles fully explained and defended. See Storey on Equity Jurisprudence, vol. ii. 365–383.
[2] 1 Merivale, 94. [3] 2 Merivale, 171; 2 Jac. & Walk. 1, 190.

meaning, must be its meaning everywhere. A Court of Equity may supply defects in the execution of a power; but I can not understand how the question, whether a power is well or ill executed, can receive a different determination in different Courts." Lord Eldon, however, said: "If a series of uniform authorities, through a course of centuries, prove that this Court has undertaken the difficult task of judging whether the execution of a power was reasonable or not,—using expressions more or less vague and loose, as, 'that the share must be reasonable, fair, a substantial share, a provision,—that the power is to be exercised consistently with justice,'—expressions that must distress the mind of any Judge required to act upon them,—I should pause in giving judgment, if bound to decide upon those authorities, with reference to the principle stated in the cases now before me, which, in effect (and it would be better to do it in words), destroys all the authorities, as no two cases will probably ever be the same. If the Court has this authority to consider whether the execution of such a trust, or a power coupled with a trust, is reasonable, it seems to me better to deny the doctrine at once than to lay down a rule that will destroy it in effect,—looking only to sums and figures, and considering in each case whether the motives and circumstaances by which the judgment among the different objects was regulated were the same."[1] —The Legislature has adopted the reasoning of Sir William Grant; and, by an Act which I had the honor to introduce in the House of Commons, it is declared that no appointment shall be set aside in equity on the ground of its being *illusory*.[2]

Once, at least, Lord Eldon changed his opinion,—in *Exparte Notte*,[3] the question being, whether where several firms are engaged in a joint adventure the creditors of the adventure, in the event of bankruptcy and there being no joint property, may prove against the estates of the firms, or are confined to the estates of the individuals? Lord Eldon being much pressed with his own decision in Exparte Wylie, in which he had held, under similar circumstances, that the estates of the individuals only were liable, he said, "I feel bound to add, with respect to the

---

[1] Butcher v. Butcher, 9 Ves. 393; Box v. Whitbread, 16 Ves. 18.
[2] 1 W. 4, c. 46, s. 1.   [3] 2 Glynn & Jameson, 307.

case of Exparte Wylie, which has been so repeatedly appealed to during the argument, that as the first duty of a Judge is to endeavor, in the case before him, to decide rightly, and that his next is, if in any future case of the like kind he has reason to apprehend that his judgment was not upon such sound principles as it appeared to be when he pronounced it, that he should not hesitate to rectify his error;—looking at both these obligations, I feel myself bound to state that I must, when I decided that case, have seen it in a point of view in which, after most laborious consideration, I can not see it now." Accordingly the proof was ordered against the estates of the several firms engaged in the joint adventure.[1]

When legal questions arose before Lord Eldon, he would send the case for the opinion of a Court of Law. He used to say that he had " all *possible* respect " for the Common Law Judges, which ought to have been high, for most of them were of his own nomination. But he treated them rather like school-boys, always pleased when he could tell a good story against them. He took particular delight in relating how, to ascertain what estate passed to trustees under a settlement, he sent a case to the Court of King's Bench, who told him they took an estate in fee; and how he then sent the same case to the Court of Common Pleas, who certified that the trustees took no estate at all. " Now, I was impertinent enough to think," he used to proceed, " that they were both wrong; I held that the trustees took a chattel interest; and, what is more, my decision satisfied all parties."[2]

He often said, that although when sitting in the Court of Chancery he felt himself bound by former decisions, it would be otherwise if an appeal were brought in the House of Lords,—and he would offer facilities for obtaining a hearing there,—but he was still found to adhere to the opinion he had originally expressed. I am aware only of two cases in which his judgment was reversed, and in each of these it was on the motion of Lord Redes-

---

[1] Lord Hardwicke *palinoded* more briefly, and perhaps more gracefully,—merely saying, " Upon this case being re-argued and re-considered, I am thoroughly convinced that my former degree was wrong." Walmsley *v.* Booth, 2 Atk. 27.

[2] 1 Swanst. 32 ; 1 Wils. Ch. Cas. 45 ; 18 Ves. 325 ; 11 East, 458 ; 3 Taunt. 316 ; 10 Ves. 495 ; 1 N. R. 116 ; 7 East, 97 ; Dow, 102.

dale. Neither of them involved any point of general interest. The first was *Stuart* v. *Marquis of Bute*, on the construction of a will. The testator had devised and bequeathed " all and every the wagon-ways, rails, staiths, and all implements, utensils, and *things* used and employed," with certain collieries, to trustees, on certain trusts; and the question was, whether, under the word " things," coals actually raised, debts due to the concern, and money of the concern in the hands of a banker, passed?—Lord Loughborough, shortly before his resignation, having held that they did, there was a re-hearing before Lord Eldon, who, after expressing much doubt, said, " Upon the whole, it is better for me to affirm the decree; not as being satisfied with the principle of it, but as I can not make a decree with which I could be better satisfied." [1]

An appeal being brought to the House of Lords, Lord Redesdale said, that although horses, hay, and corn used in the colleries would pass, the meaning of the word " things" must be restrained to " things *ejusdem generis;*" and therefore that the coals, debts, and money in dispute must go to the executor. *Lord Eldon:* " I think myself highly fortunate in having the assistance of my noble and learned friend, in whose view of the question I completely concur." [2] So the decree was reversed.

The other case was *Jackson* v. *Lunes*, turning on considerations still more technical, and decided by Lord Eldon on a supposed recollection of an unreported dictum of Lord Thurlow, which (according to the precedent of Anthony and Cæsar's will) he was in the habit of resorting to when at a loss for an authority.[3] But after the hearing at the bar of the House of Lords, Lord Redesdale having expressed a clear opinion that the decree was wrong, Lord Eldon said: " I conceive it to have been the opinion of Lord Thurlow that, in order to dispose of the equity of redemption of the wife in an estate, it was absolutely necessary there should be in the recitals of the instrument some expression that the parties meant it so ; that it was not enough to collect the intention from the limitations; but that there must be something more upon the face of the deed, to lead the wife to understand what those limitations were. It does, however, occur to me, on

[1] Feb. 1806. 11 Ves. 607. [2] 1 Dow. 73. [3] 16 Ves. 356.

looking into the cases which have been referred to, that such a proposition can not be supported, and therefore I am of opinion that the decree must be reversed."

The non-reversal of decrees (as I have often had occasion to observe) is but a poor proof of the merits of a Chancellor. Lord Eldon's judicial fame rests on the surer basis of the universal respect of the profession. Amid the war of jarring factions, while he was still on the woolsack, he was considered an oracle of law, both by foes and friends; since then his authority has in no degree declined; and there is no rashness in prophesying, that, for ages to come, his opinion, where it can be discovered, will rule the cases to which it is applicable.

To prove, however, that I do not reverence him like the blind worshiper of an idol, I will mention two or three of his decisions which were not quite satisfactory to Westminster Hall, and which possibly may hereafter be overturned.[1]

He had such a horror of "forestalling and regrating," by which he had heard his grandmother at Newcastle, and afterwards his tutor at Oxford say, " the price of provisions is cruelly enhanced to the poor," that all agreements *savoring* even of forestalling or regrating he held to be immoral, contrary to public policy, illegal, and void. Thus, an association of wholesale grocers, instituted under the title of the " Fruit Club," for the purpose of making purchases of imported fruits, and supplying the general trade, having brought an action against a person to whom they had sold a cargo, for the price of it, the purchaser, contending that they had not duly performed their part of the contract, filed a bill praying a discovery and an injunction. On a demurrer to the bill, Lord Eldon said, "This is not, according to the legal definition of the term, *forestalling*, much less *regrating*, still less *monopolizing;* but in the consideration of a Court of Equity it contains the mischief of all the three. First, there is a conspiracy against the vendors; next a conspiracy against the world at large, enabling those persons to buy at any price they may think proper; and then it is true they can if they please sell at a lower price than a fair competition in the

[1] Of course I do so without prejudice to my right fully to concur in them after argument and further consideration, if I should ever be called upon judicially to review them in the House of Lords.

market would produce ; but it must also be recollected that they can sell on their own terms ; and the manner in which that discretion would be exercised is obvious. Then, as between these parties, the complaint is, that it is immoral in the vendors not to let the purchaser have his bargain. What is that but an agreement that they shall be partners in a transaction in which they know they are acting illegally?" So the demurrer was allowed ;—and on the same principle, the action at law could not be maintained, although the purchaser might have resold, and received payment for the whole of the fruit he had bargained for ;—because the partnership he dealt with was called the " Fruit Club," instead of " Smith, Tompkins, and Co."[1]

I must likewise doubt some of his decisions respecting "Grammar Schools," which have had the effect of preventing these institutions in country towns from being adapted to the wants of society, and have rendered their funds of no use whatever, except to pamper a sinecurist padagogue.[2] Collecting from his friend Dr. Johnson's definition, that a " Grammar School, *n. s.* is a school in which the learned languages (exclusively) are grammatically taught," he decided that the instruction to be given in those institutions must in every instance be strictly limited to Greek and Latin. He had imbibed a strange notion that they all had their origin in the Reformation, and were distributed by King Edward VI. over the country, as instruments eminently calculated to promote the new opinions. Now, grammar schools had nothing to do with the Reformation ; and many of them where established in Catholic times,—every cathedral church or other ecclesiastical establishment of any importance having annexed to it a grammar school to teach the laity their A B C, and to qualify the clergy to go through their Latin Breviary. The Newcastle Grammar School may have been founded in the reign of Edward VI., but the Chancellor might have recollected the charge brought by Jack Cade in the reign of Henry VI. against the Lord Say, " Thou hast most traitorously corrupted the youth of the realm in erecting a GRAMMAR SCHOOL: it will be

[1] Cousens *v.* Smith, 13 Ves. 542.
[2] See the Attorney-General *v.* Earl of Mansfield, the Highgate School Case, 2 Russ. 501.

proved to thy face that thou hast men about thee that usually talk of a *noun* and a *verb*, and such abominable words as no Christian ear can endure to hear: moreover, thou hast put them in prison; and because they could not read thou hast hanged them." [1]

Lord Eldon fell into a more serious error from the excess of orthodox zeal, in declaring that since the repeal of the statute of 9 and 10 William III., imposing penalties upon persons who deny the doctrine of the Trinity, Unitarians may be punished for blasphemy at common law, and are not to be treated as Christians.[2] The doctrine he lays down would equally exclude from the pale of Christianity, Milton and Sir Isaac Newton, and all who have the misfortune to entertain any opinion in any respect at variance with the true notion respecting the Trinity, although their belief may be unexceptionable in every other article of Christian faith.[3] But this was contradicted by all the Judges in the House of Lords in Lady Hewley's case, for they held, that since the repeal of 9 and 10 William III., Unitarians, for civil purposes, are not to be distinguished from any other sect of Dissenters—was condemned by the Right Reverend Prelates who supported the "Dissenters' Marriage Bill,"—and was renounced by Queen, Lords, and Commons, in the year 1845, when, under the advice of Lord Chancellor Lyndhurst and Sir Robert Peel, they passed the "Dissenters' Chapel Bill," which allowed Unitarian congregations to retain possession of Trinitarian endowments.

But the decisions of Lord Eldon which I most object to, are those by which he erected himself into a Censor of the Press, and gave himself the power to protect or to extinguish all literary property at his pleasure. From the time when copyright was vested in authors by the statute of Queen Anne,[4] till Lord Eldon received the Great Seal, Equity Judges had guarded it from piracy by injunction; and without this remedy the right would be a mockery, as actions at law to recover damages from hawk-

[1] This does not argue much learning beyond the "neck-verse" to be entitled to "benefit of clergy,"—or more than substituting the "primer and horn book" for the "score and the tally."
[2] Attorney General *v.* Pearson, 3 Merivale, 353, 409.
[3] Although Milton and Newton were not Unitarians, they were Arians; and Lord Eldon's doctrine would equally apply to them.
[4] 3 Anne, c. 19.

ers and peddlers, who may sell pirated editions of any work, in city or country, would only add to the author's loss. The authorship and the piracy being established, the injunction had always gone as a matter of course, without any question being made respecting the nature of the publication; for under Lord Cowper, Lord Macclesfield, Lord King, Lord Hardwicke, Lord Camden, Lord Thurlow, and Lord Loughborough, it never had been imagined that the defendant could be permitted to allege, as a justification of his piracy, that he had been committing a crime by publishing something for which he was liable to be punished, as injurious to private character, or dangerous to religion, morality, or the good government of the state. Accordingly injunctions had been granted against the piracy of the " Dunciad," of Swift's " Miscellanies," of the " Beggar's Opera," of the " Life of George Anne Belamy," and of other works containing passages which if strictly examined might be considered very censurable — no one suggesting that these should be culled as a repast for the Lord Chancellor, or that he should be required to waste his valuable time in trying to find them out,—and all who thought upon the subject being convinced, that if the work pirated were in any degree exceptionable, a benefit was conferred upon the community by restraining the circulation of it, instead of proclaiming to all the world that it might be published with impunity, in any form, and at any price.

But within a year after Lord Eldon's appointment as Chancellor, DR. WOLCOTT, better known as PETER PINDAR, having a dispute with his booksellers respecting the construction of an agreement for publishing two editions of his works, and these editions being published,—as he contended, contrary to the agreement,—filed a bill, and prayed an injunction — which was granted in the first instance, till answer. The defendants by their answer admitted that they had published in one of these editions some of the plaintiff's works *contrary to the agreement*, and as to that edition, therefore, *they submitted*. With respect to the other edition they insisted that they were justified by the agreement.—The pleading at the Bar being finished, the conduct of the Lord Chancellor appears to me, I confess, to be most extraordinary and unaccountable. No charge is made by answer or affidavit, or *vivâ voce* statement, that the work in question contained anything exceptionable, and the Judge had no judicial knowledge of its contents, nor was he (as far as I can discover) judicially called upon to form any opinion upon its merits, for it was at any rate to be presumed to be innocent. But he, privately knowing that Timothy Wolcott was Peter Pindar, and that Peter Pindar had written some ribald verses respecting his "royal master,"—upon the authority of a *nisi prius dictum* of Lord Chief Justice Eyre at the trial of Dr. Priestley against the Hundred for the value of his furniture and books burnt in the Birmingham riots,—"that if any of the books were seditious, the plaintiff was not entitled to recover for them," of his own mere motion refused to decree an injunction or an account of profits, even with respect to that edition as to which there was a submission in the answer, saying,—"It is the duty of the Court to know whether an action at law would lie; for if not, the Court ought not to give an account of unhallowed profits of libelous publications. At present, I am in total ignorance of the nature of this work, and whether the plaintiff can have a property in it or not." After showing how with respect to the disputed edition there must be an action, he continued:—"But even as to the other edition, before I uphold any injunction, I will see these publications and determine upon the nature of them; whether there is question enough to send to law as to the property in those copies; for if not, I will not act upon the submission in the answer. If upon inspection the work appears innocent, I will act upon that submission; if criminal, I will not act at all; and if doubtful, I will send that question to law." As to the disputed edition, the injunction was very properly dissolved,—but as to the other edition, contrary in my opinion to all propriety, an order was made to dissolve the injunction, unless in a week the books should be brought into court for the perusal of the Lord Chancellor.[1]

Such is the foundation of the Eldonian doctrine, that the Judge before granting an injunction against literary piracy is himself *ex mero motu* to read through the whole of the work, that he may see whether it contains anything which in his opinion may possibly be construed into a libel—a doctrine which must apply equally to an Encyclo-

[1] Wolcott *v.* Walker, 7 Vesey, 1.

pædia of fifty folios as to a collection of fugitive poems in one duodecimo. I know not whether there may be a reference to the Master to report on the character of the work, but one Master may be wholly insufficient for the undertaking; and at any rate in analogy to the proceeding upon a question of title he must be allowed to avail himself of the opinions of divines, philosophers, and politicians, and exceptions may be taken to his Report to be argued before the Court. More astounding it is that in this case the Lord Chancellor, professing "total ignorance of the nature of the work," should, without any impeachment of it, have imposed upon himself the necessity of reading the whole of it before granting the injunction. The bill and answer showed it to have been printed and published at least six years—during the greater part of which he had himself filled the office of Attorney-General, so that if it was libelous it would have been his duty to prosecute it. For my own part I can not help suspecting that he was well acquainted with its contents,—that, notwithstanding his propensity to prosecute libels, he had been afraid to bring the author before a jury, and that he now thought it a more convenient course to unite in his own person the functions of prosecutor and of judge.

In the next case which occurred the Lord Chancellor was relieved from the awkward necessity of volunteering to read the work. Southey, the poet, in early youth, had written a dramatic poem, entitled "Wat Tyler," which he had placed in the hands of Ridgway, a bookseller, with the view of publishing it, but it had not been published, and the MS. remained many years in Ridgway's hands. By some means not explained, Sherwood, another bookseller, having got possession of it, printed it, and advertised it for sale. The illustrious author thereupon filed a bill, and moved for an injunction—on the acknowledged principle that "independent of the statute, an author has a property in an unpublished work, which is to be protected by injunction."[1] The defendant's counsel, not denying the authorship or the piracy, resisted the application on the *libelous tendency* of the work, and referred to *Wolcott* v. *Walker*, as an authority in his favor. The Lord Chancellor, after saying that he had read the affidavits and the book entitled "Wat Tyler,"

[1] Macklin *v.* Richardson, Amb. 694.

and that he remained of the same opinion respecting the law as when he decided the case referred to, thus proceeded:—"It is very true that in some cases it may operate so as to multiply copies of mischievous publications, by the refusal of the Court to interfere; but to this, my answer is, that sitting here as a judge upon a mere question of property, I have nothing to do with the nature of the property or with the conduct of the parties, except as it relates to their civil interests; and if the publication be mischievous, it is not my business to protect it, either for the sake of the author or the bookseller." So the injunction was refused, and hundreds of thousands of copies of Wat Tyler, at the price of one penny, were circulated over the kingdom.[1]

Of the next case, which ought to have been very interesting, we have only the following meager note:—"In *Murray* v. *Benbow*, Mr. Shadwell, on the part of the plaintiff, moved for an injunction to restrain the defendant from publishing a pirated edition of Lord Byron's poem of CAIN. The Lord Chancellor, after reading the work, refused the motion."[2] In this "MYSTERY," which, Lord Jeffrey says, "abounds in beautiful passages, and shows more *power* than any of the author's dramatic compositions," there are sentiments very much to be condemned; but so there are in the speeches of PARADISE LOST, and it must have been a strange occupation for a judge who for many years had meddled with nothing more imaginative than an Act of Parliament, to determine in what sense the speculations of Adam, Eve, Cain, and Lucifer are to be understood, and whether the tendency of the whole poem be favorable or injurious to religion.[3]

Soon after came a case which showed, in a still more striking point of view, the alarming nature of the new

---

[1] Southey *v*. Sherwood, 2 Merivale, 435.   [2] Jacob's Reports, p. 274, *n*.

[3] The poem was dedicated to Sir Walter Scott, who, ever an observer of decency, and a friend to religion and morality, thus acknowledged the compliment in a letter to Mr. Murray, the bookseller:—"I accept, with feelings of great obligation, the flattering proposal of Lord Byron to prefix my name to the very grand and tremendous drama of CAIN. I may be partial to it, and you will allow I have cause; but I do not know that his muse has ever taken so lofty a flight amid her former soarings. He has certainly matched Milton on his own ground. The fiend-like reasoning and bold blasphemy of the fiend and of his pupil lead exactly to the point which was to be expected, —the commission of the first murder, and the ruin and despair of the perpetrator."

censorship which the Chancellor had conferred upon himself. Mr. Lawrence, a most eminent surgeon, although (he will allow me to say) not a profound metaphysician, had delivered, at the College of Surgeons, "Lectures on Physiology, Zoology, and the Natural History of Man," in which he had powerfully combated the theory of one species of animals progressing into another, and proved that the different races of man, instead of being monkeys, were varieties of the same species, all derived from the same stock; but in his speculations on mind, he had fallen into some mistakes which may be easily refuted. Having finished his course of lectures without censure, he published them, and a bookseller printing a pirated edition, he filed a bill and obtained an injunction *ex parte*. The defendant moved to dissolve the injunction, and his counsel relied entirely on certain passages in the work, which they said impugned the doctrine of the immateriality of the soul. The plaintiff's counsel, on the other hand, denied that the tendency of the work was such as had been represented,—endeavoring to explain the passages objected to, and to show that they did not bear the interpretation imputed to them. The Lord Chancellor, after truly observing that he had nothing to do with those lectures being delivered at the College of Surgeons; that his jurisdiction was founded upon the consideration that an action at law is no adequate remedy for an invasion of literary property; and that he could only give relief where the law would give damages,—thus continued: "I take it for granted that, when the motion for the injunction was made, it was opened as quite of course; nothing, probably, was said as to the general nature of the work, or of any part of it, for we must look not only at the general tenor, but at the different parts; and the question is to be decided not only by seeing what is said of *materialism*, of the *immortality of the soul*, and of the *Scriptures*, but by looking at the different parts, and inquiring whether there be any which deny OR WHICH APPEAR TO DENY the truth of Scripture, or *which raise a fair question for a court of law to determine whether they do or do not deny it.* . . . . The question is, whether it is so clear that the plaintiff has this civil right, that on that ground he is to have relief? If, on reading the plaintiff's work, I thought it clear that he had that right, I should feel it necessary to state the grounds of my opinion, for after the argument at the Bar I should be unwilling to part with the subject without telling you the view I take of it. But *if I feel* A RATIONAL DOUBT *whether an action would lie*, it will not be necessary to go into the grounds of that doubt: it might perhaps prejudice the trial if I did. Looking at the general tenor of the work and at many particular parts of it,—recollecting that the immorality of the soul is one of the doctrines of the Scriptures,—considering that the law does not give protection to those who contradict the scriptures, and *entertaining a doubt, I think a rational doubt, whether this book does not violate that law*, I cannot continue the injunction." [1] Injunction dissolved.

This was the last case of the sort which occurred before Lord Eldon, and so he left the doctrine which he had originated to be corrected by his successors, or by the House of Lords, or by Act of Parliament. As at present advised, I must be allowed most respectfully, but most strenuously, to protest against it.

A decision of Lord Macclesfield, which has recently been discovered in the Registrar's Book, is quite on the other side. but I do not rely upon it as an authority, for the *ratio decidendi* cannot be supported. An English translation having been published of *Burnett's* ARCHÆOLOGIA SACRA, his executor applied for an injunction, and the question was debated whether a translation is a piracy within the meaning of 8 Anne, c. 19? *Lord Macclesfield:* "Though a translation may not be the same with reprinting the original, as the translator has bestowed his care and pains upon it, and so it may not be within the prohibition of the act, yet this being a book which to my knowledge (having read it in my study) contains strange notions intended by the author to be concealed from the vulgar in the Latin language—in which it could not do much hurt—the learned being better able to

---

[1] Jacob's Rep. 471. The Lord Chancellor's reasoning is a fine example of the *Sorites*,—the first proposition, from which all the others follow, being—"I have a rational doubt whether some parts of Mr. Lawrence's book do not tend to materialism,—*ergo*, I have a rational doubt whether they are not inconsistent with the immortality of the soul,—*ergo*, I have a rational doubt whether they are not contrary to the Scriptures,—*ergo*, I have a rational doubt whether the author could maintain an action for the piracy,—*ergo*, the injunction must be dissolved."

judge of it, I think proper to grant an injunction against printing and publishing it in English. I look upon it that *this Court has a superintendency over all books, and may in a summary way restrain* the printing or publishing any that contain reflections on religion or morality." *Injunction granted.*[1]—This reasoning has no countenance, except from the dictum of Lord Ellenborough, which caused much merriment in Westminster Hall, that "the Chancellor would, on the application of the libellee, grant an injunction against the public exhibition of a libelous picture,"—and it is certainly erroneous, for the court of Chancery has no jurisdiction on the subject, except for the protection of property. But Lord Eldon's doctrine, although it may not be opposed by any well-considered prior decision, is undoubtedly at variance with the practice of the Court of Chancery for above a century,[2] and I think is contrary to the established principles of equity. Besides the objection of allowing a man to say that he has violated the law, and to allege his own turpitude, Lord Eldon seems to me to have forgotten that the author is actually in possession, and that the pirate is a stranger and a wrongdoer. Under such circumstances, even a doubtful title has a right to protection by injunction, and is constantly so protected.

Let us always recollect, that if the injunction is refused, a meritorious writer may be ruined by the "doubt" of a Lord Chancellor; and that if the injunction is granted, no injury can possibly be done to the defendant or to the public. The consideration that, by permitting the piracy of a work which is really improper it is rendered much more mischievous to society, ought not in strictness to weigh with Equity Judges; but on other occasions they are wonderfully astute and ingenious in accommodating their jurisdiction to their own notions of the public good. In how many other instances do they

[1] Registrar's Book, 1720, A, fo. 350 b. Jac. Rep. 441-42.
[2] Although Lord Eldon has no countenance from any English Judge, the Scotch Judges seem, at one time, to have inclined to his way of thinking. "When Dr. Johnson and I were left by ourselves," says Boswell, "I read to him my notes of the opinions of our Judges upon the questions of Literary Property. He did not like them; and said, 'They make me think of your Judges not with that respect which I should wish to do.' To the argument of one of them, that there can be no property in blasphemy or nonsense, he answered, 'Then your rotten sheep are mine! By that rule, when a man's house falls into decay, he must lose it.'"—*Tour to the Hebrides*, 39.

say, "You cannot set up this defence, whether true or false, at a moment when the truth of it cannot be ascertained;" "there is a personal exception to your setting up that plea."—"You are estopped by your own conduct from making such an allegation."—There can be no practical danger of the author of any grossly immoral or seditious work applying for an injunction, for,—on his own affidavit, he might immediately be prosecuted and sentenced to an infamous punishment,—while the permission to object to the character of the pirated work not only renders all literary property insecure, but holds out the strongest temptation to spoilation and fraud. If Lord Eldon's authority is so high, that even upon such a subject it can not be judicially overturned, the Legislature must interfere and rescue literature from a bondage which is light or heavy, according to the fantasy of the Chancellor for the time being, and which might become wholly insupportable.

Want of space prevents me from dwelling at length, as I had intended, on Lord Eldon's able manner of disposing of the judicial business of the House of Lords, and especially of Scotch appeals. Here he appeared to much advantage, and the Court of *dernier ressort* has never stood in higher estimation than during his time. He made himself a most profound Scotch feudalist, and he really was more familiar with the whole compass of the law of Scotland than any of the "Fifteen" in the PARLIAMENT HOUSE. His judgments in the Roxburgh case, and on the Queensberry leases, which it took him several days to deliver, were wonderful efforts of the human mind.[1] He was very bold in reversing—and although there were sometimes loud complaints against him, he was always afterwards allowed to have been right. In one case (*Stewart* v. *Agnew*) the Court of Session for some time refused to execute the reversal, and the *remit* to

---

[1] Lord Eldon not only took uncommon pains with great causes which fixed the attention of the whole kingdom, but with the most uninteresting, tiresome, irksome, perplexed details. The first appeal I ever pleaded before him was respecting the liability of landholders to a surveyor for business done under an Inclosure Act; and, in his judgment, with the most marvelous precision and accuracy he went over many items, allowing some, and disallowing others; whereas other Judges who have said truly that "they had discovered no reason to dissent, in any respect, from the opinion of the Judges below." Johnston *v.* Cheape, 5 Dow. 241. 1817.

them, authorizing them "to proceed as should be just,"—they said "Justice required that they should suspend execution till the party whom they thought entitled to succeed should have an opportunity of petitioning the House of Lords for a rehearing." A petition was accordingly presented at the commencement of the ensuing session, praying that the appeal might be reheard, —that the judgment of the House might be recalled,— and that the original sentence of the Court of Session might be set up and affirmed. Lord Eldon retained his calmness, but, assisted by Lord Redesdale, gave the Scotch Judges a very severe castigation, and they never afterwards showed any disposition to rebel.[1]

His chief fight with them was about *entails*,—they loving "a perpetuity," much as that entity is abhorred by the law of England. When he had cut down an entail for palpable defects in the fettering clauses, they tried virtually to set it up again, by holding that the purchase money of the land, when sold, must be laid out in purchasing another estate, to be settled under the same defective fetters on the same line of heirs; but he reversed their interlocutor, showing the absurdity of a perpetual series of sales, purchases, and bad entails.[2]

I have heard him cite with great glee a saying of Lord Thurlow, that the decrees of the Scotch Judges were least to be respected when they were *unanimous*, as in that case they probably, without thought, had followed the first of their number who had expressed an opinion, —whereas, where they were divided they might be expected to have paid some attention to the subject. But I must content myself with adding Lord Eldon's own account of his performances in this line, as taken from the ANECDOTE BOOK:—

"There was no circumstance that gave me greater satisfaction upon my quitting office than the strong testimonies I received in letters from the President of the Court of Session, and the Lord Justice Clerk of Scotland, testifying the sense entertained in Scotland of my administration in the House of Lords of the law of Scotland in the hearing of Scotch appeals, and the application

---

[1] See a very full and interesting account of this proceeding in Macqueen's "Practice of the House of Lords," p. 443.
[2] Ascog case; Tillicoultry case, Sandford, 110.

made to me by the Lord President, at the instance of those whom he mentioned in one of his letters, that I would continue to attend the House of Lords to assist in the decision of Scotch causes. Very early in the time of my attendance in the House of Lords, as a counsel, I expressed to the then Lord Chancellor, Lord Thurlow, my anxiety not to appear as counsel in that house in Scotch causes. This he discouraged so strongly, that I was obliged to abandon my purpose. To make myself master of such points in Scotch law as it was necessary for me to understand in order to be able to do my duty at the Bar, was what required so much time and labor, and withdrew me so much from practice in the Courts below, that I was anxiously desirous to avoid being concerned in Scotch causes. When I became Chancellor, the duty of deciding such causes was most extremely painful, and required infinite labor. I was, however, for some time, assisted by two ex-Chancellors, Lords Thurlow and Loughborough. I have the comfort of having reason to believe that my administration in this part of my duty was satisfactory; and while the number of appeals greatly increased, and by some were alluded to as proofs of delay in that administration,—by others, and those who knew best what was the fact, that increase of appeals, I was assured, was occasioned by the confidence which the lieges of Scotland had in the judgment to which they appealed. Some thought, that in decision in Scotch causes I was too much influenced by the principles of English law. There was no one danger against which I guarded myself so anxiously as the danger that I might be so influenced. Whether all the pains I took to protect myself and the Scotch suitors against this danger were thoroughly effectual, I can not determine; I believe they were. But he must know little of the operations of the human mind who can be positively certain that he can withdraw, in the administration of Scotch judicature, wholly and absolutely from that mind the influence which may have been created in it by the daily and hourly contemplation of the rules and principles of English law, through a long course of years."

Here I take a final leave of Lord Eldon as a magistrate,—with the painful consciousness that I have conveyed but a very imperfect notion to the reader either of his judicial merits or defects,—although actuated by a sincere desire to do justice to both.

He himself tells us that on the Bench he had three objects in view:—" Looking back;" he said, "to my judicial conduct, I hope with no undue partiality or self-indulgence, I can never be deprived of the comfort I receive when I recollect, that in great and important cases I have endeavored to sift all the principles and rules of law to the bottom, for the purpose of laying down, in each new and important case as it arises, something in the first place, which may satisfy the parties that I have taken pains to do my duty; something, in the second place, which may inform those who, as counsel, are to take care of the interests of their clients, what the reasons are upon which I have proceeded, and may enable them to examine whether justice has been done; and further, something which may contribute towards laying down a rule, so as to save those who may succeed to me in this great situation much of that labor which I have had to undergo, by reason of cases having been not so determined, and by reason of a due exposition of the grounds of judgment not having been so stated."[1] His first two objects were effectually attained; but I am much afraid that his successors, who are fond of ease, are little beholden to him, for it has been truly said, " a sense of duty incited him to, and supported him in, the continued toil of a quarter of a century, in erecting and forming a structure which it is the labor of a life to gain an adequate comprehension of,—

'Εν ΜΑΚΑ'ΡΕΣΣΙ πόνων ἀνταξιος εἴη ἀμοιβή."[2]

I can not more fairly finish this head than with two conflicting statements of his judicial performances—the one by a keen satirist, the other by an indiscriminating admirer.

" It would be difficult, we conceive, to deny that he more frequently gives proof of *caution than of boldness*, of *subtlety than of vigor*, in his reasonings—that, in the determination of particular cases, he seems too often to exercise his ingenuity *in raising up doubts and difficulties, rather than in clearing them away*—and, above all, that

[1] Attorney-General *v.* Skinners' Company, 2 Russell, 437.
[2] Law Review, No. IV. p. 284.

he confines himself far too rigidly to the decision of the special matters that come before him, *without aiming either at the establishment of general principles, and the improvement of the science he professes,* or at the *correction of those vices in the constitution or administration of his Court,* of which he daily hears and sees too much to make it conceivable that he should be ignorant.

"We shall find, in his judgments, a tortuous and mazy involution, parenthesis suffocated by parenthesis, *a profuse, inelegant, and cumbrous verbiage which afflicts the reader with a sense of obscurity,* and a most painful image of labor at once interminable and unproductive. Meaning, in itself never redundant or excessive, struggling in vain through a heavy and oppressive load of qualifications, and limitations, and restrictions, creeps into light, at length, in a shape and in dimensions little calculated to repay the wearisomeness of pursuit, from its first introduction, through its general attenuation and diminution, to its final extinction.

"In what part of those ample magazines of learning (bonded warehouses under double lock), to which allusion has before been made, will the painful and fainting student find any of *his* adjudications which unequivocally *enlarge, correct, or define the rules of Equity* in which he has been so long engaged? Why, *his decisions are absolutely the exclusion of all conclusion.*"[1]

But says Charles Butler—"In profound, extensive, and accurate knowledge of the principles of his Court, and the rules of practice which regulate its proceedings—in complete recollection and just appreciation of former decisions—in discerning the inferences to be justly drawn from them—in the power of instantaneously applying this immense theoretical and practical knowledge to the business immediately before the Court—in perceiving, almost with intuitive readiness on the first opening of a case, its real state and the ultimate conclusion of Equity upon it, yet investigating it with the most conscientious, most minute, and most edifying industry,—in all, or in any of these requisites for a due discharge of his high office, Lord Eldon, if he has been equaled, has assuredly never been surpassed, by any of his predecessors."[2]

[1] Edinburgh Review, Oct. 1823.
[2] Reminiscences, 1822, p. 141. The strictures in the Edinburgh Review

I am sorry to say that as I proceed I am called upon to speak of Lord Eldon much less favorably, for although he was *a great Judge* he was not *a great Man*. Deciding justly between plaintiffs and defendants, he did nothing to correct abuses or to adapt our judicial system to the altered condition of the country. Hence his defenders only make him say—

. . . . " non hæc in fœdera veni "—

insisting that, as first Judge of the land, nothing could be required of him beyond attending to the administration of justice in his own Court. But let us hear what is said on this subject by the most illustrious of Chancellors:—" Peu content de cette attention particulière qui se renferme dans le cercle étroit de la cause des plaideurs, la supériorité de son génie lui inspirera cette attention générale qui embrasse l'ordre entier de la société civile, et qui est presque aussi étendue que les besoins de l'humanité. Etre encore plus occupé du droit public que du droit privé; avoir toujours les yeux ouverts sur la conduite des ministres inférieurs de la justice; venger le client trompé de l'abus qu'on a fait de sa confiance, et punir l'avidité du défenseur infidèle, dans le temps que l'équité du magistrat fait éclater le bon droit de la partie; répandre un esprit de règle et de discipline dans tous les membres du

probably never reached the Chancellor, and if he saw them, he was no doubt told, and he believed, that they proceeded from political rancor; but Charles Butler's panegyric being eagerly laid before him by his secretary, he thus addressed the author:—

" 19th April, 1822.

" Dear Sir,

" Seeing your 'Reminiscences' offered to the public, I have placed them in my library. I wish I could satisfy myself that Lord Eldon was entitled to all the approbation which your partiality has bestowed upon him. I have ventured to think that my life exhibits a remarkable proof of what may be done, in a free country, by moderate talents and never-ceasing industry, but I have never presumed to think that I had the merit you have been pleased to think it good to ascribe to me. I have felt more consolation than I can express, in reading, in a part of your work, what a considerable person stated in answer to the imputation of being dilatory. This has been often, and I admit most fairly, imputed to me; to all who accuse me of it, I wish to give, as my answer, the passage I allude to. I must soon quit this scene: whether any memory of me will survive me, I know not; but I hope I may have descendants professing the Law; and if I have (as they must study the works of Charles Butler, if they mean to understand their profession), those descendants at least will be taught to entertain, upon very considerable authority, a favorable opinion of the character of their ancestor.

" Yours, dear Sir,
" ELDON."

vaste corps de la magistrature; arreter l'injustice dans sa source, et, par quelques lignes d'un réglement salutaire, prévenir les procès avec plus d'avantage pour le public et plus de véritable gloire pour le magistrat que s'il les jugeait: voilà le digne objet de la supreme magistrature; c'est là ce qui couronne le mérite de son application dans le temps qu'elle exerce ses jugements."[1]

Lord Eldon himself really seems once to have entertained these views; for, on taking his seat in the Court of Chancery, he expressed strong indignation at the frauds committed under cover of the bankrupt laws, and his determination to repress such practices. Upon this subject his Lordship observed, " that the abuse of the bankrupt laws is a disgrace to the country; and it would be better at once to repeal all the statutes, than to suffer them to be applied to such purposes. There is no mercy to the estate. Nothing is less thought of than the interest of creditors. Commissions, in the country particularly, are merely considered the stock in trade of the solicitor. He appoints the commissioners, and they tax his bill in return. Unless the Court hold a strong hand over such proceedings, it is itself accessory to as great a nuisance as any known in this land." Yet it was not till the reign of William IV., when the Great Seal had passed into other hands, that there was any alteration in the so severely condemned system of Commissioners of Bankrupts, either in town or country; and for a quarter of a century, under Lord Eldon, the Court continued accessory to the nuisance, which according to his own sentence, ought to have been abated.[2]

So he declared early in his career: " It is absolutely necessary that it should be perfectly understood, that the property of schools, all over the kingdom, is dealt with in a manner most grossly improvident, amounting to the most direct breach of trust." Nevertheless, while by narrow-minded decisions he prevented any improvement being introduced judicially into these institutions, he not only abstained from seeking to reform them by legislation, but sneered at an act passed by Sir Samuel Romilly for the better administration of all charities.

[1] Œuvres de D'Aguesseau, tom. i. p. 185, 8vo. ed.
[2] He encouraged Mr. Eden (afterwards Lord Henley) in preparing 6 Geo. 4, c. 16, which consolidated the bankrupt statutes, but left these abuses exactly as they were.

In no other department was he more active as a law reformer. He did not think, like one of his successors,[1] that the Chancellor alone was able, with proper vigor, to do all the business of the Court, but often truly declared that its judicial strength was wholly insufficient. Yet he took no adequate measures to remedy the deficiency. Although aware of all the facts proved before the Commission appointed in 1824, which showed that all the procedure in a cause — from the filing of the bill to the execution of the decree—was calculated to occasion delay and expense, — he never even attempted to supply a remedy, either by his own authority or by Act of Parliament. It is a curious fact that, having held the Great Seal longer than any Chancellor since the foundation of the monarchy, he left the Court exactly as he found it, and that the " New Orders," framed on the suggestion of the Chancery Commissioners, were not published till the accession of Lord Lyndhurst. The only bills he ever brought into Parliament, or cordially supported, were for suspending the Habeas Corpus — putting down public meetings—rendering persons convicted a second time for a political libel subject to transportation beyond the seas, —and extending the laws against high treason.[2]

He frustrated the efforts of Romilly and Mackintosh to mitigate and amend our penal code, and I suspect that he retarded and enfeebled those of Sir Robert Peel.

He even resented any effort of courts of law, *proprio vigore*, to improve their procedure, — as by dispensing with the production of written instruments, lost or destroyed — or by granting a commission to examine witnesses abroad, without the aid of a court of equity.[3]

" He came into power" (wrote a barrister boldly while Lord Eldon was still Chancellor[4]) " at a conjuncture when the decided change which was taking place in the texture of society, when increasing wealth, commerce, and population, indicated that a greater change in our law and legal institutions would soon become desirable than had taken place at any antecedent period of our history. Had he prompted, promoted, or superintended this great work,

[1] Lord Brougham.
[2] An exception ought to have been made of the famous statute, called *par excellence*, "LORD ELDON'S ACT,"—" to empower the Lord Chancellor to make sergeants-at-law in vacation as well as in term time !!!"—passed in 1813. [3] See 1 Swanston, 124. [4] A. D. 1824.

the length of his reign and extent of his influence would have enabled him to bring it almost or altogether to its completion, and thus to have left a monument to his memory which it falls to the lot of few individuals to have the power of erecting. Unfortunately for the country and his own reputation, he had pursued a totally opposite course. Feeling that his strength did not lie in the depth and comprehensiveness of his general views so much as in the extent of his acquaintance with the minutiæ of precedents and practice, and perceiving also that the surest way of continuing in place is to abstain from all innovation, his love of power combined with his love of superiority to induce him to withhold from all decided improvements himself, and to look with an unfavorable eye on those which were proposed by others. In this course he has invariably persevered. It is probable that at this moment Lord Eldon has no conception of the sentiments which are almost universally entertained of his judicial administration, either by the persons who frequent his court, or by those who are capable of judging out of it. He has never heard the truth spoken with that freedom and affection with which it flows from the lips of friends of equal understanding. It is one of his greatest misfortunes that through life he has made age, submisiveness, and mediocrity the passports to his favor, and has as steadily kept aloof from men of liberal and independent minds as they have kept aloof from him."[1]

An apologist says, "He saw with intuitive acuteness the abuse, but 'his heart failed him for fear' when he came to apply the remedy. Timidity of temper, and excess of official toil, are sufficient reasons for this reserve, without imputing unworthy motives, as harsh professional critics have not scrupled to do."[2] He has been compared, rather rashly, to D'Aguesseau, who, according to St. Simon, being asked whether, with his experience of the chicanery of the law and the length of legal proceedings, he had never thought of some regulation which might put an end to them, answered, "I had gone so far as to commit to writing the plan of such a regulation; but after I had made some progress, I reflected on the great number of *avocats*, *avoués*, and *huissiers* whom it would ruin,—compassion for them made

[1] Millar on the Civil Law of England, 525.   [2] 2 Townsend, 457, 458.

the pen drop from my hand." But it is a well-known fact that the virtuous French Chancellor, after due deliberation introduced most important reforms in the procedure of the courts at Paris, without respect to the profit of himself or others.

In considering Lord Eldon as a *politician*, I begin with the eulogium (using the liberty to abridge it) of one well qualified to estimate his qualities in this line:—" He possessed a consummate power of managing men, an admirable address in smoothing difficulties with princes, of whom he had large experience, and a degree of political boldness where real peril approached, or obstacles, seemingly insurmountable, were to be got over, that contrasted strongly with his habits of doubting about nothing, and conjuring up shadowy embarrassments, and involving things of little moment in imaginery puzzles—the creation of an inventive and subtle brain. The counsellor, so hesitating in answering an important case—the judge, so prone to doubt, that he could hardly bring his mind to decide one —was, in all that practically concerned his party or himself, as ready to take a line, and to follow it with determination of purpose, as the least ingenious of ordinary politicians. On great occasions—that is, the occasions which put his interest or his power in jeopardy—a less wavering actor—indeed, one more ready at a moment's warning to go all lengths for the attainment of his object—never appeared upon the political stage. His fears in this respect very much resembled his conscientious scruples, of which no man spoke more or felt less; he was about as often the slave of them as the Indian is of his deformed little gods, which he now makes much of and now breaks to pieces or casts into the fire. Let there come any real embarrassment, any substantial peril, which required a bold and vigorous act to ward it off;—let there be but occasion for nerves to work through a crisis which it asked no common boldness to face at all;—let there arise some new and strange combination of circumstances, which, governed by no precedent, must be met by unprecedented measures;— and no man that ever sat at a council-board more quickly made up his mind, or more gallantly performed his part. Be the act mild or harsh, moderate or violent,—sanctioned by the Law and Constitution, or an open outrage upon both, he was heard indeed to wail, and groan much of piteous necessity,—often vowed to God, spoke largely of conscience, complained bitterly of his harsh lot,—but the paramount sense of duty overcame all other feelings; and, with wailing and with tears, beating his breast, and only not tearing his hair, he did, in the twinkling of an eye, the act which unexpectedly discomfitted his adversaries, and secured his own power forever. He, who would adjourn a private road or estate bill for weeks, unable to make up his mind on one of its clauses, or would take a month to decide on what terms some amendment should be allowed in a suit, could, without one moment's hesitation, resolve to give the King's consent to the making of laws when his Majesty was in such a state of mental disease that the keeper of his person could not be suffered to quit the royal closet for an instant, while his patient was, with the keeper of his conscience, performing the highest function of sovereignty."[1]

But, consummate as was his skill in party manœuvres— in acquiring and retaining office, slender praise can be bestowed upon him as a statesman. It is a strange but undoubted fact, that when he had once formed a Cabinet he gave himself very little trouble about its measures. I have heard that even upon law questions he would

[1] Lord Brougham's Statesmen, 2nd series, 54, 58. Although he had no doubts where *power* was concerned, he did not act with the same decision respecting *profits*,—at least when delay did not prevent him from deciding at any time in his own favor. "He had, it appears, entertained some doubts upon the right of the Chancellor to receive, for his own use, the large fees in bankruptcy, which used, before the change in 1832, to form part of the emoluments, and which former Chancellors had never hesitated to take as a matter of right and of course. His doubts were great; he could not solve them; he could not get over them; he oftentimes consulted the officers; oftentimes chatted on the matter with Mr. Richards; often did he seek for light from Heaven, and assuredly much would he have groaned over it when found if unfavorable to the claim. But all in vain; nothing could be found satisfactory. So he would not touch the fees; but desired that they might all be carried to a separate account for a year or two. At length, and long after he had ceased to discuss the subject, or apparently to think of it, just before the Court rose for the summer he called for the Secretary of Bankrupts, and asked to how much the fund then set apart amounted? It had reached an enormous sum; and, as if that which should have added force to his doubts were sufficient to dispel them, or as if the force of temptation applied to his mind were too strong to be resisted, and powerful enough to overcome its doubting propensities, he in one word directed the whole to be transferred to his account,—in which, be it observed, he was perfectly right, no mortal but himself having ever been able to descry the shadow of a reason for questioning the claims of the Great Seal to this fund."—*Law Review*, No. 11, p. 275.

generally give no opinion — desiring Lord Liverpool, or the Premier for the time being, to consult the Attorney and Solicitor-General. He was utterly ignorant of foreign politics, and his only maxim for the domestic government of the country was to preserve all things as he found them when he first entered public life, unless where he thought he saw a necessity for new coercive laws. "Mistrusting the most specious improvements, considering any organic change as synonymous with confusion, and satified that audacity in reform was the principle of revolution, he paid too little heed to the advancing spirit of investigation, and persisted in following at the flood those ancient fords and pathways which could only be pursued with safety at an ebb-tide."[1]

His inordinate love of political prosecutions and measures of coercion seemed to be morbid and incurable. By his course of policy he no doubt thought that he preserved the Constitution of this country; but in truth he greatly endangered it. "A few more drops of *Eldonine*, and we should have had the PEOPLE'S CHARTER."[2] Notwithstanding his furious resistance to the disfranchisement of a single corrupt borough, perhaps he would now acknowledge that since the Reform Bill our representative system stands on a surer basis than in the times when he thought it unsafe to allow the nation to enjoy the Habeas Corpus, or the holding of public meetings to petition Parliament; and he could not deny that the popularity and the influence of the Church have considerably increased since all the civil disabilities of the Dissenters have been removed, although he thought it would be fatal to religion if they should be allowed to marry in their own way. My own firm opinion is, that, by the liberal measures which he so severely reprobated, we have escaped a revolution which would have been violent, bloody, and destructive.

Lord Eldon must, at all events, be allowed to be free from the suspicion of sudden political conversion. *Qualis ab incepto* he continued without flinching to his dying day. The sentiments expressed by him at the last Pitt dinner which he attended[3] varied in nothing from

---

[1] 2 Townsend, 457. [2] Quarterly Review, lxxiii. 542.
[3] Sentiments very unlike those of the statesman whose name was usurped.

his first address to the electors of Weobly.[1] "It should be recollected that his attachment to the institutions of England, as he first knew them, was one of the laws of his moral and intellectual nature: it might be narrow, bigoted, inconvenient; incapable of gracefully bending to the necessities of the times; but still it was part of his true self; an attack on Church and State was to him the same thing as a violation of his paternal roof, or an insult to a domestic affection."[2]

Yet his steadiness to his opinions did not interfere with his political intrigues, or prevent him from choosing or changing leaders or associates, according to his views of expediency. "His temporary connection," says Mr. W. E. Surtees, "with Queen Caroline when Princess of Wales, and perhaps some other incidents, suffice to show that in public life there was no deficiency, on the *proper* occasion, of a convenient versatility—an invaluable ingredient to those who would rise. It was probably from a consciousness of this that he so pertinaciously arrogated to himself the credit of undeviating consistency [in political attachments as well as principles], and that flattery, of which he was somewhat exacting, never stole more sweetly upon his ear than when it invested him with this attribute!"[3]

In weighing the deserts of a Chancellor, much consideration is to be given to the exercise of his immense patronage. Very qualified praise only can be bestowed upon Lord Eldon in this department. He was disposed to do what was right, both in lay and ecclesiastical promotion; but he had no zeal in discovering and rewarding merit, and he often allowed himself to be swayed by undue influence. "The solicitations of the royal family," says Mr. Twiss, "were his chief embarrassment."[4] While we are indebted to him for such judges as Abbott, Holroyd, Bayley, Littledale, and Richardson, he was made an instrument for advancement of others who, though honorable men, were extremely incompetent, from the want of ability, or of professional knowledge, or of both. He was thus assailed by many gibes from the witlings of West-

---

[1] I not aware of any opinion he ever changed, except that in 1795 he agreed with Lord Kenyon in the answer to George III., that the coronation oath was not binding on the King in his legislative capacity, but afterwards loudly asserted that it disqualified the King from giving the royal assent to any act mitigating the Roman Catholic penal code.
[2] Q. Rev. vol. lxxv. p. 42.   [3] Surtees, 189.   [4] Ch. lxiii.

minster Hall, one example of which I may give in a saying respecting a near connection of a court physician, whose advancement to the bench was defended on the ground that he was "a judge by *prescription*."

When Lord Eldon was pressed to make a bad appointment, his way was to delay it as long as possible, and by seeming reluctance to throw the blame off his own shoulders. He rescued one of the superior courts from having a Chief wholly unskilled in the first rudiments of law, though a man of singular natural acuteness; but he made the same individual a puisne Baron, giving him power to decide upon questions of property and life. He said himself, in conversation: "On occasion of a vacancy on the Bench, by the death of one of the puisne judges, the Prime Minister of that day took upon himself to recommend a certain gentlemen to the King as a very fit person to fill that vacancy; and finding there was a disposition in the King to take that recommendation, I very respectfully urged that it was on the responsibility of the Lord Chancellor that these judges were appointed, and that I should not consider myself worthy of holding the Great Seal if I permitted the advice of any other man to be taken,—*at the same time tendering my resignation.* The Minister gave way, and the gentleman I recommended was appointed." But, giving full faith to the story, it shows only a resistance (so far very proper) to the usurpation of the Prime Minister on the rights of the Chancellor, —not a resistance to an appointment which would be injurious to the public.

Of the degree to which he really would stand out on such occasions, we have an amusing instance in the Diary of Sir Samuel Romilly, under date 24th June, 1815:— "Amongst the other obstructions to the prosecution of suits, has been the Chancellor's delay in the appointment of a Master, in the place of Mr. Morris. That gentleman died on the 13th of April last, and it was only yesterday that Mr. Jekyll was appointed to succeed him. The Prince's favor has procured him that appointment. As soon as the vacancy happened, it was known that Jekyll was to be appointed. The Chancellor, however, has delayed all this time filling up the office, at very great inconvenience to the suitors,—only, as it should seem, to show his sense of the impropriety of the appointment,—

and a more improper one could hardly be made; for, with a thousand good and amiable qualities as a private man, and with very good talents, Jekyll is deficient in almost every qualification necessary to discharge properly the duties of a Master in Chancery. If the Chancellor had meant to show with what deliberation he could make a bad appointment to a very important judicial office, and with how strong a sense of the impropriety of it he could surrender up to the Prince that patronage which it is a duty he owes to the public to exercise himself, he could not have contrived matters better than he has done."[1]

Let us now have Lord Eldon's own account of this same transaction:—"The fact was, that Jekyll was a great favorite with everybody. He was the descendant of an eminent lawyer, Sir Joseph Jekyll, who had been Master of the Rolls. Everybody wished him to be well provided for, in a proper mode. Nobody wished *that* more than I wished it; but I hesitated for weeks and months before I made the appointment. His most anxious and most powerful well-wisher was the Prince Regent, who was very much attached to him, and with whom Jekyll had spent many convivial hours. He was a person of great humor and wit, and indulged himself in manifesting his wit and humor to a great extent, and, I believe, without having ever said an ill-natured, provoking, or rude thing, of or to any man whilst he was so indulging himself. The Prince Regent, after having applied to me repeatedly, at Carlton House, to appoint Mr. Jekyll the Master, without effect, and having often observed that a man of his sense and abilities would soon be able to learn his business (which might be very true, but the appointment would nevertheless introduce a most inconvenient host of candidates from the Common Law Bar for Chancery offices), at length, in furtherance of his purpose, took the following step:—He came alone to my door in Bedford Square. Upon the servants going to the door, the Prince Regent observed that, as the Chancellor had the gout, he knew he must be at home, and he therefore desired he might be shown up to the room where the Chancellor was. My servants told the Prince I was much too ill to be seen. He, however, pressed to be admitted, and they, very properly and respectfully, informed him that they had positive orders

[1] Life of Romilly iii. 186.

to show in *no* one. Upon which he suddenly asked them to show him the staircase, which, you know, they could not refuse to do. They attended him to it, and he immediately ascended, and pointed first to one door, then to another, asking, 'Is that your master's room?'—they answering, 'No,'—until he came to the right one; upon which he opened the door and seated himself by my bedside. Well, I was rather surprised to see his Royal Highness, and inquired his pleasure. He stated he had come to request that I would appoint Jekyll to the vacant Mastership in Chancery. I respectfully answered, that I deeply regretted his Royal Highness should ask that, for I could not comply. He inquired why I could not, and I told him simply because, in my opinion, Mr. Jekyll was totally unqualified to discharge the duties of that office. He, however, repeated his request, and urged very strongly. I again refused, and for a great length of time he continued to urge, and I continued to refuse, saying Mr. Jekyll was unfit for the office, and I would never agree. His Highness suddenly threw himself back in his chair, exclaiming, 'How I do pity Lady Eldon!' 'Good God,' I said, 'what is the matter?'—'Oh, nothing,' answered the Prince, 'except that she never will see you again, for here I remain until you promise to make Jekyll a Master in Chancery.' Well, I was obliged at length to give in,—I could not help it. Others ought really to be very delicate in blaming appointments made by persons in authority, for there often are very many circumstances totally unknown to the public. However, Jekyll got on capitally. It was an unexpected result. One of my friends met him after he was appointed, and asked him how in the world he came to be picked out for that office, and he answered that he supposed it was because he was the most unfit man in the country. Now, you see this very consciousness of his own want of ability led him in all difficult cases to consult two or three other Masters in Chancery, and, being guided by two or three experienced heads, he never got wrong. Thus he executed his office very reasonably well. He continued in office for a considerable time, till indisposition and age obliged him to retire upon the usual pension. I met him in the street the day after his retirement; when, according to his usual manner, he addressed me in a joke:—'Yesterday, Lord

Chancellor, I was your master:—to-day. I am my own master.'"[1]

At the solicitation of Lady Eldon, he made a more exceptionable appointment, to the same office, of a militia captain, who had been very useful in rescuing his family from a mob.[2] The greater number of his Masters, however, were well chosen. I have great pleasure in commemorating one of them, my lamented friend the late Lord Henley, who had well earned his promotion by editing the reports of Lord Northington's decisions, and by consolidating the statutes respecting bankruptcy. Lord Eldon thus sincerely mentioned him in a letter to Sir Robert Peel: "Mr. Eden succeeds Mr. Courteney, and the professional knowledge which he has manifested in several publications I think fully authorize[3] the opinion I confidently entertain that, with experience and diligence, he will do credit to the appointment."[4] All the Masters in Chancery had been nominated by Lord Eldon, and their emoluments increasing much in his time from the very accumulation of arrears,—by this body he was unanimously considered a most deserving and faultless judge.

Of his stingy distribution of honors to the Bar, I must speak with forbearance, having myself been one of the sufferers. Although he himself had asked and obtained a silk gown at the end of seven years after his call to the Bar, he declined to give one to me when I had been twenty years at the Bar, and had for several years enjoyed the decided lead of my circuit. This, like the far more flagrant injustice done to Scarlett, might appear to have been from political prejudice; but he treated still worse his particular friend, Charles Wetherell, who shared all his sentiments in Church and State, besides enjoying deservedly high professional eminence, and who, when well stricken in years, was allowed to remain without a

---

[1] Twiss, ch. xxxvii.
[2] At this time the Lord Chancellor appointed to the office of his own sole authority, by putting a black velvet cap on the head of the new Master in open Court. To guard against such abuses, by 3 & 4 W. 4, c. 94, the patronage was nominally transferred to the Crown, but still with the intention that the *recommendation* of the Masters in Chancery, as of the puisne Judges, should be in the Chancellor, subject to the check which the form of tacking the royal pleasure imposes. Happily the office is now abolished.—*4th Edition.*
[3] Sic.   [4] March, 1826.

full-bottom wig to cover his grey hairs.[1] These instances are probably to be explained from a mere love of procrastination, and the dislike of being driven to decide upon the pretensions of other gentlemen at the Bar of equal standing and more doubtful claims. But his conduct in not giving the rank of King's Counsel to Mr. Brougham and Mr. Denman was positively culpable, and proceeded from a sordid motive. When appointed by Queen Caroline her Attorney and Solicitor General, they actually, as of right, had worn silk gowns and sat within the Bar; but on her death they were obliged to appear without the Bar in stuff gowns—and so they remained as long as Lord Eldon held the Great Seal, because they had given offense to George IV. by an honest and strenuous defense of their royal mistress. Now it was clearly the duty of Lord Eldon to have done what Lord Lyndhurst and the Duke of Wellington afterwards nobly and effectually did,—to have respectfully but firmly represented to the King that his Majesty's resentment proceeded upon an erroneous impression, and that to act upon it was unbecoming his exalted station. When Lord Eldon had surrendered the great Seal, and Mr. Brougham first, and after some delay Mr. Denman likewise, had obtained the professional rank to which they had been long entitled, Lord Eldon tried to exculpate himself by throwing all the odium upon George IV.; but the "Keeper of the King's Conscience" was infinitely more to blame, for he had been withheld from conveying the truth to the royal ear by the dread of giving offense and losing the royal favor,—on which he gloated, perhaps, still more than on the enjoyment of office.

He was likewise accused, like Lord Hardwicke, but I think unjustly, of withholding peerages from those filling high legal offices, that he might not endanger his influence in the House of Lords. He concurred in the elevation of Lord Redesdale, Lord Ellenborough, and Lord Manners, and always cordially co-operated with them. Sir William Grant, when made Master of the Rolls, was wisely content to remain a member of the House of Commons, where, being listened to with so much respect, he did more for his party, and for his own fame, than if he had

[1] Wetherell, when at last called within the Bar, was of older standing than Lord Eldon himself had been when made Chancellor.

been *ennobled*. I know that Chief Justice Abbott was not offered a peerage till Mr. Canning was Minister; but Lord Eldon would have felt no jealousy of his oratorical powers, or his influence; and in a letter which I have before introduced,[1] he took a very sensible view of this difficult subject.[2] It could hardly be expected that he should encourage the notion of conferring a peerage upon Sir John Leach, who had been trying to undermine him by pushing on the prosecution of Queen Caroline; and I doubt whether the presence of the author of the Milan Commission would have been of much use to the deliberations of their Lordships, although he certainly would have enlivened them with some smart contests with the old Chancellor. Lord Eldon has been exposed to opposite censure for the rapid elevation of Lord Gifford, that he might ease himself from the inconvenient pressure of Scotch appeals; but this is said to have been the act of Lord Liverpool, and the favored individual, although he had not fulfilled the early expectation entertained of his abilities,—if his life had been spared, might have left behind him a distinguished name.

Lord Eldon is much to blame for his indifference to the honor of his profession, and the interests of the public, in the appointment of the law officers of the Crown. This he left entirely to the Prime Minister for the time being, who, being necessarily unacquainted with the merits of legal practitioners, sometimes selected men indifferently qualified to act as Attorney or Solicitor General, or to fill high judicial offices, although in this lottery there did turn up for the Government such prizes as Tindal and Copley.[3]

[1] Ante, Vol. IX., p. 117.

[2] The Crown certainly might grant a peerage for life; and, in some instances, this prerogative might be usefully exercised; but there would be much danger of its being abused; and, with all the defects of the hereditary branch of the legislature, there would be great difficulty in finding a substitute for it, or in altering the mode of its formation.—*Note to 1st Edition*, 1847.

In fairness I allow this note to remain, as it was cited against me in the debates on " Life Peerages " in 1856. But after the fullest consideration of the subject, I now record my solemn opinion that the Crown can not by patent grant a peerage for life to a commoner with the privilege of sitting in parliament, and that a writ of summons to the House of Lords under such a patent is a nullity, although the writ without the patent, coupled with a sitting under it, would create an hereditary barony descendible to females as well as males.—*Note to 4th Edition, September*, 1857.

[3] Lord Eldon used to declare that he had not only never seen, but had

In the disposal of his clerical patronage he looked little for extraordinary merit. "He seemed to regard literature as a light and worthless weed, and consider those, whether clerical or lay, who went in quest of it, as cast away on a barren and bleak shore."[1] Yet he gave a living to Maurice, the author of the "Indian Antiquities," and he was the first patron of Dr. Philpotts, the present Bishop of Exeter, whom, even those who differ from him on speculative questions, must admire for his talents and his learning. He likewise did kind and good-natured things in disposing of ecclesiastical preferment, although "the solicitations of Queen Charlotte were so frequent as to entrench materially on his power of serving his friends."[2] As soon as he had got back to Bedford Square from being sworn in Chancellor, he wrote the following letter to a widow lady of his acquaintance, who had been in the habit of supplying him with home-baked bread from the country:—

"DEAR MADAM,

"I am this instant returned from the Queen's House, where I have received the Great Seal. How long I may hold it I do not know; but your goodness to me in giving me so many loaves, when the loaves and fishes were at the disposal of others, makes it fit that I should say, that if the infinite and pressing importunities, which under present difficult circumstances will amazingly tie up a Chancellor's hands, should leave me the power of enabling your son to feel that he need not hereafter plague his

---

never before heard, the names of some who were appointed to the office of Solicitor-General; and he leveled severe sarcasm not only against Garrow, but others, who had been promoted without his interference. From the following letter to him it would appear that in George III.'s time he appointed always to the much less important offices of Attorney and Solicitor General to the Queen:—

"Queen's House, May 21st, 1816.

"The Queen is very sorry that her visit to Windsor prevented her acknowledging the receipt of the Lord Chancellor's letter until this morning. The Queen agrees with the Lord Chancellor, that Mr. Sergeant Vaughan should succeed Mr. Hardinge as her Attorney-General, and leaves the filling up the office of Solicitor-General to the choice of the Lord Chancellor, who has at all times been so obliging as to settle it for her; and on this, as well as on many other occasions she has experienced, she has ever found it both a pleasure and a satisfaction to abide by his decision.

"Whenever the Lord Chancellor has settled it to his mind, the Lord Morton shall have the Queen's orders to present both gentlemen.

"CHARLOTTE."

[1] 2 Townsend, 434.   [2] Twiss, ch. lxiii.

diocesan about a license, I shall be glad to avail myself of it.

"With Lady Eldon's and my family's kind regards to you and all your family, believe me, truly, yours,

"ELDON.

" April 1st, 1807."

Very soon he actually gave a good living to the young clergyman alluded to, who well deserved the advancement. He likewise appointed his old preceptor, Moises, to be one of his chaplains, and was willing to advance him high in the Church.

In the ANECDOTE BOOK, giving an account of his first election for Weobly, he says, " I lodged at the vicar's, Mr. Bridge's. He had a daughter, a young child, and he said to me, ' Who knows but you may come to be Chancellor? As my girl can probably marry nobody but a clergyman, promise me you will give her husband a living when you have the Seals.' I said, ' Mr. Bridge, my promise is not worth half a crown, but you may have my promise.' " When he had been some time Chancellor, while sitting one morning in his study, an interesting young girl broke in upon him—introduced herself as the daughter of the Vicar of Weobly—modestly informed him of an affair of the heart which she had with a poor, young clergyman— and informed him that a small Herefordshire living, which would make them happy, had the day before become vacant. The secretary of presentations was immediately called in, and she carried back with her the presentation to this living in favor of her lover.

The following was his answer to an application for a piece of preferment from his old friend Dr. Fisher, of the Charter House :—

" DEAR FISHER,

" I can not, to-day, give you the preferment for which you ask.

" I remain your sincere friend,

" ELDON.

" Turn over."

Then, on the other side,—

" I gave it to you yesterday."

He himself furnished the following narrative of another ecclesiastical appointment, redounding much to his credit :

" When I went to enjoy repose at Encombe, I gave orders

to be denied to all strangers, or I should have been beset with applicants. One of these was a country clergyman from the north of England, who found his way thither on foot, and asked for the Chancellor. The servant who opened the door said his Lordship was out shooting. 'Which way is he gone?' replied the clergyman. 'What is your business, Sir?' asked the servant. 'Never mind,' rejoined the clergyman: 'only just tell me which way your master is gone.' The servant pointed out the quarter in which the Chancellor was to be found, and the stranger, following the direction, was not long before he came up with a man carrying a gun, and accompanied by a brace of dogs, but somewhat shabbily dressed,—of whom he inquired whereabouts the Chancellor might be found. 'Not far off,' said the sportsman: and, just as he spoke, a covey of partridges got up, at which he fired, but without success. The stranger left him, crossed another field or two, and witnessed, from a little distance, the discharge of several shots as unproductive as the first. 'You don't seem to make much of that,' said he coming back; 'I wish you could tell me where to meet with Lord Eldon?'— 'Why, then,' said the other, 'I am Lord Eldon.' The clergyman fell a stammering and apologizing, till the Chancellor asked him, rather shortly, whence he came, how he had got to Encombe, and what he wanted there? The poor clergyman said he had come from Lancashire to the Bull and Mouth in London; and that, finding the Chancellor had left town, and having no money to spare, he walked from London to Encombe; and that he was Mr. ——, the curate of a small parish, which he mentioned, and of which the incumbent was just dead; and that he was come to solicit the vacant benefice. 'I never give answers to applicants coming hither,' said the Chancellor, 'or I should never have a moment to myself; and I can only express my regret that you should have taken the trouble of coming so far to no purpose.' The suitor said, 'If so, he had no alternative but to go back to the Bull and Mouth, where he expected to find a friend who would give him a cast back into Lancashire; and with a heavy heart, took leave. When he arrived at the Bull and Mouth, a letter in an unknown hand was waiting for him. He opened the cover with the anxious curiosity of a man to whom epistolary communications are rare; and had the joy of finding in it a good-humored note from the Chancellor, giving him the preferment." "But now," added Lord Eldon with a waggish smile, "see the ingratitude of mankind. It was not long before a large present of game reached me, with a letter from my new-made rector, purporting that he had sent it me, because *from what he had seen of my shooting*, he supposed I must be badly off for game! Think of turning upon me in this way after the kindness I had done him, and wounding me in my very tenderest point!"[1]

By the following letter of Lord Nelson, written from the Downs, after his attack on Boulogne, it would rather appear that the Chancellor had been compelled, although in most courteous terms, to refuse an application from that hero.

"MY LORD, "Amazon, Sept. 17th, 1801.

"I feel very much obliged by your open and very handsome answer to my request, which so exactly accords with what my friend Dawson told me of your character, and allow me to consider myself, in every respect,

"Your most obliged,
"NELSON AND BRONTE."

---

[1] I have received, from one who had ample means of observing, and on whose accuracy I can place the most implicit reliance, the following less favorable view of Lord Eldon's conduct in this department,—which I feel myself bound to lay before the reader:—" In the administration of his Church patronage he did not merit much praise. His delays in filling vacant benefices were often positively scandalous,—extending to years in some instances. I believe that he occasionally received remonstrances from bishops on this head. In selecting the objects of his patronage, he was not anxious, or at least took little or no trouble, to ascertain the fitness of the persons recommended to him. Still less did he look out for meritorious clergymen, who, by their theological works or otherwise, had established a title to the favor of the great public patron. That no man of merit was preferred by him cannot be said; doubtless there were many such. But it would be difficult to select, during the twenty-five years in which he dispensed the Crown patronage, even five persons whom he chose because of their merit. His richest benefices were bestowed either on the application of members of the Royal Family, or on his own near connections,—sometimes with a disregard of propriety which was almost, or quite scandalous.

"During the period of Lord Eldon's Chancellorship, more than twenty appointments to prebendal stalls fell vacant. Of these, few, if any, were given to men distinguished by talents, learning, or services to the Church; not to one, it is feared, because he was so distinguished.

"Lord Thurlow, shameless as he was in heaping benefices on a brother and a nephew, had yet the merit of selecting Horsley and White (celebrated in his day for his Bampton Lectures) as recipients of his more dignified preferments. They both were placed by him in stalls; 'for they,' said he 'who defend the Church, ought to be seated in its highest places'"

He jocularly complained much of the longevity of his incumbents. " I have been very unlucky," he writes to a friend, " for the gentlemen who labor to consign others to immortality seem to cling themselves most amazingly to this mortal world, and the rarity with which I have had vacancies of livings is really remarkable: certainly not in the proportion of one to a dozen, I believe, throughout all Lord Rosslyn's time." Being strongly pressed by George III. to confer a living upon the son of a court physician, he answered, " I should be able more speedily to comply with your Majesty's wishes if your Majesty would be pleased to order your physicians to prescribe for my incumbents."

From the following anecdote, we may judge that he was much pleased to hear of a vacancy. A clergyman coming to the door of his private room as he was leaving the Court of Chancery, begged to have an interview with him on important business. The secretary, purse-bearer, and gentlemen said, with one voice, " His Lordship is so deeply engaged that the thing is impossible." Clergyman: " Tell his Lordship, if you please, that I am not come to ask for a living, but to resign one " All the three simultaneously answered, " The interests of the Church being concerned, we think we may be able to obtain for you a short audience."

He gives this piteous account of the annoyance occasioned to him by his Church patronage: " From persons great and small I have had, I may almost say, thousands of applications—most of them impudently framed in effect upon some such notion as that I can not myself have in the world a clergyman that I can have any personal wishes in favor of, or a friend who has in any clergyman a friend in whose welfare he takes an interest. Many of these applications, however, come from persons whose weight throws much difficulty in my way, and more than I can easily remove. Besides this, in confidence be it spoken, the different branches of the Royal Family communicate their wishes, which are commands, that supersede even promises to others: and, upon the whole, I assure you I have little elbow-room."[1]

[1] All who have anything to do with the disposal of Crown livings must feel infinitely indebted to Lord Eldon for the excellent precedent he has left of an answer to an application for a next presentation:

In the very important function of the Lord Chancellor of the appointment and removal of magistrates, Lord Eldon was exemplary, and he exercised a vigilant control in this department over the Bishop of Durham, who then was Count Palatine of the Bishopric, as well as over the Custodes Rotulorum throughout the kingdom. He was particularly strict respecting the removal of names from the Commission of the Peace, and he would suffer no man to be dismissed till heard in his defense, and proved guilty of some offense disqualifying him for assisting in the administration of justice.[1]

Before taking final leave of Lord Eldon as an official man, I should observe that he performed in a very exemplary manner his duties as Speaker of the House of Lords. He was courteous to every one—keeping up a familiar intercourse with Opposition peers, with whom he liked to chat on the woolsack,—and to whom he would sometimes make very free strictures on his colleagues.[2]

At first he was rather too rigid in enforcing what he considered the orders of the House. He would allow no

"Sir [or Madam, or My Lord],
"I have had the honor to receive your letter respecting the living of ——. I trust that you will not impute it to disrespect that I do not express at present any intention as to the disposal of it, except in saying that no person can more strongly feel the necessity of placing, in these times, most exemplary clergymen in the Crown's benefices. I have never allowed myself to express an intention by whom I should fill up any living not actually vacant—the tenure by which I hold office, and the inconvenience of acting upon any other rule than that of forbearing to intimate any purpose with respect to benefices not vacant, appearing to me to be such as to justify my refraining from so doing. This course, I trust, will not appear inconsistent with the respect with which I am, Sir [or Madam, or My Lord],
"Your obedient Servant,
"———."*

[1] See letter to Earl Grey, March 30, 1810. Surtees, 108.
[2] This intercourse even led to his meeting a Whig party at dinner at a time when political feeling interfered much more with private life than at present.

Lord Eldon to Lady F. J. Bankes.
(July or August, 1822.)
"Wonders, they say, never cease. You will be surprised to hear that I dined at Lord Holland's yesterday, at the old house at Kensington, with Lords Grey and Lauderdale, and several of the Opposition. We had a very good and pleasant party, and I was quite delighted with the very curious old house. I never saw any that I thought better worth seeing. You must recollect the outside of it; it is old and curious, and the inside is in the same state as when it was first fitted up, about the time of James I."

* Twiss, ch. lxiii.

petition to be received which did not profess to be "humble,"—admitting no equivalent word, however submissive. He fired up exceedingly at a petition which prayed their Lordships to give some bill "a cool and deliberate discussion," which, he said, contained an impertinent insinuation that they were sometimes "hot and hasty." He once declared that, in the course of thirty years' experience, he had never seen anything so irregular and disorderly as the production of a newspaper in the House.—At last being reminded that, although he sat on the woolsack, he had no more authority than any other peer, he somewhat pettishly refused to interfere when his advice would have been useful and well received; and he allowed irregular practices to prevail among their Lordships, which have never yet been corrected. But he always continued to support the privileges of the House with a high hand. Shortly before his resignation arose the famous "Umbrella case," so frequently quoted in the recent discussions on that subject.[1] A stranger being admitted below the bar, was required by one of the doorkeepers to deposit his umbrella in an anteroom, and his property not being returned to him when the debate was over, he brought an action against the messenger for the value of it before the Westminster Court of Conscience, and recovered a verdict for 17$s.$ 6$d.$ damages, with 2$s.$ 10$d.$ costs. But on complaint of this proceeding, Lord Eldon had the plaintiff and his attorney summoned to the bar, and he refrained from committing them to Newgate only when they had made a humble apology, and renounced the fruits of the verdict;—intimating a clear opinion that the House would not allow to be prosecuted any suit brought before any other tribunal with the intent of questioning their privileges.

The following letter shows that he himself had ceased to stand much in awe of their Lordships, although he trembled before a few shopkeepers sitting round a table in the office of the Auditor of the Exchequer:—

" Westminster, April 27th, 1822 ; half-past eight.

"I am down here to give a charge to my old friends the Pix Jury, as to-day is the trial of the coin, and the Goldsmiths' dinner. I am always a little nervous before I

[1] Lord Campbell's Speeches, p. 270.

make this sort of address, and such a strange being is man, that, though I *could talk before a Parliament with as much indifference as if they were all cabbage-plants*, a new audience has ever borne an appalling appearance." [1]

Of Lord Eldon as an orator it is hardly worth while to say more. From his station, from his character, from his zeal, from his earnestness, from his protestations, from his appeals to conscience, from his old stories, from his power of shedding tears at will, he was generally listened to with attention ; but his speeches, long, involved, and obscure, really contained very little of information or of reasoning, any more than of fancy. He put forth some one subtle plea,—often some merely technical difficulty,—on which he rested his cause,—even when that cause involved principles of the gravest kind. Perhaps in the speeches of no man who spoke so often, and it must be added with so much authority, could there be found so few sayings which are remembered, or are worthy of being remembered. In its day, one sentence in a speech of his on the Roman Catholic question had a run, and was in the mouths of his many admirers. " My Lords," said he, " the union of Church and State was designed, not to make the Church political, but the State religious." But even this solitary apothegm ascribed to him was not original. It was delivered and published by the late Dean Rennell, in one of the eloquent and powerful sermons with which he delighted his legal hearers, when Master of the Temple.—If a malefactor of any taste, on having the choice, should say that he would submit to read all Lord Eldon's speeches rather than suffer death,— before he got through two on constructive treason, and

---

[1] I have lying before me a MS. copy of his first address to a Pix Jury, on the 2nd of December, 1802. It is very long and elaborate, giving an account of the history of our coin, with all the statutes upon the subject from the earliest times. Having pointed out the duties of the jury in making an assay, he thus concluded : " Public wisdom has long ago determined, that an inquiry in its consequences so important as that which is now to be instituted can only be committed, with safety to the interests which it affects, to a jury of gentlemen, by profession skilled in the subject to which the inquiry relates. You have been named as that jury without influence, and have been fairly and impartially returned by the respectable Company, to whom the precept for forming a jury has according to usage been addressed. You will therefore now, gentlemen, proceed to the discharge of this important duty, and I shall detain you only while I add, that I am perfectly satisfied that by your verdict you will enable us to record the result of an inquiry anxiously, conscientiously, and judicially made."

two on the Catholic question, he would call aloud for the executioner.

His Lordship's most successful efforts probably were at the anniversary meetings of the club professedly instituted in honor of Mr. Pitt,—when, amidst enthusiastic cheers, he declaimed in praise of the intolerant doctrines, which that great man had so powerfully combated.[1]

I have now the pleasure of presenting Lord Eldon as a poet; and it is always most refreshing to me to find a Lord Chancellor sacrificing to the Muses.[2] After a happy union of almost forty years, he thus addressed her who on the "Sand Hill" descended the ladder to throw herself into his arms:—

"Nov. 18th, 1811.

"Can it, my lovely Bessy, be,
  That when near forty years are past,
I still my lovely Bessy see
  Dearer and dearer at the last?

"Nor time, nor years, nor age, nor care,
  Believe me, lovely Bessy, will—
Much as his frame they daily wear—
  Affect the heart that's Bessy's still.

"In Scotland's climes I gave it thee,—
  In Scotland's climes I thine obtain'd,—
Oh, to each other let them be
  True, till an Haven we have gain'd.
"ELDON."

These stanzas having a higher merit than the finest versification can claim, we ought not to criticize them severely; but it is impossible not to be astounded at their flatness, when we consider the theme, for it has been finely said of him,—"the poetry of his life began and

---

[1] He seems himself to have been wholly unconscious of this discrepancy. Thus he writes 29th May, 1820:—"We had our commemoration of poor Pitt on Saturday. The company did not amount to more than 250: it ought to have been twice as many; but after the greatest and best of men have been buried fourteen years, the attention to the memory, even of those whose names will be had in everlasting remembrance, slackens and abates wonderfully. Of fifteen members of a Cabinet, some of whom, possibly none of whom, would ever have been in a Cabinet if not brought forward in public life by him, only four felt it their duty to attend, viz.: Wellington, Westmoreland, Bragge Bathurst, and myself."

[2] I almost envy the delight which the future biographer must enjoy in another generation, when, in recording the lives of Lord Eldon's successors, he is interspersing their judgments and speeches in Parliament with their metrical effusions—tender and facetious.—*1st Edition*, 1847.

O for the *vers de société, facetiæ,* and *ana* of Lords Lyndhurst, Brougham, Cottenham, Truro, St. Leonards, and Cranworth!!!—*4th Edition*, 1857.

ended with Bessy." I suppose they have been given to the world to lessen the envy of mankind at his elevation, and to console the thousands who fail in the struggle of ambition, with the thought that at any rate they could write better verses.

But we have a happier specimen of his talents in this line from his kinsman, Mr. E. W. Surtees, who thus pleasantly introduces it: — "On some occasion, when going to call on Mr. Calcraft, who resided in the neighborhood of Encombe, he saw, on passing through the grounds, two daughters of his friend and two other girls playing at 'see-saw'—two at each end of an oak tree, which had been cut down. He used, afterwards, laughingly to compliment one of the Misses Calcraft on the *pretty ankle* which he persisted she had then revealed; and he commemorated his own happy fortune in the following *vers de société*, copied from the original in Lord Eldon's handwriting:—

> "In days of yore, as Roman poets tell,
> *One* Venus lov'd in myrtle groves to dwell:
> In modern days no less than *four* agree
> To consecrate to fame our oaken tree—
> Blest tree! the monarch shelter'd by thy arms!
> The goddess from thy boughs displays her charms."

I have several times expressed deep regret that my ex-Chancellors did not employ their leisure in writing memoirs of themselves and their times; but this feeling is much weakened by Lord Eldon's "ANECDOTE BOOK," a sort of *autobiography* compiled by him in his old age. These "Tales of a Grandfather" display much good humor, but would place the narrator very low in the catalogue of "Royal and Noble Authors." It is wonderful even how he fails on paper in the *jesting line*. In society he had been considered, as far as a large assortment of professional jokes went, to have been equal to some of the most successful *diners out*—and the Prince Regent, no mean authority, professed himself as much pleased with him as with Colman or Sir Walter Scott. But in the "ANECDOTE BOOK" he is generally tedious, vapid, and pointless,—and if indicted in the Grand Court, on the Northern Circuit, for *unnaturally murdering his own jokes*, —though perhaps acquitted of the *murder*, he must be found guilty of *concealment*.[1]

[1] The Law Review, No. II. p. 276, gives the following specimens:—

The best specimen of Lord Eldon's literary powers is an inscription, designed by him for the tombstone of a Newfoundland dog named CÆSAR, buried at Encombe :—

> "You who wander hither,
> Pass not unheeded
> The spot where poor Cæsar
> Lies deposited.
>
> He was born of Newfoundland parents;
> His vigilance, during many years,
> Was the safety of Encombe House:
> His talents and manners were long
> The amusement and delight
> Of those who resorted to it.
>
> Of his unshaken fidelity,
> Of his cordial attachment
> To his master and his family,
> A just conception can not
> Be conveyed by language,
> Or formed, but by those
> Who intimately knew him.
>
> To his rank among created beings,
> The power of reasoning is denied.
> Cæsar manifested joy
> For days before his master
> Arrived at Encombe:
> Cæsar manifested grief
> For days before his master left it.

"Everyone has heard of Sergeant Davy's joke—that the 'further he went to the West (of England), he was the more convinced the wise men came from the East.' The point is thus worn away in the Anecdote Book :—' The Sergeant used to express no very high opinion of the talents of the men of that portion of the kingdom; observing that it was most true that the wise men came from the East.' Sergeant Hill having a case laid before him with a fee of one guinea, to construe a very cramp devise in a will, answered that 'he saw more difficulty in the case than, under all the circumstances, he could well solve,'—adding the year and day. The case was returned to him with another guinea, and his answer was, that 'he saw no reason to change his opinion.' The Anecdote Book makes him say, 'I don't answer such a case as this for a guinea.' which is both pointless and unprofessional. —When a richly embroidered Jew was objected to by a sergeant as bail for a certain amount, it is known that Lord Mansfield said, 'Why, brother, he would burn for the money.' The book thus dilutes an excellent jest :— '.Don't waste our time by objecting to a gentleman with such a waistcoat— he would burn for more than the debt.' "—The author of this article explains the fact that the stories in writing are "the ghosts, or rather mummies, of their originals," from Lord Eldon's "disease of doubt and hesitation," which came upon him when he took the pen in his hand; but I should rather impute the failure to his entire unacquaintance with written composition. The ex-Chancellor sitting down to write his "Anecdote Book" may be compared to a skillful dancer all at once trying to swim.

> What name shall be given
> To that faculty
> Which thus made expectation
> A source of joy,—
> Which thus made expectation
> A source of grief?"

But it was in spoken facetiousness that he excelled.—If there were allusions to the delays in Chancery in his time, he would tell a story, which he had invented or embellished, of a very old lady, a Peeress, who came into Court in person when Lord Thurlow was Chancellor, to be examined touching her consent to the transfer of some property. This business being done, Lord Thurlow told her he would not detain her. "But," said she, "I should be glad if your Lordship would let me stay a little longer, for my cause has now been in Court eighty-two years, and I want to know how they are going on about settling it." Lord Eldon used to say, " he would leave it to others to guess which first came to an end—the old lady or her cause."

The following hit at a Bishop (which he was ever fond of) he himself related:—" Lord Donoughmore came to me upon the woolsack upon a day in which something was to pass on the Catholic question, and an eminent prelate it was understood was to vote with Donoughmore. Entering into conversation with me, Lord Donoughmore said, 'What say you to us now? We have got a great card to-night.' I said, 'What card do you mean? I know the KING is not with you; there is no QUEEN; there is only another great card.' 'What,' said Donoughmore, 'the Right Reverend Prelate a KNAVE!' 'You have called him so,' said I; 'I have not.'"

He related the following anecdote, which may be taken as a fair specimen of the wit of the Court of George III.: —"On one occasion I, and the Archbishop of Canterbury, and many other Lords, were with George III., when his Majesty exclaimed, 'I dare say I am the first King whose Archbishop of Canterbury and whose Chancellor had both run away with their wives—was it not so Chancellor?' 'May it please your Majesty, will you ask the Archbishop that question first?' answered I. It turned the laugh to my side, for all the Lords were beginning to titter."[1]

[1] The Lord Privy Seal, the late Earl of Westmoreland, had done the same.

He retained the relish he had acquired at University College for bad puns. When suffering from the gout in both *feet*—where, though painful, it is not dangerous, he said, "he did not much mind gout below the *knee*—provided it were '*ne* plus ultra!'"

He caused a loud laugh while the old Duke of Norfolk was fast asleep in the House of Lords, and amusing their Lordships with "that tuneful Nightingale, his Nose," by announcing from the woolsack, with solemn emphasis, that the Commons had sent up a bill for "inclosing and dividing Great SNORING in the county of Norfolk!"

A counsel at the Chancery Bar, by way of denying collusion, suspected to exist between him and the counsel representing another party, having said, "My Lord, I assure your Lordship there is no *understanding* between us," the Chancellor observed, "I once heard a Squire in the House of Commons say of himself and another Squire, 'We have never, through life, had but *one idea between us,*' but I tremble for the suitors when I am told that two eminent practitioners at my Bar have *no understanding* between them!"[1]

Mr. Pierce Egan, the author of "Boxiana," having pleaded his own cause, and succeeded—about the granting of an injunction,—was beginning a long speech to thank him for his patience and impartiality, when the Chancellor cut short the eulogy by exclaiming, "Mr. Egan, you have gained all you want, and the sooner you take *your own head* and mine *out of Chancery* the better!"[2]

Whenever it was indicated, by a peculiar elevation of his eye-brow, that he meant to be jocular, it is said that the gentlemen of the Chancery Bar were thrown into an ecstacy of mirth, and those most anxious to have the "ear of the Court," were guilty, by premeditation, of seemingly involuntary indecorum.[3]

---

[1] When the Welsh jurisdiction was about to be abolished, two judges were appointed with *an understanding* that if it was abolished they should not be entitled to a pension; but it was said that "all the others had pensions granted to them because they had been appointed *without any understanding.*"

[2] As the language of the "ring" is now nearly obsolete, perhaps I ought to explain that, when a boxer had his antagonist's head fast under his arm, so that he could pummel it as severely and as long as he pleased, the helpless victim's head was said to be "in Chancery."

[3] I myself have actually seen one gentleman so comport himself in the Court of King's Bench under the jokes of Lord Ellenborough.

> " Well could they laugh, with counterfeited glee,
> At all his jokes, for many a joke had he."

The greatest display of wit in the Court of Chancery, while he presided there, was on the memorable day when *Metcalfe* v. *Thompson* was decided.[1] This was an application to dissolve an injunction against an invasion of the plaintiff's patent for hair-brushes, the invention being, that some of the hairs should be long and others short. No Counsel appearing for the plaintiff, the Chancellor said, " This injunction must be *brushed off*, unless some Counsel be had in a few minutes to support it."—The brush of an old wig-maker being produced on behalf of the defendant, and being the same to *a hair* as the plaintiff's brush, the Chancellor said, waggishly, " Is it a Fox's brush? [alluding to a well-known old hair-dresser in the Temple.] This old brush, Mr. Treslove, is rather an odd sort of a thing; but when you and I get as old, and our tresses have been as well worn as these, we shall look, perhaps, quite as antique." Mr. TRESLOVE: " My Lord, I advised my client not to *show his brush*." LORD CHANCELLOR: " There, I must say, that you being a *pursuer* were *at fault ;* for if an injunction is granted by this Court, the article on which the injunction is granted must be lodged with the Master. I remember in a case of *waste*, that a person who made an affidavit, actually affixed his oak trees to his affidavit, to show the Court of what nature the trees were."—The injunction was dissolved, amidst peals of laughter, that were heard all over Westminster Hall.

Lord Eldon in allusion to Lord Stowell's love of good things, which induced him to dine in the Temple Hall, at 5, by way of a whet for an 8 o'clock dinner at the West-end of the town, would say, " My brother takes regular exercise twice a day—*in eating ;*"—but Lord Stowell had his revenge by saying good-humoredly, " My brother will drink any *given* quantity of wine,"—and being asked what the Chancellor *killed* when he went out shooting, at Encombe, by answering " He kills—*time*."

Perhaps we may admire Lord Eldon's pleasantry more when he did not aim at wit. Traveling the circuit with a companion, who, according to a custom not uncommon in

---

[1] This affords a striking contrast to the " Dumb Day" in the Court of Common Pleas. Ante, Vol. IV., p. 260.

those days, always carried pistols with him and placed them under his pillow, they slept one night at an inn, and at dawn of day Mr. Scott discovered in his bed-room a man's figure, seemingly dressed in black. The intruder being sharply challenged, said, "Please your honor, I am only a poor sweep, and I believe I've come down the wrong chimney." "My friend," was the reply, "you have come down the right,—for I give you sixpence to buy a pot of beer, and the gentleman in the next room sleeps with pistols under his pillow, and had you paid him a visit he would have blown your brains out."

Once when he was looking at his own picture in the Exhibition, two lively damsels placed themselves before him, and began to criticize it, the one observing to the other, "I am sure, my dear, we have seen enough of that stern-looking Chancellor, so let us go on,"—whereupon he observed to them, with his best bow, "And yet, young ladies, if you knew him, he would be happy to convince you that he is really a good-tempered old gentleman."

On the accession of her present Majesty, he had turned his 80th year. Being still able occasionally to take exercise on foot, he was walking in St. James's street, where a crowd had gathered to see the carriages of some gentlemen goining to the Palace with an address. Amidst the throng he felt the hand of a man in one of his pockets: but as it luckily was not that which contained his purse, he contented himself with the thief's disappointment, and quietly turning to him, said, "Ah! my friend, you were wrong there: this other was the side where the *grab* lay."

It is almost with unmixed satisfaction that we behold Lord Eldon in private life. He had not a particle of the pomposity which in former times I have seen displayed by puisne Judges when they mixed with the world. To him might truly be paid the compliment of Tacitus to Agricola. "Ubi officio satisfactum nulla ultrà potestatis persona." He who had lately been seen under the bushy honors of his flowing wig, presiding in the Court of Chancery or the House of Lords, was here transformed into the light-hearted, simple-minded playfellow of his own dogs and his bailiff's children. On the first day after his arrival at Encombe, he would suddenly jump up in the drawing-room, and, dancing a step to a tune of his own singing, would observe, with a smile, to the family party around, "You don't know the luxury of playing the fool."[1]

When he had written his verses on Miss Caroline Calcraft's ankle, he was crowned by the young ladies with a wreath bearing this inscription—

"Instead of powder'd curls, let ivy twine
Around that head so full of Caroline:"

he himself entering into their fun with all the zest of boyish frolic.—"Nor was his graciousness reserved only for his family, friends, and favorites: it was with him an habitual benevolence, extending to all who came in contact with him. There was no fawning upon royal and noble persons, nor ostentation of condescension to private men; he talked as frankly and as courteously with a tenant, a clerk, a servant, a stranger, according to their respective relations to him, as with a Prince of the blood: preserving always a demeanor which was free alike from affectation and from assumption, and in which natural dignity was tempered with unfailing good-humor."[2]

We could wish, for the sake of himself as well as others, that the "Literæ humaniores" had been allowed to interest, enlighten, and refine him: but in all his correspondence for fifty years, I trace only two allusions to books. During the Christmas before he surrendered the Great Seal, which he was obliged to spend in London, he wrote to his grandson, "If I had my gun in my hand, accompanied by *Bill and Co.,* at Encombe, I should defy the gout's preventing me to-day exhibiting the ardor and vigor that I could have displayed half a century ago in the field. 'It is wiser,' Pennington would say, 'to sit musing over the authors and the papers:' so, as a prudent one, I am hunting for amusement and sport in the volumes and pages of the publications of the day, and of the days of yore,—of the modern and the olden times."[3] But I suspect that he found this a poor substitute for frightening the partridges, and that he speedily laid it aside for a gossip with an old attorney. However, once again, in the year 1834, when he had been seven years out of office, he wrote to his grandson: "I now and then peep into my old school-books. I find Tully abusing his countrymen, as heartily as I am grumbling at

[1] Surtees, p. 172.   [2] Twiss, ch. lxiii.   [3] 22nd January, 1827.

mine for their ruinous practices and projects, to make the wealthy part of the people change places with the poorer orders, and to convince the latter that exchange is not robbery, though *all* is parted with on one side, and *nothing* on the other taken." Yet, if he had looked into the treatise " De Officiis," I believe he would have expected to find how the " Master's Office," and the " Six Clerks' Office," were regulated under the Roman Prætor.

Attending public worship in the country, he tried, though ineffectually, to revive his recollection of Greek,— of which he gives this account: " I took up to Church, on Sunday, a little old Greek Testament, hoping to read in Greek when the clergyman was reading the second lesson in English,—having strong spectacles too ;—but my eyes are so altered that I found they would not do, and that I must employ my ears only for instruction of this sort."

He had never been, or desired to be, out of England, unless when he ran off with his bride to Scotland,—and he had no taste for any of the fine arts. No painting interested him, unless perhaps the portrait of a friend,—of which he judged only by the likeness. In the long-depending " Opera case," which, to his horror, placed him sometimes in the situation of a manager of a theater, and application having been made which rendered it necessary for him to inquire into the proper rate of remuneration to be allowed for certain principal singers, and especially for Madame Catalini (the Jenny Lind of that day), he said, jocularly, in pronouncing his order, " For my own part, I would not give five shillings to hear her sing for six months together."[1]

With respect to *cards*, he knew spades from clubs, and hearts from diamonds, and it was rumored that he had learned the rudiments of whist; but he was certainly altogether ignorant of all other games, even the most common and simple. " This led, on one occasion, to a rather laughable scene at the palace of King George III. The royal party were playing at 'commerce;' and, through Lord Eldon's bad luck or bad play, he had soon forfeited

---

[1] This doctrine, which was blazoned in the newspapers, brought many gibes upon him from his musical friends. When hard pressed, he one day thus defended himself: " Well, I don't deny having said so ; but which of you would listen, on any terms, to the best singer in the world *for six months together ?*"

his three lives. In perfect ignorance, however, that this catastrophe should have been the signal for his retiring from the contest, Lord Eldon kept his seat at the table and continued playing. At last Queen Charlotte, perceiving that all his counters were gone, suddenly addressed him: 'My Lord Chancellor, you are dead!' Expostulation proving vain, and Lord Eldon, to his own diversion, and that of the company, being made to understand, that, though physically alive and well, he was metaphorically defunct, they proceeded in their game without his being further allowed to join in it."[1]

Unlike his brother, Lord Stowell, who visited and revisited every exhibition in London, he cared nothing for *sights*, and never was detected at Panorama, Diorama, show of Wild Beasts,[2] or levée of Mysterious Lady. Once, however, his curiosity actually made him prefer pleasure to business. During a visit of Lord and Lady Eldon, in 1805, to Mr. Farrer, at Eltham, it happened that the Ocean, a ninety-eight gun ship, was to be launched at Woolwich; and arrangements were made that the whole party should go to witness the sight. On the morning of the day on which the launch was to take place, a letter by express was brought to Lord Eldon at the breakfast-table. When he had read it, he said it was a summons to a Cabinet Council. The company all expressed their hopes that he would not be under the necessity of going to Downing-street. With a smile, he replied: "No, I will not go; because, though I may attend other Cabinet Councils, I never can have another opportunity of seeing the Ocean launched." So he went with them, and "made a day of it."

His great delight was in the Court of Chancery,—although, towards the commencement of the long vacation, he was both satiated and fatigued with his enjoyments there, and even found a bagpipe a relief. Thus he wrote on Sunday, the 1st of August, 1824:—" I have some, and no small comfort to-day, in having my organs of hearing relieved from the eternal din of the tongues of Counsel. I am sometimes tormented by the noise of Lady Gwydir's Scotchmen playing under my windows upon the Scotch

---

[1] Anecdote related by the present Earl of Eldon. Twiss, ch. xxi.
[2] Perhaps he might be afraid that it might be reported of him, as of Lord Chancellor Guilford, that " he had been riding on a rhinoceros."

instrument vulgarly called the bagpipes; but there is music in that droning instrument compared to the battle of lawyers' tongues. This, however, I must get through, somewhat more, before they can be silenced."

When he had any leisure in London he spent it in gossip,—preferring the society of inferiors and dependants. He was not a "clubable man," and instead of imitating Thurlow by gladiatorial exercitations, on equal terms with such men as Burke, Johnson, and Horne Tooke, he gathered round him Dick Wilson, the attorney, Smith, the Accountant-General, and his old crony Campbell, the Master in Chancery, to listen to his stories—of which he was himself always the hero.[1] This taste not only made him egotistical, but gradually weakened his discrimination between the *actual* and the *ideal*. To add to the effect of his narratives, he imagined circumstances which, by frequent repetition, he himself firmly believed. Thus only can we account for his exaggeration of his early difficulties, the representation of his pecuniary losses by accepting office, and various other verbal statements, at variance with written documents under his own hand. In paliation, I must observe, that he confined himself to what he called "white lies," and that whether speaking truth, or using a little liberty with it, he was ever free from malignity.[2]

When in the country he amused himself with feeding his dogs and following the game. He professed a great contempt for *battues,* which he pronounced to be *unsportsmanlike*. But the lovers of these massacres had their revenge by asserting that the Lord Chancellor, despairing of killing birds on the wing, would fire at partridges and phesants on the ground, and he certainly always went out with his gun and dog alone—expressing much chagrin if he was followed or watched. On his return home he

[1] "Whether or not Lord Eldon were unwilling to have, in his hours of relaxation, his hard-worked intellect still kept upon the stretch, certain it is that he did not generally select his more familiar associates from men of commanding ability. They were, for the most part, worthy fellows, who had a vast respect for him, could tell or listen to a good story, and crack with him a joke or a bottle of wine."—*Surtees*, 174.

[2] An old acquaintance of his writes to me: "That he was a most engaging companion I need not tell you; thoroughly good-natured, very desirous to please, and not indifferent to the reputation of *bonhomie*. In truth, he was rather *exigeant* of incense; and those who burned it to him most profusely, however coarsely and smokily, were the most in his liking."

would sometimes show his bag pretty well filled,—leaving it doubtful whether he had taken the birds by *descent* or by *purchase*. He used to declare that he was far from being so good a shot in later life as when a young Oxonian, without a *qualification*. "By the time I got a *qualification*," said he, "I found myself *disqualified*."

Being invited in the autumn of 1822 by Sir Robert Peel to visit him at Lulworth, and to shoot over a well-stocked manor, he answered:—"As to my gun, I dare not expose myself as a sportsman—a wretched sportsman,—anywhere but at home."[1]

He wandered about the fields wearing an old shabby jacket—generally gaiters—though sometimes top-boots, and a weather-beaten hat—so that his official dignity could little be guessed at by strangers.

An old friend of his has communicated to me the following story of the great danger in which the Lord High Chancellor of Great Britain once was of being *had up* before a magistrate as *a poacher* :—" I heard that Lord Eldon was spending a few days with his friend Mr. W., whose domain was very rural and pretty, but not extensive; and on calling on him there I found him in his usual suit of black, with the addition of his well-known traveling topped boots, and with an old shotbelt over his shoulder. His countenance at once convinced me that he had something amusing to tell, and with an air of assumed alarm he related an adventure in which he had just played a principal part. 'I unfortunately crossed a lane in pursuit of my game, and in the second field from this lane I was accosted by a powerful and almost savage-looking farmer, who challenged me as the poacher for whom he had long been looking. I at once acknowledged that I might have made a mistake as to his land, and offered to turn back immediately, but this did not at all pacify him, for putting himself in front of me he declared that I should not stir until he knew who I was and where to be found. I tried to evade giving a description of myself by renewed offers of departure, and a promise not to return; but this did but increase his violence, and so I was at last forced to acknowledge that I was the Lord Chancellor,—a communication which was so far from allaying his ire that it did but increase its fury,

[1] Peel MSS.

for in language which looked very like earnest he *swore* that of all the impudent answers he ever got, mine was the most impudent, and I verily believe he would have laid hands on me if my tall footman (one of the finest young men I ever saw) had not come up to us and addressed me as my Lord."

However, in Dorsetshire he was regarded with vast veneration,—which, according to the following anecdote related by himself, was felt not only by dogs and horses, but by animals *feræ naturæ*. "When out shooting at Encombe we went through a field where a boy was employed to drive off the crows and rooks from new-sown wheat. I perceived the boy following us in our sport at least a mile from that field. 'My boy,' said I, 'how came you to leave your work?—the birds will get all the wheat.' —'Oh no, my Lord,' said the boy, 'they saw your Lordship in the field, and they won't dare come again, now they know your Lordship has been there.'"[1]

He was rather a strict preserver of his game, although always disposed to act good-humoredly to trespassers when he personally came in contact with them. "One day," he said, "as I was with my dog and gun on my grounds in my usual shooting attire, I heard two reports in an adjoining field, and saw what appeared to be, as in fact they afterwards proved, two gentlemen. I accosted them with 'Gentlemen, I apprehend you have not Lord Eldon's permission to shoot on his grounds?'—to which one of them replied, 'Oh, permission is not necessary in our case.' 'May I venture to ask why, gentlemen?' I said.—'Because we flushed our birds on other ground, and the *law* entitles us to follow our game anywhere; if you ask your Master, Lord Eldon, he'll tell you that is the *law*.' Whereupon I said, 'I don't think it will be necessary to trouble him on that account, since, to tell the truth, I am Lord Eldon myself!' They instantly sought to apologize; but I added,—'Come, gentlemen, our meet-

---

[1] This knowledge of the Dorsetshire crows of the Lord Chancellor's power to grant an injunction against their trespassing on the new-sown wheat, may be credible after the undoubted fact that, in Scotland, the crows, who take such good care to keep out of gun-shot on every "lawful day," on the *Sabbath* come close up to the houses, and seek their food within a few yards of the farmer and his men,—discovering the recurrence of the sacred day from the ringing of the bells and the discontinuance of labor in the fields,— and knowing that while it lasts they are safe.

ing has begun in good humor, and so let it end—pursue your pleasure on my grounds—only next time don't be quite so positive in your *law*.'"[1]

He one day required a half-pay captain to show his certificate. "Who are you?" said the trespasser: "I suppose, one of old Bags' keepers?" "No," replied the Chancellor, with a smile, "I am old Bags himself;" and they parted good friends.

He never appeared on horseback after having grown to man's estate, although he had actually followed the hounds when a boy. "I left off hunting," said he, "because I had a fall one day, when in full cry on Newcastle Moor. I wished to clear a broad and deep ditch, but my horse fell in, and I tumbled over him,—when there was a great chance of my being presided over by the Coroner, instead of presiding over the House of Lords. Since then I have trusted to *wheels*, and, above all, to *my own legs*."

There is some abatement from the admiration with which we are disposed to view him as a private citizen. Mr. Surtees, after alluding to his "permanent personal prejudices and resentments," adds, "that he, on some matters, was anxious to exact from his family a submission of their judgment to his own, incompatible with with proper independence:—that his tenderness was changed for anger, his confidence for distrust, the moment that he considered his interest or his authority to be invaded—is a statement which can not be disputed."[2]—It is said that he would not allow his eldest son, who was a very sound Tory, any liberty of choice as to the section of the Tory party to which he might attach himself, or any freedom even of criticising the measures of Government.—When his daughter-in-law was left a young and blooming widow, with a single child, he was indignant at her entering into a second matrimonial connection, long after the year of grief had expired, with a gentleman every way most unexceptionable.—Although he himself had run away with Miss Surtees and was rather proud of this exploit—when his eldest daughter, Lady Elizabeth, gave her hand, without his consent, to an ardent lover of respectable character and good education, but not of much wealth, years rolled away before he would

[1] Surtees, 173.   [2] Id. 731.

forgive her. Although Lord Encombe ever testified for him the warmest affection and the most devoted submission, he latterly beheld him with jealousy, suspecting that "the servants at Encombe rather looked to their future than their present master;" and he himself regarded him "more in the light of an immediate successor than in that of a young companion;"—insomuch that he capriciously made an alteration in his will, preferring the descendants of his own daughters to the daughters of his grandson. But with such slight exceptions, occurring in the lapse of three-quarters of a century, he was most exemplary in all the relations of domestic life. We have seen his pious respect for the worthy "hoastman," his father; and we may guess how strong was his affection for the good lady his mother, from observing that his elevation to the peerage only seemed to please him because it would make her happy. We read of few things, in history or fiction, more touching than the long attachment between the two brothers, John and William Scott, never relaxed in adversity, nor in prosperity, which is still more trying. What they were to each other when under the care of Mr. Moises, at the free grammar-school at Newcastle, they continued when they were presented to the King at the same levee, the one as King's Advocate, the other as Solicitor-General—when they were raised to the highest judicial offices, the one as Judge of the Admiralty, the other as Lord Chancellor—when they both sat together in the hereditary branch of the legislature, as much honored as if they had derived their titles from a long line of illustrious ancestors—and in extreme old age, when, having retired from office, they were approaching the confines of second childhood. Although the elder brother had suffered the greatest share of mental decay, yet he occasionally continued sensible of the undiminished tenderness with which "Jack" still watched over him. "It is related of Lord Stowell, that a short time before his death, having, in the deepening twilight of his powers, submitted to a less genial regimen, on a visit from his brother he resumed his glass; and as he quaffed, the light of early days flashed upon his over-wrought brain — its inner chamber was irradiated with its ancient splendor—and he told old stories with all that exquisite felicity which had once charmed young and old, the careworn and the fair —and talked of old times with more than the happiness of middle life."[1] On this occasion, probably the last time they ever met, Lord Eldon, delighted with the gleam of intellect which he witnessed, rose from his chair, embraced Lord Stowell, and imprinted a kiss upon his forehead.

But the constancy of his passion for Bessy is his brightest distinction. The devotion of the most ardent suitor could not exceed that which he continued to show her to the end of her days. He was never weary of referring to the period of their obscurity and poverty as the happiest of his life; "for then," said he, "we were all in all to each other, and she did much for me, which has never been done so well since." In his elevation, her happiness was his first care. Not even the blandishments of royal favor were enjoyed by him, if they separated him from home and Lady Eldon. Partly from ill-health, partly from shyness, partly from penurious habits contracted in straitened circumstances, she had a great dislike of giving entertainments, and he cheerfully renounced visiting society for her sake, and incurred the imputation of stinginess. In Hamilton Place, they must have seemed to an inmate to live for each other as much as in Serle Street. "She cut his hair, arranged his linen and clothes for dress, and stole to the window when he went out, to see, so neat in all his arrangements, the Chancellor pass by. His indulgence to every wish she might form was unbounded."[2]

"The influence of Lady Eldon over her husband, always great, seemed only to increase with her age. On the event of her death, Lord Eldon seemed crushed with

---

[1] Quarterly Review, vol. lxxv. p. 5. Said to be from the pen of my friend Sergeant Talfourd.

[2] To show his consideration for her, the following anecdote was circulated; but I believe it to be pure invention. When about to give a Cabinet dinner, he himself ordered a fine turbot, which cost a guinea and a half, but which he told her he had got at a great bargain, at half a guinea. When he came home at night, she said, "My dear John, I have been doing something for the family to-day as well as you, for our old friend Mrs. ———, having called upon me when you were gone, I showed her the turbot, and told her what a bargain we had got. She said *it was well worth a guinea*, and I let her have it for that money." He preserved his temper; and next day, when the Cabinet dinner was to be given, turbots being scarce, he could not get a nice one under two guineas. Still he was as good-humored to her as when he ran down to Fleet Market to buy sixpenn'orth of sprats for her supper.

grief; and though he afterwards rallied, he ever continued to mourn her loss, constant in sorrow as in love."[1]

It must be admitted that by so closely conforming to Lady Eldon's taste, he neglected a public duty (although not one of the highest order), for the great emoluments of the Chancellor are given to him (among other other good purposes) that he may maintain the exterior dignity of his office, and exercise hospitality for the benefit of the profession over which he presides, and consequently for the general good. But Lord Loughborough's two magnificent coaches, in all respects equipped alike, without which he never appeared in public, were now changed for one old battered carriage, which might have been picked up at a neighboring hackney-coach stand, and the Chancellor "working the Great Seal with a pair of horses," one of them having fallen lame, the CLAVIS REGNI was actually known to have made its progress to and from Westminster Hall in a "jarvy." By all former Chancellors levées had been held, which not only brought together the senior and junior members of the Bar, but gave them the opportunity of mixing with eminent literary and political characters, of enlarging their ideas, and of polishing their manners. These were now entirely discontinued, as being attended with trouble and expense. Worse remains behind. We know that ever since the time of Sir Christopher Hatton (and the probability is that the "good and approved usage" might be traced back to the Anglo-Saxons), the holder of the Great Seal had entertained at dinner the Judges, the King's Sergeants, the Attorney and Solicitor-General, the Benchers of the Inns of Court, and the officers of the Court of Chancery,—they in return praising his wine and his equity: But no Judge, no King's Sergeant, no Attorney or Solicitor-General, no Bencher of an Inn of Court, no officer of the Court of Chancery, ever placed his knees under the dinner-table of Lord Chancellor Eldon.[2] In consequence,

---

[1] Surtees, 167.

[2] We have seen, however, that he could give dinners to royal personages in great style ; and thinking that the stability of the Government depended on good Cabinet dinners, his were the best going. Thus he writes:

"Nov. 23rd, 1820.

"We are all well, safe, and quiet, only in a fuss, the morning after our Cabinet dinner, which was by far the handsomest that any Minister has given in my time. Mamma really did this most magnificently."

although the soundness of his judgments could not be carped at, his *modus operandi* was severely criticized; the arrear of his causes was magnified, being measured by the arrear of his dinners, and the most extravagant stories were circulated of his desire of money, and his unwillingness to part with it.

In truth, there was no foundation either for the one charge or the other, beyond the advice he once jocularly gave to a gentleman at the Bar, who, being appointed a Master in Chancery, consulted him as to whether he should resign the valuable appointment of Counsel to Queen Anne's Bounty. "I should advise you to do no such thing: the true rule, I fancy, is to get what you can, and keep what you have."[1] In his own practice, he never did anything unfairly to increase his profits, and he gave away money with great liberality. Like all men in eminent station, he had many more demands upon him for pecuniary assistance than it was possible for any fortune to supply. "I have received letters from strangers," said he, "asking relief on every imaginable ground. One man from a prison candidly stated that he had behaved so excessively ill that nobody who knew him, and none of his relations, would assist him; and therefore he hoped that I would." But he did not refuse assistance to those who had peculiar claims upon him, and he could be generous without any solicitation. Being called upon to decide whether a very old and respectable solicitor, of the name of Edmunds, was not liable to refund a sum of 82*l.* which he had incautiously paid, he said, "I have no doubt that Mr. Edmunds is liable, but he is near the latter end of his life; and I know him to be a very worthy man; an order upon him to pay would disturb the close of his life, and I

("Nov. 1820.) "Sir William heard so much of my Cabinet dinner, that he invited himself to dine yesterday on the *scraps*."

"June 16th, 1823. "Cabinet dinner went off amazingly well! Mamma had directed things in capital style. I have seen no such doings at any other Minister's."

But the account of these doings only aggravated our discontent in Westminster Hall. Even the grave Romilly observed, on Sir Thomas Plumer giving a series of dinners when appointed Master of the Rolls, "Verily, he is clearing away the arrears of the Lord Chancellor."

[1] "For why? Because the good old rule
 Sufficeth them; the simple plan,
 That they should take who have the power
 And they should keep who can."

have made up my mind to pay the money myself." So he gave a check for 100*l*., the excess being to cover the interest from the payment being so long delayed.

I can not put down to the score of *charity*, as has been done by his biographers, the 2,500*l*. a year which he was called upon to contribute to the salary of the Vice-Chancellor; receiving fees on all business done in the Court of Chancery, he was lucky in not being required to pay the whole: but he may claim some merit for indemnifying, out of a fund which was his, the officers of the Court, whose incomes were injured by an order which he made—the amount during his Chancellorship rising to nearly 30,000*l*.

Mr. Belt, a gentleman of the Chancery Bar, happened to mention, in Lord Eldon's hearing, that he had prepared with great labor, some Notes on the reports of the elder Vesey.—"You should publish them," said the Chancellor. "My Lord," replied Mr. Belt, "I have offered them to the booksellers; but they will not take the risk of the printing, and I can not afford it myself." "The Notes ought not to be lost," rejoined Lord Eldon: "let me know what the printing would cost." On learning the probable expense, which was estimated at £200, Lord Eldon sent Mr. Belt a check for that amount. The work was successful; and when it had repaid its expenses, Mr. Belt came to Lord Eldon, and proposed to repay him the £200. "No, no, Mr. Belt," said the Chancellor: "I wish to have the pleasure of making your work a present to the profession."

One day, while he was Chancellor, *more suo* he took a hackney coach to convey him from Downing-street, where he had been attending a Cabinet, to his own residence; and, having a pressing appointment, he alighted hastily from the vehicle, leaving papers containing important Government secrets behind him. Some hours after, the driver discovered the packages, and took them to Hamilton Place unopened, when his Lordship desired to see the coachman, and after a short interview, told him to call again. The man called a few days afterwards, and was then informed that he was no longer a servant, but the owner of a hackney coach,—which his Lordship had, in the mean time, given directions should be purchased and presented to him, together with three horses,—as a reward for his honor and promptitude.

His name seldom appeared in public subscriptions, but he quietly gave assistance to gentlemen in reduced circumstances, who had seen better days; in such cases the parties relieved were often kept in ignorance of the source from which their succor flowed.

He was an excellent landlord and a kind master, enjoying the great good-will of all his officers and attendants.[1] I may even mention, that although, when he lost Lady Eldon, it was too late to begin a new course of life by entering into mixed society, he thenceforth was in the habit of having parties of his relations living in the house with him both in town and country,—and the consideration of expense was never allowed to interfere with the attainment of any object which a reasonable man in his circumstances would desire.

Among his peculiarities was a habit, which, though interesting to strangers, was rather *boring* to those who lived much with him, of relating and considerably exaggerating the difficulties of his early career. When presiding at his dinner-table in Hamilton Place, and carving a leg of mutton, he had great delight in relating how long such a joint served him and Bessy in Serle Street, and the various shapes in which it appeared throughout the week. A lady once having called him a dandy for wearing broad chitterlings of fine cambric, most delicately plaited, and asked who was his laundress? his reply was, "My dear madam, they are not, in my opinion, to be compared to those which I had in the days of my poverty, when I was not able to employ a laundress, and all was done for me by her fingers," [pointing to Lady E.] And then he would go on to tell stories of "Poor Jack Scott," and how proud he was when first permitted to be the bearer of the half guinea which paid for his quarter's schooling.

He retained his early taste for homely fare. Sir John Leach, aiming at high fashion, having engaged a French cook of great celebrity, invited the Lord Chancellor to dine with him, and begged that he would name any "*plat*" of which he was particularly fond. The reply was, "Liver and bacon." Sir John was highly incensed, thinking that this was a premeditated insult on him and his *artiste;*

---

[1] Mr. Pensam, his Secretary of Bankrupts, was his esteemed friend, and has materially assisted his biographers in doing justice to his memory.

but was much soothed, though still a little shocked to be accessory to such vulgarity, when told that this same "*plat*" had been provided for the Lord Chancellor by the Prince Regent at Brighton:

" So there he sat stuck, like a horse in a pound,
While the *bacon and liver* went merrily round."

Lord Eldon disliked French wines almost as much as French principles, and abjuring such thin potations as claret and champagne, he stuck to *port*, preferring a growth remarkably rough and strong, which he called " Newcastle port." Of this he drank very copiously ; but he can not be considered as intemperate, for his liquor never disturbed his understanding, or impaired his health, or interfered with the discharge of any of his duties. Among the Persians he would almost have received divine honors.

Lord Sidmouth related that he once talked to Lord Stowell, his father-in-law, about the practice of himself and the future Lord Chancellor, at an early period of their lives, dining together on the first day of term at one of the coffee-houses near the Temple:—"You drank some wine together, I dare say." "Yes." "Two bottles?" "More." "What! three bottles?" "More." "What! four bottles?" "More,—do not ask any more questions."

The only cause of regret was, that Lord Eldon's young countrymen, not sufficiently appreciating the exceptional strength of his constitution, nor the difference between him and them, both corporeal and mental,—were apt to think that hard drinking, if it did not directly lead to the woolsack, was not inconsistent with the attainment of that eminence ; and I myself could name several promising students of the law whose prospects have been ruined by their recollecting how Lord Eldon drank port wine,—while they forgot how, at the same time, he read and re-read Coke upon Littleton.

His Lordship had some misgivings himself as to the correctness of his practice in this respect. During the session of Parliament, dining almost daily between four and five, in his private room near the House of Lords, on mutton chops brought from an adjoining coffee-house,—to set a good example to his secretaries, he began by ordering a pint of port only ;—but although the time for his repast was very short, he never finished it without a second pint, and seldom without a third. He would sometimes ask the Earl of Shaftesbury, the respected Chairman of the Committees of the Lords, with powers only inferior to his own, to partake,—and then for "pint," "bottle" was substituted;—but when they entered the House to perform their important duties, it never could have been suspected that since breakfast they had tasted anything beyond a biscuit and a glass of spring water. That drinking was with him ever a social and intellectual gratification, we may know from the following anecdote related by one of those who partook of his kindness:— "When Lord Eldon visited Lord Stowell in his season of decay, at his seat near Reading, he sometimes slept at Maidenhead on his way; and on one occasion, having dined at the inn, and learned that the Revising Barristers were staying at the House, he desired his compliments to be presented to them, and requested the favor of their company to share his wine. He received the young gentlemen—very young compared with their host—with the kindest courtesy; talked of his early struggles and successes, as much for their edification as delight; and finished *at least* his own bottle of port before they parted."[1]

He used jestingly to ascribe his occasional fits of the gout to his having been "a three-bottle man," but I believe the disease was hereditary in his family; and at other times he boasted that he had, by this assistance, confined the enemy to his lower extremities,—introducing his favorite joke: "*Ne*—plus ultra."

His general health was excellent, even to extreme old age. In the year 1822 he had to undergo an operation for a polypus in his nose, of which he sent this account to a lady of his acquaintance: "As you do me the honor to inquire after my *Nose*, I think I should be unworthy of the affectionate anxiety you express concerning that particle of me, if I did not tell you that, on Sunday last, Mr. Brodie, in the course of a very painful and bloody operation, removed what for nearly two years has been, though not painful, most teasing and troublesome. I hope it is effectually removed. I certainly have had a nose which has been a more agreeable companion last week than it has been for a long time past." He con-

[1] Quart. Rev. vol. lxxv. p. 53.

tinued all his life afraid of catching the usual diseases of infancy, which his mother told him, to his great dissatisfaction, that by her care he had escaped. When he was near seventy, he thus excused himself for staying away from the house of an old friend: "As I have not myself, to my knowledge, had the small pox, that fact will account for my not calling upon you at present."

Although I believe him to have been a sincere Christian, and really a pious man, I wish I could have been excused from taking any notice of his religion, and I have deferred it as long as possible. The subject was too often in his mouth, and by his frequent appeals to the Supreme Being, and his strong professions of a desire to conform to the Divine will, he excited a suspicion of hypocrisy to which I really believe that he was not justly liable. But I can not defend him from bigotry and intolerance. Not contented with regarding the Church of England as the purest system of Christianity which has appeared since the Apostolic times, he evidently thought that there was no salvation beyond her pale, and he looked with equal horror upon Roman Catholics and Dissenters. He not only would not on any account have entered a Presbyterian place of worship, but I believe he would have refused to accompany Dr. Johnson to hear Dr. Robertson preach from a tree. Thus he wrote in 1823, when Mr. Irving, one of the most impressive pulpit orators I ever heard, was giving lectures by which he roused many to a forgotten sense of religious duty:—"All the world, here, is running on Sundays to the Caledonian Chapel, in Hatton Garden, where they hear a Presbyterian orator from Scotland preaching, as some ladies term it, *charming matter*,—though downright nonsense. To the shame of the King's Ministers, be it said, that many of them have gone to this schism-shop with itching ears."[1] But the Chancellor himself, trusting, I suppose, to the efficacy of his private devotions, was by no means a strict observer of religious ordinances. Although Dr. Johnson, when dying, had sent him a message "to request that he would attend public worship every Sunday," he never

[1] He adds a rather indecorous sarcasm on his "royal young master," that when a lady, whose name he mentions, and with whom his Majesty was supposed to be *very intimate*, was present, the preacher, instead of a "heavenly *mansion*," spoke of a "heavenly *pavilion*," in allusion to the royal residence at Brighton.

was present at public worship in London from one year's end to the other. Pleading in mitigation before Lord Ellenborough that "he attended public worship in the country," he received this rebuke,—"as if there were no God in town!"

On an occasion when his merits were discussed among some lawyers, a warm partisan of the Chancellor extolled him as "a pillar of the Church." " No," retorted another; "he may be one of its *buttresses*, but certainly not one of its *pillars*, for he is never seen *inside* its walls."

So regardless was he of external forms and observances, that during the prayers daily said in the House of Lords —a short and beautiful service (except that we continue to thank God for having saved us from Guy Faux¹)—as soon as the Bishop began, the Chancellor pulled out of his pocket letters he had received by the post, or the cases of the appellant and respondent in the appeal that was coming on,—and upon these he employed himself till the blessing was pronounced. Indeed, this habit was so inveterate that he adhered to it when he attended the hearing of appeals as ex-Chancellor, and when press of business could not have been urged by him as any palliation.

But there are undoubted traces of his faith and of his devout feelings in various passages of his life, particularly when suffering from family bereavements. Neglect of religious ordinances is said to have been common among his contemporaries. He did attend public worship when he was in the country, and he rebuilt, at an expense of some thousands of pounds, Kingston Chapel, near Encombe, in the parish of Corfe Castle.

In his person Lord Eldon was about the middle size, his figure light and athletic, his features regular and handsome, his eye bright and full, his smile remarkably benevolent and his whole appearance prepossessing. The advance of years rather increased than detracted from these personal advantages. As he sat on the judgment-

---

¹ Strangely, the casks of gunpowder concealed under the House of Lords are here described as "the great and *apparent* dangers wherewith we were compassed in this place," for which I am not aware of any authority except Lord Kenyon's " *apparently* LATET ANGUIS IN HERBA."

I have in vain consulted the highest authorities, legal and ecclesiastical, to find out by whom the service was framed, and how this blemish may be removed from it.

seat, "the deep thought betrayed in his furrowed brow,—the large eyebrows, overhanging eyes that seemed to regard more what was taking place within than around him,—his calmness, that would have assumed a character of sternness but for its perfect placidity,—his dignity, repose, and venerable age, tended at once to win confidence and to inspire respect."[1] He had a voice both sweet and deep-toned, and its effect was not injured by his Northumbrian burr, which, though strong, was entirely free from harshness or vulgarity.

The statues and busts of him attempted from time to time are rather indifferent performances; but several excellent portraits of him, which have been engraved, have rendered his likeness familiar to the British public. Of these two are by Sir Thomas Lawrence: the first, when yet a young man, in plain clothes, with a powdered *toupet* and *ailes de pigeon*, in the possession of the present Earl; the other, when he was advanced in life, and such *coiffure* had gone out, but to please George IV.—in the same style,—which remains at Windsor Castle. A portrait of him as Lord Chancellor, by Owen, was much admired, and was copied by the same artist for many corporations and private friends. There was another fine portrait of him, as Lord Chancellor, by Pickersgill, the great ornament of Merchant Tailors' Hall, where he ate many good dinners and made many applauded Church-and-King speeches. But the most interesting portrait of him, perhaps, is that by Briggs, representing him as High Steward of the University of Oxford at the installation of the Duke of Wellington, receiving the homage of his grandson.[2]

The corporation of Newcastle, justly proud of having at the same time three natives of their town, the sons of freemen, themselves freemen, and all schoolfellows together at the Free Grammar School there under Mr. Moises, now become most eminent men in the public service,—Lord Eldon, Lord Stowell, and Lord Collingwood,—requested them all to sit for their portraits, to be hung up in the Guildhall. Lord Eldon's answer to the Mayor displays much good feeling, and (the parentheses with which it

---

[1] 2 Townsend, 496.
[2] Lord Eldon is rarely noticed by caricaturists. "H. B." and "Punch" had not yet appeared. But an Appendix of Caricatures will be necessary to illustrate the Lives of subsequent Chancellors.

had been interspersed having been struck out by a friend) no contemptible power of composition:—

"DEAR SIR,

"I beg you to be assured, and that you will be pleased to assure the Aldermen and Common Council, that I am impressed with a very warm sense of gratitude for the mark of respect and regard which is mentioned in your letter of the 13th instant. In complying with the request contained in it, which I am satisfied is dictated more by their kind partiality than by any claim which I can have to the distinction offered to me. I would willingly indulge the hope that the measure which has been proposed may occasionally and usefully suggest to the descendants of our fellow-burgesses that in this great and free country the industrious exercise of moderate talents may, under the blessing of Providence, raise them, before the close of life, to those situations in the state, to which, in the beginning of life, they could hardly aspire, and may ensure to them also the solid gratification which flows from receiving in advanced years distinction and honor from that part of the community, among whom were passed the days of infancy and youth.

"I am, dear Sir,
"Your obliged and faithful friend,
"ELDON.'

"July 26th, 1811."

---

[1] Lord Stowell's is in still better taste:—
"My dear Sir,
"I beg you will take an early opportunity of presenting my sincere thanks to the corporate body over which you at present preside, for the high and unexpected honor they have been pleased to confer upon me, in requesting me to sit for my picture, to be placed in the Guildhall in company with the pictures of the Lord Chancellor and Lord Collingwood.

"It cannot but be highly gratifying to me, on every account, to be thought worthy of such a distinction by the gentlemen of Newcastle. I received my education among them; and to that education, under God's good providence, I owe everything that can have obtained for me so flattering a declaration of their regard. I am happy in feeling that, in their opinion, I have not dishonored it, in the course of a life that has passed under some degree of public observation. It is a testimony to my character, to which I hope my family will in all future time advert with peculiar pride and satisfaction—as conveying the sentiments of those who have had the best opportunities of judging upon the general tenor of my conduct—It is with real elevation of mind that I receive the result of their favorable judgment, in their associating me upon such an occasion with two individuals who have made a more splendid use of the same early advantages in life, and whose more important

The portraits are still to be seen in the Guildhall, and it may well be a subject of debate, which of the three so commemorated is most to be admired, and best deserves the gratitude of his country. The mace and the seal have carried it for the Chancellor among his townsmen, who have named a magnificient new square after him, who often paint his head for a sign-post, and who in various ways show that they now consider him as their tutelary saint.

His arms[1] appear thrice in the heraldic ornaments of the new House of Lords, in respect of the three times when he received the Great Seal; first, as Chancellor to George III. in 1801; again, as Chancellor to the same Sovereign in 1807;—and finally as Chancellor to George IV. in 1820. Other Chancellors have received the Great Seal from the hands of the Sovereign a greater number of times—but no Chancellor from the foundation of the monarchy held it so long; and, although he was unequal to many of those whose arms are blazoned with his in eloquence, in literature, and in philosophy, he was excelled by none of them in law, and he excelled them all in political intrigue.

His two sons having died in his lifetime, the only children he left behind him to lament his loss were his daughters, Lady Elizabeth and Lady Frances, who were both respectably married.

He is worthily represented by the only son of his eldest son, whose untimely end he had lamented so deeply. Knowing the present Earl of Eldon to be a most amiable and estimable man, and having reason to think that he naturally and laudably considers his grandsire as absolutely perfect in all that he ever thought, said, or did, I have felt many a pang in writing this memoir, when I considered that, if it should meet his eye, it must often appear to him censorious and unjust. But the world may decide that I have finished my biographical labors without for-

---

public services have united for them the applause of their country with the honorable approbation of their native town.

"I have the honor to be, Mr. Mayor, with particular regard and respect,
"Your obliged and faithful humble servant,
"WM. SCOTT.

"July 27th, 1811."

[1] Argent, an anchor erect sable between three lions' heads erased gules; on a chief wavy azure, a portcullis or—Motto: "Sit sine labe decus."

feiting my claim to impartiality, and *he* may yet come to the conclusion, that as in the character of his distinguished ancestor the good so much predominates over the evil, its lustre will not be diminished by placing its conflicting qualities in opposition to each other. Bronze is more durable than tinsel, and so is truth than flattery.

POSTSCRIPT.

HAVING had occasion, in preparing this work, to examine the history of the country in every reign, from King Ethelbert to Queen Victoria, I had intended, at the conclusion of it, to point out and try to explain some of the most striking changes which have gradually taken place in the institutions, the laws, and the manners of the people; but I feel that it would not become me to trespass longer, at present, on the patience of the public with any speculations of mine. Still I venture to bring together a few facts respecting my Chancellors, which may be found not uninteresting.

I reckon the number of those whom I have had to commemorate to be 167. The names of only ten Anglo-Saxon Chancellors have come down to us—but we have a series nearly unbroken from Maurice, who received the Great Seal in the year 1067, to Lord Eldon, who died in 1838. The Conqueror had 6 Chancellors; —William Rufus, 3;—Henry I., 7;—Stephen, 5;—Matilda, 1;—Henry II., 7;—Richard I. 4; John, 3;—Henry III., 17;—Edward I., 6;—Edward II., 6;—Edward III., 20;—Richard II., 11; —Henry IV., 7;—Henry V., 2;—Henry VI., 8;—Edward IV., 5;—Edward V., 1;—Richard III., 1;—Henry VII., 4;—Henry VIII., 5;—Edward VI., 4;—Mary, 2;—Elizabeth, 5;—James I., 3;—Charles I., 5;—the Commonwealth, 15;[1]—Charles II., 5;—James II., 2;—William and Mary, 2;[2]—Anne, 3;—George I., 4;—George II., 4;—George III., 8;—George IV., 2.

Of these the far greater number were ecclesiastics. The first lay Chancellor in England was Fitzgilbert, appointed by Queen Matilda soon after her coronation, during the short time she occupied the throne,—and there was no other till Sir Robert de Bourchier, a soldier, appointed by Edward III. There were four common-law judges placed

---

[1] Lords Commissioners.
[2] Besides Lords Commissioners Manard and Trevor.

in the "marble chair" at the latter end of the same reign. The practice of appointing Bishops, however, was soon resumed, and continued, without interruption, till the fall of Wolsey. Then came Sir Thomas More and a succession of lawyers, till Mary gave the Great Seal to her two persecuting Prelates, Gardyner and Heath. Elizabeth returned to the laity, and a series of them continued till Lord Bacon was convicted of corruption—when, the lawyers being in bad odor, James I. ventured on Bishop Williams. He was the only Protestant divine who was ever in possession of the Great Seal, although the Privy Seal was held by a Bishop as late as the reign of Queen Anne.

Archbishop Arundel, during the wars of the Roses, was Chancellor five times, but no one else has been Chancellor more than four times. Turketel alone was Chancellor under four sovereigns—Edward the Elder, Athelstane, Edmund, and Edred. Lord Eldon, as Chancellor to two sovereigns, held the Great Seal for the longest period of time.

Scrope, in the reign of Richard II., is to be regarded as the first law Lord ever created. A succession of lay commoners afterwards held the Great Seal; but from the time of Lord Ellesmere they were all ennobled, except Sir Orlando Bridgman and Sir Nathan Wright. A good many have been Earls, but there has been only one Chancellor made a Marquess, Sir William Poulet, Marquess of Winchester; and one a Duke, Sir Thomas Beaufort, Duke of Exeter. Five have been Knights of the Garter: Bourchier, Earl of Essex, the Marquess of Winchester, Lord Audley, Lord Wriothesley, and Sir Christopher Hatton.

There are now sitting in the House of Lords sixteen Peers descended from Chancellors in the direct male line —Earl Fortescue, from Sir John Fortescue—the Marquess of Winchester, from Sir William Poulet—the Earl of Bradford, from Sir Orlando Bridgman—the Earl of Coventry, from Lord Coventry—the Earl of Shaftesbury, from Lord Shaftesbury—the Earl of Winchelsea and Nottingham, from Lord Nottingham—the Earl of Guilford, from Lord Guilford—Earl Cowper, from Lord Cowper—the Earl of Macclesfield, from Lord Macclesfield—Marquess Camden, from Lord Camden—the Earl of Lovelace, from Lord King—the Earl of Hardwicke, from Lord Hardwicke—Earl Talbot, from Lord Talbot—Earl Bathurst, from Lord Bathurst— the Earl of Eldon, from Lord Eldon—and Lord Erskine, from Erskine THE GREAT. The Earl of Clarendon and other Chancellors are represented in the House of Lords by decendants through females.

Only one Chancellor was beheaded while in possession of the Great Seal; this was Simon de Sudbury, murdered by the mob in Wat Tyler's riots: but the Earl of Salisbury, Sir Thomas More, and several others came to a violent end after their resignation.

During the last 300 years, six have been impeached,—Cardinal Wolsey, Lord Bacon, Lord Keeper Finch, Lord Clarendon, Lord Somers, and Lord Macclesfield,—and of these Lord Somers alone was acquitted.

One was Chancellor of Ireland at the same time that he was Chancellor of England, and another was Chancellor of England after having been Chancellor of Ireland.[1]

Prior to the reign of Edward I. there were various instances of Normans and other foreigners having the Great Seal confided to them, although, like Lord Chancellor Longchamp, they could not speak a word of English,—but since then the Chancellors have all been native-born subjects. Among these there are only two Scotchmen, Lord Loughborough and Lord Erskine. When the English and Irish bars are amalgamated, as they are soon likely to be, Irishmen, it may be hoped, will often be Chancellors of England, as well as Englishmen Chancellors of Ireland.

In the history of the Great Seal of England there is one and only one instance of its being held successively by two brothers—John and Robert de Stratford, in the reign of Edward III.

The new House of Lords has been adorned with an emblazonment of the armorial bearings of all the Lord Chancellors and Keepers of the Great Seal who have presided on the woolsack since the end of the reign of Edward III.[2] This is a proper compliment to an order

---

[1] Since the close of the period comprised in this work, there have been two additional instances of Irish Chancellors having high promotion in this part of the United Kingdom—LORD ST. LEONARD's made Lord Chancellor of Great Britain, and LORD CAMPBELL made Lord Chief Justice of England.—*Note to 4th Edition.*

[2] From Adam de Houghton to Lord Cottenham—in number 79. The

which includes many great names, and, through a long succession of ages, has been the main support of the hereditary branch of our legislature.

I hope that the line of Lord Chancellors may be continued with increasing reputation to distant generations. In any speculations for abolishing or remodeling the office of Chancellor, I wish Benthamites to consider whether, as it has subsisted since the foundation of the monarchy, it can be safely dispensed with, or materially altered. To insure the steady march of the government, there must be a great Jurist to guide the deliberations of the Peers, and to assist in the councils of the Sovereign; he can not do so advantageously without the weight to be derived from a high judicial office, and his political functions are incompatible with the administration of the criminal law. The CLAVIS REGNI must therefore be held by the first Equity Judge in the land.

I will conclude with a prophecy, that if the proposed experiment of a *tripartite* division of the Chancellorship should be tried, it will fail, and that no author will ever acquire reputation by writing the lives of the "Ministers of Justice," or of the "Lord Chief Justices in Equity," or of the "Lord Chief Justices of Appeal."

Note to Fourth Edition.—From the formation of Lord Melbourne's second administration in 1825, the Great Seal had been in imminent peril. When, to the astonishment of the public, the determination was announced that it was not to be restored to Lord Brougham, the new Prime Minister did me the honor to consult me about his law arrangements, and asked my opinion of his scheme of putting the Great Seal into commission. Among other objections, I pointed out that, according to this arrangement, the cabinet would be *inops concilii.* "Oh!" said he,

arms of all of them were found by that very learned herald and most useful officer of the House of Lords, Mr. Pulman, except those of Searle (or Scarle), who held the Great Seal at the end of the reign of Richard II. and the beginning of the reign of Henry IV., whom I had designated as "the most obscure of the Chancellors." According to the arrangement which has been adopted, the shields are 102 in number; those of each reign being preceded by the arms of the Sovereign, of which there are 26; and in order to preserve the chronological order, the arms of a Chancellor or Keeper are repeated as often as he received the Great Seal from the reigning Sovereign.

NOTE TO FOURTH EDITION.

"I will advise them on questions of law myself, and we shall do all the better without lawyers." *C.*—"You, to be sure, have had the advantage of studying the law, and being called to the bar and going a circuit; but do you mean to say that permanently the Cabinet would go on without the Chancellor being a member of it, to explain questions of international or municipal law, on which the most important measures of government may depend?" *M.*—"Yes, I do. Whoever is fit to be Minister should know enough of general principles to guide him, and when any technicalities arise we can consult the Attorney and Solicitor-General."

So Lord Melbourne went on, as long as he could, with the Great Seal in commission, and he was exceedingly annoyed by the thought of a Chancellor being intruded into the Cabinet. In the beginning of 1836 he was alarmed by the loud complaints that the Lords Commissioners were incompetent to do the judicial business of the Chancellor, as they were unable to clear off the arrears in their own proper Courts,—and he reluctantly made a Chancellor—but with an intimation that the office was to be divided as soon as possible. Accordingly a Bill for this purpose was introduced, and it was thrown out—chiefly by the opposition of Lord Langdale, who contended for a *tresection* instead of *bisection*, and that there should be a "Minister of Justice," as well as a "Lord Chief Justice in Equity," and a "Lord Chief Justice of Appeals."

Luckily Lord Chancellor Cottenham disposed satisfactorily of the business in the Court of Chancery, giving no trouble in the Cabinet,—and the *prestige* of the Great Seal revived. This quietude continued to a considerable degree in Lord Lyndhurst's last Chancellorship, and in the beginning of the second Chancellorship of Lord Cottenham. But when his health failed, arrears multiplied most alarmingly, both in the Court of Chancery and in the House of Lords; and there were loud cries for abolishing the office of Lord Chancellor, and completely remodeling the procedure for administering equity and disposing of appeals in the last resort. These controversies were long carried on in the newspapers, and many pamphlets were published upon the subject. The favorite scheme was the appointment of a Minister of Justice, to whom should be assigned many of the duties, and the whole of the judicial patronage of the Lord Chancellor. —In the mean time the Great Seal was again put into commission, and confusion was worse confounded.

Untoward events followed, to which I made allusion in a note to the first volume of this edition of the " Lives of the Chancellors,"[1] and which certainly have considerably impaired the splendor of the office. But, when we consider the perils to be encountered, perhaps we ought to rejoice that the office still survives, and that the Chancellor still presides on the woolsack, and has a seat in the Cabinet. The creation of Lords Justices of Appeal under Lord Truro may have been a necessary evil, and the complaints against the exercise of the appellate jurisdiction of the House of Lords may have arisen from fortuitous circumstances not to be foreseen,—and not likely to recur,—without any particle of blame being imputable to any of the very learned, and able, and honorable men on whom the exercise of this jurisdiction devolved.

My anxious wish is that the ascendency of the Great Seal should be fully maintained. Considering the difficulties with which the holders of it recently have been encompassed and with which I should have been unable to cope, I consider my lot felicitous in escaping it.

" Sauve mari magno," &c.

But, instead of calmly enjoying the contrast between my position and that of others, I am earnestly desirous to contribute, if I could, to the relief and safety of those who are tossed by the tempest.

Hartrigge, Sept. 22*nd,* 1857.

[1] Page 26.